D0829195

# Jim Murray's
# WHISKEY BIBLE
## ~ 2008 ~

**This 2008 edition of Jim Murray's Whiskey Bible is dedicated to
Theo
A Dragon among Lions.**

This edition published 2007

10 9 8 7 6 5 4 3 2 1

The "Jim Murray's" logo and the "Whiskey Bible" logo are trade marks of Jim Murray.

A CIP catalogue record for this book is available from the British Library

ISBN: 978-0-9554729-1-6

Printed in Peru

Written and Edited by: Jim Murray
Design: Jim Murray, Darren Jordan
Maps: James Murray
Production: James Murray, Billy Jeffrey; Dani Dal Molin, Mike Leaman, Howard Buchanan
Sample Research: Dani Dal Molin, Edna Mycawka

**Author's Note**
I have used the spelling "whiskey" or "whisky" depending on how the individual
distillers prefer. All Scotch is "whisky". So is Canadian. All Irish, these days, is "whiskey",
though that was not always the case. In Kentucky, bourbon and rye are spelt "whiskey",
with the exception of the produce of the early Times/Old Forester Distillery and Maker's
Mark which they bottle as "whisky". In Tennessee, it is a 50-50 split: Dickel is "whisky",
while Daniel's is "whiskey".

*Jim Murray's*

# WHISKEY BIBLE
~ 2008 ~

*The world's leading whiskey guide from
the world's foremost whiskey authority*

DRAM GOOD BOOKS

# Contents

Introduction . . . . . . . . . . . . . . . . . . . . . . . . . . . . . . . . . . . . .6
How to Read The Bible . . . . . . . . . . . . . . . . . . . . . . . . . . . . . .7
Bible Thumping . . . . . . . . . . . . . . . . . . . . . . . . . . . . . . . . . . .9
Review of the Whisky Year . . . . . . . . . . . . . . . . . . . . . . . . . .13
Jim Murray's Whisky Award Winners 20080 . . . . . . . . . . . . . .16
Scottish Malts . . . . . . . . . . . . . . . . . . . . . . . . . . . . . . . . . . . .22

| | | |
|---|---|---|
| Aberfeldy . . . . . . 24 | Glencadam . . . . 92 | Littlemill . . . . . . 155 |
| Aberlour . . . . . . . 25 | Glendronach . . . . 93 | Loch Lomond . . 155 |
| Allt-A-Bhainne . . .27 | Glendullan . . . . . . 94 | Lochside . . . . . . 158 |
| Ardbeg . . . . . . . . 28 | Glen Elgin . . . . . 95 | Longmorn . . . . . 158 |
| Ardmore . . . . . . . 35 | Glenesk . . . . . . . 95 | Longrow . . . . 161 |
| Auchentoshan . . 37 | Glenfarclas . . . . . 96 | Macallan . . . . . . 161 |
| Auchroisk . . . . . . 39 | Glenfiddich . . . . . 103 | Macduff . . . . . . . 173 |
| Aultmore . . . . . . . 39 | Glenflagler . . . . 106 | Mannochmore . 174 |
| Balblair . . . . . . . . 40 | Glen Garioch . . . 106 | Millburn . . . . . . 174 |
| Balmenach . . . . . 42 | Glenglassaugh . . 107 | Miltonduff . . . . . 175 |
| The Balvenie . . . . 42 | Glengoyne . . . . . 108 | Mortlach . . . . . . 175 |
| Banff . . . . . . . . . . 45 | Glen Grant . . . . . 110 | Mosstowie . . . . 177 |
| Ben Nevis . . . . . . 45 | Glen Gyle . . . . . 113 | North Port . . . . . 177 |
| BenRiach . . . . . . . 46 | Glen Keith . . . . . 113 | Oban . . . . . . . . . 178 |
| Benrinnes . . . . . . 52 | Glenkinchie . . . . 114 | Old Rhosdhu . . .178 |
| Benromach . . . . . 53 | The Glenlivet . . . 114 | Pittyvaich . . . . . 178 |
| Ben Wyvis . . . . . 54 | Glenlochy . . . . . 118 | Port Ellen . . . . . . 178 |
| Bladnoch . . . . . . 54 | Glenlossie . . . . . 118 | Pulteney . . . . . . 181 |
| Blair Athol . . . . . 56 | Glen Mhor . . . . . 119 | Rosebank . . . . . 182 |
| Bowmore . . . . . . 57 | Glenmorangie . . 119 | Royal Brackla . . . 185 |
| Braeval . . . . . . . . 63 | Glen Moray . . . . 123 | Royal Lochnagar 185 |
| Brechin . . . . . . . . 64 | Glen Ord . . . . . . 125 | St Magdalene . . 186 |
| Brora . . . . . . . . . . 64 | Glenrothes . . . . . 125 | Scapa . . . . . . . . 187 |
| Bruichladdich . . . 65 | Glen Scotia . . . . 128 | Speyburn . . . . . . 188 |
| Bunnahabhain . . 70 | Glen Spey . . . . . 130 | Speyside . . . . . . 189 |
| Caol Ila . . . . . . . . 72 | Glentauchers . . . 130 | Springbank . . . . 189 |
| Caperdonich . . . . 79 | Glenturret . . . . . 131 | Strathisla . . . . . . 192 |
| Cardhu . . . . . . . . 80 | Glenugie . . . . . . 132 | Strathmill . . . . . 194 |
| Clynelish . . . . . . . 80 | Glenury Royal . . 133 | Talisker . . . . . . . 195 |
| Coleburn . . . . . . 84 | Highland Park . . 133 | Tamdhu . . . . . . 197 |
| Convalmore . . . . 84 | Hillside . . . . . . 139 | Tamnavulin . . . . 194 |
| Cragganmore . . . . 85 | Imperial . . . . . . . 139 | Teaninich . . . . . . 195 |
| Craigellachie . . . . 86 | Inchgower . . . . . 140 | Tobermory . . . . . 195 |
| Croftengea . . . . . . 86 | Inverleven . . . . 141 | Tomatin . . . . . . . 197 |
| Dailuaine . . . . . . . 86 | Isle of Arran . . . 141 | Tomintoul . . . . . 198 |
| Dallas Dhu . . . . 87 | Isle of Jura . . . . . 145 | Tormore . . . . . . 199 |
| Dalmore . . . . . . . 88 | Kilchoman . . . . 146 | Tullibardine . . . . 199 |
| Dalwhinnie . . . . . 89 | Kilkerran . . . . . 146 | **Unspecified Singles** |
| Deanston . . . . . . 90 | Knockando . . . . 147 | Campbeltown . . 203 |
| Dufftown . . . . . . 90 | Knockdhu . . . . . 147 | Highland . . . . . . 203 |
| Dunglass . . . . . . 91 | Ladyburn . . . . . 148 | Island . . . . . . . . . 205 |
| Edradour . . . . . . . 91 | Lagavulin . . . . . 148 | Islay . . . . . . . . . . 206 |
| Fettercairn . . . . . 91 | Laphroaig . . . . . 149 | Lowland . . . . . . 209 |
| Glen Albyn . . . . . 91 | Ledaig . . . . . . . 153 | Speyside . . . . . . .209 |
| Glenallachie . . . . 92 | Linkwood . . . . . 153 | **Vatted Malts** . . . .213 |
| Glenburgie . . . . . 92 | Linlithgow . . . . 155 | **Mystery Malts** . . . 221 |

| | | | |
|---|---|---|---|
| **Scottish Grain** | 222 | | |
| **Single Grain** | 223 | Invergordon | 224 |
| Alloa | 223 | Loch Lomond | 225 |
| Caledonian | 223 | Lochside | 225 |
| Cambus | 223 | North British | 225 |
| Cameronbridge | 223 | North Scotland | 226 |
| Carsebridge | 223 | Port Dundas | 226 |
| Dumbarton | 224 | Strathclyde | 227 |
| Girvan | 224 | **Vatted Grain** | 227 |
| **Scottish Blends** | 228 | | |

| | | | |
|---|---|---|---|
| **Irish Whiskey** | 262 | | |
| **Pure Pot Still** | 263 | **Single Grain** | 270 |
| **Single Malt** | 264 | **Blends** | 270 |
| **American Whiskey** | 276 | | |
| **American Single Malt** | 278 | **Straight Rye** | 299 |
| **Bourbon Distilleries** | 279 | **Straight Wheat Whiskey** | 302 |
| **Bourbon Brands** | 280 | **Kentucky Whiskey** | 302 |
| **Tennessee Whiskey** | 297 | **American/Kentucky Blends** | 303 |
| **Corn Whiskey** | 298 | **Other American Whiskey** | 303 |
| **Single Malt Rye** | 298 | | |
| **Canadian Whisky** | 304 | | |
| **Canadian Single Malt** | 306 | **Canadian Blended Whisky** | 306 |
| **Canadian Grain Single Barrel** | 306 | | |
| **Japanese Whisky** | 314 | | |
| **Single Malts** | 316 | Shirakawa | 321 |
| Chichibu | 316 | Yamazaki | 321 |
| Fuji Gotemba | 316 | Yoichi | 323 |
| Hakushu | 316 | **Unspecified Malts** | 326 |
| Karuizawa | 318 | **Japanese Vatted Malts** | 326 |
| Komogatake | 320 | **Japanese Single Grain** | 328 |
| Miyagikyo | 320 | **Japanese Blends** | 338 |
| Sendai | 320 | | |
| **European Whisky** | 333 | | |
| Austria | 334 | Poland | 341 |
| Belgium | 336 | Spain | 341 |
| Bulgaria | 336 | Sweden | 341 |
| France | 336 | Switzerland | 343 |
| Germany | 338 | Turkey | 345 |
| Latvia | 341 | Wales | 345 |
| **World Whiskies** | 348 | | |
| Argentina | 349 | New Zealand | 355 |
| Australia | 349 | South Africa | 356 |
| Brazil | 353 | Miscellaneous | 356 |
| India | 353 | Cross-Country Vatted Malt | 357 |

| | |
|---|---|
| **Slàinte** | 359 |

**List of Maps**

| | |
|---|---|
| Scotland | 22–23 |
| Speyside Malts | 24 |
| Ireland | 263 |
| United States | 277 |
| Canada | 304–305 |
| Japan | 314–315 |

# Introduction

**A**nd so the whiskies just keep rolling in....Another 950 tasted of which a staggering 811 were new on to the whisky shelves. Incredible.

Whether the number from independent bottlers, continues is debatable in the current climate of ever-shrinking supply lines. But, such is the way of nature, where there is a will there so often appears to be a way and I don't expect to taste fewer new 'uns than this for the 2009 edition. In fact, probably something nearer the 1,000 mark. It could be that the ages go up slightly on average as malts of popular blending vintage are earmarked for elsewhere. And there are all the wine cask and other exotic finishes that once allowed to start their metamorphosis a couple of years back are likely to be left alone.

There really have been some shimmering highlights for this edition. I left the staggering new range from Glenfarclas, The Family Casks, in a which a cask every year from 1952 to 1994 was bottled, to the end of my annual marathon. Let's face it: in life it always helps to have some carrot or other before you. And I wasn't disappointed. Likewise, after four years of trying I at last managed to open a sample superhighway from the Scotch Malt Whisky Society, with 50 samples tasted this time round. Next year we are going for their complete year's bottling, and that means for all their branches worldwide. Hold on tight...

I have also been ticked off by the odd supplier for not including their whiskies. Usually it was because we are not aware of them and we ask all independent whisky companies to contact us to ensure their whiskies are included. There is not a single company in the world we ignore: if I get the whisky, I'll taste it.

Going back to the whiskies tasted for the 2008, there have been highs and lows. Certainly more lows than normal on account of the increased manifestation of whiskies either dulled or spoiled by sulphur-treated casks. My lack of joy over this matter is discussed in Bible Thumping.

But at last a single malt has pulled off World Whisky of the Year. And it just had to be an Ardbeg. The label claims 10-years-old. Reality and stock shortages means it is a lot older than that, so yet again Jim Murray's World Whisky of the Year ends up being a whisky which you don't have to re-mortgage your house to afford. And that's exactly the way it should be.

During the last year, time spent researching and writing the Bible (or Bibles, seeing as the 2007 wasn't completed until November) has kept me away from my normal round of tastings, fairs and distillery visits. Now, with the 2008 finally put to bed, I will have the chance to get out and join in the fun.

And because November 2007 sees me celebrate my 50th birthday and the launch of the 5th Jim Murray's Whisky Bible, I hope we get a chance to enjoy a dram or two together should you see me on the road..

Also, after handing out so many awards, it will be a pleasant duty to be the recipient when inducted into the Bourbon Hall of Fame during the Kentucky Whiskey Festival later in the year.. To have my name mentioned in the same breath as the Elmer T Lees and Jimmy Russells of that great industry is an extraordinary honour and one I will always hold very dear. Especially as my first-planned whiskey book of all time was supposed to be my guide to bourbon. But the publishers changed their mind at the last minute because they saw no future in the spirit.. That was way back in 1992. Another reason to share a whisky should you bump into me during my travels. And the filip I need to at last getting round to fixing the roof of my old Kentucky home.

And, finally. The last country I visited, to conduct a tasting, was Malta. Tomorrow I fly to Peru to oversee the printing of the Bible. Malta. Peru. Make an anagram of the two and you get: A Pure Malt. It could only happen to a whisky writer...

Jim Murray
The Tasting Room
Wellingborough
July 2007

# How to Read
# The Bible

The whole point of this book is for the whisky lover – be he or she an experienced connoisseur or, better fun still, simply starting out on the long and joyous path of discovery – to have ready access to easy-to-understand information about as many whiskies is possible. And I mean a lot. Thousands.

This book does not quite include every whisky on the market ... just by far and away the vast majority. And those that have been missed this time round – either through accident, logistics or design – will appear in later editions once we can source a sample.

## Whisky Scoring

The marking for this book is tailored to the consumer and scores run out just a little higher than I use for my own personal references. But such is the way it has been devised it has not affected my order of preference.

Each whisky is given a rating out of 100. Twenty-five marks are given to each of four factors: nose (**n**), taste (**t**), finish (**f**), balance and overall complexity (**b**). That means 50% of the marks are given for flavour alone and 25% for the nose, often an overlooked part of the whisky equation. The area of balance and complexity covers all three previous factors and a usually hidden one besides:

**Nose:** this is simply the aroma. Often requires more than one inspection as hidden aromas can sometimes reveal themselves after time in the glass and increased contact with air. The nose very often tells much about a whisky, but – as we shall see – equally can be quite misleading.

**Taste:** this is the immediate arrival on the palate and involves the flavour profile up to, and including, the time it reaches maximum intensity and complexity.

**Finish:** often the least understood part of a tasting. This is the tail and flourish of the whisky's signature, often revealing the effects of ageing. The better whiskies tend to finish well and longer without too much oak excess.

**Balance:** This is the part it takes a little experience to appreciate but it can be mastered by anyone. For a whisky to work well on the nose and palate, it should not be too one-sided in its character. If you are looking for an older whisky, it should have evidence of oak, but not so much that all other flavours and aromas are drowned out. Likewise, a whisky matured or finished in a sherry butt must offer a lot more than just wine alone and the greatest Islay malts, for instance, revel in depth and complexity beyond the smoky effects of peat.

Each whisky has been analysed by me without adding water or ice. I have taken each whisky as it was poured from the bottle and used no more than warming in an identical glass to extract and discover the character of the whisky. To have added water would have been pointless: it would have been an inconsistent factor as people, when pouring water, add different amounts at varying temperatures. The only constant with the whisky you and I taste will be when it has been poured directly from the bottle.

Even if you and I taste the same whiskies at the same temperature and from identical glasses – and even share the same values in whisky – our scores may still be different. Because a factor that is built into my evaluation is drawn from expectation and experience. When I sample a whisky from a certain distillery at such-and-such an age or from this type of barrel or that, I would expect it to offer me certain qualities. It has taken me 30 years to acquire this knowledge (which I try to add to day by day!) and an enthusiast cannot be expected to learn it overnight. But, hopefully, Jim Murray's Whisky Bible will help...!

**Score chart**

Within the parentheses () is the overall score out of 100.

**0–50** Nothing short of absolutely diabolical.

**51–64** Nasty and well worth avoiding.

**65–69** Very unimpressive indeed.

**70–74** Usually drinkable but don't expect the earth to move.

**75–79** Average and usually pleasant though sometimes flawed.

**80–84** Good whisky worth trying.

**85–89** Very good to excellent whiskies definitely worth buying.

**90–93** Brilliant.

**94–97** Superstar whiskies that give us all a reason to live.

**98–100** Better than anything I've ever tasted!

**Key to Abbreviations & Symbols**

**%** Percentage strength of whisky measured as alcohol by volume. **b** Overall balance and complexity. **bott** Date of bottling. **db** Distillery bottling. In other words, an expression brought out by the owners of the distillery. **dist** Date of distillation or spirit first put into cask. **f** Finish. **n** Nose. **nc** Non-coloured. **ncf** Non-chill-filtered. **sc** Single cask. **t** Taste. ❖ New entry for 2008. ⊙ Retasted – no change. ⊙⊙ Retasted and re-evaluated.

## Finding Your Whisky

**Worldwide Malts:** Whiskies are listed alphabetically throughout the book. In the case of single malts, the distilleries run A–Z style with distillery bottlings appearing at the top of the list in order of age, starting with youngest first. After age comes vintage. After all the "official" distillery bottlings are listed, next come other bottlings, again in alphabetical order. Single malts without a distillery named (or perhaps named after a dead one) are given their own section, as are vatted malts.

**Worldwide Blends:** These are simply listed alphabetically, irrespective of which company produce them. So "Black Bottle" appears ahead of "White Horse" and Japanese blends begin with "Amber" and ends with "Za". In the case of brands being named after companies or individuals the first letter of the brand will dictate where it is listed. So William Grant, for instance, will be found under "W" for William rather "G" for Grant.

**Bourbon/Rye:** One of the most confusing types of whiskey to list because often the name of the brand bears no relation to the name of the distillery that made it. Also, brands may be sold from one company to another, or shortfalls in stock may see companies buying bourbons from another. For that reason all the brands have been listed alphabetically with the name of the bottling distiller being added at the end.

**Irish Whiskey:** There are four types of Irish whiskey: (i) pure pot still; (ii) single malt, (iii) single grain and (iv) blended. Some whiskies may have "pure pot still" on the label, but are actually single malts. So check both sections.

## Bottle Information

As no labels are included in this book I have tried to include all the relevant information you will find on the label to make identification of the brand straightforward. Where known I have included date of distillation and bottling. Also the cask number for further recognition. At the end of the tasting notes I have included the strength and, if known, number of bottles (sometimes abbreviated to btls) released and in which markets.

# Bible Thumping Candles of Misunderstanding

**L**et me take you, if I may, to what is probably my favourite restaurant in the world.

We are in Portland, Oregon and a taxi has just decanted us at the entrance of the Ringside Steakhouse downtown on West Burnside.

We have just handed in our coats and are proceeding into the dark, cavernous interior. After some sparkling and witty conversation (well, from you, anyway...), and having perused the menu and wine lists and selected our heart's desire, the waiters are now guiding our respective choices between impatient knives and forks.

On my plate a rib-eye steak spits, sporting minor char scars to the outside, yet inside oozing with myriad juicy possibilities. You salivate as you marvel at the marbling, randomly criss-crossing, like tracks over Rocky foothills, the most perfectly textured cut you are likely to encounter. And beside the plate stands a glass three quarters full with Archery Summit Arcus, a local Pinot Noir whose grapes have been trodden by the feet of gods and which will perfect the melt-in-the-mouth meat with a silk-caressed fruitfest of formidable body and intensity.

Outside of a bed or sticking your head into a glass of Ardbeg, George T Stagg or 18-year-old Old Parr, (or perhaps devouring a crumbly White Stilton alongside a spicy Melton Mowbray pork pie all washed down with a pint of Grainstore Cooking bitter, as regular readers of Bible Thumping will know) the senses are rarely sent into such raptures.

But what's this? As I lift the first square of steak to my mouth, via the immediate airspace below my nose, I smell something. Experience tells me the olfactory sensation should be quite outstanding: a blending of delicate, grilled fats – some near raw, some singed – with sweet, ruby-centred beef, all to the background accompaniment of onion rings and a few molecules of the wine thrown in to stimulate the tastebuds in an expectation point of no return. But no. It is if a box of matches has exploded in my face. Instead of pure, uncluttered sensory bliss, the brain is trying to somehow make sense of this sulphurous slap in the kisser. Has Mount St. Helens gone up again?

"Waiter...!"

"Yes, sir."

"My steak. This 24 ounces of prime American boned beef. This marbled masterpiece. The reason why the west was won. It reeks of sulphur. And my friend's filet mignon is minging, too. And as for the taste... It's kind of powdery and bitter. And the aftertaste....(splutter!!!)"

"Yes, sir," repeats the waiter, bobbing slightly up and down as he adjusts his jet propulsion pack. "That's because the truck that carried the beef here wasn't refrigerated. And the meat has to travel a long way from the other side of the Rockies and in hot temperatures. But that's no problem, because what they did was burn a bunch of sulphur sticks inside to kill off any bacteria. So, honestly, sir,your steak's fine. It hasn't made any difference to your enjoyment whatsoever, because we went to the ranch, inspected the cattle and know just how good that steak was before it was put in the sulphur-fumed truck. Bon appetit...." And with that his black jacket and bowtie turning before my very eyes into a fetching lilac and green number, he puts his jet pack into full throttle and disappears head-first through the ceiling.

Of course, such a story is entirely ridiculous. Quite obviously I have made it up. The final few paragraphs above are the stuff of Lalaland, right? The Ringside, which really is my favourite restaurant, has been a fixture in Portland since during the Second World War thanks, in no small part, to the fact they never have (and doubtless never will) present their meat contaminated with sulphur or any other undesirable element. If there is to be a raised eyebrow or pursed lip, it will be over whether the degree of red, pink or grey to the meat has met one's expectations. So far at the Ringside for me, 100% success. Ditto Barberians in Toronto and Harris's in San Francisco. Establishments all that are in the business of excellence and go out of their way to achieve and preserve it. Like making sure that the very item on which they made their name and on which their reputation depends – in these instances, steak, - are brought to their customers in the finest condition possible.

In fact, surely any company with its name and reputation to protect would do the same. Right?

Now I'm sure that you don't exactly have to be a genius to see the point I am getting to here. Because back in the early '90s, disquieted and seriously concerned, I began asking questions of distillers about the way their sherry butts were being treated in Jerez. I was told not to worry, it was a perfectly natural thing to do. Burning sulphur candles inside the butt wouldn't do any harm to the whisky. In fact, if they didn't do the spoiling of the wine residue in transit would be quite ruinous to the new spirit filled into the cask, so run along now and write about something else...

Well, the cattle – err.., I mean chickens – have come home to roost.

Because this year's Bible sees the first very slight dip in form in the general standard of malts since I began writing the thing in 2003. In fact, it is the first I have seen in about 30 years. Though I was expecting this to happen some time, it was still a bit of a jolt when it came. Because the quality of Scotch whisky available to the public in general has been rising year on year for as long as I can remember. This was partly due to the single malt revolution. Not because single malts are superior to blends – because they are not, or at least shouldn't be- but because, thanks largely to the work of independent bottlers, most notably kicked off by Cadenhead's, more and more whiskies are turning up in the glass uncoloured, unfiltered and bottled at least at 46% abv.

This has been a movement that has filtered, to some extent, into the much more conservative section of the industry run by the distillers themselves. So the quality, on average, has improved owing to the fact that there is less and less caramel around per 100 bottles sold than there once was.

I remember that many times I had to shut up shop for the day when working on the 2004 Bible because my tastebuds had been silted by colouring. No amount of washing the mouth out with San Pellegrino was going to clear the blockage. Now, for the 2008 Bible, only twice whilst tasting over 925 whiskies did I have to leave my tasting lab, confounded by caramel. But sulphur...that's another story. Over a dozen times this year it has brought my work to an unpleasant and uncompromising halt. Because after tasting that, it would have been massively unfair on the poor, probably innocent, whisky that was to follow. And let's be honest here. There is absolutely nothing vaguely attractive about sulphur in your whisky, either to nose or taste. Especially to not-even-a-single-puff-in-a-lifetime non-smokers like me.

To keep things in perspective, it must be remembered and writ very large that the vast majority of casks used in maturation are ex-bourbon. For every single time I've been assaulted by sulphur, there are many dozens when I have been seduced by the beauty and charm of other single malts. So no, it is by no means doom and gloom. and if you do get a bad bottle, you have been unlucky. The trouble is, you'll not have been as unlucky as you were last year, or the year before. In the last year I have had three tastings where one of the whiskies had been wrecked by sulphur. Two years ago there were none. So this is not a rant for a rant's sake.

There are those I know in the industry, caught between a rock and hard place, who have told me, with very little conviction it must be said, that the sulphur has minimal impact on the whisky. That the public don't mind. They often don't even notice. And, memorably, I have even been told that that the odours escaping from the glass was "good sulphur."

Well, sorry, guys. There really is no such thing as good sulphur. In an industry that prides itself and goes to enormous lengths to portray the complexity of their brands, the naturalness of their product, underlining wherever possible the honey-sweet tones, the heather and the peat, how on earth can they even begin to turn a blind eye to an odour which, let us not kid ourselves, is the closest possible relation to stink bombs and rotten eggs?

And here's some news, chaps: the public do mind. Some years back I made a film for television with the former racing champion Sir Stirling Moss. He and I drove a succession of cars around a race track looking for the sulphur reek of vehicles whose owners were far from impressed by the smelly by-product of not entirely efficient engines. One car I was in, I thought, was remarkably similar to a butt I'd stuck my head in just a couple of days before up in Speyside. The owner told me she was having constantly to explain to her passengers that she really wasn't suffering from a gastric problem.

Likewise, at tastings I am regularly told by confused whisky lovers that they have found this and that whisky "dirty" - a descriptor often used. "Sulphured", not surprisingly, is another. Most, though, can't work it out. They just know there is an unpleasant dullness there which they had not expected, and the finish, in particular, often left them feeling completely underwhelmed to the point of disillusionment. Such anecdotal evidence has piled up over the years, and many have felt relieved when I told them that it was the fault of a wayward cask (or two). It was not their tastebuds, or whisky in general. And it is not only Scotch. The same problem has been happening in Japan, where the journey from Jerez is very much longer and sulphur casking is just about compulsory.

But there is a feeling of resentment, too. If someone has forked out the best part of a hundred bucks to sit back and be entertained by a bottle from a well- known distillery, they would like to think all has been done to make that experience as enjoyable as nature allows. A sulphur moment doesn't happen that often in the average whisky drinker's life, but when it does people tend to remember.

It has to be said that one cannot but have some sympathy with the whisky industry. When the sending of full sherry butts to wine merchants ended as a practice, and all bottling was instead carried out in Spain, it meant that there were immediate problems in keeping the butts fresh before filling, especially in the warmer months. Over two decades on, the problem persists. And here I do think there is cause for concern.

The current situation stems partly from distillers being painted into a corner regarding stocks. And also, I am sad to say, some bottlers not always being able to recognise the faulty butts in the first place. I know, from first-hand experience.I have been called to a distilling company whose blender admitted he had a " bit of a blind spot" detecting them and have sorted through butts for special bottlings. I know he is not alone. There is no shame in that. However, what is baffling is how a dud butt can get right the way through the system without being detected.

So from the very top there has to be better training. Old-fashioned nosers employed, trained up to detect the toe-curling whiff of a faulty butt. And, for new wood, distillers themselves must change or at least tighten their own practices. No longer can it be left to the bodega to get the butts to the distillery as quickly as possible. With each cask costing around the £450 mark and a single shipment worth £30,000 - and the potential value of the spirit poured into them a whole lot more - surely massive steps have to be taken to make it a choreographed operation? From the emptying of the butt in Jerez, to altering the filling schedule at the distillery. Sherry butts should not have to wait their turn. They should be shipped without delay, entirely free from sulphur, and filled immediately on arrival in Scotland. And it can be done.

Indeed, the section of the world's whisky industry requiring sherry butts would do well to follow the lead set by The Macallan and Irish Distillers, both of which spotted the growing problem years back and, rather than pretending it might go away, actively did something about it. Macallan's assault on the problem has been ferocious: at any one time they have £15 million worth of butts sitting in Spain, every single one of them bespoke, and, working in conjunction with Gonzalez Byass having for 18 months to two years oloroso sitting in them. The time from emptying the butts in Jerez to filling them in Scotland is rarely more than three weeks and not an atom of sulphur is required. This is a 10 month operation, with only July and most of August, when temperatures are at their highest, being silent.

Likewise, all through the 1990s I was pretty amazed by the consistency of the Irish sherry casks. At Midleton and Bushmills I could count the number of sulphur-tainted casks on one hand, testimony to the work or Brendan Monks, who for the last quarter of a century has been among the most assiduous whisky woodsmen in the world. And I can remember only one bottling – ever – being let down by matchsticks. But even that was too much for them. Since the turn of the century they have adopted a completely sulphur-free programme of having the casks made for the bodega and then being filled for six months with white wine, before they spend a similar period with red. These wines are used to season the wood and extract the more powerful tannins before the sherry is filled. After another year they are emptied and sent to Ireland. But there is, even then, a trick played. Being a smaller operation than Macallan, the emptied butts are moved during the months of January and February, and at the very latest March, when temperatures are at their lowest. The butts are then immediately filled on arrival at the distillery.

Some Scottish distillers are also looking at these methods. To copy them would result in the industry-wide eradication of the sulphur problem within a generation. But there are those that baulk at the short- term cost of such an operation. Others tell me they cannot find friendly bodegas happy to see their sherry take on the extra degree of oakiness that is the inevitable result of such a process. However, some bodegas are starting to look into blending this heavy sherry for extra depth, so perhaps there may well be hope.

What, though, to do with the many spoiled casks already in circulation? The ones that you and I are encountering on a more regular basis these days. With stocks now at a premium as open season has dawned in China and India, the situation is likely to get worse before it gets better. Especially in the case of smaller, independent bottlers whose stocks are finite and who are struggling to find new supplies.

For these, I feel, there should be a whisky amnesty. If they find that they have sulphur-tainted butts in their portfolio, the distillers who made the malts (even those who are less than pleased that these companies are, they argue, making money on their brand name) should exchange these poor casks for age-equivalent or younger clean ones.

Distillers will cry stinking fish – or casks – and ask why should they be the guys to pay for it. Well, there are two reasons. One is that it is quite possible that it was they who filled the faulty cask in the first place before it entered the open market.

The second is that the industry is already spending vast amounts of money to protect the Scotch whisky name. Currently, for instance, the SWA is hurling hundreds of thousands of dollars at an attempt legally to thump the tiny Glenora Distillery in Nova Scotia, Canada, which happens to make whisky in an area originally colonised by Scots, and still populated by their descendants, who gave the area a title of a glen. Glenora, horror of horrors, wish to trademark their name. Rather than spending such vast sums fighting a company which has never claimed to make Scotch, would not the money be better directed at truly protecting Scotch's reputation by ring-fencing the more badly sulphur-stained casks and keeping them out of the public domain, other than being blended off in minute amounts? Just a thought.

And the independents can help themselves further by resisting the temptation to round off some older, ex-bourbon malts in sherry. More often than not those butts will have been hanging around empty longer than could possibly be good for them before being used. If you have no-one in your company with the skill and knowledge to stick their nose inside and give the butt a complete and unequivocal clean bill of health, why take the chance?

My scoring has shifted in the last year or two as truly great sherry whiskies become scarcer. But they are still out there: there are still certain recent, younger bottlings of Macallan and Glenfarclas that have the ability to bring me to my knees in appreciation. The industry can get it right. But now it is up to them to get it right every single time. Perhaps if they discuss it over a faultless steak at The Ringside the penny might finally drop that by allowing damaged goods freely to circulate the whisky shelves, albeit in relatively small numbers, it is the great name of whisky that suffers in the end.

# Review of the Whisky Year

**S**wallows like distilleries. Or perhaps don't, if the number of dead ones you can find trapped in redundant maltings is anything to go by. But although a live swallow doesn't a summer make, you certainly know that when you see the first of the year a change in climate is on its way.

And there was a similar feeling of warm expectation when I heard that, finally, Indian billionaire Vijay Mallya, owner of the UB Group, had bought **Whyte and Mackay** for a few millions in loose change short of £600 million.

It was not too difficult to predict what was coming next. The chilly relationship between Scottish distillers and the Indian government had become increasingly arctic over the previous year due to the massive protectionist import duties the New Delhi government had been slapping on foreign spirits. So hostile had the impasse become that the Scots had even successfully lobbied the European Union to make an official complaint to the World Trade Organisation. And that was already on top of a very piqued US government demanding that India justify why bourbon distillers were also being hit. Seriously heavy stuff. Whisky should be more fun than this, surely...?

While this frosty state of affairs rumbled on, the Indian whisky producers achieved the impossible by exacerbating things. They decided to up their fight to get their own style of "whisky" accepted in markets outside their native country, including Europe. Seeing as 90-odd percent of all Indian whisky isn't whisky at all but rum – on the cut and dried account of it being made from molasses or cane sugar as opposed to grain, which is something of a prerequisite – for once one could understand the hackles of the **Scotch Whisky Association** bristling with cask-strength indignation.

So when Mr Mallya finally signed on the dotted to bring the Glasgow-based distillers and blenders under his colourful wing, my mobile phone went into virtual meltdown with calls from people in the industry looking for all the goss. And seeing if I could find tickets for them to be there the day Mr Mallya attends his first SWA meeting. When a man puts his fingers in two highly charged sockets, sparks have a tendency to fly.

One of the things that had intrigued the industry – and worn to a frazzle the nerves and patience of Whyte and Mackay employees – was the time it had taken for the deal to finally go through. A constant question at the end of the line was: so why now? China was the most common theory. My own, echoed by one or two I know at the sharp end of the marketing game, was that something was about to happen with India.

That was in late May. And now, in early July, guess what? Those draconian Indian import taxes of north of 500% have just been drastically cut to 150%. Still a lot. But swingeing enough for more than one marketeer I know in the industry to rub his hands in glee and start buying extra pins for his world wall map. India now looks such a viable proposition that there is talk about Scotch whisky sales in the subcontinent going up by something close to the percentage the Scots were used to being taxed at.

Now the question is: does the swallow fly to Scotland because summer is on its way? Or is summer on its way because the swallow has turned up in Scotland? It might be some time before anyone can properly answer that one.

For among the previously beleaguered staff at Whyte and Mackay, who were not quite sure what to do next whilst the company was held in limbo but who now find themselves in the vanguard of any Scotch whisky explosion in India, there is probably little chance that anyone cares. Especially as Vivian Imerman, who sold the company, has reportedly offered to pay his former staff a bonus worth three months wages as a thank you for, first, turning their fortunes round and then hanging on in during the protracted negotiations. And a odd little footnote to this little saga, apart from the fact that many thought that Whyte and Mackay's new owner bore an uncanny resemblance to a certain whisky writer, is that the UB Group was actually founded by a Scotsman in the days of the Empire.

Strange, also, when you think about it: for over a hundred years the Scotch whisky industry has been waiting for a billion-population market to turn up. Then, all of a sudden, two arrive at once.

Just as well, then, that Diageo had earlier in the year done a 180 degree about-face from their production policy of the last 25 years – and announced their intention to build a new super malt whisky distillery in the Highlands. Shortly after the monumental plans were unveiled I happened to be with Diageo's production manager whilst judging at the International Wine and Spirit Competition. He told me so far no name had been decided upon for the new distillery. I helpfully suggested they call it Rosebank. Or Port Ellen.

No-one, though, is more excited about it all than the good old P&J, the Aberdeen-based, Morning Roll-finger-greased Press and Journal, who have dubbed the £40 million project "Scotland's first new whisky distillery for 30 years." Which means I must have been dreaming the building of the Isle of Arran Distillery. Not to mention Kininvie, Speyside, Kilchoman, Glengyle and Daftmill. I just knew Arran's sensational malt I thought I'd given an award to in this year's Bible was too good to be true...

And who knows, the sad, lonely (well, lonely amongst the housing estate that's being built around it) shell of Rosebank may not have been a bad call for a name, as the site Diageo are earmarking is at Roseisle, where they already have a maltings. And if that is not a further ironic kick in the groin of the sacred memory Port Ellen, I don't what is.

Before single malt lovers start getting too excited, it must be stressed that the principal purpose of the distillery will be to keep happy the Chinese, Russians, Indians and Brazilians who are giving up their traditional spirits in their hundreds of thousands, if not millions, in favour of blended scotch. The last big boy distillery that I remember being purpose-built to serve the blended market was Auchroisk in the 1970s, and it has done that stoically because as a single malt in its own right it is famously hopeless.

And it's not just Diageo whose offices are full of blueprints and architects' fees. William Grant have also announced plans to create a new malt distillery at their Girvan grain plant in Ayrshire. Now that may sound strangely familiar to some of you. Because, yes, Grant's have also been here before with the Ladyburn distillery which was built there in 1966 and was closed just nine years later because the spirit was, well, a bit rubbish. Some are scratching their heads and wondering why a company that goes out of its way to successfully make way above average whisky is returning to the scene of a pretty gruesome crime. Well, this time Grant's are boxing clever. Where a certain lack of planning marked the building of the old Ladyburn distillery, resulting in a spirit so light and characterless it was good to neither man nor blender, this time plans are in place to create a Lowlander like no other. In fact, their full intent is to produce a Speyside-style malt, based very much on their stunning Balvenie make. The stills are styled on those found at that classic Dufftown-based distillery's and when I say stills, I mean stills: eight of them. As I write this, in the second week in July, half are already in place. If all goes according to plan, by the end of 2007 it could be that the output of Lowland malt whisky will have been increased by truly massive proportions. And not only will there be a Speyside style, don't be surprised if some peaty malt comes from there, also. William Grant own three Scottish malt distilleries, but none producing the heavier smoky stuff they need for their blends. Or a new internationally marketed single malt, come to that. It defies belief that beautifully sweet distillery-induced peak reek won't soon be borne on the winds of Girvan. Notice I keep calling it "the distillery." Like the proposed Diageo plant, it, too, doesn't yet have a name. Staff at the company have entered a competition to come up with something suitable.

Which is not a problem on Islay if Bruichladdich get planning permission to build a second distillery, as they very much hope. They intend to bring Port Charlotte back to life after 80 years of silence, having ceased production in 1929 while distilling as the Lochindaal distillery. A few of the original buildings still remain but Bruichladdich's Jim McEwan a few years back plotted for the day when maybe a great old name could be revived. So he went and brought the stills and other vital plant from the long closed Inverleven Distillery at Dumbarton just prior to its demolition. I must admit, as someone who some 25 years ago read many hundreds of pages of the old Lochindaal's copper-plate business letters at the local library, that I never really expected to see the day Bruichladdich would be producing side-by-side with its semi-vanished neighbour. Hopefully the planning permission will be granted and, if so, it will represent easily the most romantic episode in the whisky world since the historic old **Labrot and Graham** Distillery was revived in Kentucky a dozen years ago, and more than on a par with this year's re-opening of the glorious **Kilbeggan** distillery in the midlands of Ireland.

And, nipping back to America, some outstanding news from **Lawenceburg** Indiana where **Pernod Ricard's** giant all purpose distillery has been sold to a Trinidad and Tobago concern, C L Financial. Lawrenceburg is home to Jim Murray's Whisky Bible's 2008 bourbon award winner **Cougar** and also makes some of the most perfectly balanced and intense rye in the world. As the sale was completed only a day or two ago, it is too early yet to know if whiskey production has been saved, although I understand gin production will continue under contract. The 2007 Bible lamented the announced closing of this great, if little-known, distillery and the fact any distilling will be carried out there offers hope where before there was little. It may be that CL Financial has spotted one very good reason for owning a whisky distillery right now and one as enormous as Lawrenceburg: a worldwide shortage of the stuff.

And not only whisky, but grain and other materials required to make the whisky have also been in limited supply. Bean counters in Scotland have been breaking out in cold sweats over the increased prices bourbon casks now command. In the wake of the great whisky rush, demand is now beginning to seriously outstrip supply. Meanwhile, the rye situation facing Kentucky and Canada continues to be less than great with distillers having only a finite amount of high quality grain available to them. But in Scotland the situation has been less than satisfactory for years, with maltings – including those further south in England - working at full capacity and often unable to meet demand of the peated variety. Part of the problem has been lack of capacity, with three famous old maltings having closed in recent years. The other is that farmers have not been too turned on by the prices offered for malting barley and been using their fields to yield more cash-friendly crops. However, Simpsons have decided to go some way towards redressing the balance by upping their capacity at their Berwick-on-Tweed maltings by nearly 30%, at a cost of some £12 million.

Hopefully their malt will be able to feed other planned distilleries: one on their doorstep on the Scottish side of the border and another up in Huntley where Euan Shand of **Duncan Taylor** hopes to at last own a distillery – by building his own (or rather converting a creamery into one) – after his several year-long search for a distillery to buy proved fruitless. And with the way distillers are now clinging on to them for dear life he doubtless concluded that his search would not get any easier.

So, busy times in the whisky industry and especially Scotland. But amid all the hard-nosed businessing there have been sad and funny moments, too. Sad: in Dublin, **Irish Distillers** are boxing up their belongings as I write this for their move next week away from their famous old **Jameson** distillery headquarters to offices new. The visitor's centre shall, thankfully, remain. With **Green Spot** owners, Mitchell's, moving from their centuries-old home Kildare Street, a visit to the once great old distilling city really will never quite be the same again.

But laughs, too. Not least when **Glenfiddich** issued hip flasks to commemorate Robbie Burns' birthday. Sadly, or wonderfully, some of the flasks came back with the inscription of "Rdbert Bums." The ensuing apology from the company to anyone who received one would have been completely wasted: it is hard not to believe that the few that got into the public domain will soon be changing hands for the kind of money one normally associates with the distillery's 50-year-old malt.

However, quote of the year has to fall to Bob Scott of **Glenora** Distillers who, after their landmark David and Goliath victory over the SWA in the Canadian courts to protect their Glen Breton brand reacted to news that the Scottish lobbyists would be coming back for a re-match by saying: "We were hoping that the SWA may not appeal and would meet with us, have a chat, shake hands and say congratulations."

Having known Bob for a very long time, and the SWA even longer, I can tell you that he would have said that heartfelt and without the slightest trace of irony. Perhaps if he traces his ancestry far enough back he will find he is descended from Canute. Priceless.

# Jim Murray's Whisky Bible Award Winners 2008

**O**n the face of it, it looks as though I've come over all peaty. Smoke has not only got in my eyes, but also my nose..

Well, not really. Yes, having banged the gong louder and longer than most people living I suppose I could be, as one BBC presenter once introduced me: "the great grand-daddy of peaty whisky. " Thanks. And that was even before my beard went as completely white as it is today. But, in truth, the Islays had not been Hoovering up the awards in my previous Bibles like some might have expected...or predicted. That is because I judge all whiskies entirely, and strictly, on merit. And as wonderful as some Islays have been, there have been better bourbons and blends around to take the honours.

Until now. When the Ardbeg 10-year-old has come of age....or, rather, hasn't. Huh! I hear some conspiracy theorists snort: you would say that as you were the guy who actually created it when it came back on the market. Vested interest, buddy!

Well, sorry to disappoint you... The Ardbeg 10 I worked on (as a consultant and a long time ago) was malt of that exact age, and not in the same league as the present bottling. When Bill Lumsden of Glenmorangie paid his first visit to my tasting rooms a few days back I asked him: "What the hell has happened to Ardbeg 10? It has gone up a couple of extra gears. This is now supernova stuff." And he reminded me that ten years ago (1996 to late 1997) no whisky was being made at Ardbeg. So the malts being used are nearer 16 and 17 years old.

Which helps explain why it has picked up the Whisky of the Year award. But, equally, I am giving the award for the 12 Years and Under Single Malt category to a more apposite cause, if you see my logic.

To me, Ardbeg is - and always has been - the most complex malt on earth. Had the Bible been around a decade ago – and especially 20 years ago – it would have pinned to Ardbeg's proud chest a clutch of Bible awards. Not least for the brain-exploding 1974 distillate bottlings. But lack of stock and changing style as the stills thinned and the peat source altered meant it was always prone to be picked off by other ultra whiskies. Which is what happened. Until now. Mind you, one sobering thought is that this 10 year-old, deserving JMWB2008 Whisky of Year winner, is fully eclipsed by the same titled malt from 25 years ago. I know: I have just tasted the two side by side...

And the other five whiskies in the taste off? Two more of them well peated: the extraordinary Lapbeg vatted malt from my old mates at Mac Y in Denmark (whose previous foray into whisky is the pretty awful Cu Dhub) and the quite brilliant Ileach. Also in there was a pretty smoky and perfectly honeyed Highland Park from the SMWS and a dream of a peat-less Glencadam courtesy of Douglas Laing. And, of course the massive George T Stagg, which is back as top dog amongst the bourbons. Top cat, by the way, is Cougar, the 37% bottling for Australia which will doubtless make a few bourbon purists twitch at this Indiana upstart.

It appears, though, that 2008 was destined to be The Year of the Smoke in the Whisky Bible.!

# Award Winners

**2008 World Whisky of the Year**
**Ardbeg 10 Years Old**
2008 World Whisky of the Year Runner Up
**The Ileach Single Islay Malt Cask Strength**
Scotch Single Malt of the Year
**Ardbeg 10 Years Old**
Best New Scotch Whisky of the Year (single cask)
**Scotch Malt Whisky Society Cask 4.115**
Best New Scotch Whisky of the Year (multiple casks)
**Glenfarclas – The Family Casks 1952 - 1994**
Best Single Malt of the Year 12 Years and Under
**The Arran Malt Amarone Finish**
Best Single Malt of the Year 13 to 21 Years
**Scotch Malt Whisky Society Cask 4.115**
Best Single Malt of the Year 22 to 39 Years
**Old Malt Cask Port Ellen 23 Years Old**
Best Single Malt of the Year 40 Years and Over
**Glenfarclas – The Family Casks 1960 Cask No 1767**
Scotch Vatted Malt of the Year
**Mac Y Lapbeg Aged 8 Years**
Scotch Blended Whisky of the Year
**Old Parr Superior 18 Years Old**
Scotch Blended Whisky of the Year (8-12 Years)
**White Horse Aged 12 Years**
Scotch Blended Whisky of the Year (Over 12 Years)
**Old Parr Superior 18 Years Old**
Scotch Premium Blended Whisky of the Year (No age statement)
**Dewar's Signature**
Scotch Standard Blended Whisky of the Year (No age statement)
**William Grant's Family Reserve**
Best New Scotch Blended Whisky
**Black Grouse**
Scotch Grain Whisky of The Year
**Duncan Taylor Port Dundas 1973**
Bourbon of the Year & Best Bourbon Aged Over 13 Years
**George T Stagg 70.3%**
Best Bourbon Aged Under 10 Years
**Cougar Aged 5 Years**
Best Bourbon Aged 10-12 Years
**Elijah Craig 12**
Rye Whiskey of the Year
**Old Potrero Hotaling's Whiskey Aged 12 Years Essay MCMVI - MMVII**
Rye Whiskey of the Year Aged 10 Years or Under
**Jim Beam Yellow Label**
Irish Whiskey of the Year
**The Tyrconnell Aged 10 Years Madeira Finish**
Japanese Whisky of the Year
**Hanyu King of Diamonds**
Japanese Single Malt of the Year
**Hanyu King of Diamonds**
Japanese Blended Whisky of the Year
**Tsuru Aged 17 Years**
Japanese Blended Whisky of the Year (No Age Statement)
**Kakubin**
Canadian Whisky of the Year
**Alberta Premium 25 Years Old**
Best Small Batch Distillery Whisky of the Year
**Old Potrero Hotaling's Whiskey Aged 12 Years Essay MCMVI – MMVII**
European Mainland Whisky of the Year
**Mackmyra Privus 03 Svensk Single Malt Whisky**

# The Rankings (97-94)

## 97

**Scotch Single Malts**
Ardbeg 10 Years Old
Ardbeg Ping No 1 Single Cask
Old Malt Cask Ardbeg 1975 Aged 25 Years
Brora 30 Years Old
Scotch Malt Whisky Society Cask 4.115
Aged 20 Years (Highland Park)
Whisky-Doris Strathisla Aged 35 Years
**Unspecified Single Malts (Islay)**
The Ileach Single Islay Malt Cask Strength
**Blended Scotch**
Old Parr Superior 18 Years Old
**Bourbon**
George T Stagg (64.5%)
George T Stagg (68.8%)
George T Stagg Spring 2005 Release

## 96

**Scotch Single Malt**
Connoisseurs Choice Aberfeldy 1989
Ardbeg 1976 Single Cask No. 2390
Ardbeg 1977
Ardbeg Kildalton 1980
Ardbeg Provenance 1974
Ardbeg Young Uigeadail
Scotch Malt Whisky Society Cask No. 66.16
The BenRiach 1984 Ltd Release Cask Bott
Norse Cask Sn Bowmore 1993 Aged 11 Ys
Queen of the Moorlands Rare Cask
Bowmore 1991 Edition XVIII
Brora 30 Years Old
Port Charlotte 4 Years Old
Member's Legacy C'donich 1967 Agd 36 ys
Platinum Clynelish 23 Years Old
Glenfarclas 1954 Aged 46 Years
Glenmorangie Truffle Oak
Glen Moray 1986 Commemorative Bottling
Cadenhead's Authentic Collection
Glenrothes Aged 16 Years
Highland Park 25 Years Old
The Arran Malt Amarone Finish
Isle of Jura Aged 36 Years
Duncan Taylor Longmorn 1978 Agd 25 Ys
Murray McDavid Mission Macallan 1985
Aged 21 Years
Parkers Whisky Port Ellen 1982 iPert
mELLoni Bottling
The Whisky Fair Springbank Aged 35 Years
The Bottlers Teaninich 1982 Aged 21 Years
Tullibardine 1966 World Cup Edition
**Scotch Vatted Malt**
Serendipity
**Single Grain Scotch**
Duncan Taylor Collection Port Dundas 1973
**Blended Scotch**

Ballantine's 17 Years Old
Johnnie Walker Gold Label The Centenary
Blend 18 Years Old
William Lawson's Founder's Reserve Aged
18 Years
**Irish Single Malt**
Bushmills Rare Aged 21
**American Single Malt**
McCarthy's Aged 3 Years
**Bourbon**
Buffalo Trace Experimental Collection Twice
Barrelled
Elijah Craig 12 Years Old
Evan Williams 12 Years
George T. Stagg (70.3%)
Wild Turkey Russell's Reserve Aged 10
Years 101 Proof
**Single Malt Rye**
Old Potrero Single Malt Hotaling's Whiskey
Aged 11 Years Essay MCMVI-MMVI
Old Potrero Single Malt Hotaling's Whiskey
Aged 12 Years Essay MCMVIMMVII
**Straight Rye**
Rittenhouse 21 Years Old Barrel no.28
Sazerac Rye 18 Years Old Rye
**Japanese Single Malt**
The Cask of Hakushu 1989
King of Diamonds 1988
Yoichi 12 Years Old 70th Anniversary
**Swedish Single Malt**
Mackmyra Privus 03 R'kning TillÅten

## 95

**Scotch Single Malts**
Aberlour a'bunadh Batch No. 8
Aberlour a'bunadh Batch No. 19
Ardbeg 1965
Ardbeg 1974 Single Cask No. 2751
Ardbeg Airigh Nam Beist Limited Rel 1990
Ardbeg Mor
Cadenhead's Authentic Collection Ardbeg
Aged 11 Years
Cadenhead's Ardbeg Aged 12 Years
Cadenhead's Authentic Collection Ardbeg
Aged 13 Years 1993
Old Malt Cask Ardbeg 12 Years Old
The Clydesdale Aultmore 17 Years Old
The Single Malts of Scotland Aultmore
1990 Aged 16 Years
Cadenhead's Authentic Collection Balvenie
- Glenlivet Aged 25 Years
The BenRiach Curiositas Aged 10 Years
Single Peated Malt
Benriach Peated Authenticus Peated Malt
Aged 21 Years
The BenRiach Fine Wood Finishes Age

Over 15 Years Henriques Madeira Barrel
The BenRiach 1975 Limited Release Cask
Bottling
Duncan Taylor Collection Bowmore 1966
Chieftain's Brora 24 Years Old
Old & Rare Brora Aged 30 Years
Bruichladdich "Islands" Aged 20 Years
Third Edition
Port Charlotte Evolution PC5 Cask Strength
Cheftain's Caol Ila 1993 Aged 13 Years
Manzanilla Finish
Dun Bheagan Caol Ila Aged 14 Years
Old Malt Cask Caol Ila 25 Years Old
Member's Legacy Caperdonich 1967 Aged
36 Years
Mackillop's Choice Clynelish 1989
Murray McDavid Clynelish 1994 Aged 11 Ys
Old Malt Cask Clynelish Aged Over 13 Years
The Whisky Fair Clynelish Aged 32 Years
Duncan Taylor Collection Dallas Dhu 1981
The Dalmore 62 Years Old
Dalwhinnie 15 Years Old
Gordon & MacPhail Reserve Glencadam 74
Old Malt Cask Glencadam Aged 21 Years
Glendronach Aged 33 Years
Glenfarclas 15 Years Old
Glenfarclas 1960 The Family Casks
Glenfarclas 1966 The Family Casks
Glenfarclas 1994 The Family Casks
Whisky Fair Single Speyside Malt Aged 40
Glenfiddich 15 Years Old
Glenglassaugh 1973 Family Silver
Dewar Rattray Individual Cask Bottling Glen
Grant 1985 Aged 19 Years
Duncan Taylor Collection Glen Grant 1970
Duncan Taylor Special Selection No 2 Glen
Grant 1970
Glenmorangie Artisan Cask
Scotch Malt Whisky Society Cask 125.1
Glen Ord 25 Years Old
The Glenrothes 1979 Single Cask No. 3808
The Glenrothes 1979
Highland Park Aged 18 Years
The Clydesdale Highland Park 13 Years Old
Dewar Rattray Individual Cask Bottling
Highland Park 1981 Aged 24 Years
Murray McDavid Highland Park 1989
Mac Y 10th Anni Isle of Arran Agd 10 Years
Lagavulin Aged 16 Years
The Whisky Fair 'Vanilla Sky' Aged 13 Years
Laphroaig 1/4 Cask
Cadenhead's Authentic Collection
Laphroaig Aged 13 Years
Scotch Malt Whisky Society Cask 29.57
C'heads's Authentic Cn Lochside Agd 23 yrs
The Queen of the Moorlands Rare Cask
Longmorn 12 Years Old
Macallan 18 Years Old
The Macallan 1949 (53 Years Old)

The Macallan 1970 (32 Years Old)
The Macallan Fine Oak 15 Years Old
Cadenhead's Authentic Collection
Macallan-Glenlivet Aged 16 Years
Duncan Taylor Collection Macallan 1987
Scott's Selection Macallan 1985
Cadenhead's Authentic Collection
Mannochmore Aged 14 Years
Port Ellen 4th Release Aged 25 Years
Old Malt Cask Port Ellen Aged 23 Years
Old Malt Cask Port Ellen 25 Years Old
Rosebank Aged 12 Years
Cask Strength Rosebank 1990
Longrow 10 Years Old 1994
Coopers Choice Strathisla 1969 Aged 36
Years Single Cask Range
Talisker Aged 20 Years
Talisker 25 Years Old
Secret Stills Isle of Skye 1955
Chieftain's Ledaig 1973 Aged 32 Years
Tullibardine 1986 John Black Selection

**Unspecified Single Malts (Islay)**
Auld Reekie Islay Malt

**Scotch Vatted Malts**
Lapbeg 75/25 Aged 8 Years Pure Peated
Islay Malt Scotch Whisky
Wild Scotsman Aged 15 Years Vatted Malt

**Blended Scotch**
Antiquary 21 Years Old
Dewar's Signature
The Famous Grouse Scottish Oak Finish
The Royal & Ancient 28 Years
Royal Salute 50 Years Old
William Grant's 25 Years Old

**Irish Pure Pot Still**
Midleton 1973 Pure Pot Still

**Irish Single Malt**
The Tyrconnell Aged 10 Ys Madeira Finish
Bushmills Select Casks Aged 12 Years
Knappogue Castle 1994
American Single Malt
McCarthy's Oregon Single Malt Agd 3 Years

**Bourbon**
Cougar Bourbon Aged 5 Years
Daniel Stewart Aged 12 Years
Evan Williams 15 Years
Old Bardstown Aged 10 Ys Estate Bottled
Old Rip Van Winkle 15 Years Old
Wild Turkey Rare Breed
Woodford Reserve Master's Cn Four Grain

**Straight Rye**
Cougar Rye
Rittenhouse 21 Years Old Barrel no. 8
Sazerac 6 Years Old

**Canadian**
Alberta Premium
Alberta Premium 25 Years Old
Crown Royal Limited Edition

### Japanese Single Malt

The Hakushu Single Malt Whisky Aged 15
Years Cask Strength
Hakushu 1984
Yoichi Key Malt Agd 12 Ys "Peaty & Salty"
Yoichi 20 Years Old
Yoichi Nikka Single Cask Malt Whisky 1991
Japanese Vatted Malt
Pure Malt Black

### Japanese Single Grain

Nikka Single Cask Coffey Grain 1992

### Japanese Blended

Royal Aged 15 Years

### Swedish Single Malt

Mackmyra Preludium 03 Svensk Single
Malt Whisky

### Welsh Single Malt

Penderyn Welsh Rugby Union 125th
Anniversary Edition

### Australian Single Malt

Sullivans Cove Single Malt Whisky 6 YO

## 94

### Scotch Single Malts

Aberlour aíbunadh Batch 14
Aberlour W'house No. 1 HF Cask no. 1296
Aberlour W'house No. 1 HF Sh. Csk  6524
Ardbeg 1974 Single Cask No. 2743
Ardbeg 1974 Single Cask No. 2749
Ardbeg 1975 Single Cask No. 4720
C'headís Authentic Cn Ardbeg Aged 11 Yrs
Connoisseurs Choice Ardbeg 1976
Old Malt Cask Ardbeg Aged 14 Years
Platinum Old and Rare Cask Ardbeg 29 Ys
The Whisky Fair Ardbeg Aged 15 Years
Ardmore 100th Anniversary 12 Years Old
Distillery Malt Ardmore 1991
Provenance Ardmore Aged 12 Years
Cadenhead's Authentic Cn Balblair Aged 16
The Balvenie Roasted Malt Aged 14 Years
The Balvenie Merry Christmas 2005
The Single Malts of Scotland Benriach 1984
Harris Whisky Co. Benrinnes Aged 13 Years
Benromach 1968
Benromach Cask Strength 1980
Bladnoch Aged 10 Years
Chieftaní Bladnoch Aged 14 Years Rum Fin
Bowmore 30 Years Old
Bowmore Dawn
Cadenhead's Authentic Cn Bowmore 1992
Murray McDavid Bowmore 1998 Aged 8
Cadenhead's Authentic Collection The
Braes of Glenlivet Aged 17 Years
Lombard's Jewels of Scotland Brora 1982
Bruichladdich XVII Year Old
Bruichladdich 1989
Bruichladdich Infinity
Bruichladdich Infinity Second Edition
Old Malt Cask Rosebank 23 Years Old

Bruichladdich Links "Turnberry 10th Ltd Edn
Port Charlotte First Cut
Berryís' Own Sn B'laddich 1991 Aged 15 Ys
Cadenheadís Authentic Collection
Bruichladdich Aged 18 Years
Duncan Taylor Cn B'laddich 1966 Agd 39 ys
The Queen of the Moorlands Rare Cask
Bruichladdich 1991 "The Anniversary Bot"
Bunna' 1971 Aged 35 Years 125th Anni
Berryís' Own Selection Caol Ila 1996 Agd 10
Cadenhead's Authentic Cn Caol Ila Aged 15
Old Masters Caol Ila Aged 25 Years
Private Cn Caol Ila Vintage Rum Finish 1990
Scotch Malt Whisky Society Cask 53.105
Duncan Taylor Collection Caperdonich 1972
Scotch Malt Whisky Society Cask 26.50
Cragganmore 17 Years Old
Duncan Taylor Cn Dallas Dhu 1975 Aged 29
Duncan Taylor Cn Dallas Dhu 1981 Aged 14
Cadenheadís Authentic Collection Glen
Elgin-Glenlivet Aged 13 Years
Glenfarclas 1954 The Family Casks
Glenfarclas 1970 The Family Casks
Glenfarclas 1990 The Family Casks
Glenfiddich 1937
Glenfiddich 1973 Vintage
The Spirit Safe & Cask Glen Garioch 1988
Glengoyne Vintage Scottish Oak Finish 1973
Cadenheadís Authentic Collection Glen
Grant-Glenlivet Aged 16 Years
The Glenlivet Nadurra 16 Years old
John Milroy Sn Glenlivet 1975 Aged 30 Years
The Queen of the Moorlands Rare Cask
Glenlivet 30 Years Old "The Chairmanís
Bottling" Edition XVI
Scott's Selection Glenlivet 1977
Glenkeir Treasures Glen Mhor 30 Years Old
Glenmorangie 10 Years Old
Glenmorangie Golden Rum Cask Finish
Glenmorangie Nectar D'or
Glen Moray 1962 Very Rare Vintage Ad 42 Y
Glen Moray 1991 Mountain Oak Malt The
Final Release
Glen Moray Mountain Oak
The Glenrothes 1974
Glenrothes 1979 Single Cask
Old Masters Glenrothes 1988 Aged 17 Years
Duncan Taylor Collection Glenugie 1981
Rare Old Glenugie 1968
Highland Park 1967 Single Cask
Cask Strength Highland Park 1994
Gordon & MacPhail Cask Strength HP 1991
The Dormant Distillery Co Imperial 29 yo
C'head's Dumbarton (Inverleven Stills) 18 Y
The Arran Malt Single Sherry Cask
Cadenhead's Authentic Cn Arran Aged 11
Kilchoman New Spirit
Knockdhu 23 Years Old
Laphroaig Vintage 1989 Aged 17 Years

Laphroaig Aged 30 Years
Laphroaig Aged 40 Years
Premier Barrel Laphroaig 7 Years Old
Murray McDavid Mission Linkwood 1983
Croftengea Heavily Peated Cask No.1
Distillery Select
Old Malt Cask Lochside Aged 14 Years
Norse Cask Sn Longmorn 1990 Aged 15 ys
Macallan 10 Years Old Cask Strength
The Macallan 1989
The Macallan Cask Strength
The Macallan Easter Elchies Seasonal Cask
Selection Winter Choice 14 Years Old
The Macallan Fine Oak 25 Years Old
Cadenhead's Authentic Collection
Macallan-Glenlivet Aged 17 Years
Duncan Taylor Collection Macallan 1969
Duncan Taylor Collection Macallan 1986
G&M Speymalt Macallan 1938
Platinum Sn Macallan 26 YO Rum Fin
Harris Whisky Co. Macduff Aged 14 Years
Port Ellen 27 Years Old
Dun Bheagan Port Ellen 23 Years Old
Provenance Port Ellen 21 Years Old
The Whisky Fair Port Ellen Aged 25 Years
Provenance Lochnagar 12 Years Old
Duncan Taylor Collection Scapa 1977
Chieftain's Springbank Aged 31 Years
Strathisla Distillery Edition 15 Years Old
Cadenhead's Authentic Collection
Strathisla-Glenlivet Aged 18 Years
Cask Strength Strathisla 1985
Dewar Rattray Individual Cask Bottling
Strathmill 1989 Aged 15 Years
Talisker Aged 18 Years
Talisker 25 Years Old
Old Malt Cask Tactical Aged 18 Years
Blackadder Raw Cask Ledaig 13 Year Old
Murray McDavid Tomintoul 1973 Mission IV
Tullibardine 1993 Sherry Wood Finish
**Unspecified Single Malts (Islay)**
The Ileach Peaty Islay Single Malt
**Scottish Vatted Malts**
Clan Denny
Compass Box Oak Cross
Compass Box The Spice Tree
The Famous Grouse 30 Years Old Malt
**Single Grain Scotch**
Duncan Taylor Cameronbridge 1979
Chieftain's Carsebridge 42 Years Old
**Blended Scotch**
Ballantine's Original Character
Black Grouse
Chivas Brothers Oldest and Finest
Duncan Taylor Collection Rarest of the Rare
Deluxe Blend 33 Years Old
Isle of Skye 8 Years Old
Tanner's Peaty Creag Aged 8 Years
White Horse Aged 12 Years

William Grant's Family Reserve
**Irish Pure Pot Still**
Redbreast 15 Years Old
**Irish Single Malt**
Connemara Cask Strength
C'head's World Whiskies Cooley Aged 15
Knappogue Castle 1992
**Irish Blended**
Jameson 1780 Matured 12 Years
Jameson Gold
**Bourbon**
Buffalo Trace
C'head's World Whisky Heaven Hill Aged 10
Eagle Rare Single Barrel Bourbon 10 Years
Evan Williams Vintage 1995 Single Barrel
George T. Stagg
Jefferson's Reserve 15 Year Old
Old Forester B'day Bourbon Dist Spring '93
Old Forester Birthday Bourbon 1995
Old Taylor Aged 6 Years
Virgin Bourbon 15 Years Old 101 Proof
**Single Malt Rye**
Old Potrero Single Malt Straight Rye
Whiskey Essay 10-SRW-ARM-E
**Straight Rye**
Rittenhouse 21 Years Old Barrel no.14
Rittenhouse 21 Years Old Barrel no.21
Rittenhouse 21 Years Old Barrel no.23
Rittenhouse 21 Years Old Barrel no.27
Sazerac Kentucky Straight Rye 18 Years Old
**Japanese Single Malt**
Suntory Pure Malt Hakushu Aged 20 Years
Karuizawa 1979 Aged 24 Years
Karuizawa 1986 Aged 17 Years
Shirakawa 32 Years Old Single Malt
The Yamazaki Single Malt Whisky Aged 15
Years Cask Strength
Yoichi 15 Years Old
Nikka Whisky Yoichi 1986 20 Years Old
**Japanese Blended**
Nikka Master Blend Blended Whisky 12
Years Old 70th Anniversary
Nikka Whisky Tsuru Aged 17 Years
Special Reserve 10 Years Old
**Austrian Oat Whisky**
Waldviertler Hafer Whisky 2000
**French Single Malt**
Taol Esa 1999
**Swedish Single Malt**
Mackmyra Privus 02 N‰osa F?r Sprit
**Swiss Malt Whisky**
Swissky Exklusiv Abf,llung
Zurcher Single Lakeland Malt Whisky 3 yo
**Australian Malt Whisky**
Bakery Hill Classic Malt Cask Strength
Bakery Hill Peated Malt Cask Strength
**Indian Single Malt**
Amrut Cask Strength
Stillman's Dram Single Malt Whisky Ltd Ed

# Scottish Malts

**F**or those of you deciding to take the plunge and head off into the labyrinthine world of Scotch malt whisky, a piece of advice. And that is, be careful who you take your advice from. Because, too often, I hear that you should leave the Islays until you have tackled the featherlight Speysiders and the bolder, weightier Highlanders. This is just complete, patronising nonsense. The only time that rings true is if you are tasting a number of whiskies in one day. Then leave the smoky ones to last, so the lighter chaps get a fair hearing.

I know many people who didn't like whisky until they got a Talisker from Skye inside them, or a Lagavulin to swamp their tastebuds with oily iodine. The fact is, you can take your map of malt whisky, start at any point and head in any direction you feel. There are no hard and fast rules. Certainly with over 2,000 tasting notes for Scottish malts here you should have some help in picking where this journey of a lifetime begins.

It is also worth remembering not to be seduced by age. It is true that some of the highest scores are given to big-aged whiskies. But they are the exception rather than the rule: the truth is that the majority of malts, once they have lived beyond 20 years or so, suffer from oak influence rather than benefit. Part of the fun of discovering whiskies is to see how malts from different distilleries to perform to age and type of cask. Happy discovering.

ORKNEY ISLANDS

Highland Park
Scapa

Pultney

Clynelish
Brora

Balblair
Glenmorangie
Dalmore
Teaninich
*Invergordon*
Glen Ord
Royal Brackla
Inverness
Tomatin
Glen Albyn
Glen Mhor
Millburn
Speyside Distillery

Glenglassaugh
Banff
Macduff

Knockdhu

Glendronach
Ardmore

Speyside see page 24

Glen Garioch

Royal Lochnagar
Aberdeen

Dalwhinnie
Glenury Royal
Fettercairn

Ben Nevis
Fort William
Glenlochy
Blair Athol
Edradour
Aberfeldy

Glencadam
North Port
Lochside
Glenesk

Dundee

Glenturret
Perth
Daftmill
Tullibardine
*Cameronbridge*
Deanston

Loch Lomond
*Dumbarton*
Inverleven
Littlemill
Auchentoshan
Glengoyne
Rosebank
St. Magdelene
Glasgow
*Strathclyde*
*Port Dundas*
Edinburgh
*North British*
Glenkinchie

Girvan
Ladyburn

Bladnoch

### Key

- ● **Major Town or City**
- ⌂ Single Malt Distillery
- ⌂ (*Italics*) Grain Distillery
- † Dead Distillery

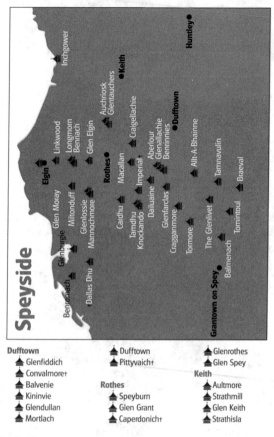

**Speyside**

**Dufftown**
- Glenfiddich
- Convalmore†
- Balvenie
- Kininvie
- Glendullan
- Mortlach

- Dufftown
- Pittyvaich†

**Rothes**
- Speyburn
- Glen Grant
- Caperdonich†

- Glenrothes
- Glen Spey

**Keith**
- Aultmore
- Strathmill
- Glen Keith
- Strathisla

## Single Malts
### ABERFELDY
**Highlands (Perthshire), 1898. John Dewar & Sons. Working.**

Aberfeldy Aged 12 Years db **(90) n**22 softly honied, rich and clean; **t**23 lighter in body than the nose suggests, a prick of first smoke, then spice, but the honey develops; **f**23 pretty long with developing vanilla and soft oils and very late, more intense and slightly burned honey; **b**22 I have long loved this malt and it shows to good effect here although I'm not sure if the strength does it any favours, though as distillery bottlings go at 40%, this has now become super-league stuff. **40%** ☉ ☉

Aberfeldy Aged 21 Years db **(86) n**24 **t**22 **f**19 **b**21. Never quite lives up to the blood orange and vaguely smoky nose. **40%**

Aberfeldy Aged 25 Years db **(85) n**24 **t**21 **f**19 **b**21. Just doesn't live up to the nose. When Tommy Dewar wrote, "We have a great regard for old age when it is bottled," as quoted on the label, I'm not sure he had as many as 25 years in mind. **40%**. *150 bottles to mark opening of Dewar's World of Whisky.*

Connoisseurs Choice Aberfeldy 1988 **(83) n**20 **t**22 **f**20 **b**21. Attractively nutty with a big digestive biscuit, mildly salty kick and dry finale. **43%.**

⋰ **Connoisseurs Choice Aberfeldy 1989 (96) n**24 breathtaking: an amalgam of feisty and laid-back barley with a sub-strata of something much more fruity. Wonderful balance; **t**24 again the barley is dual-edged and takes the lead with a ripe sultana and apples follow through; juicy and showing a very healthy sweetness and a slow gathering of delicate spice; **f24** a mildly coppery, estery lushness fuses kindly with the vanilla; long, not even a hint of tiredness and effortlessly elegant; **b24** the nose captures vividly the essence of this outstanding distillery and what follows very much continues in the same vein. A genuine must-have cracker from G&M and probably the best independent Aberfeldy bottling of all time. Long have I been waiting for a bottling to crack this outstanding distillery – and this one's done it with aplomb. One of the bottlings of the year. **43%.** *Gordon & MacPhail.*

**Connoisseurs Choice Aberfeldy 1991** bott 13/06/06 **(91) n**23 seaweedy, but without any tangible peat; **t**23 mouthwatering yet, like the nose, displaying the most extraordinary and inexplicable coastal tendencies; **f**22 the saltiness continues though some wonderful barley does re-emerge for a sweetish finish; **b**23 Aberfeldy is one of those distilleries just screaming to be discovered. Surprisingly few great casks get out there, but here is one. Though its impersonation of an old school Bunnahabhain is as impressive as it is bizarre. **46%.** *Gordon & MacPhail, US Market.*

⋰ **Kingsbury's "The Selection" Aberfeldy 1999** Hogshead cask nos. 301662/301663, dist Feb 99, bott July 06 **(88) n**22 young barley, lively, enticing; **t**22 intense, pepperminty barley; **f**22 soft oils drag out the grassiness; **b**22 refreshing and highly entertaining. **43%. ncf.** *Japan Imports System. 911 bottles.*

# ABERLOUR
## Speyside, 1826. Chivas Bros. Working.

**Aberlour 10 Years Old** db **(87) n**22 different nose to how it's been for the last decade: much more grapey-style fruit and lavender to the trademark mint: genuinely deep and brooding with a soft marzipan sweetness; **t**22 dry in parts with the oak really hitting home; the spread of delicate honey is teasing; **f**21 toffee and spice; **b**22 big stuff: a whole lot older than ten years. **43%**

**Aberlour a'bunadh Batch No. 7** db **(87) n**23 **t**20 **f**23 **b**21. Can you have too much of a good thing? Possibly. The intensity of this sherry cask is almost unbearable, but it has to be said that the cask itself is faultless and of rare quality. In some ways, it is too good... **59.9%. ncf.**

**Aberlour a'bunadh Batch No. 8** db **(95) n**23 it's the old honeycomb and teasing spices one-two. Irresistible; **t**24 stunningly intense malty shockwaves are met by seismic sherry. Imagine the results: better still, taste them...; **f**24 beautifully nutty with hints of praline and marzipan: lasts seemingly forever; **b**24 another a'bunadh that sends this distillery into the stratosphere. The best I've encountered yet. **60.2%**

**Aberlour a'bunadh Batch 13** db **(88) n**23 **t**23 **f**21 **b**22. The dull-ish finish apart, this is sheer entertainment and one for late, cold nights. **59.8%**

**Aberlour a'bunadh Batch 14** db **(94) n**23 slightly earthy but the grape is genuinely clean, intense and spicy; **t**25 truly glorious, actually quite perfect, delivery of balance between the unimpeachable grape and malt concentrate that gathers on the palate and bores into the tastebuds like a tornado into a Midwest town. One of the great moments of Speyside whisky drinking; **f**22 relatively short, but the shock waves continue amid some toffee; **b**24 it would be easy to pass this off as just another whisky from first time of trying, probably because of the relative ordinariness of the finish. But instinct should tell you to try again and watch. Try and find if there is a fault in the quality of the distillate or cask; find a winner between bitter and sweet. You will be amazed! **59.5%**

**Aberlour A'bunadh Batch 15** db **(84) n**20 **t**20 **f**23 **b**21. A rogue lightly sulphured cask has taken the edge of this one. A shame. No: bloody annoying!! **59.6%. ncf.**

**Aberlour a'bunadh Batch 16** db **(87) n**21 I don't believe it: sulphur again. Someone is becoming a bit careless here. Fortunately, the blinding brilliance of some of the other sherry butts have helped limit the damage; **t**23 the intense kumquat/orange tang to the sherry-trifle grape is pure joy and helps take the mind off the furry-interference of that single sulphur cask. Chewy...and so could have been a champion; **f**22 the odd, telling off-note remains but you can't entirely suppress the fruit; **b**21 for this to happen once is bad for a world-great dram. Twice in a row is close to being the stuff of nightmares. The real shame is that this could so easily have been 2007 Whisky Bible Whisky of the Year, because some of the other casks still bear the hallmark of greatness...I could weep. **59.6%. ncf.**

···:·· **Aberlour a'bunadh Batch No. 17** db **(88) n**22 enough thick oloroso on the nose here to make for a shortage in Jerez: the distant rumble of spice, like thunder in the air, is the one thing to edge this away from being too one-dimensional; **t**23 almost immediately those stormclouds break and spices rain down on the tastebuds in torrents; first though the sherry gathers in further clean intensity; **f**21 a fluffy, chalky finish – perhaps through a slight blemish – with grape lingering and some late toffee apple; **b**22 if you don't like sherried whiskies, give this one a miss. **60.2%**

···:·· **Aberlour a'bunadh Batch No. 19** db **(95) n**24 de rigueur big sherry but of exemplary clean-ness of butt, entirely blemish free and showing just enough lightness of touch for some barley and a bourbon-esque honeycomb to pass through the juicy grape. Exceptional... **t**24 sublime spices launch themselves on defenceless tastebuds tattooing oloroso indelibly into them; some background honeycomb represents the oak; **f**23 long, chewy, some lovely natural toffees to go with the grape and general slightly overcooked fruitcake effect; **b**24 it is a sherried malt such as this that makes my daily encounter with sulphur-ruined dross entirely worthwhile. **59.9%**

**Aberlour 12 Years Old Sherry Matured** db **(90) n**24 few latter-day sherry butts come through this clean and complete; just the right degree of spiciness; **t**23 silky, decisive oloroso again showing an uncanny excellence in spice: not a single off note; **f**21 flattens out slightly; **b**22 another vastly improved, beautiful expression displaying genuine class. **40%**

**Aberlour 13 Years Old** Sherry cask, hand fill db **(84) n**21 **t**22 **f**20 **b**21. Skimps on the complexity. **58.8%**

**Aberlour 15 Year Old Double Cask Matured** db **(84) n**23 **t**22 **f**19 **b**20. Brilliant nose full of vibrant apples and spiced sultana, but then, after a complex, chewy, malt-enriched kick-off, falls surprisingly flat on its face. **40%**

**Aberlour 15 Years Cuvee Marie d'Ecosse** db **(91) n**22 fresh sherry trace with kumquats and lime for extra zest; **t**24 beautifully ethereal with the malt drifting in all directions while the fruit offers no weight at all; **f**22 light vanilla apologetically drifts into the picture. The smoke of old has gone; **b**23 this always was a deceptive lightweight, and it's got lighter still. It is sold primarily in France, and one can assume only that this is God's way of making amends for that pretentious, over-rated, caramel-ridden rubbish called Cognac they've had to endure. **43%**

**Aberlour 15 Year Old Sherry Finish** db **(91) n**24 exceptionally clever use of oak to add a drier element to the sharper boiled cooking apple. And a whiff of the fermenting vessel, too. Love it! **t**22 the sharp fruit of the nose is magnified here ten times for some of the strangest mouth arrivals I've ever come across: the roof of the mouth won't know what's hit it; **f**23 wave upon wave of malt concentrate; **b**22 quite unique: freaky, even. Really a whisky to be discovered and ridden. Once you acclimatize, you'll adore it. **43%**

**Aberlour 16 Year Old Double Cask Matured** db **(81) n**19 **t**21 **f**20 **b**21. Pleasant, but marred by an imbalanced nose and a dreary finish. **43%**

**Aberlour 1975** cask no. 4579, bott 11 Apr 05 db **(82) n**21 **t**21 **f**20 **b**20. A little hot and cramped. **48.5%**

**Aberlour 100 Proof** db **(91) n**23 beneath this sherried, volcanic start there is something rather sweet and honied. One of the most two-toned noses you'll find in a long while; **t**23 sweet to begin and honied, too. The maltiness keeps its shape for some time. Between the middle and end an ebulliient spiciness takes hold **f**22 massively long and fruity; **b**23 stunning, sensational whisky, the most extraordinary Speysider of them all ...which it was when I wrote those official notes for the bottling back in '97, I think. Other malts have superseded it now, but on re-tasting I stand by those original notes, though I disassociate myself entirely with the rubbish: "In order to savour Aberlour 100 at its best add 1/3 to 1/2 pure water. **57.1%**

**Aberlour Warehouse No. 1 Aged 13 Years** Sherry cask no. 1947, filled Mar 93 db **(91) n**23 splash-it-on-oloroso with heavy roast Brazilian; **t**23 the tastebuds vanish under a tidal wave of ultra-fresh sherry; spices abound as mocha meets the middle; **t**23 those Exocet-style spices continue for a while before fizzing out under the oloroso; **b**22 if you are into sherry-influenced whisky, it's multiple orgasm time. My money, though, is on the malt being better still when the butt is used for a second time... **57.6%. sc ncf.**

**Aberlour Warehouse No. 1 Hand Filled** First fill Bourbon cask no. 1296, filled into cask Sept 93, bott 11 Apr 06 db **(94)** n24 mega intense malt with acacia honey and golden syrup dominating; t23 more of the same with an early oak tang; f24 settles beautifully and a coppery richness propagates the honey; b23 there are many excellent reasons for visiting Speyside. Encountering magnificent casks like this is one of them. **61.5%.** *From the distillery only.*

**Aberlour Warehouse No. 1 Hand Filled** Sherry cask 1st fill 1714, filled Nov 92, bott 11 Apr 06 db **(93)** n24 blind, this could easily pass for Demerara rum (a70/30 blend of AWM and REV, to be precise); t23 the uncanny rum theme continues on delivery; eventually some rich sherry and lighter barley begin to restore sanity; f23 back to Demerara. Fabulous: but what the hell is happening??? Softening caramel finishes the journey; b23 when I first tasted this at the distillery, it reminded me of Jamaican rum. Back in my lab, I thought Demerara. And all this from a sherry butt. This game never fails to amaze you... **57.6%.** *From the distillery only.*

**Aberlour Warehouse No. 1 Hand Filled** Sherry cask 6524, filled 26 May 89, bott April 05 db **(94)** n24 classic ultra clean and fresh Oloroso; t24 chewy. Mouthwatering and spicy. The grape/barley balance just about 60/40. 100% superb; f23 lingering and elastic; b23 if lessons are given in exactly how a 15-year-old Speyside malt matured in a sherry butt should be, then here is the demonstration model. *From the distillery only.*

**Berry's Own Selection Aberlour 1994 Aged 11 Years** casks 8847/ 8850, dist 94, bott 05 **(75)** n19 t19 f18 b19. Refreshing, malty, almost new-make. But I'm not sure someone got the cuts quite right on this one. **46%.**

**Duncan Taylor Collection Aberlour 1995** cask no. 5249, dist Sept 95, bott Mar 06 **(85)** n22 t21 f21 b21. Jammy dodgers and treacle tart. **43.1%.** *406 bottles.*

**Cadenhead's Authentic Collection Aberlour – Glenlivet Aged 15 Years** dist 89, bott May 05 **(80)** n21 t21 f19 b19. Massive ultra-sweet gristy kick to start, but the esters seem slightly out of alignment. Big enjoyable stuff, though. **58.6%.** *288 bottles.*

⋙ **Provenance Aberlour Aged 10 Years** dist Winter 96, bott Winter 06 **(79)** n21 t20 f19 b19. Seriously lightweight, pleasantly juicy blending fodder. **46%.** *Douglas Laing.*

**Scotts Selection Aberlour 1989** bott 05 **(83)** n20 t21 f22 b20. An attractive, if conservative, expression, though the hint of strawberry on the finish is as intriguing as it is delicious. **53.8%.** *Speyside Distillers.*

⋙ **Scott's Selection Abelour 1990** bott 06 **(81)** n20 t21 f20 b20. Attractive if run of the mill barley and vanilla. **52.5%.** *Speyside Distillers.*

⋙ **Wilson & Morgan Barrel Selection Aberlour 1992 Marsala Finish** bott 2007 **(77)** n20 t19 f19 b19 Decent, but never finds its legs or direction. Bottled at the wrong point in finishing. **46%**

# ALLT-A-BHAINNE

**Speyside, 1975. Chivas Bros. Working.**

**Cadenhead's Authentic Collection Allt-A-Bhainne Aged 12 Years** dist 92, bott Feb 05 **(88)** n21 t23 f22 b22. An above average offering from this distillery thanks to a degree of softening oiliness that helps intensify the rich malty middle. **57.6%**

⋙ **Cadenhead's Authentic Collection Allt-a-Bhainne Aged 14 Years** Bourbon, dist 1992, bott May 07 **(86)** n21 t21 f23 b21. A handsome malt full of sweet barley and vim. **56.2%.** *216 bottles.*

**Dun Bheagan Allt-A-Bhainne Aged 28 Years (87)** n23 young, busy and charming; a big fruity edge to this though soft oak thrives amid the barley; t24 explosive stuff with malty fireworks popping around the palate. The barley is much, much younger than its age – there is almost a new- makey freshness. Some clean sherry has also made its presence felt: the overall picture is fussy, but strikingly attractive; f20 lets the side down slightly with some very odd sherry-led incursions. Long, but confused; b20 a decent malt bowling along beautifully until it hits some very weird sherry buffers. **60.2%.**

⋙ **Duncan Taylor The NC2 Range Alt-a-Bhainne 14 Years Old (87)** n20 ungainly and slightly thin; t23 ample compensation with the barley in full flow showing gristy sweetness, a grassy juiciness and the oak adding peppery spices to the side of the tongue; f22 good vanilla follow through aided by soft, oaky salts; b22 works impressively from the moment it hits the tastebuds. **46%. nc ncf.**

⠿ **Harry's No. 5 All-a-Bhainne Aged 14 Years** Cask no. 40657, dist 1993, bott 2007 **(87)** n21 the sharp barley is concreted on; t22 blistering barley of the rock-hard, juicy variety; f22 good spice and coffee fade; b22 solid whisky in every respect. **56.4%.** *James MacArthur & Co Ltd for Sweden.*

**Old Malt Cask Allt-A-Bhainne Aged 15 Years** dist 14 Nov 89, bott 23 Mar 05 **(74)** n17 t20 f18 b19. The poor nose and unimpressive finish point towards a not very well made spirit. **50%.** *Douglas Laing & Co.*

**Old Masters Allt-A-Bhainne 1995 Aged 10 Years** cask no. 140864, dist 95, bott 06 **(89)** n21 green and fresh; new make beefed up with a dash of manuka honey; t23 the delivery is very, very young, but the thrust of the barley is wonderful. Clean, fabulously textured and gently oiled, the deft barley-sugar sweetness delights; f22 long, thanks to that youthful, oily coating. No more than trace oak involvement, but just so chewy and lip-smacking with excellent late cocoa; b23 a pretty well- used cask means that this whisky could pass for six or seven. But it is clean, fascinating and genuinely delicious fare. **58.9%.** *James MacArthur.*

⠿ **Scotch Malt Whisky Society Cask 108.7 Aged 12 Years** Refill Butt, dist Feb 94 **(88)** n23 beautiful old-school sherry with a peppery dose of soft bourbon, too; t21 typically aggressive peppers but enough in the malty-grapey locker to see the oak off; f22 soft, chewy toffee and raisin; b22 no prisoners taken. **61.5%**

## ANCNOC ( see Knockdhu)

## ARDBEG
### Islay, 1815. Glenmorangie Co. Working.

**Ardbeg 10 Years Old** db **(97)** n24 more complex, citrus-led and sophisticated than recent bottlings, though the peat is no less but now simply displayed in an even greater elegance; a beautiful sea salt strain to this; t24 gentle oils carry on them a lemon-lime edge, sweetened by barley and a weak solution of golden syrup; the peat is omnipotent, turning up in every crevice and wave, yet never one once overstepping its boundary; f24 stunningly clean, the oak offers not a bitter trace but rather a vanilla and butterscotch edge to the barley. Again the smoke wafts around in a manner unique in the world of whisky when it comes to sheer élan and adroitness; b25 like when you usually come across something that goes down so beautifully and with such a nimble touch and disarming allure, just close your eyes and enjoy.... **46%** ☉☉

**Ardbeg 17 Years Old** (earlier bottlings) db **(92)** n23 t22 f23 b24. OK, I admit I had a big hand in this, creating it with the help of Glenmorangie Plc's John Smith. It was designed to take the weight off the better vintages of Ardbeg whilst ensuring a constant supply around the world. Certainly one of the more subtle expressions you are likely to find, though criticised by some for not being peaty enough. As the whisky's creator, all I can say is they are missing the point. **40%**

**Ardbeg 17 Years Old** (present bottlings) db **(90)** n22 t23 f22 b23. The peat has all but vanished and cannot really be compared to the original 17-year-old: it's a bit like tasting a Macallan without the sherry: fascinating to see the naked body underneath, and certainly more of a turn on. Peat or no peat, great whisky by any standards. **40%**

**Ardbeg Guaranteed 30 Years Old** db **(91)** n24 t23 f21 b23. An unsual beast, one of the last ever bottled by Allied. The charm and complexity early on is enormous, but the fade rate is surprising. That said, still a dram of considerable magnificence. **40%**

**Ardbeg 1965** db **(95)** n24 how does it do it? How can an Ardbeg manage to hang together all such vivid classic Ardbegian riches after some 40 years in the cask? The earthiness of the smoke coupled with those orangey citrus notes means this can only be pre '78 Ardbeg. No other distillery can put this character together; t23 early, light arrival of citrus, then sweetening malt staving off a big surge of smoky sap; the body, so delicate to start, begins to groan under the weight, but it's all melt-in-the-mouth and improbably gentle; f24 goes back into classic Ardbeg overdrive with gentle, lapping waves of peat reek over the vanilla and cocoa oakiness; b24 it seems unreasonable to hope that one of the oldest Ardbegs ever bottled will be a classic. But prayers are answered...and with interest. A note for Ardbeg lovers of a nervous disposition: I didn't spit a drop.... **42%** *Bottled 2005 – not for release until July 2006.*

**Ardbeg 1972 Single Cask No. 2738** db **(92)** n23 anyone who has experienced the darting, wispy warmth of passing peat-reek in a storm-lashed Scottish coastal village will recognize this immediately, made all the more vivid by the slight coke-smoke, too; citrus and vanilla back up attractively; **t**23 immediate spice attack but it's the gristy, vanilla-clad peat that stars; again some orangey-citrus lightens the load; **f**23 the peats gather more heavily now, but grape thins it and helps see off any over-active oak; **b**23 charming, evocative but enough lightning and thunder to show this is still alive and kicking. **53.1%**

**Ardbeg 1974 Single Cask No. 2741** bott 20.9.05 db **(81) n**19 **t**21 **f**21 **b**20. Gin!!! Juniper, orange peel, coriander, the lot!!! What the hell is all that about? Fabulous nose for a gin, but for an Ardbeg.... Even the delivery says much the same thing. After tasting this, I retired to my lab and blended a tiny amount of high quality gin with a standard ancient Ardbeg...and got a very similar result. A bottling hall fault? Or a freak? For the record, quality-wise, if I wasn't marking it as an Ardbeg and simply gave it a score for flavour etc, it'd get 93!!! **51.9%**. *122 bottles.*

**Ardbeg 1974 Single Cask No. 2742** bott 20.9.05 db **(92) n**22 cooing vanilla and citrus; the peats are dry and dainty; **t**24 lush, beautifully textured barley, juicy sultana and a slow evolving of peat: a seduction of the highest order; **f**23 the cocoa can something so gentle last so long; the cocoa- sprinkled peats carry with them that lush fruitiness; **b**23 for a whisky of this antiquity the freshness is astounding; the peat has faded, though. But not enough for it not to plot the course. **42.7%**. *36 bottles.*

**Ardbeg 1974 Single Cask No. 2743** bott 20.9.05 db **(94) n**23 a robust delivery of Seville orange and peat reek; a touch of chocolate-covered marzipan, too; **t**24 big esters and fruit, almost rum-like in its delivery. Then spices and peat bloom and abound; **f**23 jaffa cakes and dark chocolate again; the spice buzz and barley are beautiful; b24 just one of those casks that makes you hold your glass in awe. **51.7%**. *106 bottles.*

**Ardbeg 1974 Single Cask No. 2749** bott 20.9.05 db **(94) n**24 a touch of the farm yards mixing in with rockpools and open peat fires. Wonderful...; **t**23 an unusually firm, brittle start with the barley offering a flinty yet fruity edge; the smoke is refined and delicate; **f**23 a touch oilier now with those peats showing increasing weight. Again a lovely fruity, slightly juicy edge; **b**24 this is, quite simply, great whisky. **51%**. *120 bottles.*

**Ardbeg 1974 Single Cask No. 2751** bott 05 db **(95) n**24 a crisp nose with tight, Fishermen's Friend bite and the most extraordinary coastal tang: almost a blueprint for how old Ardbegs should be...; **t**24 firm, pulsing barley and smoky and an eking out of something citrussy. This lasts only a second as a second, more emphatic wave of peat re-emerges; **f**23 a surprisingly fast drop off of action but the emerging soft oils take the mocha, toasty vanilla to its drawn out conclusion; **b**24 just stunning whisky that can be only Ardbeg. **51.8%**. *141 bottles.*

**Ardbeg 1974 Single Cask No. 2752** bott 20.9.05 db **(91) n**22 marauding fruit has done its best to dull the nose slightly: some achievement...; **t**23 astonishingly fruity with a vague hint of lychee amid the chunky smoke; **f**23 it's more of the same, only with the peat drying slightly and a lovely gristy freshness emerging; **b**23 a very different Ardbeg: just one cask along but this sibling looks nothing like the others. **52.1%**. *133 bottles.*

⋰ **Ardbeg 1975 Single Cask No. 1375** db **(84) n**22 **t**21 **f**20 **b**21. Some delightful aspects but something doesn't quite click here the way you'd think a sherry butt would. Some lovely sweet, fruity elements but... **54.4%**

⋰ **Ardbeg 1975 Single Cask No. 1378** db **(77) n**19 **t**20 **f**19 **b**19. When Ardbeg re-opened ten years ago there was the odd cask from this vintage I put to one side with a recommendation to blend them off as I thought they were not quite right,. I wondered where they had got to... **53.8%**

**Ardbeg 1975 Single Cask No. 4699** db **(92) n**23 the weightlessness of the fine and moderate smoke helps amplify the oak, but the balance remains excellent; **t**23 again, soufflé light and then a slow, growling peat presence. Detectable barley sweetness sees off any oak; **f**23 perhaps a shade tired with some dryness accentuated by cocoa and spices but the freshness of the delicate grape is wonderful; **b**23 I had to come back to this cask three times, as the palate has to be spot- on to get the story here. At first I thought it was over-oaked; on second tasting got a different reading. These third and fourth times my palate has been free of a slight blocked nose etc and the patience has paid dividends. Yes, it is on the aged side, but the shades of subtlety astound. **40.9%**. *121 bottles.*

**Ardbeg 1975 Single Cask No. 4701** db **(87) n**22 **t**22 **f**21 **b**22. Unusual mouthfeel for an Ardbeg: hard and relatively unyielding for this distillery. **46.4%**

**Ardbeg 1975 Single Cask No. 4703** db **(91) n**22 **t**23 **f**23 **b**23. A lovely Ardbeg that is quite lethargic despite its obvious riches. **47.7%**

**Ardbeg 1975 Single Cask No. 4704** ex oloroso db **(95) n**24 I have been flung back into a warehouse by the lapping shores and I have my nose stuck in a butt: coastal, salty, fresh yet ancient, barley-sweet yet oaky-dry, smoke laden yet curiously light, firm traces of bourbon despite being unmistakably Scotch: Ardbeg at its most typically paradoxical; **t**24 dissolving malt leaves the way for a rampant, raisiny-grapey depth to battle it out with the smoke; **f**23 layer upon layer of barley which defies the years and then a crushed-sultana sweetness adding fruit to the fun; **b**24 genius will out.... **47.2%**

**Ardbeg 1975 Single Cask No. 4716** db **(86) n**21 **t**22 **f**22 **b**21. Doesn't quite take off and develop like the average Ardbeg of this era. Still a little gem, though. **45%**

**Ardbeg 1975 Single Cask No. 4717** bott 8 May 06 db **(90) n**22 excellent peats try to paper over the worrying oaky cracks; **t**22 oak-starched start but saved by improbably intense and mouthwatering barley which appears almost from nowhere; **f**23 the recovery continues with soft fruits adding to the dazzling peats; long and actually softens and juices up as it keeps stretching the horizon; **b**23 perhaps no other distillery in the world could have got away with this: there is enough evidence in both nose and delivery for those of us who have been around a bit to fear the worst. Yet, somehow, this not only comes back from life support but begins to sing and dance on its deathbed. Astonishing...and mildly frightening! **46.3%.** *165 bottles.*

**Ardbeg 1975 Single Cask No. 4718** db **(83) n**20 **t**22 **f**20 **b**21. The least inspiring of the individual casks, revealing that Ardbeg is mortal after all. Still amasses a complexity other whiskies dream about but the finish, like the nose, is bitter and less than perfect. **46.7%**

**Ardbeg 1975 Single Cask No 4719** bott 29 Apr 05 db **(87) n**20 battered, peaty but failing; **t**23 worrying oak, then an avalanche of juicy malt. The sweetness levels are rising by the second, as it the peat; **f**22 long with some wonderful light roast coffee (kind of Kenyan-Indian mix), allowing the spices and roaming peats to flourish, but still enough oak just to remind you of its age; **b**22 tries the same trick as its sibling, 4717, but doesn't quite make it. Or so you think until you taste it a third and final time before signing the death certificate. And then... **44.7%.** *188 bottles.*

**Ardbeg 1975 Single Cask No. 4720** bott 16.2.06 db **(94) n**23 crushed toffee apple; the smoke no more than toys with the nose; **t**23 silky, fruity grape and barley unite for a mouthwatering entry, then soft thrusts of peat from the rear; **f**24 the two styles meet for the most erotic finale, with every single tastebuds being toyed with at different levels of intensity. Complex and sheer genius; **b**24 this must have been one hell of a sherry butt in its day: come to think of it, it was its day right up until 16th February 2006. A genuine great whisky, and for those who love both sherry and peat, well life has just got even better... **41.4%.** *207 bottles.*

**Ardbeg 1976 Single Cask No. 2390** Sherry butt, filled 24 Nov 76, hand bott at dist 27 Apr 02 db **(96) n**24 **t**25 **f**23 **b**24. When you die, have a bottle of this put beside you in the coffin to take to the afterworld: this is just one of those drams of a lifetime. **53.1%.**

**Ardbeg 1976 Single Cask No. 2395** db **(93) n**24 **t**23 **f**22 **b**24. Supremely weighted malt with more oak than it needs but enough charisma to see it off. **54.4%**

**Ardbeg 1976 Single Cask No. 2396** db **(91) n**24 **t**23 **f**21 **b**23. This was marked in the mid-80s. Then I tasted again ... and again ... and again.... Superb. **53.5%**

**Ardbeg 1976 Single Cask No. 2398** db **(89) n**23 nose-twitching stuff: the oak and peat are sharp-edged and bold; sandalwood, marshmallow and damp leather football boots add to the bitter-sweet enigma; **t**22 equally punchy on the palate with a fizzing oak dryness perfectly countered by a peaty-Demerara sweetness; **f**22 much drier now but the malt digs deep for some weighty barley; **b**22 old and noble. **52.3%**

**Ardbeg 1976 Single Cask No. 3275** db **(85) n**22 **t**21 **f**21 **b**21. A quite different, light dram highlighting the scope of the peating levels in those ownmade malt days. Those who thought the lightly peated 17-year-old vatting a recent un-Ardbegian invention and vociferously decried it are in for a reality check and a large slice of humble pie. **44.6%**

**Ardbeg 1977** db **(96)** n25 t24 f23 b24. When working through the Ardbeg stocks, I earmarked '77 a special vintage, the sweetest of them all. So it has proved. Only the '74 absorbed that extra oak that gave greater all-round complexity. Either way, the quality of the distillate is beyond measure: simply one of the greatest experiences – whisky or otherwise – of your life. **46%**

**Ardbeg 1978** db **(91)** n23 t24 f22 b22. An Ardbeg on the edge of losing it because of encroaching oak, hence the decision made by John Smith and I to bottle this vintage early alongside the 17-year-old. Nearly ten years on, still looks a pretty decent bottling, though slightly under strength! **43%**

**Ardbeg Airigh Nam Beist Limited 1990 Release** bott 06 db **(95)** n24 dark and deep yet sensuous and gentle; there is a distinctive organic quality to this (not in the health drink sense...); lots of clues to location, with a rich salty texture to the aroma; t24 big, thick with flavour, yet not oils. Huge peat, yet always allowing the sweet barley strands to filter through; f23 those coastal, salty notes at last arrive as does a dusting of cocoa; b24 there is only one distillery on earth that could make something so gigantic, yet so delicate. And mind-blowingly complex. Smoky sophistication. **46%. ncf.** ☺

∴ **Ardbeg Almost There** Third Release dist 98, bott 07 db **(93)** n23 fabulous peat and coal-gas mix with a citrus thinning and strimming things out; t24 marauding barley and orange peel combine for a grassy, mouth-watering delivery, but with the peat riding a gently oiled wave; enormous and you'll keep chewing until your jaw drops off...; f23 long, quite big smoke but some oils help disguise some of the more complex final moments; b23 further proof that a whisky doesn't have to reach double figures in age to enter the realms of brilliance... **54.1%. ncf.**

**Ardbeg Kildalton 1980** bott 04 db **(96)** n23 t24 f24 b25. Many years back, when I helped get Ardbeg back on the road, I selected certain years as vintages and created the 17-year-old by using this unpeated version as the heart, with some overly old but highly peated casks to ensure the Ardbeg style flourished and equilibrium was maintained. The one and only recommendation I made that was not carried out, though, was to launch Kildalton as a malt in its own right, showing – uniquely – the inner working of Ardbeg in much the same way as a bourbon cask version does to Macallan. Now, at very long last, they have got around to it. This is better now than when it was 17 years old, and a degree of unbalanced freshness remained (to confirm my suspicions, I have tasted it against the samples I took then). It has developed extra fruit and complexity, making it a breathtaking treat – a masterpiece map of Ardbeg – that no true whisky connoisseur can afford to miss... and proof positive that Ardbeg doesn't need peat to bring complexity, balance and Scotch whisky to their highest peaks.... **57.6%**

**Ardbeg Lord of the Isles** bott Autumn 04 db **(85)** n20 t22 f22 b21. A version of Ardbeg I have never really come to terms with. This bottling is of very low peating levels and shows a degree of Kildalton-style fruitiness. No probs there. More, it's a fact that some of the casks are leaching a soft soapy character noticeable on the nose. Enjoyable enough, but a bit frustrating. **46%** ☺☺

∴ **Ardbeg Mor** db **(95)** n24 coastal to the point of sea spray showering you, with the smell of salt all the way home until you reach the peat fire. Evocative, sharp with elements of vinegar to the iodine; t24 one of the biggest deliveries from Ardbeg for yonks; the peat appears way above the normal 50%, thickset and gloriously bitter-sweet, the steadying vanillas carried on the soft oils; f23 mocha enters the fray with a raspberry jam fruitiness trying to dampen the continuing smoke onslaught; b24 quite simply Mor the merrier... **57.5%**

**Ardbeg Ping No 1 Single Cask** cask 2780, dist 27 Oct 72, bott 14 Oct 04 db **(97)** n24 we are back to model steam locomotives with the most beguiling array of sensuous peats since the legendary OMC '75; slightly farm-yardy., a dab here and there of grape and citrus. Words never do justice, because this is all about nuance and timing: ladies and gentlemen, only Ardbeg can give you this; t24 sweet peats dissolve immediately into the palate; the barley adds a juicy layer or eight; vanilla is present, as is mocha and muscovado sugar; f24 just so long, and the sweetness that evolves towards the middle refusing to die; the peat is so fragile yet powering enough to shape and re-shape the structure and direction of the dram. This is lithe and living whisky, showing shape and form from nose to the longest of finishes; b25 there'll be another scramble to

Copenhagen when the world gets word of this one...sadly I didn't get this until just after the last Bible went to press: as an October 04 bottling this might have won Whisky of the Year, but we'll never know! **51.4%.** *245 bottles for Juuls Vinhandel, Denmark.*

**Ardbeg Provenance 1974** bott 99 db **(96)** n24 t25 f23 b24. This is an exercise in subtlety and charisma, the beauty and the beast drawn into one. Until I came across the 25-year-old OMC verson during a thunderstorm in Denmark, this was arguably the finest whisky I had ever tasted: I opened this and drank from it to see in the year 2000. When I went through the Ardbeg warehouse stocks in 1997 I earmarked the '74 and '77 vintages as something special. This bottling has done me proud. **55.6%**

**Ardbeg Single Cask 2740** db **(83)** n21 t21 f20 b21. A bit hot with lots of oak to chew on. **52.3%.** *Belgium only.*

**Ardbeg Single Cask 2782** db **(87)** n22 t22 f21 b22. Positively schizophrenic. **52.3%.** *Italy only.*

**Ardbeg Still Young** dist 98, 2nd release bott 06 db **(93)** n24 still the sizzling smoky bacon, with perhaps a salty-buttered Arbroath Smoky for company; even a touch of the dentists...; **t24** if this was any more delicate or highly strung, my tastebuds would have have a breakdown. The peats are enormous, but simply hover and then land like butterflies; the barley offers moisture; **f22** even at this age the oak begin to have an input, drying and adding a vanilla pod to the sweeter peats. Lengthy and lip-smacking; **b23** a couple of generations back – maybe even less – this would not have been so much "Still Young" as "Getting on a Bit." This is a very good natural age for an Ardbeg as the oak is making a speech, but refuses to let it go on too long. Stylish – as one might expect. And, in my books, should be a regular feature. Go on. Be bold. Be proud say it: Ardbeg Aged 8 Years. Get away from the marketing straightjacket of old age... **56.2%. ncf.**

**Ardbeg Uigeadail** db **(89)** n25 awesome package of intense peat reek amid complex fruitcake and leather notes. Everything about this nose is broadside-big yet the massive oak never once oversteps its mark. A whiff of engine oil compliments the kippers. Perfection; **t22** begins with a mind-blowing array of bitter-sweet oaky notes and then a strangely fruity peat entry; real scattergun whisky; **f20** very odd finish with an off-key fruit element that flattens the usual Ardbeg grand finale; **b22** a curious Ardbeg with a nose to die for. Some tinkering - please guys, as the re-taste is not better - regarding the finish may lift this to being a true classic **54.1%** ☺☺

**Ardbeg Very Young** db **(91)** n22 cured bacon on rye bread; a seasoning saltiness compliments the firmer peat while a second, lighter, level floats around. Complex stuff; **t24** the initial strike is sweet malt followed by spicy peat; cocoa arrival on middle; **f22** a tad oily which carries sweet, smoky malt all the way; **b23** this bottling helps demonstrate the true genius of Ardbeg's versatility. **58.9%**

**Ardbeg Very Young For Discussion 1997** bott 03 db **(82)** n19 t22 f21 b21. Some Ardbeg greatness here, even with a phenols on the low side. Just that a poor, soapy bourbon cask has damaged proceedings somewhat. **58.9%**

**Ardbeg Young Uigeadail** db **(96)** n23 a touch of fruit, a little detracting soap, serious barley sugar and prickly peat. That's just the first layer...; **t25** sumptuous, near perfectly weighted delivery with mollassed peat dried with some real toasty oak. Big and bordering on bruising, though the smoke does hold back slightly even if the spices don't; light oil keeps the wheels turning. The star turn in the late middle is the Quality Street candy hazelnut caramel – watch out for it; **f24** layers of mocha and peat...as far as the tastebuds' detection abilities stretch; **b24** forget the slight off-key nose: what really takes the breath away here is the ability to give so much yet at no stage ever be sweet or dry, just a mind-blowing mixture of both. Don't expect instant results here. Your taste buds need to learn and adapt. But by the fourth or fifth mouthful you will start getting the barely believable picture. **59.9%**

**Benedict XVI "Habemus Cerevisiam Destillatum!"** Commemorative Bottling to Honour the Pontificate **(91)** n22 t23 f24 b22. If Ardbeg wasn't blessed before, it probably has been now...this Ardbeg (though the distillery isn't mentioned on the label for some obscure legal reason) has been matured for a while in oak grown near the village of Gewekin, close to the Pope's home town of Regensburg, Germany. I take my funny hat off to the members of the local whisky club. You have excelled tourselves, herrs and fräuleins. **50%.** *Regensburger Whisky Club.*

**Cadenhead's Authentic Collection Ardbeg Aged 11 Years** Bourbon Hogshead, dist 93, bott May 05 **(95)** n24 my late old dad's allotment in Surrey: bonfires, freshly cut sticks of rhubarb, a hint of compost, freshly dug earth; t24 bitter-sweet malt that becomes more barley-sugar sweet as it progresses; the way the malt dissolves in the mouth is natural poetry; f23 a gradual build-up of fruit as the smoke delves and delivers then disappears. Long and enormously intricate; b24 touchingly evocative and beautiful; from a whisky standpoint...well, nothing short of mesmerically brilliant. **57.4%**. *270 bottles.*

**Cadenhead's Authentic Collection Ardbeg Aged 11 Years** Bourbon Hogshead, dist 93, bott May 05 **(94)** n23 rich, rugged peat with Surrey bonfires again, but fractionally less weighty and complex than its sister cask; t24 dry and intense with the malt, peat and oak arriving in one enormous tidal wave. Soft fruits eventually show. Stunning: some of the best post-maltings complexity delivered in bottle; f23 lovely cocoa and coffee notes survive with distant hints of citrus enlivening the growing dryness; b24 Ardbeg at its most unpredictable and enduring. A must for any collector. **59.5%**. *312 bottles.*

**Cadenhead's Ardbeg Aged 12 Years** dist 94, bott Sept 06 **(95)** n25 stick your head in a silent maltings kiln and you aren't too far away; the intensity appears to be on varying levels and the phenol level's high even for an Ardbeg. The grassy, citrussy sub plot adds just the right relief. Of its type, quite perfect; t24 how many peated malts do you find this crisp and mouth-watering? This is sensational because the palate is serenaded by smoke and barley in almost equal measures. Salivating and chewy; f23 now the smoke intensifies as the barley vanishes. This is all about variations of peat, being dry and clingy on one hand, and sweeter and lighter on another; b23 a second – maybe even third – fill bourbon cask allows for a warts and all look at a magnificent malt. Considering the lack of oaky input, the complexity astonishes. Ardbeg will be kicking themselves it was left to an independent to bottle something quite so revealing, sublime and different. **46%**.

**Cadenhead's Ardbeg Aged 12 Years (93)** n23 lively, gristy, farm-yardy; t23 puckering barley and then a wonderful wave of spice along with a plummy fruitiness; about as salivating as Ardbeg of this age gets; f23 back to soft grists again with loping layers of peat; b24 another Ardbeg that took over half an hour to get to truly appreciate. This really is complicated stuff. **58.2%**

**Cadenhead's Authentic Collection Ardbeg Aged 12 Years** Bourbon Hogshead, dist 93, bott Feb 06 **(93)** n22 dull, oily and hard to pick the structure. Some beautiful peats, though; t24 thumping smoke riding on a barley-gristy ticket and no shortage of cocoa; a real firecracker of an opening with brilliant juxtaposition between exploding spices and very sweet barley; f24 the vanillas and cocoa help overcome the oils and now we have some serious complexity. b23 an oily creature and early on it appears some Ardbeg magic is lost because of it. But on third and fourth inspection, that is clearly not the case: it's cranked up the finish and is never less than sheer bliss!! **59.3%**. *318 bottles.*

⠿ **Cadenhead's Authentic Collection Ardbeg Aged 13 Years** Bourbon Hogshead, dist 1994, bott May 07 **(91)** n23 big, wedges of enormous peat; t23 spiced, massive peat delivery with a big, upfront maltiness; f22 a procession of fruits, including citrus; b23 a chewy emphatic Ardbeg not much caring for airs nor graces. **58%**. *300 bottles.*

⠿ **Cadenhead's Authentic Collection Ardbeg Aged 13 Years** Bourbon Hogshead, dist 1994, bott May 07 **(92)** n24 soft, delicate, citrussy peat; t23 fabulous meeting point of lively spices, varied vanillas and sweet barley; f22 lethargic, understated smoke with soft oils amplifying the gristy barley sweetness; b23 most probably a very close relation to Cadenhead's other Ardbeg 1994 bottling, but here everything is just little more laid back and relaxed. **58.4%**. *318 bottles.*

**Cadenhead's Authentic Collection Ardbeg Aged 13 Years 1993** Bourbon hogshead, dist 93, bott Nov 06 **(95)** n22 peppery edge to smoke t25 massive: almost pure Talisker in its spiced up delivery; the barley sweetens and juices the palate and smoke rumbles beautifully as those peppers bombard the roof of the mouth: TNT in a bottle; f24 more white pepper as the barley melts towards cocoa and coffee; the peat rumbles forever; b24 the spiciest Ardbeg I've ever come across: blind this is Talisker, though the peat depth is a giveaway. Once tasted never forgotten. **61.1%**. *246 bottles.*

**Connoisseurs Choice Ardbeg 1976 (94)** n24 t24 f23 b23. Wonderful Ardbeg of the old, original school that spellbindingly defies its years. Well done G&M for giving us some classic Ardbeg. But next time can we have it at 46%, please...!! **43%**. *Gordon & MacPhail.*

❖ **Connoisseurs Choice Ardbeg 1979 (93) n**24 that uniquely Ardbegian mixture of brain-explodingly complex peat and orangey citrus tones, only here the balance and denouement are as near as damn it perfect; **t**23 light to the point that the molecules virtually fall apart on the palate; again it's citrus leading the line and the peat showing restraint to the point of good old fashioned manners; **f**22 dry vanilla; **b**24 quite beautiful malt but at 43% compared to every man and his dog bringing out Ardbeg at full strength – and at at least 46% by the owners themselves – this does at first appear underpowered. But as the strands of complexity unravel... **43%.** *Gordon & MacPhail.*

**Connoisseurs Choice Ardbeg 1995 (90) n**22 **t**22 **f**24 **b**22. Ardbeg at its most lethargic, and made at a time of enormous uncertainty at the distillery. But the finish alone projects this into Premier League status. **40%.** *G&M.*

**Connoisseurs Choice Ardbeg 1996 (88) n**21 eerily light and quiet both in terms of peat and strength: a bit like going to see Pink Floyd and the only thing unplugged are the amplifiers...; **t**22 light, gristy, juicy barley; the peat arrives at first as an afterthought but soon gathers momentum – and then vanishes again; **f**22 such a well behaved finale with soft vanilla here, a wisp of peat and heather there; **b**23 such a strange experience to find Ardbeg at 40%: I can hardly remember the last time I did. Hopefully, it will be the last....!! **40%.** *G&M.*

**Mackillop's Choice Ardbeg 1991** dist Oct 91 **(92) n**22 **t**23 **f**23 **b**24. Nothing particularly exceptional about this cask. And it gets 92. Need I say more...? **43%.** *Angus Dundee.*

**Murray McDavid Ardbeg Aged 14 Years** Matured in Bourbon casks, dist 91, bott 05 **(91) n**23 three star turn with that trademark multi-dimensional peat and citrus character; **t**23 a delightful marriage of citrus and grist; refreshing yet enormously deep; **f**22 caramel wafer with praline and, of course, sweet peats; **b**23 can this distillery do no wrong? **46%. nc ncf.** *360 bottles.*

**Old Malt Cask Ardbeg 10 Years Old** dist Oct 94, bott May 05 **(91) n**22 one of the firmest noses I've come across in bottled form for a while, with the malt showing little give despite the softness of the smoke; **t**23 the firmness transports to the palate but works wonderfully in chipping away at the oak; wonderful bitter-sweet character with pulse smoke; **f**23 long, becoming more salivating as it progresses, with some late salt; **b**23 a quality little number. **50%.**

**Old Malt Cask Ardbeg 12 Years Old** Rum finish, dist 1 Oct 92, bott 14 Oct 04 **(95) n**24 dry, with the peat showing signs of pre-78 depth and complexity. Toasty and alluring; **t**24 quite fabulous arrival of what would be ultradry oak and peat were it not for the mouthwatering, saliva-gushing input of the barley; lovely fruits and even nut in the form of semi-dry Danish marzipan; **f**22 long, pulsing peat of a once-lost style with so many enormous sub-plots of bittersweet, fruity complexity; **b**25 those lucky buggers in downtown Manhattan! If Park Avenue have any bottles left, beat a path to their shelves as soon as you read this and get as many as you can afford. **50%.** *Douglas Laing & Co. For Park Avenue Liquor, NY, USA.*

**Old Malt Cask Ardbeg 14 Years Old** dist 28 Mar 91, bott 5 Apr 05 **(93) n**24 floral and perfumed with a touch of lavender; herby and earthy. And smoky...the complexity takes some unravelling; **t**22 very sharp on the palate; almost a bite to the malt with some vanilla flooding in but kept at bay by undulating smoke; **f**23 salty and fruity with a decidedly citrussy slant. The smoke heads off in a milky-coffee direction; **b**24 a busy, slightly directionless Ardbeg that keeps you guessing..and intrigued. **50%.**

**Old Malt Cask Ardbeg 14 Years Old** dist Mar 91, bott Aug 05 **(92) n**23 gossamer-light peat couched in some of the thick stuff, quite mossy and north-facing garden-ish; **t**23 gosh! Just how juicy can Ardbeg become? Swirling smoke but really it is the ripeness of the barley that impresses; **f**23 at last the peats form some kind of shape and structure, ushering the vanillas along the longish path; **b**23 Ardbeg coming off a slightly different tack, but still no less beautiful. **50%.**

❖ **Old Malt Cask Ardbeg Aged 14 Years** dist Mar 91, bott Jan 06 **(94) n**24 crisp, tight peat but with a unique intensity and reverence: Ardbeg!! It could be nothing else...**t**23 the softest of delivery defies the nose; sweetens out and the peats become complex and crystalline; **f**24 some Java coffee tones melt into the smoke and salt; **b**23 a big whisky that threatens at times to explode but refuses to be so bold...or coarse. **50%.** *Douglas Laing. 330 bottles*

**Old Malt Cask Ardbeg 15 Years Old** dist Mar 91, bott Mar 06 **(92) n**23 heady, pungent peats battle orange peel, sultanas and even a touch of liquorice head on. The thing is, just how many layers are there?; **t**23 big and rich, the grapey theme continues until unseated by a hickory/peat stand; well spiced early but fades; **f**23 long, more hickory and Fishermen's Friend cough sweet with the sweetness holding sway throughout and the return of spice is perfect; **b**23 a dram that threatens to run amok but a sweet malty theme pervades. **50%**. *341 bottles.*

**Old Malt Cask Ardbeg 15 Years Old** Rum finish, dist Mar 91, bott July 06 **(82) n**20 **t**22 **f**20 **b**20. Austere and lacking in the usual Ardbegian grace and elegance: I'm not sure this has been bottled at a time when the Ardbeg and rum were on the best speaking terms. **50%**. *Douglas Laing. 378 bottles.*

⫶⫶ **Old Malt Cask Ardbeg Aged 15 Years** dist Mar 91, bott Oct 06 **(86) n**22 **t**22 **f**21 **b**21. Some OTT oils clip the wings of the higher-flying notes. Attractive but limited by Ardbeg standards. **50%**. *Douglas Laing. 358 bottles.*

⫶⫶ **Old Malt Cask Ardbeg Aged 15 Years** Rum Finish dist Mar 91, bott Oct 06 **(90) n**23 rock-hard smoke with a shell of sugar; **t**23 brittle barley with the peat coming in silver sugar-sweetened strata; an unmistakable rum character offers another dimension **f**22 melts at last but the recently released oils contains the complexity slightly; **b**22 wonderful stuff but underscoring that sugary sheen often found in rum finishes. Not normally a bad thing, but perhaps restrictive when it comes to something so labyrinthine as Ardbeg. **50%**. **nc ncf**. *Douglas Laing. 312 bottles.*

**Old Malt Cask Ardbeg 1975 Aged 25 Years** dist Oct 75, bott Oct 00 **(97) n**25 **t**24 **f**23 **b**25. Is this the best independent bottling of whisky of all time? I would say yes. And it would be a hard job to find a better single cask throughout Ardbeg's warehouses. I have tasted more individual casks of Ardbeg than any other whisky critic living, but never have I found one that so captures the brilliance of the world's greatest distillery – even my mark of 97 is me just nitpicking and being mean! Just one single glass at bottle strength – don't you dare add a single drop of water to this one – a quiet room, and you will be lost in the labyrinth of this great whisky for hours if not days. Will you ever get to the bottom of it? I very much doubt it. **50%**. *Douglas Laing. 702 bottles.*

**Platinum Old and Rare Cask Ardbeg Aged 29 Years** dist 75, bott 04 **(94) n**24 some marmalade and nuts freshens the delicate peat reek: classic old Ardbeg that embraces the oak; **t**24 immediately the mouth is cluttered by peat of varying enormity; just the odd flake of toasted honeycomb can be found; **f**23 beautiful mocha just so compliments the vanilla and smoke; some soft toffee leaves a gentle trail and controls the mounting oak; **b**23 holds back from going full frontal. **58.3%**. *Douglas Laing.*

⫶⫶ **The Whisky Fair Ardbeg Aged 15 Years** Bourbon Hogshead, dist 1991, bott 07 **(94) n**24 dry, gristy peat: clean, oil-free and displaying a salty-iodine coastal quality to die for; **t**23 massive delivery with the peats ganging up like sweet, smoky thugs ready to bash the living daylights out of the tastebuds only to caress them instead with molasses-tinged sweetness; remains salty and islandy; **f**23 the salts continue but an intense gristy sweetness prevents an oaky charge; **b**24 a substantial Ardbeg, absolutely brimming with malice and front but, on reflection, showing nothing but restraint and breeding. **54.4%**. *Germany.*

⫶⫶ **The Whisky Fair "Still Very Young Islay Single Malt" (Ardbeg)** Refill Sherry, dist 2000, bott 2007 **(90) n**24 gorgeous dusty, old ash of a coal and peat fire; **t**22 oily sweet peat; **f**22 sweat peat at first, dries to a dust; **b**22 very sweet peat. But the nose is legendary. **62.6%**. *Germany.*

# ARDMORE
### Speyide, 1899. Fortune Brands. Working.

**Ardmore 100th Anniversary 12 Years Old** dist 86, bott 99 db **(94) n**24 **t**23 **f**23 **b**24. This was to be one of the great whiskies of 1999. As this didn't get Allied switched on to what a truly great malt this is, nothing will. Quite fantastic.

**Ardmore 100th Anniversary 21 Years Old** db **(91) n**24 **t**22 **f**22 **b**23. A malt which simply caresses the tastebuds. The fruit influence is important but the malt and smoke are intriguingly subtle. It just gets better each time you taste it. **43%**

⠿ **Ardmore Fully Peated Quarter Casks** db **(89) n**21 the most un-Ardmore-ish nose of all time due to the thumping American oak tones. Those, plus a touch of caramel have to a degree flattened the peat-smoke so celebrated on the label; still, a rare example of where bourbon meets soft peat... **t**23 a surprisingly dull, toffee-led initial entry is compensated for by an astonishing degree of development towards the middle where the smoke battles through the double-sweet sword of intense bourbon and barley sugar, helped along the way by an unusual oiliness; something to really chew on... **f**23 the barley-fruit touch that has developed lingers for a while, as do those big, sweet tannins; soft oils continue and the smoke tries to be heard above the oaky noise and excellent, balancing spices. A touch of returning caramel flattens it out; **b**22 this is an astonishingly brave attempt by the new owners of Ardmore who, joy of all joys, are committed to putting this distillery in the public domain. Anyone with a 2004 copy of the Whisky Bible will see that my prayers have at last been answered. However, this bottling is for Duty Free and, due to the enormous learning curve associated with this technique, a work in progress. They have used the Quarter Cask process which has been such a spectacular success at its sister distillery Laphroaig. Here I think they have had the odd slight teething problem. Firstly, Ardmore has rarely been filled in ex-bourbon and that oak type is having an effect on the balance and smoke weight; also they have unwisely added caramel, which has flattened things further. I don't expect the caramel to be in later bottlings and, likewise, I think the bourbon edge might be purposely blunted a little. But for a first attempt this is seriously big whisky that shows enormous promise. When they get this right, it could – and should – be a superstar. Now I await the more traditional vintage bottlings... **46%. ncf.**

⠿ **Cask Strength Ardmore 1991 (89) n**22 rather plodding, oily, but never less than attractive; **t**23 enormous sweet punch to this one with the lighty peated oils apparently bolstering the natural sugars and citrus notes; **f**22 the smoke has been hiding somewhat but fully reveals itself towards the finale; **b**22 a much less smoky version with an astonishing sweetness. The quality is unquestionable, though. **57.9%.**

⠿ **Distillery Malt Ardmore 1991 (94) n**23 Ardmore at one of its highest peating levels – certainly more than the normal 9-14ppm. Even so, there is room for lovely profusion of vanilla and grist. Just so delicate for all its weight; **t**24 quite stunning: the weight of the peat is telling but the soft oils help both propel and even out the smokiness. Chewy yet juicy: quite fabulous; **f**23 lightens towards a smoky custard but very long with a delicate barley sugar towards the end; **b**24 this is simply brilliant whisky that no whisky lover can afford to be without. Startling. **43%.** *Gordon & MacPhail.*

**Gordon & MacPhail Ardmore Aged 16 Years** dist 90, bott 06 **(87) n**23 clean but seriously above average peat even by Ardmore standards; **t**22 pretty gristy for its age with an even radiation of smoke and spice; **f**20 smoky custard; **b**22 enjoyable; just perhaps lacking the usual complexity. **43%**

⠿ **Old Malt Cask Ardmore Aged 30 Years** dist Apr 77, bott Apr 07 **(90) n**22 delicate peat is little more than a wisp in a fruity breeze; **t**23 a passionate delivery, full of busy spice and silky barley; the fruit element is fuzzy but never less than juicy; the smoke offers little more than a haze; **f**22 excellent muscovado sugar and vanilla sign off; **b**23 a real sweetie. Elegance and understanding are key here. **50%.** *595 bottles.*

**Provenance Ardmore Aged 12 Years** casks DMG 1328 & 1329, dist Spring 92, bott Summer 04 **(89) n**22 firm malt gives full scope to the soft but gently penetrating peat; **t**23 relaxed, with the barley coating the mouth beautifully; no oaky cracks and really understated sweet smoke; **f**22 oily style continues, ensuring excellent length. Intense barley pulses to the finish line; **b**22 much less peaty delivery than the nose suggests; the oils are exquisite. **46%.** *McGibbon's.*

**Provenance Ardmore 12 Years Old** dist Oct 93, bott Summer 06 **(93) n**24 perhaps only Ardmore can offer this style of smokiness: light, but because of the delicate, intricate nature of the other aromas appears smokier than it actually is. Cream rice pudding with a splodge of raspberry jam; vanilla wafer; **t**23 apologetic oils offer a thin layer of peat around the palate; elsewhere a degree of gristiness yields a juicy sweetness; **f**23 oaks and spices play are equal to any smoke; **b**23 great to see the distillery bottled at arguably its optimum age from second fill. Charming, absorbing and complex whisky that craves time to discover. **46%.**

· **Provenance Ardmore Aged 12 Years** dist Autumn 94, bott Winter 06 **(94) n**24 the Ardmore nose at near full perfection: the gristy Port Ellen-esque smoke punching above its weight and superbly backed by mouth-watering, juicy barley. For its age the oak is supine, but there is just enough around for the vaguest vanilla edge; **t**24 beautifully sweet, ultra clean malt despite the continuous upping of the peat which starts soft yet confidentially and reaches the middle with some weight behind it; even so never less than delicate; **f**23 long with a touch of oaky bitterness to counter the lengthy sweet barley **b**23 a spot-on cask which shows the distillery at very nearly its best at this age **46%**. *Douglas Laing.*

**Scotch Malt Whisky Society Cask No. 66.16 Aged 20 Years (96) n**25 **t**24 **f**23 **b**24. Best whisky not to win an award in 2006 Bible. **54.8%**

· **Scotch Malt Whisky Society Cask 66.21 Aged 21 Years** Refill Hogshead, dist Mar 85 **(87) n**21 anthracite and peat; **t**22 sweet cough sweet with a blowtorch of spices; **f**22 remains a tad gristy and worthy; **b**22 delightful, yet perhaps over simplistic for this distillery with the complexity rarely getting beyond the smoke. **54.2%**

· **Scotch Malt Whisky Society Cask 66.22 Aged 21 Years** Refill Hogshead, dist Mar 85 **(92) n**23 an unusual coastal saltiness to this one which makes this slightly more Islay-esque than the norm. Fabulous, though; **t**23 soft and textbook-layered with the gristy smoke weaving between bitter-sweet barley and milk powder; **f**23 vanilla-peat all the way and the mandatory spices; **b**23 a soft landing towards the finish perhaps but the extra saline kick is outstanding. **52.7%**

· **Scotch Malt Whisky Society Cask 66.24 Aged 22 Years** Refill Hogshead, dist Mar 85 **(86) n**22 **t**22 **f**21 **b**21. Busy oak on the smoke and while quick dose of honey helps overcome the over-vigorous wood it's all rather too much for true greatness. **52.7%**

**The Single Malt of Scotland Ardmore Aged 11 Years Vintage 1994** cask no. 121011 **(82) n**20 **t**21 **f**21 **b**20. Very strange Ardmore: hot in part and also from a cask which is not entirely at ease with itself. That said, the oily peat positively throbs and many excellent moments are to be had. **60.8%**. *The Whisky Exchange. 789 bottles.*

**Whisky Magazine France Ardmore 1990** bott 06 **(93) n**23 lean and clean, the peats are profound yet luxuriating in a gristy lightness; **t**24 divine delivery with that grist to the fore and helping to intensify the smoke; **f**23 hardens again with crisp barley pounding with confidence and class; **b**23 curses! The French have got their hands on the best bottling of Ardmore this year. **60.2%**. *400 bottles.*

## ARRAN (see Isle of Arran)

## AUCHENTOSHAN
**Lowlands, 1800. Morrison Bowmore. Working.**

**Auchentoshan 10 Years Old** db **(81) n**22 **t**21 **f**19 **b**19. Much better, maltier, cleaner nose than before. But after the initial barley surge on the palate it shows a much thinner character. **40%** ☉ ☉

· **Auchentoshan 12 Years Old** db **(85) n**20 **t**23 **f**21 **b**21. Thicker and more chewy malt than is the norm for a 'Toshan. But don't get this one confused with the astonishing peaty number that was 43%!! The finish is OK, but the delivery is superb. **40%**

**Auchentoshan 12 years Old** db **(93) n**22 lilting malt and figs with, amazingly, some smoke: a real teasing surprise-package; **t**23 that curious smokiness hits the palate early, and then the sweetness heads in a Demerara direction; **f**24 medium roast Java combines with the sweet smoke for a spellbinding finale of extraordinary length; **b**24 this is legendary stuff. It could be a freak, smoky one-off. If so, here's a tip: get a bottle...NOW!! **43%**

**Auchentoshan Aged 17 Years Bordeaux Wine Finish** db **(82) n**21 **t**21 **f**20 **b**20. Very oily early on by 'Toshan standards with the grape dominating throughout. Intriguingly tart and sharp, but perhaps overly so. Lovely ironic bourbon thrust to nose, though. **51%**. *3,600 bottles.*

**Auchentoshan 18 Years Old** Limited Edition Selection of first and second fill oloroso sherry butts db **(89) n**22 clean and majorly complex grape; attractively dry; **t**23 brilliant fruit/barley delivery in excellent harmony. Salivating and mildly spicy; **f**22 bitter orange and vanilla; **b**22 a quite beautifully orchestrated Lowlander. **55.8%**. *4,800 bottles.*

**Auchentoshan 21 Years Old** db **(92)** n22 trich and fruity, a wonderful combination of pulped raisin and honey; t24 really stunning mouth arrival with that deliciously estered, sweet maltiness that appears to be becoming an Auchentoshan trait; f23 soft, sultry malt with a thoughtful sprinkling of oak; b23 been consistently good of late: it's now even better...!!! **43%** ☉ ☉

**Auchentoshan 1962** db **(88)** n21 t22 f22 b23. A genuinely different malt. One to get to know. **40%**

**Auchentoshan 1973** Sherry, dist 14 Mar 73, bott 08 July 05 db **(74)** n20 moist date but a big winey toffee-apple note tries to muscle in and send off –key; t19 the very first moment is a nano-second of barley-wine bliss – then it goes a bit frantic with a metallic bite sending everything out of kilter. Some dates try to return, but it's too little, too late; f17 hard and harsh; b18 just doesn't work. **55.5%**. *480 bottles.*

**Auchentoshan 1978** (*see* Auchentoshan 18 Years Old)

**Auchentoshan Select** db **(85)** n21 t22 f21 b21. A gentle, refreshing and untaxing treat. **40%** ☉ ☉

**Auchentoshan Three Wood** db **(84)** n22 t21 f21 b20. Still can't help thinking that the spirit from this distillery is simply too delicate for this type of treatment and the actual character vanishes under the welter of wood. **43%**

**Berry's' Own Selection Auchentoshan 1983 Aged 22 Years (71)** n19 t18 f17 b17. Almost a Japanese buckwheat style. But a rare off-cask from this bottler: by 'eck it's grim. **46%.**

⟐ **Berrys' Own Selection Auchentoshan 1991** Cask no. 481, bott 07 **(62)** n17 t17 f13 b15. Gruesomely off key....almost worth getting just for the horror show!!! **46%**

**Cadenhead's Authentic Collection Auchentoshan Aged 12 Years** dist 92, bott May 05 **(82)** n19 t22 f21 b19. Some seriously chewy moments, but has that old-fashioned Auchentoashan off-target feel. **57.2%.** *294 bottles.*

⟐ **Cadenhead's Authentic Collection Auchentoshan Aged 16 Years** Bourbon barrel, dist 90, bott Feb 07 **(92)** n22 pure Canadian or pure grain scotch....this is malt...?!?!? t24 the bizarre nose is followed by a similar Canadian theme on the delivery – then whoosh!!! The barley turns up in force and at its most thick, juicy and chewy and stuns the tastebuds with its uncompromising beauty; f23 long, lingering vanilla and a gentle breakdown of something Canadian blessed with sweet malt. To call it charming hardly does it justice.../ b23 'Toshan at its very best.... In fact one of the finest I've come across from this distillery for a very long time. Tasted blind I'd never have recognised it! **59.2%.** *Cadenhead's. 204 bottles.*

**Dewar Rattray Individual Cask Bottling Auchentoshan 1991 Aged 15 Years** cask no. 478, dist Feb 91, bott May 06 **(83)** n19 t22 f21 b21. It's not often you get a slightly feinty triple distilled whisky... but you have one here. On the plus side there is enough body here for you to get your tongue around... **59%.** *390 bottles.*

**Duncan Taylor Collection Auchentoshan 1999** cask no. 800003, dist Mar 99, bott Mar 06 **(73)** n21 t21 f15 b16. After textbook nose and delivery, falls apart alarmingly and bitterly as the balance with oak is lost. **43%.** *430 bottles.*

⟐ **Milroy's of Soho Auchentoshan 1990** Hogshead, cask no. 17284, dist 14 Dec 90, bott 23 Feb 07 **(84)** n20 t22 f21 b21. Not your standard Auchentoshan, this. Much more oily and displaying bigger natural caramels than usual. A competent dram. **46%.** *329 bottles.*

**Murray McDavid Auchentoshan 1992 (77)** n19 t20 f19 b19. Creamy, fruity...but somehow not on the ball. **46%.**

⟐ **Murray McDavid Auchentoshan 1999 Aged 8 Years** Bourbon/Mourvedre **(86)** n21 t21 f22 b22. One of the few whiskies in the world I suggest you take with water. Not to improve the flavour. Just to save you from dehydration...Sophisticated, though. **46%**

**Murray McDavid Mission Auchentoshan 1981 Aged 25 Years** Bourbon/ Mourvedre, bott 06 **(85)** n22 t22 f20 b21. The calm nose gives no warning of the grapey, mouthwatering turbulence ahead. **55.7%. nc ncf.** *350 bottles.*

**Provenance Auchentoshan Aged 10 Years** dist Apr 95, bott Nov 05 **(83)** n20 t22 f21 b20. An attractive interplay of solid and soft barley. Refreshing and more-ish. **46%.**

**Secret Stills Auchentoshan Aged 17 Years** Distillery no.3, sherry hogshead casks 5746/7, dist 8.12.89, bott Jun 06 **(83)** n21 t22 f19 b21. Pleasant, undemanding though perhaps thwarted rather than enriched by the sherry. **45%.** *G&M. 500 bottles.*

**Vom Fass Auchentoshan 12 Years Old (88)** n22 t23 f22 b21. Great to see the distillery living up to its regional style so eloquently. Twelve by name, six by nature! **40%.** *Austria.*

## AUCHROISK
**Speyside, 1974. Diageo. Working.**

**Auchroisk Aged 10 Years** db **(84)** n20 t22 f21 b21. Tangy orange on the nose,  the malt amplified by a curious saltiness on the palate. **43%.** *Flora and Fauna.*

**Cadenhead's Authentic Collection Auchroisk Aged 15 Years** Sherry Butt, dist 89, bott May 05 **(69)** n15 t20 f16 b18. Sulphur tainted; shame because the honey delivery is a noble waste. **59.5%.** *636 bottles.*

**Cadenhead's Authentic Collection Auchroisk Aged 16 Years** Butt, dist 89, bott Sept 06 **(71)** n17 t18 f18 b18. Sulphur-clobbered. A tragedy, as there are some great moments here – if you are able to isolate them. **58.8%.** *666 bottles.*

**Chieftain's Auchroisk Aged 11 Years Medoc Finish (79)** n20 t22 f18 b19. Salivating but thin. **43%.** *Ian Macleod.*

**Connoisseurs Choice Auchroisk 1993 (78)** n19 t21 f19 b19. Simplistic malt essay of few words. **43%.** *Gordon & MacPhail.*

⠶ **D&M Connoisseurs' Club Bottling Auchroisk Aged 14 Years** Cask no. 15576, dist Oct 92 **(77)** n20 t19 f19 b19. Only some persistent sweet barley keeps the oak from the door. **46%. nc ncf.** *US by Angus Dundee Distillers.*

**Kingsbury's New Celtic Auchroisk 15 Years Old** cask no. 3653, dist 90 **(86)** n22 t22 f20 b22. This distillery produces blending malt. Casks worthy of bottling are few and far between: this, with its intense barley, is one. **62.8%.** *Japan Import System.*

**Maverick Auchroisk Aged 12 Years Port Finish** dist 93, bott 04 **(87)** n20 poppy seeds and pepper; t23 beautiful delivery of warming fruit and juicy barley; f22 medium length, and a gentle burn of soft spice in oil; b22 maverick right enough...an Auchroisk at last that can get the pulse racing! Now this is a good example of justified cask finishing. **46%. nc ncf.** *Murray McDavid.*

⠶ **Murray McDavid Auchroisk 1992 Aged 14 Years** Bourbon/Guigal Cotes Rotie Syrah **(76)** n19 t19 f19 b19. Time for me to have a little whine... **46%**

⠶ **Old Masters Auchroisk Aged 10 Years** Cask no. 1073, dist 1996, bott 06 **(86)** n19 t22 f23 b22. One of the best Auchroisk bottlings for a while. The oak-punchy nose doesn't promise much but the fit, flighty yet ultimately intense nature of the barley is a minor treat. **59%.** *James MacArthur & Co Ltd.*

**Old Malt Cask Auchroisk Aged 16 Years (81)** n21 t20 f20 b20. Pear drops and barley. **50%.**

**Old Malt Cask Auchroisk Aged 30 Years** dist Apr 75, bott Nov 05 **(77)** n21 t19 f18 b19. A 30-y-o Auchroisk....!! I must be getting old. I remember standing outside my spirit merchants in Cross Street, Manchester, waiting for the delivery of the first-ever bottling – a distillery bottled 12 year old. But what a disappointment most bottlings have been since, and this is typically thin and lacklustre. **48.9%. nc ncf.** *239 bottles.*

⠶ **Old Malt Cask Auchroisk Aged 30 Years Bourbon Finish** dist May 76, bott Nov 06 **(74)** n19 t19 f18 b18. For a malt which, from its first distillation, began falling apart from about the age of eight onwards, this has lasted the test of time comparatively well. Obvious oaky incursions have cut short the complexity but enough malt sticks to make it interesting. **44.8%.** *Douglas Laing. 330 bottles.*

⠶ **Scotch Malt Whisky Society Cask 95.6 Aged 21 Years** Refill Hogshead, dist Mar 85 **(81)** n20 t22 f19 b20. Sharp, malty and bigger-bodied than more recent expressions. But there is still something rather hot and hostile about this. **54.6%**

**Scotts Selection Auchroisk 1989** bott 05 **(77)** n19 t21 f18 b19. Decent malt surge; otherwise dry and nondescript. **63.9%.** *Speyside Distillers.*

⠶ **Secret Stills Lowland 1989** Distillery No. 3 Release No. 2 **(86)** n19 t22 f23 b22. A very sweet rendition of one of Scotland's most temperamental malts. Just to add to the confusion there is even a degree of smoke to this one. **45%.** *Gordon & MacPhail.*

## AULTMORE
**Speyside, 1896. John Dewar & Son. Working.**

**Aultmore 12 Years Old** db **(86)** n22 t22 f20 b22. Do any of you remember the old DCL distillery bottling of this from, what, 25 years ago? Well, this is nothing like it. **40%**

⋅⋅⋅ **Cadenhead's Authentic Collection Aultmore Aged 17 Years** Bourbon barrel, dist 89, bott Feb 07 **(86)** n21 t23 f21 b21. some delightful moments, especially when it comes to the intense bourbon middle. Lovely cocoa-clad finish but at times runs a little hot. **54.4%.** 186 bottles.

⋅⋅⋅ **The Clydesdale Aultmore 17 Years Old** 18 Months Sherry Cask Finish, cask ref. 0076/3060, dist Sept 89, bott Oct 06 **(95)** n23 a wonderful duel between sharp blood orange and sweeter American oak bourboniness: sheer class t24 salivating freshness of crisp barley is pounded by juicy, fruity spice – and big spice at that; the barley is sharp and wonderfully defined; f24 again the balance is near faultless with the drying oaks never drying too far, maintaining just enough barley edge to complement the big cocoa finale. A malt to make you swoon... b24 a dram of almost surreal complexity that radiates near faultless quality. Thanks to the use of a quite fabulous sherry butt for rounding off, Aultmore rarely comes better than this. Come to think of it, Speysiders in general rarely come better than this. **55.8%. nc ncf.** Blackadder International.

**Dun Bheagan Aultmore Aged 15 Years (76)** n19 t19 f19 b19. A bit dense, monosyllabic and bitter. **43%.** Ian Macleod.

**Norse Cask Selection Aultmore 1989 Aged 15 Years (83)** n18 t23 f21 b21. Tricky vintage at this distillery, '89. Usually the nose sucks and this one's no exception. However, the intensity of the barley delivery is mind-blowingly beautiful. **55.8%.** Quality World, Denmark.

**Old Malt Cask Aultmore 16 Years Old** dist June 1989, bott Dec 05 **(66)** n17 t17 f16 b16. One for the mother-in-law. **50%.** Douglas Laing. 270 bottles.

⋅⋅⋅ **Old Malt Cask Aultmore Aged 16 Years** Sherry Finish dist May 90, bott Feb 07 **(66)** n14 t19 f16 b17. scuppered by the dreaded "S" word... **50%.** 742 bottles.

**Old Masters Aultmore 1989 15 Year Old** Cask no. 726, bott Feb 05 **(89)** n20 pretty confused; t23 wonderful, dank Jamaican ginger cake – with extra ginger. A bit of a spot the malt competition; f23 perhaps only Talisker at full throttle can match this for sheer spice wooomph!! b23 delicious gingery spice and busy throughout and though a fraction out of alignment it hardly seems to matter. For those who like their whisky hot! **54.9%.** James MacArthur.

**The Single Malt of Scotland Aultmore Aged 13 Years** Vintage 1992 cask 3852 **(90)** n23 high octane barley: as intense as it gets; t23 beautiful gloss to the ultra-intense barley shuts out any telling oak interference; f22 well integrated with vanilla forming beautiful patterns on the single-minded malt; b22 simplistic but one of the best Aultmores of the last five or six years. **57.6%.** The Whisky Exchange.

⋅⋅⋅ **The Single Malts of Scotland Aultmore 1990 Aged 16 Years (95)** n24 crushed Crunchy bars – it's honeycomb and chocolate all the way, except for a slight puff of peat smoke; t23 lush delivery with the accent on honey, though the oak ensures bitter-sweet harmony; a tad oily; f24 at first seems oak-riddled and bitter. By the third mouthful the honey has permeated so deeply that balance is restored and also some juicier barley tones radiate impressively until the cocoa arrives to give a virtuoso display; b24 at first taste I thought this was all nose with the oak doing damage further down the line. Then, slowly, you realise you are in the company of greatness and your palate has been caressed by genius. Magnificent whisky. **58.8%. sc.** Speciality Drinks, UK.

## BALBLAIR
### Highlands (Northern), 1872. Inver House. Working.
**Balblair 10 Years Old** db **(86)** n21 t22 f22 b21. Such an improved dram away from the clutches of caramel. **40%**

**Balblair Aged 16 Years** db **(84)** n22 t22 f20 b20. Definitely gone up a notch in the last year. The lime on the nose has been replaced by dim Seville oranges; the once boring finish reveals elements of fruit and spice. It's the barley- rich middle that shines, though, and some more work will belt this up into the high 90s where this great distillery belongs. **40%**

**Balblair Aged 24 Years Limited Edition** dist 1979, bott Oct 03 db **(90)** n23 t22 f22 b23. Absolutely spot-on whisky from a truly great distillery. The absence of colouring on this underlines my assertion that this is a distillery that is far too good to be tampered with at any age. **46%.** 3,150 bottles.

**Balblair 35 Years Old Limited Edition** db **(91)** n23 debonair and regal, there is wonderful confidence to the elegant ginger and citrus lead while the oak offers grey around the temples; t23 more slivers of caramelised ginger as the intense malt spices up and the oak forms almost a cloudy haze on the palate; f22 gentle and sweet, a touch of cocoa offers excellent balance, though its age really shows at the death; b23 textured and weighted almost to perfection, the malt really does display enormous depth. **45.4%**

**Balblair 38 Years Old Limited Edition** db **(93)** n23 tangerines on the turn; lavender guarding the wardrobe; t23 massive oak injection suggests that it's past its sell-by date, but a magnificent infusion of ripe fruit ranging from juiceleaking plums to grapefruit brings this back to life; f23 a pulsating finish with soft spices amid the juice and barley; b24 what a treat of a dram, always teetering at the edge of the cliff but being brought back to safety by some extraordinary fruit. **44%**

**Balblair 1989 Limited Edition** db **(82)** n21 t21 f20 b20. Good honey in places. **46%**

**Balblair Peaty 1992** cask 2932 **(88)** n21 a vague smoky buzz; youthful for its age; t22 sweet and biting at first then a wave of soft peat; f23 quite classy at the death as varying waves of bitter-sweet malt and oak delve into the light smoke; b22 Very good distillate, but don't expect an Ardbeg or even an Ardmore here. **58.8%**

**Balblair Peaty 1992** cask 3026 **(81)** n20 t20 f21 b20. Re-defines the term "peaty". The delicate smoke hides behind firm malt; takes a little time to get going though there is no doubting the overall quality. Just comes up a bit short on the complexity stakes. **61.5%**

**Balblair Elements** db **(84)** n20 t20 f23 b21. Just like the Scottish elements, this seems to change dramatically from bottling to bottling. This one starts indifferently but the finish is an essay in luxurious honey. **40%**

⋅⋙⋅ **Balblair Vintage 1979** dist 79, bott 07 db **(84)** n21 t22 f20 b21. A pretty whisky, but one which refuses to open out entirely despite the barley-rich prompting. **46%. nc.**

⋅⋙⋅ **Balblair Vintage 1989** dist 89, bott 07 db **(89)** n22 custard powder mixed into barley grist; t23 plate-cleansing from the off with the barley surging in gigantic waves; the oak is hardly shy but very much kept in check; f22 soft, juicy barley-fruit re-enters the fray as the oaks do their best to dry with that European-fruit distillate bitterness (wild cherries, to be precise) that seems to be a part of this distillery's latter-day character; b22 the key to this malt is its refreshing qualitiy: the way the oak come on board but the barley wins the day. An excellent journey. **43%. nc.**

⋅⋙⋅ **Balblair Vintage 1997** dist 97, bott 07 db **(88)** n23 an exceptionally confident nose: bursting out of the bottle with kumquats and jazzed-up barley. Just so intense and fresh; t22 again the fruits pile in, both a mixture of something citrussy and barley-related. Big yet refined with the house-style light bitterness towards the middle as the oaks absorb easily; f21 a delicate and rather simple fade pepped up by the lightest of spices; b22 this is the way I've been wanting to see Balblair at this age for a long, long time. Easily the most true to character distillery bottling for the last 20 years. **43%. nc.**

**Cadenhead's Authentic Collection Balblair Aged 16 Years** dist 90, bott Sept 06 **(94)** n23 pithy, fruit stones. Take your time here: this is very complex; t24 astonishing exhibition of sweet-dry harmonization; a wonderful early fruit edge which is then met full on by a dry, oakier blast. Pure complexity and indulgence; f23 massive cocoa arrival in tidal waves; b24 One of those stunning casks which reveals little on first meeting, but after getting to know you offers nothing but sheer elegance: a malt just oozing class. **58.8%**. *174 bottles.*

**Dewar Rattray Individual cask Bottling Balblair 1990 Aged 15 Years** cask no. 1145, dist Apr 90, bott Sept 05 **(89)** n23 exemplary balance considering the crispness of the barley; t22 juicy barley dripping off firm but unobtrusive oak; f22 softens with slices of toast and vanilla; b22 just one of those whiskies that works brilliantly, though hard to say exactly why. **62.9%**. *680 bottles.*

**Harrods Balnagown Balblair (90)** n23 busy, sharp malt; remains cheerfully green and raw; t22 at once lush and mouth-watering with the usual citrus met in a head to head with roasty barley; f23 much longer and those toasty, roasty notes persist magnificently; b22 someone has eased off on the caramel from the last bottling and we are left with a real gem. **40%** ⊙⊙

**Private Collection Balblair 1973 (90)** n22 not quite impenetrable sherry, but close; t24 chewy and spicy with moist and dry dates. Just so stunningly juicy for its age; f22 big dry mocha finish, getting roasty late on; **b**22 what an excellent sherry cask this whisky has been housed in. Bottled just in time, though. **45%**. *G&M.*

The Single Malt of Scotland Balblair Aged 40 Years Anniversary Selection Hogshead cask no. 1346 **(89) n**22 enticing, fruity nose that is exotic yet traditional. There is the most delicate puff of peat, but four decades of oak offers us mango with a dash of passion fruit. Over-ripe, but lovely; **t**22 as silky as one would expect from this type of oak development; there is a puckering element, too. But holds together against the odds; **f**23 loads of cocoa but just enough barley sweetness – and again that charming little smoke injection - to balance things out; **b**22 another cliff-hanger, with the oak threatening to get away from things, but remains stylishly impressive to the last. **42.8%. nc ncf.** *The Whisky Exchange. 152 bottles.*

⠆⠆ The Single Malts of Scotland Balblair 1965 Aged 40 Years **(76) n**19 **t**20 **f**18 **b**19. I know it's old and all that. But this does nothing for me other than provide me with soft bourbon. Otherwise, from the mildly butyric nose through the oak-induced fruitiness to the washed -out liquorice finale, it all seems...well, a whisky that is too old. **42.7%. Sc.** *Speciality Drinks, UK.*

## BALMENACH
### Speyside, 1824. Inver House. Working.

Balmenach Aged 25 Years Golden Jubilee db **(89) n**21 **t**23 **f**22 **b**23. What a glorious old charmer this is! An essay in balance despite the bludgeoning nature of the beast early on. Takes a little time to get to know and appreciate: persevere with this belter because it is classic stuff for its age. **58%**. *Around 800 decanters.*

Blackadder Aberdeen Distillery Balmenach 14 Years Old cask no. 2500, dist Apr 90, bott Nov 04 **(86) n**20 **t**23 **f**22 **b**21. Never quite hits a comfortable pitch or rhythm yet still has enough charisma to entertain. **46%**

The Bottlers Balmenach 21 Years Old Spanish oak, refill sherry, cask no. 3056, dist Dec 84, bott Dec 05 **(82) n**19 **t**22 **f**21 **b**20. Lots to chew on, clever use of distant smoke and at times attractively spiced. But we have come to expect rather more from this bottler. **57.8%**

Cadenhead's Authentic Collection Balmenach-Glenlivet Aged 17 Years Bourbon Hogshead, dist 89, bott Sept 06 **(90) n**23 sexily soft: wafer-thin oak, sultry barley and a dab of something vaguely fruity all in perfect proportions; **t**22 short, muddled delivery and then a spreading of finely-tuned, trim malt; **f**22 bigger oak say, the light bitterness balancing the juicier barley; **b**23 in many ways simplistic, but has that certain something that picks it out above the norm. **53.1%.** *312 bottles.*

Chieftain's Balmenach 15 Years Old Hogshead **(77) n**19 **t**21 **f**18 **b**19. Fruity and pleasant, but a fraction too over-oaked. **43%.** *Ian MacLeod.*

⠆⠆ Connoisseurs Choice Balmenach 1975 **(92) n**24 wonderful oloroso theme: clean and with a distinctive "cream sherry" lead-in to the roasty and very lightly smoked barley; **t**23 age is immediately apparent but such is the intensity and clarity of the sherry the balance is maintained; lovely barley sub strata; **f**22 soft toffee apple and vanilla **b**23 what a great little malt, showing just how a sherry cask should influence, and marking clearly the gap between the quality of latter -day sherry butts and the pre-sulphured hey-days of over 30 years ago. **43%.** *Gordon & MacPhail.*

Deerstalker Balmenach Aged 12 Years **(82) n**20 **t**21 **f**20 **b**21. Surprisingly and disappointingly dull, with just enough sweet malt in there to see off the worst of the big oak thanks to this being the new, natural-coloured bottling. Even so, this seems a lot older than twelve. **40%.** *Aberko.*

Deerstalker Balmenach Aged 18 Years **(89) n**23 near faultless sherry butt influence gives a zesty, mocha-tinged frame to the heavyweight malt; **t**23 superb arrival of spicy, Christmas puddings fruit that zips around the palate leaving a delicious trail of sweet barley; **f**21 the oak kicks in reluctantly, but its arrival is welcome and balancing; **b**22 perhaps the more distant hint of sulphur, but it really is acceptable here: this naturally coloured update is amazingly fresh and mouthwatering for all its age and sherry influence; a massive improvement on the old, caramel-enhanced bottlings. **46%. ncf.**

## THE BALVENIE
### Speyside, 1892. William Grant & Sons. Working.

The Balvenie Aged 10 Years Founders Reserve db **(90) n**23 astonishing complexity: the fruit is relaxed, crushed sultanas and malty suet. A sliver of smoke and no more:

everything is hinted and nudged at rather than stated. Superb; **t**24 here we go again: threads of malt binding together barely detectable nuances. Thin liquorice here, grape there, smoke and vanilla somewhere else; **f**20 Light muscovado-toffee flattens out the earlier complexity. The bitter-sweet balance remains brilliant to the end; **b**23 just one of those all-time-great standard 10-year-olds from a great distillery – pity they've decided to kill it off. **40%**

**The Balvenie Double Wood Aged 12 Years** db **(77) n**22 **t**20 **f**17 **b**18. I had hoped to report an improvement on this expression from one of the world's greatest distilleries. But, sadly, no can do. Over the top with the sherry, then later the caramel (either added or natural), this just never gets going and Balvenie's legendary complexity is buried far too deep to find. **40%**

**Balvenie Rum Wood Aged 14 Years** db **(88) n**22 excitable malt; lively almost piercing sugars; **t**23 incredible spice delivery, seriously warming and increasingly sensual as the malt fights back; **f**21 lots of toffee-barley; **b**22 tasted blind I would never have recognized the distillery: I'm not sure if that's a good thing. **47.1%**

⠠⠄ **The Balvenie Roasted Malt Aged 14 Years (90) n**21 a European style of aroma often found in the smaller distilleries being in some ways closed, offering a hard edge and, on another level, showing attractive bitter-sweet conflict; **t**23 it's the sweet element that shows the more powerful hand, especially with a delicious barley rush, though rabid peppers soon gather all the attention **f**22 dry at first, a little sinewy but the gradual build up of mocha is sublime **b**24 Balvenie very much as you've never seen it before: it takes time to settle, but when it does it becomes an absolute, mouth-filling cracker! **47.1%**

**The Balvenie Roasted Malt Aged 14 Years** dist 92 db **(94) n**23 thick, sweet, intense, vaguely floral, even more vaguely bourbony but very, very different; **t**25 salivating for all the enormity. The fruitiness is in barley concentrate form and offers a delivery as memorable as it is unique; the barley juice appears to seep into the palate in equal spurts. Breathtaking and nigh-on perfect; **f**23 warming spices develop while the oak tries to gain a foothold into the silky barley; a tad thin towards the end; **b**23 having beaten the drum for this distillery longer than any independent observer breathing, it is so rewarding to find a bottling that so encapsulates Balvenie's brilliance. To do so, though, they have used a percentage of malt briefly germinated before being massively roasted in the style of a stout beer. The result is not unlike some European mainland malt whisky styles but fortified with the usual Balvenie complexity and weight. For the first 25 seconds on the palate it is, quite frankly, probably as good as anything you are likely to taste for many years and only the quick-ish finish robs it of a certain Bible Award. **47.1%. ncf.**

**The Balvenie Aged 15 Years Single Barrel** db **(93) n**23 cracking vanilla-malt split. Complex, intriguing, something to really get your nose into. Quite maltings-floorish; **t**24 massive malt surge is invigorating and mouthwatering. Glorious; **f**22 keeps clean and relatively oak-free; **b**24 just one of those drams that should be within touching distance at strategic points around the house. **50.4%.** *Being single barrel the bottlings do change quite regularly: fortunately the magnificence of the quality rarely does.*

**Balvenie New Wood Aged 17 Years** db **(85) n**23 **t**22 **f**19 **b**21. A naturally good age for Balvenie; the nose is lucid and exciting, the early delivery is thick with rich malt. This, though, has sucked out lots of caramel from the wood to leave an annoyingly flat finish. **40%**

**The Balvenie Aged 21 Years Port Wood** db **(87) n**23 clean, mouthwatering evidence of fresh port pipes; **t**22 the wine swamps the malt for a while, but being Balvenie the complexity returns and sweet maltiness leads the way; **f**21 vanilla and toffee; **b**21 using port pipes like this can backfire on a malt as complex as Balvenie, but this one comes through with flying Scottish and Portuguese colours. **40%**

**The Balvenie Thirty Aged 30 Years** db **(92) n**24 a fusion of fruits from grape to pears, all topped off with smoke and a hint of tiring oak; **t**23 stand-your-spoon-in-the-stuff proportions and seasoned with a hint of spice; **f**22 the oak which threatens on the nose erupts slightly on the finish, but still the malt offers an intensity that softens the blow; **b**23 Balvenie is a rare Speysider that by and large manages to handle encroaching age with ease up to this type of vintage. **47.3%**

**The Balvenie Aged 50 Years** cask 191 db **(87) n**23 coffee and biscuits alongside the ultra-ripe, thick sherry, not unlike moist cherry fruitcake. Smoke remains after the sherry is burnt out; **t23** some suppressed oak does its best to escape, but has a major battle to fight its way through the layers of big grape. Lovely spices point in the direction of some peat; **f19** pretty shattered oak offers a bitter finale, but the fruit does all it can to soften things and lengthen out matters; **b22** a noble dram battered by oak but comes through with a degree of nobility. *Natural strength.*

**The Balvenie 1967 Vintage Cask** db **(89) n**24 **t**22 **f**21 **b**22. Dry and complex.

**The Balvenie 1968 Vintage Cask** db **(86) n**23 **t**22 **f**20 **b**21. The delicate sweetness accentuates the dry finale. Pretty delicious. **50.8%**

**The Balvenie 1971 Vintage Cask** cask no. 8919 db **(78) n**21 **t**20 **f**18 **b**19. Wonderfully exotic fruit (often a sign of advanced age) on the nose, and for all the undoubted complexity on show the oak has defeated even a Balvenie here. **46.8%**

**The Balvenie 1971 Vintage Cask** cask no. 8921 db **(79) n**20 **t**21 **f**19 **b**19. The barley tries its complex best, but it's an unequal struggle against the oak. **46.9%**

**The Balvenie 1971 Vintage Cask** cask 8935 db **(90) n**23 a slight Canadian whisky/bourbony element here thanks to the sweet influence of the grain against the firm oakiness. Attractive and quite complex; **t22** beautiful malt develops in both intensity and sweetness; soft natural caramel and vanillas begin to fill the middle; **f22** pulsing barley and lashings of vanilla: freeze it and you could make an ice cream from this! **b23** of the three, this was the only one worth bottling in the sainted name of Balvenie thanks to the malty sweetness seeing off the oak and in a way that offers style and enormity. This really is a beauty! And such can sometimes be the thin line between something that works (in this case wonderfully) and something that doesn't. **47.3%**

**The Balvenie 1972 Vintage Cask** db **(88) n**22 **t**23 **f**21 **b**22. A superb, lightly smoked Balvenie that shows some age but wears it well. *Natural strength.*

**Balvenie 1972 Vintage** cask no. 14811 db **(82) n**20 **t**22 **f**20 **b**20. A tiring, exotic fruited effort which glows rather than shines. **47.3%**

**The Balvenie 1973 Vintage Cask** db **(92) n**22 distinctly bourbony with sweet leathery tones sitting beside vanilla and a trickle of honey. Just a distant waft of peat brings us back to Scotland; **t24** this is the acceptable face of oak: delicate bourbony notes gush at you, then a honey spice middle with vanilla ice cream; **f22** natural caramel slows it all down but still waves of bourbony sweetness both rattle and caress the tastebuds; **b24** some purists will find too many stars and stripes to the character if this malt. Even I thought I was in a Wild Turkey warehouse for a moment or two. But sheer quality cannot be denied. **49.7%**

**The Balvenie 1989 Port Wood** db **(83) n**20 **t**22 **f**21 **b**20. The nose is remarkably undemonstrative, all the fruity action arriving up front early on the tastebuds. Good follow-through. **40%**

**The Balvenie 1991 Port Wood** db **(91) n**23 darting barley and fruit gives a feather-light alternative to the much thicker, duskier malty oak beneath; **t23** enormous weight and depth offered by the chewing malt; the fruit is a peripheral, spice-wielding addition to complexity; **f22** a few strands of caramel (natural, I hope) add to the weight of the rich malt finale; **b23** I have long argued that two of the most complex noses in the world belong to Glenmorangie and Balvenie. So, a decade after Morangie began the trend, it was interesting to see how Balvenie coped with port pipes. Well, Balvenie's bigger body means that it is a little more heavy-handed. But as for complexity, Balvenie may even shade it by continuing to head down the malt rather than fruit path, using the port only to season rather than dominate. **40%**

**The Balvenie 1993 Port Wood** db **(89) n**21 well-weighted but a trifle stifled; **t23** much busier arrival, with a lovely roastiness playing off the wine; the spices buzz gorgeously; **f22** finds a light-roast Java element; **b23** oozes class without getting too flash about it: the secret is in the balance. **40%**

**The Balvenie Merry Christmas 2005** cask 749, dist 91, bott 25/10/05 db **(94) n**24 the type of cask isn't stated. But this is like almost pure Demerara rum hob-nobbing with top-of-the-table rich Balvenie malt. The result is uniquely brilliant; **t24** more Demerara-style kick with all kinds of tangent sugary, mollased notes heading off in every conceivable direction. Again the malt holds firm and digs in with some big oak notes; **f23** roasty, hickory, toasty and some boiled fruit sweets; **b23** Balvenie as you've never seen it before. But will definitely want to see again. **58.4%**. *60 bottles.*

**Cadenhead's Authentic Collection Balvenie - Glenlivet Aged 25 Years** Bourbon Hogshead, dist 79, bott May 05 **(95) n**24 dank, north-facing gardens, earthy and rich; some zesty barley adds a telling counterpunch. Such wonderful complexity; **t**24 perhaps the most intense malt you will find on the market today: everything flawless and in concentrate. Wow!! **f**23 some natural caramels escape to flattens things down slightly, but still the malt continues its enormous way. Memorable and truly beautiful; **b**24 Cadenhead's have bravely named Balvenie as the distillery here: how apposite in the year Deep Throat revealed his own identity. I'm sure this dram will be enjoyed by those able to spot a work of art in the offices of solicitors and barristers around the UK... Quite an exhibit in anyone's living-room. **52.7%**. *234 bottles.*

**Cadenhead's Chairman's Stock Balvenie-Glenlivet Aged 27 Years** dist 79, bott May 06 **(93) n**24 such depth: you need a mini-sub to get to the bottom of the complex barley-oak interplay, rounded off with a swirl of peat smoke and apple; **t**24 sweet, almost gristy intensity to the malt; the layering of the barley-sugar and oak is mind-blowing; **f**22 a slight hint of sweet apple, just like the nose; deft vanilla brings things to a close; **b**23 although from a bourbon cask, Balvenie shown in a fruit-candy hue. Gorgeous. **52.5%**. *264 bottles.*

# BANFF
**Speyside, 1863–1983. Demolished.**

**Banff Rare Malts 21 Year Old** 2004 db **(90) n**22 tangy, salty oak with citrus and distant lavender and smoke; **t**24 sensational arrival of pulsing malt and fruit enriched by wonderful smoky spices and the most delicate oiliness; **f**22 reverts to a more docile barley and vanilla merchant; **b**22 a quietly complex but brilliantly impressive addition to the Rare Malts range. **57.1%**

**Cadenhead's Banff 29 Years Old (73) n**19 **t**19 **f**18 **b**17. Too heavily oaked: should have been bottled at **25. 52%**

⸭ **Old Malt Cask Banff Aged 32 Years** dist May 74, bott Apr 07 **(86) n**20 **t**23 **f**21 **b**22. Beautifully honeyed and silky. **47.8%**. *Douglas Laing. 272 bottles.*

⸭ **Rarest of the Rare Banff 1975** Cask no. 3416 **(91) n**23 friendliest oak imaginable, with some ginger and crushed pine nuts sweetened by profuse honey; **t**22 perfect delivery of honeyed barley which rides the oaky, softly spiced waves with nonchalance; **f**23 gentle and chalky with enough spicy verve to keep it interesting; **b**23 again Banff shows itself to be an outstanding old-timer. The continuing shards of honey radiate brilliance despite the oak's best attentions. **42.2%**. *Duncan Taylor.*

**Rarest of the Rare Banff 1975** cask 3421, dist Nov 75, bott Apr 06 **(78) n**22 **t**20 **f**18 **b**18. Lovely nose and early malt delivery. But oak, sadly, has won the battle. **43.5%**. *Duncan Taylor. 179 bottles.*

**Rarest of the Rare Banff 1980** cask 2912, dist Nov 80, bott Apr 06 **(91) n**24 like entering a cake shop; **t**23 the prominent honey on nose is immediately transferred to the palate; an oaky buzz gives way to big barley; **f**22 milky-coffee; **b**22 some Banff bottlings can be supreme and here is one. Even the oaky threat retreats with good grace. **53.1%**. *Duncan Taylor. 181 bottles.*

# BEN NEVIS
**Highland (Western), 1825. Nikka. Working.**

**Ben Nevis 10 Years Old** db **(88) n**21 enormously chunky and weighty: for a 10-y-o the oak is thick, but sweetened medley of ripe fruits; **t**22 an almost syrupy mouth feel: a tad cloying but the malt is something you can so get your teeth into; **f**23 long with traces of liquorice and hickory; **b**22 a massive malt that has steadied itself in recent bottlings, but keep those knives and forks to hand! **46%**

**Ben Nevis 30 Years Old** cask 2519 db **(86) n**22 **t**22 **f**20 **b**22. A malt living on the edge: just about over the top oak but there is enough sweetness around not only too see it through but to make for a fascinating cocoa and coffee dram. **56.9%**

**Ben Nevis 1990 Port Wood Finish** bott 04 db **(92) n**21 **t**24 **f**23 **b**24. Pouring into the glass is a startling experience: it is like a Beaujolais. In 30 years of nosing my way around whisky warehouses and labs, never have I come across something as entirely unique as this: distillery manager Colin Ross deserves a medal struck for producing something so extraordinary. Collectors around the world will eventually trade their spouse for bottles of this. **61.6%**

Cadenhead's Authentic Collection Ben Nevis 14 Year Old dist 90, bott May 05 **(87)** n22 t22 f21 b22. Borderline sherry butts where the cracks show but are repaired by the enormity of the rich malt. **66.1%.**

⋄ Cadenhead's Authentic Collection Ben Nevis Aged 16 Years Butt, dist 1990, bott May 07 **(83)** n19 t22 f21 b21. the odd butt-induced flaw, but this is one of the biggest malts of the year with the power of the barley giving the taste buds a salivating workover. **66%.** 720 bottles.

⋄ The Clydesdale Ben Nevis 10 Years Old Sherry Cask, cask ref. 0184/572, dist Nov 95, bott Sept 06 **(74)** n19 t18 f19 b18. just enough sulphur to tellingly detract, but not enough to ruin. The seaweedy nose is interesting and the malt does try to fight back. **59.9%. nc ncf.** Blackadder International.

Duncan Taylor Collection Ben Nevis 1996 cask 25, dist Feb 96, bott Mar 06 **(86)** n22 t21 f22 b21. A lovely, second used cask allowing the malt to sing to the heavens. **46%.** 386 bottles.

Murray McDavid Ben Nevis Aged 6 Years Bourbon/Vintage Port, dist 99, bott 05 **(69)** n16 t18 f18 b17. Disproves the saying: "Any port in a storm." Sinks my boat. **46%. nc ncf.** 6000 bottles.

⋄ Murray McDavid Ben Nevis 1999 Aged 8 Years Bourbon/Fortified Grenache Blanc **(82)** n19 t20 f22 b21. Excellent finish of soft-centre chocolate with superb squidgy fruit fondant. **46%**

⋄ Old Malt Cask Ben Nevis Aged 10 Years Claret Finish July 96, bott Nov 06 **(89)** n20 cumbersome harsh and off-key, though something fruity does soften the blow t23 wow!! A total transformation from the nose with the tastebuds rocking from a sublime delivery of spices couched by a sweet, winey bed and brittle barley. Astonishing...; f23 enormous depth with those spices buzzing sharper now and blending perfectly with the growing cocoa; b23 a treat of a malt that pulses with freshness and character. **50%.** Douglas Laing. 361 bottles.

Platinum Ben Nevis Aged 36 Years dist Oct 68, bott Aug 05 **(75)** n20 t19 f18 b18. A semi-butyric plot doesn't help the cause here. At first it looks as though it might be a tasty bourbon-style number but falls apart in the glass. **49.1%.** 155 bottles.

Provenance Ben Nevis Aged 9 Years dist July 96, bott Nov 05 **(77)** n21 t19 f18 b19. Pulls up a bit short, even allowing for its tender years. **46%.** McGibbon's.

Provenance Ben Nevis Aged 10 Years dist 96 **(87)** n23 rich, strands of coconut in sugar syrup balanced by chalky oak: beautiful; t22 feather-light barley delivery beefed up by a big body surge; f20 thins out towards the finale; b22 tails off surprisingly fast after such a wonderfully confident start. **46%.** Douglas Laing.

⋄ Scotch Malt Whisky Society Cask 78.37 Aged 9 Years Sherry Gorda, dist Dec 97 **(63)** n14 t17 f16 b16. A sherry gorda, eh? Good Gorda, more like. Completely wrecked by sulphur. **56.3%**

Whisky Galore Ben Nevis Aged 8 Years dist 96, bott 05 **(82)** n21 t20 f21 b20. Complexity hovers around the zero mark, but there is no denying the fresh, malty deliciousness. **46%. nc ncf.** Duncan Taylor.

# BENRIACH
## Speyside, 1898. The BenRiach Distillery Co. Working.

Benriach 10 Years Old db **(77)** n18 t22 f18 b19. Thankfully this caramelinfested disaster from the old Seagram days (an essay in how to screw up a decent malt if ever there was one) is being withdrawn. If you find any, either get it as a collector's item or simply (and preferably) ignore. **43%**

The BenRiach Curiositas Aged 10 Years Single Peated Malt db **(95)** n24 Arbroath smokies that have spent longer than usual in the reek; beautiful citrus and crystal clear malt underpin the chunkiness; t24 mesmerising, succulent malt that simply melts on the tastebuds: enormously sweet, yet the balance is contained by deft oak, mouthwatering barley and a swift volley of peppering spices; f23 long, and keeps its shape: just so clean, with vanilla and a hint of cocoa adding singing in harmony to the peaty tune with near perfect bitter-sweetness for good measure; b24 there are much lauded Islay whiskies that would dream of this kind of clarity and complexity: absolutely top-of-the-range single malt that should be on every connoisseur's must-have list **46%**

**The BenRiach Aged 12 Years** (L06046) db **(83)** n21 t22 f20 b20. Very pleasant, but just not quite there by comparison with the previous bottling. A touch of soap on the nose, some stunning honey development on the palate but it's just a touch too flat. **40%**

**The BenRiach Aged 16 Years** (L05040) db **(93)** n23 playful smoke gives a phenolic haze to the striking malt and mounting oak; t24 sensational mouth-arrival: the degree of barley sweetness is perfect as are the soft oils and harmony between smoke and spice. Stunningly beautiful; f23 starchy vanilla at the death with the oak making some form of controlled impact; b23 just one of those whiskies that makes you contemplate the bottle in awe. **43%**

**The BenRiach Aged 20 Years** (L4231BB – bott 18 Aug 04) db **(88)** n23 t23 f21 b21. Never quite lives up to the nose or early mouth arrival but at this age for a light Speysider it would have been a miracle if it had. Even so, a barnstorming beaut! **43%**

**Benriach Peated Authenticus Peated Malt Aged 21 Years** db **(95)** n24 nosing blind, this has to be Laphroaig. Maybe with a dash of salty Ardbeg (thanks to the oranges). Yet it's pure Benriach; t24 a stupendous fruit-juiciness moistens the much drier smoke; the peat is chunky yet manageable, the spices warming but controlled with a slight Bowmore-style sweetness; the malt, free of smoke, chips in with some honey; f23 classic peaty sweetness that fades almost imperceptibly slowly. Almost endless; b24 still can't get my head around Seagram sitting on this little lot and doing absolutely nothing about it. It's beyond mind-boggling. The most south-east Islay of all Speysiders (except for that dash of Bowmore), including a generous pinch of salt...! This is a previously unknown masterpiece pulled not from an attic but a warehouse where it lay forgotten and unloved and one that connoisseurs around the world are going to spend hours and days getting to know, and perhaps even longer on websites discussing! **46%. nc ncf.**

**BenRiach Origine Over 12 Years** db **(90)** n23 oranges and barley sugar; fresh cut sweet grass; t23 the controlled intensity is spellbinding: the slight nuttiness mingles with firm barley, which blends with the shards of citrus, which incorporates beautifully the evolving spice; f21 slightly duller but the spices persist and the late, fudge-barley sees off any oak intrusion; b23 another little classic from Benriach, though this one feels as though it is operating within its own limits. Could there have been more? **40%. USA.**

**The BenRiach Fine Wood Finishes Age Over 12 Years Dark Rum Jamaican Barrel** Richly Peated (Pre-bottled TN) db **(90)** n22 smouldering peat cut from the deep; t23 a sugary coating to the smoke gives way to blossoming barley; f22 remains rich and beautifully textured as the soft oak also absorbs the gentle sweetness; b23 some experiments I have carried out in my own lab, and having tasted some similarly treated Caol Ila, reveal that certain rum and peat were made for each other. This is enormous stuff. **46%. nc ncf.**

**The BenRiach Fine Wood Finishes Age Over 12 Years Pedro Ximenez Butt** Richly Peated (Pre-bottled TN) db **(93)** n23 a biting peat that is chunky, hard and bristling with personality; t23 soft oils help soften the peaty blows, early on hickory and camp coffee come into play; f24 barley-sugar and vanilla. The dryness is controlled and soft; rarely does the aging process work quite so well. The waves are large and go on for ever. Genuine class. Wonderful; b23 forget about the Pedro Ximenez finish: it has made little discernible difference and is a distraction. This is all about absolutely brilliant whisky. Embrace. **46%. nc ncf.**

**The BenRiach Fine Wood Finishes Age Over 12 Years Tawny Port Hogshead** Richly Peated (Pre-bottled TN) db **(85)** n18 t22 f23 b22. the nose is awkward, but the Port influence on the palate is telling and so refreshing. **46%. nc ncf.**

◦➤ **The BenRiach Aged Over 12 Years "Arumaticus Fumosus"** Richly Peated Style, ex-dark rum barrels db **(91)** n23 cracklingly-hard peat; embers of a crofter's fire; t23 big entry but always controlled; the peat is shackled by something non-gristy but sweet but comes and comes again in waves; the tingling spices are well harnessed; f22 a Java/Indian medium roast coffee mix with a touch of demerara to lighten it...and the smoke, of course; b23 very often finishing in rum can sharpen the mouthfeel yet at the same time add a sugary sheen. This little gem is no exception. **46%**

⚜ **The BenRiach Aged Over 12 Years "Heredotus Fumosus"** Richly Peated Style, ex-Pedro Ximenez Sherry Butt db **(84)** n20 t22 f21 b21. Perfectly respectable, perfectly drinkable, highly enjoyable and pretty more-ish. But if any whisky was to convince me that latter-day sherry butts and peat make entirely happy bedfellows...this wouldn't be it. **46%**

⚜ **The BenRiach Aged Over 12 Years "Importanticus Fumosus"** Richly Peated Style, ex-Port Hogshead db **(87)** n22 the phenols are hard enough to still be embedded in a New Pitsligo peat stack; t22 some grudging fruitiness attempts to make inroads into the solid peat base; f21 some spices chisel their way into the malt; b22 spill some of this on your foot and you'll break a toe. Hardicus asius Nailsus. **46%**

**The BenRiach Fine Wood Finishes Age Over 15 Years Henriques Madeira Barrel** (Pre-bottled TN) db **(95)** n24 such is the clarity of the wine, that you can just about spot the House; things are enlivened by the kind of soft spices you pray for and an injection of oaky vanilla that appears to be measured to the last atom. The big question here is: does it get 24 or 25...?; t24 dense fruit: you can almost chew the grape and spit out the pips. Especially beautiful are the peaks and troughs of the countering sweetness and dryness – two extremes yet somehow in complete harmony. Ting...; f22 dry oak but still the palate drips with concentrated barley and grape. Wow! b25 This is an essay in subtlety. And further proof that Madeira casks are giving malt something that sherry so often fails to do these days. If bottled in the same form as I have sampled it here, we have one of the recent truly great Speysiders on our hands! **46%. nc ncf.**

**The BenRiach Fine Wood Finishes Age Over 15 Years Pedro Ximenez Butt** (Pre-bottled TN) db **(86)** n24 t23 f19 b20. A disappointing end to a spellbinding story. With its inlay of sweeteded carrot juice, probably the most complex new aroma on Sepyside, though **46%. nc ncf.**

**The BenRiach Fine Wood Finishes Age Over 15 Years Dark Rum Jamaican Barrel** (Pre-bottled TN) db **(86)** n21 t23 f21 b21. A bit of a hotchpotch, even Canadian in style, but those with a sweet tooth will walk the plank for this one. **46%. nc ncf.**

**The BenRiach Fine Wood Finishes Aged Over 15 Years Tawny Port Hogshead** (Pre-bottled TN) db **(92)** n24 unlike the disastrous 12-y-o, this is exactly how a port pipe should influence a malt: rose petals and Turkish delight sprinkled with baked brown sugar and oozing soft grape. Add to that a sultry bourbon influence, and you have one hell of an aroma; t23 perfect weight; the barley parcelled up in gentle natural caramels and juicy wine. Soft sugars lighten the mood while spices threaten. Some over-enthusiastic oak in the middle; f22 long and becomes rather too intense; b23 another quite wondrous malt from this new range of BenRiach. I can usually take or leave cask finishes. I cannot remember ever having been faced with a succession of awesome whiskies. **46%. nc ncf.**

⚜ **The BenRiach Aged 15 Years Dark Rum Wood Finish** db **(86)** n21 t22 f22 b21. Some malts, when put into a dark rum cask, have a propensity to become enjoyable but pretty sweet. This is one such example. **46%. nc ncf.**

**The BenRiach Limited Edition Bottlings Age Over 25 Years** bott 06 db **(79)** n19 t21 f20 b19. A thread of golden syrup helps control the slightly over attentive oak. **50%.**

**The BenRiach Limited Edition Bottlings Age Over 30 Years** bott 06 db **(88)** n20 not entirely happy with itself; thin and gluey with just a touch of barley to compensate; t22 lush and fruity: ultra-ripe sultanas and then a spicy injection of barley-come-oak; f24 absolutely wonderful denouement with some liquorish notes intertwining brilliantly with the Blue Mountain coffee, grist and honeycomb in near enough perfect proportions and weight. If only all life's finishes could be this good...; b22 a finish of legend. **50%. nc ncf.**

**BenRiach Limited Release Single Cask Bottling Aged 16 Years** cask 802, dist 88, bott Sept 05 db **(85)** n22 t21 f21 b21. Excellent barley-sugar. Spiced-up oak and natural caramels make for a relatively short-haul flight. **54.7%. sc.** 675 bottles.

**BenRiach Limited Release Single Cask Bottling Aged 25 Years** Hogshead cask 10985, dist 79, bott Sept 05 db **(89)** n22 intriguing fanfare of mildly smoked bourbon; t23 hallmark gorgeous delivery; here the oaky intrusion is contained to an off-beat wave that falls between the early mouthwatering, honey-brushed malt and a middle of delightful cocoa; f22 spicy yet mouthwatering to the death; b22 isolates the one moment of over-eager oak brilliantly and enchants us with a succession of delicate tones. **57.5%. sc.** 228 bottles.

**BenRiach Limited Release Single Cask Bottling Aged 29 Years** hogshead cask 7211, dist 75, bott Sept 05 db **(87) n**20 bit of a gluepot; **t**22 muscular and malty, there is a wonderful sheen to the barley; **f**23 the finale radiates pure cocoa; **b**22 aggressive and forceful, the oak just about stays in line. **59.1%. sc.** *216 botles.*

**BenRiach Limited Release Single Cask Bottling Aged 33 Years** hogshead cask 4043, dist 72, bott Sept 05 db **(88) n**22 a delicate dusting of peat does little to dull the apple and barley freshness; **t**23 lush, intensely malty, wonderful barley-sugar and the lightest of peat. Tender and terrific; **f**21 soft, semi-exotic fruit soothes the oak; **b**22 a charming, if slightly tired, malt with a sprinkling of something for everyone – sherry apart. **49%. sc.** *261 bottles.*

**The BenRiach 1966 Limited Release Cask Bottling** Hogshead cask 2382, bott Dec 04 db **(90) n**23 kumquats and honeydew melon; the oaky tones mingle with gristy malt and the faintest whiff of smoke; **t**21 early oak dissipates as the intense, sweet malt fights back; warming and lively; **f**23 goes into complexity overdrive as the early battles are settled and now there is wave upon wave of vaguely smoked, vanilla-edged malt that is enriched further by a sliver of Jaffa cake and dark chocolate; **b**23 an eloquent and truly majestic early contribution to Scotland's 40th anniversary celebrations of England winning the 1966 World Cup. **50%**

**The BenRiach 1968 Limited Release Cask Bottling** hogshead cask 2712, bott Jun 06 db **(89) n**22 the usual oak-led nose but here softened by a light drizzle of guava and Asian pear; **t**23 wonderful, lush malt delivery; just brimming with warming – almost slightly hot – barley; **f**22 lots of vanilla and even a touch of banana. The oak makes for a forceful farewell; **b**22 subtle fruits abound despite – in fact probably because of – the oak. **52%. nc ncf.** *155 bottles.*

**The BenRiach 1970 Limited Release Cask Bottling** cask 4005, bott Dec 04, db **(88) n**23 **t**23 **f**20 **b**22. Chewy and charming, but a season or three beyond its prime. Even so, there is no mistaking a class act when you see one. **51.2%**

**The BenRiach 1972 Limited Release Cask Bottling** Re-racked sherry butt cask 1733, bott Jun 06 db **(77) n**21 **t**20 **f**18 **b**18. Too oaked. **45%. nc ncf.**

**The BenRiach 1975 Limited Release Cask Bottling** Gomez cask 7007, bott Jun 06 db **(95) n**24 toffee apple dipped in exceptionally fine, dry sherry; coal smoke, various spices and vanilla play their part, as does moist cherry cake and slightly burned raisins; **t**24 just so fresh and mouthwatering: there are a few waves of puckering oak, but they are seen off by fruitcake and sherry. Beautifully spiced and cleverly sweet; **f**23 long with lashing of vanilla and custard and sprinkled with cocoa . That coal smoke returns to add further length; **b**24 if I'm not mistaken, I happened upon a sample from this cask when I paid the distillery a visit early in 2006. It tasted sensational then and no worse in my sample room. An entirely faultless sherry butt of a style very rarely encountered today. A classic. **55%. nc ncf.**

⸬ **The BenRiach 1975 Vintage Single Cask Campaign No. 4 Ex Port Pipe,** cask no. 4451, bott June 07 db **(91) n**23 highly complex fruit salad ranging from wild strawberries to boiled rhubarb. Very earthy, too; **t**23 boiled candy: a mixture of fruit and cough ones. Gorgeous texture, though, and the gristiness excils; **f**22 sawdusty oak pokes through; a touch of something smoky and a slightly thin finale; **b**23 the Port has certainly breathed life into this old 'un. The complexity and enormity of the experience means it takes about 20 minutes to even begin to fathom this one out. **53.9%.** *650 bottles.*

**The BenRiach 1976 Limited Release Cask Bottling** Hogshead cask no. 8084, bott Jun 06 db **(84) n**20 **t**22 **f**21 **b**21. A real spicefest with the dominant oak shades at time by the excellent, though short-lived traces of manuka honey. For those who chew sweetened toothpicks. **56%. nc ncf.** *192 bottles.*

⸬ **The BenRiach 1976 Vintage Single Cask Campaign No. 4 Ex Port Pipe,** cask no. 4469, bott June 07 db **(90) n**22 ribald and rollicking – a real spiced- up ultra fruity treat; **t**22 grip your chair as the spices scorch in! Prisoners slaughtered to order here as the white peppers rip through the tangy, salivating fruits; a soft echo of barley can just about be heard; **f**23 fabulously long and the most extraordinary thing: it really does have the taste of straw to accompany the barley and fading fruit; **b**23 good grief! Another BenRiach that is almost redefining cask finishes. This one works a treat, though! **55.5%.** *750 bottles.*

**The BenRiach 1978 Limited Release Cask Bottling** hogshead cask 1589, bott Dec 04 db **(90) n**20 heavy oak; mildly spiced; **t**23 wow! The nose gives no indication of the rich honeyfest to follow. Beautifully sweet, soft fruit and a hint of burnt fudge and cocoa; **f**23 long, with more honeycomb and chocolate and pulsing spices; **b**24 ignore the nose. And to descend its astonishing depths, allow it to breathe in the glass for a little while and get to body temperature. **54.4%**

**The BenRiach 1978 Limited Release Cask Bottling** hogshead cask 1596, bott Jun 06 db **(93) n**22 slightly thin, chalky and wallpaper-gluey. But enough malt abounds to ensure attractiveness; **t**24 sublime delivery. If you want to know just what a near perfection of beautifully layered, vanilla-led oak and mouthwatering, maple-syrup sweetened barley looks like, here you go; **f**23 charming, multilayered and very long finish with more of the same, but becoming gradually drier; some late spice and even the most distant puff of smoke finish things with a flourish; **b**24 the kind of cask you want at the bottom of your bed, so you can get up in the middle of the night and pray to it. **52%. nc ncf.** *199 bottles.*

⠿ **The BenRiach 1978 Vintage Single Cask Campaign No. 4** Ex Moscatel, cask no. 4413, bott June 07 db **(81) n**22 **t**21 **f**20 **b**18. My lack of fondness for certain finishes is well documented. Where does this sit in the pantheon of finishes? Very hard to say. Certainly it aint a rip-roaring success. But on the other hand the odd succulence drifts over the palate...but not enough to make it entirely work, sadly. **52.5%.** *198 bottles.*

⠿ **The BenRiach 1978 Vintage Single Cask Campaign No. 4** Ex Tokaji, cask no. 4416, bott June 07 db **(88) n**23 buzzing spices and even a touch of tequila about this one; the fruits sits pretty and the barley is entirely relaxed; **t**21 a bit messy as the wine and barley fight; the red hot spices have to be tasted to be believed; **f**22 a mouth-watering denouement with the wine still calling the shots; **b**22 exceptionally rare for this wine style to work with whisky. But here it pulls it off. **52.7%.** *246 bottles.*

**The BenRiach 1980 Limited Release Cask Bottling** Virgin oak cask 2535, bott Jun 06 db **(88) n**24 that waxy honey and armchair leather effect one associates with bourbon; **t**23 usual near-perfect BenRiach delivery (how many of the world's distilleries have such a just-so degree of oiliness to the malt body?) with a sliver of Demerara of honeycombe coating the barley, then the oak grabs hold; **f**20 toasty, roasty, massive oak; **b**21 the nose is the stuff of dreams, the mouth arrival is the most classic of drams, then some real problems fending off the tannins. But some moments of genius here. **52%. nc ncf.** *236 bottles.*

**The BenRiach 1984 Limited Release Cask Bottling** cask 594, bott Jun 06 db **(96) n**25 mainland Scottish peat gets no more delicate or sublime than this: a truly faultless aroma, this is a nose that repays 20 to 30 minutes study. The shift in shape and form of the peat-reek is beguiling yet for all its hypnotic power its seems fragile enough to collapse into peat dust at any minute. A world-great aroma; **t**24 as the nose suggests, the malts dissolves in the mouth; the peaty deposits offer varying depth and intensity, from a sweet cough lozenge to kippers. The bitter-sweet balance is beyond reproach; **f**23 long, seductively layered and excellent oaky strands to soak up the lingering smoke; remains chewable and lip-smacking for many, many minutes dying out to strains of medium roast Old Brown Java coffee; **b**24 it is malts like this that turn whisky into an art form. An unforgettable and very rare experience: easily one of the whiskies of the year. **54%. nc ncf.** *240 bottles.*

**The BenRiach 1984 Limited Release Cask Bottling** Re-racked sherry butt cask no. 1438, bott Jun 06 db **(85) n**22 **t**22 **f**20 **b**21. Some lovely, kippery moments but the oak breaks the spell. **54%. nc ncf.** *656 bottles.*

⠿ **The BenRiach 1984 Vintage Single Cask Campaign No. 4** Ex Port Hogshead, cask no. 4049, bott June 07 db **(83) n**21 **t**20 **f**22 **b**20. Another weird assembly of peat and port. I've yet to be entirely convinced this combination works for the best. Certainly no shortage of entertainment value but the wear and tear on the tastebuds is enormous. No wonder why they call it Campaign Number 4. Because this is one hell of a battle... **54.3%.** *276 bottles.*

⠿ **The BenRiach 1985 Vintage Single Cask Campaign No. 4** Ex Oloroso Butt, cask no. 3766, bott June 07 db **(76) n**19 **t**20 **f**18 **b**19. The oloroso and gristy, smoky malt never quite find the right stride together. Pleasantish, haphazard and very dry. **54.6%.** *672 bottles.*

**The BenRiach 1986 Limited Release Cask Bottling** Original Gomez cask 9632, bott Jun 06 db **(77) n**18 **t**21 **f**19 **b**19. Hugely disappointing: not even the tidal wave of fresh barley can save this one from its undesired and off-key sherried-shackles. **55%. nc ncf.** *661 bottles.*

**The BenRiach 1988 Limited Release Cask Bottling** Butt cask no. 802, re-racked into oloroso sherry 26 Oct 04, bott Sept 05 db **(87) n**22 light, punchy sherry offering pure white grape; **t**23 charismatic delivery brimming with beautifully married fruit and barley; the confident spices tickle and tease while soft oils coat the palate; **f**20 drier, toasty oak notes, though watch out for that grape-juice effect very late on; **b**22 big whisky with fabulous early presence but too much dryness on the finish. **54.7%. nc ncf.** *675 bottles.*

⁂ **The BenRiach 1994 Vintage Single Cask Campaign No. 4** Ex Port Hogshead, cask no. 26, bott June 07 db **(88) n**22 absolutely unique: you'll either love it or hate it. I'm still not sure which...but I'm marking up for sheer entertainment value...it's like nothing on this planet: peat as you've never nosed it before; **t**21 a faltering start as the port and peat jarringly and quarrelsomely collide; massive spice blast and then, suddenly, we are past the industrial grime and into open countryside where everything is beautiful and natural; **f**24 fantastic finish entirely out of keeping with the outbreak of World War Three which preceded it. The peat is now sweet and swarthy and the gentleness of the gristiness is sublime; **b**21 good grief....!!! Those of a nervous disposition had better give this one a miss. It's like tasty TNT.... **55.7%.** *300 bottles.*

**Chieftain's Benriach 13 Years Old** Fino sherry **(79) n**20 **t**21 **f**19 **b**19. Lovely fruitcake, marzipan and delicate smoke but the feeling that something is vaguely amiss on the nose is born out on the finish. **43%.** *Ian MacLeod.*

**Craigellachie Hotel Benriach 1976** cask 8079, bott 05 **(88) n**23 profound oak of top quality; a sandalwood/barley marriage made in heaven; **t**24 just enormous: for all its age and oak influence, still the barley bubbles to the surface causing salivation and joy in equals measures; beautiful spices buzz about a bit; **f**19 on the oak-stew side, but just enough exotic fruit for it to get away with it; **b**22 thanks to the mouthwatering barley, a dram still to be reckoned with. **57.6%.** *UK.*

**D&M Connoisseurs' Club Bottling Aged 18 Years** cask 5112, dist Apr 87 **(87) n**20 traces of butterscotch, but a bit dull; **t**23 probing malt is supported by waves of intensifying fruit; **f**22 excellent delivery of very soft oil and rich mocha; **b**22 takes its time to find its range, but a second or third glass should do the trick. **55.7%.** *USA.*

⁂ **Dewar Rattray Individual Cask Bottling Benriach Aged 15 Years** Bourbon cask 50062, dist 2 Oct 89, bott 11 Nov 04 **(82) n**21 **t**22 **f**19 **b**20. Dusty bananas on the nose while sharp barley offers early juiciness. **59.9%. ncf.** *430 bottles.*

**Dun Bheagan BenRiach Aged 10 Years (86) n**21 **t**22 **f**21 **b**22. A delicate, delicious and youthful Benriach in full blending colours. **43%.** *Ian Macleod.*

**Duncan Taylor Collection Benriach 1968 Aged 36 Years** cask no. 2595, dist Nov 68, bott Mar 05 **(94) n**24 **t**24 **f**22 **b**24. One of nature's treasures. **50.7%**

⁂ **Duncan Taylor Collection Benriach 1968** Cask no. 2597 **(91) n**23 exotic fruit and ginger **t**23 busy oak but there remain loads of barley still to get your teeth into. The warming ginger does impress; **f**22 dries towards a toasty finale but enough barley survives for the requisite sweetness; **b**23 hard to believe that a Speyside can live this long in the cask and come out guns blazing. Wonderful. **48.6%.** *Duncan Taylor.*

**Mac Y 10th Anniversary BenRiach Aged 12 Years** cask no 807, dist 94, bott 06 **(89) n**22 intense, farmyardy, playfully teasing peats given extra weight thanks to sherry. That said, maybe not the best oloroso butt of all time but the smoke deals with any inadequacies comfortably; **t**23 multi-structured with an early thinnish, off-key edge to the burgeoning smoke. Develops into a massive mouthful with the barley and peats back on track and the oak pitching in beautifully; **f**22 soft spices and a youthfulness now to the peat. The grape is a bit over eager and wayward. But long, fascinating and very tasty stuff; **b**22 massive whisky offering rough and tumble. Lurches all over the palate with virtually no direction. But, my word, it's one hell of a ride!! **56%. nc ncf.** *Denmark. 700 bottles.*

**Old Malt Cask Benriach 15 Years Old** dist 27 Mar 90, bott 11 May 05 **(76) n**17 **t**21 **f**19 **b**20. For all the creamy toffee and wonderfully intense barley on delivery, the soapy oak has gone through the top. **50%.** *Douglas Laing & Co.*

⁂ **The Single Malts of Scotland Benriach 1984 Aged 21 Years** Small batch **(94) n**23 beautiful gristy peat, exceptionally well defined and sexy; **t**23 sweet start, some surprising oils but nothing drastic enough to intrude on the gradual build up of chewy phenols; **f**24 long, softly oiled smoked fudge; **b**24 a touch of the Caol Ilas here oil-wise, but the complexity of the peat really does make you swoon. Brilliant stuff. **56.7%.** *Speciality Drinks, UK.*

The Whisky Fair Benriach 1986 Aged 19 Years Bourbon Hogshead 2972, dist 86, bott 06 **(79)** n21 t21 f18 b19. Unpeated or unsherried Benriach at this age often fails to comfortably see off the oak. Like now. **54.7%**. *Germany. 297 bottles*

## BENRINNES
### Speyside, 1826. Diageo. Working.

Benrinnes Aged 15 Years db **(70)** n16 t19 f17 b18. What a shame that in the year the independent bottlers at last get it right for Benrinnes, the actual owners of the distillery make such a pig's ear of it. Sulphured and sicklysweet, this bottling has little to do with the very good whisky made there day in day out by its talented team. Depressing. **43%**. *Flora and Fauna.*

⫶ Berry's Own Selection Benrinnes 1989 Cask no. 1658, bott 06 **(82)** n20 t21 f20 b21. Firm, decent if uncomplex malt with the accent entirely on the barley. **46%**.

The Bottlers Benrinnes 1985 Aged 17 Years Old cask 1852 **(82)** n22 t19 f21 b20. Great nose, but disintegrates to a degree on the palate and never quite finds a rhythm; adore the lingering spices, though. **60.2%**. *Raeborn Fine Wines.*

Cadenhead's Authentic Collection Benrinnes Aged 18 Years Bourbon Hogshead, dist 88, bott Sept 06 **(92)** n23 a citrussy element sharpens the spices; t24 salivating from the first moment; stunning barley layering; f22 lightens dramatically with a vanilla blast; b23 a magnificent Speysider. This distillery is, at last, coming out of the shadows. **55.9%**. *246 bottles.*

⫶ Chieftain's Benrinnes 1994 Aged 11 Years Manzanilla Finish dist 94 **(79)** n18 t21 f20 b20. Rather tight and struggles to fight off its fruity shackles. **43%. nc ncf.**

Connoisseurs Choice Benrinnes 1991 **(84)** n22 t21 f21 b20. One of the new breed of Benrinnes, showing a degree of promise but still hampered by some ordinary casks. **43%**. *Gordon & MacPhail.*

⫶ Connoisseurs Choice Benrinnes 1991 **(78)** n17 t23 f19 b19. Forget the very poor nose and the indifferent, frugal and ultimately bitter finish. It's all about the lip-smacking freshness of the ultra- intense barley on delivery. **43%**. *Gordon & MacPhail.*

Dewar Rattray Individual Cask Bottling Benrinnes 1989 Aged 14 Years cask 6835, dist Nov 90, bott Nov 04 **(79)** n18 t22 f19 b20. The fish, chip and vinegar nose, though novel, doesn't bode well, but the bubble gum and malt reply is pretty tasty. Very high esters here. **59.3%**. *524 bottles.*

D&M Connoisseurs' Club Bottling Benrinnes Aged 17 Years cask 913, dist Mar 89 **(91)** n23 light with a sexy barley texture on several levels. Outstanding complexity; t23 fresh, bitter-sweet barley. Grain and oak have locked horns but the battle is refined and mildly salivating; f22 lots of vanilla and sweetening barley sugar; b23 a rare example of Benrinnes in stunning and most complex form. Bloody well done D&M!! **43%. nc ncf.** *US by Angus Dundee.*

⫶ D&M Aficionados' Club Bottling Benrinnes Aged 18 Years Cask no. 2858, dist Oct 88 **(78)** n20 t20 f19 b19. A malty, simplistic offering which shows signs of tiring towards the finish. **54.2%. sc ncf.** *US by Angus Dundee Distillers.*

⫶ Dun Bheagan Benrinnes 1993 Aged 12 Years Muscatel Finish dist Dec 93 **(80)** n19 t20 f21 b20. An attractive sweetness drives the character beyond the odd blemish and the mouth-watering middle displays an enticing softness. **43%. nc ncf.** *Ian Macleod.*

Gordon MacPhail Reserve Benrinnes 1974 cask 3870, bott 10 Apr 04 **(85)** n23 t22 f20 b20. A distillery which always draws the short straw when it comes to casks. Despite wallowing in real full-bodied and – for once – exceptionally clean sherry, it's too much. Balance has been not so much lost as obliterated. But enjoyably drinkable? Oh, yes... **46%**. *For Juuls Vinhandel, Denmark. 234 bottles.*

Harris Whisky Co. Benrinnes Aged 13 Years cask 7014, dist Sept 92, bott Jan 06 **(94)** n23 light, grassy barley sprinkled with custard powder. Just so delicate and inviting; t24 an equally delicate sweetness combined with a soft yet more pronounced oil than you might expect from a 3D malt; the timbre of the barley is divine; f23 long with luxurious and slow fade of glorious barley; b24 proof that the skilled distillers of Benrinnes have not often been well served by those supplying the casks. This is decent wood and the result is a delicate, clean, complex, salivating and fascinating malt of the highest grade sprinkled with star quality throughout. **55%. nc ncf.** *The Harris Whisky Co.*

Mackillop's Choice Benrinnes 1989 Cask Strength cask no. 912, dist Mar 89 **(88)** n22 t23 f21 b22. I was wondering when I'd see this distillery's make in a half decent cask and able to express itself properly. Well done, Lorn!! **58.8%**. *Angus Dundee.*

⌐ Norse Cask Selection Benrinnes 1994 Aged 12 Years Hogshead cask no. 601, dist Jan 94, bott May 06 **(74)** n18 t20 f18 b18. Tries hard to sparkle, but shows why this is blending fodder. **59%**. **nc ncf**. *WhiskyOwner.com, Denmark. 290 bottles.*

Old Malt Cask Benrinnes Aged 14 Years dist Nov 90, bott Nov 04 **(77)** n19 t20 f20 b18. Barley-rich and buttery if a little banal. **50%**. *Douglas Laing. 655 bottles.*

⌐ Scotch Malt Whisky Society Cask 36.36 Aged 13 Years Sherry Butt, dist Feb 93 **(87)** n21 significant oak t22 the depth of orangey-grapey fruit really does hold its own; f22 really lovely chocolate and no little fruitcake fade; b22 sound, chewing whisky, **53.9%**

# BENROMACH
## Speyside, 1898. Gordon & MacPhail. Working.

Benromach 22 Years Old Finished in Port Pipes db **(86)** n22 t23 f20 b21. Slightly Jekyll and Hyde. **45%**. *3,500 bottles.*

Benromach 25 Years Old db **(92)** n24 seriously sexy with spices interplaying with tactile malt: the bitter-sweet balance is just so.There is even the faintest flicker of peat-smoke to underscore the pedigree; t22 an early, surprising, delivery of caramel amongst the juicy barley; f23 lots of gentle spices warm the enriched barley and ice-creamy vanilla; b23 a classic old-age Speysider, showing all the quality you'd hope for. **43%**

Benromach Classic 55 Years Old dist 49, bott 04 db **(93)** n24 sheer brinkmanship: the first signs of a perhaps too much bitter oak, until it softens and smiles in the glass as gentle Canadian-style corny-caramel notes gather intensity and bulk. The countering sweetness is charming. Next a soft delivery of clementines lightens things further. And even the strains of vanishing peat A 23.5 if ever there was one... what the hell, let's round it up...; t23 the citrus arrives first, then increasingly large waves of salivating, highly intense barley. A big oaky storm brews, but keeps a distance but the vibrancy is astonishing; f22 maltesers and latte, remains silky soft and when the oak does break the bitterness adds rather than subtracts; b24 only distillery owners G&M could come up with something like this. Scotland had a King in those far off days. In fact, so did the British Empire – and there was still an Empire (just) in 1949. And this has to be a king of aged whiskies because it bears virtually no scars of time. Charlie Hewitt was back as manager of recently relegated Millwall; my parents were in their first year of marriage; Surrey were on the cusp of forming a cricket team to dominate the English game for the next decade and some guy in Scotland, possibly long dead and his name lost to history, laid down one cask that a generation and a half on would delight and astound a lucky few. That's whisky for you. **42.4%**. *83 bottles.*

Benromach 1968 db **(94)** n25 hands up all those who would mark this as just about the perfect sherry butt? Apples, liquorice, orange peel – all the usual suspects. Clean, no off-notes, and just the right degree of oak. Pheeew!!; t24 no spitting here as the intense barley links seamlessly with the fat fruit. The oak is more upfront, but it's chalky challenge is restrained enough; f22 honeycomb arrives like thunder after a hot spell; bitters up as the oak demands a final say; b23 an absolutely stunning cask which just cracks under the oak at the end. But the build up until then is unforgettable. **41.8%**

Benromach Cask Strength 1980 db **(94)** n23 almost Highland Parkesque in its clever, not to mention delicious, honey-gentle smoke overture. Just missing the heather; t24 bloody hell!! If you have a sweet tooth then don't bother with a bottle: buy a case! The intensity of the honey is shocking, but once you have acclimatized, then wallow in its hidden, spicy depths. As enormous as any Speysider gets; f23 wonderful delivery of oak; and then that soft waft of smoke returns: some surprising hints of citrus amid the powering malt; b24 they were probably led to the cask by the bees: clazzzzic! **58.6%**

Benromach Organic db **(91)** n23 massive oak input and the freshest oak imaginable. But sits comfortably with the young pulsing malts. Wow!!; t23 oak arrives first again, but has enough deftness of touch to allow the rich, mouthwatering malts to prosper; f22 plenty of vanillins and natural, sweet toffee; b23 young and matured in possibly first fill bourbon or, more likely, European (even Scottish) oak; you cannot do other than sit up and take notice of this guns-blazing big 'un. An absolute treat! **43%**. **nc ncf**.

⸭ **Benromach Peat Smoke** db **(88) n**21 very clean and sweet; the smoke isn't big yet dominates...; **t**23 a wonderful, clean, gristy feel – even a touch of drinking the mash about this; **f**22 minimal oak interference as the smoke gently simmers down; the sweetness holds well; **b**22 nothing overly complex about this. Just wonderfully distilled and sympathetically matured malt. **46%**

⸭ **Benromach Sassicaia Wood Finish** bott 07db **(86) n**23 **t**20 **f**22 **b**21. Benromach in very different clothing here – in fact, there is no other malt with the elements so portrayed. Particularly pleasing is the beauty of the balance between the soft smoke and the varied oaky tones – very European. The arrival is a little confused (a touch of the Italian tantrums at one point) but it eventually pans out into an attractively sweet, and again softly peated, little charmer. Unique. **45%**

**Benromach Traditional** db **(88) n**23 young, lively but very clean peat smoke; **t**22 a natural harmony between smoke, barley and light vanillins; **f**22 the gristy sweetness fades for more bitter oak; **b**21 a much more comfortable and complete malt than it was a couple of years back with the peating level upped slightly but, vitally, finding much better balance. **40%**

**Benromach Vintage 1969** db **(73) n**19 **t**19 **f**17 **b**18. They were dancing on the Moon when they made this: sadly, nothing out of this world about it now. **43%**

**Benromach Tokaji Wood Finish Aged 21 Years** db **(69) n**17 **t**16 **f**17 **b**16. An interesting experiment: one, let's hope, never to be repeated. **45%**

## BEN WYVIS
### Highland (Northern) 1965–1977. Demolished.

**Ben Wyvis Aged 27 Years** cask 1061, dist 72 db **(78) n**21 vanilla, soft oak with a sweet structure and the malt is intact – amazing for a light whisky for this age – with some softening caramel; **t**20 big malt, toffee presence then becoming gradually hotter, not peppery, simply from the way it has been distilled; **f**18 very thin, surprisingly little oak, meagre malt and more bite: the finale is sweet and coated with late oil; **b**19 this is by no means great whisky, but it is certainly among the most rare you will ever locate. There are hints here of why the distillery closed: certainly even after all these years the oak cannot paper over the cracks. That said, you are drinking history and romance and it should be enjoyed with due reverence. **43.1%**. *146 bottles.*

## BLADNOCH
### Lowland, 1817. Working.

**Bladnoch Aged 10 Years** db **(94) n**23 lemon and lime, marmalade on fresh-sliced flour-topped crusty bread; **t**24 immensely fruity and chewy, lush and mouthwatering and then the most beguiling build-up of spices: the mouthfeel is full and faultless; **f**23 long, remains mildly peppery and then a dryer advance of oak. The line between bitter and sweet is not once crossed; **b**24 this is probably the ultimate Bladnoch, certainly the best I have tasted in over 25 years. This Flora and Fauna bottling by then owners United Distillers should be regarded as the must-get-at-all-costs Bladnoch. If the new owner can create something even to hang on to this one's coat-tails then he has excelled himself. For those few of us lucky enough to experience this, this dram is nothing short of a piece of Lowland legend and folklore. **43%**. *For those of you with a nervous disposition, the author would like to point out that not a single drop of this whisky was spat out during the creation of these tasting notes.*

**Bladnoch Aged 13 Years** (Distillery View) db **(81) n**19 **t**21 **f**20 **b**21. The malt and oaky-chewiness make the right sounds, but it's all a little muffled. **40%. ncf**

**Bladnoch Aged 13 Years** (Beltie) db **(89) n**21 confident, striding vanilla but the oak is enlivened by an intriguing malt-citrus mix; **t**23 brilliant! The arrival is immediately enveloped in fresh, grassy malt weighted by an estery oiliness and simple oak; **f**23 wave upon wave of soft malt turning into pure cocoa; **b**22 by no means a complex dram, just one that works if anything because of its faultless, vigorous simplicity. **55%. ncf sc.**

**Bladnoch 15 Years Old** db **(88) n**21 barely ripe pears; **t**23 mouthwatering, fresh barley and virtually no oak; **f**22 bitters out slightly as some vague vestiges of oak get amongst the barley, apples and pears; **b**22 this distillery's whisky is unquestionably as good now as at any time in living memory. The liberal use of second fill casks here has accentuated the lively fruitiness. **40%**

**Bladnoch 15 Years Old (The Sheep)** db **(88) n**22 much thinner nose than of old but the barley is lovely; **t**22 the barley imposes itself in a different manner from previous bottling, being a drier style adorned with peppers; **f**22 quality oak frames the malt beautifully; **b**22 strikingly attractive whisky, but lost some of its estery sheen and charisma since I tasted an early bottling of this. **55%**

**Bladnoch 15 Years Old Rum Finish** cask no. 5144 db **(76) n**23 **t**20 **f**16 **b**17. The hugely complex nose is misleading as to regard the rest of the whisky. This has spent 18 months rounding off in rum cask: it should have been either a shorter time, or more, because it has hit a stage in its development where it has entirely lost balance, especially on the viciously bitter finish. **55%**

◈ **Bladnoch Aged 15 Years** Sherry cask no. 1056 db **(81) n**17 **t**22 **f**21 **b**21. Perhaps not the best sherry influence of all time here but the juicy malt experience on the palate compensates for the nose. **46%. ncf.**

◈ **Bladnoch Aged 16 Years "Spirit of the Lowlands"** db **(88) n**22 vaguely salty, digestive biscuit; very firm and attractive with pleasing barley edge; **t**22 salivating and entire: the age doesn't detract from the richness of the barley one iota; **f**22 continues in the same vein though the oak does dry things out; **b**22 really lovely whisky and unusual to see a Lowlander quite this comfortable at such advanced age. **46%. ncf.**

**Berry's Own Selection Bladnoch 1992 Aged 13 Years (84) n**21 **t**22 **f**20 **b**21. This is a very strange Bladnoch. There are certain richly-malted aspects which are wonderful. But I cannot help wondering if this was bottled after a gin run. Because there are definite elements of juniper on the nose and finish. **46%.**

**Cadenhead's Authentic Collection Bladnoch Aged 16 Years** dist 89, bott Sep 05 **(89) n**22 greengages and custard, sprinkled with gristy malt; **t**23 lip-smacking, mouthwatering honey-roast barley, waves and waves of the stuff; **f**21 roasty, dry and finely spiced; **b**23 a quality cask of Lowland with some serious guts and attitude. **54.9%.** 276 bottles.

◈ **Cadenhead's Authentic Collection Bladnoch Aged 18 Years** Bourbon Barrel, dist 1989, bott May 07 **(90) n**23 some Ancient Age 10 years old...no perhaps more of a 12-y-o Wild turkey, or somewhere between the two...no, hang on, there is some barley in there, too...; **t**22 yet, it really is malt but that slips in gently from a sandwich of sweet bourbon notes; **f**23 loads of honey and a hint of liquorice – the bourbon-barley fun continues; **b**22 one assumes this is from first fill bourbon because there is more Kentucky here than Wigtown. Lovely stuff. **47.8%.** 156 bottles.

**Chieftan's Bladnoch Aged 14 Years Rum Barrel Finish** casks nos. 2073 & 2077, dist May 90, bott Jun 04 **(94) n**23 some may remember a candy in Britain (and the Empire) called Black Jacks. I can even remember when they were a farthing each...groan. Sniff this to recall your early childhood. Fabulous! **t**24 the malt remains absolutely resolute and unruffled as a sweet Demerara thread weaves intricate patterns; the middle is an explosion of complexities as all oaky-maltyrummy factions meet; **f**23 soft and chewy with a touch of milky-liquorice and we are back to Black Jacks once again; **b**24 I have a sneaking suspicion I may have unwittingly contributed to this while I blended Sea Wynde Rum. I'm not letting those casks go so easily next time...!! **46%. nc nc.** Ian Macleod. 318 bottles.

**Connoisseurs Choice Bladnoch 1991 (83) n**20 **t**22 **f**21 **b**20. Unusually oily for Bladnoch; grassy, green, mouthwatering, but complexity at a premium. **40%.**

**James MacArthur Bladnoch 1992 12 Year Old** bott Mar 05 **(81) n**20 **t**22 **f**19 **b**20. Rich malt, not unlike an old Lincoln biscuit. Shards of Demerara for good measure. **43%**

**John McDougall's Selection Bladnoch Aged 14 Years** cask no. 3317 **(93) n**23 varying levels of chalky oak sweetened by barley sugar; **t**24 a stunning and malt-encrusted riot of apricot, butterscotch and raspberry jam; **f**23 stays on the sublimely sweetened theme, though the oak plays a delicate anchoring role; **b**23 I can just imagine John McDougall wandering around the warehouse on the banks of the eponymous river and happening across this cask: a secretly chalked x on a stave and the owners wouldn't have stood a chance... **55.8%.** 250 bottles.

◈ **Old Malt Cask Bladnoch Aged 14 Years** dist Dec 91, bott Sept 06 **(86) n**20 **t**22 **f**22 **b**22. Despite its great age for a Lowlander, retains a grassy freshness bolstered by delicate spice. Quite charming. **50%.** Douglas Laing. 777 bottles.

Old Malt Cask Bladnoch 15 Years Old dist Nov 90, bott May 06 **(86)** n22 t22 f21 b21. Steady as a rock: eschews complexity for sheer malty delight. **50%.** *333 btls.*

Old Malt Cask Bladnoch 21 Years Old dist 31 Dec 83, bott 22 Mar 05 **(88)** n21 t23 f22 **b**22. Relentless and remorseless, the jaw-achingly chewy malt goes on and on and on! **50%.** *Douglas Laing.*

Old Masters Bladnoch 1992 13 Years Old cask 752, bott 05 **(87)** n21 t23 f21 b22. Shimmering. **56.9%.**

Provenance Bladnoch 14 Years Old dist Nov 90, bott July 05 **(79)** n22 t20 f18 b19. Pleasant and malt-fresh to start, but soon runs out of steam and collapses at the finish. **46%.**

⁕ Scott's Selection Bladnoch 1993 bott 07 **(87)** n21 spiced custard tart; t23 under-ripe gooseberries by the bowlful early on then clean-as-a-whistle barley radiating in all directions; f21 a bit thin and stilted but the cocoa's a bonus; **b**22 honest and no frills. **59.5%.** Speyside Distillers.

## BLAIR ATHOL
### Highlands (Perthshire), 1798. Diageo. Working.

Blair Athol Aged 12 Years db **(77)** n18 t19 f21 b19. Thick, fruity, syrupy and a little sulphury and heavy. The finish has some attractive complexity among the chunkyness. **43%.** *Flora and Fauna range.*

Cadenhead's Authentic Collection Blair Athol Aged 15 Years dist 89, bott Feb 05 **(84)** n21 t22 f20 b21. No shrinking violet, but the barley sugar start sets the dram up well. **55.6%.** *198 bottles.*

Cadenhead's Authentic Collection Blair Athol Aged 16 Years Bourbon Hogshead, dist 89, bott May 05 **(75)** n18 t20 f18 b19. High esters, dubious oak but oversweet and ungainly. **56.2%.** *312 bottles.*

Connoisseurs Choice Blair Athol 1993 **(89)** n23 refreshing, new-mown straw and citrus; t23 gorgeous clarity to the barley despite the early intensity. Refreshing, excellently balanced sweetness; f21 gets a bit bitter and furry towards the end; b22 I remember then distillery manager Mike Nicholson telling me he had cleaned up this distillery's act. Now living in western Canada, I know he'll be reading this. So, what can I say? Well done, Mike. Absolutely great job: this – even taking the untidy finish into account - is very good whisky. And well done, G&M for selecting a sympathetic cask and giving the malt a chance. **43%.**

⁕ The Dram Blair Atholl Vintage 1989 bott 06 **(76)** n19 t22 f17 b18. Some decent moments on arrival but a pretty dull experience, especially at the death. **43%. nc ncf.** *Whisky-Doris, Germany. 120 bottles.*

⁕ Duncan Taylor Collection Blair Atholl 1977 Cask no. 36853D **(84)** n21 t20 f22 b21. made at the distillery when it was churning the stuff out for Bells as if there was no tomorrow. Evidenced through a distinctive hotness and lack of body but there have been compensations from the oak over the years, especially when the gristy sweetness begins to take shape around the vanilla and custard powder. A mixed bag, but enjoyable nonetheless. **54.4%**

Old Malt Cask Blair Athol Aged 21 Years dist Feb 84, bott Aug 05 **(79)** n22 t20 f18 b19. The flat delivery doesn't match the attractive nose. **50%.** *271 bottles.*

⁕ Old Malt Cask Blair Athol Aged 21 Years Rum Finish dist Feb 85, bott Nov 06 **(79)** n19 t20 f20 b20. Improbably sweet for a malt this age, but then this is from a weird distillery. The nose is a mixture of wallpaper paste and barley and the rest follows suit. **50%.** *Douglas Laing. 286 bottles.*

⁕ Platinum Blair Athol Aged 40 Years dist 66, bott 06 **(86)** n24 t22 f19 b21. Just one of those malts you have to go out and get just to nose. Hold the glass long in the hand and sniff deeply and often: there is oak present but the accent is on varying degrees of honey and how they interplay with the under-ripe kiwi fruit and myriad other delicate scents. The silky, malty delivery is eventually over-run by the drying oak, but not too much to prevent a really lovely experience. It's the nose, though, that will win your heart. **49.5%.** *Douglas Laing. 184 bottles.*

Premier Barrel Blair Athol 11 Years Old Sherry, dist Nov 94, bott Feb 06 **(85)** n21 t22 f21 b21. A neat and tidy malt with grist 'n' grape. One of the cleaner, juicier examples I've come across. **46%.** *Douglas Laing. 867 bottles.*

⁘ **Provenance Blair Athol Aged 11 Years** dist Winter 95, bott Winter 06 **(85) n**21 **t**22 **f**21 **b**21. Great to see a bottling unencumbered by a dodgy cask, which has often been the problem. Also, a cleaned-up spirit with the attractive emphasis on mouth-watering, juicy malt. Limited depth, perhaps, but genuinely good whisky. **46%.** *Douglas Laing.*

**Provenance Blair Athol Aged 12 Years** dist 1 Feb 93, bott 5 May 05 **(75) n**18 **t**20 **f**18 **b**19. Silk purses. Sows ears. **46%.** *Douglas Laing & Co.*

**Provenance Blair Athol 12 Years Old** Sherry, dist Dec 93, bott Feb 06 **(77) n**19 **t**19 **f**20 **b**19. Underwhelming. But a little bit of smoke sneaks in from somewhere. **46%.**

**Provenance Blair Athol 12 Years Old** Sherry, dist May 94, bott Aug 06 **(70) n**16 **t**18 **f**18 **b**18. Gosh! How this takes me back to the sulphurous old days at the distillery. **46%.**

⁘ **Provenance Blair Athol Aged 12 Years Sherry Matured** dist Winter 93, bott Autumn 06 **(84) n**21 **t**22 **f**20 **b**21. A chewy beast, must be nearer a Trinidadian rum in character than a Highland malt. Pretty estery, with a touch of rubber and playful sweetness. Perfect for those looking for something outside the box. **46%.** *Douglas Laing.*

## BOWMORE
**Islay, 1779. Suntory. Working.**

**Bowmore 12 Years Old** db **(85) n**21 **t**22 **f**21 **b**21. Revealing greater peaty youth than of old. **40%** ⊙

⁘ **Bowmore 12 Years Old Enigma** db **(82) n**19 **t**22 **f**20 **b**21. Sweet, molassed and with that tell-tale Fisherman's Friend tang representing the light smoke. This Enigma hasn't quite cracked it, though. **40%.** *Duty Free.*

⁘ **Bowmore 15 Years Old Darkest** db **(74) n**18 **t**18 **f**19 **b**19. An improvement on the dreadful original. Just. **43%.**

⁘ **Bowmore 15 Years Old Mariner** db **(79) n**19 **t**21 **f**19 **b**20. There are two ways of looking at this. As a Bowmore. Which is how I have marked it. Or a something to throw down your neck for pure fun. Which is probably worth another seven or eight points. Either way, there is something not entirely right here. **43%.** *Duty Free.*

**Bowmore Aged 16 Years Limited Edition** dist 89, bott 05 db **(90) n**21 a youthful aroma with smoking peat embers; **t**23 dazzling, multi-layered peat offers varying degrees of intensity and sweetness, from Fishermen's Friends cough candy to Tyrolean smoked cheese; **f**23 long with excellent vanilla involvement and a dash of buttery kipper; **b**23 the nose promises little but the complexity and sure-footedness of this malt is truly wonderful. **51.8%**

**Bowmore Aged 16 Years Limited Edition** Oloroso sherry, dist 90, bott 06 db **(89) n**24 if you stick your head in the malt kiln, this – exactly - is what you get. When it's not alight, I mean...; **t**22 a surprising degree of fruit takes the lead but that incredibly pungent peat does all it can to resist and gain control. Enormous, though hardly structured; **f**21 semi-sweetened hickory; **b**22 It has peat. And fruit. And never the two do meet. But the battle for supremacy is engrossing. **53.8%**

**Bowmore 17 Years Old** db **(83) n**22 **t**21 **f**20 **b**20. Once upon a time, 17-y-o Bowmore was this distillery at its optimum. A whisky which could just about look any other in the world directly in the eye. No more. Pleasant, yes. But Bowmore 17-y-o shouldn't be about pleasant. **43%.** *Duty Free.* ⊙ ⊙

⁘ **Bowmore 18 Years Old** db **(79) n**20 **t**21 **f**19 **b**19. Pleasant, drinkable Fisherman's Friend style – like every Bowmore it appears around this age. But why so toffee-dull? **43%.**

**Bowmore 25 Years Old** db **(86) n**21 **t**22 **f**21 **b**22. Not the big, chunky guy of yore: the age would surprise you if tasted blind. **43%** ⊙ ⊙

⁘ **Bowmore 30 Years Old** db **(94) n**23 intense burnt raisin amid the intense burnt peat; a deft rummy sweetness strikes an improbable chord with the sweetened lime; the oak is backward coming forward but binds beautifully with both peat and fruit; **t**24 near flawless delivery showing a glimpse of Bowmore in a form similar to how I remember it some 25 years ago. The peat, though intense - much bigger than you will find today - does have a hint of the Fisherman's Friend about it, but not so upfront as today. For all the peat this is clean whisky, moulded by a craftsman into how a truly great Islay should be; **f**23 dries sublimely as the oak contains the peat and adds a touch of coffee to it in unsugared form. Gentle oils cling tightly to the roof of the mouth but it is at once gentle yet enormous; **b**24 frankly, a Bowmore that no Islay scholar should be without. Shows the distillery at its most intense yet delicate; an essay in balance and how great oak, peat and fruit can combine for those special moments in life. Unquestionably one of the best Bowmores bottled this century. **43%**

**Bowmore Aged 37 Years 1968 Limited Edition** db **(90)** n22 you can hardly see the peat for the exotic fruit, which means only one thing...; t23 so juicy and non-specific fruity, except maybe some mango. The peat finally arrives like the 7th Cavalry; f22 long and subtle with vanilla stratas of varying intensity; b23 one of those casks that's past its sell-by date, yet somehow works to glorious effect. Most of the peat has been kicked out, but it's as gentle a ride as you'll find. **43.4%**.

**Bowmore 1957** db **(91)** n23 t23 f22 b23. Nothing from 1957 has the right to be this well preserved and sophisticated. It appears I have a challenger... **40.1%**

**Bowmore 1964 Vintage Bourbon Cask** db **(86)** n23 t21 f21 b21. Just about holds together for a very enjoyable dram. The peat has been absorbed to create an unusual rye effect. **43.2%**

**Bowmore 1964 Vintage Fino Cask** db **(90)** n21 t23 f23 b23. Sheer quality. Curiously, much more Bushmills in style than Bowmore. Exquisite stuff. **49.6%**

**Bowmore 1971 Vintage 34 Years Old** Sherry cask db **(86)** n23 t22 f20 b21. Loses it on the finish. But one for those who like their whisky big and with splinters aplenty. **51%**. *960 bottles.*

**Bowmore Claret Bordeaux Wine Cask** db **(62)** n16 t16 f17 b13. When this first came out the then distillery boss Jim McEwan and I fell out (temporarily, of course!): he loved it, I loathed it. For the sake of this book (and it needed a good reason) I re-visited this whisky. And I still loathe it. The whisky has been swamped by the wine, is raw and the character of a distillery I love has been obliterated with all balance sacrificed. Oh dear, oh dear. **56%**

**Bowmore Dawn** db **(94)** n23 young, raw, yet complete peat in a style unique to Bowmore; t24 the arrival on the palate is momentous: it is sweet yet the intensity of the peat and oak crashing wave upon giant wave upon the palate acts as the perfect foil; f23 much drier with that excellent and highly distinctive chocolate swiss roll (unique to Bowmore) kicking in. Still room for lots of malt and a sliver of fruit; b24 none other of the distillery-bottled range quite nutshells Bowmore as well as this. Fabulous and markedly improved in recent years, this is a must-have malt for any true Islayophile. Overtaken the 17-y-o as the flagship brand. **51.5%**

**Bowmore Dusk** db **(80)** n18 t19 f23 b20. Another youngster, almost a mirror image to the Oddbins exclusive bottling of Bowmore or Islay (can't remember) of about 15 or 16 years ago. Memorable for the astonishing finish.. Love it!! **50%**

**Bowmore Legend** db **(80)** n21 t21 f18 b20. Refreshing, clean malt and raw, young-ish smoke. **40%**

**Bowmore Surf** db **(82)** n23 t21 f21 b21. Still a ripple. But a slightly bigger one now. The retreat of caramel has really helped accentuate the complexity on the finish. More than decent, well weighted malt, if a touch over-sweet. **43%** ☉ ☉

**Berry's Own Selection Bowmore Aged 11 Years (84)** n20 t23 f21 b20. To see Bowmore like this from a second- (or even third) - filled bourbon cask makes for interesting tasting: such is the mouthwatering malt intensity, and so retiring is the peat, this could almost pass for lightly smoked Speyside. **56.2%**. *Berry Bros & Rudd..*

**Cadenhead's Authentic Collection Bowmore Aged 13 Years** Bourbon Hogshead, dist 91, bott May 05 **(81)** n23 t21 f18 b19. Quite hot and peppery but the complexity of peat on the nose is exceptional. **60%**. *300 bottles.*

**Cadenhead's Authentic Collection Bowmore 14 Years** dist 91, bott Sep 05 **(87)** n21 firm and closed; t22 lovely oils help develop the sweet peat; f21 good length with smoke attached to the cocoa; b23 understated and impressive, it overcomes a lazy nose to offer excellent Islay. **59.1%**. *288 bottles.*

**Cadenhead's Authentic Collection Bowmore Aged 14 Years** Bourbon Hogshead, dist 91, bott Feb 06 **(84)** n22 t23 f19 b20. Nose and delivery exquisite with outstanding peating level. But the finish is too dry and dusty. **56.1%**. *294 bottles.*

**Cadenhead's Authentic Collection Bowmore Aged 14 Years 1992** Bourbon hogshead, dist 92, bott Nov 06 **(94)** n23 unusual, almost uncharted style: Fisherman's Friends have gone, replaced by drier, more refined smoke; t24 the best Bowmore delivery for a year or two: juicy barley fits like a glove with the crunchy peat; **f**23 long, spiced, so clean and charismatic; **b**24 a charmer with sweet barley a perfect foil for the smoke. Bowmore at its very best. **54.4%.** *294 bottles.*

⋰ **The Coopers Choice Bowmore Aged 12 Years** dist 1994, bott 07 **(87) n**21 a crofter's fire; **t**22 sweet barley followed by sumptuous waves of soft peat: simplistic but attractive; **f**22 vanilla brushed with smoke; **b**22 a good, honest Islay. **46%.** *The Vintage Malt Whisky Co.*

⋰ **The Coopers Choice Bowmore 1990 Aged 16 Years** **(79) n**20 **t**20 **f**19 **b**20. Well oaked and some sweet barley residue. But you'd hope for more. **46%. sc ncf.** *The Vintage Malt Whisky Co.*

**Dewar Rattray Individual Cask Bottling Bowmore Aged 14 Years** Sherry butt cask no. 2054, dist 15 July 91, bott 28 Sept 05 **(86) n**21 **t**22 **f**21 **b**22. Some 20-30 years ago Bowmore was famed for its high quality sherry casks. This is not quite up with the legendary stuff especially with the peat being a little shy. **59.6%.** *575 bottles.*

**Dewar Rattray Cask Collection Bowmore 14 Years Old** cask 2056, dist 15 July 91, bott 15 May 06 **(87) n**22 chunky and a bit of a thug. The unstable peats lash out at everything; **t**20 rough and ready; hot, peppery stuff with Fishermen's Friends abounding; **f**23 a zillion waves keep the tastebuds busy; the peat is pretty loud and screams long into the distance; **b**22 For those wanting a bit of rough. **57.8%.**

**Dewar Rattray Individual Cask Bottling Bowmore 1989 Aged 17 Years** Sherry cask 1095, dist Feb 89, bott May 06 **(66) n**15 **t**18 **f**16 **b**17. From a sherry cask, apparently. But the nose and finish suggests something metallic got into that cask and given it a strange, seriously flawed personality. A shame. **49.6%.** *180 bottles.*

**Duncan Taylor Collection Bowmore 1966** cask no 3312, dist May 66, bott May 06 **(93) n**24 coal dust, distant peat reek and mango chutney in near perfect proportions. Stunning; **t**24 a velvet delivery of something vaguely bourbony then a steady procession of soft peat and delicate fruit; the level of sweetness could not be better; **f**22 the oak is a friend here as it tops off proceeding with wonderful, semi-sweet vanilla; **b**23 just one of those wonder casks. The line is so very fine between greatness and plain ordinary when you get to exotic fruit time. Here it has kept both feet in greatness. **43.2%.** *130 bottles.*

**Duncan Taylor Collection Bowmore 1966** cask no. 3317, dist May 66, bott May 06 **(95) n**23 well aged, very high quality bourbon. The peat is no more than a foil to the leather and ripe cherries; **t**25 yes... yes... yes... yessssss! Meg Ryan wouldn't have to fake this one as soft, pulsing waves of pleasure build up in intensity. It starts sweet and slightly peaty, then various degrees of fruit surf in. All the time the barley is simply melting on every taste bud on the palate and warming spices are added to the intensity that guarantees glory; **f**23 tires very slightly; ample compensation with those playful spices digging deep under the sugary skin and receding as the light cocoa notes arrive. From first to very long last, this is the type of whisky we pray we will one day find. It just makes tender love to you from the moment it caresses your nose; **b**24 my last whisky of the day, and what a colossus; what an all-time memorable dram to take to bed with me. No cleaning of the teeth tonight. A Whisky of the Year contender? We'll see. Curiously Duncan Taylor had another high quality 66 (distilled especially by the Scots to commemorate the impending victory by England in the World Cup Finals, a few weeks later – thanks guys!) which came out at exactly the same strength. That, after 40 years, is very weird. However, this is the darker of the two and suggests it comes from a better bourbon cask, hence less fruit and more balance. I was going to savour this after England lifted the World Cup again in Germany. Only my hopes were Swede-bashed. Still, I can toast 40 years of supporting Millwall, instead. Anyway, there are pitifully few bottles of this. Are you in your mother-in-law's will...? **43.2%.** *171 bottles.*

**Duncan Taylor Collection Bowmore 1968** cask 1429, dist Feb 68, bott July 05 **(80) n**20 **t**21 **f**19 **b**20. Like the other DC 68 Bowmore, this has been divested of its peaty status thanks to time: regard this as very lightly smoked. **42.8%.** *182 bottles.*

**Duncan Taylor Collection Bowmore 1968** cask 3826, dist Oct 68, bott May 06 **(83) n**21 **t**22 **f**20 **b**20. We are again firmly into exotic fruit territory here, which reveals a degree of over-aging. Occasionally, if the Whisky Gods are smiling, that can turn into a true superstar – as it did with the Bowmore 66 (see above). Not this time, though it has its moments. **41%.** *150 bottles.*

∴ **Duncan Taylor Collection Bowmore 1968** Cask no. 3827 **(86)** n22 t21 f22 **b**21. Thanks to the exotic fruit, the peat is so scarce that it's just oak, fruit and barley all the way. **42.7%.** *Duncan Taylor.*

**Duncan Taylor Collection Bowmore 1969 Aged 35 Years** cask 6089, dist Nov 69, bott Jan 05 **(77)** n20 t20 f18 **b**19. The nose hints at the soapy oak having gone through the top and the finish confirms it. Very mild. Japan only. **42.7%**

**Duncan Taylor Collection Bowmore 1969** cask 6089, dist Nov 69, bott Nov 05 **(89)** n22 perky peat, fruit candy; t23 rounded with the smoke forming guard of honour for the starring pomegranate and vanilla; f21 oak thunders on, but some underlying barley sweetness maintains the balance; **b**23 does exceptionally well to hold its line in the face of a full oaky charge. Great stuff. **42.7%.** *226 btls.*

**Duncan Taylor Collection Bowmore 1982** cask 89545, dist Oct 82, bott Mar 05 **(87)** n22 curious: like a bourbon make from peated corn! t22 oily sweetness still has that corn effect and then the malt arrives; f21 vanilla and malt; **b**22 very sweet, malty and only moderately peated. **62.6%**

**Duncan Taylor Collection Bowmore 1982** cask no. 89545, dist Oct 82, bott Mar 05 **(74)** n19 t20 f17 **b**18. Like its sister bottling (above) there is bourbon on the nose, and displays the same lack of rhythm and elegance. Only here it has lost shape and direction, as well. Not a whisky happy with itself. **62.2%.** *157 bottles.*

**Duncan Taylor Collection Bowmore 1982** cask 85014, dist Oct 82, bott 15 Mar 06 **(79)** n21 t19 f20 **b**19. Jam and cream Swiss role amid the ungainly peat. An awkward customer. **58%**

∴ **Duncan Taylor Collection Bowmore 1982** Cask no. 85059 **(83)** n21 t21 f20 **b**21. A 25-year-old cough sweet...!! Some delicious sweet elements, but there is just something about this house style of the time... **56.7%**

**Duncan Taylor Collection Bowmore 1987 Aged 17 Years** cask no. 18020, dist Oct 87, bott Mar 05 **(86)** n21 t22 f23 **b**20. At Bowmore's optimum age, but this one falls all over the palate like it was drunk. Take the figure one away from the 17, and you might have the age of the style. **57.9%**

**Duncan Taylor Collection Bowmore 1987** cask 18027, dist Oct 87, bott Apr 06 **(81)** n21 t22 f18 **b**20. Distinctly pungent and peppery in that uniquely and un-unnervingly fresh Bowmore style; just runs out of legs at the finish. **58.4%.** *252 bottles.*

∴ **Duncan Taylor Collection Bowmore 1987** Cask no. 18052 **(84)** n21 t21 f21 **b**21. Steady as she goes with the distillery's unmistakable peat character. But there is no fourth gear. **52.1%**

∴ **Duncan Taylor Collection Bowmore 1987** Cask no. 18054 **(80)** n20 t19 f21 **b**20. Enjoyable, but with more natural toffee which makes for a duller, less integrated and characterful version of the 18052 (above). **54.3%**

**Dun Eideann Bowmore 10 Years Old** cask 4250 **(91)** n22 good sweet/dry balance to the smoke; t22 a light, citrussy flourish to the gathering peat; heads towards hickory near the middle; f24 molassed and sweetening, the finish gathers weight, cocoa and delicate oils impressively; **b**23 a charming, well-mannered Bowmore benefiting from a sensible upbringing in a good home. **46%.** *Signatory.*

∴ **John Milroy Selection Bowmore 1996 Aged 10 Years (76)** n19 t20 f18 **b**19. Decent sweetness but some tobacco notes and unhelpful bitterness towards the end. Yet another Bowmore that disappoints. **46%**

**Kingsbury's Single Cask Bowmore 17 Years Old** cask 2849, dist 87 **(89)** n22 the youthfulness of this nose is more like a classic Bowmore at 7 rather than a present-day 17. Only with a Bowmore from this era are you likely to find this phenomenon. Lovely, though! t22 here we go again: everything I would expect from a youthful version of the malt. The sweetness offers pure barley; the smoke is Fishermen's Friend at its warmest. This can come from one distillery only; f23 multiple layers of teasing peat, each at varying intensity. The oak plays a relaxed, tempering part; **b**22 the youngest 17 year old you'll ever see. Until you find another Bowmore... **46%.** *Japan Import System.*

∴ **Kingsbury's "The Selection" Bowmore 2001** Hogshead cask nos. 20037/20038/20040, dist Mar 01, bott July 06 **(90)** n23 pure smoked grist: stunning!! t22 new-makey oils and barley enjoy some slapstick moments with sweet peat; f23 more thoughtful with a liquorice element to the smoke; **b**22 remarkable how happy this distillery is while still in its infancy. Beautifully made whisky. **43%. ncf.** *Japan Imports System. 1,390 bottles.*

**Mackillop's Choice Bowmore 1990** dist Apr 90 **(92)** n22 t24 f23 b23. On the nose, I'd have sworn this was Caol Ila. But rarely does that distillery quite hit this level of sweet complexity. **43%. *Angus Dundee.***

**Murray McDavid Bowmore Aged 9 Years** Matured in Bourbon/Syrah casks enhanced in Guigal Hermitage Rouge casks, dist 96, bott 05 **(91)** n22 sprightly only tells the half of it; so pink is this stuff you half expect essence of panther, or even paraffin. Instead you get clipped barley and even more sharply clipped peat. The grape is bristling, too, but seems under-ripe. Very, very different; **t24** the peat goes AWOL for the first five seconds, entirely incapable of getting through the barley-fruit mix; then the smoke surges through, taking few prisoners en-route before intermingling gloriously and adding to the beautiful confusion on the palate; **f22** relaxes for the first time and at last the youthfulness of the malt begins to reveal itself, especially as the oak just about entirely gagged; **b23** wow! Now that was different – and there aren't that many whiskies in Scotland I can call a first! **46%. nc ncf. *1,500 bottles.***

⁘ **Murray McDavid Bowmore 1995** Bourbon/GuigalCondrieu Viognier **(92)** n22 tight, almost crisp peat, entirely kept in place by even tighter, crisper fruit; **t23** the veneer of fruit is eroded away by wave upon wave of peat, which splendidly grows in intensity; **f24** a grapey return which is completely at one with the smoke: muscular but delicate and, late on, quite spicy; **b23** not normally a fan of peat and fruit. This, though, works wonders. **46%**

⁘ **Murray McDavid Bowmore 1998 Aged 8 Years** Bourbon/Quart de Chaume Chenin Blank **(94)** n23 firm grape does its best to outshine the peat-shed earthiness. And fails...; **t23** smoked malt is first to arrive then builds into something altogether sweeter with the green grape oozing juice; **f24** becomes a much more delicate, thoughtful creature towards the end; **b24** wonderful Bowmore which shows so brilliantly when not trying to impersonate a particular brand of cough candy. A genuine treat that does the reputation of Bowmore no harm whatsoever. **46%**

⁘ **Norse Cask Selection Bowmore 1985 Aged 21 Years** Hogshead ref. QW7023, dist 85, bott 07 **(89)** n23 spikey peat and crushed gorse: pretty floral; **t23** beautifully full on the palate with immediate spices battling against a honeyed barley thread: a chewy mouthfiller; **f21** toffees out annoyingly as the oak intercedes and makes for a dull fade; **b22** beautiful, curiously fruitless malt for all the barley flying about. The peat offers an unmistakable Bowmore fingerprint. **57.5%. *WhiskyOwner.com, Denmark. 293 bottles.***

⁘ **Norse Cask Selection Bowmore 1989 Aged 17 Years** Sherry Hogshead, cask no. 1096 **(91)** n24 perfect, clean, intact, thick and intense sherry face-to-face with chunky peat; **t23** again, perfect delivery with the sherry revealing its juicy nature and then peat, in that mega Fisherman's Friend style unique to this distillery, rampages about; **f22** more FF; **b22** I fall prostrate in awe before this unvilified sherry butt. But I cock a withering snook at the unsubtle FF. Works, though! **52.8%. *WhiskyOwner.com, Denmark.***

**Norse Cask Selection Bowmore 1993 Aged 11 Years (96)** n24 a picnic by the sea: plenty of ozone and salt, the most beautiful peat-reek with clear iodine form rock pools. Man, this is soooo Islay...!!!; **t24** a meal in itself: thick, intense layering of 90% cocoa chocolate with sludgy peat and gorgeously sweet barley, all sprinkled with a little sea salt; the degree of oiliness just about hits perfection; **f24** long and sweetens as the gristiness to the barley comes through, shuddering layers of more cocoa and peat that go on ad-infinitum. **b24** why do we so rarely see casks of this distillery's malt exactly the way I remember it some 25-years ago? This is a true classic destined to be one of the talked-about all-lifetime greats. Sod the sample: I'm off to find a bottle...!! **65.5%.**

⁘ **Old Malt Cask Bowmore Aged 10 Years Claret Finish** dist June 96, bott Nov 06 **(85)** n23 t21 f21 b20. Nothing wrong with the Claret – for once. This time it's the Bowmore that refuses to play ball, offering no more than a puff of peat. Languid – but a great nose. **50%. *Douglas Laing. 365 bottles.***

⁘ **Old Malt Cask Bowmore Aged 12 Years** dist Jan 95, bott Jan 06 **(86)** n21 t22 f21 b22. So clean even the peat is polished...! **50%. *Douglas Laing. 359 bottles.***

⁘ **Old Malt Cask Bowmore Aged 18 Years** dist Oct 88, bott Nov 06 **(82)** n20 t21 f20 b21. People talk about whisky vintages – which seldom makes sense. But this was one distillery that went with a less than perfect vintage at this time: perhaps just a Fisherman's Friend phase it was going through. **50%. *Douglas Laing. 309 bottles.***

**Old Malt Cask Bowmore 21 Years Old Sherry Finish** dist Oct 84, bott Sept 06 **(86)** **n**21 **t**22 **f**22 **b**21. With its molassed Fisherman's Friend and Ovaltine, this is such a direct ancestor of the 6-years-old bottled in 1992 for Oddbins that's it's almost scary. You would never believe its age otherwise. **50%.** *309 bottles.*

**Old Masters Bowmore Aged 12 Years** cask no. 20100, dist 94, bott 06 **(83)** **n**20 **t**21 **f**22 **b**20. Decent, delicate whisky for those who prefer their peat toned down a little. **57.8%.** *James MacArthur.*

**Old Masters Bowmore 1990 Aged 15 Years** cask no. 1168, bott 05 **(84)** **n**21 **t**22 **f**21 **b**20. A sugary sweetness glazes the soft peat but for all its charm complexity is at a minimum. **51.1%.** *James MacArthur.*

⋯ **Provenance Bowmore Aged 9 Years** dist Spring 97, bott Winter 06 **(86)** **n**22 **t**22 **f**21 **b**21. Clean, refreshing delicate and very light for all its peaty charms. **46%.**

⋯ **Provenance Bowmore Aged 9 Years** dist Winter 97, bott Winter 06 **(86)** **n**22 **t**22 **f**21 **b**21. Lively, refreshing, well peated and beautifully made. **46%.** *Douglas Laing.*

⋯ **Provenance Bowmore Aged 10 Years** dist Spring 97, bott Spring 07 **(89)** **n**22 crisp barley and firm peat; a lovely controlled sweetness; **t**23 mouth filling with a real gristy freshness and even an echo of new make; **f**22 clean sherbet sweetness to the prevailing oak and citrus-juicy barley; **b**22 an honest dram that delivers on the sweet-peat front. Much closer to the 10 year old Bowmores of 25 years ago. **46%.** *Douglas Laing.*

**Provenance Bowmore 13 Years Old** dist 10 Apr, bott 21 Mar 05 **(86)** **n**20 **t**22 **f**22 **b**22. Untaxing and unsophisticated, it's one for simple pleasures. **46%.**

⋯ **Queen of the Moorlands Rare Cask Bowmore 1991 Edition XVIII (96)** **n**24 layers of pugnacious, spicy peat of varied intensity attempt to knock the crap out of layers of high quality sherry of equally contrasting hues: it's an honourable draw; **t**25 so massive my palate sends out for extra tastebuds: a deluge of opaque sherry carries with it that wondrous peat – and spice. For a Bowmore of this age it simply cannot be bettered; **f**23 by the standards of before just a fraction tame, but the bitter-sweet balance remains true and some molassed burnt raisin really does help calm things; **b**24 an exceptional shock to the system. By the third mouthful you know you are experiencing a true Islay moment never to be forgotten. And by the fifth I'd given up spitting...The 400th new whisky for the 2008 Bible... and what a way to celebrate! **57.7%. nc ncf.** *Available at The Wine Shop, Leek & Congleton, and Islay Whisky Shop.*

**The Queen of the Moorlands Rare Cask Bowmore 1995** cask 271035 **(90)** **n**22 Bowmore at its most bonfiresque; **t**22 young, sweet and well smoked with the body an attractive dual personality of softness and extreme rigidity; **f**23 goes into overdrive here with the intensity of the peat now building up above the Bowmore norm and the accompanying spices letting rip; **b**23 a rock solid and above average version of this distillery at 10. **57.2%. ncf sc.** *The Wine Shop, Leek. 108 btls.*

**Royal Mile Whiskies Bowmore Young Peaty Islay** cask 20022, dist 17 Feb 99, bott Mar 05 **(84)** **n**21 **t**22 **f**22 **b**19. Brilliant to see Bowmore in this Bambi-like state. So sweet, the peat goes in every direction. Fond memories of the old Oddbins bottlings of 15 years ago, when they still knew how to have fun... **61.5%.** *322 btls.*

⋯ **Scotch Malt Whisky Society Cask 3.125 Aged 17 Years** Refill Hogshead, dist Dec 88 **(84)** **n**21 **t**22 **f**21 **b**20. Sweet, plenty of now trademark Fisherman's Friends on what was once the optimum age for the distillery. **53.7%**

⋯ **Scotch Malt Whisky Society Cask 3.126 Aged 18 Years** Refill Hogshead, dist Dec 88 **(85)** **n**22 **t**21 **f**21 **b**21. Pretty oily, which perhaps accounts for the lack of real complexity in a malt this age. The peat, though, is a rumbling treat. **52.8%**

⋯ **Scotch Malt Whisky Society Cask 3.127 Aged 10 Years** Refill Hogshead, dist Mar 97 **(88)** **n**22 peppery and sneezy; clean, crisp, a tad salty; **t**23 much sweeter, gristier style than the nose suggests; peat is below average in density but offers excellent weight; **f**22 long, some developing oil and vanilla joins peat fade; **b**21 the cough sweet peat has gone (thank heavens!) and a crisper, more Islay-defined dram has taken its place. **59%**

**Secret Stills Bowmore Aged 17 Years** Distillery no.4, release no. 1, casks 7049/7050, dist 19 Aug 89, bott Jun 06 **(92)** **n**24 dogged peat whimpers and snarls with a bi-polar display of softness and aggression. Lovely salt attaches to the gristier element; **t**23 perfect sweetness in having dry oak assuring a cut-off point to the developing demerara-laced peat; **f**22 bitter-sweet; some coffee with the smoke **b**23 not too much secret about Bowmore, being one of the more eponymous Islays. Great, though, to see it at arguably its best age. And in such great nick. **45%**. *Gordon & MacPhail. 650 bottles.*

⋯ **Secret Stills Islay 1989** Distillery No. 4, Release No. 3, sherry hogshead casks no. 7042, 7043, 7045 & 7056, dist 19 Sept 89, bott June 06 **(87) n**23 peat hides behind thick fruit and barley: heavy stuff; **t**22 voluptuous barley with smoke of the non-islandy style; **f**20 toffee, oil and vanilla; **b**22 almost a secret Islay: tasted blind I'd never have recognised it. **45%**. *Gordon & MacPhail.*

**The Spirit Safe & Cask Bowmore 1990 Aged 15 Years** Hogshead, dist 90, bott May 06 **(83) n**20 **t**22 **f**21 **b**20. Lethargic peat and honey dependent. Clean but oaky towards the finish. **53.1%. nc ncf.** *Celtic Whisky Compagnie, France.*

**Vom Fass Bowmore 12 Years Old (85) n**20 **t**21 **f**22 **b**21. For those who prefer their peat to whisper rather than shout. **40%.** *Austria.*

⋯ **Wilson & Morgan Barrel Selection Bowmore 1997 Extra Strength** bott 07 **(89) n**22 apologetic peat on clean barley; still weighty, though; **t**23 spot-on delivery with exceptional weight; bit of a confused middle but the soft oils and touches of honey delight; **f**22 long, still a touch oily but a good chew; **b**22 peaty, despite the nose. **50%**

⋯ **Whisky-Doris Bowmore Aged 16 Years** Bourbon cask, dist 24 Apr 90, bott 1 Feb 07 **(88) n**22 buttered kipper; emptied coal sacks; **t**23 lively, punchy smoke with reserves of sweet barley; **f**21 enough oil for the Pentagon to get interested; **b**22 disappointing end to a lovely malt. **58.4%. ncf.** *Germany. 88 bottles.*

# BRAES OF GLENLIVET (see Braeval)

# BRAEVAL
**Speyside, 1974. Chivas. Silent.**

⋯ **Cadenhead's Authentic Collection The Braes of Glenlivet Aged 17 Years** Sauterne hogshead, dist 89, bott Feb 07 **(94) n**22 an odd twosome of bourbony notes and over-ripe fruit. Strange...; **t**25 Gadzooks! No-one could possibly expect such a confused nose to come up with something so confident and vivid! Remains bipolar, with amazingly intense wine in one corner and a rip-roaring roasty barley in the other, with spices and high cocoa content chocolate somewhere in between. Sublime...faultless; **f**23 enormously long and uncompromising. The oak does fade towards a sultana sweetness and the barley gathers oils as well as more cocoa. But it's a long, long fade...and just as well; **b**24 simply stupendous and quite enormous whisky by any standards. **55.9%.** *276 bottles.*

**Deerstalker Braeval Aged 10 Years (91) n**23 ripe gooseberries and fat watermelon balance beautifully with the no less refreshing malt; **t**23 just so stunningly clean and uncluttered, giving the malt a clear, mouthwatering path to dazzle and shimmer; **f**23 gloriously long and chewy for a malt so light, with a slow procession of oak adding spice at the death; **b**22 can hardly be called complex, but the allure is its simple, honest, delicate, mouth-cleansing intensity. The secret, though, is its near perfect degree of sweetness. The youngest of the Deerstalker range, but the best by a long way – and another reminder of what we are missing from this very good distillery. **40%**

⋯ **Dun Bheagan Braeval 1995 Aged 11 Years** Butt, dist June 95 **(90) n**22 freshly quartered lemon squeezed onto the purest barley grist; **t**23 just so mouth-watering you can drown in your own juices: fresh, gristy sweet and refusing to show a single off note; **f**22 about now the oak should offer something bitter, but it doesn't. It plays along with the gristy-sweet game and does little to head off the citrus; **b**23 Bravo for Braeval! I just so love this distillery, especially when it's in this cooing, wooing mood where it just caresses your tastebuds with disarming gentility. **46%. nc ncf.** *Ian Macleod Distillers.*

**Old Malt Cask Braes of Glenlivet Aged 13 Years** Refill Hogshead 1498, dist Nov 90, bott Oct 04 **(83) n**21 **t**22 **f**20 **b**20. Some very decent barley-oak combinations, but a bit fierce in part. **50%. nc ncf.** *Douglas Laing.*

**Old Malt Cask Braeval 16 Years Old Wine Finish** dist May 90, bott Sept 06 **(84) n**20 **t**21 **f**22 **b**21. Pretty closed on nose and arrival but finally opens up to let loose some firm barley and oak. **50%.** *Douglas Laing. 327 bottles.*

Provenance Braeval Aged 8 Years dist Nov 96, bott Nov 04 (87) n22 beefed up barley as you might expect, but the oak thrust is a surprise; t23 what wonderful barley intensity. Youthful, but showing greater age than the norm; f21 slightly off-key with the oak offering a bitter finale; b21 unmissable youth, but probably a first fill cask has helped here. 46%.

## BRECHIN (see North Port)

## BRORA
### Highland (northern), 1819–1983. Diageo. Closed.

⁑ Brora 30 Years Old Special Releases 2006 db (92) n23 just the odd shaving of oak too many to make for a truly great nose but the soft coal-tar layering with the hickory and liquorice really is so lovely; t24 big, big, BIG!! A triumphant landing of massive peat with an oaky backbone; spices buzz both contentedly and with a touch of menace; f22 retains its hickory/peat course with some much drier elements; b23 showing a degree of age decay but even so the sheer beauty of this malt leaves you gasping. 55.7%

Brora 30 Years Old db (92) n23 supremely balanced and intact after all these years. The full-on smoke offers a sweet counter to the well-behaved oak. An apologetic hint of pine reveals some of the age. Majestic, nonetheless; t22 the full strength plays into the hands of the beguiling oak-peat character. Despite the wood chippings, the sweetness of the barley keeps the tastebuds panting: this is sexy stuff; f23 good breeding here as the oak backs off to offer nibbling vanilla and marmalade and just the right percentages of smoke-fuelled spice; b24 oh, it does the heart such good to find aged malts like this. Near sublime. 55.7%

Brora 30 Years Old db (96) n25 near enough faultless smoke, less seaweed than farmyard. But there are countless layers here with malt and oak visible, so to speak. Perfect harmony; t24 the sweetness of the malt defies time: you could be running your finger along the mill at the old Broro distillery in the days when it was probably Scotland's prettiest working distillery; f24 just so long and relaxed. Try and count the layers of smoked malt, then lightly smoked oak as one by one they strike against the tastebuds. You can't: there's too many. For good measure, there is a very low surge of fresh, mouthwatering malt as well; b23 I'll dock it a mark as it doesn't quite have that extraordinary (almost immeasurable but profound) extra depth, complexity and balance that all the top Ardbegs possess. I'm a heartless bugger, me. But being purely analytical, I think that's a fair call. Scotch of the year? It's up there. Just a Rosebank and maybe a fluke vatting to battle with. I understand they are getting very low on Brora now. The lab has done the distillery proud with this one: nothing like its age and then best I've seen it since it was in its prime at 12. Sensational and a lifetime must-have. 56.6%

Brora 30 Years Old db (97) n24 that stunning Brora farmyard again, perhaps with a touch of extra fruit this time round. Beautiful structure, layering and harmony; t25 Gosh! Perfect or what? How can something be this old yet offer such a gristy sweetness? Chewy, smoky, barely oaky but 100 okay-dokey; f24 some late peat spice buzz adds a bit of bite to the smoke-fuelled serenity of this dram. A touch of something citrus helps thin out the layers; b24 here we go again! Just like last year's bottling, we have something of near unbelievable beauty with the weight perfectly pitched and the barley-oak interaction the stuff of dreams. And as for the peat: an entirely unique species, a giant that is so gentle. Last year's bottling was one of the whiskies of the year. This even better version is the perfect follow-up. 56.4%

Chieftain's Brora Aged 23 Years Pedro Ximenez Sherry butt cask 1510, dist Nov 81, bott Mar 05 (93) n23 lt24 f22 b24. The sherry is profound but doesn't overwhelm the intricate character of the malt. 46%. nc ncf.

⁑ Chieftain's Brora 24 Years Old Cream sherry butt, dist June 90 (95) n23 buttered kippers and steaming, unsugared cocoa; t23 near perfect weight and oils as the coffee and peat go head to head. Spice kicks off aggressively but pacified by oak-instated demerara; f25 one of the longest – and most complete – finishes of the year with the sherry at last getting a look in. The spreading of the soft sugars, as they mix in with the Jamaican Blue Mountain will become the stuff of legend amongst whisky lovers. A truly perfect finale to a near perfect malt; b24 most probably the best bottling ever under the Chieftain's label. This whisky is marks a great distillery at its very peak. 46%. nc ncf. Ian Macleod Distillers.

∴ **Connoisseurs Choice Brora 1982 (86)** n21 t22 f22 b21. A curiously tight Brora where the peat gets up to sing and only a squeak is heard. Some decent buttery-oaky waves, but something is muffled here. The odd fruity spark and a fabulous range of complex smoky notes, yet an unfulfilled pleasure. **43%**. *Gordon & MacPhail*.

**Dun Bheagan Brora Aged 23 Years** Sherry butt **(86)** n22 t23 f20 b21. Some uncommonly good sherry influence at work here. **48%**. *Ian Macleod*.

∴ **Dun Bheagan Brora 1981 Aged 24 Years** Fino Sherry Butt, dist Dec 81 **(82)** n21 t21 f20 b20. the dryness of the Fino does absolutely nothing to help the barley battle against the oak. Thin and disappointing by Brora standards. **48.5%. nc ncf**. *Ian Macleod*.

∴ **Lombard's Jewels of Scotland Brora 1982 Aged 22 Years (94)** n23 thick, sploshed on all over smoke with a pleasing degree of vanilla; t24 enormous, mouth-filling and charismatic delivery with tidal waves of peat crashing over the barley concentrate: sweet, dense and enormously delicious; f23 if it took any longer you'd have to get life insurance for it: just a continuation of the stunning peat/barley/grist middle only now with a light spread of raspberry jam; b24 when they call this a Jewel of Scotland, for once there is no overstatement in the marketing. **50%**. *Lombard Brands*.

∴ **Old & Rare Brora Aged 30 Years** dist Oct 76, bott Apr 07 **(95)** n23 strumming smoke in perfect tune; t24 enormous delivery with the silkiest peat imaginable, oaky dry at first then sweetening out as a beyond- the- grave gristiness kicks in; f24 the usual molassed finale, except it's not quite that simple with the layering oscillating between spice and honey, oak and smoke; b24 once more a dram from a distillery that leaves you spellbound. No descriptors entirely do justice. And as I am just completing this edition and space is at a premium, I'll not even try. **57.5%**. *Douglas Laing. 109 bottles*.

**Old Malt Cask Brora Aged 22 Years** dist Mar 83, bott Sept 05 **(84)** n21 t22 f20 b21. Intense oaked-barley-toffee apple but the peat is notable for its absence, though a coal-dusty smokiness is apparent. **50%**. *Douglas Laing. 224 bottles*.

**Old Malt Cask Brora Aged 22 Years** dist 17 Mar 83, bott May 05 **(78)** n19 t21 f19 b19. Another curiously smokeless expression. **50%**. *Douglas Laing. 421 bottles*.

## BRUICHLADDICH
### Islay, 1881. Bruichladdich Ltd, Working.

**Bruichladdich 10 Years Old** db **(90)** n22 beautifully clean and zesty, the malt is almost juvenile; t23 sweet, fruity then malty charge along the tastebuds that geets the mouth salivating; f23 the usual soft vanilla and custard but a bigger barley kick in the latter stages; b22 more oomph than previous bottlings, yet still retaining its fragile personality. Truly great stuff for a standard bottling. **46%**

**Bruichladdich 12 Years Old 2nd Edition** db **(88)** n23 big barrage of fruit; crisp barley beautifully integrates with oak; t22 an uneven, mildly uncertain, delivery due to the grape being out of sync with the big barley; give it about eight-ten seconds and they have found a delicious degree of harmony; f22 long with the intense, chiselled flavours still slightly at odds, but calming down with some oils; b21 a similar type of wine involvement to "Waves", but this is oilier in the old-fashioned 'Laddie style and lacks a little of the sparkle. The fruit on the finish is outstanding, though, and I don't think you or I would turn down a third glass... **46%**

**Bruichladdich 15 Years Old 2nd Edition** db **(86)** n22 t23 f20 b21. Delicious, as usual, but something, possibly fruity, appears to be holding back the show. **46%**

**Bruichladdich XVII Year Old** db **(94)** n23 gentle citrus-led fruit caresses the nose; soft malt counters the spice; t23 mild malt offers both a sharp barley thrust and a much softer gristy sweetness; f24 the mouthwatering richness continues to the very end with some spices suggesting oak but the malt remaining in control; b24 there has been a quite enormous jump in quality between "official" tastings of this malt. Where once it was just delicate, it is now delicate and raucous: soft and rough lovemaking to the palate. A dram dedicated to Laddie blender Jim McEwan's sex life, one assumes! Lucky bugger! **46%**

**Bruichladdich Flirtation 20 Year Old** db **(88)** n23 t22 f21 b22. All the fun is in the chase with this one.... **46%**

**Bruichladdich Flirtation Aged 20 Years Second Edition** db **(86)** n21 t22 f22 b21. Hi sugar! A Laddie for those with a sweet tooth. **46%**

-∴- **Bruichaladdich 1970 Anniversary Bottling 125th** Bourbon cask, mature enhanced in Zind Humbrecht Selection de Grains Noble Pinot Gris Alsace white wine casks db **(95) n**24 Good grief!! You don't sniff many aromas like this during the course of a year...decade...lifetime...!!! Initially you think: aha! loads of passion fruit and other exotics = great age. Then you think: hang on a mo... what's all that vaguely paprika-esque spice doing? Then you start detecting the most delicate of smoke notes and then spices, boiled plums and stewed apples and even something peculiarly boiled-crab-like. I kid you not...see for yourself... **t**24 think of the softest delivery you ever tasted in your life...then multiply that softness by a factor of about 1.5. Silk doesn't do this justice, nor does the simple descriptor of varied, lightly spiced Pacific fruits. There is a distinctive boubony edge to this as if Kentucky's finest has galloped in to town. An absolute treat; **f**23 incredibly light with just a smattering of roasty over-the-top oak, but it's so refined it sits very comfortably amid the bourbon, fruit and barley; **b**24 an unbelievably complex malt that defies time. A must- experience malt. **40.1%**

-∴- **Bruichladdich Blacker Still 1986** Sherry cask db **(87) n**21 a not entirely un-flawed cask but before treatment this must have been a peach of a butt as the intensity of the sherry makes your hairs stand on end; **t**22 again ribbons of something that shouldn't quite be there, yet such is the totality of the grape and spice that you cannot do other than be entertained with its sweet and juicy brilliance; **f**22 that nagging S word continues, but now a gorgeous hickory tone wades in and stirs the pot; **b**22 mildly flawed but you can forgive it its trespasses on account of its utterly juicy deliciousness. **50.7%**

-∴- **Bruichladdich 1989** Bourbon/Tempranillo db **(94) n**23 not dissimilar to African violet petals crushed in the fingers, though this is no shrinking violet. Floral, fruity but very firm; **t**24 cracking delivery: crisp and mouth-watering with an excellent involvement of barley sugar and soft fruit juices; the spices are weighted with rare diligence; **f**23 a light silver sugar sprinkling over gorgeous custard and coffee; and still those playful spices persist; **b**24 stunning structure: a malt that feels as if it has been carved into shape by the most gifted of hands. Wonderful. **46%.** *Scanlines, Denmark.*

-∴- **Bruichladdich Ghost Ship Valinch 1990** db **(92) n**23 on the surface a drier than most Laddie cask with almost a background touch of Riesling; the balance and charm never waver; **t**24 part-dissolves on the palate with barley just pulsing through, building in sweetness and chewability: one of the best deliveries of the year. Of its type, absolutely amazing... **f**22 a little more conventional with its mocha fade once the oak digs in but the sheer class cannot be diluted; **b**23 what an honest and wonderful cask this came from. Some moments offered are to die for. **54.5%.** *Available exclusively from distillery where drawn directly from cask.*

-∴- **Bruichladdich 1994** Bourbon/PX Sherry db **(78) n**19 **t**20 **f**19 **b**20. Love the distillery. Love the shop. Just don't particularly love this bottling. Sorry. **59.7%.** *Special Bottling for Potstill, Austria.*

**Bruichladdich Infinity** db **(94) n**24 lazy smoke slowly disengages itself from the thick barley. Seriously sexy; **t**24 enormously viscous as the honeycombed barley grips to the roof of the mouth while sweet peat thuds around the palate; **f**22 some timid vanillins shove their head above the peaty parapet; **b**24 from a distillery that has been known to distil more than twice, here's something that might have been in the pot only once, such in the enormity and intensity of the malt. Knife, fork and spoon needed for this one...and you could stand them up in it. To infinity, indeed...and beyond...!! **55.5%**

-∴- **Bruichladdich Infinity Second Edition** Bourbon/Rioja db **(94) n**24 Jesus H....a nose to both rock you back in your chair and getting you springing to your feet at the same moment. Cured bacon (though there was probably nothing wrong with it) and peppered kippers; barley grist and roasted oatmeal: staggering bitter-sweet combination with no imbalance at all. Simply a wondrous nose... **t**24 A spicier affair than the first edition with just a little extra oil to coat the mouth, not quite Caol Ila style but getting there. The fruit also plays a big part with those blatant spices; but it's juicy also and ultra chewy; **f**23 real smokiness to the finish which dries in the same way as when you swallow the fumes of your cottage's peat fire; mildly dusty towards the finish...and classy; **b**23 Wasn't it Daffy Duck who used to put on his cape and shout: "Infinity and Beyond" ? Oh, no... it was Buzz Lightyear. Anyways, he must have been thinking of this. And there's certainly nothing dethspicable about this one... **52.5%**

**Bruichladdich "Islands" Aged 20 Years Third Edition** Aged in Madeira db **(95) n**23 sublime balance between keen grape and drier vanilla. A light-heavyweight; or is it a heavy-lightweight; **t**24 immediate buzz to the mouth and then, on secondary impact, the most luscious fruity delivery which entirely cleanses the palate; sweet but some lovely spices counter perfectly; **f**24 long, lithe and light, again its that soft pepper and barley which sits so happily with the grape; **b**24 just perfect for those looking to spice up their whisky lives. **46%**

**Bunnahabhain Islay Festival Bottling 2006 14 Years Old** Pedro Ximenez Finish db **(78) n**18 **t**19 **f**21 **b**20. Call me an old misery guts. But only trace elements of the distillery style survive – a salty blast about three quarters in. Has some good moments, but not enough. And too many fault lines. **52.6%**.

**Bruichladdich Legacy 1965** db **(90) n**22 **t**23 **f**22 **b**23. Well, I don't now how it did it, but a malt as gentle as Bruichladdich has survived nearly 40 years in the cask with barely a wrinkle. Not a single off note! **41.8%**. *1,500 btls*.

**Bruichladdich Legacy 1966** db **(92) n**23 **t**23 **f**23 **b**23. No sappiness or bitterness here, just grace, charm, melting malt: that's my laddie! **40.6%**

⋇ **Bruichladdich Legacy V Aged 33 Years** dist pre–72 db **(87) n**21 some panting, exhausted oak is kept alive by resuscitating fruits; **t**22 a no-less exhausted delivery and then the light bourbony tones pitch in deliciously; the spices have " Ol' Kentucky" written through the centre... **f**22 the finale is pure Blue Grass... **b**22 the single malt that will win over bourbon-only drinkers! **40.7%**. *1,600 bottles*.

⋇ **Bruichladdich Links K Club Ireland "16th Hole" 14 Years Old** Bourbon/Syrah, dist 1992, bott 07 db **(93) n**23 **t**23 **f**23 **b**24. I quite like this, though as hard as I try I can't quite love it. The spices offer great entertainment value and the juiciness on delivery is astonishing, but..... My tongue is investigating every crevice in my mouth with some urgency, so I know it's complex – and very unusual, but..... It's gossamer light. It kind of teases you. It's playful. But it's not beautiful. Is it...? Third mouthful in and I'm getting hooked. Oh, sod it! I've just upped it from a 86 to 93. What can I do? I'm in love... **46%**. **nc ncf**. *12,000 bottles*.

**Bruichladdich Links "Royal Liverpool Hoylake" 14 Years Old** db **(89) n**23 another wonderful compendium of varying fruit nuances...and barley; **t**23 astonishing freshness to the delivery massages every single taste bud; **f**21 oily, gentle fruits, but a little flat; **b**22 a conservative malt by 'Laddie's recent standards: should go down in the Clubhouse well... **46%**

**Bruichladdich Links "Turnberry 10th Limited Edition" 14 Years Old** db **(94) n**24 as soft, tantalizing and teasing as fingernails down the spine. And just as fruity...; **t**24 oh yes....the softness of delivery, the valuation of the fruit, only to be attacked and overcome by the voluminous and unstriated barley... words simply fail me...; **f**22 a sombre finish with a more bitter edge to the complex fruit and cocoa; **b**24 at first I thought this was the first scotch whisky to be named after roads of British housing estates for the nouveau riche...then I realised they were golf courses....Majorly complex malt; I could nose and taste there was some Port in there somewhere, but something else was happening. Research reveals that something is Pedro Ximenez. Talented bloke is Pedro... **46%**

**Bruichladdich Rocks** db **(82) n**19 **t**22 **f**20 **b**21. Perhaps softer than you'd imagine something called "rocks"! Beautiful little malty charge on entry. **46%**

**Bruichladdich 3D 2nd Edition Moine Mhor** db **(91) n**22 bigger age and the peat comes chunkier rather than the soft wafts of the 1st edition; **t**23 almost in-your-face delivery of smoke-encrusted fruit: this is enormous and the intensity is furthered by the delicious cocoa towards the middle and a burst of spice; **f**23 softer than the 1st edition with the smoke making a soft landing for the vanilla and; the sweetness at the death reminds me of the raspberry jam in a Swiss role...yummy! **b**23 The re-creation kind of underlines that the 1st edition was, perhaps, a one-off. This is top-rate whisky and no mistake. But falls short of the 1st edition's near genius. This will be an interesting set to collect over the years. **50%**

⋇ **Bruichladdich 3D Third Edition** A marriage of Bruichladdich, Port Charlotte & Octomore, Bourbon/Madeira db **(91) n**23 a Bowmore-ish style of sherry-kippery peat, perhaps exaggerated by a certain youthful trait; the phenols are prickly and at times attractively stark; as near as damn it like sticking your head into the pagoda as the smoke from the densest, darkest peat is wafting through; **t**22 soft, sweet delivery with a deliberate ramping up of the smoke yet the barley is still there to add a juicy dimension; **f23** superb balance at the finish with that thick knot of smoke now evening out allowing fruit, barley and mild hickory tones to play off the light spices. Charming; **b23** an incredibly old-fashioned style of high-class Islay malt... taking me back to my first-ever visits to the island over 25 years ago. In fact, about the time I first met the Norrie Campbell, peat cutter extraordinaire and now, sadly, lost to us...So, those of you who taste this – or any other Islay, come to that – please share with me a smoky toast to his memory. **46%.** *Norrie Campbell Tribute.*

**Bruichladdich 1970** db (79) **n**21 **t**20 **f**19 **b**19. Plucked from the warehouse just in time; lovely fruits on the nose and delivery, but becomes a bit sappy as the finish works overtime to regain lost ground. **40.2%.** *Taiwan.*

**Bruichladdich Vintage 1973** db (88) **n**22 **t**22 **f**21 **b**23. First sight suggests that the oak is too intrusive; give it time and instead you get a genuinely delicious bourbony strata to a fabulously complex whisky. **40.2%. nc ncf.** *4200 bottles.*

**Bruichladdich Waves Aged 7 Years** db (90) **n**21 young, with clipped fruit and smoke; **t**23 mouthwatering barley at first, soon swamped in light grape; **f**23 stylish finale with the gathering smoke really feeling at home with the Madeira. Seriously classy despite the obvious youth; **b**23 compact, tasty little fruitfest lengthened by evidence of soft smoke and extra clean grape. Proof absolute that whisky at 7 years old can offer just as must delight as something twice or three times its age. **46%**

**Bruichladdich WMD II - The Yellow Submarine 1991** db (75) **n**20 **t**19 **f**18 **b**18. Sorry guys. But by this distillery's normally orbital standards, while quite drinkable, this one just doesn't have the balance and sinks. **46%**

⸭ **Port Charlotte Evolution PC5 Cask Strength** db (95) **n**24 enormously heavy going with the thick grape and the 40ppm peat (actually, it seems a lot bigger than that) arm-wrestling for control. Perhaps the peat wins, but only after it has spent ten minutes oxidizing in the glass... **t**23 a spice kick on the nose is no less evident on delivery where again the sherry and peat arrive in one massive and very sharp tangle. Only with the introduction of a touch of oak do matters become a little clearer and less confused; **f**24 wonderful denouement as finally the palate finds space to make sense of it all. The grape thins out sufficiently to at last add colour to the haze of the peat smoke while the phenols begin to grasp gently the custard tart oakiness to help lighten and sweeten the load; **b**24 a bit like a David Lynch movie: you are caught in the dazzling genius of it all, not exactly knowing what is going on, yet never doubting that you are experiencing something very special; and only at the very end does the plot make any sense at all. One thing is for certain: even the most experienced peat whisky lovers are unlikely to have encountered anything quite like this....simply because Port Charlotte offers a style of peating different from any other not only on Islay but in the world. **63.5%.** *6,000 bottles.*

**Port Charlotte 4 Years Old** dist 12th Jun 01, bott 25th Nov 05 (96) **n**25 quite possibly the most coastal whisky I have ever nosed: it is as if the peat has been diluted only by seawater. This smells of rotting distilleries and malt kilns. It is unique and unquestionably the most evocative thing I have ever sniffed. I close my eyes and I am on undiscovered Islay, before I ever wrote about the place; when I could wander around barely-known distilleries alone. No matter how it tastes, it cannot paint a picture so vividly, or bring back such a lost joy as the nose, or even a sense of loss of how things used to be. ...I don't know if you believe this or not, but it has actually brought a lump to my throat and a slightly moistened eye. I think I should pause before tasting...; **t**24 salty, fruity, even – eventually – wild raspberries and banging on the door all the time, massive peat wanting to be let in; **f**23 dry despite its age though enough mollased mocha to keep the  rumbling peat sweet and company; **b**24 so stupendous – and moving – is the nose that it takes time to focus on what happens palate-wise. Not quite so good, as one might suspect. But still a unique and astonishingly pleasurable take on Islay. **61.4%.** *The Whisky Shop, Gordon Homer's Private Stock. 39 bottles.*

⸭ **Port Charlotte First Cut** 27/05/07 Bourbon cask no. 007, dist 28 May 01, bott May 07 db (94) **n**23 dry, clumpy peat; a sweet pipe tobacco balances things slightly; an entirely different peat-reek aroma from any other whisky on this planet: there is an intensity to this that borders on the manic; **t**24 big: a slow dissolving of thick peat on the palate; always sweet and mildly gristy; given the conditions, spices are expected – and arrive in force; **f**24 a light involvement of vanilla helps and at last the intensity softens to something much more delicate and even sophisticated. But it is never less than a white knuckle ride...; **b**23 great whisky, even if it does, through youth, struggle slightly to get its legs and balance. For best results, leave in the glass to settle and oxidise for a while before tasting. A malt for extremists. **61.5%**

**Berry's' Own Selection Bruichladdich 1991 Aged 15 Years (94) n**24 greengages, honey, salt and a vague smokiness combine for something rather wonderful; **t**24 a stunning honey thread weaves through the crystal-clear barley; threatens to be mouthwatering, but prevented at the last minute by drier vanilla. The weight and delicacy of the sweetness defy the odds. 'Laddie, you feel, unplugged...; **f**23 raspberry jam raps itself around that renegade peat; **b**23 unexpected little gems like this make you feel so lucky to do this job... **46%.**

**Cadenhead's Authentic Collection Bruchladdich 12 Years** Bourbon Hogshead, dist 93, bott Sep 05 **(85) n**20 **t**22 **f**22 **b**21. Oily, hugely barley-intense, straight-down-the-line 'Laddie. Not even the hint of a deviation. **55.8%.** *312 bottles.*

⸭ **Cadenhead's Bruichladdich Aged 15 Years** Bourbon, dist 1991, bott May 07 **(86) n**23 **t**22 **f**20 **b**21. A detailed tapestry of gently salted barley notes and varying shades of oak make this a dram to take your time over. **46%.** *312 bottles.*

**Cadenhead's Authentic Collection Bruichladdich Aged 18 Years** Bourbon Hogshead, dist 86, bott May 05 **(94) n**24 peat reek? A soft wisp of it here and there? Surely not. It is, though. But that is not all: wonderful saltiness and grandstanding oak. Fabulous; **t**23 succulent wave upon wave of mouthwatering barley sugar and treacle. Vanilla gathers towards the middle, as does cocoa – surprisingly early on; **f**23 that hint of smoke on the nose is confirmed at the smouldering death; **b**24 what a glass of class... **55.8%.** *270 bottles.*

**Cask Strength Bruichladdich 1990 (83) n**20 **t**21 **f**21 **b**21. Oaky and salt encrusted; a lovely honey edge, too. But forget the strength: this is hot whisky; a wave of glistening barley cools it – to a degree. **54.9%.** *Gordon & MacPhail.*

**The Coopers Choice Bruichladdich 1991 Matured for 14 Years** bott 06 **(82) n**22 **t**21 **f**19 **b**20. The oily richness to the early barley is stunning. **46%.**

**Dewar Rattray Individual Cask Bottling Bruichladdich 1993 Aged 12 Years** cask no. 1558, dist Apr 93, bott Sept 05 **(86) n**21 **t**23 **f**21 **b**21. An enjoyable if straightforward expression. **55.1%.** *329 bottles.*

**Duncan Taylor Collection Bruichladdich 1966 Aged 39 Years** bott Jan 05 **(94) n**23 **t**24 **f**23 **b**24. An awesome cask that has withstood the test of time with barely a blemish. A quite mesmerizing and near unbelievable malt. **41.4%**

**Duncan Taylor Collection Bruichladdich 1990** dist Jun 90, bott Sept 05 **(90) n**22 enormously hard barley with a rummy-liquorice-hickory depth to the fruit. All prisoners slaughtered; **t**23 rock-hard, vivid barley yet salivating and sharp; **f**22 the undulating sweetness pans out to something nutty, almost marzipan in style; **b**23 blind-tasted, I'd never have recognized this as a 'Laddie in a 100 years. In fact, I'd have no idea what the hell this was. In some eyes, possibly a faulty cask. But what faults...!!! Very different, and rather excellent to boot. **54.7%.** *736 bottles.*

**Dun Eideann Bruichladdich 10 Years Old** cask 3036 **(89) n**22 a squeeze of lemon and a shake of salt on the transparent barley; **t**23 simplistic, softly oiled and salivating young barley pans out into something much more complex; **f**22 lovely vanilla tints as it dries; **b**22 an honest, delightfully complex cask. **46%.**

**James MacArthur's Bruichladdich Aged 14 Years** dist 91, bott 05 **(90) n**22 lively citrus thins out the intense barley; **t**23 deft, playful barley offers a grassy lightness which allows in some early, excellent vanilla and spice; **f**22 long, multi-layered barley of just the right weight; **b**23 a honey of a cask. **43%.**

⸭ **Murray McDavid Bruichladdich 1989** Sherry **(93) n**23 like opening a bag of fresh organic sultanas; wonderful fruit and a tang of something spiced; **t**23 mmm! Juicy! Outstanding meeting of yielding barley and less yielding fruit; the spices on the nose quickly translate to something more substantial on the palate; **f**23 comfortable layers of oak add weight and counter dryness in the boiled candy grape; **b**24 when I moan at the front of the Bible about the lack of decent sherry bottlings – this isn't one I have in mind! Excellent. **46%**

**Old Malt Cask Bruichladdich 15 Years Old** Bourbon finish, dist Dec 90, bott July 06 **(88) n**21 curious vanilla/suet pudding/sultana, yet lacking balance; **t**23 busy with mouthwatering spices and gathering barley intensity; **f**22 soft oils guide the gentle oak to calmer waters and onto cocoa; **b**22 lurches drunkenly all over the palate but the main thrust really is beautiful and big. Very different. **50%.**

Provenance Bruichladdich **11 Year Old** dist 25 Nov 93, bott 23 Feb 05 **(87) n**22 **t**22 **f**21 **b**22. At its cleanest and unpeatiest. Unusual but fun. **46%.** *Douglas Laing.*

Provenance Bruichladdich **Aged 8 Years** dist 2 Dec 93, bott 21 Apr 05 **(87) n**22 **t**22 **f**21 **b**22. An enjoyable Laddie with less oil than usually found from this era. **46%.**

⁖ **The Queen of the Moorlands Rare Cask** Bruichladdich 1991 "The Anniversary Bottling" **(94) n**22 an old-fashioned traditional Laddie nose with a light, attractively salty edge; **t**24 powering barley with breathtaking integrity; the oak acts only as a foil to the tidal waves of juicy grist; lovely fruit notes help complete mouth-watering deliciousness; **f**24 coffee cake, drying towards a more chocolately finale. Long and just wonderful; **b**24 a quite stunning bottling very much in the style that made this the islanders' choice. A light viscosity holding the most delicate sweetness makes for an unmistakable fingerprint. Glorious and in part near faultless. I'm blown away... **52.8%. nc ncf.** *Available at The Wine Shop, Leek & Congleton, and Islay Whisky Shop.*

⁖ **Scotch Malt Whisky Society Cask 23.55 Aged 17 Years** Refill Hogshead, dist Apr 89 **(85) n**21 **t**22 **f**21 **b**21. Just on the change from a young malty lass with semi-hidden puff of smoke to something a little more middle aged, fruity and exotic: neither one thing nor the other, though a bit temperamental. **54.1%**

⁖ **Scott's Selection Bruichladdich 1990** bott 2007 **(80) n**21 **t**21 **f**19 **b**19. Pretty coarse from nose to finish. There are some rich seams of barley concentrate but a real bruiser, this. **57.4%.** *Speyside Distillers*

**Scott's Selection Bruichladdich 1990** bott 05 **(91) n**22 **t**24 **f**22 **b**23. A wonderful cask with not a single blemish or off note. Very true to the distillery. And with a touch of attitude, too. **56.5%.** *Speyside Distillers.*

Vom Fass Bruichladdich **14 Years Old (84) n**19 **t**22 **f**21 **b**22. A hint of soap on the nose, but the stewed apples and malt concentrate compensate wonderfully. Pleasantly oiled and spiced. The odd hint of smoke, too! **46%.** *Austria.*

Whisky Galore Bruichladdich 1991 **Aged 12 Years (87) n**22 **t**22 **f**21 **b**22. Unusual to find Laddie in a second (ot third) fill cask: the distillery's output in its most natural, naked state. **46%**

# BUNNAHABHAIN
### Islay, 1881. Burn Stewart. Working.

Bunnahabhain **Aged 12 Years** db **(89) n**23 very sharp malt, almost nosepinchingwith a distinctly salty, softly sherried bite; **t**23 tangy fruit, then a wave of salted oak and crisp barley. Busy and bracing and teasingly sweet in places; **f**21 soft malt and salted vanilla; **b**22 much back to its old, eye-watering self: less emphasis on sherry and more on its coastal roots. Brilliantly evocative and very true to the distillery. One sad note: this is from a new bottling that has been re-designed. It is elegant and attractive, keeping close to the original. But I must say that the label which served the Bunna for the last quarter century always reminded me of when I used to holiday at the distillery in the early 80s, with the bottle waiting on the table by a peat fire as the rain relentlessly lashed the cottage. I loved the fact that the label never changed and the reference to "Westering Home" which we would sing, Bunna in hand, once safely inside and away from the gale. There was a permanency about the label, as there is the distillery. Little things...but at least the whisky is almost back to top form. **40%**

Bunnahabhain **XVIII Aged 18 Years** db **(86) n**20 **t**23 **f**22 **b**21. The nose puts you on the back foot but by the third mouthful it is easier to pick up the nuances of this decently weighted dram. **43%**

Bunnahabhain **XXV Aged 25 Years** db **(93) n**22 some serious coastal saltiness here...and grape; **t**24 big saline kick as the oak offers some early latte; mouthwatering barley also impresses, topped off with brown sugar and damson tart; **f**23 more milky coffee with an oatcake side dish; **b**24 a fruity Bunna, but jam-packed with all the big barley-salt notes which set this distillery apart. One of the few bottlings around at the moment that us Bunna Old Timers can hold up and say: "Yeah, this is the business." Quite superb. **43%**

**Bunnahabhain 1971 Aged 35 Years 125th Anniversary** bott Oct 06 db **(94)** n25 close your eyes and you can breath in the warehouses in the shadow of the Paps of Jura: a stunning combination of sea-salt and the cleanest, most high quality sherry butts imaginable. Smokeless Bunna just exactly as it should be and faultless; t24 near spot-on delivery of juicy, mouth-watering grape again sprinkled liberally with sea-salt and dried with lightly pulsing oak yet enough barley escapes the intensity for balancing lightness while deft spices abound; f22 dries, but never too much, though there is a spicy rumble amid the gathering oak; b23 when I stayed at the distillery on holiday in both 1983 and 1984 – long before I let on the secret of it being a must-experience whisky destination – the 12 year-old Bunna that sat on my table before the peat fire came from sister casks of what we are tasting here. Previous owners Highland lost the plot with Bunna when they strangled it with sherry, often sulphured, and though the grape shapes the malt here, there is enough of the old clean signature to take me back to those wonderful days. Frankly, it is doubtful this great distillery's anniversary could have been celebrated in finer style. **44.9%. ncf.** *750 bottles.*

**Berry's' Own Selection Bunnahabhain 1974 Aged 31 Years (77)** n19 t20 f19 b19. Entirely drinkable and fruitily enjoyable. But just the wrong side of the oaky line to be a great. **46%.**

**Cadenhead's Authentic Collection Bunnahabhain Aged 26 Years** Bourbon Hogshead, dist 79, bott May 05 **(71)** n19 t18 f17 b17. Tangy and off-key. **49%.** *216 bottles.*

**Celtic Heartlands Bunnahabhain 1966** bott 25 Apr 05 **(80)** n19 t20 f21 b20. A fascinating dram: almost an experiment to see how long a whisky can remain just that in cask. And discover its state just before it dips below 40%. Here we have, as suspected, a degree too much oak, especially on the nose and very early mouth delivery. But you cannot but be impressed by the finish which somehow conjures essences of a sweet, estery, Jamaican-style rum from stills sitting on the Sound of Islay. **40.1%.**

**Chieftain's Bunnahabhain Aged 10 Years Sherry Finish (79)** n20 t21 f19 b19. Bit of a half-way house with the sherry seemingly scrubbing out much of the bourbon complexity, but not quite imparted enough of its own character. **46%.**

**Dun Bheagan Bunnahabhain Aged 10 Years Manzanilla Finish (86)** n22 t22 f20 b22. Distinctive fruity bite to this. **46%.** *Ian Macleod.*

**Dun Bheagan Bunnahabhain Aged 10 Years Rum Finish (88)** n22 cleansed barley; t23 lush, sugar-coated malt retaining some mouthwatering moments; f22 remains sweet, gristy, clean and easy going; b21 hardly complex but the rum has impacted with an agreeable sweetness. **46%.** *Ian Macleod.*

⋅∷⋅ **Duncan Taylor Collection Bunnahabhain 1966** Cask no. 4878 **(80)** n22 t21 f18 b19. Interesting. Not true whisky, apparently, if the strength is correct. I would have been tempted to vat this off because, for all its fruity promise, on its own there is not quite enough depth to see off the oak. **39.9%.** *Duncan Taylor.*

**Duncan Taylor Collection Bunnahabhain 1967** cask no. 3328, dist Mar 67, bott Nov 05 **(89)** n23 rich bourbon backbone; waxy barley sugar; t22 slightly eye- watering where the oak has got through, but the mouthwatering coffee-barley qualities are sublime; f22 a whole pack of caramelized biscuits and late, gristy barley; b22 big, refined and has stayed honest. **40.8%.** *209 bottles.*

⋅∷⋅ **Lombard's Jewels of Scotland Bunnahabhain 1979 Aged 25 Years (68)** n17 t19 f16 b16. I remember going through the Bunna warehouses in the early 80s and finding a nest of less than perfect sherry butts. Hullo again.... **50%.** *Lombard Brands Ltd, UK.*

⋅∷⋅ **The MacPhail's Collection Bunnahabhain 1991 (86)** n22 t21 f22 b21. Bunna in reflective, barley-rich mood with a shake of salt making an interesting contrast to the gentle raspberry preserve at the death. Deliciously curious. **43%.** *Gordon & MacPhail.*

**Murray McDavid Mission Bunnahabhain 1966** Oloroso sherry **(86)** n21 t23 f20 b22. Creaks a fair bit, but never goes snap... **40.3%.** *500 bottles.*

**Old Malt Cask Bunnahabhain Aged 12 Years** Hogshead cask 2132, dist Nov 92, bott Sept 05 **(93)** n23 beautiful oak-salt interaction; the barley as clear and crisp as the Paps on a sunny January morning; t24 stunning delivery with perfect sharp-sweet tones getting the juices flowing big time; great oak-spice buzz at back of the tongue; f23 pretty long with that gentle vanillas taking control; b23 so good to see the distillery at probably its best age and away from sherry butts...the way it used to be..!! **50%. nc ncf.**

⋰ **Old Malt Cask Bunnahabhain Aged 15 Years** dist Feb 91, bott Sept 06 **(89) n**22 salt and vinegar; **t**23 massive fresh barley attack with a gorgeous semi-sweet viscosity which helps keep in the salt; **f**22 jelly babies and barley; **b**22 no shortage of tang and intensity with this. Wonderful. **50%.** *Douglas Laing. 328 bottles.*

**Old Malt Cask Bunnahabhain Aged 15 Years** cask 1056, dist. Mar 89, bott May 04 **(79) n**19 **t**21 **f**20 **b**19. Clean but tame fare. **50%.** *Douglas Laing. 159 bottles.*

**Peerless Bunnahabhain 1967** (*see* Duncan Taylor Bunna 67)

**Provenance Bunnahabhain Aged 12 Years** dist Nov 92, bott Aug 05 **(84) n**22 **t**21 **f**20 **b**21. Gristy and soft, but lacking some of the distillery's more bracing qualities. **46%.**

**Royal Mile Whiskies Bunnahabhain 1971** cask 6249 **(87) n**22 **t**21 **f**23 **b**21. A shade too much age but the finish is memorable. **46%. ncf.**

**Scott's Selection Bunnahabhain 1977** bott 05 **(84) n**21 **t**22 **f**20 **b**21. Predictably salty and perhaps a touch tart. **49.6%.** *Speyside Distillers.*

⋰ **The Single Malts of Scotland Bunnahabhain 1979 Aged 27 Years (76) n**21 **t**19 **f**18 **b**18. A peculiarly furry beast with a good nose. **46%. sc.** *Speciality Drinks, UK.*

**Vom Fass Bunnahabhain 9 Years Old (83) n**20 **t**23 **f**21 **b**19. Curiously lightly peated with the odd thread of honey. Wonderfully mouthwatering throughout, struggles to find a balance. An elegant and delicate rarity. **40%.** *Austria.*

⋰ **The Whisky Fair Bunnahabhain Aged 29 Years** Bourbon Hogshead, dist 1977, bott 07 **(85) n**23 **t**19 **f**22 **b**21. Salt 'n' honey nose offers exceptional poise and charm but an uncomfortable landing on the palate with the oak not entirely in sync. **53%.** *Germany.*

## CAOL ILA
**Islay, 1846. Diageo. Working.**

⋰ **Caol Ila (Highland) 8 Years Old** dist 97 db **(87) n**22 massive oak injection for something so relatively young with the malt coming into a world of dry toast and cardboard dust. Good spices; **t**22 mouth-filling barley of decent, juicy intensity at first; then surprisingly dry; **f**21 the oils I had expected don't materialise and instead the spices zing; **b**22 I remember tasting this when new make and being impressed and hopeful (both for its development and that they wouldn't make unpeated malt at Caol Ila too often!). Perhaps hasn't quite complexed out the way I had hoped. But no faulting its structure and depth. Scores higher on novelty than genuine thrills – but entirely enjoyable malt. **59.8%**

**Caol Ila Aged 12 Years** db **(89) n**23 a coastal, salty biting tang (please don't tell me this has been matured on the mainland!) with hints of rockpools and visions of rock pipits and oystercatchers among the seaweed; **t**23 enormously oily, coating the palate with a mildly subdued smokiness and then a burst of gristy malt; **f**21 caramel and oil; **b**22 a telling improvement on the old 12-y-o with much greater expression and width. **43%**

**Caol Ila Aged 18 Years** db **(80) n**21 **t**20 **f**19 **b**20. Another improvement on the last bottling, especially with the comfortable integration of citrus. But still too much oil spoils the dram, particularly at the death. **43%**

**Caol Ila 25 Years Old** dist 78 db **(90) n**24 **t**23 **f**21 **b**22. A wonderful Caol Ila in so many respects: truly great. Yet another, like most it has to be said, that noses better than it tastes because of the massive oiliness. Still some genuine quality here, make no mistake. **59.4%**

**Caol Ila 1979** db **(74) n**20 **t**19 **f**17 **b**18. Hugely disappointing. I could go on about tropical fruit yada, yada, yada. Truth is, it just conks out under the weight of the oak. Too old. Simple as that. **58.6%**

**Caol Ila 1996** Refill AM 406 db **(92) n**24 spot-on bourbon casks have allowed full reign to the complexity here. None of the usual attendant oils, and an enticing degree of gist to some fruity barley; some wonderful farm-yardy stuff; **t**23 great body with just enough oil to lightly coat the palate; peat is slightly bolder than usual for this distillery and also two-toned with variation on weight; **f**22 long, lacking in complexity but the sugared peat fade is very attractive; **b**23 Oh!! If only all Caol Ila's could be quite so light on their feet and sophisticated... **43%.** *For Juuls Vinhandel, Denmark. 445 bottles.*

⋰ **Caol Ila Distillery Bottling** bott May 07 db **(88) n**24 a curious inflection to the nose makes for an un-Caol Ila-ish aroma. Something of the south-east coast to this one:

both at once oily and dry. Strange...and rather beautiful... **t22** some thumping spices; the peat is a dry force trying to overcome the early sweet barley dominance; **f20** runs out of steam slightly balance-wise and bitters out as the oak and peat go their different ways; **b22** like most bottlings from this distillery, it's a dram that refuses to run a natural path. Never lives up to the nose, but still enough to delight Islay lovers. **58.4%.**

⠿ **Adelphi Caol Ila Aged 13 Years** Cask no. 9154, dist 1993, bott 07 **(85) n23 t21 f20 b21.** Perhaps a touch too heavily oaked for total comfort. But the nose has the refined earthiness of a dank Surrey bluebell wood. **59.4%.** *Adelphi Distillery Ltd. 282 bottles.*

⠿ **Berrys' Own Selection Caol Ila 1982** Casks no. 727/8 **(85) n21 t22 f21 b21** Deliciously sweet, fat... and a little flat maybe. **46%**

⠿ **Berry's Own Selection Caol Ila 1991** Casks no. 486/487, bott 07 **(93) n23** that rare beast: a Caol Ila that's multi-stratum in the peat department: excellent complexity; **t23** hard and hot with enough late, citrussy sharpness to the barley to make for rounded experience; **f23** long and well layered coffee and smoke and even a spoonful of demerara to keep it going; **b24** one of the few Caol Ilas this year to really get my pulse racing. **51.8%.**

⠿ **Berry's Own Selection Caol Ila 1991** bott 07 **(88) n21** attractive smoke fails to cover the thinness of the malt; **t23** entirely different on delivery with a honeyed thread helping to add weight as well as charm to the rich smoke and butterscotch middle; wonderful layering; **f22** more of the same but dries with a sawdusty, bourbony-vanilla charm; **b22** some serious lustre to this bottling. **46%.**

**Berrys' Own Selection Caol Ila 1996 Aged 10 Years (94) n23** with its hints of apple and celery, this pretty subtle by Caol Ila standards; even a touch of the gristy Port Ellens about it. Spooky; **t24** beautifully delivered peat on a base of sugared black pepper. This is so big for this distillery, but also just so mercurial; **f23** long, remains lush and the slow development of the cocoa is pure tease; **b24** so often the malt from this distillery passes my heart by. Excellent blending malt, usually, but a bit of a plodder in the glass. Here Dougie McIvor has pulled a stunner out of the hat. A must have collector's item for those who want to wallow in ultra delicate and complex Islays. **57%.**

**Cadenhead's Authentic Collection Caol Ila Aged 11 Years** Bourbon Hogshead, dist 95, bott Feb 06 **(86) n20 t22 f23 b21.** A particularly oily expression that rewards patience. **60.5%.** *330 bottles.*

**Cadenhead's Caol Ila Aged 12 Years** dist 93, bott Feb 05 **(92) n24 t23 f22 b23.** Drips with quality and finesse. **46%.** *390 bottles.*

**Cadenhead's Authentic Collection Caol Ila Aged 15 Years** Bourbon Hogshead, dist 91, bott Sept 06 **(94) n23** chunky with some serious peat embers; above average phenol levels and excellent clarity; **t23** juicy barley and stunning spices. But it's the richness to the honeycomb sweetness that really impresses, allowing the oak to integrate charmingly; **f24** long and pulsing with grace and balance. Some toasty notes absorbed by the lingering sweetness of the barley while the peat continues to fill every crevice it can find; **b24** oh, if only all Caol Ilas could be this gloriously structured. The distillery at it's best. **56.3%.** *318 bottles.*

⠿ **Cadenhead's Caol Ila Aged 16 Years** Bourbon, dist 1991, bott May 07 **(84) n20 t22 f21 b21.** Another Caol Ila this season which hasn't quite got it's all- round act together. Plenty of smoke but lacking fire when it comes to complexity. **46%.** *360 bottles.*

⠿ **Cadenhead's Authentic Collection Caol Ila Aged 22 Years** Bourbon hogshead, dist 84, bott Feb 07 **(92) n22** drier than the Bible belt of America... **t24** bursts into an immediate sweet rhapsody that entirely defies the nose; the smoke is shovelled on thick, but the barley retains the upper hand; **f23** long, lovely mocha and reverting to dry; **b23** ultra complex? Hardly. Something I've never come across before? Most probably not. A genuinely well made whisky that has matured as well as might be expected for its age and makes all the right noises? Most certainly. **55.5%.** *Cadenhead's. 246 bottles.*

**Cadenhead's Caol Ila Bond Reserve Aged 25 Years (93) n24 t24 f22 b23.** Good ol' Cadenhead! They've turned up trumps again!! **53.4%.**

**Cask Caol Ila 1991 (93) n23 t23 f23 b24.** Unusual, drier, fruitier, spicier, quite memorable Caol Ila. Good old G&M: they certainly know how to pick a belter! **57.4%.**

**Cask Caol Ila 1993 (80) n19 t21 f20 b20.** Rock-hard, sweet, metallic and unforgiving. **57.8%.** *Gordon & MacPhail.*

⠿ **Cask Strength Caol Ila 1995 (77) n**19 **t**21 **f**18 **b**19. Strangely lethargic and a pinch of bitterness on nose and finish. **57.6%.** *Gordon & MacPhail*

**Cask Strength Caol Ila 1994 (90) n**23 profound fruity nose: plums and some hidden citrus balancing out the dull peat; **t**22 quality arrival with soft barley forced ahead of massive spice; liquorice and natural caramel softens the oak delivery; **f**22 a long, fruity finale cannot disguise the medium roast Java and toast; **b**23 a lovely cask with a few surprises up its sleeve; refuses to take the normal Caol Ila route. **58.2%.**

**Chieftan's Caol Ila Aged 9 Years Medoc Finish** casks 90441/90444, dist Jun 95, bott Feb 05 **(86) n**20 **t**22 **f**22 **b**22. Hardly one for the purists. **50%. nc ncf.** *1,674 btls.*

**Chieftain's Caol Ila 10 Years Old** Hogshead **(78) n**20 **t**20 **f**19 **b**19. A hard-as-nails nose and delivery: I have seen more give from a taxman. **43%.**

**Chieftain's Caol Ila Aged 11 Years** Hogshead **(89) n**23 an unlikely and quite delicious combination of violets and diffused peat reek; **t**22 excellent barley sweetness allows the peat to drop in gently and confidently; **f**22 some hickory dryness but remains gentle and discreet; **b**22 a wonderful cask of Caol Ila which accentuates the understatement. **43%.**

**Chieftain's Caol Ila Aged 12 Years** Hogshead **(77) n**19 **t**20 **f**19 **b**19. Pleasant and plodding in its own way, but has little to say. **43%.** *Ian Macleod.*

**Chieftain's Caol Ila 12 Years Old Rum Finish (83) n**22 **t**20 **f**20 **b**21. Slightly too oily and thick to fully take advantage of the proffered rum influence. But the peat is more polished than it might be. **46%.** *Ian Macleod.*

⠿ **Cheftain's Caol Ila 1993 Aged 13 Years St Emilion Finish** dist 93 **(87) n**22 smoked bacon with tomato ketchup; **t**21 sharp, unbalanced fruit- burst then settles as the peat grabs hold; **f**22 long with beautiful smoke depth and as soft as a malt gets; **b**22 a surprise package: I didn't expect this to work quite so attractively! **46%. nc ncf.** *Ian Macleod.*

⠿ **Cheftain's Caol Ila 1993 Aged 13 Years Manzanilla Finish** dist 93 **(95) n**24 improbably delicate with the peat kept at bay by a complex medley of fruit and herbal notes. It doesn't always work but intrigues and sometimes astounds; **t**23 a big Islay further tamed by an assortment of fruit notes and a bitter crushed pip effect. And yes there is complexity: by the bucket load. The sweetness arrives relatively late and in mercurial – and fruity –form; **f**24 that fruity sweetness holds its ground until a slightly spiced oaky cavalry arrives. The unravelling of the textures and varied fruit elements is sublime; **b**24 here's an admission: on the first and second tastings I didn't think too much of this. "Oh, Gawd, not another crap finish", I thought. Only by going back to it did I begin to understand the picture. Don't hunt for the big smoke here. This is exclusively for those seeking sophistication. **46%. nc ncf.** *Ian Macleod.*

⠿ **The Clydesdale Caol Ila 13 Years Old** Cask ref. 0001/6980, dist May 93, bott Sept 06 **(84) n**21 **t**21 **f**22 **b**20. Prim and proper, neat and tidy: allowing the peat out in precise bursts. Unusually un-oily! **56.5%. nc ncf.** *Blackadder International.*

⠿ **The Coopers Choice Caol Ila 1991 Aged 16 Years (85) n**21 **t**22 **f**21 **b**21. Clean, pleasant and surprisingly undemanding for a 16-y-o. Good gristy sweetness throughout. **46%. sc ncf.** *The Vintage Malt Whisky Co.*

**Connoisseurs Choice Caol Ila 1993 (81) n**21 **t**20 **f**21 **b**19. The nip and bite to the nose is hardly matched by the supine, oily delivery to the palate. **40%.**

**Connoisseurs Choice Caol Ila 1994 (72) n**17 **t**19 **f**18 **b**18. Misses the target: just never feels right either on nose or palate. **40%.** *Gordon & MacPhail.*

**Connoisseurs Choice Caol Ila 1995** bott 18 Apr 06 **(91) n**23 soft oils, but the peats are of varying depth; **t**23 excellent weight and richness to the malt; the smoke refuses to take the sweet route; **f**22 plenty of vanilla and coffee; **b**23 now that's a Caol Ila on song and balanced. **46%.** *G&M. US Market.*

**The Coopers Choice Caol Ila 1984 Years 21 Old** bott 06 **(84) n**22 **t**22 **f**20 **b**20. An interesting bottle for those with a literary bent. Especially George Orwell fans. He wrote his novel "1984" on Jura, and it is almost inconceivable that he spent time on the island without looking out onto the Caol Ila distillery, across from him and the Sound of Islay. The whisky then was made in different stills and would have been a lot weightier than this. But for all its oaky flaws, not too a bad dram to keep the book company. The spices, in particular, are a page turner. **46%.**

**Coopers Choice Coal Ila 1990 14 Years Old**, Single Cask Range, bott 05 **(76) n**18 **t**20 **f**18 **b**18. Harsh and disappointing. **46%. ncf.** *Vintage Malt Whisky Co.*

⠿ **Demijohn Caol Ila 1991 Single Malt (91)** n23 superb and unlikely balance between the deftest vanilla and dolloped-on peat; t23 stilted sweetness, first heading towards grist, then thicker oiled and back to much softer grist again; f22 long, a touch lethargic; b23 tip top Caol Ila at its gristiest. **46%.** *Demijohn Ltd, UK.*

⠿ **Dun Bheagan Caol Ila 10 Years Old** Hogshead, dist June 96 **(79)** n18 t21 f20 b20. Sweet and distinctly new makey, though avoid the nose. **43%. nc ncf.** *Ian Macleod.*

**Dun Bheagan Caol Ila Aged 11 Years (82)** n21 t21 f20 b20. The tastebuds get a good peaty buffeting, but plenty of oil on hand to soften the blows. **43%.**

⠿ **Dun Bheagan Caol Ila Aged 12 Years** Hogshead, dist 93 **(86)** n22 t22 f21 b21. Soft oils help fuse the smoke into the roof of the mouth. But for all the alcohol it's a light ride with plenty of delicious charm but limited complexity. **55%. nc ncf.** *Ian Macleod.*

**Dun Bheagan Caol Ila Aged 12 Years** Hogshead **(85)** n20 t23 f21 b21. Some delicious coffee notes crystallise at the finale as the peat calms down. A pleasant, if sometimes bumpy, ride. **43%.** *Ian Macleod.*

**Dun Bheagan Caol Ila Aged 14 Years** Hogshead **(95)** n24 a much drier nose than the norm, yet allowing the barley and peat to surface. Also a lack of oil – thankfully!! What remains is custard powder and dry banana. Easily one of the most complex and confident noses from this distillery for many a year; t23 just enough oil to ensure a gentle landing for the marauding, juicy barley and enough oomph for the peat to race full throttle into each and every taste bud; f24 fabulous complexity to the finish here because – so rarely with this distillery – the oiliness has gone and we are left behind with varying, complex layers of encrusted phenols, rock salt and freshly ground peppers. Yet the barley remains fresh and salivating; b24 sheer quality all the way. Easily one of the finest Caol Ilas I have tasted in over 25 years... **53.8%.** *Ian Macleod.*

⠿ **Dun Bheagan Caol Ila 15 Years Old** Hogshead, dist Mar 91 **(88)** n22 dry and cindery; farmyardy t23 first a sweet, gristy intro then beautiful mocha notes display the oak's involvement; f21 dry, soft smoke b22 delicate and relaxed. **43%. nc ncf.** *Ian Macleod.*

**Dun Bheagan Caol Ila 16 Years Old** Hogshead **(83)** n21 t22 f20 b20. Astonishingly sweet for its age; the odd touch of marzipan on the smoke apart, hardly taxes the tastebuds. **46%.** *Ian Macleod.*

**Mackillop's Choice Caol Ila 1990** dist Feb 90 **(91)** n23 t22 f23 b23. Such a relief to see a Caol Ila stripped mainly of its oily vineer. What lies behind is high class and of considerable depth. **43%.** *Angus Dundee.*

⠿ **Milroy's of Soho Caol Ila** 1989 **Aged 17 Years** Ex Bourbon, cask no. 4542, dist 27 Nov 89, bott 6 Oct 06 **(86)** n22 t21 f22 b21. Like silk running over your chest. Don't go hunting complexity but the overall effect is a delight. **46%.** *204 bottles.*

⠿ **Murray McDavid Mission Caol Ila 1984** Gold Series, Bourbon/Grenache Vincent Le Grand **(91)** n24 perhaps the ultimate seaside rock pool experience in a whisky glass. You half expect to see a starfish and sea urchin in the glass; t22 as is so often the case with wine casks, the peat is backed into a corner and shy; mainly fruit, the smoke is tight and nervous; f23 relaxes as the fruit recedes, the vanillas shine and the peat returns in respectable but, crucially, un-oiled waves; b22 the big question is: is it an Islay or a French rock pool? I'm sure this is near the Singing Sands... **54.1%**

**Murray McDavid Caol Ila 1991 Aged 15 Years** Bourbon/Mourvedre/Syrah **(88)** n24 freshly cracked oysters by a peat fire and glass of heavy, opened-too-early red; t22 big juicy start with the peat pushed far into the background, bizarrely thirst-quenching; f21 as the smoke finds its feet some balance is lost; remarkably light finish, if slightly too bitter; b21 you get the feeling that no whisky can live up to that extraordinary and quite unique nose; and this one doesn't quite make it. The freshness of the grape is wonderful, but it never quite finds a way of entirely gelling with the smoke. That said, it's worth the experience as this is something very different and offers many plusses. **46%. nc ncf.** *2600 bottles.*

⠿ **Murray McDavid Caol Ila 1991 Aged 16 Years** Bourbon/Mourvedre **(70)** n17 t18 f17 b18. Really a mess. The dreaded S word at work, it appears. **46%**

**Murray McDavid Caol Ila 1993 Aged 12 Years** Bourbon/Chenin Blanc **(89)** n23 rock pools: about as salty as Caol Ila gets; t22 major spat between fruit and smoke with some delicious arm-wrestling; f22 smoke wins, and celebrates by calling up vanilla and a touch of spice; b22 charming and unusual. **46%.** *2,700 btls.*

⫶ **Murray McDavid Caol Ila 2000 Aged 6 Years** Bourbon/Ridge Zinfandel **(90)** n22 surprisingly dry and oil-less. In fact on of the most floral Caol Ilas I've come across in the last decade; t23 attractively sweet delivery – sweet that is in a fruity sense with few OTT sugars; the smoke is lethargic and happy to string along with the grape; f22 vanilla brushed with smoke on a field of light fruit; b23 not yet another six-year-old Caol Ila in a Ridge Zinfandel cask! I keep telling these scotch guys: "Look, when you've tasted one six year old Islay in a Zinfandel cask, you've tasted them all." Why is this industry so bloody predictable...? **46%**

⫶ **Old & Rare Caol Ila Aged 28 Years** dist Feb 79, bott Mar 07 **(93)** n24 salty but the peats have structure and variations. Complex; t23 big spice delivery and uplifting citrus notes abound. None of the usual oils, so the gristy nature is unearthed; the vanillas complement, the spices attack like Port Askaig hotel midges.; f22 medium length with spices and smoked vanilla; b24 great to see a CA with this kind of attitude. One of the rare un-oily versions and worth investigating for its delicate but unrestricted beauty. A recent Caol Ila classic. **54.6%.** *Douglas Laing. 272 bottles.*

**Old Malt Cask Caol Ila Aged 10 Years For A Fine Cigar's Pleasure** Bourbon Hogshead **(88)** n22 "Earthy, oily with smoke and pepper" says the label. Correct; t23 "round and spicy with peaty smoke." That only tells the half of it: spices get in early as the barley really cranks up the sweetness and there's a saline kick from the digestive biscuit. The peat rumbles deliciously with malcontent; f21 "salty, coastal and coffee'd" Perhaps: I'd certainly go with the coffee. But for me just fizzles out under an oily avalanche – as this distillery's whisky is so often apt to do; b22 I don't smoke, so can't vouch for its ability to keep a cigar good company. But as Caol Ila casks go, this is a cut above. **50%. nc ncf.** *Douglas Laing.*

**Old Malt Cask Caol Ila 12 Years Old** Wine finish, dist Mar 94, bott July 06 **(92)** n23 firm barley and peat: this could almost go snap; t24 is this really Caol Ila? The fruit is a shrinking violet to the massive peat attack which is crisp and lean; f22 usually the palate is by now swamped in oil; instead there is smoke-flavoured cocoa and a sprinkle of mollased sugar; b23 is it the wine at work here? Something appears to have removed the usual gushing oil and this crisper Caol Ila is a charmer, a real class act. **50%.**

**Old Malt Cask Caol Ila 15 Years Old** dist 10 Jan 90, bott 14 Jun 05 **(84)** n22 t21 f21 b20. A bit of a spitfire: hot stuff but unquestionably entertaining. **50%.**

⫶ **Old Malt Cask Caol Ila Aged 17 Years** dist Mar 90, bott Mar 07 **(83)** n20 t22 f20 b21. Some grizzle and attitude, but just a shade on the oily side. **50%.** *365 bottles.*

⫶ **Old Malt Cask Caol Ila Aged 21 Years** dist Apr 85, bott Jan 07 **(84)** n21 t22 f20 b21. The oak has leapt in here and made some bitter marmalade statements. A touch of salt and docile smoke: seems older than its 21 years. **50%.** *Douglas Laing. 327 bottles.*

**Old Malt Cask Caol Ila 25 Year Old** dist 2 May 79, bott 13 Apr 05 **(88)** n21 t22 f23 b22. A very curious, mildly out of tune Caol Ila that thrives on the lack of oil. **50%.**

**Old Malt Cask Caol Ila Aged 25 Years** dist Nov 79, bott Aug 05 **(75)** n20 t19 f18 b18. Strangled by the oak. **50%.** *Douglas Laing. 271 bottles.*

**Old Malt Cask Caol Ila 25 Years Old** dist Apr 80, bott Jan 06 **(95)** n24 firm and lucid, the peat-oak symbiosis is about as much as you could ask for at this age. Very few Caol Ilas offer this type of grace and nutty beauty; t22 decent body and jumbled messages. Takes time to get going; f25 it is all about the unbelievably long finale. It is all there: fresh barley, the most playful fruity notes under honeyed almonds. And all bathed in cocoa-dusted peat. Take your time with this one: about three hours should do the trick; b24 it is impossible not to become besotted with this one. **50%.** *Douglas Laing. 327 bottles.*

⫶ **Old Masters Caol Ila Aged 25 Years** Cask no. 731, dist 1982, bott 07 **(94)** n23 an avalanche of smoke with much oak caught in its path; t23 buzzing, zippy spices that enliven the peat but fall respectfully quiet when the coffee and flecks of raspberry jam arrive; the subtlety of the sweetness is divine; f24 glorious finish with layer upon layer of complex oak showing its feminine side: the coffee remains soft, the smoke understated and the texture is textbook; b24 this is Caol Ila at its very best. **55.5%.**

**Premier Barrel Caol Ila 10 Years Old** dist Jan 95, bott Dec 05 **(92)** n23 brilliant! Parcels of peat waft effortlessly around; there is a sweet mocha element and all softened by well oiled barley; spotted dick abounds...; t23 melt-in-the-mouth stuff: both barley and peat home in on the tastebuds relentlessly but both caress rather than smother. The waves are countless; f23 a wonderfully orchestrated finale:

somewhere some vague hints of lime dovetail in with the banana and vanilla. But it all relative: the smokey barley continues to pull the strings; **b**23 a premier barrel by name and nature. **46%.** *Douglas Laing. 401 bottles.*

⊱ **Premier Barrel Caol Ila Aged 10 Years** bott Winter 06 **(88) n**23 if you ever thought of mixing banana with clean young peat, you'd end up with this.... **t**23 powering, super-clean delivery with superb grist; **f**21 bitters out; **b**21 it's all about the amazing nose and delivery! **46%.** *Douglas Laing. 372 bottles.*

**Private Collection Caol Ila Demerara Rum Finish 1990** casks 99/103 2,3, dist 31 Jan 90, bott June 05 **(86) n**20 **t**23 **f**22 **b**21. Lots to chew on but never quite finds its length. **45%.** *Gordon & MacPhail. 650 bottles.*

**Private Collection Caol Ila Vintage Rum Finish 1990** casks 99/103 1, dist 31 Jan 90, bott June 05 **(94) n**24 such is the enormity of the nose, so well does the rum and peat combine that, for reasons I can't even begin to understand or explain, the first punches of the aroma are very similar to a freshly opened First Growth Bordeaux prior to oxidization. The riches are near unfathomable; **t**23 the sweetness of the peat forms glorious layers amply supported by barley and an unusual element – probably rum; **f**23 there is very little house cooking oil to this, so the more complex oaks and barley have a chance to shine; **b**24 Works a treat but, curiously, has more Demerara character than an actual Demerara!! **45%.** *G&M. 865 bottles.*

**Private Collection Caol Ila Cognac 1991** bott 02 Feb 06 **(86) n**22 **t**22 **f**20 **b**22. Brittle and sweet: probably the least oily Caol Ila on the market and not easily recognisable from this distillery at all. **46%.** *Gordon & MacPhail US Market.*

**Private Collection Caol Ila Marsala Wood 1995 (88) n**23 floral and fruity; oily peat reek; **t**22 excellent bitter-sweet delivery – edging on the sweet side as it always should; **f**21 pretty oaky and oily. Just a tad too bitter; **b**22 always a touch nervous when encountering such wine finishes, as they have a propensity to end in tears. But, the dull finish apart, this is a real entertainer. **45%.** *G&M.*

⊱ **Provenance Caol Ila Aged 8 Years** dist Winter 98, bott Winter 07 **(88) n**20 hmmm: not great but the uninterrupted, oakless smoke lets you know you are in for something unusual...; **t**23 quite gorgeous arrival with spot on oils helping to fix the salivating barley to every quarter of the palate; the smoke builds and builds in weight; **f**23 very long, with nothing quite so boring as oak to get in the way: just the slow disappearance of smoke into the horizonless background; **b**22 another warts-and-all bottling from a well used cask (to put it mildly) – and you can only applaud its naked beauty. **46%.** *Douglas Laing.*

⊱ **Provenance Caol Ila Aged 10 Years** dist Winter 96, bott Winter 06 **(86) n**21 **t**23 **f**22 **b**20. can a malt whisky be too sweet? Get some of this and look for the answer. A joy, whatever way you decide. **46%.** *Douglas Laing.*

**Provenance Caol Ila Aged Over 10 Years** hogshead DMG 1714-1715, dist Aut 94, bott Wint 05 **(89) n**22 teasingly layered peat operates off both sweet and drier levels; **t**23 hallmark oiliness works so much better when not hauling oak around: it's peat and barley all the way; **f**22 vaguely toasty yet sweet...and long thanks to those oils. The shortage of oak really does give this a lift; **b**22 a dream of a Caol Ila – about as uncluttered a bottling you'll ever find. **46%. nc ncf.**

**Provenance Caol Ila 10 Years Old** dist Feb 96, bott Autumn 06 **(84) n**21 **t**21 **f**21 **b**21. Ultra clean Caol Ila with firm smoke and a decent barley development from the late middle. **46%.** *McGibbon's.*

**The Queen of the Moorlands Rare Cask Caol Ila 10 Years Old** dist 6 Jun 95, bott 16 Jun 05 **(88) n**22 sweet and oily. Oh, and peaty...; **t**23 lush delivery and a fine development of fresh barley and the deeper smoky tones; **f**21 tails off as the oak gives it a bitter tweak; **b**22 does what it says on the tin. **46%. sc.** *The Wine Shop Leek, UK. 318 bottles.*

⊱ **Scotch Malt Whisky Society Cask 53.104 Aged 13 Years** Refill Butt, dist July 93 **(86) n**22 **t**21 **f**22 **b**21. Faultless Caol Ila, clean, decently peated, sweet and a tad gristy. Lovely, but perhaps missing that vital spark. **61.3%**

⊱ **Scotch Malt Whisky Society Cask 53.105 Aged 15 Years** Refill Hogshead, dist Aug 91 **(94) n**23 coal and peat smoke combined with a superb kumquaty-black cherry fruit kick; **t**24 no sign of those dispiriting oils and instead we again have those fruits, by the kilo, and a stunning peat interplay; **f**23 trace oil as spices arrive for a late battle. Excellent! **b**24 the fruit offers something a touch different from this distillery. And what a better malt this is without those soggy oils! **55.1%**

⋄ **Scotch Malt Whisky Society Cask 53.106 Aged 10 Years** Refill Hogshead, dist Mar 96 **(82) n**19 **t**22 **f**20 **b**21. The nose and finish are as dull as a rain-threatening sky hanging over Islay. The delivery, though, has more than its fair share of juicy, smoky charms. **59.6%**.

⋄ **Scotch Malt Whisky Society Cask 53.107 Aged 10 Years** Refill Hogshead, dist Mar 96 **(82) n**21 **t**20 **f**21 **b**20. Further frustrating proof that as a single malt, this would be better off in a blend. Don't get me wrong: well made, full of peat etc etc. But those bloody oils and the monotony of the smoke makes this style a much inferior malt, in terms of complexity, to Lagavulin, Laphroaig and, of course, Ardbeg. In this guy's favour is the squirt of citrus on the nose and the feeling that this was brilliantly made. But... **60.4%**.

⋄ **Scotch Malt Whisky Society Cask 53.113 Aged 11 Years** Refill Hogshead, dist Mar 96 **(88) n**22 warm engine oil and a nearby peat fire; vague fruits, too; **t**23 stunningly structured degree of soft fruit that joins forces first with a gristy sweetness then oil-saturated smoke; **f**21 the oils continue, but with enough bite to ward off the developing vanillas; **b**22 rather excellent despite having enough oil for Bush to send the troops in to secure the distillery from perceived tyrannical forces... **60.7%**.

**Scott's Selection Caol Ila** dist 84, bott 06 **(85) n**20 **t**23 **f**21 **b**21. The mintiness to the nose is a pretty useful air sock. Pretty major oak interference throughout, but there is enough juice remaining in the gristiness to ensure some delicious, quality moments. **53.5%**. *Speyside Distillers.*

**Signatory Un-Chill Filtered Collection Caol Ila Aged 14 Years** dist 15 Jul 90, bott 2 Mar 05 **(86) n**23 **t**21 **f**21 **b**21. Oily smoked Rupp; attractively inert. **46%**.

⋄ **The Single Malts of Scotland Caol Ila 1991 Aged 16 Years (90) n**22 clean, softly oiled peat, nosing a lot younger than its age; **t**23 attractive early oak involvement restricted to thick vanilla, soon overcome but soon met head on by a wonderful injection of juicy barley; **f**22 gorgeous barley continues, with some unfurling butterscotch on the smoke; **b**23 way above average for this distillery thanks, mainly, to its lightness of touch with the salivating barley. **57.9%**. *Speciality Drinks, UK.*

**The Wee Dram Caol Ila Aged 12 Years (93) n**23 attractive mixture of peat reek and burning coal: a free Scottish fireplace in winter with every sniff; **t**24 a shade estery with the clean, faultless, mildly grassy malt leading the way; the peat arrives first as an afterthought and, once established, builds by degree; the sensational middle even displays some brave honey; **f**23 some oak arrives to slightly lighten the peat intensity. But it is never less than very big; **b**23 so many Caol Ila bottlings of recents years have been dull and workmanlike. For once we have a cask that shows life and elegance despite the enormous weight: Caol Ila as it should be – except the strength! **40%**. *The Wee Dram, Derbyshire, UK.*

⋄ **Whisky-Doris Caol Ila Aged 16 Years** Bourbon cask, dist 15 Jan 91, bott 1 Feb 07 **(88) n**21 big, yet thin: strange... **t**23 juicy malt with some serious bite amid the lemon curd tart and smoke; **f**22 long, silky and still that lingering touch of citrus to the smoke; **b**22 beautifully made, big-hearted Islay. **57.4%**. *Germany. 115 bottles.*

**The Whisky Fair Caol Ila Aged 13 Years** Bourbon Hogshead 4734, dist Mar 91, bott Feb 05 **(84) n**21 **t**21 **f**22 **b**20. Oily and mildly on the hot side. **54.2%**. **nc ncf**. *359 bottles.*

⋄ **The Whisky Fair Caol Ila Aged 22 Years** Sherry Hogshead, dist 1984, bott 2007 **(73) n**19 **t**19 **f**17 **b**18. Sometimes sherry (especially poor sherry) and peat don't mix. Like here. Not bad farmyardy nose, though. **55.9%**. *Germany.*

⋄ **The Whisky Fair Caol Ila Aged 23 Years** Bourbon, dist 1984, bott 07 **(92) n**23 dry peat, beautifully crisp with a touch of hickory; **t**23 seriously intense, again dry with the peat showing full respect to the oaky vanilla; clean and with a seriously appealing bitter-sweet personality; **f**22 a touch of coffee and demerara sugar to the lingering smoke and oak **b**24 an excellent bottling devoid of the usual spoiling oiliness. Not overly complex in variety of flavours, but certainly in the way they are delivered. **55.9%**. *Germany.*

**The Whisky Fair Caol Ila 26 Year Old** Bourbon Hogshead, dist May 79 **(88) n**22 the oaky onslaught is soft and full of bourbon character: the peat hardly gets a look in ...!; **t**23 buzzing spices impact immediately, showing the oak really is alive. Again the peat has to take a back seat as, finally, some barley sweetens things out **f**22 lots of liquorice and chocolate hazelnut; **b**21 a remarkable malt: my guess is that you have a barely used first-fill bourbon barrel at work here. The results are near unique. **57.2%**. *212 bottles.*

**Whisky Galore Caol Ila 1992** dist Mar 92, bott 23 Mar 06 **(90)** n23 busy, structured and gristy: not your typical Caol Ila; t23 again waves of mounting intensity and, though oily, the sweetness is kept in check; f22 back to smoke and vanilla; also a trace of attractive coffee; **b**22 as with most Caol Ilas, the thick oil forms a gravity field that lets little really take off. But look closely enough and distinct charm and complexity can be found close to the surface. **46%**. *471 bottles.*

⸬ **Wilson & Morgan Barrel Selection Caol Ila 16 Years Old** dist 1990, bott 06 **(91)** n22 dry, chunky smoke with vanilla custard; t23 thick, but not overly oily with the smoke hanging beautifully off the lychee and barley sugar centre; f23 long, chewy with soft, well balanced oils pervading; the oak almost hangs in the air; **b**23 a stupendous cask full of all kinds of smoky trickery. **57.1%**

⸬ **Wilson & Morgan Barrel Selection Caol Ila 1996 Limited Edition** bott 07 **(86)** n21 t23 f20 **b**22. A sleepy and docile nose is rocked back by the fabulously explosive delivery. The bitter finish is out of keeping but hold on to something tightly when you take your first, fantastic, mouthful! **48%**

# CAPERDONICH
**Speyside, 1898. Chivas. Silent.**

**Caperdonich 16 Years Old Cask Strength Edition** dist 88, bott 05 db **(88)** n23 t21 f23 **b**22. The first actual distillery bottling I can remember from this distillery in my drinking lifetime – some 30 years. And this isn't half bad, though the early heat on the palate gives some indication as to why we have been waiting so long. I'd not be surprised if it surprised one or two in the Chivas lab! **55.8%. ncf.**

**The Bottlers Caperdonich 1976 Aged 27 Years** cask 8965 **(89)** n22 t22 f23 **b**22. Another outstanding Caperdonich that has come alive in old age. **54.3%**.

**Connoisseurs Choice Caperdonich 1968** **(84)** n21 t22 f20 **b**21. A lovely golden, mildly honied malt is spoilt slightly by a degree of over-enthusiastic oak. Having said that, it's a real charmer. **46%**. *Gordon & MacPhail.*

⸬ **Duncan Taylor Collection Caperdonich 1968** Cask no. 2616 **(89)** n22 polished oak with hints of hickory and crisp barley; t23 mountainous oak, but scaled sublimely by the most deft malt fashioned with a touch of barley sugar; f22 the soft sugars remain, keeping at bay the encroaching burnt, toasty oak. All played out with a degree of sophistication; **b**22 a touch of quiet class. **56.3%**.

**Duncan Taylor Collection Caperdonich 1968** bott 5 Apr 06 **(81)** n21 t20 f21 b19. Oaky-dokey. Enough barley hangs on to make interesting. **40.3%**

⸬ **Duncan Taylor Collection Caperdonich 1972** Cask no.3246 **(94)** n24 a Pacific fruit cocktail with a small shake of oaky allspice on the mashed banana and passion fruit; t23 busy delivery with the oak threatening then lying low as the barley garners all the eclectic fruit it can find; f24 really classy with a vanilla drying out the barley; quite sawdusty in places but the juicy instincts of the barley continue; liquorice and burned honeycomb completes one enormous experience... **b**23 any number of distilleries reach the "exotic fruit" stage of old age, but none seem to master the genre with such panache as Caper. What a treat! **46.5%**

⸬ **Duncan Taylor Collection Caperdonich 1972** Cask no. 7435 **(84)** n22 t22 f19 **b**21. So many good things to say about this, especially in the buttery, spiced butterscotch department. But, ultimately, just a shade too old. **55.6%**

**Lonach Caperdonich 33 Years Old** **(86)** n20 t22 f22 **b**22. Kept itself in good shape. **42.3%**. *Duncan Taylor.*

**Lonach Caperdonich 37 Years Old** **(90)** n21 sponge pudding with a dab of maple syrup; t23 fills the mouth superbly with the golden/maple syrup continuing to evolve; wonderful spices are then unleashed; f23 varying degrees of oak pan out into a wonderful Jamaican Blue mountain finale; **b**23 on first taste, seems to be doddering. On third and fourth the true character emerges. Give it time...and it'll give you 37 years. **41.5%**. *Duncan Taylor.*

**Lonach Caperdonich 1972** cask vx2, dist Oct 72, bott Mar 06 **(86)** n22 t22 f21 **b**21. An enjoyable but ultimately tired imitation of the great '67 casks. **41.9%**.

**Member's Legacy Caperdonich 1967 Aged 36 Years** cask 4945 **(95)** n24 Sensational aroma: blind tasted we've a bourbon-old fashioned Canadian on our hands. Also cream toffee with faintest dab of smoke; **t**24 big, big, big: prisoner-slaughtering stuff, with at first a golden thread of barley, then runs through several layers of gathering oak; **f**23 dries with liquorice as the oak that has given us that big bourbon arrival digs in; **b**24 one of four consecutive spell-binding casks. **57.2%**

Member's Legacy Caperdonich 1967 Aged 36 Years cask 4947 **(96) n**24 this sister aroma of cask 4945 and the all-conquering Platinum Old and Rare has a very different dimension: this is coastal, with a salty, seaweedy tang to it, maybe through some covert peat. Mazy, complex, confusing and perhaps scored down in the end only by a splinter of oak too many; **t**24 a pea from the same pod as the platinum old with a sexy, silky, see-through marmalady fruitiness that coats the very back of the roof of the mouth whilst that astonishing briny bourbon character kicks open the doors and makes a swaggering entrance; this is all high-octane, rather hot stuff where the oak is taken to its ultimate level without ruining the fun; **f**24 just, so long you could read the first part of War and Peace whilst its still deciding just what its going to do....in the end it settles of a bourbn theme of startling honeycomb sweetness tempered wonderfully by those drier, saltier oaky notes. All topped with wondrous chocolate; **b**24 alongside its sister cask, above, and last year's all-conquering cask, this represents one of the most extraordinary batches of malt of all time. **57.6%**

Murray McDavid Mission Caperdonich 1968 Sherry/Madeira **(85) n**23 **t**20 **f**21 **b**21. A wondrous, sniffed-to-be-believed nose; then real fruity fireworks with probably the spiciest dram of all time and big malty finish. Some people may rate this one as a lifetime best. Others will hate it. I'm somewhere in between, although I suspect, given time, I could become hooked... **46.2%**. *500 bottles.*

Old Malt Cask Caperdonich 32 Years Old Wine Finish dist Dec 73, bott Sept 06 **(89) n**22 some punchy oak filtering through the grapey (though not customary exotic!) fruit; **t**23 manic delivery of intense but delicious oak with barley-fruit. Dense and chewy; **f**22 tongue-tingling spices and, at last, a thickening of the barley; **b**22 rather map-less with some gung-ho oak and bruising barley. Great fun in its tired but rebellious way. **50%**. *272 bottles.*

Peerless Caperdonich 1968 (*see* Duncan Taylor Caperdonich 1968)

Peerless Caperdonich 1970 (*see* Duncan Taylor Caperdonich 1970)

⫶⫶ Platinum Caperdonich Aged 32 Years Rum Finish dist 73, bott 06 **(87) n**23 a sugary sheen sticks to the ripe fruits; **t**22 bliss as the barley melts in the mouth, though the usurping oak is in too much of a hurry for power; **f**21 aggressive oak tempered by the last remnants of fruity barley **b**21 deprived of greatness by, simply, far too great an oak delivery. But some wonderful moments to savour. **49.2%**. *336 bottles.*

Platinum Caperdonich 37 Years Old Rum finish, dist Nov 67, bott Oct 05 **(75) n**20 **t**19 **f**18 **b**18. Big, unforgiving oak. **56.4%**. *Douglas Laing. 133 bottles.*

⫶⫶ Scotch Malt Whisky Society Cask 38.16 Aged 12 Years Refill Hogshead, dist May 94 **(74) n**19 **t**18 **f**19 **b**18. Hot, harsh, thin and pretty unforgiving: so not bad for a Caper of this age... **58.7%**

# CARDHU

### Speyside, 1824. Diageo. Working.

Cardhu 12 Years Old db **(90) n**23 just about the cleanest, most uncluttered, pure, sweet malt you will ever find, a touch of apple, perhaps, giving an extra dimension; **t**24 again the malt is pure and rich, just a thread of oak adding some dryness and depth; **f**21 vanilla and malt; **b**22 a classic: welcome back! **40%** (*see also Cardhu Pure Malt*)

# CLYNELISH

### Highlands (Northern), 1968. Diageo. Working.

Clynelish 14 Years Old (old Flora and Fauna label) db **(86) n**22 **f**20 **t**22 **b**22. A lovely dram with a sweet malt dependency rather than the usual Clynelish complexity. **43%**

Clynelish 14 Years Old (new "Coastal Highland" label) bott lott no. L4316 db **(79) n**18 **t**21 **f**20 **b**20. How bloody annoying! Just this week I write in a top-selling American magazine what a consistent dram this is (and have just spotted, bizarrely, that the label claims the very same thing) when a few days later I taste this... Just a miniscule sulphur blemish, but enough to drop this down a few points despite the lovely depth to the delicate smoke. A one-off, I'm sure. **46%**

**Clynelish Aged 15 Years "The Distillers Edition"** Double matured in Oloroso-Seco casks Cl-Br: 169-1f, bott code L6264CM000 03847665, dist 91, bott 06 db **(79) n**20 **t**20 **f**19 **b**20. Big in places, distinctly oily in others but the overall feel is of a potentially brilliant whisky matured in unsympathetic barrels. **46%**

**Adelphi Clynelish 1995 Aged 10 Years** Sherry butt cask 12783, bott Jun 06 **(85) n**22 **t**21 **f**22 **b**20. A curious Clynelish offering boldness and thrust though harmonization is a bit awry due, mainly, to a soft sulphur buzz. **59.3%. 698 btls.**

**Boisdale Clynelish 1992** Cask no. 7169, bott 06 **(81) n**20 **t**22 **f**19 **b**20. Surprising for a Clynelish. Pleasantish and all that. But refuses to fire on all cylinders – especially on the so-so finish. **46%**

**The Bottlers Clynelish 1984 16 Years Old** cask 4016 **(91) n**23 **t**23 **f**23 **b**22. Not the normal guise for Clynelish, but looks in its pomp in this powerful sherry-spice romp. **58.5%. Raeborn Fine Wines.**

**Cadenhead's Authentic Collection Clynelish Aged 12 Years** dist 93, bott Feb 06 **(91) n**21 brusque barley, lazy oak and teasing snatch of something vaguely smoky; **t**24 velvety entrance for all the strength with intensity of the lush barley quite startling; subtle hints of white pepper and citrus ride on a slightly viscous wave: exuberant and quite brilliant; **f**23 at last some serious complexity as cocoa-oak weaves deliciously through firm two-toned barley; **b**23 charming barley-rich and proud: underlines the beauty of a simple bourbon refill. **60%. 630 bottles.**

**Cadenhead's Authentic Collection Clynelish Aged 13 Years** Bourbon Hogshead, dist 92, bott Sept 06 **(91) n**22 citrus and vague bubble gum clings to the rich barley; **t**23 intense with a non-specific fruitiness dovetailing with the mammoth barley; **f**23 long with touches of mocha; **b**23 charming Clynelish that works the oak so beautifully you almost wouldn't notice. **57.2%. 294 bottles.**

**Cadenhead's Authentic Collection Clynelish Aged 15 Years** Bourbon Barrel, dist 90, bott May 05 **(90) n**22 **t**23 **f**22 **b**23. Just one of those genuinely complex and sexy casks that thrill you to the core. **56%. 162 bottles.**

**Cadenhead's Authentic Collection Clynelish Aged 15 Years** Bourbon Barrel, dist 90, bott May 05 **(84) n**23 **t**22 **f**19 **b**20. Wonderful, bourbontouched nose, but over-egged on the oak all round. **56.1%. 144 bottles.**

**Cask Strength Clynelish 1990 (94) n**23 **t**23 **f**24 **b**24. I had no idea sherry butts like this still existed. **57.6%**

**Chieftain's Clynelish 12 Years Old** Sherry wood **(84) n**19 **t**22 **f**22 **b**21. Recovers well from the less than impressive nose and benefits from an attractive viscosity and decent sweetness. Quite charming. **43%. Ian Macleod.**

**The Clydesdale Clynelish 14 Years Old** Cask ref. 0264/7164, dist May 92, bott Sept 06 **(92) n**23 more than just a thread of bourbon to the malty, toasty aroma; **t**22 a sweet, honeyed, kick to the delivery, but it's short lived as a touch of orange introduces the barley concentrate; the oak begins to stir quickly; **f**24 probably the most chocolatey finish you'll come across for a year or two: astonishing... **b**23 genuinely well-made malt from an excellent bourbon cask. Ultra-subtle bitter-sweet balance here. A malt that repays a search for finer detail. **60.4%. nc ncf. Blackadder International.**

**The Coopers Choice Clynelish Aged 9 Years** dist 97, bott 06 **(91) n**23 a fascinating combination of young bourbon, slightly older Canadian and delicate malt all put in a blender with under-ripe banana a dash of acacia honey. Yummy... **t**23 a delivery to die for: silky barley topped with exactly the right amount of silver sugar with the sweetness immediately countered by drying staves of oak; **f**22 very mildly estery and a resurgence of the juicy barley; **b**23 a nine-year-old scoring more than 90 marks: who would have thought it, eh? Well, anyone who knows that great whisky isn't all about massive age. It's about style, charisma, class and balance: and this little babe has them all...! **46%. ncf. The Vintage Malt Whisky Co.**

**Connoisseurs Choice Clynelish 1993 (89) n**22 beautifully delicate with a waft of dry marzipan on the crisp barley; **t**23 initially every bit as clean, mouthwatering and refreshing as the nose suggests, then a shard of soft peat can be chewed towards the middle; **f**22 dies at the death but with some late strands of oak and peat offering belated and surprising weight; **b**22 feigns to fade after a glorious start and middle but carries on to a wonderful conclusion. **43%**

**Dun Bheagan Clynelish 13 Years Old** Hogshead **(79)** n20 t21 f19 b19. Some pleasant shards of honey and butterscotch cannot disguise the relatively hot nature of this one. **46%.**

⠿ **John Milroy Selection Clynelish 1992 (87)** n21 clean with a hint of smoke? Lightly spiced; t23 juiced- up barley that flies off the salivameter. Lots of marmalade and a dash of spice; f21 soft landing for the barley, helped by the sawdust; b22 a close relation to the Boisdale, except this one has 240 volts of barley running through it! **46%**

⠿ **Kingsbury's "The Selection" Clynelish 1999** Hogshead cask nos. 305314/305315/305316, dist Apr 99, bott July 06 **(91)** n22 big, big barley; soft mallow; t23 wonderfully unmolested barley with increases in sweetness as, oddly, the vanilla slowly builds; f23 gentle spice and vanilla pods; b23 no oak, no sherry, absolutely nothing to detract from the brilliance of the malt. **43%. ncf.** *Japan Imports System.* 1316 bottles.

⠿ **Lombard's Jewels of Scotland Clynelish 1982 Aged 21 Years (88)** n21 clean, surprisingly fresh barley for its age with a sliver or two of ginger, pine nut and diced, unripe yam; t23 a real juiceball of a malt with waves of salivating barley helped along by big oaky spice; f22 remains a real spicefest; b22 a busy and quite joyous bottling. **50%.** *Lombard Brands.*

**Mackillop's Choice Clynelish 1989** cask 1140, dist Feb 89 **(95)** n24 brilliant. On the nose this is not only pure Clynelish, but the distillery nutshelled better than I have ever seen it in bottle. Wonderful honey buttress against the developing oak; t25 yikes! What can you say? The fabulous honey is found on several levels: there is both acacia and manuca in there; but it's sexily spiced up. The malt runs through with a refreshing clarity that could be easily missed. Just so close to getting full marks here...oh what the hell...!! f22 gentle honeycomb and spice with soft vanilla oak; b24 just such wonderful honey structure to this, but there is much more to it than that. Better than sex: sorry, ladies, but it's true! **56.7%.** *Angus Dundee.*

**Murray McDavid Clynelish 1994 Aged 11 Years** Bourbon/Viognier, bott 05 **(95)** n23 t23 f24 b25. The most subtle of drams offering ever-increasing body and spices; the usual Clynelish sweetness is kept in check and the fruit has accentuated the drier oak. Makes for a decent aperitif. Perhaps I may not be the world's greatest advocate for cask finishes and I continue my call for restraint, but when something this complex, intriguing and so thoroughly enjoyable turns up in the glass, I can only stand, applaud and say "bravo"... **46.2%. nc ncf.** *1,800 bottles.*

⠿ **Murray McDavid Clynelish 1995 Aged 11 Years** Bourbon/Port **(86)** n21 t21 f22 b22. Highly unusual both as a Clynelish and Port finish. The port is offering a slightly restrained character and the Clynelish has none of its usual honeyed charm. Enjoyable and attractive to those who prefer their malts dry enough to be stirred but not shaken. **46%**

**Murray McDavid Mission IV Clynelish 1976 Aged 28 Years** drawn 25 Apr 05 **(93)** n23 t24 f23 b23. A peach in every sense. **46%**

**Old Malt Cask Clynelish Aged 13 Years** Refill hogshead 1499, dist Jan 91, bott Oct 04 **(90)** n22 a hint of smoke on the sherry; t23 delicate oils and bracing malts with a salty, vaguely smoky tang; f22 gentle spices are in keeping with an unusually measured production; b23 beautifully soothing: this is all about grace and elegance. **50%. nc ncf.**

**Old Malt Cask Clynelish Aged Over 13 Years** Rum Finish, dist July 89, bott Feb 03 **(95)** n25 sexy and delicate with infused poppy seed and rose petal. The dynamics of the spiced barley/wood are nigh-on perfect. Something to stick your nose in and keep there; t23 the rum is wonderfully understated but there is unquestionably something of unusual origin latching onto the intense barley; the barley-oak layers are numerous and of astounding subtlety; f23 only at the very death does the rum come into its own, with a vague hint of non-coloured Demerara, though such is the integrity of the crisp barley, it is just about impossible to be sure of the rum's origin; b24 This is a masterpiece! Damn it, why didn't Douglas Laing send this to me when they bottled it? It could well have been an award winner. My thanks to Duncan Chisholm for sending me something very special. Should you see this around anywhere, rip the shop owner's arm off. **50%. sc nc ncf.**

⠿ **Old Malt Cask Clynelish Aged 23 Years** dist Apr 83, bott Dec 06 **(88)** n21 a curious interplay between exotic fruit and a floor of pine needles, but the message of age is clear; t22 the first punch is with an age-withered, oaky hand, then comes a stream of varying honey tones; f23 excellent balance between good oak and very healthy barley and those honey notes become a little toastier but stay the course; b22 a malt which becomes more content with itself as it develops. The exotic fruitiness hints at decay and the arrival reinforces this, but there is enough strength in depth to see it home as an elderly statesman rather than a clapped-out journeyman. **50%.** *Douglas Laing. 303 bottles.*

⋅⋅⋅ **Old Malt Cask Clynelish Aged 24 Years** dist Apr 83, bott May 07 **(88) n**22 celery and linseed; **t**23 wonderful deftness to the lush barley **f**21 vanilla wafer; late spice; **b**22 elegant and clean. **50%.** *Douglas Laing. 305 bottles.*

⋅⋅⋅ **Old Masters Clynelish Aged 10 Years** Cask no. 2774, dist 1995, bott 06 **(82) n**20 **t**20 **f**21 **b**21. Not entirely happy with itself, but certain honey elements are so damn good that it still makes for a sporadically more than delicious dram. **58.9%.** *James MacArthur & Co Ltd.*

**Platinum Clynelish 23 Years Old** Rum finish, dist Apr 83, bott Aug 06 **(96) n**23 a strange, early off-ish note is encircled and over-run by an increased delivery of kumquat and barley. Leave in the glass for a good five minutes before nosing: the improvement is astonishing; **t**25 a quite perfect delivery of intense fruit coupled with sparkling barley; the freshness belies the great age and the development of spices is faultless; **f**24 long with not a single blemish. Only now does something on the rum side make itself known, but is so delicate it is impossible to declare exactly the extent of its influence, or even what rum it may be; **b**24 it seems like rum finishes are working pretty well this year. What a treat! This is a classic. **55.3%.** *Douglas Laing. 254 bottles.*

**Platinum Selection Clynelish Aged 32 Years** dist Mar 73, bott Aug 05 **(80) n**19 **t**23 **f**19 **b**19. There is a fine line in whisky between success and failure and this malt is standing right astride it. **55.1%.** *232 bottles.*

**Private Collection Clynelish 1969 (82) n**20 **t**21 **f**21 **b**20. Just hangs onto its integrity by the width of an oak's bark; enough mocha-themed fruit and spicy complexity and charm to see it through some dodgy moments. **45%**

⋅⋅⋅ **Provenance Clynelish Aged 11 Years** dist Autumn 96, bott Winter 06 **(88) n**22 surprising footprints of a young bourbon; **t**22 clean, almost textbook weight to the soft oils and developing oak; **f**22 long and much drier than the norm; **b**22 the usual subtle complexity from this distillery, though less sweet than you might expect. **46%.**

**Provenance Clynelish 14 Years Old** dist 26 Feb 90, bott 1 Feb 05 **(83) n**20 **t**22 **f**20 **b**21. Gentle, undemanding malt with the spotlight on clean, uncluttered barley. **46%**

**Provenance Clynelish 15 Year Old** dist 18 May 89, bott 14 Apr 05 **(83) n**22 **t**21 **f**20 **b**20. Marmalade on thick buttered bread. **46%.** *Douglas Laing.*

⋅⋅⋅ **Scotch Malt Whisky Society Cask 26.50 Aged 23 Years** Refill Hogshead, dist May 83 **(94) n**23 sugar puffs anchored by soft but significant smoke; **t**23 classic Clynelish with honey spread by the knife onto a slightly buttered hot cross bun, the spices turning to smoke towards the middle; **f**24 drier with toastier traits but still those spices bite and pound; the smoke resurfaces with a sweet, if kippery, fade; **b**24 get a bottle of this and you have Clynelish nutshelled. **57.1%**

**The Single Malt of Scotland Clynelish Aged 11 Years Vintage 1994** Sherry butt **(79) n**19 **t**22 **f**19 **b**19. Blood oranges and magnificent spice but the butt is a big but... **58.9%.** *The Whisky Exchange. 367 bottles.*

**The Single Malt of Scotland Clynelish Aged 13 Years Vintage 1992** cask 7156 **(90) n**22 delightfully bourbony, though the malt projects a 3D sharpness and strands of honey; **t**23 brittle, mouthwatering malt impact, mega salivating and never distracted despite the slow arrival of custard tart; **f**22 lovely spices abound; **b**23 a fabulous bottling which shows this great distillery at its malty best. **58%.** *The Whisky Exchange.*

**The Single Malt of Scotland Clynelish Aged 32 Years Vintage 1972** Hogshead cask 15619, dist 13 Dec 72, bott 02 Nov 05 **(88) n**22 exotic fruit underscores the big age on this; **t**23 the delivery is a triumph with truly salivating malt coursing through the oak; **f**21 tires as the nose suggests it might but still holds together attractively. Teasing smoke and cocoa add ballast; **b**22 a cask that has just – but only just – held together and any oak flaws are enormously outweighed by the brilliance of the barley. **49.9%. nc ncf.** *The Whisky Exchange. 226 bottles.*

⋅⋅⋅ **The Single Malts of Scotland Clynelish 1972 Aged 34 Years** Small batch **(83) n**20 **t**22 **f**21 **b**20. Such is the honeyed grace before it is crushed under the weight of oak, that this must have been a stunner ten years ago. **50.5%.** *Speciality Drinks, Ltd.*

**Tanner's Clynelish 10 Year Old 1992 (90) n**23 oakier, spicier, altogether punchier than the age suggests. Intriguing layers of peat and orange entertain; **t**22 enormous attitude as it hits the palate slogging. The taste-buds barely stand a chance against repeated blows from the frenzied oak-studded barley; the spices fizz leaving a distant trail of something smoky; **f**22 good length; pleasing and surprising depth to the bitter chocolate and mildly over-aged citrus. You can chew your jaw off; **b**23 good grief! I didn't expect this – not from a ten-year-old! The evidence is weighed towards a first-filled bourbon cask. Having said that. It probably isn't a 10-y-o: it was distilled in 1992, not '95 or '96. A corking Clynelish at its most belligerent and revealing a depth some insist it doesn't possess. Oh yeah? Well try this – if you're man enough. **45%.** *Tanners, UK.*

The Whisky Exchange Clynelish 1972 Aged 32 Years **(89) n**20 **t**22 **f**24 **b**23. The nose suggests little of the sheer brilliance that is to follow. **49.4%.**

The Whisky Fair Clynelish Aged 32 Years dist Feb 74, bott Apr 06 **(95) n**24 probably the optimum aroma for a malt of this age and style: the oak is big and rules the roost, but the richness and range and the barley-spice combination is something to marvel at; **t**24 three different types of honey, starting with acacia, moving towards honeycomb and getting into full throttle manuka. Strands of toffee apple and then soft smoke offer both lightness and depth; **f**23 enormous length and depth; complexity continues unmolested; **b**24 just one of those malts that it is a rare privilege to come across in life. Whoever found the cask should be given the Freedom of Germany. **58.6%. nc ncf.** *266 bottles.*

⋯ Wilson & Morgan Barrel Selection Clynelish 1992 Sherry Finish bott 07 **(79) n**20 **t**21 **f**19 **b**19. Unusually flat for a Clynelish. Jam tarty in part, but you get the feeling the sherry finish has done the complexity no favours. **46%**

# COLEBURN
### Speyside, 1897–1985. Diageo. Closed.

Connoisseurs Choice Coleburn 1981 **(81) n**21 **t**21 **f**19 **b**20. Usual thin, hot stuff from Coleburn but benefits from a big malt kick. Way above the norm. **43%**

⋯ Connoisseurs Choice Coleburn 1981 **(74) n**20 **t**19 **f**17 **b**18. The barley is sparse and stretched thinly over the hot body **43%.** *Gordon & MacPhail.*

Old Malt Cask Coleburn Aged 25 Years dist Feb 80, bott Aug 05 **(68) n**20 **t**17 **f**15 **b**16. Best Coleburn nose in years, but spectacularly disintegrates on the palate as is its wont. **50%.** *Douglas Laing. 661 bottles.*

# CONVALMORE
### Speyside, 1894–1985. Closed.

Convalmore 1977 bott 05 db **(91) n**23 wonderfully layered barley offering many hues of intensity and tartness, embracing fruit gums, bourbon and even very gentle peat; **t**23 mouth-puckering barley is sharp and intense, then a softening sweetness radiates out as both soft- and hard-edged oaks home in; **f**22 mildly out of sync for the first time, but settles as some soft butterscotch and liquorice arrives; **b**23 must be blended with Botox, as there is no detrimental ageing to either nose or delivery. A quite lovely and charming whisky to remember this lost – and extremely rare - distillery by. **57.9%.** *3,900 bottles.*

Convalmore Rare Malt 24 Years Old dist 78, db **(88) n**23 Peaches and cream ... and pretty juicy peach at that. One of the fruitiest noses on the market; **t**23 not even a straffing of searing spices can reduce the peachy onslaught. About as juicy and salivating as it gets for a malt so old; **f**20 an abrupt entry of cocoadusted oak plus some lingering barley; **b**22 another stunning version of a muchmissed distillery, begging the question as to why it was ever closed. **59.4%**

⋯ Dun Bheagan Convalmore 30 Years Old Hogshead, dist Dec 75 **(83) n**19 **t**21 **f**22 **b**21. Thin, crisp and angular but displaying a pleasing malty bent for all its age. **46%. nc ncf.** *Ian Macleod.*

⋯ Old Malt Cask Convalmore Aged 30 Years dist Oct 76, bott Apr 07 **(88) n**23 plasticine, gooseberries, custard; so light..; **t**22 early barley juice augmented by something fruity; dries and spices up slightly; **f**21 sawdusty; **b**22 a charming and unusual expression of this rare malt. **44.1%.** *Douglas Laing. 192 bottles.*

⋯ Scott's Selection Convalmore 1975 bott 06 **(89) n**23 taken the exotic fruit – and floral – path, but enough barley residual to add good weight; **t**22 that barley really hammers itself home with force; the oak is zippy rather than spicy though does help to dry out the middle; **f**22 after an uncomfortable second or two the sweet barley reestablishes itself for a decent, chewy if lethargic finale; **b**22 nose apart, hard to know how something so old can have such limited complexity. But, that said, what it does it does well and with confidence. **46.1%**. *Speyside Distillers.*

## CRAGGANMORE
### Speyside, 1870. Diageo. Working.

Cragganmore 10 Year Old dist 93 db **(84)** n20 t23 f20 **b**21. The sheer beauty of the softly fruited malt on the mouth arrival is glorious. But the oak hasdone the whisky few other favours. **60.1%**

Cragganmore 12 years old db **(89)** n23 a weirdly coastal, salty slant to this, with ripe sultanas; t23 beautiful banana delivery, custard and malt but with lush, grapey undertones; f21 thins out with some vanilla at the death; **b**22 the best Cragganmore 12 I've come across for a while, though the original Cragganmore of a dozen or so years ago was so much better. And still could be: much more bourbon-cask oriented. "The most complex aroma of any malt," boasts the label. As wonderful as it is, I really don't think so. Obviously no-one at Diageo has stuck their nose in a glass of Glenmorangie. Or Ardmore. Or Glen Elgin.... **40%**

Cragganmore 17 Years Old Special Releases 2006, dist 88 db **(94)** n23 squelched, juicy sultana; many layers of vanilla of varying sweetness; the most delicate strand of smoke; t24 so impressively together in both delivery and immediate follow-through: the malt is very big and intense with, again, that distinctive fruitiness. Holds together perfectly allowing excellent spice bite to serenade and embolden rather than scatter; f23 long, luxurious and still the balance shows no sign of wavering; **b**24 for those of us who have been in love with this distillery for the last 30 years, it's a bit of a shock to the system to see it in this massively fruity form. But what a real treat, too, because this is as dynamic as a usually controlled and crusty Speysider gets...! **55.5%**

Cadenhead's Cragganmore-Glenlivet Aged 15 Years dist 89, bott Feb 05 **(91)** n24 t23 f21 **b**23. Deft, relaxing and quite classic, most probably second-fill Cragganmore from outstanding distillate. **46%**. *306 bottles.*

Cadenhead's Authentic Collection Cragganmore-Glenlivet Aged 15 Years dist 89, bott Feb 05 **(89)** n21 t22 f23 **b**23. Bold oak strokes on the malty canvas. **57.8%**. *606 bottles.*

Cadenhead's Authentic Collection Cragganmore-Glenlivet Aged 16 Years dist 89, bott Sep 05 **(94)** n24 fabulous: the most delicate fruit imaginable adds pith to a sweet and salty barley base; the range of the oak is mind-boggling; t23 fantastic spice buzz pitches in harmony with the waxy barley and burnt honeycomb; f23 lots, lots more of the same, except the honey sweetens slightly as the oak grip lessens; **b**24 a sublime cask has extracted every last ultra-complex nuance it can find. **58.6%**. *678 bottles.*

Dewar Rattray Individual Cask Bottling Cragganmore 1993 Aged 12 Years cask 1911, dist Apr 93, bott Jan 06 **(86)** n20 t22 f22 **b**22. A pretty standard version of a high-class Speysider. The complexity does shine through eventually. **59.3%**. *311 bottles.*

Murray McDavid Cragganmore Aged 12 Years Bourboun/Syrah enhanced in Guigal Cotes Rotie, dist 93, bott 05 **(89)** n23 crisp barley encased in clipped fruit and spice; t23 firm and clean, the barley-grape act really does show delicious harmony; f21 bitters down slightly as the oak ups the pace; **b**22 charming and sophisticated: the near perfect aperitif. **46%. nc ncf.** *2,100 bottles.*

Murray McDavid Mission Cragganmore 1985 Aged 21 Years Guigal Côte Rôtie. Bourbon/Syrah **(82)** n23 t21 f19 **b**19. When they say bourbon, they aren't kidding: parts of this is pure Kentucky, especially on the glorious nose. But the truth is that it's gone through the wood and after the brain-blowing entry, things slip downhill. **56.5%. nc ncf.** *665 bottles.*

Old Masters Cragganmore 1993 Aged 13 Years cask 1905, dist 93, bott 06 **(79)** n19 t20 f21 **b**19. Decent, but overly sweet and one might expect a bit more from this distillery. **61%**. *James MacArthur.*

Scotch Malt Whisky Society Cask 37.31 Aged 28 Years Refill Hogshead, dist June 78 **(86)** n21 t22 f21 **b**22. At first appears shot through with oak but a grapey recovery confounds and the natural caramels help soften things further. Still, this is a brave attempt by Cragganmore at taking it into pretty unknown territory. At times looks as though its willing to lay down and die, then picks itself up for a fruity encore. Such entertainment! **52.7%**

# CRAIGELLACHIE
**Speyside, 1891. Dewar's. Working.**

**Craigellachie 14 Years Old** db **(82)** n21 t22 f19 b21. Complex nose and battles deliciously and maltily before the indifferent finish; quite a bit of bite. **40%**

⸭ **Cadenhead's Authentic Collection Craigellachie-Glenlivet Aged 12 Years** Bourbon Hogshead, dist 1994, bott May 07 **(80)** n19 t21 f20 b20. Big barley and biscuity fare. **58.3%.**

**Connoisseurs Choice Craigellachie 1988 (90)** n21 t24 f22 b23. A shimmering beauty: probably the best bottled expression from this distillery at this age I have ever tasted. **43%.**

**Connoisseurs Choice Craigellachie 1989 (87)** n21 indulgent oak plays brinkmanship. It's foot slips over the edge a few times but there is just enough coal-smoked barley to pull it back; t21 a delivery of pure silk also heads quickly to oak; f23 at last harmony is found as kumquats, passion fruit and spice surf on the tides of gentle oils. Some late smoke wraps things up well; b22 the developing exotic fruit suggests a whisky almost twice its age. Quite a surprise package. A cheapskate could shove on a fake label claiming to be a 30-year-old and who the hell would know ...??? **43%.** *Gordon & MacPhail.*

⸭ **Connoisseurs Choice Craigellachie 1990 (86)** n21 t22 f21 b22. Enjoyable dual personality being at once lush and barley rich and on another plane firm and crisp. Clean and well-balanced. **43%.** *Gordon & MacPhail.*

**Dewar Rattray Individual Cask Bottling Craigellachie 1989 Aged 15 Years** cask 3882, dist Oct 90, bott Sept 05 **(79)** n20 t21 f18 b19. A furry, bitter finale points towards a lacking cask. A shame, as the delivery offers barley at its most eye-watering. **54.2%.** *315 bottles.*

⸭ **Milroy's of Soho Craigellachie 1989 Aged 16 Years** Hogshead, cask no. 3883, dist 9 Oct 89, bott 18 Jan 06 **(83)** n19 t21 f22 b21. Without its trademark smoky edge, though the gentle oils remain. A sweet expression very much sticking to a simplistic malty route. **46%.** *358 bottles*

**Murray McDavid Mission III Craigellachie 1970** Refill sherry **(93)** n23 oaky spice off-set by damson plums in custard; t24 stunning!!! The arrival simply glimmers with fabulous barley in that sweet custardy setting; an usual form of sweetness, this, fruity and refined, though not in a sugary way; f22 natural caramel blunts the richer tones but there is soft sherry back-up; b24 when I tell people that Craigellachie can be a God, I'm looked upon with incredulity. Well, get your lips around this! Also rare to find this distillery in any form of sherry. **46%**

**Old Malt Cask Craigellachie Aged 13 Years** Hogshead 1613, dist Aug 91, bott Jan 05 **(86)** n21 t22 f22 b21. A simple malt. **50%. nc ncf.** *Douglas Laing.*

**Old Malt Cask Craigellachie Aged 14 Years** cask 1037, dist Oct 89, bott Oct 03 **(80)** n19 t21 f20 b20. Soft, delicate oils, which always used to be a feature of this distillery, have returned to lay the citrus sweetness on with a trowel. **50%.** *318 bottles.*

**Platinum Selection Craigellachie Aged 32 Years** dist May 73, bott Aug 05 **(84)** n20 t23 f21 b20. Almost a relative of the Connoisseur's Choice '89, except the fruit here – and we are talking market places of the stuff – has just a little too much oak on the finish for this to be up there with the stars. For a few glorious seconds, though... **42.7%.**

**Provenance Craigellachie 10 Years Old** dist Feb 96, bott Jan 06 **(83)** n22 t21 f20 b20. Gristy, grassy and pure Speyside. **46%.** *McGibbon's.*

**Provenance Craigellachie 13 Years Old** dist 21 Aug 91, bott 20 Jan 05 **(83)** n21 t22 f21 b20. Intensely malty and slightly oily fare from an oft-used bourbon cask that is beginning to creak a bit. **46%.** *Douglas Laing.*

**The Wee Dram Craigellachie 15 Years Old** db **(89)** n23 fascinating meeting of ultra-lazy smoke and slightly less lazy grapey fruit. Rounded off with a layer of intense malt and shyer citrus; t21 chewy, big and increasingly fatty; f22 breaks down into more complex characters, with fruit at the fore and cocoaoak towards the finale; b23 takes its time to get into gear on the palate, but once it does it backs up the nose in proclaiming a beaut! **43%.** *The Wee Dram, Bakewell, UK.*

# CROFTENGEA (see Loch Lomond)

# DAILUAINE
**Speyside, 1854. Diageo. Working.**

**Dailuaine Aged 16 Years** bott lot no. L4334 db **(79)** n19 t21 f20 b19. Syrupy, almost grotesquely heavy at times; the lighter, more considered notes of previous bottlings have been lost under an avalanche of sugary, over-ripe tomatoes. Definitely one for those who want a massive dram. **43%**

Berry's' Own Selection Dailuaine 1974 Aged 31 Years **(83) n**23 **t**21 **f**19 **b**20. Sparkling, salivating bitter-sweet barley at first then a heavy oak portcullis shuts off the fun. **46%.**

⫶⫶ Berry's Own Selection Dailuaine 1985 Cask no. 1964, bott 06 **(79) n**19 **t**21 **f**19 **b**20. Meaty and less uncompromisingly sweet than usual; still a big chew – and one that can be hard work at times. **46%.**

Chieftain's Dailuaine Aged 10 Years **(88) n**21 the barley and oak barely gel; **t**23 rock-solid malt: no compromising at all!; **f**22 barley sugar and mallows; **b**22 hard-nosed malt, takes time to unravel. Ignore the occasional flat bit. **43%.**

⫶⫶ The Clydesdale Dailuaine 20 Years Old Cask ref. 0220/4566, dist Dec 85, bott Sept 06 **(82) n**20 **t**22 **f**19 **b**21. A much more elegant and uncluttered barley character to this bottling, pointing towards a pretty decent cask. The finish is its usual ungainly self. **53.3%. nc ncf.** *Blackadder International.*

Connoisseurs Choice Dailuaine 1991 **(78) n**21 **t**20 **f**18 **b**19. Another Dailuaine felled by oak. **43%.** *Gordon & MacPhail.*

⫶⫶ Connoisseurs Choice Dailuaine 1993 **(82) n**21 **t**22 **f**19 **b**20. Some attractive touches that show this distillery in its more expansive and barley-sugary light. Not too bad at all. **43%.** *Gordon & MacPhail.*

⫶⫶ John Milroy Selection Dailuaine 1996 Aged 10 Years **(72) n**17 **t**19 **f**18 **b**18. Good Dailuaines are pretty rare – and this ain't one of them. Cloying at best, the feinty nose is especially worth avoiding. **46%**

Norse Cask Selection Dailuaine 1989 Aged 14 Years **(79) n**20 **t**19 **f**21 **b**19. Diamond-hard and revealing exactly why this is such good blending malt. **60.4%.** *Denmark.*

⫶⫶ Old Malt Cask Dailuaine Aged 35 Years dist Dec 71, bott Apr 07 **(79) n**19 **t**20 **f**20 **b**20. Tangy. The oils keep the gathering oaks at bay. **45.6%.** *Douglas Laing. 152 bottles.*

# DALLAS DHU

### Speyside, 1899–1983. Closed. Now a museum.

⫶⫶ Cadenhead's Chairman's Stock Dallas Dhu Aged 27 Years Bourbon Hogshead, dist 1979, bott May 07 **(89) n**23 shortbread and oaky, roasted barley; **t**22 the oak gathers like storm clouds but the palate explodes with barley sugar, butterscotch and manuka honey...then the oaks rain in; **f**22 the storm clears to leave a dusty, burnt toasty finale. But just enough barley-led sweetness to even the scores; **b**22 this distillery never fails to amaze me. Yes, the oak is a little too emboldened but such is the chemistry of the barley and butterscotch foreground, you have to be impressed. **59.2%.** *198 bottles.*

Duncan Taylor Collection Dallas Dhu 1975 cask no. 2481, dist Dec 75, bott Apr 06 **(85) n**18 **t**22 **f**23 **b**22. Avoid the nose of a clapped-out cask: the unperturbed grace of an unsophisticated but beautiful malt is there to be chewed. **51%.**

Duncan Taylor Collection Dallas Dhu 1975 Aged 29 Years cask 2484, dist Dec 75, bott Feb 05 **(94) n**23 **t**23 **f**24 **b**24. You have to be impressed with this. Dallas Dhu wasn't built to make whisky of this age, but sheer quality has persevered. We have a minor classic here: a must-have whisky, though one to taste and revere rather than let sit and gather dust. **47.1%**

Duncan Taylor Collection Dallas Dhu 1981 Aged 14 Years Sherry cask 387, dist Apr 81 **(94) n**23 concentrated barley with well-matured farmhouse cake thrown in; **t**24 a delivery to die for: faultless, concentrated barley – again with that peculiar tart citrus kick that appears to attack the fillings! – and then oak ushering in a hint of Jameson chocolate truffle; **f**23 almost too long for belief: wave upon wave, layer upon layer of increasingly intense barley and burnt fudge; **b**24 could this be one of the last bottlings that – at cask strength and not tampered with by cask finishing – shows this great distillery in its full glory...? **58.3%.** *523 bottles.*

⫶⫶ Duncan Taylor Collection Dallas Dhu 1981 Cask no. 419 **(95) n**24 a tapestry of honey: just how many soft, sweet barley notes can you spot? It is a nose that defies belief...and age; **t**24 the barley dissolves on the palate and although the oak tries to bustle through there is enough acacia honey and spice in reserve to regain the balance; **f**23 a quiet, teasingly spiced finish where the vanquished oak gives way to more soft barley: astonishing... **b**24 It's almost as if this old distillery is sending a message: forget about me being a bloody museum...just fire up my stills again!!! Just marvellous...incredible...a thing of total beauty! **57.9%**

Gordon & MacPhail Dallas Dhu 1982 (89) n22 almost mash-tun barley clean and sweet; t23 intense barley with a peculiar and attractive citrus tartness; f22 lengthy for something so soft, and unremittingly malty; b22 it's a sombre and sobering thought that whisky from the penultimate year of distillation at this distillery is now close on 25 years old. 40%. Gordon & MacPhail.

Murray McDavid Mission Dallas Dhu 1979 Bourbon/Marsanne, bott 06 (73) n19 t18 f18 b18. Off-key and unforgiving. Not the way a lost treasure like Dallas Dhu should be remembered. 57.8%. nc ncf. 240 bottles.

∹· Scotch Malt Whisky Society Cask 45.19 Aged 31 Years Refill Barrel, dist Aug 75 (77) n21 t19 f18 b19. Most Speyside casks have problems dealing with this kind of age. Here's one of them. 45.6%

The Whisky Fair Dallas Dhu 23 Years Old Bourbon Hogshead dist May 81 (90) n23 whole-hearted kippery peat dovetailing with lemon and lime; t22 massively oily and rich, the peat clings to every crevice. Some citrus tries to thin it out; f23 lychees and white grape juice weighted down with youthful peat; b22 last year I raised my eyebrows at this smoked-up version. They have sent me another sample...and yes, it really is the kippery brute I described. What a fabulous find by the boys from the Whisky Fair!!! Well done, chaps! 53.5%. Germany. 164 bottles.

# DALMORE
## Highand (northern), 1839. Whyte and Mackay. Working.

Dalmore 12 Years Old db (91) n22 big, fruity, firm, a threat of smoke, weighty; t24 well-muscled malt surge followed by clean fruity tones, immaculate mouth-presence and bitter-sweet balance; f22 long, tapering fruit-malt residue, some brown sugar coating and uncomplicated oak; b23 simply one of the great Highland malt whiskies at just about the perfect age: what I would do to see this unplugged at 46% minimum and no bottling hall interference. 40%

The Dalmore 21 Years Old db (87) n22 just how many citrus notes can we find here? Answers on a postcard ... on second thoughts, don't. Just beautifully light and effervescent for its age: a genuine delight; t23 again, wonderfully fruity though this time the malt pushes through confidently to create its own chewy island: fabulous texture; f20 simplifies towards toffee slightly too much in the interests of great balance. A lovely coffee flourish late on; b22 bottled elegance. 43%

The Dalmore 30 Years Old Stillman's Dram db (89) n23 nuts, oranges in a rich fruitcake; lime marmalade adds to the fruit cocktail: seductive; t22 enormous fruit explosion, silky malt then an injection of bitter oak; f22 medium length; the emphasis is on the malt as the oakiness burns off. Complexity levels rise as the fruit recedes and spices arrive late; b22 in some ways the ultimate bitter-sweet dram, with the burnt-toast oak fighting against the sweet fruit and malt. 45%

∹· The Dalmore Forty Years Old db (82) n23 t20 f19 b20. Doubtless my dear friend Richard Paterson will question whether I have the ability to spot a good whisky if it ran me over in a ten ton truck. But I have to say here that we have a disappointing malt: I had left this too late on in writing this year's (2008) Bible as a treat. But it wasn't to be. A soft delivery: but of what? Hard to exactly pin down what's going on here as there is so much toffee and fruit that the oak and barley have been overwhelmed. Pleasant, perhaps, but it's all rather dull and passionless. Like going through the motions with an old lover. Adore the sherry-trifle/toffee mousse nose, though... 40%

The Dalmore 50 Years Old db (88) n21 buxom and bourbony, the oak makes no secret of the antiquity; t19 oak again arrives first and without apology, some salty malt creaking in later. Ripe cherries offer a mouthwatering backdrop; f25 comes into its own as harmony is achieved as the oak quietens to allow a beautiful malt-cherry interplay. Spices arrive for good measure in an absolutely has-it-all, faultless finish: really as much a privilege to taste as a delight; b23 takes a while to warm up, but when it does becomes a genuinely classy and memorable dram befitting one of the world's great and undervalued distilleries. 52%

The Dalmore 62 Years Old db (95) n23 PM or REV marked demerara potstill rum, surely? Massive coffee presence, clean and enormous, stunning, topdrawer peat just to round things off; t25 this is brilliant: pure silk wrapping fabulous moist fruitcake soaked in finest oloroso sherry and then weighed with peat which somehow has defied nature and survived in cask all these years. I really cannot fault this: I sit here stunned and in awe; f24 perfect spices with flecks of ginger and lemon rind; b24 if I am just half as beautiful, elegant and fascinating as this by the time I reach 62, I'll be a happy man. Somehow I doubt it. A once-in-a-lifetime whisky – something that comes around every 62 years, in fact. Forget Dalmore Cigar Malt – even I might be tempted to start smoking just to get a full bottle of this. **40.5%**

The Dalmore 1966 db **(86)** n23 t22 f20 b21. A remakable dram for the years that it has kept its fruity integrity despite the big age. **44.6%**

The Dalmore 1973 Gonzalez Byass Sherry Cask Finish db **(93)** n24 t23 f22 b24. What happens when you get one of Scotland's greatest – if entirely undervalued – drams and fill it into what what was obviously a special, handpicked, clean and flawless sherry butt? You get this this ultra-complex gem **52.3%**

The Dalmore Black Isle db **(77)** n19 t20 f19 b19. Very little of the complexity I automatically associate with Dalmore; slightly furry and a little drab. **40%**

⋯ The Dalmore Cabernet Sauvignon db **(79)** n22 t19 f19 b19. Too intense and soupy for its own good. **45%**

The Dalmore Cigar Malt db **(71)** n17 t20 f16 b18. For me, flat and un-Dalmore-like. But there again I have never smoked as much as a cigarette in all my life. **43%**

Cadenhead's Authentic Collection Dalmore Aged 14 Years Bourbon Hogshead, dist 92, bott May 06 **(88)** n23 delightfully structured with barley holding sway; t22 firm oak adds backbone to the juicy barley; f22 remains firm; b21 exceptionally malty. **62%**. *306 bottles.*

Cadenhead's Authentic Collection Dalmore Aged 15 Years dist 89, bott Feb 05 **(91)** n22 t23 f22 b23. Dalmore at its most deliciously devilish. **57.5%**. *198 bottles.*

Cadenhead's Authentic Collection Dalmore Aged 16 Years dist 89, bott Sep 05 **(91)** n22 moist malt cookies; t24 superb delivery of high- octane barley: fresh, lively and clean; f22 long, relying on vanilla; b23 pretty simple. But pretty superb, too... **56.7%**. *216 bottles.*

Chieftain's Dalmore Aged 10 Years Hogshead **(78)** n19 t21 f19 b19. A bit of a sweaty armpit nose and the malt meanders aimlessly, if sweetly and fruitily, around the palate. **58%**. *Ian Macleod.*

Chieftain's Dalmore Aged 10 Years Medoc Finish casks 90431 & 90434, dist Nov 94, bott Feb 05 **(80)** n19 t21 f20 b20. Seriously lethargic. **43%. nc ncf.**

Old Malt Cask Dalmore Aged 14 Years dist Feb 91, bott Aug 05 **(78)** n20 t19 f20 b19. A touch of tiring, fizzy oak kicks it out of orbit. **50%**. *Douglas Laing. 340 bottles.*

Old Malt Cask Dalmore Aged 14 Years Refill Hogshead 2094, dist Feb 91, bott Sept 05 **(88)** n23 gooseberries and custard; t22 sublimely clean and soft malt; f21 crème brulee; b22 excellent body and charisma. **50%. nc ncf.** *340 bottles.*

⋯ Old Malt Cask Dalmore Aged 15 Years dist May 91, bott Feb 07 **(86)** n21 t22 f21 b22. Quite simplistic despite – or maybe because of – its barley-concentrate character. Decent spices and a touch of mocha at the death. **50%**. *Douglas Laing. 357 bottles.*

⋯ Provenance Dalmore Aged 10 Years dist Autumn 96, bott Winter 06 **(77)** n19 t19 f20 b19. Barley-led but tobacco present, too. Not dissimilar to some German malts. **46%**.

Provenance Dalmore 14 Years Old dist 25 Feb 91, bott 24 Mar 05 **(86)** n21 t22 f21 b22. Very decent second-fill bourbon Dalmore. **46%**.

⋯ Scotch Malt Whisky Society Cask 13.39 Aged 21 Years Refill Hogshead, dist Sept 84 **(93)** n23 it maybe a cliché, but this really is butterscotch and honey... oh, with a bit of salted shortbread thrown in for good measure... t24 outstanding arrival with maple syrup impacting in just-so quantities to counter the brain-exploding spices and intense barley body; f23 more conservative finale with the balancing vague oaky bitterness trying to bring the curtain down...it takes a very long time...! b23 so old Dalmore does come without caramel....what an unforgettable improvement! **52.7%**

# DALWHINNIE
### Highlands (central), 1898. Diageo. Working.

Dalwhinnie 15 Years Old db **(95)** n24 sublime stuff: a curious mixture of coke smoke and peat-reek wafts teasingly over the gently honied malt. A hint of melon offers some fruit but the caressing malt stars; t24 that rarest of combinations: at once silky and malt intense, yet at the same time peppery and tin-hat time for the tastebuds, but the silk wins out and a sheen of barley sugar coats everything, soft peat included; f23 some cocoa and coffee notes, yet the pervading slightly honied sweetness means that there is no bitterness that cannot be controlled; **b**24 a malt it is hard to decide whether to drink or bath in: I suggest you do both. One of the most complete mainland malts of them all. Know anyone who reckons they don't like whisky? Give them a glass of this – that's them cured. Oh, if only the average masterpiece could be this good. **43%**

⟨⟩ **Dalwhinnie 20 Years Old** Special Releases 2006, dist 86 db **(70) n**18 **t**17 **f**18 **b**17 Hot and sulphured. **56.8%**

**Dalwhinnie 29 Years Old** dist 73 db **(85) n**21 **t**20 **f**23 **b**21. Fighting whisky; an old bruiser for its age with plenty of tongue-pulverising oomph; one for those hunting the atypical. **57.8%**

## DEANSTON
### Highlands (Perthshire), 1966. Burn Stewart. Working.

**Deanston 6 Years Old** db **(83) n**20 **t**21 **f**22 **b**20. Great news for those of us who remember how good Deanston was a decade or two ago: it's on its way back. A delightfully clean dram with it's trademark honey character restored. A little beauty slightly undermined by caramel. **40%**

**Deanston 12 Years Old** db **(78) n**19 **t**21 **f**19 **b**19. A fabulous transformation has taken this from one of the worst distillery bottled malts in Scotland to a dram that can hold it's head up with something approaching pride. Still some distance to go to reach the quality levels of a decade ago: there remains a thinness to the nose and finish, but some of the old honey and lustre has returned. **40%**

**Deanston 17 Year Old** db **(68) n**17 **t**17 **f**17 **b**17. A 17-year-old anorexic with agoraphobia: painfully thin and goes nowhere. **40%**

**Deanston 1967** casks 1051-2, filled Friday 31st Mar 67 db **(90) n**23 the very faintest hint of peat rubs shoulders with high fluting honey and polished pine floors; **t**23 the loud oak influence is perfectly tempered by rich barley concentrate. Sweet towards the middle with hints of honey and peat; **f**21 spiced and softening towards vanilla; **b**23 the oak is full on but there is so much class around that cannot gain control. A Perthshire beauty. **50.7%**

**The Whisky Shop Deanston 12 Year Old** Oloroso Finish **(71) n**18 **t**18 **f**17 **b**18. I wonder if I'll ever drink an enjoyable Deanston again... **40%**

## DUFFTOWN
### Speyside, 1898. Diageo. Working.

**Dufftown Aged 15 Years** db **(69) n**16 **t**19 **f**17 **b**17. Rubbery, syrupy and sickly sweet: Dufftown in a nutshell. **43%**. *Flora and Fauna range.*

**Dufftown Rare Malts Aged 21 Years** dist 1975 db **(59) n**14 **t**17 **f**14 **b**14. Not rare enough. **54.8%**

⟨⟩ **Singleton of Dufftown 12 Years Old** db **(71) n**18 **t**18 **f**17 **b**18. A roughhouse malt that's finesse-free. For those who like their tastebuds Dufft up a bit... **40%**

⟨⟩ **Connoisseurs Choice Dufftown 1993** db **(80) n**19 **t**21 **f**20 **b**20. Sweet, malty and stylish, this is a very drinkable dram. Simplistic, maybe. But infinitely better than the dirty, rubbery stuff hurled at us for the last 20-30 years... **43%**. *Gordon & MacPhail.*

⟨⟩ **Kingsbury's "The Selection" Dufftown 1999** Hogshead cask nos. 2622/2623, dist May 99, bott July 06 **(83) n**21 **t**21 **f**20 **b**21. So rare to find this beast uncaged. A much better prospect when young and well casked. Obvious limitations and still a propensity to do battle all over the palate but the pure barley elements are a treat. **43%. ncf.** *Japan Imports System. 926 bottles.*

**Murray McDavid Maverick Dufftown Aged Over 10 Years** Bourbon cask W0405, Syrah finish from Languedoc region, dist 93, bott 04 **(79) n**20 **t**21 **f**19 **b**19. Pretty good. And probably the fruitiest expression I've ever come across. Falls out of sync towards the finish, but trying to guide a Dufftown is like  attempting to stop a 100mph train by holding your hand out and closing your eyes. **46%. nc ncf.**

⟨⟩ **Murray McDavid Dufftown 1993 Aged 14 Years** Bourbon/ Guigal St. Joseph Syrah **(79) n**20 **t**19 **f**20 **b**20. Big malt that lumbers about the palate rather slobbishly. Dufftown is rarely known for finesse and you'll do well to find any here, despite the best efforts of some pretty decent casks. **46%**

⟨⟩ **Murray McDavid Dufftown 1997** Bourbon/Syrah **(76) n**18 **t**19 **f**20 **b**19. My poor 'ol tastebuds! Having just been duffed-up for the second time in 20 minutes by a Dufftown, I can hear them pining for a non ex-Bell's behemoth. **46%**

⫶⫶⫶ **Old Malt Cask Dufftown Aged 30 Years** dist Mar 77, bott Apr 07 **(76)** n18 t20 f19 b19 There is an unwritten law that says that malts that are a bit rubbish when they are young (Fettercairn, Littlemill, Caperdonich et al) can be quite brilliant when older. Here is a syrupy exception. **50%**. *Douglas Laing. 303 bottles.*

⫶⫶⫶ **Provenance Dufftown Aged 12 Years Sherry Finish** dist Winter 95, bott Winter 07 **(86)** n21 t22 f21 b22. From a distillery that is so often a dud, this has more than its fair share of charming, even delicate, moments with a very attractive clean barley theme – despite the sherry intervention. And it's not often you can say that – with or without the sherry! Highly drinkable. **46%**. *Douglas Laing.*

**Vom Fass Dufftown 11 Years Old (73)** n18 t20 f18 b17. Mildly soapy cask redeemed by a big bourbon kick and some curiously raisiny malt. Typical, unwieldy Dufftown scruffbag. **59.4%**. *Austria.*

## DUNGLASS ( see Littlemill)

## EDRADOUR
**Highland (Perthshire), 1837. Signatory. Working.**

**Edradour 10 Years Old** db **(86)** n21 t22 f22 b21. A better version of one of the most inconsistent drams in the world. **40%**

**Edradour 'Straight from the Cask' Aged 10 Years Sauternes Finish** cask 04/457/5, dist 20 Apr 94, bott 22 Feb 05 db **(77)** n19 t21 f18 b19. This does have its moment of sheer brilliance, about five seconds in, but it is gone in a trice. The whole secret to great whisky is that it must have balance and if this malt were a trapeze artist it'd be dead by the time it reached half way across. **56.2%**.

## FETTERCAIRN
**Highland (Eastern), 1824. Whyte and Mackay. Working.**

**Fettercairn 12 Year Old** db **(66)** n14 t19 f16 b17. If the nose doesn't get you, what follows probably will...Grim doesn't quite cover it. **40%**

**Fettercairn 1824** db **(69)** n17 t19 f16 b17. By Fettercairn standards, not a bad offering. Relatively free from its inherent sulphury and rubbery qualities, this displays a sweet nutty character not altogther unattractive – though caramel plays a calming role here. Need my arm twisting for a second glass, though. **40%**

⫶⫶⫶ **Cadenhead's Authentic Collection Fettercairn Aged 13 Years** Bourbon Hogshead, dist 1993, bott May 07 **(78)** n19 t19 f20 b20. Hot and boiled candy but more barley than rubber this time. **59%**. *318 bottles.*

**Part Nan Angelen Fettercairn 25 Years Old (79)** n19 t20 f20 b20. Decent sherry influence, but rather thick and muddled. **40%**

**Scott's Selection Fettercairn 1989** bott 05 **(76)** n18 t20 f19 b19. Big barley sugar kick; cumbersome, awkward and cloying; could well appeal to liqueur lovers. **55.9%**.

## GLEN ALBYN
**Highland (Northern) 1846–1983. Demolished.**

**Gordon & MacPhail Rare Vintage Glen Albyn 1966 (87)** n19 t23 f22 b23. Not sure this malt was ever built for this kind of age, but a sophisticated degree of exotic fruit and smoke-induced spice defies the odds for a delicious trip down Memory Lane. **43%**

**Gordon & MacPhail Rare Vintage Glen Albyn 1975 (78)** n19 t20 f19 b20. Too much soapy age, though the sweet malt and soft smoke linger. **46%**

**Old Malt Cask Glen Albyn 35 Years Old** dist 26 Sept 69, bott Jul 05 **(90)** n24 a star-studded aroma for something this ancient: the oak weaves delicate vanilla patterns around the apple-honey-barley lead. As aromas go, a veritable gold nugget for its age; t23 early barley absolutely rips through the tastebuds helped along the way by a glossy sweetness and a puff of smoke and cocoa; f21 the drying oak lays claim with tolerable force; b22 understandable signs of longevity, but overall this is simply wonderful. **50%**. *229 bottles.*

**Rarest of the Rare Glen Albyn 1979** cask 3960, dist Dec 79, bott Mar 06 **(91)** n23 melon and barley play host to a clever, nose-nipping spiciness. So relaxed: supreme confidence here; **t**23 the incredibly fresh, salivating barley intertwines with glorious vanilla to give a drier tier to the delicately sweet malt; **f**22 some chalky vanilla and mocha but the barley holds true; **b**23 of Scotland's disappearing malts, this is going with flourish. **57.3%.** *Duncan Taylor. 244 bottles.*

## GLENALLACHIE
### Speyside, 1968. Chivas. Working.

Glenallachie 15 Years Old Distillery Edition db **(81) n**20 **t**21 **f**19 **b**19. Real battle between nature and nurture: an exceptional sherry butt has silk gloves and honied marzipan, while a hot-tempered bruiser lurks beneath. **58%**

Glenallachie Cask Strength Edition 15 Years Old dist 89, bott 05 db **(86) n**21 **t**23 **f**20 **b**21. You should never expect too much from this distillery, but this is an unusual expression this does little to impress but much to entertain. **58%. ncf.**

Cadenhead's Authentic Collection Glenallachie Aged 17 Years Bourbon hogshead, dist 89, bott Feb 07 **(88) n**22 distinct tangerine thread amid the firm oak and deft barley. A delightful surprise as the balance is lovely **t**23 the charm offensive continues as the rich barley counters the usual hotness to deliver an impassioned maltiness; **f**21 good length and a biscuity delivery before the natural caramels and bitterness intervene; **b**22 the best Glenallachie bottled? Certainly I have never tasted a superior expression and for once I have to say this is a malt that unquestionably delights. **58.5%.** *Cadenhead's. 240 bottles.*

Connoisseurs Choice Glenallachie 1992 **(69) n**16 **t**19 **f**17 **b**17. Scotch malt whisky's version of Dickensian gruel. And badly made gruel at that... **43%.** *Gordon & MacPhail.*

Connoisseurs Choice Glenallachie 1992 **(67) n**18 **t**17 **f**16 **b**16. Sweaty armpits: this really isn't Scotland's finest distillery, is it. **46%.** *Gordon & MacPhail.*

Dun Bheagan Glenallachie Aged 13 Years Sherry finish **(68) n**19 **t**18 **f**15 **b**16. Just dreadful. Further confirmation, hardly that it's needed, that here is a distillery which should rarely be bottled. **43%.** *Ian Macleod.*

Provenance Glenallachie Aged 12 Years Refill Hogshead DMG 1879, dist Spring 93, bott Winter 06 **(83) n**19 **t**21 **f**22 **b**21. A rare beast: an attractive and drinkable Glenallachie. Vindaloo-esque but the barley is clean, crisp and precise with a sexy little sweetening of the malt. A really enjoyable experience...and it's not often I've said that about one of these Johnnies. **46%.**

## GLENBURGIE
### Speyside, 1810. Chivas. Working.

Glenburgie Aged 15 Years Bott code L00/129 db **(84) n**22 **t**23 **f**19 **b**20. Doing so well until the spectacularly flat, bitter finish. Orangey citrus and liquorice had abounded. **46%**

Dun Bheagan Glenburgie 1992 Aged 14 Years dist May 92 **(87) n**21 delicate and clean: pure essence of Speyside; **t**22 youthful barley at its most mouth-watering and zingy; **f**22 what little oak there is finally catches up to offer a drier element; **b**21 another delightful little essay from a well made malt maturing in a well-used cask. **43%. nc ncf.**

Gordon & MacPhail Reserve Glenburgie 1990 bott 09 Aug 05 **(91) n**24 stupendous! Classic aroma of over-ripe dates and mellow spices. Just so rare these days...; **t**23 big, bitter-sweet with loads of toffee-apple and a sub-plot of oily malt. A real chewathon; **f**22 relatively flat, but a soft retreat with caramel lingering about; **b**22 for those looking for big, nutty in-your-face chestnut-coloured sherry, time to use up a few air miles to the USA. **40%.** *US Market.*

Kingsbury's "The Selection" Glenburgie 1999 Hogshead cask nos. 2859/2860, dist Feb 99, bott July 06 **(85) n**20 **t**23 **f**21 **b**21. Thick, clean barley but with limited complexity and development. **43%. ncf.** *Japan Imports System Co. Ltd. 883 bottles.*

## GLENCADAM
### Highland (Eastern), 1825. Angus Dundee. Working.

Glencadam Aged 15 Years db **(84) n**19 **t**22 **f**22 **b**21. The first distillery-bottled Glencadam I can remember thanks to new owners and the brakes are never taken off. The middle and early finale are really quite sublime with that glorious malt-intense signature that offers the kind of irresistible drive and style to the tastebuds that Frank Lampard gives to Chelsea...and it's worth getting just for that. But something, a roasty caramel maybe, is holding back on the start and finish: oh, what might have been! Delicious all the same! **40%**

⁘ **Berry's Own Selection Glencadam 1973** Cask no. 706, bott 06 **(90) n22** quite a fat nose with a puff of unexpected smoke for extra weight; **t22** distinctly fruity with no little citrus battling it out with the uncompromisingly rich barley; **f22** relatively stark, but some bourbony elements kick in to ensure great complexity at the death – especially when the smoke returns; **b24** what a great little Highlander: Glencadam is little known but many more superbly balanced bottlings like this just might see it become a sought-after malt. Excellent. **46%**.

**Cadenhead's Authentic Collection Glencadam Aged 17 Years** Bourbon, dist 89, bott May 06 **(81) n20 t21 f20 b20**. A pulsing, pounding malt that's big on barley but wants for development **57.8%**. *234 bottles*.

**D&M Aficionados' Club Bottling Glencadam Aged 31 Years** cask 2, dist Dec 74 **(86) n22 t23 f20 b21**. Holds together despite the splinters; the bourbon theme is never less than attractive. **43%. nc ncf.** *US by Angus Dundee* .

⁘ **D&M Connoisseurs' Club Bottling Glencadam Aged 14 Years** Cask no. 1453, dist May 92 **(88) n21** more than a sprig of mint to this one; the oak has been busy but the malt refuses to crack; **t22** light but exceptionally firm, brittle even; the intensity of the oak begins surprisingly early, but it's of the dry cocoa variety and delicious, especially when the spices kick in; the sweetness is sparse but what little there is barley-led; **f23** one of the best renditions of a bourbony-bitter chocolate finishe for years; almost like an old-fashioned Scapa in its pomp; **b22** just lovely malt which is perhaps limited complexity-wise, but what it does do is accomplished with a touch of class. **46%**. *US by Angus Dundee Distillers*.

**Dun Bheagan Glencadam 20 Years Old** Hogshead **(80) n20 t19 f21 b20**. For all its age it remains hot stuff. The honey influence will win friends, though. **48%**

**Gordon & MacPhail Reserve Glencadam 1974** dist 2 Sep 74, bott 28 Oct 05 **(95) n24** high calibre honey-oak dovetailing; Battenburg cake; **t23** wonderful firmness to both the barley and oak with hints of acacia honey and so much more, including the orangey bit in a Jaffa Cake; **f24** long, exceptionally rich with marzipan – Danish, one presumes – and dark chocolate; **b24** Copenhagen has become even more wonderful with the best Glencadam I've ever come across. This is a masterpiece malt. **46%**. *182 bottles*.

⁘ **Old Malt Cask Glencadam Aged 21 Years** dist June 85, bott Apr 07 **(95) n24** super-complex: butterscotch, marzipan with apricot filling, lightly salted barley.....and so much more; **t24** those apricots deliver on arrival then a wave of vanilla-led barley; spices sweep in...as they must!! **f23** drier but with the fruits and barley still haggling for presence; excellent pepper tingle; **b24** a true gem of a cask with a nose that, alone, could seduce a eunuch. **50%**. *Douglas Laing. 311 bottles*.

**Platinum Glencadam 1985** dist Jun 85, bott Nov 05 **(84) n19 t22 f21 b22**. A typically curious malt, as one expects from this distillery from this time. The heat in the whisky suggests hard-pressed stills, but there is a sheen to the honey-barley intensity that is quite beautiful. **54.2%**. *Douglas Laing. 306 bottles*.

**Vom Fass Glencadam 13 Years Old (83) n21 t21 f20 b21**. Charmingly fruity and light with emphasis on citrus and barley sugar. **40%**.

**The Whisky Fair Artist Edition Glencadam Aged 32 Years** Bourbon Hogshead, dist Apr 1973, bott Feb 06 **(81) n19 t21 f20 b21**. Some chewy chocolate pudding for desert but the main course is a feisty, oaky affair. **46.4%. nc ncf.** *Germany. 87 bottles*.

⁘ **The Whisky Fair Glencadam Aged 32 Years** Sherry Wood, dist 1974, bott 07 **(83) n22 t22 f19 b20**. Some lovely red berry fruits are crushed latterly under oak. **57.3%**.

# GLENDRONACH
### Speyside, 1826. Chivas. Working.

**Glendronach Original Aged 12 Years Double Matured** db **(88) n23** dense, ripe plummy fruit: serious touches of fruitcake, complete with brown sugars. Oak does give a vanilla topping but barley also punches through. Some coal smoke buzzes around, too. Needs some time to get the full story; **t21** some serious infighting here, some of it off-key, between grape and grain. The grape wins but is not entirely unbloodied as the mouthwatering barley has some juicy moments; **f22** the lull after the storm; much more measured doses of bitter marmalade and vanilla, softening towards a gentle spice within the cocoa. Very different; **b**22 vastly improved from the sulphur-tainted bottling of last year. In fact, their most enjoyable standard distillery bottling I've had for many years. But forget about the whisky: the blurb on the back is among the most interesting you likely to find anywhere. And I quote: "Founder James Allardice called the original Glendronach, 'The Guid Glendronach'. But there's no need to imitate his marketing methods. The first converts to his malt were the 'ladies of the night' in Edinburgh's Canongate!" Fascinating. And as a professional whisky taster I am left wondering: did they swallow or spit... **40%**

**Glendronach 15 Years Old** db **(83)** n20 t22 f20 b21. Chocolate fudge and grape juice to start then tails off towards a slightly bitter, dry finish. **40%**

**Glendronach Aged 33 Years** db Oloroso Sherry **(95)** n24 it's as if your head is stuck in a sherry butt still in the bodega; be transported back in time to when soft, very gently smoked malt still had the wherewithal to link with the grape and offer something teasing yet profound, ripe yet beautifully fresh. Majestic...; **t**24 sublime sherry arrival with a wonderful toffee-apple, honeycomb and leather (almost very old bourbon) theme; the malt is almost thick enough to cut, and the softest smoke imaginable combines to add extra weight to the fruit; **f**23 the oak now arrives, but offering layers of vanilla to complement the fruit; still the smoke drifts and this adds further to the near bitter-sweet perfection; **b**24 want to know what sherry should really nose like: invest in a bottle of this. This is a vivid malt boasting spellbinding clarity and charm. A golden nugget of a dram, which would have been better still at 46%. **40%**

**The Glendronach 1968** db **(92)** n23 nuts, clean sherry of the highest order; **t**22 exceptionally together with the most vibrant oloroso: not a single off note; **f**23 astonishing depth, with more than a touch of pot still Demerara (PM mark to be precise); **b**24 an almost extinct style of sherry that is faultless in its firmness and clarity. This was bottled in 1993 – I remember it well. Astonishingly, some bottles have just turned up in Whisky of the World Duty Free in UK and this is how it tastes now. Grab while you can. **43%**

**Murray McDavid Mission IV Glendronach 1976 Aged 27 Years (87)** n21 t23 f21 **b**22. A curiously attractive dram from an enigmatic distillery. **46%**

**Murray McDavid Glendronach 1990 Aged 16 Years** Bourbon/Port, bott 06 **(84)** n22 t22 f19 **b**21. I admit this is a distillery I have long failed to get my head round in its normal state. But when confronted by something that looks like paraffin and surely from Pipes on express delivery from Oporto, then my horizons are widened again. If anything the Port is too good, as the malt is lost without trace towards the finish. But the juicy arrival to that point is a delight, as are the soft spices that offer needed ballast. **46%. nc ncf.** *3,500 bottles.*

**Old Malt Cask Glendronach 20 Years Old** dist 2 Feb 85, bott 18 Apr 05 **(88)** n23 t22 f21 **b**22. A rum cove. **50%.**

# GLENDULLAN (see also below)
### Speyside, 1898–1985. Closed.

⊰⊱ **Singleton of Glendullan 12 Years Old** db **(87)** n22 significant oak hides some of the Jamaican ginger; **t**22 a gutsier barley character with stifled honey and the oak dives in again; **f**21 dry with a slight return of ginger; **b**22 much more age than is comfortable for a 12-y-o. **40%**

⊰⊱ **Murray McDavid Glendullan 1993 Aged 14 Years** Bourbon/Rioja **(79)** n21 t19 f20 b19 Weird, eh? I adore Glendullan. I have a house in Kentucky, such is my love for bourbon. And my wine of the season I had served in any football boardroom during 05/06 was a Rioja at Coventry City. Yet put these together...works in part, but too bitty. Though I love the chocolate finale. **46%**

**Murray McDavid Glendullan 1996** Bourbon/Grenache, bott 05 **(81)** n20 t21 f20 **b**20. Curious, salted celery to the nose; the behaviour on the palate is no less singular. Clean, spicy and confused – and that's just the guy writing these notes. **46%. nc ncf.** *3,600 bottles.*

**Old Malt Cask Glendullan Aged 14 Years** Refill Hogshead 2131, dist Aug 91, bott Sept 05 **(86)** n22 t23 f20 **b**21. An oily expression. **50%. nc ncf.**

**Provenance Glendullan Aged 10 Years** Sherry finish, dist Nov 94, bott Dec 04 **(80)** n22 t21 f18 **b**19. Finishing in sherry has bigged-up the nose, but at what cost to the delivery and finish on the palate? **46 %.** *McGibbon's.*

**Provenance Glendullan 14 Years** dist Aug 91, bott Aug 05 **(89)** n22 light, clean barley; **t**23 a salivating freshness that pulses ripe barley; **f**22 soft oils help sweeten and lengthen the finale with a touch of cocoa at the death; **b**22 impeccably behaved and makes all the right noises. **46%**. *McGibbon's.*

## GLENDULLAN (see also above)
### Speyside, 1972. Diageo. Working.

Glendullan Aged 8 Years db **(89) n**20 fresh, gingery, zesty; **t**22 distinctly mealy and malty. **f**24 brilliant – really stunning grassy malt powers through. Speyside in a glass – and a nutshell; **b**23 this is just how I like my Speysiders: young fresh and uplifting. A charming malt.

Glendullan Aged 12 Years (new stock circa 03, bottling mark – on reverse of label – L19R01457997, dark green print) db **(77) n**19 **t**20 **f**19 **b**19. Oily, flat and bitter towards the finish. Really disappointing. **43%**. *Flora and Fauna range.*

Glendullan Aged 12 Years batch no. 00195262 db **(85) n**22 **t**22 **f**20 **b**21. Intriguing and a good example of where oak starts to lop points off what had recently been excellent stuff. **43%**

Glendullan 1978 Rare Malt db **(88) n**23 exceptional piquancy to this with the quietness of the oak shattered by a lemon-citrus shrill. Genuinely wonderful; **t**22 a lovely, tart start with that citrus making a crashing entry but the oak barges in soon after and coffee is soon on the menu; **f**21 more coffee and lemon cake, though it by now a very small slice; **b**22 Sherlock Holmes would have loved this one: he would have found it lemon-entry. **56.8%**

## GLEN ELGIN
### Speyside, 1900. Diageo. Working.

Glen Elgin Aged 12 Years db **(89) n**23 blistering, mouthwatering fruit of unspecified origin. The intensity of the malt is breathtaking; **t**24 stunning fresh malt arrival, salivating barley that is both crisp and lush: then a big round of spice amid some squashed, over-ripe plums. Faultless mouthfeel; **f**20 the spice continues as does the intense malt but is devalued dramatically by a bitter-toffee effect; **b**22 absolutely murders Cragganmore as Diageo's top dog bottled Speysider. The marks would be several points further north if one – rightly or wrongly – didn't get the feeling that some caramel was weaving a derogatory spell. Brilliant stuff nonetheless. States Pot Still on label – not to be confused with Irish Pot Still. This is 100% malt... and it shows! **43%**

Glen Elgin Aged 32 Years db **(68) n**15 **t**19 **f**17 **b**17. Unacceptably soapy and sappy, even for its age. Really disappointing. **42.3%**

Cadenhead's Authentic Collection Glen Elgin-Glenlivet Aged 13 Years **(94) n**24 probably a second-fill bourbon cask allows unfettered insight into the green apple fruitiness that mingles with grist and coal dust. Complex and seductive; **t**24 much younger than its 13 years, and that's great news for Glen Elgin which peaks earlier than most. Salivating and green, some watered honey sweetens the juicy, sharp grass; **f**23 layers of chewability and even the oak-flaked vanilla cannot dampen the freshness; **b**23 when asked what is my favourite Speysider, I often consider Glen Elgin before plumping for Balvenie. If more truly genius casks like this were around, the answer might be different. **59.5%**. *672 bottles.*

Connoisseurs Choice Glen Elgin 1968 **(84) n**23 **t**21 **f**20 **b**20. Expressive nose full of diced pineapple and suet: loses it in the telling of the tale. **46%**. *G&M.*

Mackillop's Choice Glen Elgin cask 3542, dist Jul 76 **(88) n**22 **t**23 **f**22 **b**22. Gloriously textured whisky: reminds me of a fruit trifle of the mid '70s! **42.6%**.

Old Malt Cask Glen Elgin Aged 20 Years dist Apr 85, bott Oct 05 **(83) n**21 **t**21 **f**21 **b**20. Surprisingly salty for an Elgin; an oaky tang has also got in to disrupt the high quality malt harmony. **50%**. *Douglas Laing. 302 bottles.*

## GLENESK
### Highland (Eastern), 1897–1985. Closed.

Connoisseurs Choice Glenesk 1984 **(78) n**19 **t**21 **f**19 **b**19. Still too syrupy for its own good, but so much better than other G&M bottlings from this less than distinguished late distillery. **43%**. *Gordon & MacPhail.*

⸫ **Connoisseurs Choice Glenesk 1984** db **(83)** n19 t21 f21 b22. A very rare malt this, but the style is consistent. Here the sweetness is down slightly and hangs together and harmonises much, much better than in many previous bottlings. An attractive, surprise package. **43%**. *Gordon & MacPhail.*

# GLENFARCLAS
## Speyside, 1836. J&G Grant. Working.

**Glenfarclas 8 Years Old** db **(89)** n23 soft, intense malt under a gentle layer of clean grape and blood oranges; the most distant and surprising hint of freshly grilled kipper; t22 luxurious and gentle, the sweetness is Demerara oriented; f22 much more oak than one might expect from a youngster; some quite excellent fruit follow-through; b22 just such a much more together, harmonious and confident dram than the old bottling: an absolute little cracker. A taste of their final bottling under the old label shows all the above except the kipper on the nose. **40%**

**Glenfarclas 8 Years Old** db **(86)** n21 t22 f22 b21. Less intense sherry allows the youth of this malt to stand out. Mildly quirky as a Glenfarclas and enormous entertainment. **40%**

**Glenfarclas 10 Years Old** db **(80)** n19 t20 f22 b19. Always an enjoyable malt, but for some reason this version never seems to fire on all cylinders. There is a vague honey sheen which works well with the barley, but struggles for balance and the nose is a bit sweaty. Still has distinctly impressive elements but an odd fish. **40%**

**Glenfarclas 105 Cask Strength 10 Years Old** db **(91)** n22 perfect fresh sherry influence; clean, intense, charismatic, fruity and precise; t23 rather confusing as the might of the malt and sherry battle for supremacy: takes time to settle and the drier oak helps enormously to accentuate the honied qualities of the malt; f23 a fine, layered oak seeing off the sweeter honeycomb theme for a distinguished finale; b23 this, for various reasons, has been a regular dram of mine for over 20 years. It has been at its very best in recent bottlings, though the nose here doesn't quite hit the heights. **60%**

**Glenfarclas 12 Years Old** db **(89)** n22 oops! Nothing like its usual near brilliant self early on, but some golden strands of honey compensate handsomely; t23 recovers superbly to offer lashings of the trademark honeycomb amid a riot of gentle oaky spice; the light sprinkling of muscovado sugar is sublime, as is the crushed raisins; f22 more burned honeycomb and some subtle extra oak offers dry vanilla; b23 from this sample just the odd cask has tarnished the usual brilliance, but it's still good enough to offer moments of Speyside most glorious. **43%**

**Glenfarclas 15 Years Old** db **(95)** n23 such is the intensity of the fruit and sugar-rich barley, there is an element of medium ester Jamaican pot still rum to this, a feeling intensified by an orangey-oak influence that seems greater than 15 years. The top-shelf sherry, though, is of a classical type rarely found these days, though common 30 years ago; t24 succulent and stupendous. Barley sugar shows first then a sherry input that borders on intense but dissipates as the spicy oak digs in; f24 long, chewy, a tad oily and fades with a wonderful coffee-vanilla combination and a late surge of something bourbony; b24 Eureka!!! The 15-y-o back to how I can remember it in the past. Some of you may have been scared away by some less than impressive recent bottlings. It's safe to come back because now it has been returned to its position as one of Scotland's most sublime malts. The quality of the sherry is astonishing; its interaction with the barley is a wondrous joy. Go find and get... **46%**

**Glenfarclas 17 Years Old** db **(93)** n23 just so light and playful: custard powder lightens and sweetens, sultana softens, barley moistens, spice threatens...; t23 the relaxed sherry influence really lets the honey deliver; delightfully roasty and well spiced towards the middle; f23 when I was a kid there was a candy – pretend tobacco, no less! – made from strands of coconut and sweetened with a Demerara syrup. My, this takes me back...; b24 an excellent age for this distillery, allowing just enough oak in to stir up the complexity. A stupendous addition to the range. **40%**

**Glenfarclas 21 Years Old** db **(83)** n20 t23 f19 b21. A chorus of sweet, honied malt and mildly spiced, teasing fruit on the fabulous mouth arrival and middle compensates for the blips. **43%**.

**Glenfarclas 25 Years Old** db **(88)** n22 a heavy, impervious nose with the sherry and oak providing a cleanly-built wall; t23 much softer with an immediate mouthwatering delivery full of prime, sweet barley and then toasted raisins; **f21** soft vanilla; fruitcake and cream; **b22** an distinct improvement on previous bottlings with the finish here having much more to say. **43%**

**Glenfarclas 30 Years Old** db **(85) n**20 **t**22 **f**21 **b**22. Flawed yet juicy. **43%**

**Glenfarclas 40 Years Old Millennium Edition** db **(92) n**23 **t**23 **f**23 **b**23. An almost immaculate portrayal of an old-fashioned, high-quality malt with unblemished sherry freshness and depth. The hallmark of quality is the sherry's refusal to dominate the spicy, softly peated malt. The oak offers a bourbony sweetness but ensures a rich depth throughout. Quite outstanding for its age. **nc ncf.**

**Glenfarclas 1954 Aged 46 Years** dist 16 Jun 54, bott 27 Jul 00 db **(96) n**24 the clarity of the sherry defies belief; just a fraction too much oak for perfection but the kumquats and most subtle coriander give this such a delightful lift. A squirt of soft peat balances it out gloriously; **t**25 Faultless. Absolute perfect harmonisation on the palate as the dissolving oloroso integrates seamlessly with the rich barley and developing spices. The chewiness is provided by German-style caramelized biscuit, the elegance by a clever mixture and intriguing of Muscovado and Demerara sugars; **f**23 edges towards oak-fuelled bitterness, but some soft peats generate an excellent sweet, earthy repost; the oak is big and slightly bitter towards the end; **b**24 sincere apologies for missing out on this in earlier editions of the Bible. Apparently, though, this can still be found. Buy two: one to drink, the other to be buried with. **43%.** *1,193 bottles.*

**Glenfarclas 50 Years Old** db **(92) n**24 Unique. Almost a marriage between 20-y-o bourbon and intense, old-fashioned sherry. Earthy, weighty stuff that repays time in the glass and oxidization because only then does the subtlety become apparent and a soft peat-reek reveal itself; **t**23 an unexpected sweet – even mouthwatering - arrival, again with a touch of peat to add counter ballast to the intense richness of the sherry. The oak is intense from the middle onwards, but of such high quality that it merely accompanies rather then dominates; **f**22 warming black peppers ping around the palate; some lovely cocoa oils coat the mouth for a bitter-sweet, warming and very long finish; **b**23 Most whiskies cannot survive such great age. This one really does bloom in the glass and the earthy, peaty aspect makes it all the more memorable. It has taken 50 years to reach this state. Give a glass of this at least an hour's inquisition, as I have. Your patience will be rewarded many times over. **44.4%**

⠿ **Glenfarclas 1952 The Family Casks** Cask no. 1712, plain Hogshead db **(78) n**21 papaya fruit and crushed cherry stone; **t**19 the oak has taken over, leaving enough for a Fisherman's Friend sweetness; **f**19 cough sweet. Or, a sweet that makes you cough... **b**19 perfectly drinkable. Quite enjoyable. But this is old whisky. And tastes like it. **56.5%.** *110 bottles.*

⠿ **Glenfarclas 1953 The Family Casks** Cask no. 1678, Sherry Butt db **(87) n**23 fruit spirit: cherry and raspberry brandy softened by burnt honeycomb; **t**21 excellent malt delivery then a sinus-attacking wave of oak; **f**22 recovers superbly for a tangy grapey finale; **b**21 myriad battles are fought to keep the oak in check. Most are won. **53.7%.** *480 bottles.*

⠿ **Glenfarclas 1954 The Family Casks** Cask no. 444, Sherry Butt db **(94) n**22 more oak than an Elizabethan man-of-war. Except this is far from sunk... **t**24 oak scorches into the back and roof of the mouth; countering muscovado tries to douse the flames. The ensuing battle is fabulous.. **f**24 long, ultimately on the dry and mildly bitter side, but not before some mocha and Melton cake have made their fabulous marks, as well as marmalade and cherry preserve; **b**24 simply defies time and belief. Carries the scars of 52 summers, for sure. But with the same pride a legionnaire would wear his trophies of combat. **52.6%.** *406 bottles.*

⠿ **Glenfarclas 1955 The Family Casks** Cask no. 2211, Sherry Butt db **(88) n**23 medium roast Brazilian and crushed hazelnuts adds complexity to dried dates; **t**21 big oak start, off balance slightly but stabilised by a pinch of Demerara; **f**22 recovers for an impressive finale with outstanding vanilla camp coffee; **b**22 a proud dram gallantly hanging on to its last sweet traces. **46.1%.** *545 bottles.*

⠿ **Glenfarclas 1956 The Family Casks** Cask no. 1758, Sherry Butt db **(83) n**24 amazingly similar to the '58 but with a shot of extra oak; **t**21 short oloroso blast, soft oils and spice; dries quickly; **f**19 pretty well oaked and bitters up; **b**19 great nose but relentless oak. **47.3%.** *435 bottles.*

⣿ **Glenfarclas 1957 The Family Casks** Cask no. 2111, Sherry Hogshead db **(91) n**23 a hickory/Java coffee combo, only not so camp; the fruit is almost opaque; **t**23 the inside of your mouth puckers as your tastebuds try to negotiate the minefield laid by the massive oak and the intense, sharp sherry; **f**22 traces of molassed barley filter through, as does sherry concentrate; bitter fruit stones abound; **b**23 I left this as the last whisky before finishing the tasting notes to the 2008 edition (this is the 811th and final brand new dram fresh to market to be included this year, and exactly the 950th to be tasted in all). I was born in 1957. And in four and half months I shall be celebrating (?) my 50th birthday. So it had to be. Great whisky. Unquestionably: if you have the balls to take a fourth or fifth mouthful. Enjoyable? Hugely. Providing you strap yourself into your chair first. Ladies and gentlemen. The tasting notes for 2008 are finished. **54%.** *158 bottles.*

⣿ **Glenfarclas 1958 The Family Casks** Cask no. 2245, Sherry Butt db **(88) n**24 outrageous aroma for its age: walnut oil coated on ripe greengage and mildly burnt Dundee cake and sprinkled with demerara...swoon!..; **t**22 lush, juicy delivery then, after about ten seconds, in comes the oak. With a vengeance... **f**20 brown sugars try to head off the oak's excesses; **b**22 keeps its head above the oaky water - just. **51.6%.** *455 bottles.*

⣿ **Glenfarclas 1959 The Family Casks** Cask no. 1816, Sherry Hogshead db **(83) n**22 **t**21 **f**20 **b**20. The nose with its fabulous array of latte coffee, saves this one. The delivery is as searingly oaked as you'll find. **52.5%.** *194 bottles.*

⣿ **Glenfarclas 1960 The Family Casks** Cask no. 1767, Sherry Hogshead db **(95) n**23 thumping blood orange, grape and a sliver of bourbon; **t**25 enormous delivery but absolutely sublime in the honeycomb and molassed mix to the barley and fruitcake, chewy and a touch salty; **f**23 Mysore medium roast coffee under-sprinkled with molassed sugar; long and bitters out; **b**24 yes, there is no doubting the oak is present. The trick is making it sing, which it does almost without a crack'd note. The secret is warming it right up to body temp. Simply marvellous whisky. **52.4%.** *228 bottles*

⣿ **Glenfarclas 1961 The Family Casks** Cask no. 4913, Sherry Hogshead db **(79) n**19 **t**21 **f**19 **b**20. A '61 vintage yet appears to have vague, weird sulphur-type traces....nah, must be my imagination. Something very bitty about it, though. **46%.** *159 bottles.*

⣿ **Glenfarclas 1962 The Family Casks** Cask no. 2645, Sherry Hogshead db **(91) n**23 clean demi-sec oloroso keeps the oak honest; **t**23 warming oloroso: soft grape counters the stinging oak; **f**22 some major age here plus liquorice-lime to balance; **b**23 another summer may have broken this one. **54.8%.** *166 bottles.*

⣿ **Glenfarclas 1963 The Family Casks** Cask no. 4098, Sherry Butt db **(87) n**24 stunningly floral with crushed, dank petals, marzipan and hickory...phew!! **t**22 dry and spiced for all the grape; **f**19 a tad too oaked; bitter; **b**22 borderline. The oak really is big, but the grape holds out – just. The nose is a different matter. **56.7%.** *420 bottles.*

⣿ **Glenfarclas 1964 The Family Casks** Cask no. 4717, Sherry Butt db **(92) n**23 signs of creaking oak but clean, sweetish oloroso stands firm; **t**24 juicy, tangy marmalade and spice; **f**22 gentle, refined finale with grape in ascendant; **b**23 a gentleman dram which speaks quietly despite the obvious power at hand. **53.1%.** *415 bottles.*

⣿ **Glenfarclas 1965 The Family Casks** Cask no. 3861, Sherry Butt db **(86) n**22 **t**21 **f**22 **b**21. No shortage of active, tangy oak. A non-phenol version of Fisherman's Friend. **60%.** *417 bottles.*

⣿ **Glenfarclas 1966 The Family Casks** Cask no. 4177, Sherry Butt db **(95) n**25 faultless. Exactly how you dream a 40 year old sherry butt should be. Curves everywhere, not a jagged edge, just caresses, hints, whispers and innuendoes. A king – or perhaps queen - among casks; **t**23 surprising lightness with some raspberry amid the juicy grape; **f**23 soft honey and spice. Absolutely no evidence of oaky deterioration; **b**24 how fitting this whisky is the same colour as Alan Ball's hair. Because there is no greater way of toasting the memory of the man who was 1966. **51.5%.** *514 bottles.*

⣿ **Glenfarclas 1967 The Family Casks** Cask no. 5118, Sherry Hogshead db **(90) n**23 wonderful fino-style dryness, bite and freshness; **t**22 oaky incursions met by chocolate and grape; **f**22 remains fresh and fruit salady mouth-watering; **b**23 diced plain chocolate on the plummy nose; a fruity mishmash on delivery. Tasty, though. **58.5%.** *181 bottles.*

⣿ **Glenfarclas 1968 The Family Casks** Cask no. 1316, Sherry Butt db **(84) n**21 **t**20 **f**22 **b**21. Despite the massive strength for its age, has a slightly metallic resonance. **65.1%.** *483 bottles.*

**Glenfarclas Vintage 1968** db **(92)** n23 t23 f23 b23. Just one of those sherry casks that was destined for greatness in Scotland. **43%**. *USA*.

⫶⫶⫶ **Glenfarclas 1969 The Family Casks** Cask no. 3184, Sherry Hogshead db **(89)** n22 knots of oak and sweetish liquorice; t22 a real battle between the dry oak and honeycomb; f23 increasingly dry and oaky...then those rich rays of golden syrup breaking through the oaky cloud – unbelievable. Especially when it looked as though age had won; b22 bravo this brave and proud cask. Fights back from the brink with absolute class. **56.2%**. *148 bottles*.

**Glenfarclas 1969** cask 2895, dist 16 May 69, bott 02 Sep 03 db **(85)** n21 t21 f22 b21. An unbelievably relaxed malt for one so old. **40.1%**. *205 bottles*.

**Glenfarclas 1969** cask 2898 dist 16 May 69, bott 02 Sep 03 db **(89)** n23 t24 f21 b21. If it had been able to continue at the pace achieved on mouth arrival we would have had a major classic. **41.7%**. *197 bottles*.

**Glenfarclas 1969** cask 2899, dist 16 May 69, bott 02 Sep 03 db **(92)** n23 t22 f24 b23. Sophisticated and full of honeycomb/Demerara depth. **41.1%**.

⫶⫶⫶ **Glenfarclas 1970 The Family Casks** Cask no. 566, Sherry Butt db **(94)** n24 Jamaica Ginger Cake doused in beautifully clean oloroso; t23 massively mouth-filling with heavyweight fruit punctuated by lazy spice; f23 back to the moist ginger again with black peppers and molassed sugar in equal measures; b24 seriously elegant and complex malt that shows not a single blemish despite the extraordinary great age. A Glenfarclas Great. **53.6%**. *497 bottles*.

**Glenfarclas 1970** db **(83)** n20 t20 f22 b21. Rich and spicy. **50.1%. nc ncf.**

⫶⫶⫶ **Glenfarclas 1971 The Family Casks** Cask no. 140, Sherry Butt db **(93)** n24 Demerara rummy with enormous depth: bitter-sweet heaven with slow build up of big fruit; t24 sandalwood, toffee and berry fruit; f22 thins quite fast, allowing in the vanilla; b23 a noble dram. **57.1%**. *459 bottles*.

⫶⫶⫶ **Glenfarclas 1972 The Family Casks** Cask no. 3546, Sherry Butt db **(83)** n21 t21 f21 b20. Dry, a tad dull and much more natural toffee here. **51.1%**. *645 bottles*.

**Glenfarclas 1972** db **(92)** n23 t23 f23 b23. A steady-as-a-rock malt that never alters course from its deliciously clean-sherried path; some real sophistication here. **43%**

⫶⫶⫶ **Glenfarclas 1973 The Family Casks** Cask no. 2578, Sherry Butt db **(92)** n24 ginger and honeycomb; t22 soft, yielding grape; usual spices abound; f23 vanilla stirs up the complexity; b23 a more gentle expression than most from the mid 70s: one for the faint hearted. **58.8%**. *457 bottles*.

**Glenfarclas Vintage 1973** db **(89)** n24 t21 f22 b22. A deceptively delicate malt where some complexity is over-ridden by oil. **46%**. *Germany*.

⫶⫶⫶ **Glenfarclas 1974 The Family Casks** Cask no. 5786, Sherry Butt db **(93)** n23 salty and seasoned; t23 wonderful orangey-grapey-spicy infusion; Warming spices become positively vicious; f23 some old citrus sinks deeply into the vanilla; the pugilistic spices are positively puckering; b24 what a real brawling dram! A kind of Oliver Reed of malts; shows that touch of class despite those rough diamond edges. **60.8%**. *555 bottles*.

**Glenfarclas 1974** bott 12 Dec 05 db **(89)** n22 heavy duty sherry, and the oak is no less imposing; t23 beautiful, spiced up delivery of intense oloroso leaving space enough for some demerara sweetness to filter through; f22 soft, vanilla wafers with sweetened mocha; b22 almost too indulgent in sherry, but the stunning dark sugar balance offers the perfect counter to the big oak. A real late night dram of substance. **57.4%**. *USA*.

**Glenfarclas 1974 Single Cask** Cask no. 6042, dist 11 Jul 74, bott 26 Oct 04 db **(90)** n22 a curious, unique and highly attractive intertwining of soft sherry and asparagus! t22 asparagus-free development of warming grape that edges towards the Glenfarclas trademark of honeycomb; f23 very long and increasingly roasty: the honeycomb remains a constant and some almondy nuttiness furthers the complexity; b23 one of those beautiful malts that repays careful study. **53.3%**. *288 bottles*.

⫶⫶⫶ **Glenfarclas 1975 The Family Casks** Cask no. 5038, Refill Hogshead db **(92)** n23 chunky marmalade with the oak at full throttle; t22 dry yet salivating. Only a wonderful stratum of juicy grape absorbs the blows; f24 so long, so spicy: so get stuck in...!! b23 dry yet balances wonderfully. Another spicy number. **51.4%**. *187 bottles*.

⫶⫶⫶ **Glenfarclas 1976 The Family Casks** Cask no. 3111, Refill Butt db **(92)** n23 wallows in a Dundee cake fruit richness, complete with nuts and perhaps with a curl of butter;

**t**23 melts on impact to leave a grapey residue. Burnt raisin and plump sultana dominate; **f**23 dries with a suety dryness but barley water and a sprinkle of silver sugar maintains the balance; **b**23 no whisky that's 30 years old has any right to be this juicy and fresh. A malt to take your time over. **49.4%.** *595 bottles.*

⠿ **Glenfarclas 1977 The Family Casks** Cask no. 61, Refill Butt db **(90) n**22 slight, crushed sultana; **t**23 wonderful amalgam of barley sugar and grape juice: light, but on a waxy body; **f**22 delicate banana custard; **b**23 a class, understated act from nose to finale. **59%.** *582 bottles.*

⠿ **Glenfarclas 1978 The Family Casks** Cask no. 587, Refill Hogshead db **(85) n**21 **t**21 **f**22 **b**21. Chewy and fat. Not a hint of bitterness on the well-oiled grape. **50.3%.** *257 bottles.*

**Glenfarclas 1978** db **(83) n**22 **t**21 **f**20 **b**20. Sweet chestnuts and malt to nose; hot, sweet and malty to taste. **53.3%.nc ncf.**

⠿ **Glenfarclas 1979 The Family Casks** Cask no. 146, Plain Hogshead db **(92) n**22 sherbet lemon; lively vanillas; **t**23 eye-watering, mouth-watering sharpness that reveals the distillery's grassy, Speyside roots; **f**24 continues in the same manner with the barley frothing about the palate, light spices teasing and weak golden syrup balancing out the drier oaks; **b**23 for its age, a real surprise cask. Has more life than I do, that's for sure... Sheer class. **52.8%.** *225 bottles.*

**Glenfarclas 1979** db **(89) n**22 big, sweet, chocolate pudding and fruit; **t**23 spicy from the off and a lovely fanning out of chewy malt and burnt fudge; **f**22 very long with some toasted honeycomb in there; **b**22 a big, bruising, fullflavoured malt that takes no prisoners. **51.8%. nc ncf.**

⠿ **Glenfarclas 1980 The Family Casks** Cask no. 1942, Refill Sherry Butt db **(80) n**19 **t**21 **f**20 **b**20. Soft toffee apple, but not entirely flawless. **50.1%.** *681 bottles.*

**Glenfarclas 1980** db **(69) n**16 **t**19 **f**17 **b**17 . Rich but sulphur-stained. **55%**

⠿ **Glenfarclas 1981 The Family Casks** Cask no. 29, Refill Sherry Hogshead db **(86) n**20 **t**22 **f**22 **b**22. Enjoyable, especially the explosive delivery. **52.4%.** *234 bottles.*

**Glenfarclas 1982 Vintage** db **(90) n**22 fat sultanas and fresh-cut grass; **t**22 immensely sweet by Glenfarclas standards with a big barley rush; **f**23 stunningly layered with delicate vanilla found with varying levels of toastiness; **b**23 a good choice for the market as there is extraordinary youth for a malt so old. Just so clean and quietly sophisticated. **43%.** *Spain.*

⠿ **Glenfarclas 1982 The Family Casks** Cask no. 2213, Refill Sherry Hogshead db **(82) n**19 **t**21 **f**21 **b**21. Silky, lush, toffeed and well spiced. **58.3%.** *258 bottles.*

⠿ **Glenfarclas 1983 The Family Casks** Cask no. 50, Refill Hogshead db **(88) n**20 tight, a tad untidy; **t**22 firm barley which slowly blossoms into a wonderful, bitter-sweet spicefest; **f**24 better balance as the barley shines and muscovado sugar sorts out the oak; **b**22 a sunshine after a rainy afternoon malt **56%.** *302 bottles.*

⠿ **Glenfarclas 1984 The Family Casks** Cask no. 6028, Plain Hogshead db **(93) n**23 citrus!! What's all this about? Nostrils-full of barley...; **t**23 more citrus on delivery with soft, mildly chalky oak dovetailing with the grassy, mouth-watering barley; **f**23 lemon then a light dusting of cocoa; **b**24 at first I thought I had been poured malt from the wrong distillery until I saw the cask type. By no means the first non-sherry Glenfarclas, but perhaps the most lemony-fresh and palate-cleansing at this age. So, so lovely! **51.3%.** *267 bottles.*

⠿ **Glenfarclas 1985 The Family Casks** Cask no. 2826, Refill Sherry Hogshead db **(91) n**23 apple crumble and near cinnamon; **t**23 lush, warmed plum pudding on a caramel base; **f**22 custard pie and light spice; **b**23 what a tart! And a fruity one at that... **46.3%.** *329 bottles.*

**Glenfarclas 1985 18 Years Old** Refill Sherry Hogshead cask no. 2823, dist Sept 85, bott Oct 03 db **(83) n**21 **t**19 **f**23 **b**20. Hot whisky: a strange choice for a single cask, though the fabulous honey theme that tries to develop may be a clue. The finish is outstanding. **48.5%.** *308 bottles.*

⠿ **Glenfarclas 1986 The Family Casks** Cask no. 3434, Refill Sherry Puncheon db **(87) n**22 fruity, but with nip and bite; **t**22 the spices initially rise above the laid-back sherry-toffee theme; some honeycomb notes counter the drier oaks; **f**21 genuinely lethargic finale with very light oak; **b**22 the fight on the nose and delivery isn't matched by the sleepy follow through. **56.5%.** *521 bottles.*

**Glenfarclas 1986 Fino Sherry Cask** db **(90) n**22 **t**22 **f**23 **b**23. An eye-closing, think-about-it dram. A laid-back classic. **43%**

**Glenfarclas 1987 The Family Casks** Cask no. 1010, Refill Sherry Hogshead db **(90)** n22 floral with violets et al; t23 lovely silky delivery with restrained spices but no shyness to the stewed plum and toffee; f22 more caramel trifle; b23 an honest to goodness cask with not a hint of a fault. **55.1%.** *262 bottles.*

**Glenfarclas Vintage 1987 Refill Oloroso** Cask db **(93)** n23 t23 f23 b24. Sherry bottlings of this integrity and class are appallingly thin on the ground. I have come all the way to Europe to track it down: and worth every mile travelled, too. **46%.** *Mahler-Besse, Bordeaux.*

**Glenfarclas 1988 The Family Casks** Cask no. 7033, Sherry Butt db **(85)** n21 t21 f22 b21. Clean, if a tad soapy. Significantly oily. But good barley richness. **56.3%.** *572 bottles.*

**Glenfarclas 1989 The Family Casks** Cask no. 11721, Sherry Butt db **(94)** n23 almost identical to the 1990 bottling; t24 see 1990 f23 slight change here with more of a molassed, old bourbon accent here, otherwise identical; b24 the 1989 and 1990 could be twins born a year apart – astonishing! **60%.** *600 bottles.*

**Glenfarclas 1989 14 Years Old** Plain Oak Hogshead cask no. 505, dist 89, bott Oct 03 db **(92)** n23 t24 f22 b23. Exceptionally well-made whisky where the malt positively glows. **58.7%.** *307 bottles.*

**Glenfarclas 1989 Oloroso Sherry Cask 1st Fill** db **(90)** n24 cream toffee, mocha, brown sugar – and not an off-note in sight; t23 mouthwatering sweet malt despite the forming dry notes. The oak is chunky for its age, but the malt and sherry are wonderfully sure-footed. Not dissimilar to a demerara pot-still rum in mouthfeel; f21 the oak gathers pace to offer liquorice and soft oils; b22 it says "1st fill Sherry" on the label. A waste of ink. Just one sniff will tell you! **43%**

**Glenfarclas Vintage 1990** db **(88)** n23 t22 f21 b22. Just refuses to go that extra mile for complexity. **46%.** *Germany.*

**Glenfarclas 1990 The Family Casks** Cask no. 9246, Sherry Butt db **(94)** n23 big thickish, faultless sherry well padded with oak; t24 another fruit 'n' spice blitz with oloroso oozing into every pore; f23 long, lush, sensibly spiced and that house chocolate style coming through loud and clear; b24 this is how every sherry butt should be. It almost brings a tear to the eye. **58.9%.** *617 bottles.*

**Glenfarclas 1991 The Family Casks** Cask no. 5623, Sherry Butt db **(92)** n24 exemplary display of highly complex fruit and toffee tones; some over-ripe cherry, a touch salty and some crushed pine nut; t23 mildly aggressive arrival, mainly thanks to early spices; again complexity rules and the brief raspberry stratum is a treat; f22 simplifies out with the natural toffee; b23 an entrancing malt which has your tastebuds on full alert. **57.9%.** *613 bottles.*

**Glenfarclas 1992 The Family Casks** Cask no. 264, Sherry Butt db **(89)** n23 wonderful marmalade and botanicals; t22 the fruit is voluptuous, the body curvy and soft; f22 long, traces of cocoa and massive chewing power; b22 big, gutsy, oily stuff. **55.5%.** *669 bottles.*

**Glenfarclas 1993 The Family Casks** Cask No. 11, Sherry Butt db **(77)** n19 t20 f19 b19. The three Ss: sherry, spice and sul\*\*\*\*. Shame. **58.9%.** *592 bottles.*

**Glenfarclas 1994 Aged 12 Years** cask no. 3847 db **(92)** n23 fabulous mix of oloroso sherry and Demerara rum. Heady, fruity and vibrant; t24 the big strength is lost in the velvet body; again a rummy theme continues. Pulsing and mouth-watering, the barley battles through; f22 spices and liquorish; b23 a wonderful, unspoiled oloroso cask at its clean, nutty best. **58.3%. sc.** *Germany.*

**Glenfarclas 1994 The Family Casks** Cask no. 2935, Sherry Butt db **(95)** n24 an orangey on a warm, sunny day; beautifully botanical; t24 staggeringly complex from first arrival with the fruit and barley hamming it up and harmonising to the nth degree; f23 lively spices rumble on as the cocoa goes crackers; b24 a fabulous cask choice which appears perfectly to encapsulate the excellence of the distillery. **59.6%.** *628 bottles.*

**Glenfarclas Heritage** db **(91)** n22 an unusually clipped nose with firm and precise malt though the oak does give a suety backdrop; t22 surprisingly mouthwatering despite the dull fruitiness at first then ups the barley voltage; f23 a really classy follow through natural toffee offering a creamy late surge; vanilla and barley intermingles beautifully, as does that understated fruitiness that has been shyly apparent throughout; b24 a real treat of a malt offering stylish intensity. Lucky French! **40%.** *The Heritage Malt Collection, France.*

**Blairfindy Raw Cask 39 Year Old** Sherry butt cask no. 4552, dist 65, bott May 05 **(89)** n23 t21 f22 b23. An intriguing sherry butt with very little colour – or fruit. **55.6%.** *Taiwan.*

**Blairfindy Raw Cask 39 Year Old** Sherry butt cask no. 4003 dist 66, bott June 05 **(88)** n24 t22 f21 b21. A haphazard beast full of fun. **46.6%**. *Taiwan*.

**Blairfindy Raw Cask 40 Year Old** Sherry butt cask 4711, dist 64, bott May 05 **(86)** n22 t21 f21 b22. Phew! A malt bristling with age and chunky intent. **55%**.

**Cadenhead's Authentic Collection Glenfarclas Aged 17 Years** Bourbon Hogshead, dist 88, bott May 05 **(90)** n23 waxy wooden floors, pepper, diced apple and spiced pears: quite superb; t23 shimmering malt of profound intensity; wonderful esters propel the barley-sugar sweetness to every corner of the palate; f22 enormously long with the gristy barley freshness actually upping in tempo; b22 so rare to see Glenfarclas in ex-bourbon form, and on this evidence we are being denied a Speyside classic. Beautifully made and matured, not a blemish to be found. **57%**. *288 bottles*.

**Cadenhead's Authentic Collection Glenfarclas Aged 18 Years** Bourbon Hogshead, dist 88, bott May 06 **(87)** n20 not entirely happy with itself: some farmyardy notes confuse the rich barley; t23 big, semi-thuggish malt offers countless waves of salivating complexity; the oak plays a clever, restrained and spicy part; f22 oak to the fore; b22 firebrand malt that for all its rawness delivers intense quality by the mouthful... **55.2%**. *276 btls*.

꒐꒐꒐ **Cadenhead's Glenfarclas Aged 19 Years** Bourbon, dist 1988, bott May 07 **(86)** n21 t21 f22 b22. An attractive malt offering light – almost green – grape and a radiance to the pulsing barley. **46%**. *306 bottles*.

**Cadenhead's Chairman's Stock Glenfarclas Aged 33 Years** Bourbon Hogshead, dist 72, bott Sep 05 **(78)** n20 t21 f18 b19. The oak has too great a say and isn't really worth listening to. **43.4%**. *132 bottles*.

**Cadenhead's Chairman's Stock Glenfarclas Aged 33 Years** Bourbon Hogshead, dist 73, bott Sept 06 **(93)** n23 zesty, Seville orange with a squeeze of kiwi fruit and blackberry. Yum! t24 for all the fruit nose, it's unmolested barley which arrives first. Soon the fruits are lining up again, not least pithy grape and blackberry; spices abound and astound; f22 oak has a big say after all this time but the cocoa-vanilla dryness counters the earlier fruit with aplomb; b24 as you might expect, a malt of such antiquity takes time to settle and is helped by oxidization. But when it hits its stride becomes a class act of the first order. **42.6%**. *120 btls*.

**The Lord Balliol Single Cask Aged 20 Years** cask no. 1 **(89)** n23 soft grape but with a feisty malt kick; t22 chewy, big, well-matured fruitcake character; f22 molassed sweetness topped with singed raisins; b22 big, knife and fork malt. There is no way of telling which of the two bottlings they have had so far is cask one or two. Hopefully these not [these notes?] will help. **46%. sc.** *282 bottles*.

**The Lord Balliol Single Cask Aged 20 Years** cask no. 2 **(87)** n21 crushed sultana but a little unsettled; t22 immensely sweet barley outperforms the chewy grape; f22 light, golden syrup on fruit chocolate; b22 not the best of starts on the nose, but the sweet character complements the drier, more roasty elements. There is no way of telling which of the two bottlings they have had so far is cask one or two. Hopefully these not will help. **46%. sc.**

**The MacTarnahan Pure Highland Single Malt 1994 Distillation Season Aged Nine Years (87)** n21 t22 f22 b22. Wonderful to see a Speysider this fresh and confident. High quality distilling evident. **46%**. *MacTarnahan's Brewing*.

**The MacTarnahan Pure Highland Single Malt Aged 15 Years (78)** n17 t21 f19 b20. Big, sherried bruiser with enormous burnt raisin and spice but a sulphury shadow spoils the party. **46%**. *MacTarnahan's Brewing, Portland, Oregon*.

꒐꒐꒐ **Milroy's of Soho Tomfarclas 1971 Aged 35 Years** Ex Sherry Hogshead, cask no. 3946, dist 1 Oct 71, bott 7 Dec 06 **(87)** n22 curiously smoked; t22 enormously sweet start – as one sometimes gets from peated malt - with the fruit slowly ingratiating itself; f21 malty, then metallic; b22 odd whisky by any standards. **46%**. *93 bottles*.

꒐꒐꒐ **Scotch Malt Whisky Society Cask 1.134 Aged 36 Years** Sherry Butt, dist Jan 70 **(81)** n19 t22 f20 b20. Sporty and spicy. But slightly out of harmony. **53%**

꒐꒐꒐ **Scotch Malt Whisky Society Cask 1.135 Aged 36 Years** Sherry Butt, dist Nov 70 **(91)** n23 minty sherry; kumquats; t23 brooding oak but some bitter-sweet grape and delightfully soft oils pull it through; f22 unusual chocolate mint finale; b23 only to be drunk After Eight. **54.7%**

⊱ The Whisky Fair Single Speyside Malt Aged 35 Years Oloroso Sherry Butt, dist 1971, bott 2006 **(87)** n23 powering oaks lightened by a sugary coating; t22 I happen to like creosote – which is just as well – wow!!! f21 some pretty weathered strands of oak tie together the muscovado sugar and fruit; b21 a touch of the creosotes reveals a tad too much age. **51.4%**. *Germany*.

⊱ The Whisky Fair Single Speyside Malt Aged 40 Years Oloroso Sherry, dist 1966, bott 2007 **(95)** n24 roasty-oaked but perfectly matched with grape; t24 fabulous sweet delivery allows the barley top billing; more wonderful roasty elements, including coffee and molasses; f23 long, more coffee, slightly less sugar, gorgeous burnt fudge...sigh... b24 well: 1966 must have been one hell of a bloody year at the Glenfarclas distillery...!! **52.4%**. *Germany*.

⊱ The Whisky Fair Single Speyside Malt Aged 41 Years Sherry Wood, dist 1965, bott 2007 **(85)** n21 t21 f22 b21. Heaps of character and attitude. But a bit tight and remarkably similar in cough-sweet style to the distillery's own '65 vintage. **53.5%**

## GLENFIDDICH
### Speyside, 1887. William Grant & Sons. Working.

Glenfiddich Special Reserve (no age statement) db **(88)** n21 t23 f22 b22. No longer produced and now a malt for collectors: one that brings a tear to the eye of us 40-somethings. This is malt that kept us going when none others were obtainable. Never has the term "familiarity breeds contempt" ever been more apposite to any whisky as this. It's become de rigueur in recent years for connoisseurs to rubbish this whisky (though, it has to be said, never by me) as a poor man's malt. A brilliant, effervescent whisky missed more sorely than words can describe. I never thought I would find myself writing those words, but there you have it. I believe in honesty: I have built my reputation on it. And in all honesty, the whisky world is poorer without this unpretentious, landmark malt. The official "Bring Back The No-Age Statement Glenfiddich Special Reserve" campaign starts here. **40%**

Glenfiddich Aged 12 Years Caoran Reserve db **(81)** n20 t22 f19 b20. Pleasant enough, but duller and sweeter than before with complexity at a premium. **40%**

Glenfiddich Aged 12 Years Special Reserve db **(80)** n20 t22 f19 b19. Delicious malt but perhaps a touch too much caramel subtracts from the otherwise juicy maltfest. Just not the same as the old (younger) version. Much flatter and less fun than its predecessor. **40%**

Glenfiddich 15 Years Old db **(95)** n23 beautifully sculpted nose: barley is firm, the oak bourbony, the sweetness controlled; t23 as intense as the nose suggests, again with compartmentalization. Early spices flit about while the malt is in concentrate form. Again the sweetness is allowed to progress only so far; f25 as deft as it's long, some lovely dark fudge and soft liquorice brushed with high roast Java guarantees the weight; b24 one of those stunning expressions this distillery is apt to come up with from time to time to underline the pedigree of its malt. Probably the best and most complete finish of the year: an essay in pure magnificence. **56.8%**

Glenfiddich Aged 15 Years Cask Strength db **(80)** n21 t21 f19 b19. Very toffeed: is it the oak or possibly caramel? Big dram, all the same. **51%**

Glenfiddich Aged 15 Years Solera Reserve db **(93)** n24 a marriage of citrus notes (especially oranges) subtle spices and oak; t23 honey leads the way with balancing spices and oak. The malt remains fresh and refreshing; f23 medium to long with soft sherry and gently building cocoa; b23 this is one of my regular drams, and the one I immediately display to people who rubbish Glenfiddich. Over the years I have noticed a shift in quality in both directions, the best being two marks higher, the worst cropping six points, mainly due to traces of sulphur on the sherry. However, this sample is pretty representative of a quite brilliant Speyside malt of awesome complexity. Just wish they'd up the strength and make it nonchillfiltered and noncoloured. **40%**

Glenfiddich Aged 18 Years Ancient Reserve db **(92)** n24 blood oranges, apples, the most gentle of smoke and oaky saltiness: delicate, complex and enormously sexy; t23 those oranges are there again as the malt melts in the mouth. Quite salty still but sherry and sultanas to fatten things up, brown sugar sweetens things a little; f22 a dry finale of medium length with unsweetened mocha: clean, chewy and well-defined; **b**23 another nail in the coffin of those who sniffily insist that Glenfiddich can't make good whisky. Taste this – and Solera Reserve – then find me two distillery-bottled malts of this age anywhere on Speyside that offers this enormity of complexity and sheer élan.

**Glenfiddich Aged 21 Years Havana Reserve** db **(76)** n20 t20 f18 b18. I know a lot of people are jumping up and down about this one in excitement. But, sorry, I just don't get the picture. Cuban rums tend to be light in character, so in theory it should marry with the distillery's elegant character. However, we seem to have everything cancelling each other out leaving a pleasant experience with a decent cream coffee-toffee middle/finish, but little else besides to really get the pulses racing. **40%**

**Glenfiddich 1974 Aged 29 Years** cask 2336 db **(88)** n23 t23 f19 b23. Not all old Glenfiddich casks show such class: this is a minor gem of almost hypnotic complexity **48.9%** *The Whisky Exchange*

**Glenfiddich 30 Years Old** db **(89)** n22 exotic fruit in custard; t23 a sprightly fruity sweetness gives way to powering waves of barley and chalky vanilla; f21 soft and the most distant echo of smoke; **b**23 a much happier bottling than previously with barley still rampant and some charming complexity. **40%**

**Glenfiddich Rare Collection 40 Years Old** db **(92)** n23 curiously and attractively smoked, lots of sweet vanilla and stunning spices: remarkable and beautiful; t24 brimming with oaky, toasty vanilla, malt punching through for silky, rich and mildly honied middle. Signs of oaky wear and tear, but do not detract from the overall beauty; f22 remains silky with a return of peat, mixed with cocoa; **b**23 quite brilliant for a Glenfiddich of this antiquity: rarely does it survive to this age. In fact, brilliant for any distillery. **43.6%**. *600 bottles.*

**Glenfiddich 1937** db **(94)** n24 smoky, almost agricultural farmyardy, with kippers spitting on the range, salted butter melting into them. Quite beautiful, the peat almost hitting perfection. Truly unique; t23 sweet malt that just dissolves around the mouth but leaving traces of the most elegant oak, almost too soft to be true. Again the smoke is just stunning in its elegance; f23 long, silky, soft oak and – amazingly – clean barley; **b**24 when this was distilled my football team, Millwall, reached the FA Cup semi final. My late dad went to the game in my old mate Michael Jackson's country, 'uddersfield. We lost 2–1. They haven't reached the FA Cup semi finals since. I'll taste this again the next time we do … it could be a long wait. From a sheer whisky perspective, proof – alongside some older Macallans – that Speyside once made a much peatier dram, one which perhaps only Ardmore can today match. How this whisky has remained this truly fabulous for so long has been entirely in the lap of the Gods. To whoever, whatever, is responsible: thank you!! NOTE TO 2005 EDITION: On April 4th, 2004, Millwall did, miraculously, reach another FA Cup semi-final. And beat the team they lost to in 1937. So my wait to taste it was shorter than I could even dream … **40%**. 61 *bottles only (going for in the region of £10,000 each).*

⠿ **Glenfiddich 1955 Vintage** Cask no. 4221 db **(93)** n23 pumped up oak, but deflated somewhat by the subtle nuances of the barley which, somehow, have enough breeziness to breathe a doughy freshness into the proceedings; t23 brilliant, entirely schizophrenic, delivery of honey-oak and big spice, all on a base of a coppery sheen: very much the sma' still character to this one; f23 long, lush with drying, oak-vanilla and still that wonderful barley/coppery gloss. Oh, and a dribble of smoke bleeding into the late honey; **b**24 a real surprise package, because even without sherry or peat to hide behind there is enough complexity and, at times, utter brilliance to dazzle the most demanding of commentators. And, believe me; this is one sample I didn't spit.... Over 50 years old and quite majestic. Truly classic stuff. **52.6%**

⠿ **Glenfiddich 1958 Vintage** Cask no. 8642 db **(78)** n23 t18 f18 **b**19. Oak can be such an unforgiving master. Fabulous old oloroso nose, though. **46.3%**

⠿ **Glenfiddich 1959 Vintage** Cask no. 3934 db **(89)** n23 big age here: this one is creaking with oak and oloroso but the harmony is excellent. Pans out with spiced toffee apple and dates: superb; t22 stunning delivery with big fruit at first then several layers of spice over the burned fudge; the oak is less than discreet but does limited damage; f22 long, toasty and a fade of cremated raisins; some lovely esters last the pace; **b**22 from the year Jacky Cox led Ayr United to the old Scottish Second Division Championship, something equally as rare! Glenfiddich showing something of a rummy side to its character with lots of copper and ester in the mix. The oak is profound, but sits comfortably in the scheme of things. One for late at night, closed eyes and memories of long-lost days at Somerset Park. **48.1%**

Glenfiddich 1961 Vintage Reserve db **(75)** n20 t19 f18 b18. Hasn't withstood the test of time quite as well as might be hoped. **43.2%. sc.**

⠿ Glenfiddich 1964 Vintage Cask no. 13430 db **(80)** n22 t22 f17 b19. The nose is pure bourbon – and very old bourbon at that. Wobbles a bit in both aroma and delivery but for all its oaky over- zestfulness – and even a touch of the soaps (especially on the finish) – you still cannot help but enjoy this one. To say it is a character is something of an understatement...!! **45.6%**

Glenfiddich 1967 Vintage Reserve db **(87)** n23 t22 f21 b21. An unusually refreshing dram for such age. **43.6%. sc.**

Glenfiddich Vintage Cask 1972 db **(82)** n20 t19 f22 b21. On the sappy side throughout but good honey depth. **48.9%**

Glenfiddich 1972 Vintage Cask cask no. 16031 db **(84)** n19 t22 f22 b21. Quite outstanding spices take weight off the oak and even allow the malt to show. Fights valiantly for its delightful identity with continuous arrivals of increasingly sweet malt. **47.3%**

Glenfiddich 1972 Vintage Cask cask no. 16032 db **(78)** n19 t21 f19 b19. Further evidence that this great distillery often struggles at these advanced ages. Apart from a wonderful delivery of exotic fruit and lush malt, this rapidly disappears in a forest of oak. **47.3%**

Glenfiddich 1973 Vintage Reserve db **(88)** n23 t23 f21 b21. Intense, crisp and spicy. **49.8%. sc.**

Glenfiddich 1973 Vintage cask no. 9874 db **(94)** n23 citrus - made from concentrate: hard as nails nose really pumps out the barley-fruit marriage; **t**23 mouth-filling, luxuriously mouthwatering and barley, fruit and spice all at full throttle; **f**24 the oak is driven like a stake through the barley, but there is a fabulous molassed edge to it. The late viscosity carries a delightful hint of liquorice. Wow!; **b**24 I've been tasting these special casks from this distillery since before my hair went grey. I've sampled some good 'uns. This is possibly the best of the lot. **48.1%**

⠿ Glenfiddich Vintage Reserve 1973 Cask no. 9874 **(92)** n23 very few Glenfiddich casks of this age stand quite so tall: wonderful hot-cross bun theme, even with a sliver of salted butter; the fruit-barley element excels; **t**23 exquisite delivery and mouth-feel: the oak is pounding at the door but that glorious fruit/bourbon/barley core refuses to budge; some wonderful strands of smoke disappear into the middle's demerara depths **f**22 appears for a while to be sliding under the oak, then bucks up as the honey-barley breathes fresh life back into it; **b**24 whisky picked at its very ripest! The juices are still flowing despite a massive oak threat. But such is the sheer élan and fruit and sweet edges that an astounding and beautiful experience is assured. **46.5%**

Glenfiddich Private Vintage 1976 Exclusively for Queen Mary 2, cask 21229, bott 04, db **(79)** n18 t22 f19 b20. For all the lovely honey touches, there is so much oak it would have been better designated for the Mary Rose.... **50.3%**

Glenfiddich Reserve 1984 db **(90)** n21 t24 f22 b23. Glenfiddich at its most exuberant defying its age with a nonchalant charisma. **40%**

Glenfiddich Vintage Reserve 1991 db **(88)** n22 t22 f22 b22. Exceptionally even and elegant, this is from 200-odd bourbon casks...and it shows. Just could have done with being bottled at 43 or 46% to take it up an extra notch. **40%**

Cadenhead's Bond Reserve Glenfiddich-Glenlivet Distillery Aged 32 Years **(83)** n19 t21 f22 b21. The nose and early arrival are oaksoaked, but the malty richness on the finish, plus the gathering spice, makes for a decent, if wrinkled, old 'un. **46.9%**

⠿ Glenfiddich Toasted Oak Reserve Aged 12 Years **(89)** n22 toasty alright, but with a butterscotch spread and a dollop of bourbon extract; **t**23 cleverly sweet with delicate bourbon-style honies blending beautifully with the fatted-up barley; **f**22 again a toasty bite to the finale which balances well with the persistent sweetness of the barley and butterscotch; **b**22 an elegant, bourbony, not overly complex, malt for those with a slightly sweet tooth. **40%**

## GLENFLAGLER
### Lowland, 1965–1982. Demolished.

**Glenflagler 29 Years Old** db (**88**) **n**22 pretty ripe tangerines on vanilla ice cream. The oak makes for just about perfect bitter-sweet balance; **t**23 massive fresh fruity to start – citrus again – then an astounding intense and clean malty follow-through; **f**21 a quiet finale with the malt remaining confident, the oak adding a slight bitterness, but all under control; **b**22 I've tasted some Glenflagler over the years, but nothing quite as accomplished as this. Lowlander it might be, but this has seen off the years with the grace and élan of the noblest Highlander. Forget about collector's item: eminently drinkable in its own right. **46%**. *A unique malt, as it was run through a Kentucky-type beer still before entering a pot still: a Lowlander made the American way.*

**Killyloch 35 Years Old** db (**80**) **n**20 thin, malty nose, but strong enough to see off the oak; **t**20 again a thin, wispy start wth the malt offering sweetness but always in the shadow of something oaky; **f**20 holds together reasonably well: the oak does play the major role but behaves itself while again the malt makes a valiant stand.; **b**20 only the fourth Killyloch I have ever tasted – even including lab sample form – and, I admit, a lot better than I thought it might be. It doesn't have either the muscle or complexity to guarantee a great malt, but very few faults, either. Rather, it hangs on in there proudly – like a frail old lady successfully crossing a busy road – so you can relax and enjoy it for the pretty decent dram it is. **40%**

## GLEN GARIOCH
### Highland (Eastern), 1798. Suntory. Working.

**Glen Garioch 10 Years Old** db (**80**) **n**19 **t**22 **f**19 **b**20. Chunky and charming, this is a malt that once would have ripped your tonsils out. Much more sedate and even a touch of honey to the rich body. Toffeed at the finish. **40%** ⊙

**Glen Garioch 12 Years Old** db (**86**) **n**21 **t**22 **f**22 **b**21. Little complexity, but just sits very comfortably on the palate. **43%** ⊙

**Glen Garioch 15 Years Old** db (**86**) **n**20 **t**22 **f**22 **b**22. The peat, that once familiar distillery trait, which previously tied this malt together has gone. Leaving behind a big, very well made malt that offers liquorice as well as toffee. **43%** ⊙ ⊙

**Glen Garioch 16 Years Old** db (**88**) **n**20 fruity and spiced: a real heavyweight with a hint of peat thrown in; **t**23 clean, fresh oloroso character massively chewy with a fine malt thread; **f**22 lengthy, sweetening malt, a hint of peat and spice returns; **b**23 lovely whisky, setting off a bit like a Dufftown but heading into a galaxy that poor old Speysider can only dream of. Really high grade malt with bags of character and attitude. **55.4%**

**Glen Garioch 16 Years Old Wine Finish** SL06.002, bott 13 Feb 06 db (**87**) **n**20 sweetish, wine-dulled and not entirely unlike a Portuguese rose; **t**23 an "after you, Claude" gentility to the melt-in-the mouth malt, though an on-rush of spice livens things up in towards the middle; **f**22 very long and works well considering the bitter almond note to the oak. The very faintest of smoke signals gives extra value; **b**22 you have to check the label to confirm this is a 'Garioch! **53.8%**

**Glen Garioch 21 Years Old** db (**91**) **n**21 a few wood shavings interrupt the toasty barley; **t**23 really good bitter-sweet balance with honeycomb and butterscotch leading the line; pretty juicy, busy stuff; **f**24 dries as it should with some vague spices adding to the vanilla and hickory; **b**23 an entirely re-worked, now smokeless, malt that has little in common with its predecessors. Quite lovely, though. **43%** ⊙ ⊙

**Glen Garioch 1958** db (**90**) **n**24 what a brilliant, heady, almost eccentric mix of once chunky peat, once vivid malt and now beautifully varnished oak; **t**21 loses its early balance but settles on a waxy honey thread to complement the slowly reasserting peat; **f**23 elegance in abundance as the oak plays lip-service to the sweet, chewy malt. Just so charming! **b**22 the distillery in its old clothes: and quite splendid it looks! **43%**. *328 bottles.*

**Glen Garioch Highland Tradition** db (**83**) **n**20 **t**22 **f**21 **b**20. Struggling to find complexity a bit, but so much better than previous bottlings. The delivery is a real toasted malt, ultra-sweet chewfest. **40%** ⊙ ⊙

**Glen Garioch 12 Years The National Trust for Scotland** db (**77**) **n**18 **t**21 **d**19 **b**19. Mouthwatering, and would be even more so but for a toffeed intrusion. **43%**

Cadenhead's Authentic Collection Glengarioch Aged 13 Years Bourbon Hogshead, dist 93, bott Sept 06 **(82) n**20 **t**22 **f**21 **b**19. Big barley at times yet just a shade on the thin side. And hot. **57.6%.** *264 bottles.*

⸭ **D&M Connoisseurs' Club Bottling Glen Garioch Aged 16 Years** Cask no. 10291, dist Dec 90 **(93) n**23 glorious infusion of toasty vanilla and dried ginger just bristles with lively barley, though softened somewhat with fresh buttered toast; **t**24 barley concentrate helped along by a silky, buttery sheen and roaming spices; the sweetness from the barley is of almost perfect proportions; **f**23 the oak digs in but finds the richness of the barley too big to shift: long and lithe; **b**23 always great to see this grand old distillery being shown off to its full potential: a minor classic. **57.1%. sc ncf.**

⸭ **Duncan Taylor Collection Glengarioch 1988** Cask no. 1557 **(87) n**21 flour and biscuits sweetened with maple syrup **t**22 sugar-coated barley **f**22 a dash of vanilla and some rapidly drying oak **b**22 a pussy cat of a Glengarioch, much sweeter than the norm and with the customary fires completely doused. Highly attractive. **52.8%**

**Duncan Taylor Collection Glen Garioch 1988** cask no. 1554, dist Apr 88, bott May 06 **(80) n**19 **t**21 **f**20 **b**20. Sweet with banana and lime. But a bit leaden-footed and plateaus out. **55.8%.** *283 bottles.*

⸭ **Murray McDavid Glen Garioch 1993** Bourbon/Banyuls Grenache Rouge **(80) n**19 **t**19 **f**22 **b**20. Pleasant, if limited in complexity. **46%**

**Old Malt Cask Glen Garioch 14 Years Old** dist Nov 91, bott May 06 **(91) n**23 just like the old days: soft peats trundle about the nose though now with a salty, citrussy edge; **t**22 lovely weight with some smoky depth to the sweet, gristy barley. Some spices on this chewathon; **f**23 long with ultra-clean barley and soft cocoa notes to the smoke; **b**23 curiously oily, but so satisfying and sweet. Geary as God intended!! **50%.** *326 bottles.*

**Old Masters Glen Garioch 1988 Aged 18 Years** cask no. 1535, dist 88, bott 06 **(90) n**22 an intriguing Bowmore-type peat edge to this: curious as that is its sister distillery...; **t**23 the Bowmore-esque theme continues as the malt generates a freshness not normally associated with such relative old age; **f**22 excellent smoked vanilla and wonderful bitter-sweet balance; **b**23 handsome, weighty yet fresh. A real meal of a malt. **53.9%**

**Park Avenue Liquor Store Glen Garioch 24 Year Old** db **(90) n**23 lavender and moist ginger cake; **t**23 an eruption of warming spices and calming sweet malt; some herbal notes pitch in for the fun and even the strangest delivery of rye on a malt I've ever seen; **f**21 peat trickles from the base of toasted rye bread and vanilla; **b**23 another Glen Garioch that just heads off on a tangent and that you never quite get to the centre of. Weirdly fascinating, typically unique and genius in a bottle. **52.1%.** *New York.*

**Provenance Glen Garioch Aged 11 Years** Refill Hogshead 1880, dist Autumn 94, bott Winter 06 **(85) n**20 **t**22 **f**21 **b**22. The refreshing fruits of a Garioch matured in a clapped-out third-fill cask, I assume. Not instantly recognizable as malt from this distillery, a burst of smoke gives some clue. Deliciously light...in every sense. **46%. nc ncf.** *McGibbon's.*

**Signatory Glen Garioch 1988 Aged 16 Years** cask 4107 dist 28 Oct 88, bott 27 May 05 **(90) n**23 **t**22 **f**22 **b**23. Only a touch of smoke, but as much barley sugar as you'll ever need. That said, the complexity is stunning. **55.3%.** *272 bottles.*

**The Spirit Safe & Cask Glen Garioch 1988 Aged 18 Years** Hogshead, dist Apr 88, bott May 06 **(94) n**23 a breakfast of chocolate spread on slightly burnt toast with kippers on a side-dish; **t**24 one of the best deliveries of a 'Garioch I've encountered for year or three: mouthwatering with a fabulous degree of barley-sodden demerara and manuka honey mixing with the smoky grist; rounded body holds exceptionally wonderful weight; **f**23 pulsing spices that begin halfway through the cycle continue towards the death; more vanilla and singed butterscotch generate a fabulous sweet balance to the drying oak; **b**24 almost the complete whisky experience. Wonderful! **56.1%. nc ncf.** *Celtic Whisky Compagnie, France.*

## GLENGLASSAUGH
### Speyside, 1875. Edrington. Silent since 1986.

**Glenglassaugh 1973 Family Silver** db **(95) n**23 fruity and exceptionally complex: quite coastal with something vaguely citrussy, orange in particular; **t**24 melt-in-the-mouth malt that intensifies by the second. Never becomes either too sweet or vaguely woody. There is a soft hint of peat around the spices; **f**24 virtually without a blemish as the malt continues on its rich and merry way. Some sublime marmalade follows through on the spice; **b**24 from first to last this whisky caresses and teases. It is old but shows no over-ageing. It offers what appears a malt veneer but is complexity itself. Brilliant. And now, sadly, almost impossible to find. Except, possibly, at the Mansefield Hotel, Elgin. **40%**

**The MacPhail's Glenglassaugh Selected Single Distilleries Collection Aged 18 Years** dist 86, bott 04 **(85) n**23 **t**21 **f**21 **b**20. The nose may be like walking past a Surrey garden in August after a downpour but a meandering malt that struggles to focus. **40%**

⋅⋅⋅⋅ **Milroy's of Soho Glenglassaugh 1976** Ex Bourbon Hogshead, cask no. 2373, dist 17 Dec 76, bott 7 Dec 06 **(89) n**23 the most playful puff of smoke adds excellent weight to the potpourri of floral tones that sits so well with the maple syrup; **t**23 gorgeous, pouting malt makes a seductive sweet of the tastebuds; the weight and mouth-feel as good as a 30-year-old gets but perhaps thins out too readily towards the middle; **f**21 surprisingly lazy with the soft oak holding sway; **b**22 another charming and very high class malt from beyond the grave. **46%**. *318 bottles.*

**Murray McDavid Mission Glenglassaugh 1978 Aged 28 Years** Fresh Sherry/Syrah, bott 06 **(86) n**24 **t**20 **f**23 **b**19. What balance? One of the challenges of cask finishing is that you never know when it will get better or worse: the nature of the beast there is nothing with which you can compare the whisky. This works and fails on two massive levels, but it is worth experiencing for the astonishing nose and charming finale alone. **46.6%. nc ncf.** *500 bottles.*

**Old Malt Cask Glenglassaugh Aged 27 Years** dist Jan 78, bott Nov 05 **(85) n**22 **t**20 **f**22 **b**21. Straight up and down stuff for something of this antiquity. Plenty of class, though, and the bourbon dimension is appealing. **50%.** *Douglas Laing. 213 btls.*

⋅⋅⋅⋅ **The Whisky Fair Glenglassaugh Aged 27 Years** Sherry Hogshead, dist 1987, bott 06 **(85) n**22 **t**22 **f**20 **b**21. Highly drinkable for its age, but being 'Glassaugh I expect a little bit more. Rich, but no shattered chandeliers. **56.8%.** *Germany.*

⋅⋅⋅⋅ **The Whisky Fair Glenglassaugh Aged 40 Years** Fino Sherry Butt, dist 1965, bott 06 **(89) n**24 big complexity but delicately delivered: a riot of varied fruit tones from apple peelings to crushed sultana; **t**23 again big grape before the barley bustles in...so, so soft!! **f**20 chocolate fudge but a little oily; **b**22 rather lovely. **46.7%.** *Germany.*

# GLENGOYNE
**Highlands (Southwest), 1833. Peter Russell. Working.**

**Glengoyne 10 Years Old** db **(90) n**22 beautifully clean despite coal-gas bite. The barley is almost in concentrate form with a marmalade sweetness adding richness; **t**23 crisp, firm arrival with massive barley surge, seriously chewy and textbook bitter-sweet balance; but now some oils have tucked in to intensify and lengthen; **f**22 incredibly long and refined for such a light malt. The oak, which made soft noises in the middle now intensifies, but harmonises with the intense barley; an added touch of coffee signals some extra oak in recent bottlings; **b**23 proof that to create balance you do not have to have peat at work. The secret is the intensity of barley intermingling with oak. Not a single negative note from first to last and now a touch of oil and coffee has upped the intensity further. **40%** ☉☉

**Glengoyne 12 Years Old Cask Strength** db **(88) n**21 **t**23 **f**22 **b**22. The sulphur that has been mentioned in previous bottlings of this has returned, but in such tiny amounts it doesn't detract from the enjoyment....yet. Need to keep an eye open that it doesn't get any worse, though, as it would be a shame to see a quite lovely whisky undermined. **57.2%. sc, nc, ncf.** ☉☉

**Glengoyne Limited Edition 15 Years Old Scottish Oak** db **(86) n**22 **t**21 **f**21 **b**22. perhaps not quite as complex as you might expect, but there is good balance and impressive clarity to the simplicity. **43%. nc.**

**Glengoyne 17 Years Old** db **(86) n**21 **t**23 **f**21 **b**21. Some of the guys at Glengoyne think I'm nuts. They couldn't get their head around the 79 I gave it last time. And they will be shaking my neck not my hand when they see the score here...Vastly improved but there is an off sherry tang which points to a naughty butt or two somewhere. Elsewhere mouth-watering and at times fabulously intense. **43%** ☉☉

**Glengoyne Single Cask LE Aged 19 Years** Sherry cask no.1227 db **(93) n**24 sherry as it should be: clean, fully of grapey weight yet light enough for the barley to sing a tune or two; **t**23 brilliant barley on the charm offensive then some real chewy grape kicks in; **f**23 plenty of liquorice seasoned with Demerara sugar: the way old oak should behave; **b**23 absolute bliss. **55.8%. sc.**

**Glengoyne 21 Years Old** db **(90) n**21 closed and tight for the most part as Glengoyne sometimes has a tendency to be nose-wise, with the emphasis very much on coal gas; **t**22 slow to start with a few barley heads popping up to be seen; then spices arrive with the oak for a slightly bourbony feel. Gentle butterscotch and honey add a mouth-watering edge to the drier oaks; **f**24 a stupendous honey thread is cross-stitched through the developing oak to deliver near perfect poise and balance at finish; **b**23 a vastly improved dram where the caramel has vanished and the tastebuds are constantly assailed and questioned. A malt which builds in pace and passion to delivery a final, wonderful coup-de-grace. Moments of being quite cerebral stuff. **43%** ☉ ☉

⊹ **Glengoyne 21 Years Old Sherry Edition** db **(93) n**22 heavy, nutty oily, slightly sweaty and not entirely faultless. When warmed the full, brooding oloroso gamut comes into play. Seriously big, if somewhat cumbersome; **t**24 much sweeter arrival than you might have thought possible from the nose, and less sticky too. The richness of the oloroso coats every crevice and a playful spice teases while a mollased, toasted oaky/barley sub plot develops delightfully; **f**23 not dissimilar to an excellent Demerara rum on the finish with no shortage of coffee-tinted roasty notes on the death. A real chew; **b**24 the nose at first is not overly promising, but it settles at it warms and what follows on the palate is at times glorious. Few whiskies will match this for its bitter-sweet depth which is pure textbook. Glengoyne as few will have seen it before. **43%**

**The Old 'Glen Guin' Glengoyne 21 Year Old** db **(85) n**21 **t**22 **f**20 **b**22. Another summer would have been one too many for this old chap. A fascinating, juicy improvement on the old 21-y-o version, though. **43%. nc.**

**Glengoyne Single Cask LE Aged 32 Years** White Rioja cask no.985 db **(92) n**25 unique. In 30-odd years of nosing this stuff, no other whisky has offered such a style which moves across so many oak types. Despite the obvious grape, it is the bourbony theme which underpins the style; next, light and heavy spices buzz the nose.....and then there is the dryness to the grape offset by the naturally sweet barley and bourbon. Fabulous; **t**23 bumbling and somewhat brusque, there is a discreet harshness which is softened by bourbon and barley; **f**23 still quite juicy yet hot and uncompromising; a little milky Java softens the finale; **b**21 Wow! What was all that about? Either there was no balance at all, or it was perfection... **48.7%. sc.**

⊹ **Glengoyne 33 Years Old 1972 Single Cask Limited Edition** db **(87) n**23 egg custard tart, seasoned and with a fruity side-dish; **t**21 soft landing but the accent is on spice; **t**22 back to fruit again and more vanilla-custard; **b**21 the cask may be from somewhere near Rotorua, but the fruity, simplistic qualities are disarming. **50%.** *Exclusive for Taiwan.*

⊹ **Glengoyne Vintage Scottish Oak Finish 1973 Age 33 Years** Cask no. 90941, dist Mar 73, bott Nov 06 db **(94) n**24 supremely weighted, with the lighter lemon-lime and gristy notes underpinned by the deftest of peats (yes peat!!).There is a real dexterity to this nose with the fruitiness always fresh and pleasing and wonderful inter-mingling between citrus and heavier fruits; **t**23 again the peat is very early to show, but does so with the lightest of sprinklings. The oak chugs in next but becomes wonderfully servile to the ever-thickening barley; **f**23 thins out slightly as the oak re-forms towards something slightly more exotic in its fruitiness while the peats add excellent length; **b**24 the neck label proudly boasts an unpeated malt. This is anything but, however. And the understated sublime smokiness helps lift this malt into the higher echelons of older single casks. A malt much younger than its years suggest, yet benefitting from all the complexity. Quite sublime. **43%** *348 bottles*

⊹ **Glengoyne 34 Years Old 1972 Single Cask Limited Edition** db **(92) n**24 unspoiled fruit is complemented by soft cinnamon and sweet barley tones; **t**23 mouth-watering delivery that astounds for its age: how can barley remain so beautifully fresh for so long? The oaks are omnipresent but reveal themselves only in spice form; **f**22 medium length finale, concentrating mainly on spice and vanilla and interplay between simple malt and something juicier; **b**23 one of those lovely whiskies that you just have to spend a little time alone with... **55%.** *Exclusive for Taiwan.*

**Glengoyne Single Cask LE Aged 37 Years** Sherry butt cask no.975 db **(91)** n24 no ifs to this butt: absolutely as clean and beautifully structured as they come, though oak and barley is at a premium; t23 mouthwatering and majestic, the wine digs deep; f22 simplistic, though a little barely does peak through; b23 in some ways the sherry works too well: so rich and soft is the wine, you cannot help think that some of the complexity has been washed away. **47.6%. sc.**

⁙ **Glengoyne Stillman Duncan's Choice 15 Years** Sherry hogshead, cask no. 1024, dist 4 July 89, bott May 05 **(66)** n16 t18 f16 b16. Oh, Duncan!!! What about the sulphur.?!?!?!? **55.7%**

⁙ **Glengoyne Stillman Ewan's Choice 19 Years** Sherry Puncheon, cask no. 441, dist 13 July 86, bott May 05 **(93)** n23 ye olde-style oloroso from days of yore: slight treacle effect to the over-ripe plums and the oak drives in to offer natural caramels and coffee tones; something of old demerara rum about this one; t23 pounding spices from the off ensure this isn't a sherry fest; beautiful sweetness oozes around the palate but just the right dry oakiness to match; f24 long, remains spiced and runs from ripe juicy to entirely dried dates. A stunner...; b23 just so wonderful to come across a sherry style common 25 years ago and nearly gone today. Too much sherry influence? Maybe. But there again when it is this good - and absolutely 100% free of sulphur - who can complain? **51.5%**

⁙ **Glengoyne Stillman Ronnie's Choice 22 Years** Bourbon barrel, cask no. 449, dist 23 Dec 82, bott May 05 **(90)** n23 some real Kentucky notes starting to pile in; mildly gluey but the vanilla/acacia honey blend does the trick; t22 beautiful delivery with again honey lurking about, but a bit more toasty now; f22 touches of liquorice and barley: long and poised; b23 a stonking bourbon cask that shows not the slightest sign of degradation. Great stuff! **53.6%**

**Old Malt Cask Glengoyne Aged 16 Years** dist Nov 88, bott Aug 05 **(89)** n23 barley and coal fires. Beautifully balanced; t22 salivating delivery; slightly uneven towards the middle and a little bitter, but it is the barley that continues to star; f22 bitter-burnt raisin and vanilla; b22 hints of sophistication, but just a slightly bitter edge. **50%.** *331 bottles.*

**Provenance Glengoyne 10 Years Old** dist Jun 96, bott Aug 06 **(80)** n19 t21 f20 b20. Young, clean, malty: pure blending fodder. **46%.** *McGibbon's.*

⁙ **Provenance Glengoyne Aged 11 Years** dist Autumn 95, bott Winter 06 **(88)** n21 sweet, docile barley perked up by a youthful element; t23 genuinely radiant delivery with layers of golden syrup amid the grassy, juicy barley; f22 long, just a dab here and there of vanilla and remains velvety and yielding; b22 a sensationally sweet malt but never loses its shape. Or softness. **46%.** *Douglas Laing.*

**Provenance Glengoyne Aged 11 Years** Refill Hogshead DMG 2403, dist Winter 95, bott Winter 06 **(88)** n22 daises and dank grass; t23 charmingly refreshing with simple barley tones; f22 soft vanillas over barley; b21 clean and simple. **46%. nc ncf.** *McGibbon's.*

# GLEN GRANT
## Speyside, 1840. Campari. Working.

**Glen Grant** db **(89)** n22 young, clean malt doesn't come much cleaner, maltier – or even younger than this: drooling stuff; t23 crisp, brittle grain nibbling at the tastebuds, lovely and mouthwatering; f22 more of the same: the intensity of the malt is stunning, yet it remains delicate throughout; b22 little oak, so not much complexity, but the balance and quality is nothing short of superb. **40%. nc.** *France.*

**Glen Grant 5 Years Old** db **(84)** n21 t21 f21 b21. Enormous malt, much more oily than the non-age-statement version with an unusual lack of crispness for a Glen Grant. Still mouthwateringly delicious, though! **40%. nc.** *Italy.*

**Glen Grant 10 Years Old** db **(87)** n21 fine, flinty grain, quite hard and with limited oak interference; t23 really mouthwatering, clean and fresh: not an offnote in sight; f21 gentle, almost half sleeping, just malt and a faint buzz of oak; b22 a relaxed, confident malt from a distillery that makes great whisky with effortless charm and each mouthful seems to show that it knows it. **43%. nc.**

**Glen Grant 14 Years Old Distillery Edition** db **(89)** n22 Scandinavian cracker bread; a touch salty and big oak; t23 you could cut diamonds with the barley: flinty hard with a distant golden sugary glow; f21 back to the salt and oak; b23 those of you expecting a soft, dreamy, Speyside ride will be in for a shock. Ride the punches and enjoy. **59.5%**

**Cadenhead's Authentic Collection Glen Grant-Glenlivet Aged 16 Years** Bourbon Barrel, dist 89, bott May 05 **(94)** n23 granite-like, rock solid malt; just so clean and crisp; **t24** like geological layers on a cliff face, one flinty note peels aways before another. Mouthwatering barley concentrate. Tastebud invigorating. And entirely mind-blowing; **f24** successive strata of green-malty, mouthwatering, lip-puckering delight; **b23** have you any idea how long I have been waiting for Chivas to unleash on us a malt of this stature? Almost a lifetime, it seems. Those of us in the know are aware that fabulous, unsherried casks like this exist from Glen Grant: why must we wait for an independent to show the world just how magnificent this distillery really is? **61.6%.** *216 bottles.*

⁘ **Cadenhead's Authentic Collection Glen Grant-Glenlivet Aged 18 Years** Bourbon Barrel, dist 1989, bott May 07 **(90)** n22 for a bourbon barrel, the degree of soft grape with the barley effect is astonishing; **t23** big, booming barley, unusually yielding in places but a firmness to the malty sheen; **f22** those gentle fruit notes resurface with the vanilla; sharp and eye watering; **b23** beautiful malt that is much fruitier than it has any right to be. **60.8%.** *204 bottles*

**Cask Strength Glen Grant 1990** bott 01.02.06 **(85)** n21 t22 f21 b21. Ultra- intense barley sugar, but the oak keeps tabs on the sweetness. Good spice and body. **59.3%.** *Gordon & MacPhail. USA.*

⁘ **The Coopers Choice Glen Grant 1977 Sherry Wood Aged 30 Years (91)** n22 clean, faultless oloroso – almost too clean and faultless as the barley battles to stake a claim; **t23** amazingly sweet for a sherry butt with lashings of molassed sugar amid the juicy mildly toasted raisin; **f23** long, a hint of spice; a touch of barley on the grape helps integrate the oak; **b23** quite beautiful whisky. **46%. sc ncf.** *The Vintage Malt Whisky Co.*

**Dewar Rattray Individual Cask Bottling Glen Grant 1985 Aged 19 Years** cask no. 16914, dist Nov 85, bott Sept 05 **(95)** n24 if it wasn't for the firmness of the barley, this could have been raised in Kentucky: just stick your nose in this to discover the meaning of complexity; **t24** shimmering barley forces the pace but is soon surrounded by those expected bourbony notes, complete with a rye spiciness – weird!! And beautiful; **f23** strands of liquorice dipped in muscovado sugar. So elegant; **b24** the new owners of Glen Grant better take a pretty close look at this. This will be hard pressed to produce anything finer. **58.4%.** *240 bottles.*

⁘ **Distillery Malt Glen Grant 1990 (88)** n22 apple blossom and Chinese pears amid the barley; **t23** firm, beautifully structured with the malt arriving in layers of varying sweetness and tempered slightly by an oaky-vanilla and mildly spiced weightiness; **f21** a touch of toffee and bitters while the deft spices continue; **b22** only a slight bitterness to the finale detracts from an otherwise excellent malt. **40%.** *Gordon & MacPhail.*

**Duncan Taylor Collection Glen Grant 1969** cask no. 6232, dist Oct 69, bott Mar 06 **(88)** n23 butterscotch tart – I have just been transported back over 40 years to my primary school in Surrey ...; **t23** masterful delivery of gently honeyed barley complete with body you that you so want to explore; dries a tad too quickly; **f20** over oaked; **b22** delicious at times but bottled about five or six years too late for greatness. **52.3%.** *143 bottles.*

⁘ **Duncan Taylor Collection Glen Grant 1970** Cask no. 818 **(95)** n24 classic oloroso of the very highest order: anyone who has come across Chivas sherry butts from this era will know the score; almost a touch of the old Demereras about this one; **t23** enormous fruit – mainly over-ripe plums and dates – sticks to the palate while soft spice and drier oak dig in; **f24** long, with a gradual delivery of slightly sweeter malt notes, then a drying effect; **b24** where demerara meets oloroso. But for all the enormity of the sherry, the trick is that it is complex enough to allow full development of the juicy barley, too... as well as oak. Simply gorgeous. **53.6%.** *Duncan Taylor.*

**Duncan Taylor Collection Glen Grant 1970** cask no. 827, dist Feb 70, bott Apr 06 **(92)** n23 lashings of natural toffee lightened by a bourbon-style small grain buzz. Highly complex and rich; **t23** big, mouth-filling and immensely chewy early on. Fabulous structure to the barley which is firm enough to hold the oak and spice with comfort; a some lightly roasted Cuban also makes an entry; **f22** the cracks that began to appear in the late middle begin to widen; still a lovely bourbon sheen to this; **b23** a fascinating bourbony element has appeared. **53%**

**Duncan Taylor Collection Glen Grant 1970 Aged 36 Years** cask no. 830, dist Feb 70, bott 17 May 06 **(89)** n23 one assumes sherry, but the enormity of this almost suggests a pre-carameled Demerara rum; t23 seriously big: requires a second mouthful to get a bearing on this: the intensity of the oak with all its burnt fudge tries to confuse, but there is something else in this swamp. Kind of fruity. Miraculously, some barley actually punctures through and salivates the tastebuds; f21 do you know those brown and black liquorice allsorts? Imagine that in concentrate with some extra oak for good measure; b22 good God! What the hell was that? If it was a sherry butt, then that was pretty strange fruit coming from it. A must for whisky clubs all over the globe to muse over. **54.1%.** 140 btls.

Duncan Taylor Special Selection No 2 Glen Grant 1970 cask no. 122, dist 1970, bott Nov 05 **(95)** n24 more along the same lines of the 54.1% above, except the oak is less aggressive and the fruit is softer and slightly more raisiny; t24 if I was in my lab blending a rum, I wouldn't bat an eyelid at this: I have seen several species of these from Guyana. Thrillingly intense, with a stunning sweetness, the oak plays a wonderful spicy part. The usual coffee and cocoa notes are there, plus a mild bourbony overture. It is hard to find a glass big enough for this one ...; f23 enormous yet relaxed, sumptuous waves of varying intensity and sweetness wash over the tastebuds for ages; b24 just one of those great old whiskies that pops up from time to time. In exchange for eternal life, it has sold its soul for a rummy depth. But when the result is this astonishing, who the hell cares??? **57.1%.** 548 bottles

⸫ **Gordon & MacPhail Glen Grant 1948** Rare Vintage range **(91)** n24 something to be experienced, with a nod towards exotic fruit, a distant smokiness and a shake of salt. Changes countless times through temperature and oxidisation in the glass: a real moving target; t22 the arrival is silk, what follows is warming oak in spicy form and kept honest by a very gentle and delicious smokiness; just a dab or two of light molasses for good measure; f22 bitter-sweet with just a hint of marmalade before the oak and delicate smoke dry proceedings; b23 the guys at G&M did exactly right bottling this now, rather than waiting until it reached 60. I'm not convinced there was another summer in this one to keep the peaty structure intact. Genuinely inspiring malt. **40%**

⸫ **Gordon & MacPhail Glen Grant 1953** Rare Vintage range **(92)** n23 just a catch of smoke attached to the faultless sherry. The oak lets everyone know its about; t24 excellent weight to the oloroso and the spices are spot on; particular wonderful is the interplay between the grape and honeycomb sweetnesses; again a wisp of smoke towards the middle; f22 shows a degree of oaky stress but there is enough weight and finesse to see it through to a sultana-rich finale; b23 same age as my brother, David, this; except has worn better and, because it doesn't ceaselessly drone on and on and on about bloody Chelsea, has a lot more interesting things to say...One of the great super oldies of the last few years. The whisky, I mean. Not my brother... **48%**

⸫ **Gordon & MacPhail Glen Grant 1964** Rare Vintage range **(89)** n22 spotted dick pudding; heavily toasted raisins; t23 vibrant fruit and barley very much in tandem; f22 a decent viscosity and sweetness to the fruit sees off the oak; b22 has stood up to time with uncanny depth. What a treat!! **48%**

⸫ **Gordon & MacPhail Glen Grant 1966** Rare Vintage range **(88)** n23 French toast, a touch of salt and toffee apples; t22 stupendously well balanced delivery with barley and fruit profound and in sync; a touch of over-eager oak towards the bitter-coffee middle f21 again the oak pushes a little too hard but enough firm malt in reserve to see off the worst; b22 yes, there are a few cracks showing here, but for such age the overall picture is a pretty one. **40%**

⸫ **Gordon & MacPhail Glen Grant 1967** Rare Vintage range **(86)** n23 t22 f20 b21. Curious how this works far better on the nose than the '68, yet, for all the lovely honey apparent, tires much more quickly. Funny ol' game, this whisky lark. **40%**

⸫ **Gordon & MacPhail Glen Grant 1968** Rare Vintage range **(89)** n21 a mild hint of sap; exotic fruit on oxidisation; t23 such beautiful barley: the oak is around but the structure of the malt is propped up by several layers of lightly coated maple syrup; f22 long, beautifully gentle with the accent return to the barley; b23 one whiff of the nose suggests a possible problem, but the palate confounds. **40%**

James MacArthur Glen Grant 1993 11 Year Old, bott Apr 05 **(84)** n21 t22 f20 b21. Beautiful malt crescendo. **43%. ncf.**

James MacArthur Glen Grant 1993 Aged 11 Years bott 05 **(88)** n22 intense, brittle barley overwhelms the slightest oak overture; t22 mouthwatering; limited sweet development; f22 more relaxed with subtle oil just softening the barley and traces of golden syrup towards the finale; **b**22 precise, clipped malt. Would you expect anything else? **43%**

    **John Milroy Selection Glen Grant 1984 Aged 22 Years (83) n**20 **t**22 **f**20 **b**21. Unusually sweet. Raisin concentrate. **46%**

    **Lonach Glen Grant 31 Years Old (84) n**21 **t**22 **f**21 **b**20. Exceptionally firm barley for its age; enjoys a sugar-coated lustre and good depth. **42.3%.**

    **Lonach Glen Grant 35 Years Old (83) n**20 **t**21 **f**21 **b**21. Creaks a bit, but some lovely barley sugar and liquorice. **41.8%.** *Duncan Taylor.*

    **Lonach Glen Grant 1970** cask no. 3487, dist May 70, bott Apr 06 **(78) n**22 **t**19 **f**19 **b**18. Exotic fruit early on, but age catches up with it. **41.5%.** *168 bottles.*

    **MacLeod's Extremely Rare Glen Grant 1949** cask no. 3447 **(83) n**24 **t**21 **f**19 **b**19. A lost cask found a few summers too late for true greatness, although the nose is fabulously complex. For those born in 1949 a fascinating annual dip into the past. **46%.** *80 bottles: one can be found at TasTToe, Kampenhout, Belgium.*

    **Milroy's of Soho Glen Grant 1995 Aged 11 Years** Fino Sherry Butt, cask no. 142920, dist 14 Sept 95, bott 8 Nov 06 **(87) n**22 a hard marriage of firm grape and malt; **t**22 clean, a touch salty with vivid barley; the fruit comes in as an afterthought; **f**21 carries on down that same mouth-watering line with minimal complexity; **b**22 the austere crispness of the Fino is entirely in sympathy with the house style. **46%.** *878 bottles.*

    **Norse Cask Selection Glen Grant 1965 Aged 40 Years (84) n**22 **t**22 **f**20 **b**20. The nose is a mildly drier version of the G&M '66; enough early sweetness but dries big time. **52.5%.** *WhiskyOwner.com, Denmark.*

    **Norse Cask Selection Glen Grant 1967 Aged 38 Years (86) n**21 **t**23 **f**21 **b**21. One of those ancient malts hanging on by the slenderest thread to attractiveness and elegance. Another month or two in the cask and this would have gone. **44.2%.** *Denmark.*

    **Old Malt Cask Glen Grant** Wine finish, dist Nov 92, bott Oct 05 **(92) n**23 crushed green and white peppers give an unexpected twist to the fruity barley; **t**23 beautifully clean delivery and sweet. The crispness of the barley ensures that shape and direction is maintained; **f**23 this has to be one of the cleanest finishes to any wine cask I've ever come across: the barley is pristine and the soft fruits juicy; **b**23 easily one of the better wine finishes around: a malt that is in the pink in every sense... **50%.** *272 bottles.*

    **Platinum Glen Grant Aged 30 Years** dist 76, bott 06 **(80) n**19 **t**20 **f**21 **b**20. One of those big fellows where the malt wallows in the sherry and structure and complexity are in part compromised. A pleasant middle, however, and the alacrity of the spice is a boost. **49.4%.** *Douglas Laing.* 308 bottles.

    **Provenance Glen Grant Aged Over 10 Years** Refill hogshead DMG 2746, dist Spring 96, bott Summer 06 **(87) n**22 you'll never find cleaner barley; **t**22 sparkling malt with little else beyond the fabulous, juicy freshness; **f**21 pretty short but again it's pure grist; **b**22 thanks almost certainly to a third fill cask there is astonishing clarity and mouth-watering properties to this near colourless gem. **46%. nc ncf.** *Douglas Laing.*

    **Provenance Glen Grant Aged 11 Years** dist Summer 95, bott Winter 06 **(85) n**22 **t**22 **f**20 **b**21. Untaxing, something of a Lincoln biscuit sub plot and wholly enjoyable, if a tad bitter at the death. **46%.** *Douglas Laing.*

## GLENGYLE (*see* Kilkerran)

## GLEN KEITH
**Speyside, 1957. Chivas. Silent.**

    **Glen Keith 10 Years Old** db **(80) n**22 **t**21 **f**18 **b**19. A malty if thin dram that finishes with a whimper after an impressively refreshing, grassy start. **43%**

    **Connoisseurs Choice Glen Keith Aged 36 Years** Sherry Hogshead, dist 67, bott 03 **(85) n**22 **t**22 **f**21 **b**20. A clean dram brimming with cream toffee and attractive spices. Attractive and very drinkable but a bit too closed on the finale and lacking development. **46%.**

    **Connoisseurs Choice Glen Keith 1993 (91) n**22 freshly cut rhubarb, barely ripened apple and crisp barley; **t**24 a real malt storm, with a blizzard of barley melting 'gainst the tastebuds – a real and rare hard-soft complexity; **f**22 an almost Glen Grantish follow through of rock hard grain: clean and revitalizing; **b**23 I had to look twice to check the distillery!! You don't see Glen Keiths like this every day – alas! **46%.**

**Coopers Choice Glen Keith 1969 36 Years Old** Single Cask Range, bott 05 **(89)** n22 t23 f22 b22. Well, yawl, I plumb had no idea that this here critter distillery was found smack in middle of Blue Grass country. I'll be a son of a gun.... **49.8%.** *Vintage Malt Whisky.*

**Duncan Taylor Collection Glen Keith 1971 Aged 33 Years (78)** n21 t20 f18 b19. One of those malts that sherry lovers will shoot me down in flames about. Massive sherry, but for me that's exactly the problem: the distillery character has been obliterated and it's all too one-dimensional. **50.8%**

⫶ **Old Malt Cask Glen Keith Aged 33 Years** dist June 73, bott Mar 07 **(83)** n21 t22 f20 b20. A tendency towards thinness and a hot nature, but just enough barley juice to stir the adrenalin. Some deft exotic fruit via the oak also weighs in a large early on. A pretty attractive if raw proposition. **50%.** *Douglas Laing.*

⫶ **Scotch Malt Whisky Society Cask 81.12 Aged 12 Years** Refill Butt, dist Feb 94 **(86)** n20 t22 f22 b22. A malt that rarely rises above blending fodder has its best suit on here: deliciously sprightly barley on delivery, some soft oils and excellent cocoa on death. Impressed. **61.5%**

# GLENKINCHIE
**Lowland, 1837. Diageo. Working.**

**Glenkinchie 10 Years Old** db **(79)** n20 t20 f19 b20. No great shakes on the nose; one-dimensional sweetness on the palate. What the hell was all that about? **43%**

**Cadenhead's Authentic Collection Glenkinchie Aged 18 Years** Bourbon Hogshead dist 87, bott February 06 **(88)** n21 lazy butterscotch; t23 juicy, sharp, tangy barley; f22 spiced vanilla with a late barley sheen; b22 good to see a Lowlander offering so much life at this age – lovely! **56.5%.** *246 bottles.*

⫶ **Cadenhead's Authentic Collection Glenkinchie Aged 19 Years** Bourbon Hogshead, dist 1987, bott May 07 **(84)** n20 t23 f20 b21. A magnificent show by the barley against the oaky odds. At times the mouth-watering elements offer an unexpected citrus joy. **54.8%.** *234 bottles.*

⫶ **Old Malt Cask Glenkinchie Aged 27 Years (83)** n22 t21 f20 b20. Feels the strain from carrying the oak, but the nose of salty fish with rosemary and citrus makes for a good aperitif; **50%. nc ncf.** *Douglas Laing. Miniature bottle.*

⫶ **Scotch Malt Whisky Society Cask 22.26 Aged 19 Years** Refill Hogshead, dist Oct 87 **(85)** n22 t21 f21 b21. Over-zealously sugared though the ability to cut through the oils and clear and clean the palate is rather charming. Most enjoyable, if limited in scope. Some decent oak notes, though, especially on the nose. **52.4%**

# THE GLENLIVET
**Speyside 1824. Chivas. Working.**

**The Glenlivet Aged 12 Years** db **(83)** n20 t22 f20 b21. A surfeit of apples on both nose and body. The malt is quite rich at first but thins out for the vanilla and thick toffee at the death. **40%**

**The Glenlivet Aged 12 Years American Oak Finish** db **(86)** n21 t22 f22 b21. Stylish and under-stated in every department. **40%**

**The Glenlivet Aged 12 Years French Oak Finished** db **(83)** n21 t22 f20 b20. The oak is extraordinary and offers an unusual style of spiciness, though the finish is flatter than might be expected. Good bitter-sweet sync. **40%.**

**The Glenlivet 12 Years Old First Fill Matured** db **(86)** n23 t21 f21 b21. Delightful, playful malt that is slightly underpowered. **40%**

**The Glenlivet Aged 15 Years** db **(84)** n22 t21 f20 b21. Good spice and complexity. Very well-weighted throughout. **43%**

**The Glenlivet 15 Years of Age** db **(80)** n19 t21 f20 b20. There is an undeniable charm to the countless waves of malt and oak. But don't expect much in the way of complexity or charisma. **40%**

**The Glenlivet Aged 15 Years French Oak** bott 04 db **(86)** n21 t22 f21 b22. A by no means straightforward Glenlivet with an accentuated bitter-sweet theme. **43%**

**The Glenlivet French Oak Reserve 15 Years Old** db **(77)** n20 t20 f18 b19. Half-decent honey, but for me this style is a definite "non". **40%**

**The Glenlivet Distillery Edition 16 Years Old** db **(84) n**19 t23 f21 **b**21. Very mildly flawed nose translates elsewhere, but the oily, mildly estery kick is really excellent. **58.1%**

**The Glenlivet 18 Years Old** db **(87) n**22 t22 f21 **b**22. Another Glenlivet that starts beautifully but lacks stamina. **43%**

**The Glenlivet Aged 21 Years Archive** bott 07 db **(87) n**23 wonderfully lively and making a lie of its age: apples and grape vie with juicy barley. Any cleaner and you'd use it as air freshener; **t**22 lovely barley kick to the silky delivery with mini waves of spice, though the gathering toffee makes for a candy-like middle; f20 disappointingly flat and toffeed; **b**22 almost on its way to the most improved single malt of the year. Then the toffee kicked in. Certainly moving in the right direction and worth a second shot in anyone's books. **43%** ⊙ ⊙

⁖ **The Glenlivet XXV 25 Years Old** db **(91) n**24 blindfolded, I might have marked this down as a bourbon with a gender crisis: on the one hand hairy and blokey with muscular oaks, on the other showing feminine nimbleness of grain and mature fruits. Superb... **t**22 some real grapey signs on delivery and again this is a super-soft show, but one that bitters out towards the middle; f22 low key with lots of rumbling toffee and spice; **b**23 the nose sends this into superstar status, though for all its brilliance it's a bit like driving a Mercedes E320 with the engine of a Ford Anglia. **43%**

**The Glenlivet Cellar Collection 1959** bott 02 db **(90) n**22 t23 f22 **b**23. No malt has any right to be this good at this kind of age. Oak has done very little damage, apart from giving a mildly bourbony feel amid some indulgent liquorice, and that can hardly be construed as damage at all. It is the élan of the fruitiness jousting with the rich malt that impresses most. If anyone was born in 1959, this is the bottle you must buy: a 2cl nip every birthday should be enough to see you through to the end in style. **42.28%**

**The Glenlivet Cellar Collection 1964** bott 04 db **(82) n**23 t20 f19 **b**20. Curious, delightful nose with memories of school at that time: polished floors and plasticine with oranges at break. Too oaky on the palate, though. **45.05% ncf**

**The Glenlivet Cellar Collection 1964** Bottle code 2LBF901, bott 04 db **(93) n**24 unequivocal excellence. The sherry is entirely sulphur free and pulses with grape and sultana richness. This is old-time sherry influence but the barley and oak play their part in maximizing complexity. A treat; **t**23 lush, soft and melts into the tastebuds to offer a chalky, peppered fruitiness. Mouthwatering and mesmerizing, even after 40 years; f23 tannins and leather abound, but there is enough muscovado sweetness to edge out the growing oaky-vanilla; **b**23 former distillery manager Jim Cryle selected the casks for this one: he knew exactly what he was doing. **45.1%**. *1,824 bottles.*

**The Glenlivet Cellar Collection 1972** bott Aug 05 db **(93) n**22 pleasing honeycombed fusion of oak and barley also encompasses spice; just a hint of oak tiredness detracts; **t**24 monumental arrival with searing spices pressing home a slightly bourbony theme. Languid liquorice and honeycomb delight; f23 dries towards cocoa and vanilla; **b**24 there is a brilliance to this which will delight bourbon lovers every bit as much as Scotch drinkers. **52.3%**

**The Glenlivet Cellar Collection 1983** Finished in French Oak, bott 03 db **(88) n**22 t23 f21 **b**22. Sophistication and attitude rolled into one. **46%**

**The Glenlivet Nadurra 16 Years old** db **(94) n**22 caramelised ginger wrapped in bitter chocolate; **t**24 enveloping, spellbinding, shocking...an immediate outbreak of Deremara sugar before the tastebuds are crept up on by stealthy malt and coshed by a voluptuous outbreak of Fox's ginger chocolate biscuits; the middle arrival of faintly chilli-ish spice combines beautifully with the warming ginger; f24 lengthier and with more ginger than a very lengthy, gingery thing; **b**24 in some respects one of the sweetest single malts of all time. It would be too sweet altogether except for a balancing ginger-led spice attack that drags the oak into action. The closest thing to a liqueur whisky you will ever find: pure entertainment, sheer class and immeasurable fun. **48%**

**The Glenlivet Vintage 1967** db **(85) n**21 t22 f21 **b**21. excellent cocoa-sherry complexity and no over-ageing.

**The Glenlivet Vintage 1968** db **(82) n**20 t22 f20 **b**20. Firm oak, interesting bite.

**The Glenlivet Vintage 1969** db **(89) n**22 t24 f21 ; **b**22. Fruitcake whisky with great but controlled age.

**The Glenlivet Vintage 1970** db **(93) n**24 t23 f22 **b**24. One of the most delicate distillery-bottled Glenlivets I have tasted.

**The Glenlivet Vintage 1972** db **(84) n**21 **t**22 **f**20 **b**21. Very dry sherry ensures complexity and maximum spice.

**Adelphi Glenlivet 1991 Aged 15 Years** Bourbon Hogshead cask 55486, dist 91, bott Jun 06 **(90) n**21 intense, as if there is a high degree of first-fill bourbon influence; **t**23 stunning! The weight and intensity of the barley works perfectly with the richness offered by the oak. Busy and biting the chewy harmonisation is engrossing; **f**23 chocolate fudge and walnuts; **b**23 what a glorious bottling this is. Compare this to the lacklustre 15-year-old distillery bottling: you could weep! **59.7%**. *258 bottles.*

**Berry's' Own Selection Glenlivet 1972 Aged 32 Years (86) n**19 **t**23 **f**22 **b**22. A fascinating cask which cherishes its vitality. **46%**

**Berry's' Own Selection Glenlivet 1974 Aged 32 Years (84) n**19 **t**22 **f**21 **b**22. A well-mannered dram offering barley-sugar in all the right places. But has a few bags under the eyes. **46%**

**Berry's' Own Selection Glenlivet 1975 Aged 31 Years (77) n**19 **t**21 **f**18 **b**19. A fraction bland on the nose, shapeless and hard, and early mouthwatering spiced-delivery apart, all background noise and too little structure. **54%**

**Cadenhead's Chairman's Stock Glenlivet (Minmore) Aged 30 Years** Sherry butt, dist 76, bott Sept 06 **(95) n**24 sumptuous, seasoned grape; moist fruitcake with the odd burnt raisin. Like sticking your head in a fabulous sherry cask; **t**24 a delivery to die for: pure grapey silk. The accompanying spices also inject an oaky dryness, but the balance is sublime; **f**23 much drier now with the oak having the major say through a cocoa-dusted finale. Thins out, too; **b**24 I have nosed so many dud sherry casks today this almost brings a tear to the eye when the real thing comes along. Hunt a bottle of this unspoiled nectar down at all costs! Nigh faultless malt. **57.1%**. *432 bottles.*

**Cadenhead's Glenlivet (Minmore) Chairman's Stock Aged 35 Years** Sherry butt dist 70, bott Sep 05 **(63) n**15 **t**18 **f**14 **b**16. Iffy and a not very good butt. **58.2%**. *275 bottles.*

**Cask Strength Glenlivet 1990** American Hogshead casks 26928/9, dist 21 Nov 90, bott 21 Apr 05 **(84) n**19 **t**22 **f**22 **b**21. Only toward the finish does this ultimately satisfying dram begin to talk complexity: the arrival is all about uncomplicated and delicious juicy barley. Quite lovely. **59.4%. ncf.** *G&M*

**Celtic Heartlands Glenlivet 1968 (90) n**22 rickety, creaking oak but bound together by a honey core; **t**23 again it is the honey that binds this malt together, with burnt toast bitterness offering a strangely attractive counterbalance; **f**22 a more civilised landing of doughy grain and custardy oak; **b**23 this is one hell of a journey...hang on to your hats and take a deep breath before setting out on this one. **41.2%**. *Jim McEwan/Bruichladdich. American Oak Hogshead.*

∵ **The Clydesdale Glenlivet 13 Years Old** Cask ref. 0262/350684, dist June 93, bott Sept 06 **(83) n**21 **t**21 **f**20 **b**21. Absorbed oak aplenty but the sweeter barley notes delight. **63.3%. nc ncf.** *Blackadder International.*

**D&M Aficionados' Club Bottling Glenlivet Aged 27 Years** cask 6097, dist Mar 79 **(91) n**21 a touch lazy, but sandpaper and barley make an interesting mix; **t**24 absolutely top-of-the-range arrival with an intensity to the sweet malt that has to be tasted to be believed; hints of Demerara and leather sit comfortably with the natural fudge. The spongy mouth-feel orbits perfection; **f**23 a really classy fade-out with hints of honey balancing out the gathering oak; **b**23 a corker of a dram whose arrival on the palate is as profound as it is beguiling. **43%. nc ncf.** *USA.*

∵ **Distillery Malt Glenlivet Aged 21 Years (92) n**23 serious complexity with fresh, newly exposed oak teaming up perfectly with a fruitier, citrussy lead. Lovely; **t**24 light, delicate malt with varying layers of thickening oak but the emphasis on diluted maple sugar; **f**22 oak-rich; takes on some late, controlled bitterness; **b**23 a very feminine dram full of curves, elegance and grace. **40%**. *Gordon & MacPhail.*

**Duncan Taylor Collection Glenlivet 1968** cask 5240, dist Sept 68, bott Mar 06 **(84) n**19 **t**23 **f**21 **b**21. Put your nose too close to this and you'll get splinters. Creaky, but lip-smacking sophistication on the arrival. **53.4%**. *113 bottles.*

∵ **Duncan Taylor Collection Glenlivet 1968** Cask no. 6199 **(87) n**23 clean grape given an oaky boost; **t**22 signs of wear and tear but the climax of the oloroso is a sexy diversion; **f**21 showing the oaky strain, but some Java helps the cause; **b**21 hangs on in there....just! **52.1%**

Duncan Taylor Collection Glenlivet 1968 Cask no. 8227, dist Dec 68 **(73)** n19 t19 f17 b18. Once mighty sherry sinks beneath the oaky waves. **50.9%**

Duncan Taylor Collection Glenlivet 1970 cask 1999, dist Feb 70, bott Apr 06 **(81)** n20 t22 f19 b20. A bit furry around the finish but the arrival radiates spiced barley. **54.8%.** 112 bottles.

Duncan Taylor Collection Glenlivet 1988 dist Sept 88, bott Oct 05 **(85)** n20 t22 f21 b22. Enjoyable to the extent of almost being a cliché for the distillery. **46.1%.** 1,806 bottles.

George & J.G Smith's Glenlivet 1974 **(78)** n19 t20 f20 b19. Friendly, docile, liquorice-oak controlled. **40%.** Gordon & MacPhail.

John Milroy Selection Glenlivet 1975 Aged 30 Years **(94)** n24 fizzy spice punctuates the intense oloroso; a stream of soft molasses and figs helps make for real complexity; sublimely weighted; t23 graceful delivery: sheer velvet as the sherry slides to every point on the palate; the barley-sultana sweetness mocks the oak which fails to get a real foothold; f23 long, no less complex and a touch of latte to complete the job; b24 style and class by the bodega-load... **46%**

Lonach Glenlivet 37 Years Old **(86)** n21 t21 f22 b22. Chic and fruity. **43.1%**

Lonach Glenlivet 1968 **(90)** n22 touches of guava and passion fruit; t22 any softer and it'd never quite land on the palate; the barley really is almost too light for belief; f23 vanilla and red liquorice b23 at first it seems it doesn't quite have the legs. By the third mouthful you review things a little... **41.7%.** Duncan Taylor.

Milroy's of Soho Glenlivet 1990 Aged 16 Years Bourbon Hogshead, cask no. 17146, dist 13 July 90, bott 6 Oct 06 **(83)** n21 t22 f19 b21. The lightness of Glenlivet these days really does accentuate the oak. I'd bet a grand that this was an even better whisky when there wasn't a one in front of the six... **46%.** 330 bottles.

Old Malt Cask Glenlivet Aged 16 Years dist May 90, bott Feb 07 **(84)** n22 t22 f19 b21. A beautiful ginger nose. Some fierce oak at times. **50%.** Douglas Laing. 742 bottles.

Old Malt Cask Glenlivet 20 Years Old dist Dec 85, bott Oct 05 **(86)** n20 t22 f22 b22. Enjoyable, but further proof that this distillery stubbornly refuses to surprise. **50%.** Douglas Laing. 331 bottles.

Old Malt Cask Glenlivet Aged 25 Years dist Apr 80, bott Oct 05 **(92)** n23 a flamboyant aroma (for a Glenlivet) with the vaguest nod towards passion fruit and lime; t23 silky-textured, the barley coats the mouth before a teasing fanfare of exotic fruit, which never quite arrives; f23 lovely balance to this with a wisp of smoke, the oak never offering dryness and the barley and semi-fruit sailing off into the sunset; b23 often you can tell a malt that is OTT: all kinds of exotic fruit abound. Here it has been nipped in the bud and the result borders true excellence. **50%.** Douglas Laing. 260 bottles.

Old Malt Cask Glenlivet Aged 27 Years dist Apr 80, bott Apr 07 **(82)** n20 t22 f20 b20. Makes the right noises early on, but somehow doesn't set the pulse racing. **50%.** Douglas Laing. 277 bottles.

Old Masters Glenlivet 1996 Aged 9 Years cask 906678, dist 96, bott 06 **(88)** n21 soft banana amid intense barley; t22 gushing, mouthwatering barley-sugar jazzed up with spice; f23 lovely delivery of passing honey preludes the light oak as the complexity intensifies; b22 refreshing to see an honest dram like this at such a sprightly age. A little dazzler. **58.5%.** James MacArthur.

Old Masters Glenlivet Aged 10 Years Cask no. 906680, dist 1996, bott 07 **(88)** n21 thin barley; stretched by vanilla t23 more voluptuous and pounding with clean, beautifully rich malt; f22 the sugared gloss slowly vanishes as delicate, chalky vanilla drives home; late natural toffee; b22 shows more signs of age than you might expect but the barley impact is a scorcher. **57.6%.** James MacArthur for Milan Fair 2007. Italy only.

Old Masters Glenlivet 28 Years Old cask 19753, dist 77, bott 06 **(89)** n22 crunchy, sprightly barley; t23 just so juicy with a soft honey hint adding to the zesty barley; f22 soft oils, lingering malt; b22 hardly the most complex of malts, but the refreshing youthfulness is a real turn up for the book. **53.6%.** 150 bottles.

The Peated Malt Old Ballantruan Speyside Glenlivet (see Tomintoul )

Provenance Glenlivet Aged 11 Years dist Autumn 95, bott Autumn 06 **(87)** n22 polished wooden floor and aquirt of barley water; t22 clean, angular barley; f21 a touch of sandalwood; b22 clean, satisfying, untaxing. Would be well appreciated in a blending lab. **46%.** Douglas Laing.

The Queen of the Moorlands Rare Cask Glenlivet 30 Years Old "The Chairman's Bottling" Edition XVI **(94)** n24 from the toffee-apple school of sherry butt brilliance; fresh, clean and ripe and just the right degree of herbs and spices for balance. A stunner; **t**24 mouth-watering, melt-in-the mouth delivery which starts sweetness and kind but peppers up spectacularly; **f**23 back to toffee apples and burst of lush barley to boot; **b**23 one of those wonderful sherry casks that leaves most of today's in the shade. An absolute must – even for non-sherry lovers! **54%**. *The Wine Shop Leek and Congleton, UK.*

⸬ **Scotch Malt Whisky Society Cask 2.71 Aged 21 Years** Refill Hogshead, dist Aug 85 **(89)** n20 an oak note identity parade – with a few ugly customers in there; **t**24 wonderful delivery with a to-die-for combo of barley juice and complex oak – both bitter and sweet simultaneously; to cap it all there are wondrous spices on butterscotch; **f**22 bitters out as some of those aggressive oaks appear, but excellent cocoa, too, to counter; helped along by some barley concentrate; **b**23 the togetherness of the delivery following the nose is one of the biggest shocks of the whisky-tasting year. **56.2%**

⸬ **Scott's Selection Glenlivet 1977** bott 06 **(94)** n23 thick, citrussy barley takes little shrift from even thicker oak; **t**24 if there was an award just for weight and mouth-feel, this'd win a golden gong in the first six seconds of delivery: massive barley but softly oiled (yes, old-timers – remember when this distillery once had a viscosity?) and proffering apples and spiced, tangy marmalade, too; **f**23 mainly much drier but with no shortage of dried fruit; **b**24 from a lost era when Glenlivet had so much more body and pizzazz, rather than the Size 0 bag of bones it so often is today. **50.8%**. *Speyside Distillers.*

**Scott's Selection Glenlivet 1977** bott 05 **(93)** n23 a soft, citric accent to the refreshing barley; **t**24 just unbelievable! Twenty-eight years old and all the freshness of a malt less than half that age. The barley really is about as mouthwatering as it comes at that age and the malty waves bounce against the tastebuds seemingly for ever. Gentle spices add complexity; **f**23 just a soft vanilla feel to this, but it's the rich malt that remains on show; **b**23 this is how I dream of old Glenlivets: unmolested by fancy casks and shouting its ultra-intense, mouthwatering barley from the highest, time- and weather-beaten peaks of Speyside. **49%**. *Speyside Distillers.*

**Scott's Selection Glenlivet 1977** bott 05 **(93)** n23 a soft, citric accent to the refreshing barley; **t**24 just unbelievable! Twenty-eight years old and all the freshness of a malt less than half that age. The barley really is about as mouthwatering as it comes at that age and the malty waves bounce against the tastebuds seemingly for ever. Gentle spices add complexity; **f**23 just a soft vanilla feel to this, but it's the rich malt that remains on show; **b**23 now this is how I dream of old Glenlivets: unmolested by fancy casks and shouting its ultra-intense, mouthwatering barley from the highest, time- and weather-beaten peaks of Speyside. **49%**. *Speyside Distillers.*

⸬ **Wilson & Morgan Barrel Selection Glenlivet Thirty One Years Old** dist 1975, 06 **(88)** n23 a good oaky crutch for bold fruit; **t**22 a mildly spiced battled between oloroso and oak; bitters out towards middle; **f**21 milk toffee; **b**22 slightly flat perhaps, and the oak isn't shy, but such a delight to find such clean, old-time sherry. **46%**

# GLENLOCHY
## Highland (Western), 1898–1983. Closed.

⸬ **Scotch Malt Whisky Society Cask 62.15 Aged 26 Years** Refill Hogshead, dist May 80 **(91)** n23 heads towards exotic fruit but tempered by honey; excellent weight aided by a dab of the most distant smoke; **t**23 perfect delivery belying the years: barley arrives first with a gooseberry backup; textures changes from dry to oily back to dry as the spices evolve; **f**22 dry toast and barley water; **b**23 there's exotic fruit and exotic fruit. Some work. Others don't. This does. There are many worse ways to discover this lost distillery. **59.2%**

# GLENLOSSIE
## Speyside, 1876. Diageo. Working.

**Blackadder Raw Cask Glenlossie 29 Year Old** cask 5949, dist 8 Aug 75, bott Apr 05

**(89) n**20 **t**23 **f**23 **b**23. Honey is the trademark of this wonderful Speysider, and there is enough here to feed the world's bear population. Remarkable for its age. **52.2%**

**Connoisseurs Choice Glenlossie 1978 (91) n**22 Turkish delight; **t**23 fabulously intense malt with barley sugar leading into some boiled fruit sweets; **f**23 wonderful honey refrain and links beautifully with the late chocolate; **b**23 it's like delving into a candy store! 'Lossie flying at full golden colours. **43%**. *G&M.*

⋰ **Duncan Taylor The NC2 Range Glenlossie 1993 (79) n**21 **t**21 **f**18 **b**19. This one must have smoked 30 a day, spent its summers in the sun without cream, been a Millwall supporter, or been a whisky writer some time in its life because, my word, it has aged way beyond its years... **46%. nc ncf.**

**Peerless Glenlossie 1978** (*see* Duncan Taylor Glenlossie 1978)

**Provenance Glenlossie 12 Years Old** dist 18 Nov 92, bott, 17 Feb 05 **(84) n**21 **t**22 **f**21 **b**20. Malty, sharp, simplistic: pure undemanding Speyside. **46%.**

**Provenance Glenlossie 12 Years Old (90) n**22 intriguing waft of distant smoke on the fine barley; **t**23 a stunning malt explosion with crystal clarity to the grassy barley and then a seismic wave of cocoa-spicy oak. The oil is on a slow burner; **f**22 long with those soft, sweet oils; **b**23 say what you like: a well-used cask and would make brilliant blending whisky. All true. But the ebullience of the malt is something to cherish. **46%**

## GLEN MHOR
### Highland (Northern), 1892–1983. Demolished.

**Glen Mhor 1976 Rare Malt** db **(93) n**23 pure barley sugar but any excess sweetness is trimmed by a luxuriant oaky-vanilla thread that is dipped in honeydew melon; **t**24 the delivery on palate edges close to perfection as the natural barley lushness is pricked by oak-induced spice. Oak is very often a detracting factor in an old malt: here it adds depth to the effortless elegance and adds luxuriance to the sweetness; **f**22 long, lithe and lengthened by a surprising puff of peat popping up from nowhere; **b**24 you just dream of truly great whisky sitting in your glass from time to time. But you don't expect it, especially from such an old cask. This was the best example from this distillery I've tasted in 30 years....until the Glenkeir version was unleashed! If you ever want to see a scotch that has stretched the use of oak as far it will go without detriment, here it is. What a pity the distillery has gone because the Mhor the merrier... **52.2%**

⋰ **Duncan Taylor Collection Glen Mhor 1975** Cask no. 4037 **(77) n**21 **t**20 **f**17 **b**19. Rich and voluptuous to start and no little fruit but I'm still picking the splinters out of my taste buds. **41.8%**

**Glenkeir Treasures Glen Mhor 30 Years Old** dist Apr 75, bott Nov 05 **(94) n**24 curiously and attractively rummy: a touch of 13/14 year old Jamaican Long Pond about this. Those esters also help to accentuate the residue barley against the oak. There is a freshness that belies the age; **t**24 lush with stunning esters coating the palate with coffee-crème brulee. The balance between the sugar-coated, ultra-juicy barley and the deepening oak takes some believing, as does the melt-in-the-mouth quality; **f**23 long and perhaps slightly over- dependent on a thick chocolate ice cream theme; **b**23 you just can't fault sensational whisky like this. This distillery is hitting super stardom very late in the day. **51.2%**. *The Whisky Shop. 270 bottles.*

⋰ **Rarest of the Rare Glen Mhor 1975** Cask no. 4031 **(76) n**20 **t**20 **f**17 **b**19. More or less ditto the Duncan Taylor version above. **42.6%.** *Duncan Taylor.*

## GLENMORANGIE
### Highland (Northern), 1843. Glenmorangie Co. Working.

**Glenmorangie 10 Years Old** db **(94) n**24 perhaps the most enigmatic aroma of them all: delicate yet assertive, sweet yet dry, young yet oaky: a malty tone poem; **t**22 flaky oakiness throughout but there is an impossibly complex toastiness to the barley which seems to suggest the lightest hint of smoke; **f**24 amazingly long for such a light dram, drying from the initial sweetness but with flaked almonds amid the oakier, rich cocoa notes; **b**24 remains one of the great single malts: a whisky of uncompromising aesthetic beauty from the first enigmatic whiff to the last teasing and tantalising gulp. Complexity at its most complex. **40%** ☉

**Glenmorangie 15 Years Old** db **(89)** n23 t23 f21 b22. Rich by Glenmorangie standards and very warming. **43%**

**Glenmorangie 15 Years Old Sauternes Wood Finish** db **(68)** n14 t17 f19 b18. Only the intense fruit and finish saves this sulphury one ... to a degree. Not a patch on the standard Sauternes. **46%**. *Duty Free.*

**Glemorangie 18 Years Old** db **(85)** n20 t22 f22 b21. Changed its flavour map considerably from a couple of years back: now much more oaky and a tad oilier. Beautiful honeyed spice, though. **43%** ⊙⊙

**Glenmorangie 25 Years Old** db **(84)** n21 t22 f20 b21. Soft as a baby's bum, but for all its clean tones needs an injection of complexity. **43%**

⠐⠂⠄ **Glenmorangie Quarter Century 25 Years Old** db **(92)** n23 complex, multi-layered oak segmented by barley of varying sweetness; t23 massive delivery with a threat of OTT oak dispelled by nuggets of lightly sweetened cocoa and a soft barley serenade; f23 chocolate honeycomb that must have taken every bee in Scotland to produce, as this goes on for a very long time; b23 one of those great whiskies where the genius that shaped the picture becomes clear only on fifth or six time of viewing. **43%**

**Glenmorangie 30 Years Old** db **(72)** n17 t18 f19 b18. From the evidence in the glass the jury is out on whether it has been spruced up a little in a poor sherry cask – and spruce is the operative word: lots of pine on this wrinkly. **44.1%**

**Glenmorangie 30 Years Old Malaga Finish** db **(92)** astonishing: a very similar type of nose to the 25-y-o version, though there is some chalkier oak; t23 ditto; f23 a slight change here, with the smoke vanishing and light liquorice talking its place; b23 a very strange experience: it is so similar to the 25-y-o to be almost untrue, yet that little extra age has upped the quality a notch or two as the components seem to fit that little bit better. **43%**

⠐⠂⠄ **Glenmorangie 1977** db **(92)** n24 you know that saying about the oranges in 'Morangie....? t23 beautifully soft, and sweet with a breathtaking build- up of ever-sweetening malt – and spices to guarantee balance; salivating; f22 spices remain and the barley bows out slowly as vanilla arrives; b23 excellent, but a trifle underpowered....what would this have been like at 46%...??? Shows little of its great age as the oak is always subservient to the sweet barley and citrus. **43%**. *Exclusively at Harrods.*

**Glenmorangie Artisan Cask** db **(95)** n24 playful, teasing malt, very distant carrot juice and evening primroses among other fruity/floral notes. "En perfum de jardinair" my former French girlfriend may have called it, and quite rightly, too (seeing as this most Scottish of malts wants to use French-derivated appendages to its brand names); t24 the arrival doesn't disappoint, with the malt expectedly leading the way with aplomb; in its wake soft spices stir and also a breathtaking revelry of balancing golden sugars; f23 here these is another change, with the whole finale being a lighter, more sweet gristy affair with less oak and a sublime, fabulously understated final encore; b24 from a seriously disarming former bottling to a totally seductive latest. Those who enjoyed the Golden rum Glenmorangie will find similar threads to enjoy here, too. **46%** ⊙⊙

**Glenmorangie Burgundy Wood Finish** db **(76)** n19 t20 f18 b19. Such an improvement on the first, disastrous, bottling (keep a wary eye out for that one by the way – was lucky to get 69 in the last Bible), yet still I can't see the point of this expression. By Glenmorangie's great standards it is (save for an all too brief, mouthwatering purple patch) dull, listless, unimaginative and takes the malt and imbiber absolutely nowhere. **46%**

**Glenmorangie Burr Oak Reserve** db **(92)** n24 burr by name and nature: prickly, nipping, biting but enormous and not without a passing resemblance to a very high quality bourbon; t24 capow!! The enormity of the oak-thrusted malt leaves little to the imagination: the mouth is coated in its radiance and the bitter-sweet richness positively glows; could easily mistake this for a bourbon; f22 relatively bitter and twisted, but a bourbony liquorice-cocoa character; b22 fades on the finish as a slightly spent force, but nose and arrival are simply breathtaking. Wouldn't be out of place in Kentucky. **56.3%**

**Glenmorangie Cellar 13 Ten Years Old** db **(90)** n22 the very first threads of bourbon notes are filtering through; the butterscotch and honey notes mentioned on the label are spot on; t22 more glorious honey makes for an unusually intense maltiness; f23 that wonderful honey swarms all over the finale. The vanilla picks up in weight, as do some spices; **b**23 oddly enough, as much as this is the most honey-rich Glenmorangie of them all and a tastebud pleaser from first to last, the use of 100% first-fill bourbon has slightly detracted from the all round brilliance and complexity of the standard 10-y-o. **43%**

**Glenmorangie Cote de Beaune** db **(63)** n10 t18 f19 b16. Hard to get past the disastrous nose. Improves towards the end, but too little, too late. **46%**

**Glenmorangie Elegance** db **(92)** n22 quite herbal and soothing; t24 the thinnest layer of icing sugar coats the silk-soft malt; every bit as gentle as the nose suggests; f22 medium to short with some attractive rolling vanilla; **b**24 a surprise package that is not entirely dissimilar to the Golden Rum, only a tad sweeter. **43%**

**Glenmorangie Golden Rum Cask Finish** db **(94)** n23 much of the usual 'Morangie complexity except there is also a syrupy sweetness to this one; t23 after a hesitant first second or two, the flavours sing in diverse harmonisation like a morning chorus: any more delicate it would snap; f24 some honeyed strands are coated in soft rum notes while the vanilla purrs along contently; **b**24 as limited a fan of finishes as I may be, a standing ovation here is richly deserved. The complexity fair boggles the mind. **40%**. *Glenmorangie for Sainsbury's.*

⸭ **Glenmorangie Lasanta** Sherry Finish db **(79)** n19 t21 f19 b20. Bugger. Some sulphur has crept in here. Not a lot. Some may even struggle to find it. But there is enough working behind the scenes to completely throw the show and flatten the experience. **46%**

**Glenmorangie Madeira Matured** db **(93)** n21 big, wilful, spiced fruit and, despite carrying a slight blemish, big, bruising and belligerent; t24 the enormity of the flavour takes some serious map-making. A moderately-spiced grape leads the way, but beneath this the pulse of the barley beats strongly; sweetens fabulously and unexpectedly around the middle. The most mouthwatering 'Morangie of all time? f24 long, with less flaws now but the marrying and then slow fade of the fruit, barley and oak is a treat; **b**24 this is like a scarred, bareknuckled, fist-fighter knocking 50 types of crap out of a classically trained world champion boxer: not one for the purists, but you cannot but admire and gasp in awe ... **56%**

**Glenmorangie Madeira Wood Finish** db **(82)** n17 t22 f22 b21. Like all the Glenmorangie wood finishes the quality can vary dramatically. It's all part of the fun. Here a poor nose is rescued by a wonderful fruit-pastel, candy, mouthwatering arrival. Succulent and sweet. **43%**

⸭ **Glenmorangie Margaux Cask Finish** db **(88)** n22 dark, a bit moody and the odd vinegar note. But, overall, impressive; t22 soft with a soupy barley-grape feel; f22 sweet at first, bitters up; **b**22 even taking every whisky with an open mind, I admit this was better than my subconscious might have considered. Certainly better than the near undrinkable Ch. Margaux '57 I used to bring out for my birthday each year some 20-odd years ago... **46%**

**Genmorangie Millennium Malt Aged 12 Years** db **(83)** n21 t22 f20 b20. This is from entirely 100% first fill bourbon barrels and because of this – and the extra two years – the enchanting spell that makes Glenmorangie the most complex malt on mainland Scotland has been broken. Delicious, make no mistake, but simply too much of a good thing. **40%**

⸭ **Glenmorangie Nectar D'or** Sauternes Finish db **(94)** n23 delicate cinnamon on toast and a drizzle of greengage and sultana; t24 equally refreshing and dense on the palate as the bitter-sweet battle goes into overdrive; excellent weight and body; f23 remains clean and precise, allowing some custard onto the apple strudel finale; **b**24 great to see French casks that actually complement a whisky – so rare! This has replaced the Madeira finish. But there are some similar sweet-fruit characteristics. An exercise in outrageously good sweet-dry balancing. **46%**

**Glenmorangie Port Wood Finish** db **(87)** n22 t21 f22 b22. A big improvement but still not in the league of its first expressions a decade ago. **43%**

⸭ **Glenmorangie Quinta Ruban** Port Finish db **(92)** n24 typical Morangie complexity, but the grape notes added act almost like a prism to show their varied hues; t23 fruit and spice about as the oak goes in search of glory: barley stands in its way; f22 light, deftly sweetened and juicy to the end; **b**23 this replacement of the original Port finish shows a genuine understanding of the importance of grape-oak balance. Both are portrayed with clarity and confidence. This is a form of cask finishing that has progressed from experimentation to certainty. **46%**

**Glenmorangie Sherry Wood Finish (80) n**21 **t**23 **f**17 **b**19. The finish here is more cream toffee than sherry: somewhat disappointing, knowing how good it can be. The initial mouth arrival is superb, though. **43%**

**Glenmorangie Speakeasy** db **(89) n**22 enormous vanilla, dense malt and sawdust; **t**23 bitter-sweet with sharp, acidic fruit hand in hand with even sharper barley; **f**22 some wonderful zesty orange; **b**22 just creaking a little under the oak, but the chewability of the malt is amazing. **63.3%**

**Glenmorangie Speakeasy 1990** db **(83) n**20 **t**22 **f**20 **b**21. Fine malt, as usual, but curiously dry with natural caramel not helping either. **60.2%**

**Glenmorangie Speakeasy 1990** db **(91) n**22 dusty blackboards and floral; even a hint of bourbon here; **t**23 crystal-clean malt launches with a strangely raisiny payload; **f**23 wonderful balance of softly spiced oak and confident malt – again hints of young bourbon towards the finale; **b**23 more oak than normal for a Morangie. But a real delight. **59.7%**

**Glenmorangie Tain L'Hermitage** db **(88) n**22 a busy aroma, full of darting coal gas (at times an improbable hint of very weak peat reek), wild berries crushed in the hand and vanilla-tangerine; **t**21 flat at first, then a rush of ultraripe fruity notes: the middle merges effortlessly into the finish; **f**23 much more together here, with pleasing, mouthwatering fruit outlines against a deepening chocolate kick and those bizarre peat tones again; **b**22 a see-saw of a dram full of rich, mouth-bulging entertainment. **46%.**

**Glenmorangie Traditional** db **(87) n**21 **t**23 **f**22 **b**21. Young, faultless and probably from second-fill bourbon, it reveals how the extra oak turns this from first-rate blending material into a masterpiece. **57%**

**Glenmorangie Truffle Oak** db **(96) n**24 a significant aroma: big, powering oak yet controlled with no sign of bitterness or tiredness. Some golden syrup on the barley is toned down by age. If you can find a flaw or off-note, e-mail me; **t**24 bloody hell!!! Now the golden syrup comes out to play, but the intensity of that plus the barley fair takes the breath away. Something very breakfast- cerealy about this experience. But for grown ups...; **f**25 burning embers of honey-nut cereal last forever. Keeping them company are varying shades of golden to molassed sugar. One of the longest un-peated finishes you'll ever find; **b**23 the Glenmorangie of all Glenmorangies. I really have to work hard and deep into the night to find fault with it. If I am going to be hyper-critical, I'll dock it a mark for being so constantly sweet, though in its defence I have to say that the degree of sweetness alters with astonishing dexterity. Go on, it's Truffle oak: make a pig of yourself...!! **60.5%**

**Glenmorangie Vintage 1975** db **(89) n**23 clementines! It must be Christmas...; **t**23 improbably clean malt for something so aged, then a layer or three of fruit and spiced vanilla; **f**21 bitters out as an oaky trench is found; **b**22 a charming, fruity and beautifully spiced oldie. **43%**

**Glenmorangie Warehouse Three Reserve** db **(92) n**22 dry, yet effervescent malt offers a fruity barley thrust; **t**23 slightly oily perhaps, it's all about thrusting barley and a mouth-puckering sharpness; **f**23 excellent arrival of light oak adding a touch of extra class and charisma to the finale. Lovely cocoa notes radiate warmly; **b**24 another genuinely outstanding expression, a cathartic catalogue of complexity, from a distillery that shows its greatness when allowed. **40%.** *Glenmorangie for Asda.*

⠿ **Scotch Malt Whisky Society Cask 125.1 Aged 13 Years** Designer Hogshead, dist May 93 **(95) n**24 rich, deep pomegranate and bubble gum; some hints of bourbon with red liquorice: absolutely unique; **t**23 silk with attitude: appears to be slipping down with a fruity flourish and then some spices kick in; **f**24 long, lithe, lush and liberally littered with fruit gum; a soft latte/mocha denouement is tinged with demerara; **b**24 just a peach of a cask that re-defines fruitiness as far as whisky is concerned. **51.2%**

⠿ **Scotch Malt Whisky Society Cask 125.2 Aged 11 Years** Designer Hogshead, dist June 95 **(90) n**21 pleasant vanilla if a touch gluey; **t**23 busy, spicy, massive oak delivery but in a useful, friendly manner that apparently ups the barley big time; **f**23 mouth-watering finale with an icing sugar crust to the grassiness; **b**23 very sweet but countered by wonderful spice. Another chance to see the distillery in a light it has rarely been seen in before. **53.5%**

⠿ **Scotch Malt Whisky Society Cask 125.11 Aged 11 Years (84) n**22 **t**21 **f**20 **b**21. A curious one: for all its very obvious barley-led charm missing the normal Glenmorangie complexity on the nose or typical orangie lightness. A bit of a pudding in places with a pleasant sprinkling of something a little sweet. **57%**

# GLEN MORAY
## Speyside, 1897. Glenmorangie Co. Working.

**Glen Moray** (no age statement) db (82) n19 t22 f21 b20. Young, vibrant, fresh malt, beautifully made. Has the feeling of a young blend – without the grain! **40%**

**Glen Moray Classic 8 Years Old** db (86) n20 t22 f21 b23. A vast improvement on previous bottlings with the sluggish fatness replaced by a thinner, barley-rich, slightly sweeter and more precise mouthfeel. **40%**

**Glen Moray 12 Years Old** db (91) n23 a comfortable straddle between very light, teasing malt and soft vanilla; t22 lazy flavour entry: the malt saunters round the palate as if it owns the place, perfect harmony between sweet malt and drier oak; f23 here's where we get to business with the delicate complexity between malt and oak which is simply sublime. Some minor bourbony notes make a subdued approach; b23 one of my favourite Speyside malts for the last 17 years simply because it is so unfailingly consistent and the delicate nature of the whisky has to be experienced to be believed. **40%**

**Glen Moray 16 Years Old** db (88) n23 t21 f22 b22. Seriously easy drinking with not a single note out of tune. **40%**

**Glen Moray 16 Years Old Chenin Blanc Mellowed in Wine Barrels** db (85) n20 t22 f22 b21. A fruity, oak-shaded dram just brimming with complexity. **40%**

**Glen Moray 20 Years Old** db (80) n22 t22 f18 b18. With so much natural cream toffee, it is hard to believe that this has so many years on it. After a quick, refreshing start it pans out, if anything, a little dull. **40%**

**Glen Moray 30 Years Old** db (87) n22 t21 f22 b22. A malt that seems conscious of its old age and delivers carefully and within itself. **43%**

**Glen Moray 1959 Rare Vintage** db (91) n25 t23 f21 b22. They must have been keeping their eyes on this one for a long time: a stunning malt that just about defies nature. The nose reaches absolute perfection. **50.9%**

**Glen Moray 1962 Very Rare Vintage Aged 42 Years** db (94) n23 the thick oak offers something of the farmyard, but there is a hint of apple, rhubarb and citrus to thin it out a little; t24 the orangey/citrussy notes defy the years as the malt delivers some early and surprising blows for youth; by the time the middle arrives the oak has caught up and we have a mishmash of liquorice, bitter chocolate and beautifully controlled spices; f23 some banana milkshake and a very late surge of a vague orangey fruitiness as well; b24 the first temptation is to think that this has succumbed to age, but a second and a third tasting reveal that there is much more complexity, integrity and balance to this than first meets the tastebuds. The last cask chosen by the legendary Ed Dodson before his retirement from the distillery: a pretty perceptive choice. A corker! **50.9%. sc.**

**Glen Moray 1984** db (83) n20 t22 f20 b21. Mouthwatering and incredibly refreshing malt for its age. **40%**

**Glen Moray 1986 Commemorative Bottling** cask 4698 db (96) n25 take your time over this: like a week or so! The bourbon notes are unmistakable (nosing blind I might have plumped for Kentucky!) with a series of rich and sharp blood orange/kumquat notes interlaced with dark chocolate. A peculiarly coastal saltiness has also crept in. Amid all this can be found a sharp maltiness. Just one of the great noses of this and many other years; t24 spectacular bitter-sweet arrival on the palate shows a glorious harmony between the malt and bourbony oak. Beyond this gentle spices about, as do mouthwatering, candy-fruit riches; f23 one of the longest non-peaty fade-outs since "Hotel California"...the ripeness of the malt, enriched by the most fabulous of bitter-sweet molasses lasts until finally replaced by a toasty vanilla; b24 Ed Dodson hand-picked this cask from the warehouse to mark the opening of the distillery's visitor centre in late 2004. Ed has now retired but – and this bottling proves the point entirely – he should be brought back to the distillery, as Elmer T. Lee has at Buffalo Trace, and be given his own named brand. You simply cannot buy the experience and natural feel Ed has for Glen Moray. This astonishing single cask proves the point with a delicious and unforgettable eloquence. **64.4%. ncf.**

**Glen Moray 1989** db **(86)** n23 t22 f20 b21. Doesn't quite live up to the fruit smoothie nose but I'm being a little picky here. **40%**

⋅❁⋅ **Glen Moray 1991 Mountain Oak Malt The Final Release** dist 15 Mar 91, bott 5 Feb 07 db **(94)** n24 a wonderful liquorice/kumquat mix with diluted maple syrup toning down the honey; t24 again that syrup/honey combo is first out of the blocks then we are back to barley – well spiced – and a myriad of vanillins; f23 lots of oaky notes, some bitter, but now encased in soft oils which contain a balancing sweetness; b23 another Scotch malt masquerading as bourbon. Massive and quite beautiful. Until the 1986 edition was released, the previous Mountain Oak was the best Glen Moray I had ever happened upon – and if memory serves me correctly that had a decidly bourbony bent, too. This is up there among the distillery's best ever. **58.6%.** *1,158 bottles.*

**Glen Moray 1992 Single Cask No 1441** Sherry butt db **(74)** n17 t21 f18 b18. Oops! Didn't anyone spot the sulphur ...? **59.6%**

**Glen Moray Classic** db **(79)** n22 t20 f18 b19. Sweet, malty, amiable, but a bitter finish and short of ideas. **40%**

**Glen Moray The Fifth Chapter Distillery Manager's Choice** cask filled 25 Mar 92, bott 12 Sept 05 db **(87)** n18 bugger! Sulphur alert...; t23 an early lick of sulphur is overwhelmed by, at first, salivating barley, and then marauding spices. Enormous and prisoner-free; f23 now drops into cocoa overdrive as the fruit at last finds a voice amid the barley sugar and soft molasses. The elegance is breathtaking; b23 this bottling was to mark the event of Graham Coull becoming only the fifth (and prettiest) man to put his legs under the Glen Moray Distillery Manager's desk. I'd love to have given him a top-notch welcome, but bloody sulphur has struck again. Still, the recovery on the palate is already the stuff of distillery legend! **59.6%. ncf sc.** *430 bottles.*

**Glen Moray Mellowed in Chardonnay Barrels** db **(84)** n20 t22 f21 b21. Cramped on the nose, it is much more expansive on the palate with juicy grape detectable amid the refreshing, busy malt. **40%**

**Glen Moray Mountain Oak** db **(94)** n24 it must be the Appalachians, because there is a distinct bourbony aroma here; t22 a mixture of fresh, lip-smacking barley crashes head-first into something brimming with liquid spice and a smoky, biscuity depth; f24 astonishing length and weight; cut-glass barley sparkles to the very end; b24 Unquestionably the best Glen Moray I have ever tasted: a masterpiece Speysider that, if this quality can be maintained, is set to become a legend through its sheer complexity and depth. **60.5%**

⋅❁⋅ **Cadenhead's Authentic Collection Glen Moray-Glenlivet Aged 16 Years** Bourbon Hogshead, dist 1991, bott May 07 **(81)** n20 t21 f20 b20. Leached so much toffee and tannin out of the oak, it's more like Canadian. **57.1%.** *258 bottles*

**Dewar Rattray Individual Cask Bottling Glen Moray 1990 Aged 16 Years** cask no. 4556, dist May 90, bott May 06 **(88)** n22 reminiscent of toasted oak at a Kentucky cooperage; you can almost taste the charred tannins and caramel; t23 soft liquorice and hickory feed into the barley, tries to be salivating but the warming oak won't let it; f21 buckles slightly under the tannin; b22 a classy, individualistic bottling which for the most part holds the oak well. **55.8%.** *64 bottles.*

**MacLeod's Highland Aged 8 Years (89)** n22 t21 f23 b23. Wow! This may be a Highlander by name on the label, though the source of the whisky is Speyside. But it is Highland by nature with some enormous earthy, resonance. Absolutely top-class stuff that bites and teases deliciously. Love to have seen this at 46% nonchillfiltered: might have had a minor classic on our hands. Glen Moray, though not stated on label. **40%** ⊙

⋅❁⋅ **Murray McDavid Glen Moray 1992** Bourbon/Madeira **(88)** n23 dig deep and be patient enough and you'll find some marzipan and apricots here; t20 at first a bit bitter and untidy, early vanilla; f22 balances better here, and now some interplay between malt and grape; a well integrated finish; b23 the rich malt canvas of the Glen Moray gives the Madeira an unrestricted medium to do its stuff. **46%**

**Norse Cask Selection Glen Moray 1990 Aged 13 Years (78)** n19 t20 f19 b20. A little feinty, which is unusual for this distillery but it is missing its normal charm and is even a tad oily. Still plenty of barley to grip on to, though. **62.1%.** *Denmark.*

## GLEN ORD
### Highland (Northern) 1838. Diageo. Working.

**Glen Ord Aged 12 Years** db **(81)** n20 t23 f18 b20. Just when you thought it safe to go back....for a while Diageo ditched the sherry-style Ord. It has returned. Better than some years ago, when it was an unhappy shadow of this once-great self, but without the sparkle of the vaguely-smoked bottling of a year or two back. Nothing wrong with the rich arrival, but the finish is a mess. I'll open the next bottling with trepidation... **43%**

**Glen Ord 25 Years Old** dist 78 db **(95)** n24 the most narrow seams of peat offer backbone to deeply impressive arrays of fruits, including kumquats, unripe figs and greengages. The oak is firm, as is the malt; t24 nectar-plus!! The astonishing mouthfeel is matched only by the perfectly presented fruit, mainly a citrussy affair, that battles for supremacy against grassy malt and spiced oak. Waiting in the wings is wonderfully gentle smoke. A faultlessly choreographed production; f23 slightly more simplistic here thanks to some caramel being sucked from the oak, but the spices continue as does a fruity tang; b24 some stupendous vatting here: cask selection at its very highest to display Ord in all its far too rarely seen magnificence. **58.3%**

**Glen Ord 28 Years Old** db **(90)** n22 malt and mint bound together by soft liquorice and dark fudge; t23 delightful barley-sugar theme that forms a stupendously rigid middle with the most delicate hints of smoke and coffee. The body weight is perfect; f22 amazingly long finale with lashings of cocoa to go with the mollassed sugar and powering barley; b23 this is mega whisky showing slight traces of sap, especially on the nose, but otherwise a concentrate of many of the qualities I remember from this distillery before it was bottled in a much ruined form. Blisteringly beautiful. **58.3%.**

**Glen Ord 30 Years Old** db **(87)** n22 shaped by oak, there is a peppery element to the floral thrust; t21 molten barley spearheads the arrival before a cumbersome oakiness interferes. Plenty of spice and underpinning sweetness; f23 settles down for a really long and delightful finish with a glorious interaction between delicate, velvety barley and vanilla. Charming; b21 creaking with oak, but such is the polish to the barley some serious class is on show. **58.8%**

⋅⋅⋅ **Singleton of Glen Ord 12 Years Old** db **(83)** n21 t22 f20 b20. Pleasant with some attractive blood orange notes. But, overall, it's all rather flat and fails to take off the way it should. **40%**

**Cadenhead's Authentic Collection Ord Aged 22 Years** Bourbon Hogshead, dist 83, bott Feb 06 **(88)** n21 healthy oak entanglement; t23 quite lovely barley richness, with beautifully disguised biscuity sweetness; f21 estery and a tad salty but otherwise thin; b23 a clever and attractive malt that carries its advancing years with aplomb. **55%.** 210 bottles.

⋅⋅⋅ **Kingsbury's "The Selection" Ord 1999** Hogshead cask nos. 304154/304155, dist Mar 99, bott July 06 **(88)** n22 youthful, exuberant, light; t22 mouth-watering, clean, barley water; f22 more of the same but now with an extra dose of maple syrup; b22 deliciously and delightfully gristy. **43%. ncf.** Japan Imports System Co. Ltd. 938 bottles.

**Old Malt Cask Glen Ord Aged 15 Years** cask 1335, dist Jan 89, bott Sept 04 **(83)** n21 t22 f20 b20. A well-used bourbon cask allows this one to pass off as a juicy and clean 10-year-old. **50%. nc ncf.** Douglas Laing. 604 bottles.

⋅⋅⋅ **Old Malt Cask Glen Ord Aged 18 Years Sherry Finish** dist Jan 89, bott Feb 07 **(90)** n24 multiple layers of barley and sultana dovetail with lemon-ginger and oak. Sublime; t23 more mouth-watering on delivery than any 18-year-old has a right be to; again it's the barley and grape at full play, with the very lightest wisps of smoke. The oak crashes in mid stream; f21 lots more oak, this time with a natural toffee/dried date edge b22 just shows how stupendous this distillery can be when left to its own devices. **50%.** 808 bottles.

## GLENROTHES
### Speyside, 1878. Edrington. Working.

**Glenrothes 1972** db **(88)** n23 t23 f20 b22. A shy malt for its age, releasing all its complexity on the intrinsic, suety/fruity nose and mouth arrival that is simply to die for. Old age catches up on the flat finish, though. **43%.**

**The Glenrothes 1974** bott 03 db **(94)** n24 t24 f23 b23. I know people who are Glenrothes aficionados: their lives revolve around this distillery. Without this truly classic dram, those lives will be incomplete. **43%**

⊹ **The Glenrothes 1979 Single Cask No. 3808** db **(95) n**24 a near faultless nose with the clarity of the fruit, presumably sherry (though maybe not first fill), is enough to bring a tear to the eye: a sweet nougat kick is matched by rich, spiced sultana, the most elegant wisp of smoke and a polished, leathery edge that is not entirely like a well-aged bourbon: absolutely something for everyone... **t**23 the malt dissolves on impact letting in several shockwaves of spice; almost brutally fruity yet the honeyed seam is a thick one; **f**24 long, the most playful vanillas and with a confidence bordering on arrogance as the spices re-ignite, as if telling you that it'll end when it feels like it...not when it theoretically should...meanwhile, the very lightly smoked honey and burned fudge just go on and on and on... **b**24 a pearl of a malt that has me scratching my head in wonder. Although from a single cask, there are elements in this which are pure bourbon and others which are pure sherry – in every sense. In the end, it doesn't much matter because the tastebuds are almost too overwhelmed to take in all that is on offer. Stunning. **55.2%**

⊹ **The Glenrothes 1979 Single Cask No. 13458** db **(68) n**18 **t**19 **f**15 **b**16. Wrecked by sulphur. In whisky terms, tragic. **57%**

⊹ **The Glenrothes 1979 Single Cask No. 13459** db **(75) n**20 **t**20 **f**17 **b**18. This twin cask to 13458 has also seen a sulphur stick at work, but it wasn't kept inside anything to lie so long. Even so, enough damage to the finish undoes the promising big fruit start. **56.6%**

**Glenrothes 1979 Single Cask** cask 13466 db **(94) n**23 leather armchairs, gentlemen's clubs, dusty libraries, polished oak, oloroso evaporating from a sleeping octogenerian's chair; traces of a burnt match; **t**24 dry oloroso crashing head-first into rich, honied malt; a welter of spicy punches are jabbed around the tastebuds; **f**23 burnt fudge, strings of dark liquorice and hints of coffee-infused Demerara pot still rum; **b**24 creaks around the palate with effortless class. **57%**

**The Glenrothes 1979** cask 13470 db **(95) n**24 a basket of toffee apples sitting under a spice rack. Awesome; **t**24 massive spice and hickory start, sweetened with mollased sugar and honeycomb; **f**23 long, with the spices remaining playful and the vanilla intervention soft and empathic; **b**24 that's what you call a sherry cask: big, yet everything just-so. Classic. **57.5%. sc.**

**Glenrothes 1979** bott 05 db **(91) n**22 **t**23 **f**23 **b**23. An understated gem, simply because the complexity unfolds almost imperceptibly. **43%.**

**Glenrothes 1984** bott 05 db **(87) n**22 **t**22 **f**21 **b**22. Well weighted malt with confident, spicy character. **43%.**

**The Glenrothes 1985 Vintage** dist 21 July 85, bott 31 May 05 db **(88) n**23 great complexity, offering salty, buttered crumpets and toasted hot cross buns; **t**23 silky sultanas; the spices begin to bombard as the barley and oak jostle for supremacy; **f**20 toasty and ever-drying; **b**22 a lovely old whisky which fades fast. **43%**

**Glenrothes 1987** bott 05 db **(83) n**20 **t**21 **f**21 **b**21. Enticing marmalade on toast, but never quite hits the heights expected. **43%.**

**The Glenrothes 1991** dist 7.9.91, bott 24.5.05 db **(85) n**20 **t**22 **f**21 **b**22. It is as if this distillery wants to challenge your tolerance levels: a malt that should ebb in the healthy 90s has been pegged back by guess what. **43%**

⊹ **The Glenrothes 1994** dist Oct 94, bott 11 Apr 06 db **(89) n**20 heavy, ponderous and mildly off-key fruit lightened with by a dash of honey and a topping of butterscotch; quite spicy; **t**23 fantastically busy arrival with a good smattering of spices to lift the big malt and liquorice middle; gentle Java tones arrive with the vanilla; **f**23 no little latte coffee as the differing oak tones merge **b**23 nose apart, a seriously good choice of cask with no stinting on the complexity. **43%**

**The Glenrothes Select Reserve (87) n**20 just when you wonder if a touch of sulphur has crept in, all is lost under an avalanche of over-ripe oranges. Jury's out ...; **t**24 one of the softest deliveries in Speyside, the silky barley and citrus caress the tastebuds with rare tenderness; a drop of honey assists; **f**21 again, there is a strange note to the coffee and cocoa finale; **b**22 definitely flawed greatness. **43%**

**Cadenhead's Authentic Collection Glenrothes-Glenlivet Aged 14 Years** Sherry Butt, dist 90, bott May 05 **(80) n**20 **t**19 **f**22 **b**19. One of those big, spicy butts which completely consume the whisky. Some people like this style. I must admit I don't. No off notes but, excellent finish apart, just nothing interesting going on. **58.8%.** *636 bottles.*

**Cadenhead's Authentic Collection Glenrothes Aged 15 Years** Sherry butt, dist 90, bott May 06 **(71) n**18 **t**18 **f**17 **b**18. Sulphur tinged. **59.5%.** *582 bottles.*

⋰· **Cadenhead's Authentic Collection Glenrothes Aged 16 Years** Rum butt, dist 90, bott Feb 07 **(96) n**24 weird sherry-type aroma, with a weird Demerara-style kick and weird burnt raisin without the bitterness, probably because of barley...beautiful in its very own very weird and slightly bourbony-rummy way... **t**23 entirely off-key delivery steadies itself quite quickly with the aid of in-rushing spices. Loads of burnt fruit and toasty barley abound; **f**25 Java coffee by the teaspoonful, embracing spices and then the coffee sweetened by Demerara sugar. Good grief... **b**24 you don't many of these to the dozen. A very different shape and delivery from most malts with the balance at times slipping and sliding like a one-legged man on a skate... and then suddenly everything falls wondrously into shape. A malt that shows that the line between madness and genius is so very thin...and genius this genuinely is... **573%.** *588 bottles.*

⋰· **Chieftain's Glenrothes 13 Years** Old Hogshead, dist June 93 **(88) n**20 musty; not the most impressive; **t**22 that off-key note sounds first and is then completely over-run by a gathering of the most sublimely intense malt imaginable; **f**23 goes into fruity-malty-spicy overdrive...and those spices do get deliciously prickly **b**23 the entire tasting experience makes a lie of the nose. Thoroughly enjoyable malt. **46%. nc ncf.** *Ian Macleod.*

**Dun Bheagan Glenrothes 12 Years Old** Sherry finish **(79) n**20 **t**21 **f**19 **b**19. A cleanish, sound sherry cask but short changes in the complexity department. **43%.** *Ian Macleod.*

⋰· **Duncan Taylor Collection Glenrothes 1969** Cask no. 381, dist Jan 69 **(73) n**19 **t**19 **f**17 **b**18. This doesn't need water...just a Zimmer. **40.7%**

⋰· **Duncan Taylor Collection Glenrothes 1969** Cask no. 383, dist Jan 69 **(80) n**21 **t**21 **f**19 **b**19. It may be the twin to cask 381 (above), but this one is still breathing. Collapses at the end but does a neat barley-honey shuffle before the oxygen mask is applied. **41.5%**

**Duncan Taylor Collection Glenrothes 1970** cask 10574, dist July 70, bott Apr 06 **(79) n**20 **t**19 **f**20 **b**20. Pleasant, but a touch jaded and enormous natural toffee. **43.5%.** *162 bottles.*

**Lonach Glenrothes 35 Years Old (93) n**23 heading into exotic fruit territory; **t**24 about as soft a delivery as you'll ever get. Not sure which direction to take at first, though it has to be said the bitter-sweet balance during contemplation and dissolving just couldn't be finer. Decides to pan out, as you might expect, towards drier oak; **f**22 a vague hint of something smoky and mocha and cream brings the curtain down on this most elegant of old gentlemen; **b**24 Takes time to really get to understand and appreciate this whisky: once you pick up what it's all about you will be charmed, I'm sure. **40.2%.** *Duncan Taylor.*

⋰· **The MacPhail's Collection Glenrothes 1965 (83) n**20 **t**22 **f**20 **b**21. A distinctively bourbony air to this one with no little liquorice amid the honey. Good spice, too. But maybe the odd splinter too many. **43%.**

**MacPhail's Collection Glenrothes 1965 (87) n**22 **t**23 **f**21 **b**21. Loses it on the finish somewhat, but the early complexity is a treat. **43%**

**Murray McDavid Mission Glenrothes 1968** Bourbon/Mourvedra/Syrah **(84) n**23 **t**21 **f**20 **b**20. The vivid nose of barely ripened blood oranges is not quite matched by the confused delivery which follows. Still clean and tasty, though. **45.5%.** *300 bottles.*

⋰· **Norse Cask Selection Glenrothes 1994 Aged 11 Years** Hogshead cask no. 186, dist Dec 94, bott Jan 06 **(89) n**22 dry marzipan topped with custard; **t**22 crisp, firm and with an excellent gloss to the barley; **f**22 a lovely lime tinge to the warming oak and barley; **b**23 an exceptionally demure and finely balanced malt that makes the most of a very decent bourbon cask. **58%. nc ncf.** *WhiskyOwner.com, Denmark. 320 bottles.*

**Norse Cask Selection Glenrothes 1988 Aged 15 Years (84) n**21 **t**22 **f**20 **b**21. Rich and pleasantly honeyed. **55.4%.** *Denmark.*

⋰· **Old Malt Cask Glenrothes Aged 16 Years Rum Finish** dist Nov 90, bott Mar 07 **(92) n**23 for all the obvious rum involvement it is probably the bourbon oakiness that holds sway; excellent weight and balance – slightly Jamaican in style; **t**22 warm, biting and at once bracing delivery with a massive barley surge that battles against the peppers; **f**24 settles down for something a little special with a glorious marriage of coffee and spice which only sets the scene for the delicate but distinctive echoes of rum and real – or imaginary Jackfruit. Beautifully oiled and quite superb; **b**23 a malt that lives long on the finish and in the memory. Wonderful! **50%.** *Douglas Laing. 318 bottles.*

⋰ **Old Malt Cask Glenrothes Aged 21 Years Rum Finish** dist Feb 85, bott Nov 06 **(89) n**23 the oak cranks up the weight big time, though the rum involvement is anything but token; **t**23 near perfection to the delivery and first big toffee-apple thrust; goes through the burnt honeyed gears until it reaches dried dates; **f**21 rather too enthusiastic oak that has a somewhat singed toast feel to it; **b**22 really lovely whisky but all the rum's excellent input fails to entirely disguise some over-aging. **50%.** *372 bottles.*

**Old Malt Cask Glenrothes 27 Years Old** Wine finish, dist Apr 79, bott July 06 **(66) n**17 **t**18 **f**15 **b**16. Suicide or murder? Was the sulphur there with an early sherry butt or was it the wine cask that did it? **50%.** *Douglas Laing. 363 bottles.*

⋰ **Old Masters Glenrothes Aged 12 Years Old** Cask no. 826089, dist 1994, bott 07 **(91) n**23 very clean and rich sherry with a honeyed, plummy aside; **t**23 outstanding oloroso effect with an immediate build up of spice; the oak then suggests something a lot older; **f**22 almost a bourbony-style vanilla alongside grape; **b**23 bit of an oddity this: begins life as uncompromising and rare unspoiled sherry... and finishes as something from Kentucky! Fabulous. **51.9%.** *James MacArthur for USA only.*

**Old Masters Glenrothes 1988 Aged 17 Years** cask no. 6995, bott 06 **(94) n**24 beautiful strata of acacia honey, maple syrup and Lubeck's finest, with just enough chalky oak to balance; **t**24 the sweetness generated is enormous yet somehow controlled with vivid barley sugar in concentrated form. Remarkable freshness remains; **f**23 a gentle reduction of all the starring qualities as the oak adds a quality riposte; **b**23 for that extraordinary number of Glenrothes fans out there, here is a must have...! **54.1%.**

**Platinum Glenrothes 25 Years Old** dist 21 Apr 79, bott May 05 **(87) n**23 the hint of sulphur is outweighed by the intensity of the toffee apple from what must, originally, have been one helluva butt; **t**23 more chewy toffee and dried dates: this is sherry influence at its most enormous. A slight flaw detectable, but you cannot be butt amazed; **f**19 a trace of sulphur tang, butt what toffee-treacle influence we have, right to the bitter end! **b**22 no ifs or butts here: genuine flawed genius. **51.9%.** *325 bottles.*

**Provenance Glenrothes Aged 10 Years (86) n**22 **t**21 **f**22 **b**21. Clean, re-vitalising malt. But the grappa nose is a real surprise! **46%.** *Douglas Laing.*

**Provenance Glenrothes 14 Years Old** dist 20 Nov 90, bott 5 Apr 05 **(83) n**22 **t**21 **f**20 **b**20. Busy, chewy, with mouthfilling fruit. **46%.** *Douglas Laing*

**Scott's Selection Glenrothes 1980** bott 05 **(84) n**20 **t**22 **f**21 **b**21. Such a light malt, the character is changing distinctly in the direction of spicy bourbon. **53.1%.**

## GLEN SCOTIA
### Campbeltown, 1832. Glen Catrine. Working.

**Glen Scotia Heavily Peated**, cask 518, dist 23 July 99 db **(92) n**22 moist marzipan adds a sweet, nutty element to the pre-pubescent, vaguely Bowmore-style peat. Deliciously young; **t**23 fresh, enormously sweet and surprisingly oily for this distillery: but, for all this, it is stunningly balanced and charismatic; **f**23 dries very impressively; there is an imperious flourish to the peaty signature; **b**24 this is pretty big and quite beautifully made malt. Forget the age. Enjoy a touch of class. **45%**

**Glen Scotia Heavily Peated**, cask 525, dist 23 July 99 db **(85) n**21 **t**22 **f**22 **b**20. Tasty, but relatively blunt, nothing like so together or complex as cask 518. **45%**

⋰ **Glen Scotia Aged Over 5 Years** cask no 337, dist 30 June 00, bott 16 June 06 db **(86) n**21 **t**23 **f**21 **b**21. A youthful and quite delicious maltfest. Hardly complex, but in classier clothing than it's appeared in for some time. **45%. nc ncf.** *350 bottles*

**Glen Scotia Aged 12 Years** db **(81) n**23 **t**21 **f**18 **b**19. What a whisky: you could write a book about it, a thriller. It'd be called "Murder by Caramel." The early signs on the nose and palate arrival are genuinely awesome. But then...then.....!!! I can't say for sure if it's natural from the oak, or has been added. Unmolested, this malt would be in the very high 80s, possibly low 90s: there is something wondrous in there, not least the richness of the diced apple and honey on the nose: you don't have to hunt too hard to see what I mean. Let's hope I'll be able to give it that score next year. **40%**

**Glen Scotia 14 Years Old** db **(90) n**23 complex, with darting malty notes nipping around, almost like the small grains in a bourbon: really top-quality stuff; **t**22 busy, light maltiness with flickering intensity. The malty sweetness is never more than a passing illumination amid the gathering cocoa oakiness; **f**22 gristy malt and soft oak intertwine;

**b**23 if Glen Scotia had been this good in the past it wouldn't have suffered such a chequered career. Absolutely engrossing malt with fabulous complexity. **40%**

⠿ **Glen Scotia Cask No. 78** American Oak, dist 31 May 99, bott 24 Apr 07 db **(85)** **n**22 **t**22 **f**20 **b**21. Juicy and chewy; perhaps a slight conflict when the oak gets close and personal. **45%**. *345 bottles.*

⠿ **Glen Scotia Cask No. 404** American Oak, dist 18 July 01, bott 23 Apr 07 db **(89)** **n**23 though so young there is a distinct touch of the bourbons here amid the clean, intense malt; **t**22 further evidence that a malt can sing on the palate even at these tender years with wonderful waves of unrushing sweet barley sugar; **f**22 lovely spices abound; **b**22 remarkable isn't it? Put some people into a distillery who know how to make whisky and...hey presto!! A five-year-old beauty! **45%**. *410 bottles.*

⠿ **Glen Scotia Cask No. 511** American Oak, dist 23 July 99, bott 26 Apr 07 db **(90)** **n**22 a sprig of mint lightens the peat; **t**23 the lightness of the body allows the smoke to show bigger than it might; so delicate for a peaty guy with the sweetness of the barley not afraid to show itself; **f**22 remains light with spices suffusing into the building vanilla; **b**23 not every cylinder fires here, but enough to make for a pretty profound and unforgettable dram. **45%**. *360 bottles.*

⠿ **Glen Scotia Cask No. 546** American Oak, dist 23 July 99, bott 25 Apr 07 db **(84)** **n**21 **t**22 **f**21 **b**20. Considering this is from the same distillate as 511, we have chalk and cheese here. In this bottling the oak is rather niggardly and closed. Very pleasant but... **45%**. *325 btls.*

**Cadenhead's Authentic Collection Glen Scotia Aged 14 Years** Sherry Hogshead, dist 91, bott Feb 06 **(84)** **n**21 **t**19 **f**23 **b**21. A bear-hug of a whisky at times threatening to crush the tastebuds; just enough honey to ease the sherry-oak grip. Fine spice and the odd second or two here is simply sublime. **57.7%**. *198 bottles.*

⠿ **Cadenhead's Authentic Collection Glen Scotia Aged 15 Years** Sherry hogshead, dist 91, bott Feb 07 **(87)** **n**22 Any heavier and it'd have a heart attack; really dense oloroso; meaty; **t**23 punchy delivery with the big thick malt in cahoots with the big thick sherry; **f**21 bitters out with burnt raisin; **b**21 about as subtle as a poke in the eye, but equally as noticeable. **57.8%**. *Cadenhead's. 210 bottles.*

⠿ **The Clydesdale Glen Scotia 15 Years Old** Cask ref. 0233/1080, dist May 91, bott Sept 06 **(75)** **n**19 **t**19 **f**18 **b**19. Not one of the better bottlings. **62.1%. nc ncf.** *Blackadder.*

⠿ **Dun Bheagan Glen Scotia 1975 Aged 31 Years** dist June 75 **(88)** **n**23 tinned peaches and custard **t**23 massively sharp and mouth-watering; the juicy barley is in concentrate form early on but hits an oaky wall; **f**20 pretty dry and tired but just enough malt to see it through; **b**22 a close shave here: a cask on the edge, but you can only marvel at the superb early delivery. **51.4%. nc ncf.** *Ian Macleod.*

⠿ **The MacPhail's Collection Glen Scotia 1991 (72)** **n**19 **t**18 **f**17 **b**18 The distillery not quite at its co-ordinated best. **43%**. *Gordon & MacPhail.*

⠿ **Scotch Malt Whisky Society Cask 93.25 Aged 14 Years** Refill Hogshead, dist Mar 92 **(90)** **n**22 thin, but there is good humour between the firm barley and gritty oak; some dried orange peel offers a degree of fruit and complexity; **t**23 initially warming and sharper so the sudden development of the barley into something clean and mind-bogglingly intense is almost shocking; **f**22 a few rough edges but it's cocoa all the way; **b**23 distilled during one of the more grisly periods of this distillery's history. And for all its obvious lack of breeding, this one has most certainly blossomed into something a little special. **63.9%**

⠿ **Scott's Selection Glen Scotia 1992** bott 07 **(75)** **n**19 **t**18 **f**20 **b**18. Hot and fractured in part; the finish has its odd decent cocoa-rich moment. **57.2%**. *Speyside Distillers.*

**The Whisky Fair Glen Scotia Aged 30 Years** Rum barrel, dist June 75, bott June 06 **(74)** **n**19 **t**19 **f**18 **b**18. The bubble gum nose gives due warning to the rather messy ride that is to come. **47.5%. nc ncf.** *Germany. 96 bottles.*

**The Whisky Fair Glen Scotia (Heavily Peated)** 1999 casks 541/542, dist Jul 99, bott June 06 **(89)** **n**22 firm peat gathering depths it warms in the glass; drier than many Islays of its age and a flash of hickory for extra weight. But lovely and young, nonetheless; **t**23 every bit as big as the nose suggests and again the sweetness, though momentarily intense, is kept under leash; more oak depth than might be expected for a 6-y-o; **f**22 chewy peat allows through some firm barley. A touch of coffee simmers, but youth has its way; **b**22 always a treat to come across a dram so brimming with the vitality of youth. **52.7%**. *Germany. 464 bottles.*

# GLEN SPEY
### Speyside, 1885. Diageo. Working.

**Glen Spey Aged 12 Years** db **(90) n**23 the kind of firm, busy malt you expect from this distillery plus some lovely spice; **t**22 mouthwatering and fresh, a layer of honey makes for an easy three or four minutes; **f**22 drier vanilla, but the pulsing oak is controlled and stylish; **b**23 very similar to the first Glen Spey I can remember in this range, the one before the over-toffeed effort of two years ago. Great to see it back to its more natural, stunningly beautiful self. **43%.** *Flora and Fauna range.*

**Adelphi Glen Spey 1977 Aged 28 Years** cask 3655, bott 05 **(93) n**23 light malt and a plate of crushed Alpine flowers; **t**24 poised, classy interaction between absolutely pristine malt and a variety of spices. And even the shyest hints of smoke. Brilliant; **f**23 long, soft development of citrus, orangey fruit and grassy malt: Speyside at its most playfully sublime; **b**23 I have long adored this underrated and little-known distillery, and when a bottling arrives so true to its character I can only sit here and applaud! **51.2%.** *154 bottles.*

**Connoisseurs Choice Glen Spey 1995 (76) n**19 **t**19 **f**19 **b**19. Vapid blending fodder. **43%.** *Gordon & MacPhail.*

**James MacArthur Glen Spey 1992 Aged 12 Years** bott 05 **(85) n**22 **t**22 **f**20 **b**21. In so many ways this is the distillery crystallised: one of the cleanest of all Scotland's malts and with an exceptionally sweet barley-sugar kick. But steadfastly refuses to kick on and develop. **43%**

**Murray McDavid Glen Spey Aged 9 Years** Bourboun/Madeira, dist 96, bott 05 **(87) n**21 robustly meaty; **t**22 lethargic start then, from out of the blue (or pink in this case), a whoosh of oily malt and fruit; **f**22 moist fruitcake and still oily; **b**22 absolutely no other whisky to compare this to: a unique fingerprint to this one. **46%. nc ncf.** *2,400 bottles.*

⠿ **Murray McDavid Glen Spey 1996 Aged 11 Years** Bourbon/Madeira **(78) n**20 **t**20 **f**19 **b**19. The wafer-thin malt appears to buckle under the weight of the fruit. Not at all unpleasant, but appears to find balance hard to come by. **46%**

**Murray McDavid Mission Selection Number 4 Glen Spey 1974 Aged 30 Years (84) n**21 **t**20 **f**22 **b**21. Some fresh mango developes with the white-hot peppers to make for a fascinating and entertaining dram. **46%.**

⠿ **Norse Cask Selection Glen Spey 1995 Aged 11 Years** Hogshead cask no. 421 **(79) n**18 **t**21 **f**20 **b**20. Glen Spey has always, traditionally, been one of the lightest and cleanest of the Speyside malts. This, though pleasant, is hardly representative. **59.7%** *WhiskyOwner.com, Denmark.*

⠿ **Norse Cask Selection Glen Spey 1995 Aged 11 Years** Cognac Finish Hogshead cask no. 421 **(84) n**20 **t**22 **f**21 **b**21. A fascinating experiment: part of exactly the same cask which failed above has been finished in Cognac. The result is sweeter, cleaner malt all round. Though, for all its added charms, still falls a little short of excellence. **59.7%.** *WhiskyOwner.com, Denmark.*

**Old Malt Cask Glen Spey 28 Years Old** dist Dec 77, bott Oct 05 **(91) n**23 there must be a shortage of bananas somewhere. And oak... and smoke... ???; **t**22 tied down with some early oak but slowly blossoms, helped along the way by some surprising – but welcome – gentle peat notes that build in intensity; **f**23 with the smoke giving weight and length, everything else falls into place; exotic, silky fruit links beautifully with the juicy barley; **b**23 a surprise package. I have nosed and tasted peated Glen Spey before, and it was usually from this period, but it is a long time since I have seen it take a leading role. Quite beautiful. **50%.** *Douglas Laing. 233 bottles.*

# GLENTAUCHERS
### Speyside, 1898. Chivas. Working.

**Gordon & MacPhail Distillery Label Glentauchers 14 Years Old** bott 15.02.05 **(87) n**22 the barley bristles about the nose; vanilla and coal dust interject; **t**22 simmering, mouthwatering barley of stunning freshness; **f**21 cream toffee; **b**22 not the most complex expression but the early delivery has so much energy. **43%.** *US Market.*

**Old Malt Cask Glentauchers Aged 12 Years** dist Mar 93, bott Aug 05 **(89) n**22 don't often get hints of carrot on the nose: you do here; **t**22 bristling malt and a subtle layer of maple syrup; **f**22 a lovely touch of hickory and vanilla rounds off a busy encounter; **b**23 a delightful, ever-shifting malt that plays teasing games with the tastebuds. **50%.**

✧ **Old Malt Cask Glentauchers Aged 12 Years** dist Nov 94, bott Feb 07 **(88) n**22 clean, cement-hard barley softened by oak **t**23 juiced-up barley attack with a sweetish, gristy edge; **f**21 oakier, making just the right drier noises **b**22 fabulous blending whisky that doubles up as an unerring single malt of crisp substance. **50%.** 354 bottles.

**Old Malt Cask Glentauchers Aged 15 Years** dist Aug 90, bott Nov 05 **(86) n**22 **t**22 **f**21 **b**21. 'Tauchers in its most simplistic mood. **50%.** Douglas Laing. 270 bottles.

✧ **Old Malt Cask Glentauchers Aged 30 Years** dist Oct 76, bott Nov 06 **(86) n**21 **t**23 **f**21 **b**21. A malt not particularly built for this type of oaky incarceration but has enough guts and charisma to weave a wonderful barley-fruit thread through the oak. The spices delight. **50%.** Douglas Laing. 310 bottles.

**Old Master's Glentauchers 1990 14 Year Old**, cask 14426, bott Feb 05 **(92) n**22 **t**23 **f**24 **b**23. Absolutely tip-top stuff, full of fizz and vitality. One of the longest Speyside finishes of the year. I have long adored this distillery and it's great to see it back up its sister bottling with such blistering panache. **58.5%.** James MacArthur.

**The Queen of the Moorlands Rare Cask Glentauchers 1990 Edition No. 10** Hogshead 14431, dist 21 Nov 90, bott 21 Nov 05 **(92) n**23 the clarity here is invigorating: no off notes, no fussiness from the oak. Just Speyside-style malt at its finest; **t**24 cut-glass barley cleanses the palate; the bitter-sweet elements are sublime, the drizzle of oak, just so; **f**22 maintains shape, poise and bristling barley to the last embers; **b**23 if you ever wanted to know exactly what a very good cask from this great distillery tastes like, look no further. **58.6%. sc.** Available at The Wine Shop, Leek, UK. 195 bottles.

✧ **Scotch Malt Whisky Society Cask 63.18 Aged 17 Years** Refill Barrel, dist Dec 89 **(89) n**21 clean, curiously fruity, freshly planed oak; **t**23 beautiful, mouth-filling malt with a wonderful degree of juicy barley bite; **f**22 vanilla, relatively tame; **b**23 a fine expression which shows this distillery off in impressive colours. **55.0%**

**Whisky Galore Glentauchers 1990** cask no. 14430, dist Nov 90, bott 27 May 05 **(89) n**22 a touch of coal dust on the grist; **t**23 the tastebuds go into salivatory overdrive as the barley lets rip; **f**22 oak interjects as a chalky dryness develops; **b**22 firm and steady as a rock. **46.1%.** Duncan Taylor.

# GLENTURRET
### Highlands (Perthshire), 1775. Edrington. Working.

✧ **Glenturret Aged 8 Years** db **(88) n**21 some sma' still randomness; **t**22 silky honey, a few feinty oils perhaps, but attractive; **f**23 honey overdrive with spice; **b**22 technically no prizewinner. But the dexterity of the honey is charming, as this distillery has a tendency sometimes to be. **40%**

**The Glenturret Aged 10 Years** db **(87) n**20 **t**23 **f**22 **b**22. Really does appear to have something about the "sma' still" about it, which is hardly surprising. A slightly wider cut than normal has has upped the weight all round. And even emphasises a wonderful honey depth. **40%**

**Glenturret 10 Years Old** db **(75) n**18 **t**21 **f**18 **b**18. Disappointingly feinty. **40%**

**The Glenturret Aged 15 Years** db **(87) n**21 **t**22 **f**22 **b**22. A beautifully clean, small-still style dram that would have benefitted from being bottled at a fuller strength. A discontinued bottling now: if you see it, it is worth the small investment. **40%**

✧ **Glenturret 1991 Aged 15 Years** Cask no. 638 db **(82) n**20 **t**21 **f**21 **b**20. Honeycomb and chocolate: liquid fruit jelly. Heavyweight stuff and at times a little stodgy. **55.3%**

✧ **Glenturret 1992 Aged 14 Years** Cask no. 855 db **(72) n**18 **t**19 **f**17 **b**18. A tad feinty and never quite finds the right key despite the best efforts of the honey and spice. **59.7%**

**Cadenhead's Authentic Collection Glenturret Aged 18 Years** Bourbon Hogshead, dist 87, bott February 06 **(77) n**21 **t**19 **f**18 **b**19. Pretty tight and hot, bouncing between OTT sugar and bitterness. **52.1%.** 234 bottles.

✧ **Cadenhead's Authentic Collection Glenturret Aged 20 Years** Bourbon hogshead, dist 86, bott Feb 07 **(83) n**21 **t**21 **f**20 **b**21. Starts with great promise and just the right degree of honey and bourbon-esque influence. **50.3%.** 222 bottles.

**Chieftain's Glenturret Aged 11 Years Port Finish (87) n**22 if all noses were like this, I'd never get this book finished: where does the fruit start and end, how much is the spice due to oak or Port; where the heck is the barley? So many questions...; **t**22 palate entirely cleansed by a thin layer of wine which slowly fills in body as the malt catches up. Half-hearted spices begin to assemble; **f**21 remains light and wine gummy; **b**22 something this outrageous could come from only one company these days...and you can't help loving it. **43%.** Ian Macleod.

⭐ **Cheftain's Glenturret 1993 Aged 12 Years Port Finish** dist 93, bott 06 **(91) n**21 the port wood has unnerved the barley somewhat; **t**23 but it's total relaxation now as the sweet malt melts in the mouth and swoons into the arms of the firm fruit: a superb delivery and middle; **f**23 remains entirely true with the oaky vanilla offering just the right amounts of dryness to balance; **b**24 it had been a bad day and I'd tasted more poor whiskies than I should have done: this understated and sophisticated little beauty, however, has cheered me up. **43%. nc ncf.** Ian Macleod.

⭐ **Chieftain's Glenturret 13 Years Old** French Oak Finish, dist Oct 93 **(67) n**18 **t**18 **f**15 **b**16. Whoever invented the sulphur stick to treat wine casks deserves to be horsewhipped. Or, worse, forced to drink sulphur-ruined malt for the rest of his miserable life. **43%. nc ncf.** Ian Macleod.

⭐ **Dun Bheagan Glenturret 1990 Aged 15 Years** Hogshead, dist Oct 90 **(89) n**22 busy malts assisted by blood orange and garden scents; **t**23 a really fruity arrival with the barley juices really pulsing through; **f**22 sour dough and sultana; **b**22 a very unusual malt, this, with ample evidence of a small still at work. **43%. nc ncf.** Ian Macleod.

**Kingsbury's Single Cask Glenturret 11 Years Old** cask no. 819, dist 92 **(88) n**21 big, bludgeoning body; not always in tune but worth listening to; **t**23 massively chewy malt that begins with a peck of sugar which blossoms into very mild acacia honey; **f**22 vanilla and custard; **b**22 very attractive sma' still malt, revealing the copper-rich intensity to body and finish usually found on stills below a certain size. Delightfully rich. **46%.** Japan Import System.

**Murray McDavid Mission Glenturret 1980 Aged 26 Years** Bourbon/Rioja **(83) n**23 **t**22 **f**19 **b**19. I thought, at first, that this was the best Rioja I had come across since I was in the boardroom at Coventry last season: the clarity of nose and early delivery are scintillating. But, just like my beloved Millwall that afternoon, it promised much then fired blanks. **47.3%. nc ncf.** 680 bottles.

**Old Malt Cask Glenturret Aged 15 Years** Hogshead cask 1744, dist Sept 90, bott Nov 05 **(86) n**23 **t**22 **f**20 **b**21. Forget the disappointing finish: concentrate on the big barley nose and arrival. **50%.** Douglas Laing. 302 bottles.

⭐ **Old Malt Cask Glenturret Aged 16 Years** dist Sept 90, bott Dec 06 **(79) n**20 **t**20 **f**19 **b**20. Honeyed but a bit furry. **50%.** Douglas Laing. 277 bottles.

# GLENUGIE
### Highland (Eastern). 1834–1993. Closed.

⭐ **Duncan Taylor Collection Glenugie 1981** Cask no. 5158 **(94) n**23 butterscotch embedded with ginger and lemon-juiced pancakes: genuinely deep, fun and fascinating **t**23 despite the age the malt still offers juice and grist and fizzing spices which accentuate the vanilla; the sugar types are varied and plentiful and perfectly counter the oak; **f**24 long with the vaguest hint of smoke and now the gristiness dries at last. But never is there a hint of bitterness to be found: this is near perfectly balanced whisky and a miracle for its age; **b**24 sightings of Glenugie are about as common as instances of Gordon Brown leaving those around him in helpless mirth. But, unlike politicians, this distillery never seems to let you down. The rule of thumb is: find a bottle of Glenugie and you'll find liquid gold. This is no exception. In fact, it's probably the best of the lot! **51.5%**

**Old Malt Cask Glenugie 25 Years Old**, dist 18 Oct 79, bott 14 Mar 05 **(87) n**22 **t**22 **f**21 **b**22. Highly individualistic, truly unique malt that no other distillery can begin to imitate – or now ever will. **50%.** Douglas Laing & Co.

**Rare Old Glenugie 1968** dist 68, bott 04 **(94) n**23 absolutely clapped out oak. But it somehow happens it has reconstituted itself as a very passable imitation of a Pacific island fruit salad; **t**24 stunningly soft and melt-in-the-mouth with hints of mangos and pawpaws, but enlivened, somehow, by untainted barley; **f**23 light and uncomplicated. That is if you can't be bothered to unravel the late fruits and coffee; **b**24 one of those displays of exotic fruit that works almost too beautifully to be true. By rights should be oak-infested and in its grave. Yet we have here a genuine classic whisky – Peterhead's finest! **43%.** Gordon & MacPhail.

## GLENURY ROYAL
### Highland (Eastern), 1868–1985. Demolished.

Glenury Royal 36 Years Old db **(89)** n21 oak interference damages the fruit balance; t23 starts worryingly dull then takes off to fabulous heights on fresh, beautifully textured barley; f22 begins to fall out of sync as some heavyweight hickory is driven home, but lightens with a succession of gentle waves of cocoa; b23 an undulating dram, hitting highs and lows. The finish, in particular, is impressive: just when it looks on its last legs, it revives delightfully. The whole package, though far from perfect, is pretty astounding. **50.2%**

Glenury Royal 50 Years Old dist 53 db **(91)** n23 marvellous freshness to the sherry butt; this had obviously been a high quality cask in its day and the intensity of the fruit sweetened slightly by the most delicate marzipan and old leather oozes class; a little mint reveals some worry lines; t24 the early arrival is sweet and nimble with the barley, against the odds, still having the major say after all these years. The oak is waiting in the wings and with a burst of soft liquorice and velvety, understated spice beginning to make an impression; the sweetness is very similar to a traditional British child's candy of "tobacco" made from strands of coconut and sugar; f22 masses of oak yet, somehow, refuses to go over the top and that slightly molassed sweetness sits very comfortably with the mildly oily body; b22 I am always touched when sampling a whisky like this from a now departed distillery. **42.8%**

⋇⋇ Rare Old Glenury Royal 1972 **(90)** n22 there is little doubting the 30-odd years on the clock here but some molassed fruitcake ensures the wrinkles don't show; t23 sublime delivery with a velvet caress as it stokes the tastebuds; lovely burnt fudge takes me back to my earliest childhood and a touch of liquorice, too; f22 molasses see off the oak to leave a languid finale; b23 a thumping malt showing good age but wears it effortlessly. Just beautiful. **40%**. G &M.

## HIGHLAND PARK
### Highland (Island–Orkney), 1795. Edrington. Working.

Highland Park 8 Years Old db **(87)** n22 firm young, honied malt with food coke/peat smoke; t22 silky honey and excellent complexity for a malt so young; f22 complex layers of vanilla and soft peat at first then caramel grabs hold; shame; b21 a journey back in time for some of us: this is the orginal distillery bottling of the 70s and 80s, bottles of which are still doing the rounds in obscure Japanese bars and specialist outlets such as the Whisky Exchange. **40%**

Highland Park Aged 12 Years db **(92)** n24 sublime: the peat is almost hand-sprinkled in exact measures; honey and vague molasses guaranteeing contolled sweetness, salt, old leather and apples in there, too; t22 moderately weighty mouth arrival, sweet yet enough oak to offer some bitter complexity. This fabulour bitter-sweet balance pans out in favour of the honey though there is enough peat around to add extra weight; f22 long, spicy, some earthy heather and more oak than usual. Excellent cocoa hangs about with the peat; b24 it defies belief that an international brand can maintain this quality, more or less, year in year out. Few drams are as silkily enveloped as this gem. **40%**

Highland Park Aged 15 Years db **(80)** n20 t22 f19 b19. The new kid on the block has yet to show the voluptuous expansiveness of its brothers. The nose is surprisingly closed and the flavours never fully open on the palate, either. Even the spice and smoke have deserted it. Indubitably pleasant, but you are left wanting so much more. **40%**

Highland Park 16 Years Old db **(88)** n23 softly softly strains of oranges, honey and vanilla; t23 mouthwatering and delightfully weighted barley with soft nuances of liquorice and smoke; f20 toffee-vanilla: just a little too quiet; b22 I tasted this the day it first came out at one of the Heathrow whisky shops. I thought it a bit flat and uninspiring. This sample, maybe from another bottling, is more impressive and showing true Highland Park colours, the finish apart. **40%**. *Duty Free.*

Highland Park Aged 18 Years db **(95)** n24 an empty honey jar which once held peaty embers. An enormous nose of excellent consistency, with salty butter and burnt honeycomb is always present; t23 beautifully sweet, in some ways sweeter than even the 12-y-o thanks to some manuka honey, which is accentuated against the drier oaky tones and rumbling peat towards the back of the palate: beautifully chewy, a touch oily and wholly substantial; f24 some citrus, heathery notes, controlled oak and outstanding cocoa and peat: long and rewarding; b24 a consistent dram of enormous weight and complexity, bottle after bottle, and never short of breathtakingly brilliant: the ace in the Highland Park pack. **43%**

**Highland Park Aged 25 Years** db **(89)** n23 emphasis on the heatherhoney though significant fruit – apple especially – abounds. Some pulsating oak, but the theme is sweetish and gently spiced. No more than a hint of smoke; t23 firm bodied with soft, smoky spices forming a guard around the burnt honey and barley; much more rigid and crisp than normal HP but this doesn't detract from the radiating complexity; f21 layers of vanilla and rich honey. Pretty short, though; b22 a very different animal to the 50.7% version with less expansion, depth and expression. Not a bad dram, though... **51.5%**

**Highland Park 25 Years Old** db **(96)** n24 nectar. Hang on? Is nectar this good? Honeycomb and toffee-apple combined and lightened slightly with a squeeze of tangerine and a near perfect stratum of delicate smoke. As I once, apparently famously, described a younger HP: not a jagged edge to be found...; t24 sits on the palate as if owning the place and sings: the weight is perfect so both the big barley notes are at full throttle, yet remain on the lightish side and heavier oaky-nutty-marzipan offers the weight. Meeting in the middle are warming spices and a swirl of smoke; f24 the age shows, but as if botoxed. There are no cracks in the sheened honeycomb and in the balance, as any great HP should be, the bitter-sweet battle is won hands down by the sweetness; b24 HP Ambassador Gerry Tosh's hit man has got me and I've gone to heaven....this is the best bottling of HP25 I've ever come across, in this form eclipsing the astonishing 18. You have to work overtime to find fault with this. I suggest you grab a bottle and try... **50.7%**

**Highland Park 30 Years Old** db **(89)** n22 honey and marzipan help keep the oak at bay; t23 surprisingly fay with such wondrous softness to the waxy honey; a mild nutty character to the gathering oak; f22 remains soft and coy with the vanilla thickening; honey returns as the finish develops a life of its own; b22 this has genuinely surprised me. I expected this to be a tired oldie, but though it shows understandable signs of wear and tear, the general effect is quite outstanding. **48.1%**

**Highland Park 1967** cask 10252, db **(87)** n22 t22 f21 b22. the sum is better than the parts but this is massive whisky caught at the moment it falls over the oaky edge. **49.7%.** *Exclusive to the Whisky Exchange.*

⌁ **Highland Park 1967 Single Cask** Split cask 10255, bott Nov 06 db **(94)** n23 several oak trees sandwich Seville oranges, dry marzipan and smoke; t24 the early delivery is pure barley-sugar concentrate – in concentrate form...!!! The oak immediately flies in, both as spices and something much more aggressive but enough honeycomb lustre keeps it at bay for a while; some wonderful kumquaty citrus thins things out slightly; the seam of smoke is a wide one; f23 bitter chocolate and probing, equally bitter oak; b24 Do you remember the 1967 bottled in about 1992? This is nothing like it...The oak has many inroads to the point of taking the Michael. But such is the massive depth the malt just about copes. The first two or three mouthfuls will be a struggle because this takes oak involvement to the very precipice. But once you acclimatise...stunning! **55.5%**

**Highland Park Ambassador's Cask 2** cask 1071, dist 96, bott 06 db **(79)** n19 t20 f20 b20. There are some lovely coastal qualities to this and the rich honey touches are a delight. But not, I'm afraid, from the best cask ever to hold whisky, this displaying the surprising characteristics of a mild sulphur taint and on the nose in particular a peculiar C02 tun room kick. If dear Jerry Tosh is still speaking to me I'll try and get a sample of Cask 1 from him. **58.8%.** *594 bottles.*

⌁ **Highland Park Ambassador's Cask 3** db Cask no. 9035, dist 1974 **(84)** n22 t21 f21 b20. At times in the realms of Caperdonich-esque exotic fruit maturity. But Caper was a nothing malt finding an aristocratic bent in very old age. This is from a great distillery where the unique style is obscured. There is a difference. Needs warming to release latent smoke. **45%**

**Highland Park Bicentenary Vintage 1977 Reserve** db **(93)** n24 herbal and salty. The heather is in full bloom; t25 the early peat dissolves in the mouth allowing the honey and vanilla the stage. Lovely greengages and salt add to the complexity: truly fantastic, to the point of faultless; f21 cocoa and Jamaican coffee compensate for an otherwise lazy though lightly spiced finale; b23 should have been bottled at 46–50% for full effect: they were making great whisky at this time at HP and this is a pretty peaty version. **40%**

**Highland Park Capella Special Edition** db **(87)** n23 that unique buzz of smoke that so comfortably sits with distinctive heather/gorse and honey. Genuinely awesome how this distillery does it; **t**23 smoke and some grapey, fruity notes, then thick fudge; **f**20 spice but dampened and embittered by toffee; **b**21 the caramel (natural or otherwise) that has arrived towards the middle and end flattens an until then intensely glorious bottling. **40%**

**Alchemist Highland Park Aged 15 Years** dist May 90, bott Jul 05 **(90) n**22 heathery sophistication with soft fruit as it oxidizes; **t**23 mouthwatering and zingy, there is a distinct citrus kick to the malt and late-developing honey; **f**23 some soft smoke swirls around barley and delicate oak; **b**22 this is just how I like to see H: lots of sheen to the barley, plus some tantalizing smoke. **46%. nc ncf.**

**Battlehill Highland Park 1997** cask no. 5306, dist Sept 97, bott Apr 06 **(76) n**20 **t**20 **f**18 **b**18. Highly usual: slightly feinty, massive esters and a metallic finish. Some lovely rich honey, but never quite finds its feet. **43.1%.** *Duncan Taylor. 447 bottles.*

**Berry's' Best Orkney Highland Park Aged 14 Years (87) n**23 buttery, but soft honey and smoke; **t**23 the delivery is as clear as church bell in midwinter: crisp, precise barley with just the right amount of acacia honey; **f**20 some bitter elements to the oak hard, but softened by natural caramel; **b**21 one of the few under 15 HPs bottled this year that is entirely unambiguous regarding its style and origin...though the finish is a bit rough. **43%**

**Cadenhead's Authentic Collection Highland Park Aged 16 Years** Bourbon Hogshead, dist 89, bott Feb 06 **(92) n**22 coal dust and custard; **t**24 bracing barley fans out into various honey variants, from early acacia to manuka as the oak involves itself; **f**23 playful peats and natural toffee vie for dominance over the spicy barley; **b**23 could be the house dram at a honey conference. Wonderful! **51.6%.** *210 bottles.*

**Cadenhead's Authentic Collection Highland Park Aged 17 Years** Bourbon Hogshead, dist 88, bott May 05 **(81) n**21 **t**20 **f**21 **b**19. From a tired cask which dulls the honey somewhat. **56.8%.** *288 bottles.*

**Cadenhead's Authentic Collection Highland Park Aged 18 Years** Sherry butt, dist 88, bott Sept 06 **(76) n**19 **t**20 **f**18 **b**19. There are worse sulphur taints around but pity it's a HP. **58.2%.** *678 bottles.*

**Cask Strength Highland Park 1994** bott 14 Jun 06 **(94) n**23 a confident amalgam of citrus and honey; quite tart but the peat reek is discreet though telling; **t**23 no less lucidity on the palate where rich honey replaces the early barley bite; just a flash of smoke; **f**24 long, toffee-honeycomb and finally a peat flourish to the signature; **b**24 take your time with this cask: astonishingly subtle and complex – at full strength. One of G&M's Casks of the Year! **57.8%.** *G&M. USA.*

∴ **Cask Strength Highland Park 1995 (89) n**22 spiced up nougat, a dab of smoke; **t**22 you don't often see HP this creamy-textured; mouth-watering for all its heavy weight with an early move towards cocoa while the spices ping and zip with gusto; **f**22 serious complexity here as fruity, smoke and mocha notes harmonise; **b**23 not immediately recognisable as from Orkney. What is genuinely amazing is that here we have a not entirely spotless cask, yet despite the odd trace of it, we still have a true corker. **57.2%.** *G & M.*

∴ **The Clydesdale Highland Park 13 Years Old** Cask ref. 0028/20571, dist Nov 92, bott Sept 06 **(95) n**23 cramped by tight sherry but just a hint of smoke and spice pokes through and, as it warms, the honey gauge rises...; **t**24 oh yes....!!! Maximum impact manuka honey helped along by boiled apples, a stratum of peat and the most gorgeous viscosity: few malts come so perfectly weighted; **f**24 the dovetailing of drier vanilla and confident chocolate honeycomb keeps the palate entertained for years; **b**24 whisky of the gods. **61.5%. nc ncf.** *Blackadder International.*

∴ **The Coopers Choice Highland Park Aged 16 Years** dist 1990, bott 2006 **(92) n**23 classic understated smoke and heather – and honey; **t**24 textbook HP with a flavour explosion including all the usual distillery suspects; **f**22 lighter with a surge of vanilla; **b**23 a cracker of a cask, so true to the distillery. **46%.** *The Vintage Malt Whisky Co.*

**Coopers Choice Highland Park 27 Years Old** Single Cask Range, bott 05 **(91) n**24 **t**22 **f**23 **b**22. Extraordinary and quite memorable for its ordered confusion. **52.1%**

**Dewar Rattray Individual Cask Bottling Highland Park 1981 Aged 24 Years** cask 6061, dist Sept 81, bott Sept 05 **(95) n**23 lemon tart, banana milkshake and peat trace; **t**25 sumptuous, about as curvaceous as HP gets; the mouth filling with lightly salted and cured barley that moulds itself to the tastebuds. The bitter-sweet ratio ponders perfection; **f**23 sweet vanilla and smoke begin to gain an oily weight. Long, pulsing and nothing lost to age; **b**24 an attractive if slightly unprepossessing nose offers no warning of the unforgettable beauty that is about to unfold on your palate. For seven or eight mercurial seconds you are entirely enveloped in faultless malt, with no beginning or end to it – in other words, orgasmic... An absolute must have for HP devotees. And not a bad choice for those who aren't. And, perhaps even more germane, it is interesting to note that the best HP of the year does not come from any kind of cask finish or wine involvement... **52.3%.** *263 bottles.*

**Duncan Taylor Collection Highland Park 1966** cask no. 4630, dist May 66, bott May 06 **(82) n**19 **t**20 **f**22 **b**21. Recovers wonderfully from a shaky start. The nose, for its hints of smoky exotic fruit, does the malt no favours but such is the deftness of the barley after the first biting oak that you cannot help but close your eyes and enjoy, especially when the spices arrive. **41%.** *156 bottles.*

**Duncan Taylor Collection Highland Park 1980 Aged 24 Years** cask no. 9266, dist Nov 80, bott Feb 05 **(87) n**21 **t**23 **f**22 **b**22. The nose suggests that time may have defeated this one. But it comes back to life on the plate with aplomb, though a drier HP. **55.1%**

**Duncan Taylor Collection Highland Park 1992** dist Mar 92, bott Mar 06 **(88) n**21 sluggish if unusually firm; **t**23 outstanding explosion of intense malt and peat; **f**22 gentle whispers of spiced-up smoke on the toffee; **b**22 allows the peat an open road. **46%.** *471 bottles.*

**Glenkeir Treasures Highland Park 21 Years Old Refill** sherry butt, dist May 84, bott Nov 05 **(91) n**21 toffee and raisins; **t**23 the oily creaminess is a lovely backdrop to the spotted dog pudding lead and delightful light smoke; soft honey waves in and out; **f**23 lots more cream toffee and a fabulous crescendo of mouth-watering malt and warming spice; **b**24 a genuinely pulsing HP choc-a-bloc with intense barley and the late spices are a joy. **54.1%.** *The Whisky Shop. 450 bottles.*

**Gordon & MacPhail Cask Strength Highland Park 1991 (94) n**22 linseed and hickory with perhaps the slightest touch of smoke; **t**24 close your eyes and lie back for the most wonderful delivery of classic heather-honeysmoke. HP not so much in essence as in pure form; **f**24 now goes into orbit as the complexity confounds. All those well-known HP points, but flighting around the palate with bitter marmalade for company; **b**24 slow coming out of the blocks so far as the nose is concerned, but what happens next is pure joy! **59%**

⋯ **Milroy's of Soho Highland Park 1989** Ex Bourbon, dist 7 Mar 89, bott 24 May 06 **(87) n**22 Tizer; a sweet, fruity mix with zero smoke; **t**21 sluggish start with a gradual sweetening of the 100% barley; **f**22 at last some HP-style honey; **b**22 a second gear malt. **46%.** *270 bottles.*

**Murray McDavid Mission Highland Park 1967 (93) n**22 creaking under the oak but holds out enough for a gently-matured barley twinkle; **t**24 stupendous! The entire Highland Park works: it is all here, acacia honey in hotel-sized pots with a distinctly heathery drizzle and just the right depth of smoke. This, ladies and gentleman is Orkney at its most auspicious: HP dressed up to the nines; **f**23 the oak which threatens on the nose has now gone home. Instead we have honeycomb ice-cream, with the sweetness beautifully controlled by the vanilla; **b**24 it's drams like these that makes falling in love with whisky such an easy affair. A celebration of a great distillery. **40.1%.** *500 bottles.*

**Murray McDavid Mission IV Highland Park 1979 Aged 25 Years (91) n**23 **t**23 **f**22 **b**23. So delicate, a malt that could snap in half on your tastebuds. **46%**

**Murray McDavid Mission Highland Park 1979 Aged 27 Years** Bourbon/Syrah, bott 06 **(78) n**22 **t**19 **f**18 **b**19. Decent nose and the first few nano-seconds of the delivery. But, frankly, I don't get the point of this. HP luxuriates in a unique style of honey and peat and the odd brush with heather. This, though, after such a promising nose, leaves you with a pleasantish but disjointed malt that could be from any inferior distillery and, by HP standards, is pretty one dimensional. One of the leading lights of Murray McDavid comes from an exceptional wine background. I have known him years and have much time and respect for him. But, as a friend, I say to him this: how would you feel if I was tipping a splash of Highland Park into a '82 Margaux? **46.2%. nc ncf.** *500 bottles.*

⋯ **Murray McDavid Highland Park 1989** Sherry/Port **(95) n**23 complex, well-weighted and possessing a pleasant chalkiness to counter the fruit; the most gentle waft of smoke reminds you of the distillery at the centre of this experience; **t**24 black and red Jelly Babies send the palate into salivation overdrive. Some HP character finally arrives towards the middle with a swathe of honey cutting through the barley-fruit proceedings. Good grief...! **f24** an improbably long finale with the honey hanging on for dear life, the fruits trying to edge their way back into pole position (and failing) and the smoke bringing some gravity to proceedings; **b24** my tastebuds, having recovered from the unpleasant shock of having to analyse not one but two Dufftowns, have been amply rewarded by this truly magnificent malt. Stunningly haphazard, but everything – thorough either luck or design – falls into place gloriously. **46%**

**Murray McDavid Highland Park 1989 Aged 16 Years** Bourbon/Grenache Blanc, bott 06 **(86)** n23 t22 f20 b21. The voluptuous body of HP perhaps takes to Grenache better than other malts; the curious bonfire/coal/peat smokiness guarantees a complex nose. **46%. nc ncf.** *2,500 bottles.*

❊ **Norse Cask Selection Highland Park 1991 Aged 14 Years** Hogshead cask no. 4495 **(88)** n22 a touch of the Rupps, with a honey side dish; t22 sweet honey-barley but with a strange furry note; compensated by rich, highly- smoked honey; f22 the light fur feel continues, but so does the honey and peat: are you getting a pattern here?; b22 one of the smokier HPs you are likely to find. **57%.** *WhiskyOwner.com, Denmark.*

❊ **Old & Rare Highland Park Aged 29 Years Sherry Finish** dist 1978, bott 07 **(90)** n22 burnt fruitcake softened by a puff of peat; t22 thick oak but the splinters are individually coated in honeycomb; f23 soft latte again detracts from the oak while the late smoke does wonders; b23 creakier than a sinking ship, but somehow rides the tidal waves of time. **56.7%.** *Douglas Laing. 328 bottles.*

**Old Malt Cask Highland Park Aged 10 Years** Refill Hogshead 2168, dist June 95, bott Oct 05 **(79)** n20 t22 f18 b19. Bright barley start but a dull follow-through. **50%. nc ncf.**

❊ **Old Malt Cask Highland Park Aged 11 Years** dist Feb 96, bott Feb 07 **(87)** n21 clean barley sugar; t22 juicy, pulsing barley with that honey-tinged sweetness unique to HP; f22 the usual cocoa-smoke finale; b22 Douglas Laing are cornering the market in eminently drinkable third filled casks by the looks of it. **50%.** *Douglas Laing. 362 bottles.*

**Old Malt Cask Highland Park 12 Years Old** dist 30 Nov 92, bott Jul 05 **(85)** n21 t22 f21 b21. Rich, estery and mildly metallic; very little smoke to this one. **50%.** *370 bottles.*

❊ **Old Malt Cask Highland Park Aged 16 Years** dist Apr 90, bott Oct 06 **(90)** n22 heather, honey, peat etc. etc.; t22 lovely orangey edge to the bitter-sweet barley and smoke; f23 a slow, gristy evolution of heather-honey and peat in the true HP tradition; b23 tasted blind this could possibly be the offspring of only one distillery.... **50%.** *Douglas Laing. 271 bottles.*

**Old Malt Cask Highland Park Aged 21 Years Sherry (92)** n22 caramel wafers and dank sultana; t23 lively delivery but is becalmed by waves of softening honey; f23 the spice picks up beautifully and goes hand-in-hand with the juicy malt and wispy smoke; b24 a not dissimilar bottling to the Glenkeir expression. A really big HP to take as much time as you like over. **54.1%.** *Exclusively for Vintage House.*

❊ **Old Malt Cask Highland Park Aged 25 Years Claret Finish** dist Sept 81, bott Nov 06 **(69)** n18 t18 f16 b17. The problem with a sulphured Claret finish is that it gives me something to whine about... **50%.** *Douglas Laing. 306 bottles.*

**Old Malt Cask Highland Park 13 Years Old** dist Mar 91, bott Aug 04 **(89)** n21 malty but surprisingly neutral; t22 the honey doesn't take long to kick into action, though some vanilla seems to hold it back a little; f24 absolutely comes into its own as some smoke drifts in to add depth and balance; a touch of sweet liquorice also adds weight to the gathering malt; b22 takes a little time to get going, but once it does, it's a real corker. **50%**

**Park Avenue Liquor Store Highland Park 24 Years Old (75)** n17 t20 f19 b19. The intense sherry fights valiantly against the annoying (and, in whisky terms, tragic) suphur. Oh, for what might have been.... **59%.** *Old Malt Cask.*

❊ **Private Cellar Highland Park 1985** bott 06 **(85)** n22 t23 f20 b20. A honeyed toffee candy. **43.0%.** *Speyside Distillers.*

**Provenance Highland Park 10 Years Old** dist 13 Jun 94, bott 23 Mar 05 **(85)** n22 t22 f20 b21. Enjoyable, but virtually nil oak input is compensated for by peat: a must for HP collectors. **46%.** *Douglas Laing & Co.*

**Provenance Highland Park 10 Years Old** dist Jun 95, bott Oct 05 **(79)** n21 t20 f19 b19. The nose is pure grist; nascent peat adds weight but otherwise thin. **46%.** *McGibbon's.*

**Provenance Highland Park 10 Years Old** dist 29 Mar 95, bott 21 Jun 05 **(84) n**22 **t**21 **f**20 **b**21. An almost identical story to the June bottling, except this has just a little extra bounce and balance. **46%.** *McGibbon's.*

⋄ **Provenance Highland Park Aged 10 Years** dist Winter 96, bott Winter 06 **(87) n**21 grist; **t**22 light, salivating with the usual honeyed barley eventually offering up something lightly smoked; **f**22 very long with a touch of cocoa balancing the honey; **b**22 Astonishing for a third-fill cask: you have only the bones of the distillery here and yet still the shape is honeyed and sexy. It has no right to be this good...! **46%.** *Douglas Laing.*

**Provenance Highland Park 12 Years Old** dist Jun 94, bott Autumn 06 **(86) n**22 more from the HP gristmill; **t**22 excellent controlled sweetness to the barley; **f**20 disappointingly dull and fragmented; **b**22 this would have been so good at a fuller strength. **46%.** *McGibbon's.*

⋄ **Scotch Malt Whisky Society Cask 4.112 Aged 24 Years** Refill Hogshead, dist Nov 82 **(92) n**23 dying embers of peat in a mainly wood fire, ashey and dry; **t**22 firm barley drills into the roof of the mouth, buzzing spices abound and then a vaguely honeyed vanilla streak; the weight and deftness of the slight oil astonishes; **f**23 much drier, soft smoke, cotton-dry vanilla and burnt Crunchie aftertaste; **b**24 a great old cask from a great old distillery. Hugely complex. **55.3%**

⋄ **Scotch Malt Whisky Society Cask 4.115 Aged 20 Years** Refill Hogshead, dist Dec 86 **(97) n**24 the absolute classic heather-honey-smoke combination you expect from this distillery in near enough (though not quite) perfect proportions. Just so understated and sophisticated. Wondrous; **t**24 less a delivery, more of an pronouncement: its honey, folks!! Pots if it and of varying, bedazzling degrees of haughtiness and depth; the smoky spices sting and prickle mischievously and complete the balance. Heather? Not sure, but there is something in there unquestionably floral; **f**24 do finishes come any longer?: lingering smoke of varying depth, the dryness is born from oak with the usual wafer-vanilla theme but there is something else besides; a shy citrus afterthought to help lighten the load. Quite amazing... **b**25 when I nosed this amongst a set of four, I pushed the glass back against the sample bottle. That means: "Watch this one – it's a bit special." I than came back to it in time and I was right. The best scotch of the year? So far, it has to be. The best whisky of the year? Quite possibly. If you are not a member of the SMWS join now and get this...and then build a machine gun post to protect the thing. It is the most balanced single malt I have come across in a very long time. Take as much time over a glass of this as you can spare: at different temps and varying degrees of oxidisation. Best, ultimately, at body temp, of course. But the journey there is no less revealing. **49.4%**

⋄ **Scotch Malt Whisky Society Cask 4.119 Aged 8 Years** 1st Fill Barrel, dist Apr 99 **(87) n**22 biting barley, youthful; **t**22 explosive spice with soothing golden syrup **f**21 a touch oily, barley-heavy and flat; **b**22 Anybody remember back a quarter of a century ago and more when HP was available at 8? From G&M, I think. Bit more devil about this one. **60.2%**

⋄ **Scott's Selection Highland Park 1986** bott 07 **(91) n**21 dank sugar and freshly emptied barrel! A tad soapy; **t**24 a near perfect dual soft/hard landing on the palate, the barley is in playful, rich mood with an intensity to the sweetness which hit the g spot; **f**23 light oak shavings amid that barley stream and developing cocoa and honeycomb – real Crunchie candy stuff; **b**23 some quite wonderful moments of intensity. **54.5%**

**Scott's Selection Highland Park 1986** bott 05 **(79) n**19 **t**21 **f**19 **b**20. Mildly hot and lacking the distillery's usual grace and charisma: at times rather rum-like. **55.7%.**

⋄ **The Single Malts of Scotland Higland Park 1990 Aged 16 Years** **(83) n**21 **t**21 **f**20 **b**21. honeyed but a mild oak imbalance; **46%. sc.** *Speciality Drinks, UK.*

**Vintage House Highland Park Aged 16 Years** Natural Cask Strength **(87) n**22 esters that wouldn't be out of place at Jamaica's Hampden Distillery...!!; **t**23 a real mouthful of toffeed barley and lemon cake; **f**21 burnt fudge and a vague marzipan depth; the smoke appears as an almost apologetic afterthought; **b**21 charming, but almost too well behaved for its own good. **50.1%.** *from Douglas Laing for Vintage House. 159 bottles*

⋄ **The Whisky Fair Highland Park Aged 25 Years** Bourbon, dist 1981, bott 06 **(83) n**22 **t**21 **f**20 **b**20. Pleasant... but should be so much more! The smoke has vanished and the trademark honey has buzzed off. Attractive, but limited... and very flat. **43.0%**

**Whisky Galore Highland Park 1989 (58)** n18 t15 f12 b13. If the whisky was attached to a cardiograph, there would be a straight line. **40%.** *Duncan Taylor.*

**Whisky Galore Highland Park 1994 Aged 11 Years** cask 1, dist Feb 94, bott Mar 05 **(87)** n22 t23 f21 b21. A honey barrel in every sense but pretty simplistic. **46.1%.**

⬩ **Whisky Galore Highland Park Aged 12 Years Port Finish** dist 94, bott 06 **(82)** n20 t22 f20 b20. Never less than pleasant but curiously flat and lethargic for an HP. **46%.**

## HILLSIDE (see Glenesk)

## IMPERIAL
### Speyside, 1897. Chivas. Silent.

⬩ **Imperial Aged 15 Years "Special Distillery Bottling"** db **(69)** n17 t18 f17 b17. At least one very poor cask, hot spirit and overly sweet. Apart from that it's wonderful. **46%**

**Berry's' Own Selection Imperial 1976 Aged 29 Years (91)** n23 tight little nose, excellent firm honey edge. Shows virtually no sign of wear and tear; t23 again there is a clipped and polished element to the barley, steadfastly refusing to allow the oak to get too dominant; lovely hints of melon on the soft manuka honey; f22 some toasty notes show just how this whisky does doff its cap, if only briefly, to advancing years; b23 unbelievably comfortable in old age; in human terms you'd have expected this to have had the full nip and tuck treatment. A wonderful cask. **46%**

⬩ **Cadenhead's Chairman's Stock Imperial-Glenlivet Aged 29 Years** Bourbon Hogshead, dist 1977, bott May 07 **(92)** n22 excellent weight; the oak-barley interaction is spot- on; t24 beautiful, near perfect delivery with masses of barley offering excellent variations of sweetness; the spices arrive on cue as does a touch of latte; f23 the oak adds a drier touch, as it should after 30 years, but the toastiness fits well with the barley lead; b23 Imperial by name and nature. **54.7%.** *228 bottles.*

⬩ **Chieftain's Imperial 24 Years Old** Fino Sherry Butt, dist June 82 **(84)** n20 t22 f21 b21. Finished in Fino, I'd say. The gentle grape effect generates a juicy vibrancy to the intense barley. A dram not lacking in style but perhaps thins out a tad too much. **46%.**

**D&M Connoisseurs' Club Bottling Imperial Aged 15 Years** cask no. 11968, dist Dec 90 **(93)** n25 one of the noses of the year: just stick your beak in a glass of this for about half an hour and discover just how astonishing Speyside can be. The balance between barley and oak is textbook, the levels of sweetness offered by the barley defies belief; t23 envelops the tastebuds in enormous waves of barley which span between marmalade and under-ripe apple. All brushed with honey; f22 some bitterness to the fade, but a buttery oil; b23 what a fabulous advertisement for this unjustly silent distillery. **60.4%. nc ncf.** *US by Angus Dundee Distillers plc.*

⬩ **The Dormant Distillery Company Imperial 29 Years Old** Refill Sherry Butt, dist 8 Oct 76, bott June 05 **(94)** n23 distant but delicious smoke acts like a siren; citrus and barley offer the lighter balance; t24 totally perfect arrival with that same smoke jousting in uncanny harmonisation with the beautifully oiled, tangy barley; f23 peat intensifies slightly as the barley fades, with a touch of cocoa-rich mocha taking its place; b24 so rare to find one of these lightly peated Imperials outside the blending lab. Not only shows the distillery in its very best light, but perfectly demonstrates how Speyside whisky tended to be 60 or 70 years ago. **46.8%.** *Royal Mile Whiskies. 408 bottles.*

⬩ **Duncan Taylor Collection Imperial 1990** Cask no. 352 **(88)** n21 crisp, clean barley underscored by the dry custard powder; t22 mouth-watering and again barley- rich with decent oils and oak buzz; f22 delicious mocha fade; b23 A juicy, sparkling Speysider with few pretensions and excellent overall style. **55.7%**

**Duncan Taylor Collection Imperial 1994** cask no. 2111, dist Mar 94, bott Mar 06 **(74)** n19 t20 f17 b18. An entirely unsympathetic cask which does the distillery few favours. **46%.** *286 bottles.*

⬩ **Duncan Taylor The NC2 Range Imperial 1994 (86)** n21 t22 f21 b22. just the right sprinkling of muscovado sugar accentuates the clean barley. Simple, clean and charming. **46%. nc ncf.**

**Gordon & MacPhail Imperial 1991 (77)** n21 t20 f18 b18. Hmmmm. After the initial sweet burst, curiously flat or out of tune. The citric-laced nose needs some time to settle. **43%**

Old Masters Imperial 1976 Aged 27 Years cask 10171, bott 04 (90) n22 curious, peaty edge takes a little time to unravel. Also some odd fruit on there. Highly unusual combination and needs oxidization to work; t23 a sweeter more intense barley than you might expect for a whisky of this vintage; the smoke arrives in mid stream and the mouthwatering properties are close behind; f22 some of the coffee notes are rather spellbinding; b23 to be honest, I didn't much care for this when I first tasted it. However, I was drawn back, for I realized there was something very different about it and it needed longer investigation. A wise choice. A particularly idiosyncratic cask. 57.2%

⠿ Platinum Imperial Aged 25 Years dist 81, bott 07 (67) n17 t17 f16 b17. Another one from the sulphur mines of Jerez. 57.2%. Douglas Laing. 270 bottles.

Private Collection Imperial Calvados 1990 bott 28.06.05 (83) n22 t21 f20 b20. The punchy aroma has no little bourbon but after a big malty chewfest the finish is lacking. 46%. G&M. USA.

The Single Malt of Scotland Imperial Aged 11 Years Vintage 1994 Sherry butt cask no. 1537 (83) n20 t22 f21 b20. Imperial in sherry is as rare as hen's teeth. And appears to have more bite as this is a full-on no holds barred, old-fashioned duff up of the tastebuds. And, for its rock hardness and imbalance...it's wonderful...!! 59.2%. 165 bottles.

Whisky Galore Imperial 1994 Aged 12 Years cask nos. Part 2112, 2113, dist Mar 94, bott 28 Jun 06 (85) n22 t21 f21 b21. Big barley theme that remains clean and chewy throughout. 45.98%. Duncan Taylor. 480 bottles.

# INCHGOWER
## Speyside, 1872. Diageo. Working.

Inchgower Aged 14 Years db (77) n19 t20 f19 b19. A vague hint of peat and a sprinkling of spice lifts the dram above something treacly and over-sweet. 43%. Flora and Fauna.

Inchgower 27 Years Old Rare Malts 2004 db (84) n21 t22 f20 b21. Oily, decently spiced, but at times heavy going. Some charming, sharp barley, though. 55.6%

Adelphi Inchgower 1980 Aged 24 Years Sherry butt cask no. 14152, dist 80, bott Jun 06 (86) n22 t21 f22 b21. Usually my memo to independent bottlers – and drinkers – is: stay away from this distillery for anything casked in the late 70s and early to mid 80s. The wood policy was, at best, horrific. But there are always exceptions, and here we have a chunky expression with just enough Demerara on the nose and early bite to make for an unusually enjoyable experience from this distillery. 60.4%. 576 bottles.

⠿ Berry's Own Selection Inchgower 1974 Cask no. 877, bott 06 (78) n19 t18 f21 b20. Sweet with succulent sultana. But that's late on after the viciously red hot delivery has subsided. Worth the pain, though. 46%

The Coopers Choice Inchgower 1980 Sherry Wood 24 Years Old (75) n18 t21 f18 b18. A shuddering nose is offset by the silky mouth arrival. But the finish is pure Inchgower from this period. Or perhaps I should say impure... 46%. The Vintage Malt Whisky Co.

⠿ Demijohn Inchgower 1980 Single Cask (84) n20 t22 f21 b21. Inchgower at its most quarrelsome: a touch rubbery and swimming in spicy and mildly sulphured fighting sherry. That said there is a honeyed glow that compensates deliciously. 59.9%. Demijohn, UK.

Dewar Rattray Individual Cask Bottling Inchgower 1980 Aged 25 Years Sherry cask no. 14161, dist Dec 80, bott May 06 (65) n15 t18 f15 b17. I originally gave this 69. What was I thinking? That might have suggested that something went down here as even vaguely enjoyably... 53.2%. 486 bottles.

Duncan Taylor Collection Inchgower 1968 Aged 36 Years cask no. 5575, dist Oct 68, bott Feb 05 (88) n21 t23 f22 b22. That rarest of beasts: an Inchgower made in the days before it had been run into the ground and the warehouses had been swamped with sub-standard wood. Charming and delicious. 46.3%. 142 bottles.

⠿ Duncan Taylor Collection Inchgower 1969 Cask no. 6129 (88) n23 Melted moist ginger cake. Weird, bizarre...unique; t20 falls about slapstick style as the sweetness tries to outdo the oak: little shape or rhythm... but still works; f23 now comes back into line with a return of the ginger, liberally sprinkled with moscovado sugar: fabulous... b22 if, like me and my sons, you have a penchant for Jamaican ginger cake, here's a malt that will leave you aghast. Question is, was this whisky baked or distilled...? 46.2%.

Usquebaugh Society Inchgower Aged 20 Years cask no. 5633, dist Jun 85, bott 16 Aug 05 (80) n22 t20 f18 b20. Technically not great. Raw and "dirty" in that old-fashioned

Bells style, there is still a wonderful resonance – some of it distinctly bourbony – that bites and nips and swamps; a whisky where the sum is infinitely better than the parts. **60.8%. ncf sc.** *250 bottles.*

## INCHMOAN ( see Loch Lomond)

## INCHMURRIN ( see Loch Lomond)

## INVERLEVEN
**Lowland, 1938–1991. Demolished.**

Cadenhead's Dumbarton (Inverleven Stills) 18 Years Old **(94) n**22 old parchment and barley water; **t**25 beautiful, intact malt that starts confidently but with a dozen graceful, mouthwatering sweeps of the palate becomes something intense and glorious. With a charming citric and barley fruitiness, too, this is sheer perfection as far as an 18-year-old Lowlander goes; **f**23 the vanilla never overdoes it, though the barley backs off with the same grace with which it initially sweeps the palate; unsalted butter coats toasted fresh bread; **b**24 while the label might be somewhat confusing, what isn't is the élan of this glorious bottling. Often the malt from this distillery was too light to withstand too long an inquisition from the oak; here it has not only survived but thrived. Not just stunning. But also outranked only by an exceptional Rosebank as Scottish Lowlander of the year. **57.9%**

Duncan Taylor Collection Inverleven 1977 cask 3099, dist Sept 77, bott Mar 06 **(85) n**20 **t**23 **f**21 **b**21. Some lovely lemon-zesty life still in this one. A bit battered, but in much better shape than the distillery. **56.5%.** *175 bottles.*

Gordon and MacPhail Inverleven 1989 **(79) n**19 **t**20 **f**20 **b**20. Though thin and shy, it is also clean, barley-rich and refreshing. **40%**

Gordon and MacPhail Inverleven 1990 **(84) n**21 **t**22 **f**21 **b**20. Delicate, malty, playfully sweet and grassy. Such a soft, courteous, unassuming yet charming memory of this recently demolished distillery. **40%**

Old Malt Cask Inverleven 16 Years Old dist 17 Jan 89, bott 24 Feb 05 **(84) n**19 **t**23 **f**21 **b**21. Attractive, if simplistic, fare where the oak has gone through the nose slightly but is compensated for by the wonderful mouthwatering quality of the concentrated malt arrival: a delicious requiem for a recently lost distillery. **50%.**

Peerless Inverleven 1977 (*see* Duncan Taylor Inverleven 1977)

⏤ Rarest of the Rare Inverleven 1979 Cask no. 5662 **(84) n**20 **t**21 **f**22 **b**21. Gravelled well in time. Won't trouble you so far as complexity is concerned. But you cannot be other than impressed with its sweet, malty confidence. A really charming Lowlander sadly lost to us. **53.7%.** *Duncan Taylor.*

## ISLE OF ARRAN
**Highland (Island–Arran), 1995. Isle of Arran Distillers. Working.**

Arran First db dist 95, bott Apr 04 **(87) n**21 melt-in-the-nose gently sweetened malt; **t**22 a double layer of malt – one hard, juicy and purposeful, the other soft, sweet and undisciplined; **f**22 some almost chalky vanilla puts the brake on the malty celebrations; **b**22 quite beautifully made malt. **46%.** *2,784 bottles.*

⏤ The Arran Malt Under 10 Years Old db **(89) n**22 limp, lush barley of the butterscotch variety; **t**23 those stunning soft oils are working overtime to spread the sweet barley; **f**22 long, biscuity and balanced; **b**22 this one's kicked its shoes and socks off... **43%**

The Arran Malt Aged 10 Years L140206 db **(93) n**23 charming, delicate; varying citrus notes hand-in-hand with rich, butterscotch-barley; the odd youthful note thins things out; **t**24 the palate coated in caressing oils, to which stick the cleanest and most profound barley. You can chew your jaw off here; **f**23 developing vanillas dovetail with some of those younger new-makish notes but still cannot escape the clutches of the fat barley. Some fizzing spice decides to make an appearance; **b**23 at last! The distillery feels confident enough to put an age statement to their malt, although it's been good enough to do that for the last four or five years. This bottling of some of Arran's first casks entertains and delight. It won't be long before the world's malt connoisseurs add Arran to their list of must haves. Because if it's character and quality you want, it's here by the malt shiel load. **46%. ncf.**

**The Arran Malt 100° Proof** L210806 db **(91)** n23 complex not just in aroma but weight: both firm yet soft; the barley offers varying degrees of intensity. Youthful and deeply desirable; t23 just so barley rich! That lovely hint of youth embracing something older and more oakily complex as it develops; the early barley offers a fruit edge, some natural toffees and then cocoas develop; f22 much drier, though with enough moistening barley, and waves of mocha; b23 different, intriguing, style of Arran; some excellent use of bourbon cask allows a relaxed meeting of barley and oak. Sheer class. **57%. ncf.**

⸫ **The Arran Malt Amarone Finish** db **(96)** n24 perhaps the best Arran nose of all time: dry rose-petaly Turkish Delight moistened with grape and toasted almond…then it starts getting really complex…! t23 melt-in-the-mouth arrival with succulent grape and bitter-sweet apricot and nuts; f24 beautiful chocolate and latte mix as the soft fruit tantalises even further; so long your tastebuds will be tested like they have never been tested before… b25 a true gold nugget of a bottling. I'm astonished at its total brilliance. Trust the Italians to have a hand in something of such style. The Whisky Gentlemen of Verona will be very proud. **55%**

**The Arran Malt Bordeaux Finish** db **(90)** n22 awkward and cumbersome, though the salty element appeals; t23 wonderful delivery on gently fruited malt, but then it unravels clumsily and falls apart to reveal its intricate workings; f22 the eclectic style here continues with a burnt raisin and chocolate finale; b23 bloody hell! I'm exhausted after that lot. Whatever balance it has is by fluke rather than design. Never settles down and the palate can't quite get a grip. Yet we have a slapdash masterpiece. Arran has gone all French with its Calvados, Bordeaux and Cognac finishes. This is probably the most intriguing of the lot. And the unconventional colour should appeal in San Francisco, Soho and Sydney… **59.6%.**

⸫ **The Arran Malt Bourgogne Finish** db **(74)** n18 t19 f18 b19. Arran Malt Vinegar more like… **56.4%**

**The Arran Malt Brandy Finish** Lepanto Px Brandy cask from Gonzalez Byass, bott 17.1.06 db **(74)** n18 t19 f19 b18. Intense but irritatingly off-key. **59.4%.** *705 bottles.*

**The Arran Malt Cream Sherry Cask** from Gonzalez Byass, bott 01.2.06 db **(90)** n22 chunky malt with spicy apple and sour under-ripe cherry; t24 a delivery from heaven with perfect weight to the barley; a bitter-sweet delivery to die for. The natural oiliness of the barley sits comfortably with the "cream" grape, the most enormous spice explosion blasting apart any chance of a cloying nature; f21 surprisingly lightweight grape; b23 make sure your chair has arm-rests… **57.5%.** *812 bottles.*

**The Arran Malt Finished in Port Cask** bott 28.6.05 db **(90)** n23 the port shines from the very first; perhaps the most distant waft of sulphur but fails to significantly detract; t23 well structured and calm – behaved fruit suddenly gives way to a rip-tide of pulsating pepper; some malt-fruit notes intertwine towards the late middle. Fabulously mouthwatering throughout; f22 firm traces of oak dry this one out, but it's a long journey; b22 at a tasting in Canada, where both this and the 4th July bottling can be found, I at first favoured the lighter-coloured bottling of just 218. However, on reflection, this one may just edge it – if you find them side-by-side, it's a close call!! **58.4%.** *770 bottles.*

**The Arran Malt Finished in Port Cask** db **(89)** n22 mildly peppered fruit; delicate and with youthful, malty resonance; t23 simple, brilliant, very young arrival: suppressed fruit on the nose arrives in concentrated form before backing off to allow those peppers full play; f22 lightens out dramatically with cocoa and vanilla leaning towards dryness; b22 genuinely lovely whisky showing both youth and maturity in its broad-sweeping mouthfeel. **58.5%.** *218 bottles.*

⸫ **The Arran Malt Grand Cru Champagne Finish** db **(87)** n21 dry; t22 bitter-sweet winey-oak then a breakthrough of trad Arran; f22 that barley oiliness continues with the fruitiness all but lost, other than a late dry soft wine echo; b22 recognisable as Arran. And the ghost of champagnes past hang unmistakably on the palate. **58.9%**

⸫ **The Arran Malt Lepanto PX Brandy Finish** db **(85)** n22 t22 f20 b21. Tight, unusually thin for an Arran, but some lovely sweet fruit amid the confusion. Pretty oaky, too. **59%**

**The Arran Malt Non-Chill Filtered** db **(89)** n22 quite feisty barley kicking up a rumpus; good age now and some real character to the mildly gristy freshness; t23 massive barley delivery, a few half-hearted spices and then a lovely oiliness creeps in to intensify the malt; f22 gentle vanilla, greengages and dry but big barley; b22 a vastly improved dram with some apparent extra age and body, though less spice. A real meal from the real deal. **46%**

The Arran Malt Premier Cru Bourgogne Cask Finish db **(86) n**21 **t**22 **f**21 **b**22. An entertaining dram which some would do somersaults for, but marks docked because we have lost the unique Arran character. **56.4%**

⋰ The Arran Malt Sauternes Finish db **(84) n**21 **t**22 **f**20 **b**21. Strap yourself in for this one: eye-watering sultana and 240 volts of spice. Choked with oak, though. **56%**

The Arran Malt Single Cask **(92) n**22 very thinly spread marmalade, vanilla and fresh malt; this freshness even hints slightly at sliced cucumber; **t**23 a breathtaking assortment of malty notes of varying sweetness and intensity; oak also pounds through and a gentle, citric fruitiness is woven into the rich tapestry; **f**24 a gentle wave of salt to go with the gentle oak and vanilla; late hints of cocoa on the death; **b**23 the bottle doesn't give the vintage or cask number (something to be addressed?) but this malt is only about eight and shows maturity way beyond those years. The depth of intensity is outstanding and from first to last not even the whimper of an off note: a glorious advert for a distillery just coming of age. For the record, it was a 1998 vintage and cask no. 640. **58.9%**. *Drawn from cask at the Isle of Arran Distillery and available only in visitor centre.*

The Arran Malt Single Bourbon Cask Strength db **(88) n**23 **t**22 **f**21 **b**22. On this evidence Arran is confidently formulating its own style. **56.6%**

Arran Single Malt Calvados Finish, bott 03 Feb 05 db **(86) n**19 **t**22 **f**23 **b**22. The unerring sharpness of this may make it the apple of some Arran fans' eyes, but not mine. **60.1%**. *620 bottles.*

Arran Single Malt Cognac Finish bott 08 Apr 05 db **(87) n**22 **t**22 **f**21 **b**22. The Cognac plays no role whatsoever here (unless it once boasted a phenol level): the star – and real shock – is the gentle peat. **59.4%**. *506 bottles.*

The Arran Malt Single Cask Strength Marsala Finish db **(82) n**21 **t**20 **f**21 **b**20. Pleasant, gentle spiced fruit but otherwise flat and charisma-free by Arran standards. **56.9%**

The Arran Malt Single Cask Strength Rum Finish db **(87) n**20 **t**22 **f**23 **b**22. A tastebud-provoking extrovert – but only on the palate. **58.5%**

The Arran Malt Single Sherry Cask Strength db **(91) n**23 tangy orange and crushed grape; has come from top-draw cask because there is still enough clarity to see the usual Arran trademark intense malt; **t**23 weighty and takes time to really find its bearings: when it does, the tastebuds are crushed under an avalanche of enormous malt and fruit in equal measures; **f**22 lightens to allow vanilla and spice to flourish; **b**23 heartening to see a latter-day sherry butt come through so brilliantly; the complexity and bitter-sweet balance is fabulous. **57.3%**

The Arran Malt Single Sherry Cask cask 98/44, dist 19 Jan 98, bott 7 Nov 05 db **(94) n**24 freshly opened conkers; nutty with a jaffa/marzipan/cocoa complexity. Wonderful; **t**25 the best Arran delivery yet. Tastebuds blitzed by a relentless barrage of high propane barley notes; mouthwatering and beguiling as the grape finds a various fissures to gain a toe-hold. Almost, but not quite overwhelmed: total brinkmanship and brilliance; **f**22 surprisingly hard and metallic; **b**23 there is not a whisky even close to this in character. A stunning one-off. **58.3%**

The Arran Malt Single Cask Finished in Calvados db **(83) n**19 **t**22 **f**21 **b**21. A strange, indecisive whisky that never quite settles on the character it wishes to be. Undermined by a slight soapiness on the nose it still has one or two astonishing moments of wanton wild, fruity passion, especially on the early mouth arrival. One that may terrify you at first but will grow on you. **62.1%**

The Arran Malt Single Montepulciano D'Abruzzo Sherry Cask bott 06 db **(76) n**19 **t**20 **f**18 **b**19. The odd butyric note reveals a cask not entirely in sympathy with the distillery. **56.9%**. *315 bottles.*

The Arran Malt Trebbiano D'Abruzzo Cask Finish db **(93) n**22 a jazzed-up, fruity, spicy number, but astonishingly clean; **t**24 thundering, spiced malt but entirely in sync with the massive, chewy body; **f**23 long with subtle re-emergence of fruit and a hint of honeycomb; **b**24 a cask finish that works uncommonly well with the malt and fruit being very much on the same wavelength. If enormous complexity doesn't come naturally to this distillery, then it certainly has the weight and charisma to absorb agents that will help. **56%**

The Arran Malt Vintage Collection 1996 db **(88)** n22 t22 f21 **b**23. All the early promise from this distillery is coming to fruition. **46%**. *6,000 bottles*.

**Robert Burns World Federation Arran Single Island Malt** db **(84)** n19 t22 f22 **b**21. Fat, creamy, full-bodied. The malt sweetens by the second to become something like a good old-fashioned American malt milkshake: amazing but there is enough oak for a drying balance. One of the most intense young malts on the market, only the naivety of the nose preventing it from hitting the heights. A delightful, tastebud-massaging malt experience. **40%**

**Cadenhead's Authentic Collection Arran Aged 10 Years** Bourbon Hogshead, dist 95, bott Feb 06 **(93)** n23 a flawless aroma of the most intense barley imaginable, yet friendly and lightly oiled; t24 the palate is swamped with barley at its most concentrated, charismatic yet clean; the degree of sweetness hits perfection; f23 soft spices appear as does vanilla and natural cream toffee; **b**23 this distillery has so come of age. Spectacular! And a more intense, if less complex, version of the distillery's own 10-year-old. **53.6%**. *348 bottles*

⁘ **Cadenhead's Authentic Collection Arran Aged 11 Years** Fino Sherry Hogshead, dist 1996, bott May 07 **(94)** n23 unsmoked bacon sizzling beside grits and grapes; t24 perfect barley with the most sublime and varied sweet tones imaginable; almost Warholesque the way the malt is painted in so many shades; f23 long with a scaled down version, except now some spice and vanilla; **b**24 Arran can always be relied on for beauty, though not always complexity. This has both – and in buckets. **56%**. *330 bottles*.

⁘ **The Clydesdale Lochranza 10 Years Old** Cask ref. 0236/07006, dist July 96, bott Sept 06 **(77)** n19 t20 f19 **b**19. Despite the obvious faults, remains very drinkable and you can only admire the pluck of the malt as it battles against an unfriendly butt. **55.5%. nc ncf.** *Blackadder International*.

⁘ **Connoisseurs Choice Arran 1998 (88)** n21 lime squeezed over barley; t23 that big Arran malt kick; f22 a trickle of custard into the barley; **b**22 not the most complex Arran, but no faulting its barley breeze **43%**. *Gordon & MacPhail*.

⁘ **Duncan Taylor The NC2 Range Isle of Arran** db **(80)** n20 t21 f19 **b**20. Clunks around a bit for all the heavy oils. **56%. nc ncf.**

**Mac Y 10th Anniversary Isle of Arran Aged 10 Years** cask no. 718, dist 96, bott 06 **(95)** n23 firm barley and sultana softened by a sprinkling of grist and most distant rumblings of peat. Proud, high quality stuff; t24 immediately crisp and salivating with a glorious crescendo of intense barley; the layering is cleverly structured with the malt offering varying intensity of sweetness. Just so subtle and perfectly weighted...; f24 long with a late grapey reprise; fades as the spices and cocoa arrive. Again, supreme structuring and complexity; **b**24 this is the kind of malt, when writing a book like this, you have to wait a long time to find. In this case, it's among the very last whiskies tasted and is on new ground as Arran is still finding its feet. And was it worth the wait! Arran in one of its most compelling guises yet; a stunning way for Danish whisky importers Mac Y to mark their first ten years. And further, indisputable, evidence of Arran taking on the status of one the Great Distilleries. **48%. nc ncf.** *Denmark. 450 bottles*.

**Old Malt Cask Isle of Arran Aged 9 Years** Sherry butt 2309, dist July 96, bott Jan 06 **(87)** n19 intense barley despite the butt, but also a tad feinty; t23 one of the richest most intense barley deliveries in the business with echoes of marmalade and butterscotch; f23 long, oily and just the faintest speck of peat to add body. Lovely whisky; **b**22 don't be put off by the very slight feintiness on the nose as, is so often the case, it is followed by untold riches on the body. **50%. nc ncf.** *Douglas Laing*.

⁘ **Old Malt Cask Arran Aged 11 Years** dist Nov 95, bott Feb 07 **(91)** n22 clean, buzzy malt; t23 sparkling, spicy then usual thick maltfest middle; faultlessly intense and so delicious... f23 an endless strand of barley intertwines with the peppery fade; **b**23 if this whisky was a person, it'd be that bloke who puts you to shame because he's so damned nice... **50%**. *Douglas Laing. 422 bottles*.

⁘ **Provenance Arran Aged 10 Years Sherry Finish** dist Spring 97, bott Spring 07 **(91)** n23 more rum than sherry; t23 again the influence appears to be from a sweet, high quality rum cask as the varying sugars collide; f22 vanilla cream; **b**23 for a sherry- casked whisky, this is as rummy as it gets. Beautiful malt. **46%**. *Douglas Laing*.

⁘ **Scotch Malt Whisky Society Cask 121.19 Aged 9 Years** Refill Butt, dist Jan 98 **(92)** n22 a soupcon of lychee lightens the tight barley; t24 good lord...at one stage it appears as though the tastebuds will be crushed under the weight of the concentrated malt, whose increments in sweetness are only just discernible to the human nerve ending; f23 oils kick and spread dry toast and vanilla around; b23 one of the most intensely malty island drams you are ever likely to unearth. **57.4%**

‍ **Scotch Malt Whisky Society Cask 121.20 Aged 9 Years** Refill Butt, dist Jan 98 **(91) n**23 lamb tikka korma; **t**23 immediate oil impact and with it one or two bourbon-style oak traits; **f**22 I must be going mad: but there really are some curry oils attached to the finish here, too; **b**23 don't let the owners of Whyte and MacKay get hold of this, or bang goes Arran's independence....!! **56.5%**

**Vom Fass Isle of Arran 6 Years Old (87) n**22 **f**22 **b**21. A bit of a wimp whisky-wise, with no spice or telling oak. But if your tastebuds want a sweet, barley-laden massage, this is your boy. Or girl. **40%**. *Austria.*

## ISLE OF JURA

**Highland (Island–Jura), 1810. Whyte and Mackay. Working.**

**Isle of Jura 5 Years Old 1999** db **(83) n**19 **t**23 **f**21 **b**20. Absolutely enormously peated, but has reached that awkward time in its life when it is massively sweet and as well balanced as a two-hour-old foal. **46%** *The Whisky Exchange*

**Isle of Jura 10 Years Old** db **(77) n**18 **t**19 **f**21 **b**19. A tangy malt that seems younger than its 10 years. The finish is long and offers the faintest hint of smoke on the rich malt. **40%**

**Isle of Jura 16 Years Old** db **(80) n**18 **t**22 **f**20 **b**20. Some lovely, mildly salty honey thorugh the middle. But an indefinable something is missing. A variable dram at the best of times, this expression is pleasant but ... variable. **40%**

**Isle of Jura Aged 21 Years** db **(78) n**20 **t**21 **f**19 **b**18. Pleasant enough, but surprisingly short of charisma. **40%**

**Isle of Jura 21 Years Old Cask Strength** db **(92) n**22 something hard and grainy against the ultra-clean fruit; **t**24 fabulous mouth arrival, just such a brilliant fruit-spice combo held together in a malty soup; **f**23 long and intensely malty; **b**23 every mouthful exudes class and quality. A must-have for Scottish Island collector ... or those who know how to appreciate a damn fine malt **58.1%**

‍ **Isle of Jura Aged 36 Years** (dist 1965) db **(96) n**25 **t**25 **f**23 **b**23. I remember 20-odd years ago being taken into a corner of Jura's warehouse and tasting a cask of something big and smoky. It was different to all the other Juras around, but had none of this honey. Is this the same cask, a generation on? Most probably. I then returned to the hotel opposite for a dram (and a bottle) of their own Jura and wondered what would become of that peaty one-off. Now I know. **44%**

‍ **Isle of Jura 40 Years Old** Finished in Oloroso sherry wood db **(90) n**23 a different species of Jura from anything you are likely to have seen before: swamped in sherry, there is a vague, rather odd smokiness to this. Not to mention salty, sea-side rockpools. As a pairing (sherry and smoke), the odd couple... which works and doesn't work at the same time. Strange... **t**22 syrupy sweet delivery with thick waves of fruit and then an apologetic ahem from the smoke, which drifts in nervously. Again, everything is awkward... **f**22 remains soft and velvety, though now strands of bitter, salty oak and molasses drift in and out; **b**23 throw the Jura textbooks away. This is something very different. Completely out of sync in so many ways, but... **40%**

**Isle of Jura 1984** db **(69) n**15 **t**18 **f**18 **b**18. Big brother ... with sulphur. All whiskies are equal, but some are more equal than others. Oops, wrong book. **42%**. *Bottled to commemorate George Orwell who wrote the book 1984 while on the island.*

**Jura Festival of Malt and Music Distilled 1989** dist Mar 89, bott 04 db **(87) n**19 the two year influence of the young "Anada" sherry butt has left a slight blemish though an agave pepperiness is interesting; **t**23 very unusual delivery of barley, almost glass textured at first and mildly cooling before thse massive peppers return to torch the outside of the tongue; **f**23 opens up later on to reveal a saltier tang to the storming spice and a distant waft of smoke; **b**22 not entirely flawless but one of the most unusual, fascinating and, it must be said, at times delicious drams of the year. **57.9%**. *850 bottles.*

**Isle of Jura Legacy** db **(82) n**19 **t**22 **f**20 **b**21. Some very chewy honeycomb on the middle. Pretty big stuff. **40%**

**Isle of Jura Stillman's Dram Limited Edition Aged 27 Years** db **(90)** n24 t23 f21 b22. One of the most complex Juras yet bottled. **45%**

**Isle of Jura Superstition** db **(86)** n21 t22 f20 b23. A rare case of where the whole is better than the parts. Wins through with superb balance between peat and sweeter barley. Distinctive to the point of being almost unique. **45%**

**Cadenhead's Authentic Collection Isle of Jura Aged 13 Years** Bourbon Hogshead, dist 92, bott May 05 **(87)** n21 t22 f22 b22. Jura at its most islandy. **54.8%**. *270 btls.*

**Cadenhead's Authentic Collection Jura Aged 14 Years** Bourbon Hogshead, dist 92, bott May 06 **(78)** n20 t21 f18 b19. A bitter, metallic experience, though not too unusual for this distillery. **56.3%**. *276 bottles.*

**Dun Bheagan Isle of Jura Aged 17 Years (76)** n19 t20 f18 b19. Another off-key offering: by and large, not a classic period for Jura. **43%**. *Ian Macleod.*

**Dun Bheagan Isle of Jura 18 Years Old (92)** n24 gorgeous citrus and marzipan; t23 melt-in-the-mouth malt offering perfect, understated sweetness; f22 decent vanilla offers a sexy, soft landing; b23 hurrah! A delightful, delicate Jura absolutely worth investing in...!!! **43%**. *Ian Macleod.*

**Old Malt Cask Jura 15 Years Old** dist 4 May 90, bott Jul 05 **(69)** n17 t18 f17 b17. Sulphur... so bad... **50%**. *Douglas Laing. 718 bottles.*

**Old Malt Cask Jura 16 Years Old** dist 16 Nov 88, bott 23 Mar 05 **(87)** n21 t23 f21 b22. An above average Jura with loads of intense malt character. **50%**. *Douglas Laing & Co.*

⁘ **Old Malt Cask Jura Aged 17 Years** dist Nov 88, bott Sept 06 **(71)** n17 t19 f17 b18. Not a good cut: the stillman had an off day. **50%**. *Douglas Laing. 357 bottles.*

⁘ **Scotch Malt Whisky Society Cask 31.16 Aged 18 Years** Refill Hogshead, dist Sept 88 **(78)** n18 t21 f19 b20. Jura at its most peaty for that period. But I still despair: this is not particularly well made and for all the sweet gristiness on delivery some of the intensity comes from feints that detract on the nose and finish. Mind you, if you love rough, sweet, peaty stuff offering a tad of honeycomb – it's faultless. **57.7%**

⁘ **Scott's Selection Isle of Jura 1989** bott 06 **(77)** n17 t21 f20 b19. Sweet, mildly syrupy and not short of feints. **56.3%**. *Speyside Distillers.*

**The Whisky Fair Isle of Jura 5 Year Old** cask 144, dist 27 Jan 99 **(88)** n22 imagine raw peat reak, barley rubbed with lashings of salt, armpit sweat and wild young oak being tossed mindlessly together: that gives you some idea of the chaos involved here; t23 enormous launch of myriad young notes with praline binding together the sweetness and the drier tones; f22 long and lush with the peat continuing its fiery dance. Wonderful fun; b21 young, robust, raw and eclectic, it holds together very well. **61.3%**

# KILCHOMAN
## Islay, 2006. Working.

⁘ **Kilchoman New Spirit** Bourbon/ Sherry, dist 6 Dec 06 db **(94)** n23 curiously attractive as there is as much coal smoke on the nose as there is peat. Quite a homely and attractive combination, nutty, a touch herbal and reminiscent of some of the early work carried out at Makmyra in Sweden; t24 sweet, as peated new make has a tendency to be, but wonderfully weighted with exceptional oil to barley ratio; f23 long and continues the same excellent course, drying laterally but with the soft peats continuing to delve in and out of the tastebuds b24 not whisky at all, but new make that has, I understand, spent a few weeks in wood and is for sale at the distillery. And there is no doubting: this is quite beautifully – and, technically, faultlessly - made spirit, far better than the owner could possibly have hoped for, and which, if this is an average sample of this new Islay make, bodes exceptionally well for the future. **63.5%**

# KILKERRAN
## Campbeltown, 2004. J&A Mitchell & Co. Working.

⁘ **Kilkerran Single Malt** db **(80)** n19 very young, slightly Shredded Wheaty, a touch of tobacco leaf, mint and some heavy oils; t20 ungainly arrival with big barley, big oils, big natural caramel; f21 settles towards a light, slightly sweeter and gristier fade; b20 Glyngyle's first offering doesn't rip up any trees. And maybe the odd flaw to its character that you won't see when the distillery is fine-tuned. But this is the first-ever bottling from this brand new Campbeltown distillery and therefore its chances of being a worldbeater as an untried and untested 3-y-o were pretty slim. I will be watching its development with relish. And with heart pounding... **46%.** *Available exclusively from distillery direct from cask.*

⫶⫶ **Kilkerran Single Malt** bott 22 May 07 db **(84) n**20 bit of an oily, vaguely feinty beast with the odd note that is bit rowdy and coarse. But the malt intensity cannot be denied; **t**21 massive delivery of barley aided and abetted by puffed- up oils and a delightful coppery sharpness unique to new stills; **f**22 better balance with the very first signs of oak intrusion in the barley which is showing some sugary teeth; **b**21 sadly, I was out of the country and couldn't attend the Coming of Age of Kilkerran, when its first casks turned three and became whisky. Very kindly, they sent me a bottle as if I was there and, therefore, these are the notes of the very first bottling handed out to visitors. Interestingly, there is a marked similarity in distillery style to the 46% bottling in that the malt offers a crescendo of quality. This is only three year old whisky, of course, and its fingerprints will alter as it spends longer in the cask. **62%. nc ncf.**

## KNOCKANDO
### Speyside, 1898. Diageo. Working.
**Knockando Aged 18 Years** Sherry casks, dist 87 db **(77) n**19 **t**21 **f**18 **b**19. Bland and docile. Someone wake me up. **43%**

**Knockando 1990** db **(83) n**21 **t**22 **f**20 **b**20. The most fruity Knockando I've come across with some attractive salty notes. Dry, but a little extra malty sweetness these days. **40%**

⫶⫶ **Duncan Taylor Collection Knockando 1980** Cask no. 1912, dist July 80 **(81) n**21 **t**21 **f**19 **b**20. Sharp and exotically bitter. **46%.**

## KNOCKDHU
### Speyside, 1894. Inver House. Working.
**AnCnoc 12 Year Old** db **(90) n**22 an aggressive pepperiness bites deep into the usual grassy maltiness and coal smoke. Excellent depth and complexity, though slightly more aggressive, if younger, in style than of old; **t**23 absolutely fabulous, near-perfect, malt arrival, perhaps the most clean, yet intense of any in Scotland. The complexity is staggering with not only multi-layers of malt but a distant peat and oak infusion; **f**22 deliciously spicy; **b**23 if there is a more complete 12-year-old Speyside malt on the market, I have yet to find it. A malt that should adorn a shelf in every whisky-drinking home.

**AnCnoc 13 Year Old Highland Selection** db **(85) n**21 **t**23 **f**20 **b**21. A big Knockdhu, but something is dulling the complexity. **46%**

⫶⫶ **An Cnoc 1975** bott Sept 05 db **(92) n**24 a graceful aroma that allows the nose fleeting glimpses of myriad delights; the oak displays in many colours, the most striking being a crusty, gently spiced custard tart, the malts offering a barley nip while some distant, exhausted phenols hang on and blend in with the sugar-dusted Turkish delight; **t**23 it was unlikely the taste would live up to the nose – but it has a damn good try: the barley still refreshes early on, some honey dives in as do some estery, Jamaica pot still rum-type notes. It hits a pretty thick oaky wall about half way but a coating of muscovado sugar helps it through; **f**22 the oak continues to dominate, allowing only the odd wisp of smoky demerara to flit by but remains long and quite regal; **b**23 curious to see how the time between my first ever visit to a Scottish distillery (in 1975) and now has passed. In the case of this malt from Knockdhu, with more than a degree of magic going on: in fact, it is rare to find casks of this great age pretty much intact. The nose in particular deserves great attention as the complexity simply stuns. Look out, too, for the tell-tale signs of a slightly peatier spirit than is made there today. **50%**

**AnCnoc 1991** bott Aug 05 db **(76) n**18 **t**22 **f**17 **b**19. Some eloquent and delightful moments early on but for a true World Great distillery, there is something very wrong here with the odd sub-standard cask having somehow made its way to the bottling hall and spoilt the party. As disappointing, flawed and under par as an England World Cup performance. **46%. ncf.**

⫶⫶ **An Cnoc 1993** db **(89) n**22 butterscotch on shortbread pastry and barley sugar interweaves attractively with the trademark soft honey note and the very lightest whiff of something vaguely smoky; **t**21 surprising oak charge arrives early, bringing with it spices and soft oils; **f**24 it's the finish that makes this one with a late – and highly unusual – intervention of citrus to help lighten the oaky load and emphasise the richness of the barley; **b**22 quite an odd one this. I have tasted it a couple of times with different samples and there is a variance. This one takes an oakier path and then invites the barley to do its stuff. Delicious, but underscores the deft touch of the standard 12-year-old. **46%**

AnCnoc 26 Years Old Highland Selection db **(89)** n23 profound. Everything is big, but perfectly proportioned: massive grapey fruit and malt concentrate; **t**22 pure Knockdhu: intense malt carrying some beautiful spices and an obscure but refreshing fruit; **f**23 the lull after a minor storm: rich vanilla and echoes of malt; **b**21 there is a little flat moment between the middle and finish for which I have chipped off a point or two. That apart, superb. **48.2%**

AnCnoc 30 Years Old db **(85)** n21 pipe smoke, old leather armchairs and a sprig of mint: this seems older than its years; **t**23 wonderfully thick malt, beefed up in intensity by drawing in as much oak as it comfortably can; the honeycomb and molassed sweetness adds a lovely touch; **f**19 big natural caramel and some pretty rough-stuff oak; **b**22 seat-of-the-pants whisky that is just on the turn. Still has a twinkle in the eye, though. **49%**

Knockdhu 23 Years Old db **(94)** n23 t24 f23 b24. Pass the smelling salts. This is whisky to knock you out. A malt that confirms Knockdhu as simply one of the great Speysiders, but unquestionably among the world's elite. **57.4%**.

Cadenhead Authentic Collection Knockdhu 16 Years Old dist 89, bott May 05 **(88)** n22 mint on malt; **t**23 immediate spices and then, of course, the honey thread and fresh plucked grass; **f**21 lush, vanilla laden and oiled; **b**22 independent versions from this distillery are rarer than hens' teeth, but I can't remember, even in the lab, the last time I came across a Knockdhu with such an oily grip. **50.1%**. *282 bottles.*

Harrods Knockdhu Aged 12 Years db **(84)** n19 t23 f21 b21. One can assume only that caramel (or an exceptional dull sherry cask) has been added here because it is otherwise impossible to find such a flat nose from a Knockdhu. However, the arrival on the palate is bliss, with dates combining with glossy honey and marzipan, but again the finish is only a dull echo of what it should be. Shackled greatness. **40%**. ☉

Provenance Knockdhu 10 Years Old dist 12 Dec 94, bott 21 Feb 05 **(88)** n23 t22 f21 **b**22. The nose is nothing short of amazing. **46%**.

Provenance Knockdhu Aged Over 10 Years, dist Spring 94, bott Winter 05 **(91)** n23 t23 f22 b23. The subtlety and complexity of this show exactly why it is so outstanding, both as a blending and a single malt. **46%. nc ncf.** *Douglas Laing.*

# LADYBURN
### Lowland, 1966–1975. Closed. Demolished.

Ladyburn 1973 db **(60)** n15 varying shades of light oak have not entirely dimmed the malt, just a tad spirity but pleasant with minimum complexity; **t**15 oak, oak and more (spicy) oak; **f**17 oak; **b**13 this has lost all trace of shape and form. Pretty one-dimensional yet easily drinkable thanks to a singular malty sweetness, especially towards the very end. Don't bother opening.

# LAGAVULIN
### Islay, 1816. Diageo. Working.

Lagavulin 12 Years Old db **(93)** n24 disarmingly gentle peat, much of its younger oils have miraculously vanished, lots of fresh fruit – including mandarin – available and mildly nutty, too. Pretty faultless material; **t**23 the smokescreen of the nose is laid bare on the palate: oil enough for heart attacks, peat laid on thickly and the oak offering an extra surge of spice that is man-marked by gristy, sweet barley; **f**23 long and at times almost too soft to be heard. Impressive vanilla to thin out the smoke, but the peat with the cocoa still lingers for a good five or ten minutes; **b**23 really, all you can ask from a Lagavulin at this age: weighty yet delicate enough for impressive complexity. Just try not having a second of this ... **57.8%**

Lagavulin 12 Years Old db **(92)** n24 clean sea-brine and peat: first class; **t**23 explosive peat and soft barley make delicious bedfellows; **f**22 cocoa and smoke. The barley hangs sweetly around; **b**23 really charming Islay with a frisky peatiness that is sweet and lingering. One to savour and reminisce for those of us who were hooked on the Lagavulin in pre-Classic Malt era. **58%**

**Lagavulin 12 Years Old** db (**91**) n22 marauding peat on a very greasy base – compelling but lacking complexity; t23 sweet malt arriving in droves and sliding around the palate on a pan of oil; some wonderful liquorice and toasty notes add depth; f23 sweetens out with a nutty dimension to the coastal feel; b23 some extra oil makes this a slightly less complex beast than its predecessor. And the last one was only enough! **58.2%**

⸬· **Lagavulin 12 Years Old** Special Releases 2006 db (**90**) n23 a touch of oil in the air, old engineering works and smoky grist; t22 spiced- up delivery and then one very sweet delivery with hickory on the smoke f22 long with a touch of Camp coffee to the Java and vanilla-peat; b23 the peat is of lighter intensity than the old-fashioned 12-y-o some of us cut our teeth on, remember. **57.5%**

⸱ **Lagavulin Aged 16 Years** db (**95**) n24 wave upon surging wave of giant peat; delicate spices interject with hints of malt and liquorice. Heavy roast Jamaican Blue Mountain coffee and medium roast Java blend (35/65) help spin out the smoke; t24 the chewiest of sweet peats, a touch of burnt grist and sugared smoke, with maximum chewing required; f23 bitter chocolate on the death, almost a touch of chocolate cup cake, but with layers of sweet peat reek to add extra sturdy depth; b24 much more like the Lagavulin of old with unfettered development and delivery. Befitting the great distillery this unquestionably is. Forget some recent disappointing bottlings: this is the real thing! **43%**

⸬· **Lagavulin 30 Years Old** Special Releases 2006, dist 76 db (**91**) n22 vague citrus notes help break up the peat dominance; t23 dry, oaky kick and some mega prickly spices that tattoo themselves into your tastebuds suggest a spoiled malt. But the malt regroups and with the aid of gentle and gutsy smoke creates a sweeter balance; f23 liquorice and coffee show the age but that gristy sweetness compensates perfectly; b23 a malt that at first sniff appears a shade past its best repays closer inspection. **52.6%**

⸱ **MacLeod's Islay 8 Years Old** (**90**) n24 an astonishing array of citrus (lime and orange) battles with some success against the crashing waves of clean peat that is iodine-rich and enticingly green. Something that no true whisky lover should fail to experience; t22 fresh-faced and tender, there is an enveloping sweetness that is like liquid grist. The peat almost pings around the mouth, so crisp is it. Only on the middle does the lack of age seem to offer an unfilled hole; f21 lengthy and luscious, it is still spritely and fun and boasts massive liquoricey chewability, but so very green and immature – fabulous all the same! b23 the nose is Islay, pure Islay. At half the age of what you would normally taste Lagavulin this effervescent malt helps you learn so much more about this great distillery. No Islay malt on the market comes cleaner than this: only the old Bowmore 5-y-o used to show such childish abandon. This dram should be in every serious collector's or Islay-phile's home. I'm 100% certain this is Lagavulin. **40%** ⊙

**The Whisky Fair "Vanilla Sky" Aged 13 Years** (Lagavulin) Hogshead no. 5341, dist Nov 92, bott Mar 06 (**95**) n23 get a chisel to cut through the dense peat, though a touch of citrus helps. Islay in a sniff...; t24 enormous delivery, yet clean, mouthwatering and barley rich over and beyond the obvious smoke; f24 just stays on course with countless waves of iodine sweetened with a small dab of maple syrup and barley sugar; wonderful vanillas arrive late on and see it through – with the smoke – to the glorious end; b24 Lagavulin on cruise control: definitely no ice with this one... **53.6%**. *Germany. 138 bottles.*

⸬· **The Whisky Fair Lagavulin "Vanilla Sky" Aged 14 Years** Bourbon Hogshead, dist 1992, bott 06 (**74**) n19 t19 f18 b18. Sulphur is sulphur – even in a big peated malt. What a shame! **53.0%**. *Germany.*

# LAPHROAIG
## Islay, 1820. Fortune Brands. Working.

**Laphroaig 10 Years Old** db (**92**) n24 impossible not to nose this and think of Islay: no other aroma so perfectly encapsulates the island – clean despite the rampaging peat-reek and soft oak, raggy coast-scapes and screeching gulls – all in a glass; t23 one of the crispiest, peaty malts of them all, the barley standing out alone, brittle and unbowed, before the peat comes rushing in like the tide: iodine and soft salty tones; f22 the peat now takes control for a sweet, distinguished finish; b23 has reverted back slightly towards a heavier style in more recent bottlings, though I would still like to see that old oomph at the very death. Even so, this is, indisputably, a classic whisky. The favourite of Prince Charles, apparently: he will make a wise king ... **40%**

⫶ **Laphroaig 10 Years Old** db **(91) n**22 less intense smoke; **t**24 much silkier delivery than usual with the sweetness all up front as the peat dovetails in and out of the barley – more complex; **f**22 a drier finale with a shade more caramel; **b**23 I discovered these 20cl 43% bottlings just after it was announced they were to be phased out. I also noticed that the whisky inside them had a slightly different character from the standard bottlings... **43%**

**Laphroaig 10 Years Old Original Cask Strength** db **(80) n**20 **t**20 **f**21 **b**19. Would never have marked this down as a Laphroaig. For all the oil, thin and disappointing. **57.3%**

**Laphroaig 10 Years Old Original Cask Strength** db **(90) n**22 an alluringly precise, almost dense smokiness with lovely strands of chocolate marzipan oak; **t**23 overtly sweet as the malt really goes to town, but the peat digs deep, chewy trenches; **f**23 more semi-bourbony oak, then slow delivery of a late wave of peat; **b**22 it is amazing when compared with different expressions of the same whisky (see below). Where the 57.3% version fires blanks, this presses just the right buttons in the right order to ensure this one is a treat of a dram and so worthy of the great Laphroaig name: just so sophisticated. **55.7%**

**Laphroaig 10 Years Old Original Cask Strength** (with UK Government's Sensible Drinking Limits boxed on back label) db **(92) n**22 a duller nose than usual: caramel reducing the normal iodine kick; **t**24 recovers supremely for the early delivery with some stunning black peppers exploding all over the palate leaving behind a trail of peat smoke; the controlled sweetness to the barley is sublime; **f**23 again there is a caramel edge to the finish, but this does not entirely prevent a fizzing finale; **b**23 caramel apart, this is much truer to form than one or two or more recent bottlings, aided by the fresh, gristy sweetness and explosive spices. Wonderful! **55.7%**

**Laphroaig Aged 15 Years** db **(79) n**20 **t**20 **f**19 **b**20. A hugely disappointing, lacklustre dram that is oily and woefully short on complexity. Not what one comes to expect from either this distillery or age. **43%**

⫶ **Laphroaig Vintage 1989 Aged 17 Years** dist Dec 89 db **(94) n**23 distinctly salt and seaweedy; oak makes inroads into the smoke; **t**24 voluptuous, mouth-filling and wonderfully balanced; the middle hits the high notes with a superb gristy sweetness meeting a crescendo of spice: fabulous; **f**23 lightens as the vanillas cool things; **b**24 bottled to mark the occasion of the opening of the new Friends' Lounge at the distillery. Keep producing bottles like this and they'll have to create a few enemies just for space... **50.3%**

**Laphroaig Aged 30 Years** db **(94) n**24 **t**23 **f**23 **b**24. The best Laphroaig of all time? Nope, because the 40-y-o is perhaps better still... just. However, Laphroaig of this subtlety and charm gives even the very finest Ardbeg a run for its money. A sheer treat that should be bottled at greater strength. **43%**

**Laphroaig Aged 40 Years** db **(94) n**23 **t**24 **f**23 **b**24. Mind-blowing. This is a malt that defies all logic and theory to be in this kind of shape at such enormous age. The Jane Fonda of Islay whisky. **43%**

**Laphroaig 1994 Islay Festival of Malt and Music 2006** db **(90) n**22 no shortage of salt and a twist of lemon to the sturdy smoke; **t**23 a beautifully refreshing citrus edge accentuates the clarity of the barley; the peat hovers but refuses to attack; **f**22 delicate and remains mouthwatering; soft spices compensate for the lazy peat; **b**23 a beautifully complex malt and one not depending on peat alone for charm and charisma. A pleasant touch, this coming from casks filled (as an apprentice) and emptied by new distillery manager John Campbell. **56%**. *600 bottles.*

**Laphroaig 1/4 Cask** db **(95) n**22 burning embers of peat in a crofter's fireplace; sweet intense malt and lovely, refreshing citrus as well; **t**24 mouthwatering, mouth-filling and mouth-astounding: the perfect weight of the smoke has no problems filling every crevice of the palate; builds towards a sensationally sweet maltiness at the middle; **f**24 really long, and dries appropriately with smoke and spice. Classic Laphroaig; **b**25 a great distillery back to its awesome, if a little sweet, self. Layer upon layer of sexed-up peatiness, this is the closest to how I remember it some 30 years ago! **48%**

**Cadenhead's Authentic Collection Laphroaig Aged 13 Years** dist 91, bott Feb 05 **(95) n**24 **t**24 **f**23 **b**24. Miss out on this bottling and you'll regret it for the remainder of your days: an absolute 24 carat gem. **55%**. *228 bottles.*

**Cadenhead's Authentic Collection Laphroaig Aged 13 Years** dist 91, bott Feb 05 **(82)** n22 t21 f19 **b20.** A half-decent cask, but one I would have earmarked for blending. **55.4%.** 234 bottles.

**Cadenhead's Authentic Collection Laphroaig Aged 14 Years** dist 91, bott May 06 **(93)** n23 pure Laphroaig!; **t24** the gristy sweetness is the perfect balance to the rumbling oak and smoke; mildly molassed but the coastal tang to the barley is sublime; **f23** long, clean, layered with vanilla and the smoke just keeps on rolling; **b23** Authentic...??? And some!!! **56.1%.** 234 bottles.

**Cadenhead's Authentic Collection Laphroaig Aged 16 Years** Bourbon Hogshead, dist 90, bott Sept 06 **(87)** n20 pretty closed and hard to recognize at a typical Laphroaig; **t23** sweetish delivery with some pounding barley and a lucid, light oiliness to the smoke; **f23** long, a touch of the Bowmores with hickory and smoke; **b21** without seeing the cask numbers (we'll get them later) this appears to be a sibling of the 53% version: very much as usual but this one has an extra degree of attitude and complexity. **58.4%.** 246 bottles.

**Cadenhead's Authentic Collection Laphroaig Aged 16 Years** Sherry Hogshead, dist 90, bott Sept 06 **(86)** n21 t22 f22 **b21.** Very different from the norm with almost a Bowmore-ish style peat to it. Restricted in development but always drinkable. **53%.** 156 bottles.

**Murray McDavid Laphroaig Aged 17 Years** dist 88, bott 05 **(69)** n19 t17 f16 **b17.** Noses wrong and tastes....well, that's me done for an hour or three. **46%**

⋇ **Norse Cask Selection Laphroaig 1987 Aged 18 Years** Hogshead ref. DL1763 **(92)** n24 peat and acacia honey have rarely gone so fittingly hand in hand...dank bluebell woods for good measure; **t23** how cruel: the brain is immediately engaged by that honey first spotted on the nose then...kaboom!! An explosion of spices of legendary dimensions; **f22** still tingling and warming, though things settle for the peat to have a louder say; **b23** someone dropped a jar of honey into this cask...! **48.3%.** WhiskyOwner.com, Denmark.

**Old Malt Cask Laphroaig 10 Years Old** dist 28 Sep 94, bott 22 Jun 05 **(85)** n22 t21 f21 **b21.** Gentle, clean and gristy. **50%.** Douglas Laing. 632 bottles.

**Old Malt Cask Laphroaig Aged 12 Years (89)** n23 two-toned peat both light and ashy and with deep base; **t23** very young style with mouthwatering fruitiness to the barley and a spice bite to the peat; **f21** thins out fast; **b22** probably a third-fill blending cask showing Laphroaig in un-oaked beauty. Light, but early on fantastic. **50%.**

**Old Malt Cask Laphroaig Aged 14 Years** dist Mar 89, bott Sep 03 **(79)** n19 t21 f19 **b20.** Astonishing, delicate Laphroaig with about the lowest phenol level I have seen in a bottle. Sugary in part with the smoke drifting around the palate. The bitter finale doesn't help. **50%. nc ncf sc.** Douglas Laing. 300 bottles.

**Old Malt Cask Laphroaig Aged 15 Years** dist Apr 88, bott Jan 04 **(93)** n23 liniment; a leaking bottle of bromine; a hint of salt; **t23** the peat dissolves on the palate with ripples of clean malt carrying with it a spicy flotsam; **f23** the sweetness continues for a minute or two more before some drier wafer-notes start dissolving again; the spices are persistent but harmonious; **b24** a memorable Laphroaig in top form. **50%. nc ncf sc.** Douglas Laing. 162 bottles.

**Old Malt Cask Laphroaig Aged 15 Years** dist Apr 88, bott Mar 04 **(83)** n22 t21 f20 **b20.** An oily, machine-room nose but the palate, though sweet, never quite gets out of third gear. **50%. nc ncf sc.** Douglas Laing. 112 bottles.

**Old Malt Cask Laphroaig Aged 15 Years** dist Mar 89, bott Apr 04 **(90)** n23 farmyards and haystacks plus plenty of cottage peat-reek **t22** sweet oils even catch a honeyed strand amid the ultra-clean peat; **f23** one of the softest finishes to a Laphroaig for quite a few years: the malt and peat are inextricably intertwined, it is all very soft yet the oak advances no more than a distant hint of vanilla while the peat becomes supremely assertive; **b22** Laphroaig at its cleanest and best behaved while still displaying its unique charms. **50%. nc ncf sc.** Douglas Laing. 289 bottles.

**Old Malt Cask Laphroaig Aged 15 Years** dist Feb 87, bott Jan 04 **(90)** n18 tainted and sweet, not exactly the perfect nose; **t24** time to sit down: the intensity of the sweet sherry backed to the hilt by writhing peat makes this one hell of an experience; **f24** big sprinkling of spices still cannot dampen the enormous, mind-blowing sherry-peat theme; **b24** if you went by the nose alone, you'd probably not go any further. But do.

Your reward will be a one-off, an oral orgy, for all bottlings in the last year. Brilliant ... very few whiskies have been awarded a 90 after such a poor start on the nose. Hey, but that's whisky ...! **50% nc ncf sc.** *Douglas Laing. 309 bottles.*

**Old Malt Cask Laphroaig Aged 16 Years** dist Feb 87, bott Sep 03 **(83) n22 t20 f20 b21.** A strangely synthetic nose while the malt is dazzlingly sweet. **50%. nc ncf sc.** *Douglas Laing. 270 bottles.*

⠿ **Old Malt Cask Laphroaig Aged 16 Years** dist Nov 90, bott Dec 06 **(85) n21 t22 f21 b21.** Just about the sweetest Laphroaig of this age I've ever come across. **50%.** *295 btls.*

**Old Malt Cask Laphraoig 17 Years Old** dist 16 Mar 88, bott 27 Apr 05 **(91) n23 t23 f23 b22.** A fascinating Laphroaig and as delicate as they come: rarely do you find one of this age with so little oak attached. Here we get a great view of the workings of the malt – and it is something beautiful to behold. **50%.** *141 bottles.*

**Old Malt Cask Laphroaig Aged 18 Years** dist Nov 87, bott Oct 05 **(89) n21** undemonstrative, relaxed; **t22** crisp barley; a touch of coffee to the smoke; **f23** restrained but drying oak tinged with excellent citrus; **b23** one of those drams that gets better as it goes along. **50%.** *Douglas Laing.*

**Old Malt Cask Laphroaig 18 Years Old** dist Apr 88, bott Sept 06 **(83) n20 t21 f22 b20.** Laphroaig coming in any kind of finish is rarer than nominations for George W Bush to receive the Nobel Peace Prize. But to turn up in rum...!!! It is both rock-hard and at times syrupy sweet. Some very drinkable moments, but a real collector's item to Laphroaig lovers. **50%.** *Douglas Laing. 327 bottles.*

⠿ **Old Malt Cask Laphroaig Aged 18 Years** dist Dec 87, bott Nov 06 **(83) n20 t22 f20 b21.** Not yet sure how or why. But the odd Laphroaig turns out much closer in style to a Bowmore with a middling peat that gives a nod to a cough candy style. This is one of them. Hard as nails (fitting as it does have a metallic feel) and strangely alluring. **50%.** *638 bottles.*

⠿ **Old Malt Cask Laphroaig Aged 18 Years Rum Finish** dist Mar 88, bott Dec 06 **(87) n22** sharp, tight: as if the peat has been herded into a small space...; **t22** sugary delivery with some warming smoke. Again, very cramped; **f22** long, Maltesers...; **b21 50%.** *Douglas Laing. 328 bottles.*

**Premier Barrel Laphroaig 7 Years Old** dist Oct 98, bott Nov 05 **(87) n21** kiddies' plasticine; **t22** gentle oils intensify the grist; **f22** citrus lightens the gentle smoke further; **b22** compare a bottle of this with the March 06 bottling and discover first hand how peating intensity and effect can vary at an Islay distillery. **46%.** *Douglas Laing. 406 bottles.*

**Premier Barrel Laphroaig 7 Years Old** dist May 98, bott Mar 06 **(94) n23** gristy, cold malt kilns; **t24** mouthwatering, fresh barley seems to be kept apart from the cindery peat which fills the palate. The controlled sweetness is excellent; **f23** medium length and cotton soft; **b24** just so wonderful to see this distillery bottled at an age it should have been available at for the last 20 years and showing so much zest. **46%.** *385 bottles.*

⠿ **Premier Barrel Laphroaig Aged 8 Years** dist Nov 05 **(86) n21 t22 f22 b21.** Sparkling, gently spiced and lazily peated. **46%.** *Douglas Laing. 371 bottles.*

⠿ **Provenance Laphroaig Aged 8 Years** dist Autumn 98, bott Winter 07 **(90) n22** defies belief just how downy-soft peat can sometimes be; **t23** grassy barley and dissolving peat on entry. Like being caressed in your half-sleep; **f23** long, softly smoked with green, almost limey tinge to the peat; **b22** distilling and maturation of the top order allowing the true charisma of the distillery to shine. **46%.** *Douglas Laing.*

**The Queen of the Moorlands Rare Cask Laphroaig 12 Years Old** dist 25 Mar 93, bott 10 Jun 05 **(81) n21 t20 f20 b20.** Too subtle for its own good: remains closed where it should be open and developing; most telling contribution is from a fruit-jam attack, rather than the uninspiring peat. Drinkable and enjoyable. But Laphroaig should offer more. **54.7%. sc.** *The Wine Shop, Leek, UK.*

⠿ **Scotch Malt Whisky Society Cask 29.57 Aged 12 Years** Refill Hogshead, dist Nov 93 **(95) n24** fresh-faced, blemish-free peat having just cleared puberty and unsoiled by oak; for its age, perfect (oh, and there are some lilacs in there, too!!); **t24** massive but with a cute gristy sweetness that piles on the sugars – and the spice; **f23** long with a touch of Camp coffee; **b24** proof that you really don't have to take a distillery into great ages to produce great whisky. Classic stuff and a true must for Islayphiles. **58.8%**

Scotch Malt Whisky Society Cask 29.59 Aged 17 Years Refill Butt, dist Mar 89 **(84) n**20 **t**22 **f**21 **b**21. Delightful and chewy, but just a bit sharp and Caol Ila-esque in its oil and sludginess, though if it's a slightly off-key salivating depth to the peat you're after, help yourself..! **58.9%**

Whisky-Doris Laphroaig 1996 Bourbon cask no. 5366, bott 06 **(76) n**19 **t**20 **f**18 **b**19. By Laphroaig standards, slumming it a little here with an off note from nose to finish. The big, juicy grist does its best to compensate. Good whisky filled into a poor cask, I'm afraid...and it doesn't stand a chance. **55.7%. ncf**. Germany. 120 bottles.

The Whisky Fair Artist Edition Laphroaig Aged 8 Years Bourbon Hogshead, dist Apr 98, bott June 06 **(88) n**21 a strange mixture of the $CO_2$ from the tun room and dying peaty embers in the furnace; **t**23 brilliant distribution of softly oiled, sweet peats, all enriched by golden-syrup sweetened barley; **f**22 drier and a tad oakier than one might expect − or hope − for; **b**22 lovely malt that lacks a little in balance but makes up for with an enchanting peatiness. **48.5%**. Germany. 420 bottles.

The Whisky Fair Laphroaig Aged 16 Years dist 88, bott Feb 05 **(69) n**16 **t**18 **f**17 **b**17. A feinty number. **50.1%. nc ncf**. 150 bottles.

## LEDAIG (see Tobermory)

## LINKWOOD
**Speyside, 1820. Diageo. Working.**

Linkwood 12 Years Old db **(79) n**21 **t**22 **f**17 **b**19. Not a patch on previous bottlings, with the usual clarity lost to a very confused fruit-caramel theme. Especially on the finish. **43%**

Linkwood 1974 Rare Malt db **(79) n**20 **t**21 **f**19 **b**19. Wobbles about the palate in search of a story and balance. Finds neither but some of the early moments, though warming, offer very decent malt. The best bit follows a couple of seconds after − and lasts as long. **55%**

Berry's Own Selection Linkwood 1985 Casks no. 4545/4546, bott 07 **(87) n**21 floral and fresh, the clean grassiness of the barley charms; **t**22 typically hot for the distillery, but the palate is cooled by the intense maltiness aided by soft citrus; drying oaks also have a gentle part to play earlier than normal; **f**22 wonderfully biscuity with an oat-meal dryness amid the barley; **b**22 delicate and simplistic malt at first with a heavy emphasis on barley. But the richness of the malt, coupled with the gradual build up of prickly spices cannot do other than impress. Really charming stuff. **46%.**

The Bottlers Linkwood 31 Years Old Refill sherry cask 12228, dist Aug 74, bott Dec 05 **(87) n**22 sultanas, vanilla and barley refreshed by freshly sliced cucumber; **t**22 big barley and muscovado delivery with spices fizzing in all directions; the sweetness intensifies for a while then some grape lightens the load; **f**21 soft vanilla and hickory; **b**22 these guys don't bottle much. But what they do has a tendency to be way above the norm. So I was intrigued to see how they would tackle one of the trickiest distilleries of them all. And I have to say: the Bottlers did good... **54.3%**

Cadenhead's Authentic Collection Linkwood-Glenlivet Aged 15 Years dist 89, bott 05 **(80) n**20 **t**20 **f**21 **b**19. Lots of natural caramel. **53.5%**. 246 bottles.

Cadenhead's Authentic Collection Linkwood Aged 16 Years Bourbon Hogshead, dist 89, bott May 06 **(79) n**20 **t**19 **f**20 **b**20. Hot stuff: the stills must have been screaming when they made this. Decent balance, though, and even an enjoyable touch of marmalade. **55.8%**. 264 bottles.

Cadenhead's Authentic Collection Linkwood Aged 18 Years Sherry butt, dist 88, bott Feb 07 **(64) n**17 **t**16 **f**15 **b**16. The kind of sulphur taint that made this a distillery worth avoiding for so long. **58.7%**. 660 bottles.

Cask Strength Linkwood 1991 **(86) n**22 **t**21 **f**22 **b**21. There is a difference between spicy and hot whisky: this is hot. Even so, there is an intriguing and wholly delicious clump of peat attached to this − very unusual for Linkwood. Flawed in its making but you cannot but love its attitude or its odd brush with genius. A must experience malt. **52.5%**. Gordon & MacPhail.

Chieftain's Linkwood Aged 13 Years French oak **(72) n**19 **t**18 **f**17 **b**18. Overly sweet and latterly furry. **43%**. Ian Macleod.

⚬ **The Clydesdale Linkwood 17 Years Old** Cask ref. 0033/1839, dist Apr 89, bott Sept 06 **(86)** n21 t22 f22 b21. Runs a bit hot but there's certainly a glint to the barley. Warming, but enjoyable. **56.5%. nc ncf.** *Blackadder International.*

**Dewar Rattray Individual Cask Bottling Linkwood 1985 Aged 20 Years** cask no. 4544, dist Nov 85, bott Jan 06 **(85)** n21 t22 f21 b21. A biting, sugary maltfest. Eye-wateringly intense but for its ability to stay fresh at this age, complexity, as ever, remains at a premium. **60.2%.** *231 bottles.*

⚬ **Dun Bheagan Linkwood 10 Years Old** Hogshead, dist Dec 96 **(85)** n21 t22 f21 b21. Genuinely clean nose and delivery with a wonderful accent on barley and zest. Just flattens at the finish, though. **43%. nc ncf.** *Ian Macleod Distillers.*

**Dun Bheagan Linkwood 10 Years Old American Oak (85)** n21 t22 f21 b21. An attractive, light cask but the real star quality is found on the arrival and soft cereal-cocoa fade. **43%.**

**Dun Bheagan Linkwood 11 Years Old Port Finish (91)** n22 some peppery prickle to the fruit; t23 spectacular arrival on the palate, about all you could ask from a Port finish: enormous complexity and variance in weight, flipping between light and heavy in a nanosecond; f23 mocha and raisin – which make themselves heard earlier – really now play out a slow finish; b23 a complex, seductive dram played out at first in double quick time and then slows for the finish. Wonderful. And it ain't often I can say that about Linkwood... **46%** *Ian Macleod.*

**Gordon & MacPhail Linkwood Aged 15 Years** First fill and refill sherry **(76)** n18 t19 f20 b19. Some decent gristy maltiness links with the toffee. **40%.**

**Gordon & MacPhail Linkwood 15 Years Old (82)** n21 t21 f20 b20. By far one of the better Linkwoods around. A bit aggressive and hot in places, but some lovely natural caramel and, dare I say it, a touch of elegance to the barley sugar. **43%.**

**Gordon & MacPhail Linkwood 1972 (87)** n22 burnt raisin, crisped barley; t22 juicy fruit and barley mix: salivating but remains rock-hard; f21 sharp, flinty, metallic at death; b22 no yield to this hard-as-nails but fun bottling. **43%.** *Rare Vintage range.*

⚬ **Kingsbury's "The Selection" Linkwood 1999** Hogshead cask nos. 3622/3624/3652, dist Mar 99, bott July 06 **(83)** n19 t22 f21 b21. Mouth-watering. Unmistakable Speyside with an early barley tornado. **43%. ncf.** *Japan Imports System. 1,348 bottles.*

**Kingsbury's Single Cask Linkwood 13 Years Old** cask 10432, dist 91 **(76)** n20 t19 f18 b19. A bit more complexity than the average Linkwood, but... **46%.** *Japan Import System.*

**Kingsbury's Valdespino Linkwood 16 Years Old (84)** n23 t21 f20 b20. Clean, well structured; caramelized biscuit. The nose, though, stars by displaying sufficient raw oak to get into the sharp barley. **46%.** *Japan Import System.*

⚬ **Mac Y 10th Anniversary Linkwood Aged 10 Years** Hogshead no. 3986, dist 96, bott 06 **(86)** n20 t22 f22 b22. Lively, lemony and effervescent. Its lipsmackingly juicy, youthful qualities show the distillery in a better light than the norm. **48%.** *400 bottles.*

**Murray McDavid Mission Linkwood 1983 Aged 23 Years** Bourbon/Madeira, bott 06 **(94)** n23 forget the Madeira; the age really comes through with traces of exotic fruit amid the grape and malt; t23 a concoction of golden sugar, sultanas, ultra-intense barley sugar and even a touch of coconut milk makes for controlled sweetness; f24 levels out with the fruity touch of a truffle bar and searing white pepper; b24 leave in the glass for a full five minutes to allow the complexity to settle. On of the best cask finishes of the year. **52.1%. nc ncf.** *700 bottles.*

**NMWL Single Cask Malt Whisky Linkwood** Hogshead cask 1835, dist 4 Apr 89, bott 6 Apr 05 **(84)** n21 t22 f20 b21. Pssst! Looking for some decent Linkwood? Try Norway. Revels in the usual weird combination of big barley sweetness and hot distillate. But this one appears to have been nurtured in a way above average cask, allowing the malt to blossom. Still don't expect too much, though... **58%.** *Norsk MaltWhisky Lag, Oslo. 388 bottles.*

**Old Malt Cask Linkwood 16 Years Old** dist Dec 89, bott June 06 **(82)** n21 t20 f21 b20. Some wonderful lavender spruces this one up. **50%.** *302 bottles.*

⚬ **Old Malt Cask Linkwood Aged 18 Years** dist May 88, bott Jan 07 **(85)** n21 t21 f22 b21. Too hot off the still ever to be a classic, but you can't but help loving the crushed Maltesers. **50%.** *Douglas Laing. 336 bottles.*

**Old Malt Cask Linkwood 22 Years Old** dist 24 Apr 83, bott Jul 05 **(78)** n21 t19 f18 b20. A remarkably soft Linkwood which battles hard to find a rhythm and depth and not entirely with success. **50%.** *Douglas Laing. 213 bottles.*

⌐ **Provenance Linkwood Aged 10 Years** dist Winter 96, bott Spring 07 **(84)** n21 t21 f21 b21. Clean, malty fare. Perfect for blending. **46%**. *Douglas Laing.*

⌐ **Scotch Malt Whisky Society Cask 39.59 Aged 22 Years** Refill Hogshead, dist Oct 94 **(83)** n21 t22 f19 b21. Estery and lush. **53.9%**

**The Single Malt of Scotland Linkwood Aged 12 Years Vintage 1993** Sherry butt cask 3517 **(76)** n20 t19 f18 b19. Intense, syrupy and a little hot. Pretty normal early 90s Linkwood, then. **59.1%**. *The Whisky Exchange. 180 bottles.*

⌐ **The Single Malts of Scotland Linkwood 1990 Aged 16 Years (78)** n19 t21 f19 b19. Tired and unemotional stuff. **58.7%. sc cs**. *Speciality Drinks, UK.*

**Vom Fass Linkwood 10 Years Old (78)** n20 t19 f20 b19. Good natural weight and malty chewability. But pretty underdeveloped for its age. **40%**

**Wilson & Morgan Barrel Selection Linkwood 1991 Sherry Wood** dist 91, bott 05 **(70)** n18 t18 f17 b17. It's sherry, Jim. But not as we know it... **46%**

## LINLITHGOW (see St. Magdalene)

## LITTLEMILL
### Lowland, 1772. Demolished.

**Littlemill Aged 8 Years** db **(84)** n20 t22 f21 b21. Aged 8 Years, claims the neck of the dumpy bottle, which shows a drawing of a distillery that no longer exists, as it has done for the last quarter of a century. Well, double that and you'll be a lot closer to the real age of this deliciously sweet, chewy and increasingly spicy chap. And it is about as far removed from the original 8-y-o fire-water it once was as is imaginable. **40%**.

**Littlemill 1964** db **(82)** n21 t20 f21 b20. A soft-natured, bourbony chap that shows little of the manic tendencies that made this one of Scotland's most-feared malts. Talk about mellowing with age ... **40%**

**Berry's' Best Lowland Littlemill 12 Years Old (71)** n17 t19 f17 b18. Astonishingly tame by Littlemill standards. But, though bad form to speak ill of the dead, pretty naff. **43%**.

**Cadenhead's Authentic Collection Littlemill Aged 16 Years** Bourbon Hogshead, dist 89, bott Feb 06 **(82)** n19 t23 f19 b21. Classically fiery as the delivery is, it has to be said, a fabulous ultra intense malt delivery of near perfect sweetness. Then tapers away towards something more off-key. **59.7%**. *294 bottles.*

**Coopers Choice Littlemill 1984 20 Years Old** Single Cask Range, bott 05 **(81)** n21 t22 f19 b19. Early, graceful malt, then becomes a roughhouse. **56.7%**

**Dun Bheagan Littlemill Aged 21 Years Sherry Finish (74)** n20 t19 f17 b18. Mutton dressed as lamb. **46%**. *Ian Macleod.*

**Old Malt Cask Littlemill Aged 16 Years (89)** n22 a rum, surely? t23 no, the fist-fighting barley confirms the distillery, though the juiciness of the barley is a shock; f21 thins down in house style but none of the usual rough edges; b23 Littlemill as never seen before. It is passed the hell-fire days of its youth that brought its demise. But there is enough attitude to jab through the barley-rum theme to land some delicious punches. A little cracker. Had only the distillery bottled such malt when still standing. **50%**

⌐ **Scotch Malt Whisky Society Cask 97.8 Aged 16 Years** 1st Fill Barrel, dist Mar 90 **(83)** n22 t21 f20 b20. Oak – and 16 long and hard years - have done their best to tame this fire-spitting beast. The fruity nose offers hope but still the pugilistic streak within dominates. Highly drinkable, though. And you wouldn't have been able to say that about this cask five or six years ago. **55.9%**

**Scott's Selection Littlemill 1984** bott 05 **(86)** n22 t21 f22 b21. Just great, lip-smacking fun. **61.1%**. *Speyside Distillers.*

## LOCH LOMOND
### Highland (Southwestern), 1966. Glen Catrine. Working.

**Craiglodge** American oak barrel 223, dist 26 Feb 01, bott 8 Sept 05 db **(84)** n19 t22 f21 b22. Big, intense malt coats the palate entirely for a seriously delicious chew. The nose isn't great, though. **45%**. *442 bottles.*

**Craiglodge** American oak barrel 329, dist 13 Sept 92, bott 15 Sept 05 db **(80)** n19 t21 f20 b20. A vaguely Fettercairnish rubbery nose picks up with the sweet smoke on the palate. Craiglodge should be – and usually is – a whole lot better than this. **45%**. *191 bottles.*

**Craiglodge** Sherry wood cask 139, dist 26 Mar 98 db **(72) n**17 **t**19 **f**18 **b**18. Cloying, off-key, rough...and they're the good points. The nose of sherry and smoke don't gel and it never recovers. **45%**

**Craiglodge Distillery Select Peated Malt** cask 061, dist 19 Feb01, bott 14 Apr 05 db **(91) n**22 **t**23 **f**23 **b**23. A little-known style of whisky from Loch Lomond that is likely to become world-famous in future years. Astonishingly compact and stable for its age. **45%. nc ncf.** *400 bottles.*

⋰⋱ **Craiglodge Peated Cask No.137 Distillery Select** Sherry Hogshead, dist 26 Mar 98, bott 9 May 07 db **(85) n**18 **t**24 **f**21 **b**22. Good grief!! Have you even been run over and then re-trampled on by a sherry-peat steam roller? Well, now I know for a fact I have. I've been in this game a long, long time. But I haven't, ever, encountered anything quite like this.... The sherry (oloroso presumably) must still have been slightly sloshing around the bottom of the butt when the big, smoky whisky was filled into it. The result is a nose that defies description but demands witnesses so the tale can be passed on to future generations and an arrival to the palate which at once amazes, charms and, ultimately, mugs. To be honest, the sheer gloss on the arrival is stunning and unquestionably beautiful but there are many issues left unresolved on the madcap (iron in the spirit-style) finish. There are only 150 bottles of this. Get one. Because you will have something to discuss at dinner parties for the rest of your life... **45%.** *150 bottles.*

**Croftengea** cask no. 18, dist 22 Jan 97, bott 09 Sept 05 db **(76) n**19 **t**19 **f**20 **b**18. Hot, less than happy with itself...or the cask it has lived in. **45%**

**Croftengea** cask no. 24, dist 22 Jan 97 db **(87) n**22 pungent young peat, bracing, clean and even mildly salty; **t**22 refreshing barley with coffee/smoke double act; **f**21 vanilla and dry toast; **b**22 what a difference a cask makes: entirely together and charming. **45%**

**Croftengea Aged Over 9 Years** Sherry finish, cask 283, dist Jan 96, bott 6 Sept 05 db **(79) n**20 **t**21 **f**19 **b**19. The sherry flattens out the contours. **45%. nc ncf.** *380 bottles.*

⋰⋱ **Croftengea Heavily Peated Cask No.1 Distillery Select** Sherry Butt, dist 3 Mar 03, bott 10 May 07 db **(94) n**23 something combustible has combusted – spewing out thick grimy, greasy plumes of something vaguely peaty. A wonderful Ugly Betty of a nose!! **t**24 an oil slick carrying various styles of peat and beautifully sweet barley; **f**23 long, still slick, a tad grimy again and then that spectacular different peat...and the way the sweet barley returns, as barley – not peat – is almost mind-blowing!! How does it do that? Amazing and beautiful in its own grim and idiosyncratic way; **b**24 fabulous knife and fork malt that doesn't even try to look pretty on the plate....let alone the palate. **45%.** *885 bottles.*

**Glen Douglas** American oak barrel no. 337, dist 27 June 01, bott 12 Sept 05 db **(89) n**22 mildly gluey, but also a staggeringly complex maltiness intrigues; **t**23 beautiful delivery with a delightful intermingling of pillow-soft esters and spice; **f**22 the precocious complexity continues with a touch of honeyed vanilla and marmalade; **b**22 not only do I love blending with this stuff, but it makes a pretty tasty single malt, even at this age! **45%.** *315 bottles.*

⋰⋱ **Glen Douglas Cask No. 1 Distillery Select** Madeira Puncheon, dist 23 Sept 02, bott 08 May 07 db **(89) n**22 busy, slightly sweaty sock but the uppercuts of barley and grape are a knockout; **t**21 soft, well structured delivery but runs into a flat in a few seconds. Recovers as some light vanilla adds weight to the barley; **f**23 really beautiful finish with spicy grape showing a delicate touch amid the cocoa; very vaguely mouth-watering; **b**23 not exactly firing on all cylinders, with the odd note way out of tune. But very different... and delicious. **45%.** *910 bottles.*

**Inchfad 2001 Heavily Peated** cask 665 dist 14 Feb 01 db **(80) n**20 **t**21 **f**19 **b**20. Pretty atypical of this particular malt. Missing the fruity ester kick that comes with the big peat. In fact, what big peat? An underwhelming example. **45%**

**Inchfad 2001 Heavily Peated** cask 666, dist 14 Feb 01 db **(87) n**22 a real youngster, but with all the charm a child can bring. Smokey, though to call it heavily peated stretches the imagination somewhat; **t**23 sweet, gristy, soft esters and a wonderful barley rounding. High quality distillate; **f**21 the oak grabs far too large a hold and the balance is compromised; **b**21 one cask on and so much more in tune. From the same distillate, but an excellent example of how a better quality cask can allow the malt to thrive. Perhaps the cask numbers are the wrong way round...!! **45%**

**Inchfad Cask No. 27 Distillery Select** American Oak, dist 15 Mar 01, bott 3 May 07 db **(90) n**22 chopped raw, under-ripe hazelnut with a vanilla-barley twist; **t**23 fat and full bodied, the malty element in this totally fills the mouth; beyond that is a wonderful structure of vanilla and muscovado sugar and even the most distant echo of smoke; **f**22 spices up attractively as the body slims; **b**23 a beautiful malt that shows stunning maturity; very individualistic. **45%**. *375 bottles.*

**Inchfad Cask No. 4359 Distillery Select** Freshly Charred American Oak, dist 18 Dec 02, bott 2 May 07 db **(83) n**20 **t**22 **f**20 **b**21. A real new- makey though the barley is slapped on thick and to eye watering effect. **45%.** *445 bottles.*

**Inchmoan 2001 American Oak Barrel no. 53** dist 5 Mar 01, bott 7 Sept 05 db **(88) n**21 a toddler of a nose with alternating wispy and punchy smoke; **t**23 the most mouthwatering malt imaginable... with glorious smoke at fore and aft; **f**22 citrussy and refreshing; **b**22 the fact this is probably a second-fill cask ensures a wonderful rawness to this. A refreshing change – in every sense. And there is probably only a handful of us in the world who can vouchsafe this: but the closest thing to peated new make Lammerlaw, from New Zealand, on the planet. **45%**. *397 bottles.*

**Inchmoan 1992 American Oak Barrel no. 151** dist 4 Sept 92, bott 14 Sept 05 db **(90) n**23 excellent smoky balance, but a lot younger than its years; **t**23 beautifully oiled and delicate, gristy sweetness to the smoked barley; **f**22 a drier send-off as oak bites; **b**22 another lovely malt from this little-known distillery. **45%**. *269 bottles.*

**Inchmoan Distillery Select** cask 48, dist 15 Mar 01, bott 14 Apr 05 db **(88) n**21 **t**23 **f**22 **b**22. Not quite in the league of Craiglodge, but worth a place in any collection. **45%. nc ncf.** *400 bottles.*

**Inchmurrin** Spanish oak butt cask 1-708, dist 20 July 01, bott 12 Sept 05 db **(76) n**18 **t**20 **f**19 **b**19. A malt equivalent of Les Dawson playing the piano. **45%.** *963 bottles.*

**Inchmurrin** American oak butt cask 1-173, dist 20 June 01, bott 13 Sept 05 db **(80) n**20 **t**21 **f**19 **b**20. A typically nutty affair. **45%**

**Inchmurrin 10 Years Old** db **(81) n**21 **t**21 **f**19 **b**20. A sturdy, sweet and indulgently complex malt that struggles very slightly on the mildly bitter finale. **45%**

**Inchmurrin Aged 12 Years** db **(80) n**19 **t**21 **f**20 **b**20. Peas from the same pod as the 10-year-old. A tad more citrus, though. **40%**

**Inchmurrin Cask No. 1 Distillery Select** Madeira Puncheon, dist May 02, bott Apr 07 db **(86) n**20 **t**22 **f**22 **b**22. Some lovely oils paint a chewy, beautifully well-balanced malt. The nose drops it down a few points, but worth a go for the curvy body alone. **45%**. *685 bottles.*

**Inchmurrin Organic Cask No. 3946 Distillery Select** Organic French Oak, dist 28 July 00, bott 01 May 07 db **(74) n**19 **t**19 **f**18 **b**18. Another poor French cask accounts for a promising malt. In terms of whisky, they should be outlawed. **45%**. *410 bottles.*

**Loch Lomond Single Highland Malt** db **(72) n**17 **t**20 **f**17 **b**18. Oh, oh.....!!! Something seriously up with this bottling: a cask or three that should have been dumped hasn't been. The result is a horribly off centre nose and car wreck of a finish. Knowing the malt as I do, keep faith as this must be a one-off. **40%.** ☉☉

**Loch Lomond 21 Years Old** db **(89) n**22 attractive, confident grape intermingling with a spiced bourbony oak and malt; **t**23 real Dundee cake properties: full of fruit and nuts, only with some extra molassed sugar stirred in; **f**22 soft liquorice and delicious cocoa; **b**22 a quality, big-hearted malt from an unfashionable distillery. To be taken by big mouthfuls only and chewed until your jaw aches! **43%**

**Old Rhosdhu 5 Years Old** db **(77) n**18 **t**21 **f**19 **b**19. Big, ungainly, molassed, caramelised chewing whisky. **40%**

**Murray McDavid Mission III Old Rhosdhu 1979** db **(81) n**20 **t**21 **f**20 **f**20. Typically well built and chewy; a handsome milk-toffee richness to the barley. **46%**

**Murray McDavid Mission Old Rhosdhu 1984 Aged 21 Years** Bourbon/Viognier, bott 06 **(82) n**21 **t**21 **f**20 **b**20. A bit fierce – especially on the nose - when first poured but calms down a treat. **49.3%. nc ncf.** *400 bottles.*

**The Whisky Fair Inchmoan 1994** cask no. 646, dist 25.11.94, bott 26.01.05 **(82) n**21 **t**20 **f**21 **b**20. A bit dirty and out of tune, but enough coffee and smoke for some fun. **54.8%.** *Germany. 210 bottles.*

## LOCHSIDE
### Highland (Eastern), 1957–1992. Closed.

**Cadenhead's Authentic Collection Lochside Aged 23 Years** dist 81, bott Feb 05 **(95)** n25 t24 f23 b24. The influence of the port pipe delivers extra spice but, really, single malt whisky doesn't come any more complex than this. Take all the time in the world over this one: just don't rush it. There are only 246 bottles of this stuff – make sure one has your name on it. **56.7%.** *246 bottles.*

**Cadenhead's Authentic Collection Lochside Aged 24 Years** dist 81, bott Sep 05 **(75)** n17 t21 f18 b19. There is something not quite 100% clean on nose or palate with this one, as if from poor sherry rather than a bourbon cask. But there is just enough versatility and fruit on the barley to make for an interesting dram. **59.1%.** *276 bottles.*

**Old Malt Cask Lochside Aged 14 Years** dist Oct 90, bott Sept 05 **(94)** n24 bedazzling with a rare firmness to the barley and lucid grassy presence which suggests a whisky considerably younger; **t**23 every bit as mouthwatering and charming as the nose suggests with a delicate digression from the barley towards a neat cocoa influx; **f**23 really beautifully balanced with a light infusion of vanilla and toast – and a dash of marmalade? – to make for a serene finale; **b**24 when a distillery capable of making whisky this good is lost to us for ever, I could almost weep. **50%.** *275 bottles.*

## LONGMORN
### Speyside, 1895. Chivas. Working.

**Longmorn 15 Years Old** db **(93)** n23 curiously salty and coastal for a Speysider, really beautifully structured oak but the malt offers both African violets and barley sugar; **t**24 your mouth aches from the enormity of the complexity, while your tongue wipes grooves into the roof of your mouth. Just about flawless bitter-sweet balance, the intensity of the malt is enormous, yet – even after 15 years – it maintains a cut-grass Speyside character; **f**22 long, acceptably sappy and salty with chewy malt and oak. Just refuses to end; **b**24 these latest bottlings are the best yet: previous ones had shown just a little too much oak but this has hit a perfect compromise. An all-time Speyside great. **45%**

·:·:· **Longmorn Aged 16 Years** bott 07 db **(78)** n19 dull and characterless. No off notes, but... **t**23 hurrah..!! There is life there as the barley piles in and the spice is not too far behind; some lovely fruit elements, too. But thickens and ultimately chokes up on toffee; **f**18 what the heck is all that about? Caramel? Dull sherry? I don't know for sure: but what is certain is that the malt and complexity are stopped dead in their tracks; **b**18 bemused...amazed...non-plussed: ultimately hugely disappointed in this expression. Let's make no bones here: Longmorn is one of the great distilleries of the world. No argument. So why a distillery bottling that is so bland when they must have such outstanding stocks of it? Yes, this is drinkable whisky with a good early delivery. But one that has undergone a charisma bypass. And as for the nose and finish...dear, oh dear. This shouldn't be just good whisky – it should be bloody great whisky of the very top order. The label talks a great game but it's back to the drawing board, I'm afraid. Because this is one of the great disappointments of the year. A bit like meeting the most beautiful woman in the bar and expecting the shag of your life...but ending up with a gum-chewer constantly checking her watch. **48%. ncf.**

**Longmorn 17 years old Distillery Edition** db **(92)** n23 exceptionally salty with big oak presence. The malt, though, remains firm and almost serene; **t**22 really good fruit, mainly orangey-citrus before the middle begins leaking big oak; **f**24 the tongue aches as the complexity not only nudges up a gear but seemingly goes on for ever; loads of cocoa and toast; **b**23 one of those drams which really knows how to milk the audience. **58.3%**

**Berry Brothers & Rudd Longmorn Aged 15 Years** Bourbon casks no. 30111 & 30112, dist 90, bott 05 **(87)** n20 bizarre...!!! Corn oil...; **t**22 lots of early oak kicks in with the oily barley; **f**22 excellent sweetness to the finale with oak now taking a back seat; **b**23 a very curious expression: lots of bourbony-oak influence yet it's almost like a corn whisky on the nose. And the oiliness on the palate is also exaggerated by this distillery's standards. That said, still quite excellent stuff!! **46%. nc ncf.**

·:·:· **Berry's Own Selection Longmorn 1988** Cask no. 010, bott 06 **(91)** n22 perhaps the odd hint of premature dementia but the oaky input is pleasantly countered by the complex barley tones; **t**23 mmmmm!! Just so refreshing with that fabulous barley now coming from all directions and in different shades; **f**23 excellent toast and marmalade a touch of something butterscotchy for good measure; the oak pans out impressively **b**23 a natural beauty. Someone from Chivas please take note.... **46%**

**Cadenhead's Longmorn-Glenlivet 18 Years Old (86)** n20 t22 f22 **b**22. The oak fails to overcome the more mouthwatering properties. **54%**. *234 bottles.*

**Chieftain's Longmorn Aged 11 Years Manzanilla Finish (83)** n19 t21 f22 **b**21. Clunks and thuds around the palate as about as an unwieldy a malt as you are likely to find from this distillery. But for all its flaws - and there a few — you cannot but help enjoy its rugged nature and bold, sweeping maltiness. A very enjoyable bit of rough and tumble. **43%**

**The Coopers Choice Longmorn 1996 Matured for 9 Years** bott 06 **(91)** n21 a surprising dose of bourbon is injected into the prime barley; t23 Enormous! The intensity of the barley is sublime while again the oak dives in much more quickly than you might expect at this age; f23 calms down to allow the malt to arrive in waves while the sluggish spices develop into something more profound; **b**24 fabulous whisky and make no mistake. What a breath of fresh air to see this distillery at such an excellent age. Faultless and fantastic. **46%**.

**D&M Aficionados' Club Longmorn Aged 31 Years** cask 3965, dist Mar 75 **(88)** n22 maybe a bit oak-tired but enough caramelized ginger, honey and even salted celery to make for an interesting sniff; t23 early confirmation of big oak but quickly gets into a honeyed stride with sweet spice and rich, telling and endearing oils; f22 long, still an extra dollop of oak but some coffee kicks in late; **b**21 from a purist and technical point of view, a cask several years beyond greatness. But here's the rub: warm the whisky well up to body temperature — and even beyond - and a quite beautiful time emerges in the glass. The score above is a midway score between traditional tasting — and the way the whisky needs to be. **46%. nc ncf**. *US by Angus Dundee.*

**Dun Bheagan Longmorn Aged 11 Years Madeira Finish (82)** n21 t22 f19 **b**20. A pretty whisky but, for all its mildly fruity make-up, lacks personality. **43%**.

**Duncan Taylor Collection Longmorn 1973 Aged 31 Years** cask 8912, dist Oct 73, bott Mar 05 **(86)** n21 t22 f22 **b**21. Hangs on for grim death as age it really caught up, but holds out for a graceful finish. **51.3%**

**Duncan Taylor Longmorn 1978 Aged 25 Years** cask 5556 **(96)** n23 dream-like complexity with near perfect salt seasoning the vanilla-dried, barley sweetened theme t24 wow...!!! No easy task to get to grips with what is happening here: that saltiness peppers the mouth but the honey edge to the barley quietens the liquorice/coffee oak f24 some fruit edges into the equation but still we have a briny quarter to the barley; the oak is dry and has weight and purpose and some late honeycomb arrives to even it up a little **b**25 ladies and gentlemen, I introduce to you complexity... **58.1%**

**Gordon & MacPhail Longmorn 1971 (91)** n22 whistle-clean sherry has soaked up rich oak comfortably; t23 again the grape is towering but such is the clarity the malt makes delicious inroads; f23 laced with cocoa and prunes, the bitter-sweet finish is a joy; **b**23 one of those exceptional Seagram sherry butts of the early '70s. Unmistakable and unmissable. **40%**. *Gordon & MacPhail*

**Murray McDavid Longmorn 1990 Aged 15 Years** Bourbon/Rioja, bott 05 **(76)** n19 t20 f18 **b**19. Full-on, fat but somewhat flat. **46%. nc ncf**. *1,200 bottles.*

**Murray McDavid Longmorn 1994** Bourbon/Tempranillo **(79)** n19 t21 f19 **b**20. Is this the way to Tempranillo, so that I can weep in my pillow; screaming dreams of Tempranillo, and sweet Longmorn who waits for me...This whisky could easily be a number one with some undoubted catchy notes. But, for us purists, there is just something that you can't put your finger on that is so bloody annoying about it. **46%**

**Norse Cask Selection Longmorn 1990 Aged 15 Years** Cognac finish, bott Aug 05 **(94)** n22 vivid barley with a light brush of fruit; t25 concentrated liquidised essence of barley-sugar. This is almost too beautiful for word paintings because it is so rare to find a malt in this near perfect, unruined form. It may have been in a Cognac cask, but that has not had the slightest jot of influence on the barley, except, maybe, for keeping off the oak, as many Cognac casks are, frankly, way over the hill; f23 just the lightest sprinkling of cocoa powder adds an aging depth to the waves of faultless malt; **b**24 only a slight tiredness to the nose and some missing complexity detracts from a glorious whisky experience. Obviously I am being picky. With that, or a touch of smoke, we would be looking at probably one of the top five whiskies of the last couple of years. **54.9%**

⚜ **Old Malt Cask Longmorn Aged 15 Years** dist Oct 91, bott Feb 07 **(86)** n22 t22 f21 **b**21. Celery on the nose and intense barley on the delivery. Fades just a little too easily towards the growling oak. **50%.** *Douglas Laing. 299 bottles.*

**Old Malt Cask Longmorn Aged 15 Years** dist Nov 88, bott Feb 04 **(91)** n23 first-class interplay between busy coal-gas/peaty smoky notes, soft honey, unripened oranges and unmalted barley flour; t22 really delicate malt with waferthin strands of oak underpinning it at first and then attempting to take control; bitter oranges and honey form a complex diversion. Mouthwatering throughout; f22 the odd waft of peat reek sweetens the lightly charred toast; **b**24 this is something to spend time over: a bitter-sweet tale if ever there was one. **50%. nc. ncf sc.** *Douglas Laing.*

**Old Malt Cask Longmorn 18 Years Old** dist Oct 87, bott Sept 06 **(89)** n22 rock solid barley; a vague Irish potstill firmness; t23 crackling barley with a wonderful diffusion of gristy sweetness; wonderfully salivating; f22 hard-as-nails barley offers late oils and oak; **b**22 lip-smacking despite the obvious rigidity. Unusual for Longmorn and an excellent early-evening dram. **50%.** *314 bottles.*

⚜ **Old Masters Longmorn Aged 14 Years** Cask no. 62552, dist 1992, bott 06 **(93)** n22 freshly chopped swede is an unusual sweet addition to the rich barley norm; t24 big, opaque barley offering several breathtaking layers of sweetness, though it is the honey-muscovado sugar mix which works best; f23 late spice and salt add piquancy to the honeyed barley; **b**24 no tricks: just excellently made and beautifully matured malt. **59.7%.** *James MacArthur.*

**The Queen of the Moorlands Rare Cask Longmorn 12 Years Old** **(95)** n24 toffee apples dipped in very high quality sherry; a fabulous buzz of spice and dank, north-facing gardens. Exquisite; t24 sweet sherry bombarded by ground white peppers; the middle thrust comprises intense barley and deft oak; the bitter-sweet ratio offers pure textbook harmony. To term it sensational hardly does all this justice; f23 long, excellent cocoa development and lashings of natural, even caramel; **b**24 I thought truly great sherry butts like this were history, but Longmorn has come up trumps again. The most startling aspect is that it has taken an excellent though barely-known little whisky outlet off the beaten track in rural England to show the world something that Chivas, with all its might, should have made available the world over. **55.4%. sc.** *The Wine Shop, Leek, UK*

**Royal Mile Whiskies Longmorn 1995 Aged 9 Years** bott 05 **(82)** n21 t20 f21 **b**20. This is one of Speyside's weightier, slower-maturing malts. Here we have a rare glimpse in bottled form of a giant just waking up and getting some curiously toffeed sleep out of its eyes. **58.4%. nc ncf.**

⚜ **Scotch Malt Whisky Society Cask 7.37 Aged 38 Years** Sherry Butt, dist Feb 68 **(72)** n19 t20 f16 b17. Bugger! I can't quite believe this. This shouldn't be happening. A 38-y-o Longmorn from sherry. Should be beyond reproach. They didn't sulphur the butts in those days...did they? Because this has been screwed by sulphur. Not by a lot – but by enough. Is it the oldest known victim of the curse? Or was this "finished" or refreshed in a newer butt to round off any oaky overload? But that butt had been ruined. I am astounded. Dash it all...if only Sherlock Holmes were still alive...This was going to be my final whisky of the night...but I can't go to bed with this infernal pollution in my mouth...next!! **53.6%**

**The Single Malt of Scotland Longmorn Aged 15 Years Vintage 1990** Bourbon cask 30091 **(92)** n23 the wood influence is striking as there is a distinct bourbon edge to this. The malt, meanwhile, shimmers; t22 stunning mouth arrival, firstly radiating rich barley and then, close behind, comes that Kentucky-style thrust. A liberal dose of spices help the two meld; f23 tingling with oak-induced mini-explosions, the barley still has intensity enough to regroup and blow you away; **b**24 left to its own devices, this distillery will come up trumps 99 times out of 100. Here's a fine example of very good whisky matured in a very good cask. But the results are way beyond very good... **60.4%.** *The Whisky Exchange. 129 bottles.*

**The Single Malt of Scotland Longmorn Aged 36 Years Vintage 1970** Sherry cask no. 28 **(78)** n19 t21 f19 **b**19. A borderline malt. This has any number of good things to be found but countless weeknesses. **56.1%.**

⚜ **The Whisky Fair Longmorn Aged 31 Years** Bourbon Hogshead no. 3494, dist Apr 74, bott Mar 06 **(74)** n19 t18 f19 b18. Lots of exotic fruit. And we know what that means. But so thin is the line between success and failure: and this isn't exactly a success... **49.8%.**

The Whisky Fair Longmorn Aged 31 Years Bourbon, dist 1976, bott 07 (87) n22 big barley, a touch of boiled apple and a vague hint of elderly Longpond Jamaican rum; t22 quite a thick mixture once the oak gets stirred in f21 just sweet enough; b22 hangs on until the nails bleed. 54.1%. Germany.

## LONGROW (see Springbank)

## MACALLAN
### Speyside, 1824. Edrington. Working.

The Macallan 7 Years Old db (89) n23 beautifully clean sherry, lively, salty, gentle peppers; t23 mouth-filling and slightly oily. Some coffee tones intertwine with deep barley and fruit; f21 unravels to reveal very soft oak and lingering fruity spice; b22 an outstanding dram that underlines just how good young malts can be. Fun, fabulous and in recent bottlings has upped the clarity of the sherry intensity to profound new heights. 40%

Macallan 10 Years Old db (86) n20 t21 f23 b22. improved by slightly thinning out and accentuating the spice. 40%

Macallan 10 Years Old Cask Strength db (94) n24 a fleck of smoke harmonises with the bitter blood orange, marzipan and ripe fig: sublime; t23 big, yet always keeping perfect shape on the palate with alternating waves of malt and fruit; f24 long, hints of spiced cocoa and Seville oranges; b23 brings tears to the eyes – and it isn't just the strength. A sherried Macallan draw from the cask coopered in heaven. Find, buy and be consumed... 58.4%

The Macallan 10 Years Old Cask Strength db (85) n20 t22 f22 b21. Enjoyable and a would give chewing gum a run for its money. But over-egged the sherry here and not a patch on the previous bottling. 58.8%. Duty Free.

The Macallan 12 Years Old Sherry Oak Elegancia db (86) n23 t22 f20 b21. Promises, but delivers only to an extent. 40%

Macallan 18 Years Old db (95) n24 compelling, crystal clear sherry notes with not a single blemish; massive fruitcake character fortified by a dry oloroso theme; t24 there are several layers working in tandem here: there is the dry oloroso forming the backbone, there is sweeter malt flitting butterfly-like around the palate; and lighter, fresher, grapey notes lighten the entire load. The whole almost overloads the tastebuds and senses; f23 just so deft and subtle: the enormity of the mouth arrival settles down now for a series of cross skirmishes between sweetened cocoa, ripe plum and even the softest wave of apologetic peat. Glorious; b24 it's been at least ten years since I've come across a Macallan 18 with such flawless depth. Beyond brilliant: a must for the Macallan purist who will be relieved by this expression following last year's unveiling of the Fine Oak range.... 43%

The Macallan 18 Years Old dist 87, bott 06 db (89) n22 marmalade and freshly trimmed rhubarb. A dab of grape, too. Not entirely without blemish, though; t22 caressing and teasing in texture, the grape, vanilla, natural caramel and barley have melted into one indistinguishable lump; f23 long and languid, the tastebuds are sent to sleep by the sheer comfortableness of it all; b22 another essay in silk. 43%

Macallan 25 Years Old db (78) n20 t20 f19 b19. After some early orangey pleasantries, goes strangely off-key and bitter. Having tasted so many classics over the years, an extremely disappointing expression. 43%

The Macallan 30 Years Old db (92) n24 orange pith and oak, really charming and incredibly sexy and complex; t23 mouth-filling with a mixture of full fruits and beguiling spices, brilliant layer of honied barley; f22 slightly medium to short after the brilliance of the palate, but lovely vanilla and lingering, silky sweet malt; b23 a greatly improved dram than a few years back. An astounding mixture of age and beauty. 43%

The Macallan 40 Years Old dist 10 May 61, bott 9 Sep 05 db (90) n23 no shortage of oak, as you might expect. But nutty, too (chestnut pure, to be precise). The scope is broadened with a distracted smokiness while oak maximizes the longer it stays in the glass; t23 soft and yielding, with a lovely dovetailing of vanillins and delicate sherry. The grape appears to gain control with a sweet barley sidekick before the oak recovers; f22 soft oils formulate with some laite and slightly salted, Digestive-style biscuit. Gentle spices delight; b22 very well-rounded dram that sees off advancing years with a touch of grace and humour. So often you think the oak will take control, but each time an element intervenes to win back the balance. It is as if the dram is teasing you. Wonderful entertainment. **43%**

**The Macallan 50 Years Old** dist 29 Mar 52, bott 21 Sep 05 db **(90) n**25 we all have pictures in our minds of the perfect grandmother: perhaps grey-haired and knitting in her rocking-chair. Or grandfather: kindly, gentle, quietly wise, pottering about in the shed with some gadget he has just made for you. This, then, is the cliched nose of the perfect 50-year-old malt: time-defying intensity and clarity; attractive demerara (rum and sugar!) sweetened coffee, a tantalizing glimpse at something smoky and sensationally rich grape and old fruit cake. So that the sweetness and dryness don't cancel each other out, but complement each other and between them tell a thousand tales. Basically, there's not much missing here... and absolutely all you could wish to find in such an ancient Speysider...; **t**23 dry delivery with the oak making the early running. But slowly the grape and grain fights back to gain more than just a foot-hold; again telling wisps of smoke appear to lay down a sound base and some oily barley; **f**19 now the oak has taken over. There is a burnt-toast and burnt raisin bitterness, lessened in effect marginally by a sweeter vanilla add-on; **b**23 loses it at the end, which is entirely excusable. But until then it has been one fabulous experience full of passion and complexity. I nosed and tasted this for over an hour. It was one very rewarding, almost touching, experience. **46%**

**The Macallan 1851 Inspiration** db **(74) n**19 **t**19 **f**17 **b**19. Uninspirational in 2007 ☉

**The Macallan 1876 Replica** db **(83) n**21 **t**21 **f**21 **b**20. Lovely oak-malt nose while the palate is silky and relaxed. **40.6%**

**The Macallan 1937** bott 69 db **(92) n**23 an outline of barley can eventually be made in the oaky mist; becomes better defined as a honeyed sweetness cuts in. Fingers of smoke tease. When nosing in the glass hours later the fresh, smoky gristiness is to die for ... and takes you back to the mill room 67 years ago; **t**22 pleasantly sweet start as the barley piles in – even a touch of melon in there; this time the oak takes second place and acts as a perfect counter; **f**24 excellent weight with soft peat softening the oak; **b**23 a subtle if not overly complex whisky where there are few characters but each play its part exceptionally well. One to get out with a DVD of Will Hay's sublime Oh Mr Porter which was being made in Britain at the same time as this whisky and as Laurel and Hardy were singing about a Lonesome Pine on the other side of the pond; or any Pathe film of Millwall's FA Cup semi-final with Sunderland. **43%**

**The Macallan 1937** bott 74 db **(83) t**19 **t**24 **f**20 **b**20. It's all about the superb, silky initial mouth impact. **43%**.

**The Macallan 1938** bott 73 db **(90) n**21 hint of apple blossoms on oak; **t**23 stupendous balance and poise as the barley rolls, wave after wave over the palate bringing with it a sweet sugar-almond biscuity quality; **f**23 fabulous finish of great length. Spices dovetail with an almost perfect barley-oak charm; **b**23 no hint of tiredness here at all: a malt that has all the freshness and charisma yet old-world charm and mystery of Hitchcock's The Lady Vanishes, which was made at the same time as this whisky. **43%**

**The Macallan 1938 (31 Years Old)** dist 38, first bott 69, re-bottled 02 db **(83) n**20 **t**22 **f**20 **b**21. Some wonderful trills of barley early on but the oak dominates. **43%**.

**The Macallan 1939** bott 79 db **(90) n**23 pleasing peaty edges to the thick malt; a touch of hickory for extra weight and Highland Park-esque heather-honey; **t**22 spot on barley gives an unmolested mouthwatering performance; the oak tags on reluctantly drying towards cocoa at the middle; **f**22 the integrity is kept as the oak backs off and little wisps of smoke re-surface; some brown sugar keeps the bitter-sweet pot boiling; **b**23 enormous complexity confidence to a whisky distilled at a time of uncertainty; one to accompany the original Goodbye Mr Chips, though the whisky seems nothing like so faded. **43%**

**The Macallan 1940** bott 75 db **(83) n**20 **t**22 **f**21 **b**20. Easily the most modern style discernible from this distillery; a Macallan recogisable as an ancestor of today's famous dram, even with one or two warts apparent. **43%**

**The Macallan 1940 (37 Years Old)** dist 40, first bott 77, re-bottled 02 db **(91) n**22 not dissimilar to an old sherried Irish of this era with the barley having a firm, crisp, almost abrasive quality. Rather lovely especially with the most subtle wisps of peat imaginable;

**t**23 bracing, full-on barley where the flintiness from the nose is transferred perfectly to the palate; a touch of spice and hint of smoke towards the middle; **f**23 clean, long finale where the barley pulsates its rock hard message; **b**23 blind-tasting I would have declared this Irish, though slightly mystified by the distant hints of peat. Hard to believe that something so sublime could have been made by a nation under siege. Obviously nothing can distract a Scotsman from making great whisky ... **43%**

**The Macallan 1945 (56 Years Old)** cask 262, bott 02 db **(89) n**22 extraordinary to the point of improbability: the sherry is fresh and keeping at bay logjams of chunky oak, though the fruitiness burns off the longer it remains in the glass; the smoke hovers and soars like pin-prick eagles on the wing; **t**23 battling oak fizzes against the sweeter, mouthwatering barley; the fruit is subtle though there is a pineapple sharpness amid the still lush grape; **f**22 really impressive, slow development of peat that offers no spice but a smoky overlay to the oak; **b**22 how can a whisky retain so much freshness and character after so long in the cask? This game never ceases to amaze me. **51.5%**

**The Macallan 1946 Select Reserve** db **(93) n**25 does peat arrive any more delicately than this? The sherry, barley and oak offer perfect harmony: perfect and faultless; **t**23 teasingly mouthwatering and fruity. Crushed sultanas cruise with the peat; **f**22 the oak makes inroads at the expense of the barley. Remains chewy and tantalisingly smoky, though; **b**23 I have never found a finer nose to any whisky. Once-in-a-lifetime whisky. **40%**

**The Macallan 1946 (56 Years Old)** cask 46/3M, bott 02 db **(84) n**21 **t**21 **f**20 **b**22. The most peat-free '46 I've come across yet **44.3%**

**The Macallan 1948 (53 Years Old)** cask 609, bott 02 db **(77) n**18 **t**21 **f**19 **b**19. Drinkable, but showing some major oaky cracks. **45.3%**

**The Macallan 1948 Select Reserve** db **(75) n**22 **t**19 **f**17 **b**17. What a fabulous nose! Sadly the package trails behind the '46. **40%**

**The Macallan 1949 (53 Years Old)** cask 136, bott 02 db **(95) n**23 wonderfully lively fruit interwoven with waxy, polished wooden floors and acacia honey; a touch of salt sharpens it further; **t**23 nothing extinct about this old Scottish volcano as oak-led spices assert their grip on the tastebuds while soft, sultry sherry tries to act as placator; **f**24 oaky-cocoa/liquorice and intense barley; remains mouthwatering yet spicy for seemingly hours; **b**24 hold on to your trilbies: this punchy malt knows exactly where it is going. What a year: Carol Reed makes the incomparable The Third Man and Macallan can come up with something like this. Oh, to swap Orson Welles for H. G. Wells and his time machine. Sheer, unrepeatable class. **49.8%**

**The Macallan 1949 (52 Years Old)** cask 935, bott 02 db **(82) n**23 **t**21 **f**19 **b**19. Faded and slightly tired, it has problems living up to the heaven-made nose. **41.1%**

**The Macallan 1950 (52 Years Old)** cask 598, bott 02 db **(83) n**22 **t**22 **f**18 **b**21. Charmingly delicate peat but probably about two or three summers past being a truly excellent whisky. **46.7%**

**The Macallan 1950 (52 Years Old)** cask no.600, bott 02 db **(91) n**20 the early fruit quickly evaporates to leave a clear path for the oak; **t**24 stunning sherry: the grape absolutely sparkles yet is soft enough to allow through a tidal wave of malt, on which peat is sensuously surfing; **f**23 spices from the middle carry through as does the chewy peat. Some fabulous undercurrents of burnt raisin and healthy malt continue; **b**24 only two casks apart, but this is almost a mirror image of the first, in the sense that everything is the other way round... **51.7%**

**The Macallan 1951 (51 Years Old)** cask 644, bott 02 db **(93) n**23 a minor fruitfest with withering grapes and raisins the main attraction but over-ripe greengages and raspberries bulk up the sub-plot: needs this to see off the firm oak. A gentle, barely discernible peatiness drifts over it all with absolutely no signs of over-aging; **t**24 fascinating detail to the barley: it is fresh and still mildly gristy at first but the sherry builds a dark path towards it. All the time the sherry remains clean and in harmony; some confident peat weaves a delicious path through the complexity; **f**23 unrefined brown sugar digs in with the barley to see off the encroaching oak; the most delicate wafts of peat imaginable caress the senses; **b**23 a malt instantly recognisable to Macallan lovers of the last two decades. Simply outstanding. **52.3%**

The Macallan 1952 (50 Years Old) cask no.627, bott 02 db (80) n20 t20 f21 b19. Good, clean sherry but it all seems a little detached 50.8%

The Macallan 1952 (49 Years Old) cask 1250, bott 02 db (74) n19 t19 f18 b18. Ye olde weirde Macallane. 48%

The Macallan 1953 (49 Years Old) cask no. 516, bott 02 db (92) n22 a shade meaty with the oak offering a big counter to the thumping sherry and delicate smoke; t24 full sherry alert as the fruitcake richness goes into overdrive, as do the spices; f23 some medium roast Santos lightens the oak while enrichening the barley; b23 deliciously big and unflinching in its Christmas pudding intensity. 51%

The Macallan 1954 (47 Years Old) cask 1902, bott 02 db (77) n19 t18 f21 b19. The line between success and failure is this: outwardly the '53 and 54 are similar but the 53 controls the oak much tighter. I love the coffee finale on this, though. 50.2%

The Macallan 1955 (46 Years Old) cask 1851 49, bott 02 db (88) n21 more burnt raisins and apples; t22 the tastebuds get a good spicy peppering as the barley rootles about the palate; the sherry is clear and intact; f23 amazingly long with the oak falling short of its desired palate domination; b22 close call: one more Speyside August and this dram would have been matchwood. 45.9%

The Macallan 1958 (43 Years Old) cask 2682, bott 02 db (86) n17 t22 f24 b23. One fears the worst from the sappy nose but the taste is sheer Highland Park in its honey depth. 52.9%

The Macallan 1959 (43 Years Old) cask 360, bott 02 db (79) n19 t21 f19 b20. The oak is giving the malt a good hiding but it just hangs on to a delicious sub-plot. 46.7%

The Macallan 1964 (37 Years Old) cask 3312, bott 02 db (86) n24 t22 f20 b20. butterscotch and honey: a real chewing whisky if ever there was one. 58.2%

The Macallan 1965 (36 Years Old) cask 4402, bott 02 db (91) n22 pretty well oaked but wonderful balance from blood oranges; t23 again lovely mouthfeel as the fabulously balanced and lush barley hits the palate; fruit and oak are dished out in even measures with the spice: this is top notch whisky; f22 after the big bust comes the ample arse: heaps of chewy barley fortified by sultanas and raisins; b24 if this was a woman it would be Marilyn Monroe. 56.3%

The Macallan 1966 (35 Years Old) cask 7878, bott 02 db (83) n21 t22 f20 b20. a malt which never quite works out where it is going but gives a comfortable ride all the same. 55.5%

The Macallan 1967 (35 Years Old) cask 1195, bott 02 db (93) n23 top notch uncompromised sherry with some lovely nutty touches; t24 the sherry deftly flicks each individual tastebud while the burnt fudge offers a bitter-sweet distraction; f23 coffee ice cream but a whole lot warmer as the spices pop about the mouth. Vanilla and raisins gather around the spicy centrepiece; some lovely salt towards the finale; b23 this is what happens when you get a great sherry cask free of sulphur and marauding oak: whisky the way God intended. Unquestionably classic Macallan. 55.9%

The Macallan 1968 (34 Years Old) cask 2875, bott 02 db (92) n21 lemon curd tart and barley; t23 full frontal barley with a grape chaperone; f22 continues to mouthwater now with late cocoa adding depth and finesse; b24 possibly the most sophisticated and delicate malt in the pack despite the strength. 51%

The Macallan 1968 (33 Years Old) cask 5913, bott 02 db (84) n17 t23 f22 b22. Flawed genius: how can a whisky with such a poor nose produce the goods like this? 46.6%

The Macallan 1969 cask 9369 db (75) n19 t18 f20 b18. One of those ungainly sherry butts that swamps everything in sight. 52.7%

The Macallan 1969 (32 Years Old) cask no. 10412, bott 02 db (76) n18 t20 f18 b20. One small sip for man, one ordinary vintage for Macallan. Splinters. anybody? 59%

The Macallan 1970 (32 Years Old) cask no. 241, bott 02 db (95) n23 another heavyweight but this time with some honey and ripe fig to offer complexity; passable impersonation of ancient bourbon blended with old Demerara rum; t24 quite massive with strands of brown sugar bringing out the best of the grape; f23 very long and so subtle: the barley and vanilla stretch a long distance with some natural toffee rounding things off; b25 Brazil win the World Cup with the finest team and performance of all time, my girlfriend born there soon after and Macallan receive a butt from Heaven via Jerez. 1970 was some year ... 54.9%

The Macallan 1970 (31 Years Old) cask no. 9033, bott 02 db **(81) n**20 **t**20 **f**22 **b**19. A butt bottled on its way down. **52.4%**

The Macallan 1971 (30 Years Old) cask no. 4280, bott 02 db **(86) n**21 **t**22 **f**22 **b**21. Imagine the trusty 10 years old from about 1980 with a grey beard ... **56.4%**

The Macallan 1971 (30 Years Old) cask 7556, bott 02 db **(91) n**22 delicate salt helps develop the barley; **t**22 vivid barley with rather soft sherry and then spice; **f**24 lengthy, subtle end with waves of rich sherry carrying a Demerara sweetness and coffee; **b**23 a complex dram that is comfortable with its age. **55.9%**

The Macallan 1972 (29 Years Old) cask no. 4041, bott 02 db **(92) n**23 hell's teeth!!! This is probably what an explosion in a bodega would smell like. The most awesomely powerful sherry I can probably ever remember on a whisky, much more one dimensional than cask 4043, though; **t**24 that trademark coffee-ness is there (in this case something of a heavy roast Costa Rican) then some tomato and burnt raisin; **f**22 bitter and slightly nutty as the oak begins to gain some control; **b**23 once, I would have hated this type of malt. But I have come across so many sulphur-tainted casks over recent years that I have learned to have fun with monsters like this. Snatched from an awesome clutch of butts. **49.2%**

The Macallan 1972 29 Years Old cask 4043, bott 02 db **(93) n**25 well, it has to be said: a quite faultless nose. The spices are entirely in true with the perfect sherry-oak balance. This is big stuff, but perfectly proportioned: seems almost a shame to drink it ...; **t**24 stupendous spice-plum-giant-boiled-Italian-tomato: enormous with a waft of smoke through the middle; **f**21 slightly bitter as the oak nibbles but still lots of complexity; **b**23 the sherry butt used for this was a classic: the intensity of the whisky memorable. If, as Macallan claim, the sherry accounts for only 5% of the flavour, I'd like to know what happened to the other 95.... **58.4%**

The Macallan 1973 (30 Years Old) cask 6098, bott 03 db **(93) n**23 the grape is brittle and nestles behind barley and honey; some ripe pears add to the freshness; **t**24 the honey is at the vanguard of a brilliant display of intense, sugarcoated barley; **f**23 the sweetness vanishes to leave the more mouthwatering, grassy malt elements; **b**23 a superbly chosen cask for those with a sweet tooth in particular. If you know any women who claim not to like whisky, seduce them with this. **60.9%**

The Macallan 1989 cask no 552 db **(94) n**23 stunningly clean sherry with wonderful nuttiness amid spice and oak; moist Melton Hunt cake at its most subtle; **t**23 explosive entrance with spices and a superbly full-on oakiness that bathes in the luxuriant, simply flawless, leathery sherry; the sweetness is not entirely unlike Demerara rum; **f**24 calms down for wave upon wave of chocolate fruit and nut ... only without the excessive sweetness; **b**24 there are countless people out there who cut their whisky teeth 20 years ago on Macallan. Battle to get a bottle of this and the grey hairs will return to black, the eyesight will improve and your clothes will fit more easily. This is timewarp Macallan it its most dangerously seductive. **59.2%**

The Macallan Cask Strength db **(94) n**22 cranked-up, sweet, clean sherry; **t**24 absolutely spot-on delivery with grape concentrate, thickened further by intense barley. Wonderful spices arrive on cue; **f**24 long with the taste buds storm-lashed by juicy sherry for some time. And still those spices rock ...; **b**24 one of those big sherry babies: it's like surfing a massive wave of barley-sweetened sherry. Go for the ride. **58.6%**. *USA.*

Macallan Cask Strength db **(82) n**20 **t**20 **f**22 **b**20. I could weep. What could have been an absolute classic is just one less-than-perfect cask away from greatness. Even so, an enjoyable and memorable ride for the most part. **57.8%**. *Canada.*

The Macallan Distillers Choice db **(80) n**21 **t**20 **f**19 **b**20. Sweeter, less sherried and more bashful than previous bottlings. **40%**

∴∴ The Macallan Easter Elchies Summer Selection 2006 Aged 8 Years **(88) n**21 musty, dusty bookshelves; **t**23 beautiful symphony of varied barley tones, each caressed by the lightest touch of fruit; **f**22 softly furred fruit with a sprinkling of cocoa; **b**22 perhaps not every cask here is faultless but the whole really does remind you how deliciously entertaining a mere 8-year-old can be. Good for Macallan for showing the way. **45.2%**

The Macallan Easter Elchies Seasonal Cask Selection Winter Choice 14 Years Old db **(94) n**24 you can almost picture the butt before it was filled: large, dripping with dampness inside and smelling as sweet as a nut. Nothing has changed in 14 years, except some exquisite marmalade and honeycomb has been added; **t**24 sizzling spices cut rapier-like through the intense grape; juicy barley seeps through the wounds; **f**23 lilting, rich-textured natural caramel and vanilla; **b**23 from a faultless cask and one big enough to have its own Postcode... **54%**. *Exclusive to visitor centre.*

⋰⋱ **The Macallan Easter Elchies Winter Selection 2006/07 Aged 15 Years** db **(90)** **n**23 the mahogany tinged with punk-orange colour is a worry, but relief is at hand at first sniff: one of the few sherry noses around these days without even a hint of sulphur. And here we are talking mega-sherry. Perhaps too one-tricked to be great, but a delight; **t**23 grape sloshes juicily around, sharply at times, but even as the oak tries to get a word in everything is so clean; **f**22 pretty long; bitter as oloroso hangs about and a late, intriguing dash of Fisherman's Friend; **b**22 Some 20 years ago I would have marked this down as over-the-top sherry. But so rare these days to find faultless butts – and this really is faultless – that I've marked it up for its ability to take you back to another era. Brings a tear to the eye of those who lament a lost whisky world... **58.5%**

⋰⋱ **Macallan Aged 12 Years Gran Reserva** db **(92)** **n**23 massive cream sherry background with well matured fruit cake to the fore: big, clean, luxurious in a wonderfully old-fashioned way. Oh, and a sprinkling of crushed sultana just in case the grapey message didn't get across... **t**24 a startlingly unusual combination on delivery: dry yet juicy! The ultra fruity lushness is dappled with soft spices; oak arriving early-ish does little to alter the path of the sweetening fruit; just a hint of hickory reveals the oak's handiwork towards the middle; **f**22 dry, as oloroso does, with a vaguely sweeter edge sparked by notes of dried date; the delicate but busy spices battle through to the toffeed end; **b**23 well, you don't get many of these to the pound. A real throwback. The oloroso threatens to overwhelm but there is enough intrigue to make for a quite lovely dram which, as all good whiskies should, never quite tells the story the same way twice. Not entirely without blemish, but I'm being picky. A Macallan soaked in oloroso which traditionalists will swoon over. **45.6%**

The **Macallan Gran Reserva 1981** db **(90)** **n**23 **t**22 **f**22 **b**23. Macallan in a nutshell. Brilliant. But could do with being at 46% for full effect. **40%**

The **Macallan Gran Reserva 1982** db **(82)** **n**21 **t**22 **f**20 **b**19. Big, clean, sweet sherry influence from first to last but doesn't open up and sing like the '81 vintage. **40%**

The **Macallan Elegancia 1991** db **(79)** **n**19 **t**21 **f**19 **b**20. Distinctly citrusy with fresh-squeezed blood orange intermingling with vanilla and fresh malt; sadly, a distant murmer of sulphur on both nose and finish docks a point or three. **40%**

The **Macallan Elegancia 1992** db **(85)** **n**19 **t**21 **f**23 **b**22. A marvellous improvement on the '90 edition **43%**

The **Macallan Fine Oak 8 Years Old** db **(89)** **n**21 entirely different to any other Macallan around: the brash freshness of the sherry appears to be magnified by the young barley, playful, kindergarten stuff; **t**23 the youthful exurberance on the nose is matched by the live-wire arrival on the palate. The shape it takes in the mouth is fascinating with the initially mouthwatering grape effect at first breathlessly rushing in and then calming to dissolve in every corner of the palate, gentle spices trickle down as does the very faintest of honey notes; **f**22 a lot of cocoa butter as the oak shows a surprising depth, burnt raisins also guarantee a bitter edge to the sweet malt; **b**23 a distinctly different, young and proud Macallan that settles into a satisfying middle and finish where the soft grapey tones break through for a mottled effect with the intense malt. Seriously tasty stuff and great fun. **43%**

The **Macallan Fine Oak 10 Years Old** db **(83)** **n**20 **t**21 **f**21 **b**21. The faintest blemish on the grass and citrus nose disappears after the bottle's been open a day or two; elsewhere soft malt dissolves leaving a more bitter biscuity oatiness in its wake. The malt-fruit combination is mouth-cleansing as it gathers in intensity. A pleasingly delicate Macallan. **40%**

The **Macallan Fine Oak 12 Years Old** db **(89)** **n**22 clean, dry sherry is bolstered by competent fresh barley and even a hint of ginger when warmed; **t**23 seriously mouthwatering with the barley coating the palate with its ultra-clean bitter-sweet charms; vanilla arrives earlier than usual – especially for a Macallan; **f**21 quite a dry, chalky finish but only after the barley is given an almost free run. If you have chewed malt, then you will recognise this beautiful character; late natural toffee muscles in on the vanilla fade; **b**23 a dram to be taken at body temp for best results: when sampled cold the balance edges towards subtle fruit and crispness; when warmed the barley makes the most stunning impact. A suave dram of near flawless character. **40%**

**The Macallan Fine Oak 15 Years Old** db **(95) n**24 over-ripe bananas on toast with freshly-picked spring grass as a side dish and plenty of floral notes to round it off: a sublime and probably unique official Macallan aroma! **t**23 the malt, complete with distant peat, simply dissolves in the mouth; beautifully weighted with the distinctive Macallan brown-sugar sweetness hitting the red zone for a while before it is pulled back by drier vanilla; **f**24 just so, so long!! Excellent playful peaty spice development late on helps punctuate the continuation of the rich barley theme that expands out into low key butterscotch/toffee; dovetailing is a distant grapey sub-plot; **b**24 true story: I have for years played about in my lab with bourbon and sherry cask Macallan and come to the conclusion that a truly great whisky was waiting to happen. This could be it. You have to travel a long way to find a whisky with quite the same refreshing all round harmony as this. The balance is the stuff of legend ... and genius. **43%**

**The Macallan Fine Oak 17 Years Old** db **(84) n**21 **t**21 **f**21 **b**21. A curious, pleasant but not entirely convincing addition to the Fine Oak family, having neither the 15-year-old's outrageous complexity or the deftness of the 18. An expression too far? **43%**

**The Macallan Fine Oak 18 Years Old** db **(91) n**23 inside the dry sherried shell is sweeter malt and vanilla; a touch of salt gives a slightly coastal air, even with some far-off peat-reek on the breeze; **t**22 myriad malt characteristics on varying levels of sweetness; there is mesmerising spice and grape varying between pungent and juicy; **f**23 remains young at heart with the barley dominating; mouthwatering to the end, distant smoke returns flanked by spineless grape juice and toffee plus oak that lays bitterness on sweet; even a touch of bourbon-style ageing at the death; **b**23 a dram much truer to the old Macallan style but with enough overt barley to make a difference. **43%**

**The Macallan Fine Oak 21 Years Old** db **(89) n**22 an attractive honeyed thread weaves through the oak and grape; some beautiful marmalade off-cuts toys with a ghostly peatiness; **t**22 oily and sultry with some stiff oak softened by the barley which is yielding and mouthwatering; **f**23 remains butter-creamy, that vague, ethereal peatiness plays peak-a-boo but the vanilla continues as does the marmalade on toast; **b**22 by far the richest textured Macallan of all time with a fascinating distant peatiness. **43%**

**The Macallan Fine Oak 25 Years Old** db **(94) n**24 probably the first Macallan since '46 to show such little shyness with peat, though here it is more fleeting; the second wave is proud, clean sherry. The third is vanilla ice-cream with pears and peaches; the fourth is pure bourbon. Speyside bliss; **t**23 the oak offers a framework in which the sherry thrives while the barley punches its weight; an assortment of fruit also make an entrance as does an almost underground spiciness; **f**23 back to vanilla for the undetectable touchdown; I can think of no whisky this age which has such a velvety feel right to the very end. Guys, if it were a woman you wouldn't know whether to make love or snuggle up in a silky embrace and go to sleep: I suggest both; **b**24 the blenders have obviously worked overtime on this: what a star! **43%**

**The Macallan Fine Oak 30 Years Old** db **(90) n**23 lots of nose-nipping oaky weight softened by crushed gooseberries and grape; a mild and deeply attractive bourbony character develops **t**23 delicate spices arrives from nowhere, there is a quick flash of half-hearted peat and then we are left in a custard-sweet and enormous world of malty-oaky-grapiness; a certain fatness to the whisky develops **f**22 where's the oak? An improbable finale that is all about barley arm-inarm with sherry and nut oil. At last the oakiness appears but immediately tapers out **b**22 the oak threatened on the nose never quite materialises. Few whiskies of this maturity are quite so polite regarding the age **43%**

⋅⁖⋅ **The Macallan Fine Oak Master's Edition** db **(91) n**23 one of the most delicate of all Macallan's house noses, depending on a floral scented theme with a sweetish malty tinge to the dank bracken and bluebells; **t**23 so salivating and sensual! The tastebuds are caressed with sugar-coated oaky notes that have a devilish buzz about them; **f**22 more malt and now vanilla with a bitter cocoa death... **b**23 adorable. **42.8%**

**The Macallan Fine Oak Whisky Maker's Selection** db **(92) n**22 good age with the oak determining a dry course; the barley carries delicate grape; **t**23 distinctively Speyside-style with an early avalanche of spice; there is a barley-juiced fruitiness and perhaps a fino touch, too; **f23** long, with all the vanilla you'd expect from such a well oaked dram; the clean-ness of the barley and grape is stunning, as is the light oily sheen that carries the dim sweetness; **b24** those who cannot see Macallan in anything other than chestnut oloroso will be having sleepless nights: this is a dram of exquisite sophistication. The ultimate pre-prandial dram with it's coy, mildly cocoaed dryness, set against just enough barley and fruit sweetness here and there to see off any hints of austerity. Some great work has gone on in the lab to make this happen: fabulous stuff, chaps! **42.8%.** Duty Free. ☉

The Macallan Millennium 50 Years Old (1949) decanter db **(90)** n23 t22 f22 **b**23. Magnificent finesse and charm despite some big oak makes this another Macallan to die for. **40%**

The Macallan Travel 1920s db **(67)** n17 t18 f15 **b**17. Does absolutely nothing for me at all. Totally off-key, no finish. Nothing roaring about this one. **40%**

The Macallan Travel 1930s db **(91)** n22 beautiful peat and sherry combo; **t23** the cleanest, most mouthwatering sherry you could pray for; **f23** soft vanilla and lingering, lazy smoke; **b23** an essay in complexity and balance. Clean sherry at its finest. You little darling! **40%**

The Macallan Travel 1940s db **(81)** n21 t22 f17 **b**21. Lovely smoke and complexity, but let down by the sherry and a faltering finish. **40%**

The Macallan Travel 1950s db **(92)** n24 intense, immaculate sherry and blood orange with playful spices adding nose prickle; **t22** massive but voluptuous sherry, then a wave of malt concentrate; **f23** more barley, a touch of smoke and then juicy sultanas and lingering spice; **b23** sit back, take a deep, mouth-filling draught, close your eyes and listen to Hogie Carmichael's "Stardust", for this is just what this whisky is. **40%**

⋙ The Macallan Woodlands Limited Edition Estate Bottling db **(86)** n21 t23 f21 **b**21. No shortage of toffee towards the finish brings a premature halt to a wonderfully mollased early delivery. **40%**

⋙ Adelphi Macallan Aged 16 Years Cask no. 14995, dist 1990, bott 07 **(79)** n19 t22 f19 **b**19. Gatecrashed by a surprising degree of oak. **57.4%.** 399 bottles.

Alchemist Macallan Aged 14 Years dist Apr 91, bott Jul 05 **(91)** n22 floral and grassy; **t23** marauding, mouth-watering barley; **f23** classy, cocoa and barley-laced vanilla; **b23** Macallan at it's unsherried best: the richness is sublime. **46%. nc ncf.**

Cadenhead's Macallan-Glenlivet Authentic Collection Aged 14 Years Butt, dist 90, bott May 05 **(75)** n19 t19 f18 **b**19. Some decent fruit and chewability despite the flaw. **57.6%.** 654 bottles.

Cadenhead's Authentic Collection Macallan-Glenlivet Aged 16 Years Bourbon Hogshead, dist 89, bott Sept 06 **(95)** n24 glorious interlinking between golden-syrup and honey on one hand and crisp barley on the other. All this is on a bed of distant smoke and ice cream cones; **t24** sweetness on nose translates automatically to palate where a mouthwatering barley middle is deeply embedded; **f23** a gathering of spices which add to the honeyed gloss of barley; **b24** showing some of the extraordinary DNA which makes Macallan Fine Oak 17 such a world-beater. Stunning. And for the thousands of Macallanophiles out there – you'd better get the next plane to Campbeltown!! **53.3%.** 282 bottles.

Cadenhead's Authentic Collection Macallan-Glenlivet Aged 17 Years dist 87, bott Feb 05 **(94)** n24 bitter orange and wild strawberries crushed in the hand; some cocoa-oak perfectly sprinkled; **t24** a bourbony oak kick, then it's back to the multi-layered fruit followed by thick malt; **f23** much drier but never too dry, returning to bitter chocolate and bitter orange; a hint of spice; **b23** very unprofessional, I know, but I just couldn't spit this one out – just too damn good! **56.1%.** 630 bottles.

⋙ Cadenhead's Authentic Collection Macallan-Glenlivet Aged 19 Years Sherry Butt, dist 1987, bott May 07 **(71)** n17 t19 f17 **b**18. A good example of sulphur influence. **56.2%.** 576 bottles.

Celtic Heartlands Macallan 1969 **(92)** n23 Macallans rarely get more exotic than this: passion fruit and gala melon. The perfect breakfast malt...; **t24** fantastic interplay between malt brushed with peat and sympathetic oak: wave upon wave of beautifully weighted malt; **f22** cocoa and smoke; **b23** proof that a Macallan from a great bourbon cask is as good as one from sherry. **40.3%.** Jim McEwan/Bruichladdich.

Dewar Rattray Individual Cask Bottling Macallan 1989 Aged 17 Years cask no. 2819, dist Feb 89, bott May 06 **(89)** n23 textbook sherried Macallan; **t21** dry toffee-nut;

f23 sweetness as barley gets a juicy grip; dries and bitters out after some while; **b**22 rich and full-bodied. **58.4%.** *256 bottles.*

**Duncan Taylor Collection Macallan 1968 Aged 38 Years** cask no. 5586, dist Jun 68, bott 4 July 06 **(79)** n23 t20 f18 **b**18. The debonair marzipan and cocoa nose raises the profile of an otherwise over-aged malt. **50.94%.** *103 bottles.*

**Duncan Taylor Collection Macallan 1968** cask 5589, dist Jun 68, bott Mar 05 **(83)** n21 t23 f19 **b**20. Beautifully sensual malty start, but tires out. **54%.** *151 bottles.*

**Duncan Taylor Collection Macallan 1969** cask no 7191, dist Jun 69, bott Dec 05 **(94)** **n**24 toffee-vanilla massages the nose; some coffee, too; t23 lush and luscious with rich barley-toffee lead; massive spices jolt the tastebuds back to life; f23 lightly roasted Java brushed with demerara; **b**24 great age, but alive and kicking to fabulous effect. **55.8%.** *116 bottles.*

**Duncan Taylor Collection Macallan 1969** cask no 8377, dist Sept 69, bott Dec 05 **(88)** n23 fruity and beautifully aged; t22 silky barley then some devilish spices: a mouthful and a half; f21 burnt toast; **b**22 a lovely malt that was just beginning its descent in the barrel. **49.3%.** *203 bottles.*

⬩⬩⬩ **Duncan Taylor Collection Macallan 1969** Cask no. 8373 **(90)** **n**22 heads in direction of exotic fruit; t22 flat delivery: takes time to wake up and overcome the oak but then a slow spreading of rich and pretty sweet barley; f23 takes forever: the barley somehow becomes even softer with gentle, doughy, vanilla; **b**23 few malts at this age show such control and poise. **44.6%.**

**Duncan Taylor Collection Macallan 1986 Aged 18 Years,** cask 10195, dist Nov 86, bott Feb 05 **(94)** n23 t24 f23 **b**24. Quite masterful whisky which gives your tastebuds one damned good seeing to.... **56.7%**

⬩⬩⬩ **Duncan Taylor Collection Macallan 1987** Cask no. 2561 **(91)** **n**21 pithy; crushed fruit stones; a touch of citrus; t23 superb delivery: this could scratch a diamond, so hard is the barley; mouth-watering, grassy, fluty notes dazzle; f23 unrealistically long and with a mind-blowing build up of cocoa and spice; **b**24 Macallan at its most refreshing. **55.3%.**

⬩⬩⬩ **Duncan Taylor Collection Macallan 1987** Cask no. 9795 **(95)** **n**24 classic blood-orange sherry notes – so clean they almost squeak; t24 lumbering fruit at first then an explosion of pure, mouth-watering barley that is beyond description; f23 the vanilla and milk gums make an interesting combo; roasted raisins mixed with fresh, juicy ones abound; **b**24 I know those who are no great fans of Macallan: try this glass of genius, guys..!! **57.7%**

**Duncan Taylor Collection Macallan 1989-91** cask vx3 **(89)** **n**24 classy and complex with soothing butterscotch and barley sugar; t21 light, varying shades of malt but big oak surge; f22 the oak calms down and behaves itself enough for the malt to return for a long, ultra-delicate finish; **b**22 surprising degree of oak in the middle but, over-all, sheer quality. **46.1%**

**Gordon & MacPhail Speymalt Macallan 1938 (94)** **n**25 can this really be over 65-years of age? How, after all these years, does the dynamic of the millroom fit so comfortably with pulped citrus and lavender? And, lurking at the very back, almost wishing not to be noticed, a waft of the softest peat imaginable. I have spent over half an hour nosing this. I cannot fault it. True legend...; t22 an oaky barrage doesn't auger well, but soon it runs out of ammunition. It doesn't take long for accompanying spices and following barley-sugar and burnt honeycomb to unite and link with the pithy orange which has kept the oak in check from the off; f23 amazingly, the oak remains on the retreat and now we get to the real serious bit. Soft peats return to offer little more than a smoky echo but the sweetness continues for dozens more waves. There is a lingering dryness, totally in sympathy with the leading malt but, most of all, the tangy orange remains sharp and delicious; **b**24 when a malt is bottled at this near unbelievable age you expect the worst. And, even if it doesn't come, you have to be hyper-critical because such whisky doesn't come cheap and tasting notes written in awe of age rather than giving a true, honest assessment of its quality is not worth the ink used to print it. So, I have taken a long time to study this. And to find fault. Naturally, there are faults: every whisky has them, and at this age is expected to have more than most. But was it the quality of the wood they used in those days, or the peat involvement? Somehow, this malt has come through the best part of seven decades without any fatal flaws. The nose, in fact, is perfect. And although it wobbles on the palate on the start of its journey, by the end you cannot but be astounded. This is nature-defying whisky, very much like the 62-year-old Dalmore. Few people will be lucky enough ever to taste this. But those that do will be one of the truly privileged. And that includes me. **41.4%**

**Gordon & MacPhail Speymalt Macallan 1950 (91)** n24 a swirl of peat beds down into the firm barley; the fruit is masterful with blood orange lightened by plums and juicy sultana. Oak is present but refuses to unbalance the delightful tranquillity and weight; t22 wonderfully fruity pulse but there is still a gristy youth hanging on in there, allowing a subtle touch of peat to weave into the fabric. Again the oak holds back from doing any damage and the off wave of tangy kumquat is there to be found; f22 does it's best to take an oaky route, but hasn't the heart to do it. Instead, light barley recovers to mingle playfully with the vanilla. Dry and sawdusty, but always in tune and balanced; b23 I always taste these ultra-ancient whiskies with trepidation. Nature suggests that they should not be that good as barley – even with the aid of sherry – can see off only so much oak. But fortified with a delightful touch of peat, this holds itself together like an old Shakespeare first in original buckskin. It creaks. It's delicate. But take the time and handled carefully, this will amaze you. **43%**

**Gordon & MacPhail Speymalt Macallan 1967 (93)** n23 fruitcake fortified, curiously, with a dash of rum; t24 stunningly soft delivery of mixed fruits – especially sultana – and almost gristy barley; f22 just the right sprinkling of chalky oak to counter the rising spice and suet; b24 a mighty classy malt which has withstood the years with aplomb. **40%**

**Harris Whisky Co. "No Ordinary" Aged 16 Years** cask 5436, dist 89, bott Jan 06 **(90)** n22 medium malt; t23 big malt; f22 little malt; b23 malty. And magnificent. **53.1%. nc ncf.** *The Harris Whisky Co. Doesn't say on label, but this is Macallan.*

**Murray McDavid Macallan Aged 8 Years** Bourboun/Syrah cask enhanced in Guigal Hermitage Rouge, dist 96, bott 05 **(73)** n18 t20 f17 b18. Guigal...but no Brueghel. Way too much polarised bitterness and sweetness. **46%. nc ncf.** *1,200 bottles.*

**Murray McDavid Macallan 1990 Aged 15 Years** Bourbon/Grenache, bott 06 **(74)** n17 t20 f19 b18. A softie, but never gets out of the starting blocks. **46%. nc ncf.**

*:::- **Murray McDavid Macallan 1996 Aged 10 Years** Bourbon/Guigal Hermitage Rouge Syrah **(75)** n18 t19 f19 b19. No Syrah-ee. Simply too sharp and disjointed. **46%**

*:::- **Murray McDavid Macallan 1997 Aged 9 Years** Bourbon/Ridge Zinfandel **(93)** n22 nippy fruit; little room in which much else can manoeuvre; t23 beautifully juiced and clean; some wonderful light fruits – pomegranates in particular – bathing and cleansing the palate; f24 barley juice fights back against the flawless, fruity onslaught: one of the cleanest battles in whisky history; b24 take your time here. At first, thought it had possibilities. On third mouthful, entirely won over. A real charmer! Perfect for the first dram of the day to restore your tastebuds and brain back into working order. An adorable nine-year-old classic. **46%**

**Murray McDavid Mission Macallan 1969** Bourbon/Marsanne/ Roussanne **(84)** n24 t21 f19 b20. Fabulous, busy and entirely unique nose. To taste, though, the malt never quite finds its compass and spends much of its time fending off the oak. Never less than juicy and enjoyable, though. **41%. 900 bottles.**

**Murray McDavid Mission Macallan 1985 Aged 21 Years** Bourbon /Sauternes (Chateau d'Yquem), bott 06 **(96)** n25 sweet, cleverly spiced (cinnamon mainly), grape underpinned by firm, rich barley. The best Macallan nose this year – by the distance from Speyside to Sauternes; t24 entirely sure-footed grape and grain in complete harmony; the tastebuds are swamped at first by the élan of this juicy, tongue-tying combination, then deft spice arrives to attack in waves and with panache; f23 long, continuing along the mouth-watering path with the oak finally getting a word in, a slightly bitter one but softened by natural caramel and tannins; b24 when I tasted this, my researcher had written only "bourbon/sauternes" after the name of the whisky (she had correctly copied directly from the label). When I had nosed, tasted, spat and found a safe route down from the ceiling, I inspected the sample bottle a little more carefully and spotted "Chateau dYquem". If all wine-finished whiskies were of this calibre you'd never hear a dissenting voice from me.

Sadly, they aren't. But this one is and all I can do is savour every last drop of a truly great malt. Oh, and put the spittoon into temporary retirement... **52.4%. nc ncf.**

⚜ **Norse Cask Selection Macallan 1988 Aged 17 Years** Hogshead cask no. 9165, dist Oct 88, bott Jan 06 **(91) n**21 a bland nose, but... **t**24 wow! What a show-stopper on the palate with as much butterscotch as you're ever likely to see on a Macallan, underpinned by sweet, gristy barley; **f**23 a touch of marzipan dipped in muscovado sugar before the cocoa **b**23 quite superb! **59.2%. nc ncf.** WhiskyOwner.com, Denmark. 271 bottles.

⚜ **Old Malt Cask Macallan Aged 12 Years Rum Finish** dist Dec 93, bott Nov 06 **(92) n**22 firm, austere but rather elegant; **t**23 a beautifully refined sweetness to the barley; excellent oils; **f**24 long, lush, bitter-sweet with a dab of cocoa here and there and ultra-late spice; **b**23 it really is amazing how rum casks work so consistently well. This malt should be wearing a cape and cane. **50%.** Douglas Laing. 307 bottles.

**Old Malt Cask Macallan Aged 13 Years** dist Jun 90, bott Feb 04 **(88) n**22 flakes of honey enrich the lazy barley and soft oak: relaxed and enticing; **t**23 sumptuous mouthfeel with that honey really making its mark from early on; soft additions of vanilla and peach work well with the faintest of smoke tones; **f**21 not quite so complex as the early arrival and dries as the oak broadens, but a lingering sweetness does the trick; **b**22 really lovely Macallan shorn of sherry and bringing about the exhibitionist in its nudity. **50%.** Douglas Laing. 307 bottles.

**Old Malt Cask Macallan 15 Years** dist 23 Jan 90, bott 15 Jun 05 **(86) n**21 t22 f21 **b**22. About as gentle and clean as they come. **50%.** Douglas Laing.

**Old Malt Cask Macallan 15 Years Old** dist 23 Jan 90, bott 6 May 06 **(87) n**21 t22 f22 **b**22. Good quality without ever testing the tastebuds. **50%**

⚜ **Old Malt Cask Macallan Aged 15 Years** dist Mar 91, bott Sept 06 **(86) n**21 t22 f22 **b**21 charming, grassy, salivating, and glossy evidence of the sma' still here. **50%.** 281 bottles.

**Old Malt Cask Macallan 21 Years Old** dist Apr 85, bott May 06 **(92) n**24 soft citrus further sweetens a gentle stem ginger-based spice buzz; **t**23 wonderfully layered, fruity barley refuses to bow to its age; the spices are busy and intriguing; **f**22 outstanding esters guarantee length and depth; **b**23 the freshness and complexity to this bottling is astounding. A real treat. But don't expect a sherry onslaught. **50%.** 302 bottles.

**Old Malt Cask Macallan 25 Years Old** dist 1 Jun 79, bott 16 May 05 **(89) n**23 t23 f22 **b**22. A thoughtful Macallan that requires and repays solitude and time. **50%.**

**Old Malt Cask Macallan 25 Years Old** dist Oct 80, bott Dec 05 **(89) n**23 rice pudding with honey stirred in; **t**23 early, crisp, lightly sugared sweetness ; big barley surge; **f**21 lazy spices and vanilla; **b**22 a laid-back joy. **50%.** 296 bottles.

**Platinum Selection Macallan 26 Years Old Rum Finish** dist 20 Oct 78, bott May 05 **(94) n**23 sherry, it ain't!! A heavy-duty bitter-sweet delight; **t**24 really lovely light sugary sheen to the barley; the deep, clean punchiness of the malt is matched by the perfectly matched oak weight; **f**23 lashings more of rich malt of near-perfect sweetness. A rare treat. **b**24 explosive and brimming with character. A bottle that has to be found and experienced. **55.4%.** 262 btls.

**Platinum Selection Macallan 27 Years Old** dist 30 May 77, bott May 05 **(88) n**23 an intriguingly rummy aroma; **t**23 exceptionally firm malt with a delicious sugary sheen; **f**20 bitters up as oak arrives; **b**22 a much flintier Macallan than most. **53.9%.** 298 bottles.

**Platinum Selection Macallan Aged 27 Years** dist May 77, bott Nov 04 **(85) n**22 t22 f20 **b**21. Attractively citrussed and malty. **49.6%.** Douglas Laing. 211 bottles.

**Platinum Macallan 29 Years Old** dist May 77, bott Sept 06 **(90) n**22 a tad tired in the oak department but some lovely floral notes (including Bluebells, the poseur in me regrets to note); **t**23 some exotic, tangy fruit darts in and then crumbles under a welter of barley-rich blows; **f**22 lovely depth to the barley-oak marriage with a vague coffee depth and warming spice. Wonderful structure and poise; **b**23 the oak is absorbed with something approaching reverence: a magnificent Macallan for its antiquity. **50.3%.** 185 bottles.

**Platinum Selection Macallan 1977 Sherry Finish** dist May 77, bott Mar 06 **(78) n**20 **t**19 f20 **b**19. The nose is a curious mixture of blood orange and spinster aunts' water closets. Old fashioned and scented. But cumbersome on the palate. **48.4%.** 249 bottles.

⚜ **Premier Barrel Macallan Aged 17 Years** dist Apr 85, bott Jan 07 **(87) n**23 gorgeous coconut dipped in golden syrup; **t**22 sweet barley arrival but the oak finds an early way through; **f**21 fades fast as the vanilla piles in; **b**21 doesn't live up to the early promise, but still a little sweetie. **46%.** Douglas Laing. 327 bottles.

❖ **Premier Barrel Macallan Aged 18 Years (89) n**22 precise, unruffled barley; **t**23 gathers in the complexity stakes as layers of fruity-sweet barley give the vanillas a good thumping; **f**22 dries demurely; **b**22 Mac at its (apparently) un-sherried best. **46%**. *312 btls*.

❖ **Private Cellar Macallan 1987** bott 07 **(75) n**16 **t**20 **f**20 **b**19. Absolutely dreadful nose but pleasantish nuttiness and vanilla-barley on the palate. **43%**.

❖ **Provenance Macallan Aged 8 Years** dist Autumn 98, bott Winter 06 **(90) n**22 sharp, grassy malt and custard tart; **t**22 mouth-watering barley, clean, refreshing if a little simple; **f**23 goes into complexity overdrive **b**23 a faultless, quite stunning cask. **46%**. *Speyside Distillers*.

**Provenance Macallan Aged 10 Years** dist 13 Dec 94, bott 12 Apr 05 **(86) n**21 **t**22 **f**21 **b**22. Naked Macallan, as you may never have seen it before: 10-y-o, not a trace of sherry, a second or even third-fill sherry cask and its maltiness exposed entirely. Fascinatingly delicious. **46%**. *Douglas Laing*.

**Provenance Macallan 12 Years Old** dist Nov 93, bott Feb 06 **(86) n**20 **t**22 **f**22 **b**22. Forget the neutral nose. Just dive into the malt!! **46%**. *McGibbon's*.

❖ **Scotch Malt Whisky Society Cask 24.94 Aged 16 Years** Sherry Butt, dist May 90 **(66) n**17 **t**18 **f**15 **b**16 Sulphured nonsense. **56.6%**

❖ **Scott's Selection Macallan 1985** bott 06 **(86) n**21 **t**23 **f**21 **b**21. Glows on the palate with no shortage of vicious barley. A scrapper. **53%**. *Speyside Distillers*.

❖ **Scott's Selection Macallan 1985** bott 06 **(95) n**24 cider brandy meets bourbon; **t**23 juicy, multi-fruity, shake-your-booty good; **f**24 long with a slow wind-down of spices and varied bourbony notes, including toffee-apple – the bitter-sweet ratio can't be bettered; **b**24 one of the most enjoyable private Macallans for a very long time: complex and exudes uncompromised class. **55.7%**. *Speyside Distillers*.

**Scott's Selection Macallan 1987** bott 05 **(91) n**23 **t**23 **f**22 **b**23. A real youngster for its age, with the freshness of the malt never failing to dazzle. **58.8%**. *Speyside Distillers*.

**Speymalt from Macallan 1973 (88) n**21 **t**22 **f**23 **b**22. A very well-behaved and flawlessly spoken malt that refuses to wallow too self-indulgently in the sherry. **40%**.

❖ **Speymalt from Macallan 1988 (88) n**23 about as delicate barley will ever get; **t**22 the clean lines and soft, buttery barley kiss continue; wonderful bitter-sweet charm **f**21 thins out too rapidly; **b**22 but for the finish this'd be a Must Have. **40%**.

**Speymalt from Macallan 1996 (79) n**21 **t**20 **f**19 **b**19. The nose is a curious embrace between green grape and green malt; the body is pretty uninspiring. **40%**.

**Speymalt from Macallan Distillery 1997** bott 15.06.06 **(85) n**22 **t**22 **f**20 **b**21. Juicy and no shortage of early barley. **40%**. *Gordon & MacPhail. USA*.

**The Vintage House Macallan (93) n**22 the input of European oak is more telling than the wine; the grapiness is gentle in and in tandem with intense barley guarantees a delicate bitter-sweet thrust. Intriguingly, there is even more than a hint of barley wine about this; **t**23 at first intense malt, then a shock wave of dry, fruity oak. Distinctive and beautifully weighted; **f**24 almost immeasurably long, with a fabulous silkiness kissing the roof of the mouth. Very dry and demanding in attention and detail; **b**24 an almost freakish one-off, the style of which I have never encountered before. The quality of the oak is beyond question; the shape and personality of the ensuing confusion will be a good reason for much study. **56.9%**

❖ **Vintage House Macallan Aged 18 Years Gran Reserva Rioja Finish** dist June 88, bott Sept 06 **(90) n**21 subtlety, subtlety, where art thou...? **t**23 brain-exploding delivery of mixed fruit and haphazard spice; the middle eventually finds a sexy rhythm to whivh sweet barley can dance; **f**23 dry but balanced with fruit and nut chocolate; **b**23 bloody hell! The wine – and a dose of blood orange – is splashed over this malt like a cheap perfume. But you can't say there is no allure or eroticism...a malt well suited to London's Soho... **50.1%**. *Douglas Laing for Vintage House*. *244 bottles*.

❖ **Wilson & Morgan Barrel Selection Macallan 1989 Marsala Finish** bott 06 **(89) n**22 weird for Macallan with a profound chocolate and blackcurrant aroma: a first for me... **t**23 hard as bricks delivery but softens as the fruit goes into boiled candy meltdown; **f**22 back to the cocoa again, but with that lingering fruit; **b**22 has "cask finish" written on it from nose to finale. Brownie points for originality – and quality! **46%**

**Wilson & Morgan Barrel Selection Macallan 1991** Refill Sherry dist 91, bott 05 **(86) n**20 **t**22 **f**22 **b**22. Exceptionally easy going. **46%**.

# MACDUFF

## Speyside, 1963. Dewar's. Working

Glen Deveron Aged 10 Years dist 95 db **(83)** n19 t23 f20 **b**21. The enormity of the third and fourth waves on delivery give some idea of the greatness this distillery could achieve perhaps with a little more care with cask selection, upping the strength to 46% and banning caramel. We'd have a malt scoring in the low to mid 90s every time. At the moment we must remain frustrated. **40%**

⊰· Glen Deveron Aged 10 Years (Macduff) dist 96, bott 06 db **(87)** n23 pure honey: a breakfast table spread including hints of marmalade and blackcurrant jam; t21 gentle barley, too gentle perhaps though again the honeys aren't shy to come forward f22 delicate vanilla and a touch of salt **b**21 pussycat whisky. **40%**

Cadenhead's Authentic Collection MacDuff Aged 16 Years dist 89, bott May 05 **(78)** n19 t21 f19 **b**19. Sherried, sweet, oily, mildly phenolic: just doesn't quite work. **59.8%.** *678 btls.*

D&M Connoisseurs' Club Bottling Macduff Aged 15 Years cask no. 7118, dist Dec 90 **(87)** n21 t22 f22 **b**22. Only less than perfect oak manages to lessen the impact of the honey. **59.2%. nc ncf.** *US by Angus Dundee.*

⊰· Duncan Taylor Collection Macduff 1968 Cask no. 8546 **(79)** n19 t19 f21 **b**20. Just a fraction too much oak to win minds as well as hearts. **46.9%**

Duncan Taylor Collection Macduff 1969 cask 3684, dist Apr 69, bott Feb 06 **(78)** n20 t20 f19 **b**19. No shortage of orange...or oak. For those who prefer their scotch bourbony. **59.4%.**

Duncan Taylor Collection Macduff 1969 cask no 3680, dist Apr 69, bott Apr 06 **(79)** n19 t21 f19 **b**20. Has some pleasant, sweet malty and spicy moments. Silky and attractive but just off the pace. **54.9%.** *197 bottles.*

Harris Whisky Co. Macduff Aged 14 Years cask no.1382, dist Mar 91, bott Jan 06 **(94)** n23 clean, green and keen; t24 stunning: mouth-watering barley begins crisp and juicy then adopts the distillery's honeyed style; f23 remains beautifully intense and salivating; vanilla almost apologetically enters the fray. Just so refined and fragile; **b**24 a stunning opening from a new whisky company which, at first attempt has succeeded in showing this under-rated distillery in all its glory and magnificence. As fresh and thirst-quenching as any malt whisky gets. One can only hope the distillery owners take a lead from this. **46%. nc ncf.**

Harris Whisky Co. Macduff Aged 14 Years cask 1383, dist 91, bott Jan 06 **(88)** n21 a dense, busy nose is somewhat claustrophobic but a gooseberry tart fruitiness does emerge; t22 that intenseness is magnified as the barley clusters around the tastebuds leading to something of an oaky cul-de-sac; f23 waves of vanilla and barley sugar; **b**22 this is the sister cask of the above. An although the oak is fractionally less impressive, this remains high quality malt. **58.7%. nc ncf.**

⊰· Harris Whisky Co. Macduff Aged 15 Years Cask no. 1375, dist Mar 91, bott Aug 06 **(92)** n23 not quite the same sheen as the sister cask which is lean, clean and keen. A baffling, distant hint of smoke, though: where on earth has that come from? t23 honey buzzes in by the beehive-full and with the odd spicy sting, too; the mouthfeel is nearly perfect with just the right density of intense barley...and there's that vague smoke again... f22 long, naturally toffeed with a hint of molassed latte; **b**24 I adore this distillery, especially when the honey comes flying through like this. There is unquestionably a tiny amount of smoke mixed up with this: I wonder if the cask once held an Islay...hardly a satisfactory explanation, but can't think of any other. Unless the casks 1375 and 1382 came from different distillations... **59.9%**

⊰· Lonach Macduff 1969 **(92)** n23 a fruit cocktail with a side dish of cold custard; a teasing herbal note complements beautifully; t23 how can something this old be so juicy? Like freshly-squeezed barley sugar; f23 the oak starts gathering forces but such is the depth of the fresh barley it nothing more than complements and balances **b**23 uncompromised star quality throughout. One of those malts that makes writing this book so rewarding...!! **40.6%** *Duncan Taylor.*

⊰· The Single Malts of Scotland Macduff 1991 Aged 16 Years **(88)** n23 custard over rhubarb; t22 bitter-sweet with juicy barley just in control; f21 splintery; **b**22 a malt on the very edge, but the pervading oily sweetness just guarantees excellence. **59.6%. sc.** *Speciality Drinks, UK.*

**Vom Fass MacDuff 23 Years Old (91)** n23 t23 f22 b23 If you ever wondered why William Lawson blends are so damn good, grab hold of this...!! **40%.**

# MANNOCHMORE
### Speyside, 1971. Diageo. Working.

**Mannochmore Aged 12 Years** db **(84)** n22 t21 f20 b21. As usual the mouth arrival fails to live up to the great nose. Quite a greasy dram with sweet malt and bitter oak. **43%.** *Flora and Fauna.*

**Cadenhead's Authentic Collection Mannochmore Aged 14 Years** Sherry butt, dist 92, bott Sept 06 **(95)** n24 top-notch sherry; no off-notes, just sublimely confident and so sexily spiced. Breathtaking...; t24 big, butch and beautiful. The grape is exploding from the glass but this is controlled quality with the barley and liquorice also having a full say; f23 barley-sugar and molasses with strands of grape. Late vanilla and dates; b24 highly unusual rendition of this little-known and criminally under-rated malt and the best I've ever found bottled. **54.6%.** *486 bottles.*

**Connoisseurs Choice Mannochmore 1990 (85)** n20 t22 f21 b22. Perhaps overly sweet and slightly featureless. **46%.** *Gordon & MacPhail.*

**Old Malt Cask Mannochmore 15 Years Old** dist 5 Feb 90, bott Jul 05 **(92)** n23 guava and pears; the fruity opening gives way to improbably soft barley; t24 little more could be asked of a malt this age; the oak remains at bay whilst the barley offers simpering waves of varying sweetness and refinement. Just so damned beautiful!; f22 lazy spice and hints of tangy oak that points to something older than its age; b23 such a gentle, refined dram, you can scarcely believe the strength. **50%.** *Douglas Laing. 339 bottles.*

**Provenance Mannochmore 11 Years Old** dist Jan 95, bott July 06 **(92)** n23 unique and unmistakable Mannoch. Flinty in the style of Glen Grant, but with a trademark weightiness that no more than hints at smoke; t23 textbook barley brittleness and then an outpouring of salivating juiciness; f23 wonderful interplay between barley and vanilla; b23 one of the few botlings I have seen that reflects the quality I find in the blending lab. **46%**

**Provenance Mannochmore Over 12 Years** dist Spring 91, bott Winter 04 **(87)** n23 fluting barley notes that never hit a bum note; textbook clarity and bitter-sweet charm; t22 green and young in part, the mouthwatering elements contrast sharply with the abrupt arrival of chunky oak; f21 more bitter than sweet, the barley-sheen remains profound although the oak has a surprisingly big say; b21 most probably a first-fill bourbon cask to the fore here: it's older than its age should suggest but the all-round complexity is quite wonderful. **46%.**

⋰⋰⋰ **Scotch Malt Whisky Society Cask 64.14 Aged 21 Years** Refill Butt, dist Dec 84 **(93)** n24 bloody hell's teeth! I have just been transported to some Atlantic-battered cove and am sitting beside a crab-ridden rock pool breathing in the salty fumes. What on earth is this nose doing on a Mannochmore...??? Sublime, and a touch fruity, too... t23 fizzy fruits do nothing to interfere with the massive malty overdose; f22 lightly salted and well spiced late on; b24 now and again a whisky turns up that makes you spring from your chair shouting Eureka. This is one such...**60.6%**

# MILLBURN
### Highland (Northern), 1807–1985. Closed.

**Millburn 1969 Rare Malt** db **(77)** n19 t21 f18 b19. Some lovely bourbon-honey touches but sadly over the hill and declining fast. Nothing like as interesting or entertaining as the massage parlour that was firebombed a few yards from my office twenty minutes ago. Or as smoky... **51.3%**

**The Bottlers Millburn 1982 Aged 20 Years** cask 1971 **(78)** n20 t21 f18 b19. The nose reminds me of freshly sharpened school pencils, and although the fruity malt shines for a short while it does, overall, succumb to age. **63%.** *Reaborn Fine Wine.*

**Cadenhead's Millburn 31 Years Old (88)** n22 an attractive sprinkling of fresh sawdust over the very softest of peats and custard tart; t23 lush malt coats the mouth before a bombardment of spicy oak keeps the barley at bay; f21 an oaky echo; b22 a rumbustuous, red-hot affair which is ensuring the distillery is not disappearing with a whimper. Now a must have cask: decent bottlings of any of the old Inverness distilleries are few and far between. **52.3%**

Mackillop's Choice Millburn 1981 cask no. 353, dist Feb 81 **(76)** n18 t18 f21 **b**19. I know some people like this type of sherry style, but I'm afraid to me it strikes a sharp, rancid tone I have major problems with, even if the malt does fight back impressively and stylishly at the very finish. Sorry. If you want to put me up against a wall, I understand. **61.5%.** *Angus Dundee.*

Platinum Selection Millburn Aged 34 Years dist Nov 70, bott 04 **(81)** n22 t19 f20 **b**20. Some pleasantly rich moments, but not faring quite as well as its sister Inverness distillery, Glen Albyn, also lost to us. **50.9%.** *Douglas Laing. 171 bottles.*

# MILTONDUFF
### Speyside, 1824. Chivas. Working.

Miltonduff Aged 15 Years Bott code L00/123 db **(86)** n23 t22 f20 **b**21. Some casks beyond their years have crept in and unsettled this one. But some real big salty moments to savour, too. **46%**

⁘ Adelphi Miltonduff Aged 26 Years Cask no. 12501, dist 1980, bott 06 **(89)** n22 shades of bourbon; nippy, spicy and yummy; t24 brilliant spiced delivery ensures a breathtaking opening; settles with varying layers of mild honey and intense, ultra-clean malt; still retains a bourbony edge f21 a damp squib by comparison but with vanilla aplenty; **b**22 assertive, high quality malt. **45.1%.** *124 bottles.*

⁘ Battlehill Miltonduff 1999 Cask no. 807 **(85)** n21 t22 f21 **b**21. Sturdy malt throughout. **43%.** *Duncan Taylor.*

Cask Strength Miltonduff 1993 Sherry butt no. 9400, dist 17/6/93, bott 21/4/05 **(91)** n21 moist Melton hunt cake; a very distant hint of something sulphurous; t24 the intense, sticky sherry is driven home into the tastebuds partly thanks to the strength. And the experience is stunning!!; f23 more of the same, except now the intensity has gone and the structure of the fruity layers become easier to detect; **b**23 not the easiest distillery to find these day. And G&M have done us proud with a very decent sherry butt (though one or two might detect the most minor flaw). **61.8%.** *Gordon & MacPhail.*

James MacArthur Miltonduff 1994 10 Year Old, bott Apr 05 **(84)** n20 t21 f22 **b**21. Deliciously clean malt with a big sweetness to the fade. **43%**

⁘ Kingsbury's "The Selection" Miltonduff 1999 Refill Hogshead, cask nos. 3571/3572, dist Mar 99, bott July 06 **(79)** n20 t19 f20 **b**20. Not from the most helpful cask but recovers late on with aplomb. **43%. ncf.** *Japan Imports System. 735 bottles.*

Old Malt Cask Miltonduff 20 Years Old dist 13 Jun 84, bott 24 Feb 05 **(89)** n23 t23 f21 **b**22. Another unsubtle reminder of how Allied have shot themselves in the foot over the years by failing to market this, like Ardmore, the way it deserves. **50%.** *Douglas Laing*

Scott's Selection Miltonduff 1987 bott 2005 **(87)** n20 caramel cake; t23 sweet barley strata but a voluminous increase in intensity: a real chewy number; f22 back to caramel notes alongside the powering malt; **b**22 rather a delicious, intense bottling that gets over its inclination towards toffee rather impressively. **58.6%.** *Speyside Distillers.*

# MORTLACH
### Speyside, 1824. Diageo. Working.

Mortlach Aged 16 Years db **(87)** n20 big, big sherry, but not exactly without a blemish or two; t23 sumptuous fruit and then a really outstanding malt and melon mouthwatering rush; f22 returns to heavier duty with a touch of spice, too; **b**22 once it gets past the bold if very mildly sulphured nose, the rest of the journey is superb. Earlier Mortlachs in this range had a slightly unclean feel to them and the nose here doesn't inspire confidence. But from arrival on the palate onwards, it's sure-footed, fruity and even refreshing ... and always delicious. **43%.** *Flora and Fauna range.*

Mortlach 32 Years Old dist 71 db **(88)** n22 t22 f22 **b**22. Big and with attitude.... **50.1%**

Cadenhead's Authentic Collection Mortlach Aged 14 Years 1992 Sherry butt, dist 92, bott Nov 06 **(82)** n22 t21 f19 **b**20. Adore the fruitcake dough nose and a rich sherry purple patch but the rest is typically roughhouse and hot. **58.3%.** *600 bottles.*

Cadenhead's Authentic Collection Mortlach Aged 16 Years dist 88, bott May 05 **(66)** n16 t18 f16 **b**16. Guess what! Spooky! Having just given it 66, I've just spotted there are 666 bottles...well, there had to be when the devil's been so busy with his matches. **58.1%.** *666 bottles.*

**Cask Strength Mortlach 1993** bott 07 July 05 **(79)** n19 t21 f20 b19. An act of bravery by G&M to offer an untreated Mortlach to the world... and they get away with it. The flaws are for all to see, but the intensity of the barley, especially in the eye-watering middle, wins the day. **60.7%.** *G&M, US Market.*

**Chieftain's Mortlach Aged 15 Years** Sherry wood **(69)** n17 t18 f17 b17. This sweet and sulphurous effort is one 69 I don't like.... **46%.** *Ian Macleod.*

⊱⊱ **The Coopers Choice Mortlach 1993 Sherry Wood Aged 13 Years (79)** n20 t21 f19 b19. A bit cluttered but the early yam is interesting. **46%. sc ncf.** *The Vintage Malt Whisky.*

**Craigellachie Hotel Quaich Bar Range Mortlach 12 Years Old** 1st release **(79)** n21 t20 f19 b19. A few moments of barley-rich lucidity, otherwise slightly over-sweet. **46%**

⊱⊱ **Distillery Malt Mortlach Aged 15 Years (69)** n16 t18 f18 b17. Fifteen years ago Mortlach was busy churning out some of Speyside's least impressive whisky. Here's some more of it. **43%.** *Gordon & MacPhail.*

⊱⊱ **Dun Bheagan Mortlach 10 Years Old** dist 96, bott for the Whisky Festival Belgium 07 **(84)** n21 t22 f20 b21. A real malty slugfest with complexity at a premium and the finish little helped by a tired cask. But it's just so great to see this once excellent distillery getting back to being its big, impressive self after so many years in the wilderness. **57.5%. nc ncf.**

**Dun Bheagan Mortlach Aged 11 Years** Port finish **(91)** n23 peaty and porty; t22 soft, barley-led delivery with a thickish amalgam of smoke and wine; f23 complex finale with the smoke drifting into delicious shapes and variants of intensity; b23 unusually smoky with big fruit and sugar. Excellent for a latter-day Mortlach. **43%.** *Ian Macleod.*

⊱⊱ **Dun Bheagan Mortlach 13 Years Old** Hogshead, dist Nov 92 **(77)** n20 t19 f19 b19. Malty but an unsympathetic cask typical of the era. **43%. nc ncf.** *Ian Macleod Distillers.*

**Duncan Taylor Collection Mortlach 1988** cask no 4743, dist Nov 88, bott Nov 05 **(74)** n18 t19 f18 b19. Dirty nose, vicious arrival on palate...but it does have some character. But then so did Billy the Kid... **57.9%.** *632 bottles.*

**Gordon & MacPhail Mortlach 1970 (83)** n23 t21 f19 b20. The nose takes me back to Niger and sumptuous dates; the confused palate and bitter finish returns me to Dufftown....with a bump. **43%.** *Rare Vintage range.*

**Gordon & MacPhail Reserve Mortlach 1991** cask no. 7880, bott 04 **(75)** n18 t20 f18 b19. Generally cloying and dysfunctional. **46%.** *For Juuls Vinhandel, Denmark. 334 bottles.*

⊱⊱ **Kingsbury's "The Selection" Mortlach 1999** Hogshead cask nos. 6444/6445/6446, dist May 99, bott July 06 **(73)** n19 t18 f18 b18. Massively sherried, flat and with little balance. **43%. ncf.** *Japan Imports System. 1,344 botls.*

**Murray McDavid Mortlach 1993 Aged 11 Years** Bourbon/Port, bott 05 **(86)** n21 t22 f22 b21. A way-above-average Mortlach, still mildly flawed from the original cask, I guess. Some of the characteristics I could recreate using a Trinidadian rum as base – and it's those impurities that help make it interesting. **46%. nc ncf.** *1,800 bottles.*

**Norse Cask Selection Mortlach 1994 Aged 10 Years (73)** n19 t18 f18 b18. Not even the citrus can save it. **58.7%.** *QualityWorld, Denmark.*

⊱⊱ **Norse Cask Selection Mortlach 1994 Aged 11 Years** Hogshead cask no. 7825, dist 94, bott 06 **(85)** n21 t22 f21 b21. An ultra-intense barley dominated malt. Some real fresh-picked dank grassiness to this: genuine green shoots to show that Mortlach's just maybe on its way back from a dark period. **58.3%. nc ncf.** *WhiskyOwner.com, Denmark. 274 btls.*

**Old Malt Cask Mortlach Aged 12 Years** dist Sep 92, bott Dec 04 **(72)** n19 t18 f17 b18. A seriously cloying dullard. **50%.** *Douglas Laing.*

⊱⊱ **Old Malt Cask Mortlach Aged 12 Years Sherry Finish** dist July 94, bott May 07 **(72)** n18 t19 f17 b18. Malt ordinaire. **50%.** *Douglas Laing. 654 bottles.*

**Old Masters Mortlach 1989 Aged 16 Years** cask no. 969 **(77)** n19 t20 f19 b19. Furry, bitter, harsh and hot: one of the better Mortlachs from this period... **56.5%.**

**The Peebles Malt Mortlach 12 Years Old (75)** n18 t20 f18 b19. A pleasant honeyed thread does its best to mend the sulphured tear. **43%.** *Villeneuve Wines.*

⊱⊱ **Premier Barrel Mortlach Aged 11 Years** Sherry Finish **(68)** n17 t17 f17 b17. Another victim of the S word. **46%.** *Douglas Laing. 776 bottles.*

⊱⊱ **Private Collection Mortlach 1968 (80)** n19 t21 f20 b20. An opaque malt with the sherry blotting out all further complexity, oak apart. If you like your sherry enormous and clean, here you go... **45%.** *Gordon & MacPhail.*

**Private Collection Mortlach 1968** Sherry hogshead cask no. 4836, dist 25.07.68, bott Mar 06 **(85)** n22 t22 f20 **b21**. Nose within first seconds of pouring – it oxidizes fast!! Fabulous sherry delivery for the first few seconds, then loses control to spicy oak; the late middle and finish is like chewing coffee liquorice allsort and Fisherman's Friend simultaneously. Some beast! **45%**.

**Raeborn Fine Wines Mortlach 1983 18 Years Old** cask 2378 **(87)** n22 t21 f22 **b22**. Uncompromising and almost too big for the glass. **51%**

⋅∴⋅ **Tanners Mortlach Aged 14 Years (69)** n19 t18 f16 **b16**. Chewy and initially sweet but displaying that furry character so typical of Mortlach at this time when the casks were dreadful and strange things were happening in the still house. Why it is used by so many companies as their own label brand is absolutely beyond me. Tanners are a much better merchant than this. **45%**. *Tanners Wine Merchants*.

**Un-Chill Filtered Collection Mortlach Aged 13 Years** Sherry butt 4776, dist 31 May 91, bott 8 Dec 04 **(74)** n19 t20 f17 **b18**. Some honey, but here is a serious case for filtration!! **46%**. **nc ncf**. *Signatory. 831 bottles*.

**Whisky Galore Mortlach 1993 Aged 10 Years (87)** n22 the second fill bourbon cask has left a clear path for the sparkling, apple-juicy, grassy barley; t23 mouthwatering and refreshing barley-sugar; f21 a touch of spice to the barley; **b21** at last! For almost the first time in a decade a Mortlach not screwed by being filled into a cask of the very crappiest order. Wonderful to show what this distillery can really do without someone doing their best to ruin it. Look forward to a few more. **46%**. *Duncan Taylor*.

**Whisky Galore Mortlach Aged 12 Years** dist 93, bott 06 **(84)** n21 t22 f21 **b20**. Even those with a sticky tooth might struggle with this one. Ultra sweet and intense barley that is always attractive and drinkable though complexity suffers. Even so, there are signs that one or two half-drinkable Mortlachs are beginning to surface. Still a long way to go, though. **46%**. **nc ncf**. *Duncan Taylor*.

## MOSSTOWIE
**Speyside, 1964–1981. Two Lomond stills located within Miltonduff Distillery. Now dismantled.**

**Connoisseurs Choice Mosstowie 1975 (85)** n22 t21 f20 **b22**. A busy dram with massive malt influence. **40%**. *Gordon & MacPhail*.

**Connoisseurs Choice Mosstowie 1979 (86)** n20 t23 f22 **b21**. Not the most complex of drams, but the weight of the malt is amazing: not entirely unlike an old-fashioned Scottish heavy ale but in sweeter form. **40%**. *Gordon & MacPhail*.

**Rarest of the Rare Mosstowie 1975** cask no. 5814, dist May 75, bott Apr 06 **(88)** **n22** takes time to open out; perfumed braised apples eventually arrive; **t22** soft barley delivery with lovely tags of honey; **f22** delicate vanillas sit comfortably with the laid-back barley and soft oils; **b22** a wonderful surprise: the nose at first indicated that it might be beyond greatness. Not a bit of it – a rare treat, indeed! **48.1%**. *Duncan Taylor. 191 bottles*.

⋅∴⋅ **Rarest of the Rare Mosstowie Aged Over 29 Years** Cask no. 5812, dist May 75, bott Sept 04 **(80)** n23 t20 f18 **b19**. Rare as hens' teeth this may be, but it has now reached the point where the style and identity of the distillery has been lost, sacrificed on an oaky altar. Enough fruit and spice for some enjoyable interludes, though, and given time to oxidise the nose is outstanding. **44.5%**. **nc ncf**. *Duncan Taylor. 161 bottles*.

## NORTH PORT
**Highland (Eastern), 1820–1983. Demolished.**

**Brechin 1977** db **(78)** n19 t21 f18 **b20**. Fire and brimstone was never an unknown quantity with the whisky from this doomed distillery. Some soothing oils are poured on this troubled – and sometimes attractively honeyed – water of life. **54.2%**

**Cadenhead's Chairman's Stock North Port (Brechin) Aged 29 Years** Bourbon Hogshead, dist 77, bott Sept 06 **(83)** n21 t21 f20 **b21**. Fishermen's Friend cough sweets by the bag-load. Hints of hotness but pretty good for this usually harsh and unforgiving malt. **51.4%**. *174 bottles*.

**Connoisseurs Choice North Port-Brechin 1981 (89)** n22 t23 f21 b23. Is this really North Port? My mouth isn't on fire and I'm still alive. What's going on? Easily the best bottled NP I've come across in over 20 years. **43%**. *Gordon & MacPhail.*

**The Whisky Fair North Port Aged 25 Years** Sherry wood, dist Apr 81, bott Apr 06 **(85)** n22 t21 f21 b21. A brave malt for any small outfit to bottle. Rips out only about half the tastebuds – great going by Brechin standards – but those left functioning will detect a genuine honey deliciousness. **56.1%. nc ncf.** *Germany. 120 bottles.*

## OBAN
**Highland (Western), 1794. Diageo. Working.**

**Oban 14 db (84)** n20 t22 f21 b21. Slick and fruity, you can close your eyes and think of Jerez. Oban seems a long way away. A very decent dram. But I want my old, bracing, mildly smoky, fruitless Oban back!! Those who prefer malts with a sheen, sweet and with enormous fruit depth won't be disappointed. **43%**

**Oban 20 Years Old** dist 84 db **(89)** n21 large oak but kept in check by salt, pepper and malt; t23 buttery on arrival, and then an explosion of massive and pretty sharp malt. Sweet mallows balance out the oak; f23 French toast and hints of light roast coffee; b22 wonderfully complex and challenging. A west coast treat. **57.9%**

## OLD RHOSDHU ( see Loch Lomond)

## PITTYVAICH
**Speyside 1975–1993. Closed.**

**Pittyvaich Aged 12 Years** db **(64)** n16 t18 f15 b15. It was hard to imagine this whisky getting worse. But somehow it has achieved it. From fire-water to cloying undrinkability. What amazes me is not that this is such bad whisky: we have long known that Pittyvaich can be as grim as it gets. It's the fact they bother bottling it and inflicting it on the public. Vat this with malt from Fettercairn and neighbouring Dufftown and you'll have the perfect dram for masochists. Or those who have entirely lost the will to live. Jesus.... **43%.** *Flora and Fauna.*

**Pittyvaich Aged 12 Years** (new stock circa 03 – bott no. L19R01941144, dark brown print) db **(84)** n22 t21 f20 b21. For a dram that will tear your throat out as soon as look at you, this has been tempered dramatically by the use of some exceptionally clean sherry casks which show to their best on the nose. Pittyvaich in a form I thought I'd never see it in my lifetime ... drinkable! And deliciously so. **43%.** *Flora and Fauna range.*

⋯ **Cadenhead's Pittyvaich 21 Years Old (68)** n18 t17 f16 b17. God help us...any Port in a storm, but little respite from the crashing waves of red-hot barley. **54.3%**

**Connoisseurs Choice Pittyvaich 1993 (79)** n21 t20 f19 b19. Decent, simple barley... though subdued: it is if the malt knows that it from the last year it was ever made. **43%**

**Duncan Taylor Collection Pittyvaich 1979** cask no. 5631, dist Apr 79, bott Feb 06 **(79)** n19 t20 f20 b20. Like an old lag who's done his time: obviously a bit rough around the edges, from the lower classes, and has relished a few scraps in his time but now, in old age, has a certain defiant dignity. **52.3%.** *189 bottles.*

⋯ **Provenance Pittyvaich Aged 12 Years** dist Winter 94, bott Winter 06 **(74)** n19 t20 f17 b18. Woefully thin, though clean: not bad by Pittyvaich's usual terrible standards. To nose this is still to become a glue-sniffer, though, while the finish is the usual firewater. **46%**

## PORT ELLEN
**Islay, 1825–1983. Closed.**

**Port Ellen 1979** db **(93)** n22 mousy and retiring; a degree of oak fade and fruit on the delicate smoke t23 non-committal delivery but bursts into stride with a series of sublime, peat-liquorice waves and a few rounds of spices; f24 a surprising gathering of oils rounds up the last traces of sweet barley and ensures an improbably long – and refined – finish; b24 takes so long to get out of the traps, you wonder if anything is going to happen. But when it does, my word...it's glorious! **57.5%**

**Port Ellen 24 Years Old** dist 79, bott 03 db **(90)** n23 t24 f21 b22. Pow!! Port Ellen at something over its usual 35ppm phenols here, acting like a 50ppm monster. On a blind tasting I'd swear it was Lagavulin! **57.3%.** *9,000 bottles.*

⁖ **Port Ellen 27 Years Old** Special Release 2006, dist 78 db **(94)** n25 the peat appears marinated the in the softest vanilla and spice possible. A near perfect score...oh, what the hell!! t24 sweet delivery: the peat alternates with soft Demerara for custody of the middle ground; spices abound; f22 fades somewhat but the death is slow and vanilla-etched; b23 a luxurious malt and worth an hour of anybody's valuable time. **54.2%**

**Port Ellen 4th Release Aged 25 Years** dist 78, bott 04 **(95)** n22 much less smoky than previous release, with greater emphasis on fruit, especially cinnamon-sprinkled apple. The oak offers perhaps the firmest thread, marginally threatening to dominate; t25 just so, so stunning! The immaculate balance between the peat-malt and oak hits home from the very first second. Somehow, after 25 years, it has retained the trademark gristiness with the peat being released in controlled waves. Hints of honey help fend off any advancement of oak, and the threat from the nose never materialises. Instead there is a steady throbbing of perfect spices; f24 honey-vanilla and more lapping waves of peat and spice bring a gentle end to proceedings...eventually; b24 for those of us who can remember it in its original younger form, this is almost something to give you a lump in the throat and a watery eye: it remains just so true to character and form, cocking the most elegant and contemptuous snook at those who decided to kill the distillery off. When they closed the distillery I remember being told by the decision-makers there was no difference in quality between PE and Caol Ila. I disagreed then, strongly. Today, my argument is mute: the eloquence belongs to the contents of this bottle. **56.2%. 5,100 bottles.**

⁖ **Chieftain's Port Ellen 24 Years** Old Hogshead, dist June 82 **(89)** n22 it appears most of the smoke has escaped from the cask over the last quarter of a century, leaving behind something attractively oaky and nutty; t23 incredibly sweet malt with the usual gristy appeal, plus a touch of oil; the peat barely registers; f22 chalky vanilla and a drizzle of smoke; b22 low-key smoke and very sweet. **59.4%. nc ncf.** *Ian Macleod.*

**Dun Bheagan Port Ellen 23 Years Old** db **(94)** n23 soft grist and vanilla; a touch of lime and the gentlest of smoke; t23 salivating, fresh barley; minimal oak interference allowing a slow crescendo of peat; f24 it appears relatively short, but if you listen, the gentle smoke rumbles on almost relentlessly; b24 Port Ellen in aspic. One of the most delicate Islays of this age to hit the market in years. **45.9%.** *Ian Macleod.*

⁖ **John Milroy Selection Port Ellen 1982 (85)** n21 t22 f21 b21. Camp coffee with no little oak. **56.8%**

**Old Malt Cask Port Ellen 22 Years Old** dist Mar 83, bott Sept 05 **(87)** n22 t22 f21 b22. An almost identical pea from an identical pod as the Provenance 22-y-o below. Spooky!! This one is perhaps a shade smokier and juicier. **50%.** *Douglas Laing. 659 bottles.*

⁖ **Old Malt Cask Port Ellen 23 Years Old** dist Mar 83, bott Oct 06 **(90)** n21 almost a crusty, Bowmore-style Fisherman's Friend bite to this, possibly thanks to the grape; t23 significant fruit kick which blends in well with the growling smoke; f23 the arrival of late muscovado sugar injects balance and brio, as does a surge in buzzing spice; b23 another one that takes time to really get to appreciate. Once you are there, what a treat...! **50%.** *549 btls.*

⁖ **Old Malt Cask Port Ellen Aged 23 Years** dist Feb 83, bott Nov 06 **(95)** n24 ground black pepper: every noseful of this produces the need to sneeze; the smoke is of just about perfect sweet/dry proportions t24 equally sublime bitter-sweet balance on arrival with a wonderful, chewy, gristy middles; some spice, but nothing like that threatened on the nose f23 long, smoked liquorice and oak dipped in watered down golden syrup; b24 a magical cask not to be sneezed at!! **50%.** *Douglas Laing. 541 bottles.*

**Old Malt Cask Port Ellen Aged 25 Years** dist 8 Sept 78, bott 6 Apr 05 **(84)** n20 t21 f22 b20. A curious bipolar attack of bourbon and peat on both nose and palate never quite harmonises, but the intensity of the smoked mocha is some treat. Very oily for a Port Ellen. **50%.** *Douglas Laing.*

⁖ **Old Malt Cask Port Ellen Aged 25 Years Sherry Finish** dist Feb 82, bott Mar 07 **(80)** n20 t21 f19 b20. Mouth filling, lightly smoked, sweet...and a tad furry. **50%.** *670 btls.*

**Old Malt Cask Port Ellen 25 Years Old** dist Nov 80, bott Apr 06 **(95)** n24 on the brink of perfection, there is a complexity to the peat that almost defies description. Those who know Fishermen's Friends cough sweets will recognise one direction it takes; there is a heathery angle to this equally. Beautiful weight and poise, this is ancient elegance; t24 melt-in-the-mouth peats with the trademark gristy barley even after all these years. Soft oils develop and expand slowly; f23 long, showing a degree of age, but the lines show maturity and grace rather than evidence of seismic turbulence. Helped along the way by some sweetened cocoa and soft vanilla; **b**24 Quite stunning; a malt to stir the emotions. How wonderful to find this truly great old distillery's whisky in a cask which allows all its natural character to sparkle. A treasure. And from this distillery, there can't be too many left... **50%**. *Douglas Laing. 201 bottles.*

**Old Malt Cask Port Ellen 26 Years Old** dist 15 May 79, bott Jul 05 **(89) n**24 light and exceptionally gristy: it is like sticking your head in a Porteus; **t**23 melt-in-the-mouth, delicate and again the grist is simply filling every last crevice with smoke and sweet barley. A joy; **f**20 rather tired as the oak bites slowly and bitterly; **b**22 a docile but proud old malt that has had a great innings, has some splendid stories to tell on the palate and is awaiting the great Spirit Receiver in the sky. A dram to salute. **50%**. *332 bottles.*

**Old Malt Cask Port Ellen 26 Years Old** dist Nov 79, bott Jul 06 **(83) n**22 **t**21 **f**19 **b**21. An odd bird, this. Chopped tobacco on nose and (I guess) delivery. There are some real mouth-watering moments, but the malt never seems to relax or find a rhythm, especially at the finish. **50%**. *Douglas Laing. 602 bottles.*

**Old Malt Cask Port Ellen 26 Years Old (92) n**24 fantastic mix of coal-peat ashes and malt kiln. Amazing...; **t**24 lively, fresh barley hits the salivation button first time; the peat is firm but keeps to the background; spices ping around happily; **f**21 oak rubs out some of the barley's finer points, though soft peat continues; **b**23 even after 26 years, this Port Ellen is still doing all it can to keep its unique, gristy style. There is such grace and near defiance in each mouthful I could almost weep! **50%**. *Douglas Laing.*

⬩⬩⬩ **Old Malt Cask Port Ellen Aged 26 Years Rum Finish** dist Dec 79, bott Nov 06 **(87) n**22 brittle, jagged smoke; **t**21 tight barley, entirely encased in a sugar-sheened oakiness; the smoke lurches about; there is a distinctive rum tenet to the overall shape; **f**22 glassy, softly sugared latte; **b**22 a very different, crisper, sweeter-edged PE than you might have seen before. **50%**. *Douglas Laing. 342 bottles.*

⬩⬩⬩ **Parkers Whisky Port Ellen 1982 "Pert mELLon" Bottling** bott 07 **(96) n**24 when God invented peaty whisky, I think he had something like this in mind for the nose: the intertwining of smoke and oak is rarely bettered; **t**25 early spices, but the star again is the just-so proportioned smoke to oak, then the weighty liquorice surge; a light shower of Demerara sugar ensures balance and charm. Yep: this is as good as it gets! **f**23 tannins and vanillins abound as the smoke tires, but that late Demerara does the trick in keeping away any threat of old age; **b**24 don't know about "Pert Mellons". But this is so arousing in many other ways. A true classic. **56.8%**. *Parker's Whisky, UK. 220 bottles.*

⬩⬩⬩ **Platinum Port Ellen Aged 27 Years** dist 79, bott 07 **(91) n**22 very light with clipped peat; **t**23 brittle, sweet barley; **f**23 remains juicy with an extra squirt of barley sugar and smokin' grist; **b**23 not entirely unlike the style of rum-cask malt. Understated and as delicate as old peated Islay ever gets. **57.1%**. *Douglas Laing. 258 bottles.*

**Provenance Port Ellen 21 Years Old** dist 3 Nov 82, bott 30 Jun 04 **(94) n**25 a miraculous nose entirely intact after all these years and for all the peat: apples and pears thin out the smoke, but it's all in perfect proportions and as enticing and delicate as a sexy 21-year-old can be; **t**22 soft layers of peat, but some oak has been given a slight head start; soft fruits sweeten things; **f**24 the tastebuds are caressed by the softest march-past of saluting peat you'll ever see; **b**23 distilled from smoked feathers.... **46%**

**Provenance Port Ellen 22 Years Old** dist Mar 83, bott Aug 05 **(87) n**22 unusual oils for a PE; cold kilns; **t**22 delicate lime and honey and lazy smoke; **f**21 bitter cocoa; **b**22 understated, lightly smoked, though much to chew on. **46%**

⬩⬩⬩ **Provenance Port Ellen Aged 23 Years** dist Winter 83, bott Winter 06 **(89) n**24 playful, teasing, gristy smoke binds the oak and barley beautifully: what complexity and weight! **t**22 surprising oils help the smoke cling to the roof of the mouth whilst the peats nibble and tickle the tastebuds **f**21 just a shade on the sweet, ungainly side; **b**22 despite some obvious oak intrusion this gorgeous expression stays the course delightfully. In style, almost a vatting of Caol Ila and PR – which is a tad ironic! **46%**. *Douglas Laing.*

⬩⬩⬩ **The Queen of the Moorlands Rare Cask Port Ellen 1982** bott 07 **(90) n**23 a dexterous, highly complex nose, at first seeming flat and graped to death but on warming the slow unravelling of vanilla and peat makes for a heady mixture.. **t**22 silky, grape-led delivery with slow evolution of smoke; **f**22 sweetens with sultana and gentle gristy peat **b**23 one of those whiskies you really have to take your time over and concentrate on. Take straight, without thinking; you might not be too excited. Peruse it, and you might just be very pleasantly surprised... **46%. nc ncf**. *The Wine Shop, Leek & Congleton, and Islay Whisky Shop.*

⦂⦂⦂ **The Whisky Fair Port Ellen Aged 25 Years** Sherry Wood, dist 1982, bott 07 **(94)** n23 plasticine and peat; coke-smoke, too; t24 delivery of soft barley first, then a wonderful wave of peat breaks over the palate; the sweetness continues to grow but vanilla keeps it within reason; f23 long, slightly peppered with some liquorice and hickory adding to the Demerara-sweetened coffee...and the smoke keeps coming... b24 an enchanting malt which captures many of the delicate – and powerful – facets of this late distillery's personality. **59.6%**

**The Whisky Fair Port Ellen 27 Years Old** dist May 78 **(89)** n22 mildly over-oaked, soft peats and butterscotch tart...with lots of crust; t23 delightful interplay between a valiantly gisty peatiness and encroaching vanilla; f22 sweetens and oils out surprisingly well though some burnt toast creeps in; b22 just starting to creak with age. But still fabulous malt. **52.3%**. *Germany. 198 bottles.*

## PULTENEY
### Highland (Northern), 1826. Inver House. Working.

**Old Pulteney Aged 12 Years** db **(82)** n20 t22 f20 b20. Much changed from the old bottlings, with greater emphasis on early brown sugar sweetness. Sadly, the finish remains dull. **40%** ☺ ☺

**Old Pulteney Aged 12 Years** db **(88)** n22 t23 f21 b22. Now this is much, much closer to what I expect from this outstanding distillery! **43%**

**Old Pulteney 15 Years Old** cask 2341 db **(91)** n22 toasty, almost like old parchment. The balancing sweetness is like French toast (on brown bread); t24 mesmerising mouth arrival: subtle citrus ranging from kumquats to lime and then wave upon wave of pounding oak, softened by something very slightly peated; f22 hints of vanilla and lime; b23 this distillery is genuinely one of the little-known, undiscovered gems of Scotland. Your reward for finding it is this: from the second cask ever sold in bottle form to visitors to the distillery. It is a better dram all round than the first! **62.8%**

⦂⦂⦂ **Old Pulteney Aged 15 Years** db **(91)** n21 pretty harsh and thin at first but some defter barley notes can be detected; t24 an attention-grabbing, eye-wateringly sharp delivery with the barley in roasty mood and biting immediately with a salty incision; the barley-sugar effect is mesmerising and the clarity astonishing for its age; f23 long, with those barley sugars working overtime; a slight salty edge there but the oak behaves impeccably; b23 only on about the fourth or fifth mouthful do you start getting the picture here: enormously complex with a genuine coastal edge to this. The complexity is awesome. **54.9%**

**Old Pulteney Aged 15 Years Old Single Cask Selection** cask 2340, dist 23 Jun 89, bott 23 Jun 04 db **(88)** n22 sharp, clean and lively; citrus abounds, with salty, bourbony notes adding further riches; t23 every bit as busy and biting as the nose suggests, only with more oil and much earlier oak than you might expect, even a hint of smoke seems to be in there, a little hot, maybe, but forgivably so; f21 long, with lashings of dark chocolate; b22 a mouthful of a dram that is delightful reward for making the long trip north. **63.2%**. *Available exclusively from distillery where drawn directly from cask.*

**Old Pulteney Aged 17 Years** db **(76)** n19 t20 f18 b19. Oh dear! Some pretty tired casks have been rolled up to the trough here. Cotton wool dry at death and not remotely representative of how this great distillery should be at this age. **46%** ☺ ☺

**Old Pulteney Cask Strength Sherry Wood 18 Years Old** cask 1500 db **(91)** n22 sharp sherry; spiced fruitcake; t22 early fresh sherry, ultra-clean green grape and lumps of brown sugar; f24 mildly bitter at first and then a clarion call of spices reverberating around the palate; b23 a malt that cleverly builds up into something a little special. **58.8%**

**Old Pulteney Aged 21 Years** db **(82)** n19 t22 f21 b21. A little less spice than of old, more estery apple but still feeling the strain. Some excellent moments, though. **46%** ☺ ☺

⦂⦂⦂ **Old Pulteney Aged 23 Years Bourbon** db **(84)** n20 t22 f21 b21. For all its great age there is a lethargy to this malt which doesn't quite work on the nose but does on the body. Intense malt, but at this age perhaps the complexity should be higher. **46%**

⦂⦂⦂ **Old Pulteney Aged 23 Years Sherry** db **(89)** n22 Party Ring biscuits and the softest of crushed raisin; t22 wonderful bitter-sweet/barley-sherry balance; an unusual style and mouthfeel with spices prominent early on; f22 again, superbly relaxed delivery of fruit before the coffee cream; dries with aplomb; **b**23 highly stylish. Not a single note out of tune. **46%**

Old Pulteney Cask Strength Sherry Wood 1983 cask 929 db **(85) n**23 **t**21 **f**20 **b**21. After the pungent sherry nose a touch too predictable on the palate. **58.4%**

Cadenhead's Authentic Collection Pulteney Aged 15 years dist 90, bott May 06 **(87) n**21 malty, but bourbon in there, too, as oak takes a firm grip; **t**22 seriously concentrated malt with lashing of oaky spice; **f**22 a defter, more subtle finale with a touch of custard to soften the spice; **b**22 in your face oak but such is the enormity of the barley it works well. Big stuff though not exactly what you expect from this distillery. **59.5%.** *228 bottles.*

Duncan Taylor Pulteney 1977 cask no. 1377, dist July 77, bott Nov 05 **(78) n**19 **t**20 **f**19 **b**20. Does its best not to be too oaky, but fails gallantly. **58.6%.**

⋮⋮ Duncan Taylor Collection Pulteney 1977 Cask no. 3976 **(88) n**21 quite soupy with thick oak lightened by salted barley; **t**23 brilliant recovery with the juicy barley and spice battling for supremacy; extremely rich with a coppery, metallic texture; **f**22 the slight saltiness returns; fabulous touches of Blue Mountain; the fade is pure vanilla **b**22 no doubting the class on show here. **55.9%**

⋮⋮ Duncan Taylor Collection Pulteney 1989 Cask no. 10260 **(91) n**22 punchy, salty barley; **t**24 enormous explosion of spicy – almost hot – barley that is sharp and almost ridiculously clean for its age; **f**22 remains mouth-watering even as the hickory arrives; **b**23 displays all the lucidity and verve missing from the distillery bottling at this age. **58%**

Gordon & MacPhail Old Pulteney 1969 **(92) n**24 aroma freshly prepared in the kitchen: slivers of cucumber, an orange and passion fruit puree, all topped with vanilla. Mmmm!!; **t**23 the mouthfeel is simply glorious, as is the slowly building intensity of the barley; toasty oaky notes offer an early vanilla and mocha counter; **f**22 medium length with more of the same; **b**23 one of those casks that threatens to go over the oaky edge, but keeps stepping back from the precipice at the very last moment. Sheer class from good ole G&M! **43%.**

⋮⋮ Private Collection Old Pulteney Sauterne Wine Finish dist 1994 **(74) n**17 **t**20 **f**18 **b**19. Some decent juiciness on arrival. But what is the French for sulphur...? **45%.** *G&M.*

Scott's Selection Pultney 1977 bott 05 **(88) n**22 **t**23 **f**21 **b**22. Some wonderful depth, but a cask dumped just in the nick of time. **55.9%.** *Speyside Distillers.*

Whisky Galore Pulteney 1989 cask no. 10254, dist Jan 89, bott Jun 05 **(89) n**22 a touch of apple to the barley; **t**23 mouth-watering and intense malt with some early spices; **f**22 remains tingling and a drop of oil adds length; **b**22 not too dissimilar to cask 10256, except this shows a touch more oil and less complexity. Still a beauty, though. **46.1%.** *Duncan Taylor. 161 bottles.*

Whisky Galore Pulteney 1989 cask no. 10256 **(91) n**22 a touch of oak and sea air amid the vivid barley; **t**23 excellent clarity and deftness of touch to the barley; mouth-watering and massively fresh and lip-smacking; **f**23 some lovely salt is detectable amid the golden syrup; a touch of spice with the developing cocoa; **b**23 what a wonderfully bright portrait of this great distillery. **46%.** *Duncan Taylor.*

# ROSEBANK
### Lowland 1840–1993. Closed. (But if there is a God will surely one day re-open.)

Rosebank Aged 12 Years db **(95) n**24 strands of honey and honeycomb entwine around a softly herbal, but enormously weighted maltiness: the type of   nose you can stick your head in and wallow about for a few minutes; **t**24 this has to be near perfection in regard to texture and not far off with the way the honeypolished malt trips around the palate with an almost apologetic spiciness for accompaniment. Just so accomplished and breathtaking; **f**23 long, more honeycomb, with hints of liquorice and soft herbs; **b**24 infinately better than the last F&F bottling, this is quite legendary stuff, even better then the old 8-y-o version, though probably a point or two down regarding complexity. The kind of whisky that brings a tear to the eye...for many a reason.... **43%.** *Flora and Fauna.*

Rosebank 22 Years Old Rare Malts 2004 db **(85) n**22 **t**23 **f**19 **b**21. One or two Rosebank moments of joyous complexity but, hand on heart, this is simply too old. **61.1%**

Berry's Own Selection Rosebank 1990 Aged 15 Years **(93) n**23 elegant, wispy barley; playful, perfectly weighted oak; barely ripened greengages and the most distant echo of coriander and....juniper?; **t**24 oh yeah, baby! Just honey me...!!!; **f**23 those beautiful waves of honey which saturate the tastebuds from the very first moment carry on, only allowing through unsweetened custard and a dash of rhubarb juice (honestly – see for yourself!); **b**23 if there is a woman in your life who says she doesn't like whisky, give her a shot of this: she'll be addicted for life. **46%**

**Cadenhead's Authentic Collection Rosebank Aged 15 Years** dist 89, bott Feb 05 **(88)** **n**21 **t**24 **f**21 **b**22. Shows signs of exhaustion towards the end, but the early complexity is awesome. **56.1%**. *318 bottles.*

**Cadenhead's Authentic Collection Rosebank Aged 16 Years** dist 89, bott Sep 05 **(87)** **n**22 fresh barley, fresh grass, freshly sawn tree; **t**23 voluptuous malt offering the normal honey sweetness and depth; the middle is a bit fuzzy due to some unexpected oils; **f**21 the oil hangs around to blur the oak/barley interplay; **b**21 the oiliest Rosebank I've seen for a long time. The result is a slight dip in complexity. **55.3%**. *294 bottles.*

**Cadenhead's Rosebank 17 years Old (90) n**22 a teasing spice buzz to this; **t**23 the hallmark honey takes little time to say hullo; **f**22 lovely fade, which is slow and befitting the gentle, yet quietly intense nature, of this lovely malt; **b**23 well mannered, gentle and classy. **54.2%**

⠶⠶ **Cadenhead's Rosebank 18 Years Old** Bourbon Hogshead, dist 1989, bott May 07 **(84) n**21 **t**22 **f**20 **b**21. Another example of this great distillery bowing too low to the intruding oak. There are moments of indisputable class here. But it's the relentlessness of the oak against the usual magic (and defiant) citrus which persists on the palate here. And as this lost whisky gets older and older, we will have to get used to it. **54.2%**. *294 bottles.*

**Cask Strength Rosebank 1990** Sherry butt nos. 1605/1606, dist 27.6.90, bott 30.3.06 **(95) n**24 confident, structured and beautifully balanced: nothing too sweet or dry despite the powering barley; **t**24 like the nose, perfect structure: controlled acacia honey, barley that is far more mouth-watering than can be possible for its age and a softening marriage of natural toffee and spices which add further solidity; **f**23 layers of vanilla of varying intensity; a late gristy maltiness and a deft sprinkling of muscovado sugar; **b**24 another cask which reinforces the fact that Rosebank has to be one of the top ten distilleries in the world. So why is it silent? **61.1%**. *Gordon & MacPhail.*

⠶⠶ **Chieftain's Rosebank Aged 16 Years** Hogshead, dist June 90 **(88) n**23 a pot pourri of spices and dank petals lean towards the oak with wisps of honey radiate from the barley; **t**23 a sublime landing of gently oiled barley dipped in maple syrup; the interplay is almost too gentle to bear; **f**21 barley and vanilla guide us to a delicate finish; **b**21 perhaps not the most complex Rosebank, but the charm is bewitching. **46%**. **nc ncf.** *Ian Macleod.*

⠶⠶ **Connoisseurs Choice Rosebank 1991 (88) n**22 lovely interplay between ripe gooseberry and peach. Delicate and subtle; **t**23 again the delivery is soft and feather-light: the oaks arrive and dissolve with the gristy barley; the bitter-sweet balance is quite perfect; **f**21 much drier with the emphasis on chalky oak; **b**22 a shade too old to be a superstar Rosebank, perhaps, but the overall charm beguiles. **40%**. *Gordon & MacPhail.*

**The Coopers Choice Rosebank 1992 Sherry Wood 14 Years Old (72) n**17 **t**19 **f**18 **b**18. Gooseberries, barley and sulphur. This is spooky: it could almost be the Chieftain's 14…!!! Except this has slightly more sulphur. Otherwise, peas in a pod! **46%**. *The Vintage Malt Whisky.*

**Chieftain's Rosebank Aged 14 Years** Hogshead **(75) n**18 **t**20 **f**18 **b**19. A fascinating unification of barley and gooseberries try to fight through the a sulphur-type off-note. Such is the brilliance of this spirit, it nearly wins… **46%**.

**Connoisseurs Choice Rosebank 1990 (86) n**23 **t**23 **f**20 **b**21. A delicious but frustrating Rosebank that for a brief moment threatens greatness but never achieves it. **40%**.

**Dun Bheagan Rosebank Aged 13 Years** Bourbon Barrel dist 91, bott 05 **(82) n**20 **t**22 **f**20 **b**21. A whiff of smoke helps iron out some of the oaky creases. **46%**. *600 bottles.*

**Dun Bheagan Rosebank 14 Years Old (91) n**23 it is as you are standing in between the doors of two shops – one a florist , the other a confectioner; **t**24 the most ingratiating arrival imaginable: the barley is about as intense as it gets, yet a perfect harmonization between oak and honey adds an extra weight and ferocity you wouldn't believe; toffee and Demerara-sweetened coffee towards the late middle; **f**21 lots of natural caramels dampens the fun; **b**23 a bold Rosebank this is slightly off the wall. But superb! **46%**. *Ian Macleod.*

∷· **Dun Bheagan Rosebank 15 Years Old** dist July 91 **(83)** n21 t22 f20 b20. Has extracted every last ounce of natural caramel from the wood it can find which somewhat dulls the finale. But the arrival offers fleeting moments of delight. **46%. nc ncf.**

**Murray McDavid Mission Rosebank 1989** Bourbon/Guigal **(91)** n22 moist earth; spiced, tangy lime peel; t22 the enormity of the barley-fruit takes time to sink in – and unravel on the palate. A real mess at first but sanity arrives with some structured barley-vanilla waves thinning out the thudding fruit; f24 now a gentlemanly and refined procession of complex oak-dusted and gently spiced and alternating waves of barley and apricot; b23 Rosebank as you have never before seen it... **55.3%**

**Old Malt Cask Rosebank 12 Years Old** dist 26 Mar 93, bott 15 Jun 05 **(79)** n21 t21 f18 b19. Attractively gristy but a touch bitter and fragile. **50%.** *Douglas Laing.*

**Old Malt Cask Rosebank Aged 15 Years** dist July 90, bott Sept 05 **(90)** n21 gooseberry perhaps, but a little closed – clean malt apart; t23 that's more like it: a silky delivery followed by a continual upping of barley intensity, topped with the softest hint of honey; f23 long and luxurious with that intense barley continuing to pulse with wonderful Java/Indian low roast blend seeing you through to the finish; b23 yet another glorious example of a great distillery. **50%.** *Douglas Laing. 242 bottles.*

∷· **Old Malt Cask Rosebank Aged 16 Years** Refill Hogshead DL 2057, dist June 90, bott Aug 06 **(80)** n22 t21 f18 b19. This fantastic old distillery just didn't have it in its armoury to go out and make old whiskies: Rosebank was always a very fast-maturing malt. This still retains echoes of genius, but the oak is simply too pervasive. **50%.** *Douglas Laing. 357 bottles.*

∷· **Old Malt Cask Rosebank Aged 16 Years Claret Finish** dist June 90, bott Mar 07 **(85)** n22 t23 f19 b21. I must admit to not being much of a Claret finish man: however this one works, up to a point. The bottlers had recognised that the original oak had probably gone a shade too far, and there is evidence of this on the finish. But the delivery in particular thrusts together, in perfect unison, very fresh fruits with bludgeoning barley. **50%.** *263 btls.*

**Old Malt Cask Rosebank 16 Years Old Rum Finish** dist July 90, bott Sept 06 **(85)** n22 t21 f21 b21. Unrecognisable as Rosebank with the usual complexity reduced significantly and bogged down in a most un-Rosebank-ish sugary squabble. Still a pretty cultured dram. **50%.** *Douglas Laing. 358 bottles.*

**Old Malt Cask Rosebank 23 Years Old** dist 26 Feb 81, bott 17 Jan 05 **(94)** n24 primroses, bluebells, the uplifting if slightly earthy aroma of a northfacing summer garden; t24 the only Lowlander that offers such glorious weight, the pristine malt seducing the tastebuds with its faultless estery riches; f23 enormous depth with a wonderful crescendo of spice; b23 sublime Rosebank: quite extraordinary for its age. **50%**

**Old Malt Cask Rosebank 28 Years Old** dist July 90 **(91)** n24 big oak, but the fabulous Kentucky/Canadian charge is met by stout marzipan-topped fruitcake resistance; t23 beautifully sweet with molten Demerara and boiled plums; f22 a darker, drier, oakier experience all round; b22 good grief! I forgot anyone ever kept Rosebank this long! Usually a malt is at its best when young though the odd old 'un does surface, and usually with excellent results. This is no exception. **50%. nc ncf sc.**

**Provenance Rosebank 11 Years Old** **(79)** n19 t22 f19 b19. Slightly soapy on the nose: the old cask refuses to further the malt's complexity. **46%.**

**Provenance Rosebank 12 Years Old** dist Mar 93, bott July 05 **(87)** n24 if all whiskies had a nose like this, this Bible would never get finished! A bowl of fruits arranged by angels. One of the most delicate noses of the year; t22 shame just doesn't quite translate as well onto the palate as the lack of oak fails to reinforce the brittle barley; f21 a sprinkling of vanilla and spice; b20 the nose is a legend: what follows is perhaps just a little too delicate. **46%.** *McGibbon's.*

**Provenance Rosebank Aged Over 12 Years** Refill Hogshead DMG 1907, dist Spring 93, bott Summer 05 **(91)** n22 fresh grist enlivened by diced apple and pear t23 wonderful weight and lift to this send the barley soaring; toasty vanilla and then a fresh wave of mouth-watering malt; f23 lovely layers of cocoa sweetened slightly by a sprinkling of brown sugar; b23 another reminder of what we will shortly never see again... **46%. nc ncf.**

∷· **Scotch Malt Whisky Society Cask 25.40 Aged 16 Years** Refill Hogshead, dist Nov 90 **(79)** n19 t21 f20 b19. It had to happen: Rosebank, a giant amongst malts at 8-y-o is a mere mortal when twice that age. Hot and aggressive in part, the oak shows exactly the same pervasive nature as in the OMC of the same age. Evidence (and time) is stacking up against it. **57.2%**

The **Single Malt of Scotland Rosebank Aged 14 Years Vintage 1991** cask no 2024, dist 01 July 91, bott 05 Apr 06 **(93)** n24 another tapestry of faint apple and cinnamon amid the near perfect fresh barley; t24 acacia honey is interwoven through the rich barley fabric; spices batter at the roof of the mouth; f22 thins out and dries as the oak interjects; **b**23 another stunning cask from this stunning distillery. **46%**. *The Whisky Exchange. 305 bottles.*

The **Wee Dram Rosebank 15 Years Old** db **(81)** n20 t20 f21 **b**20. Probably from a third-fill bourbon cask, showing early vitality and then rich cocoa-oak influence. A wafer-light dram, so reminiscent of a Scapa half its age. **40%**.

**Whisky Fair Rosebank 1974 30 Years Old Sherry Cask (92)** n23 big sherry, clean, old, nutty and faultless; t22 just slightly off-key at first, but then an explosion of honey and oloroso comes to the rescue; f24 a brilliant balance of major fruit and glossy, coppery malt; a perfection of sweetness helps to dazzle; **b**23 probably Rosebank as you've never seen it before: I can count on the fingers of one hand the times I've seen something quite like this. One of the biggest Lowlanders in recent times. **55.8%**. *The Whisky Fair, Limburg.*

**Whisky Galore Rosebank 1990** cask no. 3413, dist Nov 90, bott Apr 06 **(85)** n21 t22 f21 **b**21. As Rosebanks go, this one is pretty introverted. **55.4%**. *253 bottles.*

## ROYAL BRACKLA
### Speyside, 1812. Dewar's. Working.

**Royal Brackla Aged 10 Years** db **(73)** n18 t20 f17 **b**18. A distinct lowering of the colours since I last tasted this. What on earth is going on? **40%**

**Royal Brackla Aged 25 Years** dist 78, bott Mar 03 db **(88)** n23 t22 f21 **b**22. A very complex malt that for a light Speysider has survived the passing summers much better than can be expected and is bold enough to display its own richness of style. Some excellent cask selection has gone into this one. **43%**

**Cadenhead's Authentic Collection Royal Brackla Aged 12 Years** dist 92, bott Feb 05 **(92)** n24 t23 f22 **b**23. Sophisticated and demanding on the palate, a connoisseur's dram if ever there was one. **59%**. *234 bottles.*

∴ **Cadenhead's Authentic Collection Royal Brackla Aged 14 Years** Bourbon barrel, dist 92, bott Feb 07 **(84)** n21 t23 f19 **b**21. The early delivery of pecan nuts and barley is pretty delicious. The oaky stampede is a surprise. **57.9%**. *Cadenhead's. 228 bottles.*

**Cadenhead's Chairman's Stock Royal Brackla Aged 30 Years 1976** Sherry hogshead, dist 76, bott Nov 06 **(93)** n24 pithy, exceptional dryness counters the juicier barley: top dollar sophistication; t23 maybe the dryness is a tad too profound on delivery but a vivid bourbon/sherry hybrid develops and compensates fabulously; f22 returns to dry sherry and papery oak; **b**24 who needs Martinis? Sheer class. **53.6%**. *126 bottles.*

**Connoisseurs Choice Royal Brackla 1991 (84)** n22 t21 f20 **b**21. Wonderful honey thread on the nose, but the oak jumps in a little early. **46%**. *G&M.*

**Mackillop's Choice Royal Brackla 1976** cask no 6924, dist Oct 76 **(84)** n21 t19 f23 **b**21. Massive malt, big bold and brassy with excellent honey to soften the oaky blows; an intriguing latent smokiness adds extra depth. **59.6%**.

∴ **Provenance Brackla Aged 10 Years** dist Winter 96, bott Winter 06 **(77)** n20 t20 f19 **b**18. Bloody hell!! A 10-year-old whisky going on ten months...Very rarely have I come across a cask that has matured so little in all that time: there is more of the "new make" about his than there is "mature whisky". If you really are into sheer malt, go for it. Though, as might be expected, the finish is demanding. And as much as I love fresh, young whisky, this has been around long enough to lose its natural balance. **46%**

## ROYAL LOCHNAGAR
### Highland (Eastern), 1826. Diageo. Working.

**Royal Lochnagar Aged 12 Years** bott lott 4330 db **(83)** n21 t22 f19 **b**21. More care has been taken with this than some other bottlings from this wonderful distillery. But I still can't understand why it never quite manages to get out of third gear...or is the caramel on the finish the giveaway...? **40%**

**Royal Lochnagar Rare Malts 30 Years** Old bott 04 db **(83)** n21 t22 f20 **b20**. A wonderful thread of honey battles heroically against the invading oak. **56.2%**

**Royal Lochnagar Selected Reserve** db **(89)** n23 superb oloroso, clean and spicy with apples and pears; t23 stupendous spice lift-off which really starts showing the malts to great effect; f21 the malts fade as the toffee progresses; b22 quite brilliant sherry influence. The spices are a treat. **43%**

⬡ **Norse Cask Selection Royal Lochnagar 1977 Aged 29 Years** Cask ref no. DL863 **(75)** n20 t19 f18 b18. A touch of soap on the nose and pencil shavings on the palate. But there is still some glossy barley to be had. **50.4%.** WhiskyOwner.com, Denmark.

**Old Malt Cask Royal Lochnagar Aged 14 Years Single Cask Bottling for a Fine Cigar's Pleasure (84)** n19 t21 f22 **b22**. Curiously, before I even saw what this whisky was, I thought I was getting tobacco smoke off the nose. Strange… but a sprightly, zesty dram if ever there was one. **50%. nc ncf sc.** Douglas Laing.

⬡ **Old Malt Cask Lochnagar Aged 20 Years Rum Finish** dist Sept 86, bott Nov 06 **(76)** n20 t19 f19 b18. Struggles to find a rhythm or centre of attraction. **50%.** 229 bottles.

**Platinum Selection Lochnagar 30 Years** Old dist 10 Dec 74, bott May 05 **(83)** n22 t20 f21 **b20**. One of those suet pudding and custard jobbies; a touch of the fruitcakes, too. But it lucks out on the oak, which is altogether too forceful on landing. **60.2%.** 224 bottles.

**Platinum Lochnagar 32 Years Old** dist May 72, bott Jul 04 **(93)** n23 moist Jamaica cake with a layer of Danish marzipan; a fabulous cocoa-laced thread of smoke weaves through it; t24 busy spice throughout as the malt settles towards a Jaffa-cake fruit, honied theme; gorgeous copper and gentle peat involvement; f23 honeycomb, cocoa and a touch of smoke; **b23** as lush and rich as you could pray a whisky this age to be: really seems to have that "sma' still" body. **60.5%.**

⬡ **Platinum Lochnagar Aged 33 Years** dist 73, bott 06 **(88)** n23 sublime, estery nose; big copper presence (had they put a new still around that time, or done some other work?) with beautifully weighted barley: genuine class; t23 no less stupendous mouth arrival, with that coppery zing again: the oak arrives earlier than desired and in force, but the lime-edge to the barley helps fends off the worst of it; f21 dry, toasty oak; **b21** the oak has tried a smash and grab raid but the quality of the malt has seen off the worst of it. Breathtakingly lovely early on. **57.2%.** Douglas Laing. 245 bottles.

**Provenance Lochnagar Aged 11 Years** Sherry butt DMG 2675, dist Winter (Nov) 94, bott Summer 06 **(79)** n19 t19 f21 **b20**. A temperamental malt at the best of times, this one's a bit sulky by refusing to really get going. **46%. nc ncf.** McGibbon's.

⬡ **Provenance Lochnagar Aged 11 Years Sherry Finish** dist Spring 95, bott Winter 07 **(68)** n17 t18 f16 b17. Next…! **46%.** Douglas Laing.

**Provenance Lochnagar 12 Years Old** dist 28 Apr 93, bott 23 May 05 **(94)** n23  t25 f23 **b23**. This is the independent Lochnagar I've been waiting years to find. Absolutely spot-on, capturing the curiously delicate yet heavy style in one glass. Majestic: Queen Victoria would be very amused…. **46%.** Douglas Laing & Co.

**Provenance Lochnagar 12 Years Old** Sherry, dist Mar 93, bott Nov 05 **(84)** n20 t22 f21 **b21**. A thoroughbred of a cask showing the cleanest, most excellent sherry. But to nitpick, perhaps it could do more on the complexity side. **46%.**

**Provenance Lochnagar Aged Over 12 Years** Sherry butt no. 1790, dist Winter 93 (Spring distillation label), bott Spring 05 **(74)** n18 t19 f18 b19. Sweet barley fights to overcome a sulphured edge. **46%. nc ncf.** McGibbon's.

**Provenance Lochnagar 12 Years Old Sherry Finish** dist Jun 94, bott Autumn 06 **(86)** n21 t22 f22 **b21**. Decent, sharp barley but slightly awkward and tight at times in delivery **46%**

## ST MAGDALENE
### Lowland, 1798–1983. Closed.

**Linlithgow 30 Years Old** dist 73 db **(70)** n18 t18 f16 b18. A brave but ultimately futile effort from a malt that is way past its sell-by date. **59.6%**

⬡ **Connoisseurs Choice St Magdalene 1975** Refill Sherry cask no. 16, dist 2 June 75, bott 14 Aug 06 **(91)** n23 dappled sherry makes a sexy twosome with the oak; t23 gentle barley building and building in intensity whilst elsewhere vaguely oily grape juices things up; f22 the threatening oak now offers a toasty but controlled finish; **b23** a corker from this lost distillery — the best sherried SM I have ever tasted. **46%.** *Gordon & MacPhail for Royal Mile Whiskies. 286 bottles.*

**Gordon & MacPhail Reserve St Magdalena 1975** bott 01.11.05 **(82) n**22 **t**19 **f**21 **b**20. Slightly overcooked on the oaky front, as one might expect, but not enough to ruin those sparkling barley notes that gather attractively on the finish. **46%.** *US Market.*

**Murray McDavid Mission IV Linlithgow 1975 Aged 29 Years (81) n**20 **t**21 **f**20 **b**20. Gone fractionally through the top with oak, but recovers thanks to a relaxed malty and slightly citrussy theme. **46%.** *Bourbon Cask.*

⠐⠂ **Old Malt Cask Linlithgow Aged 24 Years** dist Dec 82, bott May 07 **(90) n**22 ultra clean and grassy; **t**23 mouth-watering with perfect juiciness and sweet/sharpness from the barley; **f**22 long, clean barley sugar: benefits from minimum oak presence; **b**23 this distillery may sound as it has a lisp, but rarely do you get such malty clarity from the mouth. Best I have tasted from here for a very long time. **50%.** *Douglas Laing. 303 bottles.*

**Old Malt Cask St Magdalene 23 Years Old** dist Dec 82, bott June 06 **(84) n**22 **t**21 **f**20 **b**21. Well preserved and really belts out the malty notes. **50%.** *329 bottles.*

⠐⠂ **Old Malt Cask St Magdalene Aged 23 Years** dist Dec 82, bott Sept 06 **(93) n**23 hint of sweetened lavender amid clean barley; **t**24 brilliant!! Just not a single hint of age as the exuberance of the spiced honey launches into the tastebuds; ridiculously juicy for its age; **f**23 long, soft, faultless vanilla; a light, spicy fruit finale; **b**23 they had better rebuild the distillery PDQ if it can come up with stuff like this... **50%.** *331 bottles.*

⠐⠂ **Old Malt Cask St. Magdalene Aged 24 Years** dist Dec 82, bott Dec 06 **(84) n**21 **t**22 **f**20 **b**21. Attractive early barley, but nose and finish scorched by oak. **50%.** *329 bottles.*

⠐⠂ **Rare Old St Magdalene 1975 (89) n**23 intriguing mix of caramelised and bourbon biscuits; **t**22 thin maple syrup over an oak-led barley thrust; soft spices enchant; **f**22 soft cocoa sheen; **b**22 a noble dram from what appears to be an excellent batch of casks. **43%.** *G&M.*

# SCAPA

**Highland (Island–Orkney), 1885. Chivas. Working.**

**Scapa 12 Years Old** db **(88) n**23 honeydew melon, soft salt and myriad styles of barley: really complex with a sprinkling of coal dust on the fruit; **t**22 truly brilliant mouth arrival: the most complex display of malt and cocoa, the fruit is ripe figs with a thread of honey; **f**21 a slight bitterness with some developing toffee, but the malt stays the distance; **b**22 always a joy. **40%**

**Scapa 14 Years Old** db **(89) n**22 hints of honey and kumquats; the sappiness from last year has gone; **t**22 relays of mouthwatering barley sprinting between the shards of honey; **f**22 toasty, a subtle bitterness blends well with the lingering barley-honey; some caramel flies in from somewhere to beat down an important degree of complexity. Otherwise the entire scoring would be two or three points higher; **b**23 the tongue works overtime trying to work out the multi-layered structure of a superb malt from a distillery at last being recognised for its excellence. **40%** ⊙

⠐⠂ **Scapa Aged 14 Years Cask Strength Edition** Batch no. SC 14001, dist 92, bott 06 db **(90) n**22 white peppers sprinkled over barley sugar and custard; **t**23 salivating with barley concentrate boosted by pounding spice and a honey hint **f**22 a soft oiliness spreads across the roof of the mouth allowing the oak to calm things down slightly; **b**23 no shrinking violet, this: an enormous statement from a usually quiet, though as often as not brilliant, distillery. And this is brilliant... **60.9%.**

**Chieftain's Scapa Aged 22 Years** Sherry **(90) n**23 one of those noses which is a bit awkward and top heavy when poured but after 5-10 mins of airing reveals a wonderful honey side to the fruit; **t**22 ditto the palate: a bit closed at first but opens up gloriously for a light fruitcake effect; **f**22 elegant, with a touch of brown sugar; **b**23 fabulous whisky deserving as much time as you can afford. **46%.** *Ian Macleod.*

⠐⠂ **D&M Aficionados' Club Bottling Scapa Aged 17 Years** dist Sept 89 **(87) n**21 a grapey, fruit edge to this one though some of the oak involvement is mildly bitter; **t**23 brilliant delivery of rich honey and burnt raisin; never quite settles but an early cocoa injection does add further complexity; **f**21 that bitterness on the nose returns to lop off the higher qualities; **b**22 usually Scapa boasts a honeyed thread: here it is a rich seam... **56.6%. sc ncf.** *Angus Dundee Distillers.*

**Duncan Taylor Collection Scapa 1977** cask no. 2831, dist Oct 77, bott Apr 06 **(83)** n20 t21 f22 b20. Sharp, tangy, lively. Has fended off obvious old age with a touch of fruity panache. **57.9%.** *164 bottles.*

**Duncan Taylor Collection Scapa 1977 Aged 27 Years** cask no. 2828, dist Oct 77, bott Mar 05 **(94)** n24 a mesmerising amalgam of ordinary and manuka honey salted down and then given a gristy, malty blast. Astonishing, and something you can keep your nose stuck in for an age; t24 the very arrival spells brilliance with the most extraordinary complexity sitting on the tongue as the saline notes are swamped by the sharp, bitter-sweet battles between oak, curvaceous malt and citrus. Spice has to arrive and it does! f22 long, but a degree of oiliness mildly dampening down the early mayhem, and some late, mildly bitter oak sees off the last of the honey; b24 I have long felt that Scapa has been poorly served by the independents. However, most of the older bottlings have been classic and this just about tops the bill. Pure drama on the tastebuds. Fabulous!!! **61.1%**

**Gordon & MacPhail Scapa 1993 (85)** n20 t21 f22 b22. If people still insist that G&M colour their standard malts, have a look at this! **40%**

⌐ **Old Malt Cask Scapa Aged 13 Years** dist Sept 93, bott Nov 06 **(87)** n20 the simple oak-barley tune shows limited harmony; t23 lush, with a soft oily sheen allowing the rich barley maximum impact alongside excellent spices; f22 soft oak delivery; b22 a bit of a curate's egg but there is no denying the brilliance of the barley. **50%.** *348 bottles.*

**Old Malt Cask Scapa 14 Years Old** dist 29 Apr 91, bott 9 May 05 **(88)** n22 t23 f21 b21. A very light Scapa that at times tries to shout but raises only a loud whisper. **50%.**

⌐ **Old Malt Cask Scapa Aged 16 Years** dist Apr 91, bott May 07 **(88)** n20 closed: dusty; t22 takes time to wake up then goes into barley juice overdrive; f24 now the complexity is cranked up to max as the malt and oak, helped along by a late citrus and honey fling, vie for supremacy. Each blow brings untold joy to the tastebuds; b22 busy with major spice. The finish is memorable. **50%.** *Douglas Laing. 335 bottles.*

**Provenance Scapa 11 Year Old** dist 4 Nov 93, bott 21 Apr 05 **(85)** n21 t22 f21 b21. Hints of papaya but very similar, if memory serves me correctly, to a Douglas Laing Macallan from a long-in-the-tooth cask which reveals a warts an' all whisky. **46%**

⌐ **Provenance Scapa Aged 11 Years** dist Winter 95, bott Spring 07 **(84)** n20 t22 f21 b21. Pleasant. A touch syrupy. **46%.** *Douglas Laing.*

**Provenance Scapa 12 Years Old** dist Nov 93, bott Summer 06 **(87)** n21 lazy: the oak is offering little sympathy to the salted barley; t22 better as the lush body generates a barley sweetness; f22 indifferent oak cramps the finer, classier notes. But there is a lovely coppery gloss that impresses; b22 attractive, as usual, for this wonderful little distillery. But the oak input could be better. **46%.**

⌐ **Provenance Scapa Aged 12 Years** dist Spring 94, bott Winter 07 **(88)** n22 youthful, gristy with absolute minimum oak interference t23 a thousand shades of barley, all of them sweet and mouth-watering. Just so clean and delicate; f21 bantamweight stuff with the oak arriving undercooked; b22 I know some well-respected names in the industry who are less than happy when whiskies from third-filled casks like this one pop up in bottlings. I tend to disagree and here is a wonderful example why: few spirits in the world can offer such delicate joys as this. A genuine lip-smacker. **46%**

## SPEYBURN
**Speyside, 1897. Inver House. Working.**

**Speyburn 10 Year Old** db **(81)** n21 t22 f18 b20. Soft, slightly smoked, sweet, syrupy, simple: Speyburn so stylish. **40%.** *Inver House Distillers.* ⊙

**Speyburn Aged 25 Years** db **(92)** n22 crisp barley sits well with the chalky oak; t24 beautiful soft honey helps thicken up the malt; exceptional mouth feel as an extra touch of maple syrup helps keeps the oak in check; a real coppery tanginess to this, too; f23 a thin spread of marmalade on buttered toast; b23 either they have re-bottled very quickly or I got the diagnosis dreadfully wrong first time round. Last year wasn't overly impressed; now I'm taken aback by its beauty. Some change. **46%** ⊙ ⊙

**Connoisseurs Choice Speyburn 1974 (77)** n18 t22 f19 b20. Pity that an off note from the cask has got in to spoil what would have been an exceptionally honied party. **43%**

⌐ **Connoisseurs Choice Speyburn 1977 (84)** n20 t22 f21 b21. Creaks its way through the oaky gears with enough malty panache to leave you wanting more. **43%.**

## SPEYSIDE
**Speyside, 1990. Speyside Distillers. Working.**

Drumguish db **(71) n**17 t19 f17 **b**18. This whisky could only improve. And, thankfully, it has. Even so, a long, long way to go on this. The nose is still flawed and, despite an injection of barley early on, it flatlines its way from the fourth taste wave to the end. **40%** ☺ ☺

Speyside 10 Years Old db **(81) n**19 t21 f20 **b**21. Plenty of sharp oranges around; the malt is towering and the bite is deep. A weighty Speysider with no shortage of mouth prickle.

Speyside 12 Years Old db **(78) n**19 t21 f19 **b**19. Gosh! What has happened to that sparkling malt that used to be Speyside 12? Still some lovely barley on delivery but a massive injection of caramel appears to have flattened all in its path. **40%** ☺ ☺

Cu Dhub **(73) n**18 t19 f18 **b**18. This is one of the few whiskies I had been trying to avoid in recent years as previous encounters had not been particularly enjoyable. Some in the past have been a touch faulty, a fault too many with so much caramel. But this is much cleaner and therefore makes for a tolerable experience. So much caramel, though, could easily be mistaken for a Scottish West Coast rum! **40%**. *Mac Y, Denmark.*

Cu Dhub 10 Years Old **(82) n**19 t22 f20 **b**21. Not too sure how they have achieved this. Threateningly dark and hardly shy of caramel but there is real juice abounding. A lot more engaging than it looks. **46%**. *Mac Y, Denmark. 100 bottles.*

⌐⌐⌐ The Whisky Fair The Speyside Aged 15 Years Bourbon Hogshead, dist 1991, bott 2007 **(88) n**20 malty, but a bit dirty with the kind of feints that pack a punch on the palate...; t24 ...bloody hell...and some!! Enormous delivery with tell-tale feints which seems to accentuate every last atom of the richest maltiness imaginable. Outstanding depth to the sweetness; f22 soft oils, a return to something a little grimy but still OK; **b**22 so many faults where do you begin? But the intensity of the delivery is among the best of the year. With this character, I assume this is from the Speyside distillery, rather than just being a Speysider. **53.7%**. *Germany.*

## SPRINGBANK
**Campbeltown, 1828. J&A Mitchell & Co. Working.**

Hazelburn Aged 8 Years 2nd Edition, release 06 db **(90) n**22 big, concentrated barley. Much more complex than first sniff suggests and there is enough oak layering to really impress; t23 kabooom!! The barley absolutely explodes around the palate; just a touch of salt brings out the full intensity; f22 soft oils help project the advancing oak. Simple, but good balance; **b**23 I adore this ultra-intense barley style: something you can devour for an age. Wonderful stuff!! **46%**. *6,000 bottles.*

⌐⌐⌐ Longrow Aged 10 Years db **(78) n**19 t20 f19 **b**20. Seeing as I was one of the first people alive ever to taste Longrow from its very first bottling and used to track down – in my comparative youth – every expression thereafter (and still have some in my personal collection), you could say I am a fan. But this has completely bemused me: bereft not only of the usual to-die-for smoke, its warts are exposed badly, as this is way too young. Sweet and malty, perhaps, and technically better than the marks I'm giving it – but this is Longrow, dammit! I am astonished. **46%**

⌐⌐⌐ Longrow Aged 10 Years 100 Proof db **(86) n**20 t23 f22 **b**21. Still bizarrely smokeless – well, maybe a flicker of smoke as you may find the involuntary twitching of a leg of a dying fly – but the mouthfeel is much better here and although a bit too oily and dense for complexity to get going, a genuinely decent ride heading towards Hazelburn-esque barley intensity. Love it, because this oozes class. But where's the ruddy peat...? Oi, mister. I want my peat back...!! **57%**

Longrow 10 Years Old 1994 db **(95) n**25 never in all the years of nosing whisky have I come across one that is a complete replica of sitting on a Scottish shore by a rock pool surrounded by seaweed and evaporating salty seawater. The pungency of the peat is deft and astonishing; t24 velvetcushioned malt gracefully coats the mouth while sweet peat offers waves of gentle intensity; f22 laid-back, with banana and caressing layers of smoky grist; **b**24 it is incredible how the present Springbank 10-y-o have problems finding their feet, yet add some peat to the mix and you have on your hands a malt of such subtlety and complexity that you need simply hours to try and fathom it out. Whisky for the gods. **46%**. *Limited availability.*

**Longrow Tokaji Wood Aged 10 Years** 8 yrs refill, 2 yrs fresh Tokaji, dist Feb 95, bott Aug 05 db **(69)** n17 t18 f17 b17. Why..? **55.6%**

**Longrow Aged 14 Years** db **(89)** n25 a strap-on-to-the-head aroma with so many barley-peat nuances at so many levels it almost defies comprehension; and it wouldn't be a Longrow if there wasn't some salty goings on, too; t21 mildly tart delivery with the smoke and oak refusing to gel; f21 where the hell is the peat on the nose? No shortage of natural toffee, though; **b**22 hard to get a bearing on this one. The nose, though... **46%. nc ncf.**

**Longrow 1995 Aged 10 Years** db **(91)** n24 distant peat reek of a coastal village carried on the wind; salty smoked bacon. Just so delicate and delicious...; t23 sweet grist and bursting spices; f22 hollows out as vanilla chimes in; again the smoke refuses to entirely vanish; **b**22 a graceful malt, almost lethargic by comparison with the legendary '94, but a whisky education in its own right. **46%**

**Longrow 1996 Aged 10 Years** db **(86)** n23 t22 f20 b21. If I was a gambling man I'd say some very fresh bourbon is involved here, because the balance has been compromised. I think this needed a few more years to find its natural balance. That said, remains very drinkable. **46%**

**Springbank 9 Years Old Marsala Wood Expression** dist Oct 96, bott Aug 06 db **(88)** n21 pungent, biting spices; a hint of something smoky and piny; t23 heavy on the wine at first, but as the barley picks up the pace and the body lightens a fabulous injection of swarming, buzzing, piny spices kick in; f22 long with lots of wine sticking to the cocoa-sprinkled finale; **b**22 easily one of the spiciest Springbanks for a long time: the Sicilian influence makes this an offer you can't refuse... **58%.** *7,740 bottles.*

**Springbank 10 Years Old** db **(74)** n18 t19 f18 b19. Woahhh...!! Way off key. But, really, that's no criticism: this is a malt on its way to greatness, but like the most glorious butterflies must go through its ugly larva stage. For these casks, this is it... **46%**

**Springbank Aged 10 Years** db **(84)** n20 t22 f21 b21. A much better fist than the 46% version, though this is dripping in natural caramels which distances it from the complexity of previous bottlings. But it pulses with its trademark malt. **57% (100 proof).**

**Springbank 10 Years Old 100 Proof Bourbon Matured** db **(85)** n19 t23 f21 b22. Another brain-busting expression. At this tender age, Springbank has no set rules: it can disappear on any tangent it sees fit. Today it has decided to take the big oak route. **57%.** *Not available in USA or Canada.*

**Springbank 12 Years Old Bourbon Wood Expression** dist 91, bott Feb 04 db **(82)** n20 t22 f21 b19. Springbank is one of the most complex and probably the slowest maturing single malt in Scotland. Here is a priceless example of a dram that cannot find its equilibrium yet at the same time generates flashes of pure genius. **58.5%.** *5986 bottles.*

**Springbank 12 Years Old 175th Anniversary** db **(86)** n20 t24 f21 b21. An unusually soft Springbank with less complexity than usual but displaying amazing intensity. **46%.** *12000 bottles worldwide from Apr 03. The age may not be stated.*

**Springbank 1989 14 Years Old Port Wood Expression** bott Sep 04 db **(89)** n22 fruity and salty, there's a bit of a directional crisis here! t23 astonishing spice explosion to start, followed by a surprisingly orderly procession of malt, fruit and coffee; f21 the malt at last finds a more gristy, sweeter gear, but that salty oak holds it back a little; **b**23 a strange beast that is nothing if not unpredictable and entertaining after an indifferent start on the nose that needs time in the glass to come alive. **52.8%.** *12 years re-fill sherry, 2 years fresh port. 7,200 bottles.*

**Springbank 15 Years Old Sherry Matured** db **(77)** n19 t21 f18 b19. Very unusual, in fact almost a first. But I think a dodgy sherry butt has got in here somewhere. **46%**

**Springbank Aged 25 Years** db **(91)** n24 t22 f22 b23. I think complex is the word. **46%**

**Springbank FFF 25 Year Old** db **(90)** n23 t22 f22 b23. The words Springbank and complexity seem conjoined: they are again here. **46%**

**Springbank 32 Years Old** bott Oct 04 db **(93)** n24 a startling and unusual overture of redcurrant jam and salted porridge; a distant hint of medium roast Java coffee underlines the complexity; t24 that unique combination of intense sweet malt and intense salty malt go into overdrive; f22 more oak and some natural crème brûlée douse the intensity somewhat; **b**23 for those Springbank diehards out there, here's a must-have for the collection. **46%.** *2,400 bottles.*

**Springbank Private Bottling for Distillery Visitors 2005** db **(79)** n21 t21 f18 b19. This is a ten-year-old but very curiously flat, especially towards the finish.

**Accura Engineering Springbank** cask no. 66, dist may 95, bott Sep 05 **(85)** n21 t22 f21 b21. A real turn up for the book Down Under, with this massive, fruit-fuelled beaut. Perhaps just a little sharp in places, especially on the finish, for greatness, but this is less a whisky and more an adventure... **57.1%. nc ncf sc.** *Australia. 12 bottles.*

**Cadenhead's Authentic Collection Longrow Aged 11 Years** dist 93, bott Sep 05 db **(91)** n23 distinct Arbroath Smokie; t23 high-class gristy delivery with all the sweetness that brings; a touch of sugared lime, too; f22 loads more fruit with a golden syrup glaze and the faintest smoke; b23 another sweetie, literally and figuratively. **54.1%.** *270 bottles.*

**Cadenhead's Authentic Collection Springbank Aged 14 Years** Sherry butt, dist 91, bott Sept 06 **(84)** n20 t20 f23 b21. Only towards the back of the astonishingly elegant and long finish do things fall into place. And how! **53.9%.** *654 btls.*

**Cadenhead's Bond Reserve Hazelburn Aged 8 Years** Sherry Hogshead, dist 97, bott May 06 db **(84)** n21 t22 f20 b21. A sherry hoggy it may be, but this behaves like a dram freshly poured from a pre-carameled PM Demerara cask, complete with give-away coffee notes. Rather lovely, but finesse is at a premium. **58.4%.** *288 bottles.*

**Cadenhead's Bond Reserve Springbank Aged 10 Years 1996** Cream sherry butt, dist 96, bott Nov 06 db **(75)** n18 t20 f18 b19. A real shame: the cream sherry has curdled. Sulphur at work. **59.4%.** *654 bottles.*

**Chieftain's Springbank Aged 31 Years (94)** n23 salty barley meets sugary barley head on: no shortage of splinters in the explosion; t24 cripes! My slumbering tastebuds – barely disturbed by the majority of the "young" Springbanks - get a rude awakening as the most astonishingly clean and intense malt crashes head first into them with myriad glorious waves of lessening intensity; f23 real complexity with the salt catching up with the golden syrup. About 20 different shades of vanilla cannot dampen the developing spices; b24 one the sweetest Springbanks I've yet across. Book a dental appointment before buying a bottle. **57.2%.** *Ian Macleod.*

**Chieftain's Springbank Aged 34 Years (86)** n21 t22 f21 b22. Just so light for its age. **43%.** *Ian Macleod.*

**Chieftain's Springbank Aged 36 Years (82)** n20 t20 f21 b21. Remarkably high strength for age but a bit raw irrespective of this. **57.3%.** *Ian Macleod.*

⁖ **Chieftain's Springbank 37 Years Old** Barrel, dist Jan 69 **(87)** n22 the most exotic of exotic fruits...and oak; t22 beautiful, crisp, eventually juicy, barley enjoys a swansong before the oak comes to get it; f21 dries until your eyes water; b22 just made it to the tape... **41%. nc ncf.** *Ian Macleod Distillers.*

**Dewar Rattray Individual Cask Bottling Springbank 1993 Aged 12 Years** cask no. 212, dist May 93, bott Jan 06 **(89)** n22 nutty, salted butter and vague smoke; t23 stunningly fresh and mouth-watering with a citrus and grist sweetness combining and a swirl of smoke adding depth; f22 lightly salted and spicy; b22 a really wonderful cask, probably second or even third fill so the caramels have been kept in check. **57.5%.** *282 bottles.*

⁖ **Dun Bheagan Springbank 38 Years Old** Sherry Hogshead, dist Apr 68 **(89)** n23 old school oloroso remains handsome for all the wrinkles; t23 sublime delivery of fruit candy and liquorice before an oaky assault; f21 fading, sweet toffee apple; b22 **43%. nc ncf.**

**Duncan Taylor Collection Springbank 1967** cask no. 1941, dist May 67, bott Dec 05 **(78)** n19 t20 f20 b19. The soft, exotic fruit doesn't quite save it from the ravages of time. **41.3%.** *196 bottles.*

⁖ **Duncan Taylor The NC2 Range Springbank 1993 (82)** n22 t21 f19 b20. Some attractive sheen to the barley. But could have done with another eight years in the cask... **46%. nc ncf.**

⁖ **Duncan Taylor The NC2 Range Springbank 1996 (77)** n20 t19 f19 b19. Sent enough for only two mouthfuls – so this is first impression only, I'm afraid. Young, flat and lacking grace - typical for this distillery in diapers. **46%. nc ncf.**

**Kingsbury's Single Cask Springbank 11 Years Old** cask no. 378, dist 93 **(84)** n21 t22 f20 b21. A short surge of honey and citrus reveals the first tentative step towards greatness. **46%.** *Japan Import System.*

**Kingsbury's Valdespino Springbank 14 Years Old (87)** n22 spiced grape; t21 grassy and grapey but toffees out early on; f22 chewy and warming if a little bitter; b22 enormously busy; the odd kink but enough plusses to make for an enjoyable and, at times, classy dram. **46%.** *Japan Import System.*

⠿ **Milroy's of Soho Springbank 1993 Aged 12 Years** Cask no. 156, dist 7 May 93, bott 1 Mar 06 **(81) n**21 **t**21 **f**20 **b**19. A notoriously difficult malt when young – and for Springbank, 12 is positively prepubescent – this expression staggers about the glass with giant malty intent but no focus. **46%.** *324 bottles.*

**Murray McDavid Springbank Aged 9 Years** Bourbon/Marsanne/ Roussane casks enhanced in Guigla Hermitage Blanc, dist 96, bott 05 **(82) n**20 **t**20 **f**21 **b**21. Considering how off the pave young Springbank can be, this thrives with the extra fruity-sweetness. **46%. nc ncf.** *480 bottles.*

**Murray McDavid Springbank Aged 12 Years** Bourboun/Marsanne Roussanne enhanced in Guigal Hermitage Blanc, dist 92, bott 05 **(84) n**20 **t**22 **f**21 **b**21. Does Springbank come softer than this? The deft fruitiness is quite enchanting. **46%. nc ncf.** *480 bottles.*

⠿ **Old Malt Cask Springbank Aged 10 Years** dist Oct 96, bott May 07 **(81) n**19 **t**21 **f**21 **b**20. A barley-fruit rant on the palate. Frustrating how this malt rarely makes the cut at this age. **50%.** *Douglas Laing. 358 bottles.*

**Old Malt Cask The Argyll Malt (Hazelburn) 1997 Aged 8 Years (82) n**20 **t**21 **f**21 **b**20. It's no secret that the malts from this slow-maturing distillery wobble about like Bambi until they get into double figures. This is no exception, though the malt intensity is marked. **58.8%.** *Exclusively for Vintage House. 296 bottles.*

**The Queen of the Moorlands Rare Cask Springbank 1991 Committee Bottling (87) n**23 mildly salty, tangy barley with a squeeze of citrus and fudge; **t**23 jarring, juicy barley; **f**20 lots of natural caramels and tannins flattens it; **b**21 hats off again to this bottler: they very rarely let you down. **46%. sc.** *Available at The Wine Shop, Leek, UK.*

⠿ **The Single Malts of Scotland Springbank 1993 Aged 13 Years (90) n**22 some light but intriguing smoke; **t**23 has every grain of barley in Kintyre been shoved into this one bottle..? **f**22 vanilla and more soft-oiled barley; **b**23 Hazelburn meets Longrow...thought the smoke vanishes after the nose. **58.7%. sc cs.** *Speciality Drinks, UK.*

⠿ **Vintage House Argyll (Hazelburn) Aged 8 Years** dist July 97, bott Apr 06 **(93) n**22 almost opaque barley; a sliver of banana steals in; **t**24 death by barley... **f**23 at least some oak arrives to make some kind of game of it; rather lovely bitter-sweet fade **b**24 the only other whisky in the world that has been equally malty as this has been...Hazelburn. Maybe the odd Swissky has come close but nothing compares in intensity. Stunning. **58.8%.** *Douglas Laing for Vintage House. 296 bottles.*

**The Whisky Fair Springbank 35 Years Old** Bourbon Hogshead, dist May 70 **(89) n**21 salty and a tad sappy; **t**23 classy entry with intense, salivating malt which is mouth-puckeringly saline; **f**22 soft spices and yet more waves of ridiculously fresh barley; **b**23 even taking the less than perfect nose into account, this is truly great stuff. The annual Whisky Fair Springbanks are becoming an important fixture in the whisky world. **59.5%.** *120 bottles.*

⠿ **The Whisky Fair Springbank Aged 35 Years** Sherry Wood, dist 1971, bott 07 **(96) n**24 a must- nose whisky – quite literally: the pressed grape softens the bourbony outline; **t**24 a wondrous delivery of fresh, juicy grape and fresh juicy barley: all age is defied here; **f**24 the dry Danish marzipan gives a nod to the advancing oak, but a fruit jelly balance is on hand; **b**24 a true golden oldie. Quite sensational. **59%.** *Germany.*

**The Whisky Fair Springbank Aged 36 Years** Bourbon Hogshead 402, dist Feb 69, bott Feb 05 **(89) n**21 **t**23 **f**22 **b**23. Typical Springbank, so polarised yet together. **45.6%.** *197 btls.*

## STRATHISLA
**Speyside, 1786. Chivas. Working.**

**Strathisla 12 Years Old** db **(87) n**21 a dab of distant peat adds even more weight to something that is malt-heavy already; **t**22 pleasant, sultana-fruity with a very rich malt follow-through; **f**22 some almost apologetic oak breaks into the rich maltiness. Some hints of cocoa and more smoke elongate the finale; **b**22 an infinitely better dram than a few years back that was a bit oily and shapeless. Today the heavily-weighted, full-bodied malt engages the tastebuds from first to last with a complexity and richness of genuine class. **43%.** *Flora and Fauna.*

**Strathisla Distillery Edition 15 Years Old** db **(94) n**23 flawlessly clean and enriched by that silky intensity of fruity malt unique to this distillery; **t**23 the malt is lush, sweet and every bit as intense as the nose; a touch of toffeespice does it no harm; **f24** just so long and lingering, again with the malt being of extraordinary enormity: these is simply wave upon wave of pure delight; **b24** what a belter! The distillery is beautiful enough to visit: to take away a bottle of this as well would just be too good to be true! **53.7%**

**The Bottlers Strathisla 1977 Aged 27 Years** cask 4472 **(90) n**23 refreshing sultanas and apple; **t**23 soft, bitter-sweet sherry influence in conjunction with developing thick malt that is never less than mouthwatering; **f**22 relatively flat thanks to some over-egging of the sherry, but makes an elegant farewell and there is even a fascinating late juniper development as it takes on a curiously ginny quality at the death; **b**22 the more I taste from the independent company, the more impressed I become. **43.9%**. *Raeborn Fine Wines.*

**Cadenhead's Strathisla Aged 18 Years** Bourbon wood **(93) n**23 lively, with a buttress of oak groaning against the wall of barley; beautifully buttery, too; **t**23 succulent: stunningly juicy with a lovely thumbprint of the delicate oils so typical of Strathisla; **f**23 much more of an oaky theme, as should be the case but still that bitter-sweet barley rumbles; **b**24 if you want to sample exactly how this excellent distillery should be at 18, here's your man....but it takes it perhaps a notch further. The sheer élan of the layers, the intensity to the body; the absolute mmmm-i-ness of this makes it among the best single malts of the year, though not quite the best Strathisla... **58.4%**

**Cadenhead's Authentic Collection Strathisla-Glenlivet Aged 18 Years** Bourbon Hogshead, dist 87, bott May 05 **(94) n**24 an astonishing complexity of bourbon-assisted citrus and barley. Oh, and apple. Both bitter and sweet, this repays a good ten minutes' sniffing; **t**24 dream-like balance between myriad malty tones and vanilla. Mouthwatering and succulent; **f**22 errs on the side of age here, with the soft oak tones having the final, softly spoken say; **b**24 Strathisla at its most tart, busy and mercurial. **58.4%**. *198 bottles.*

**Cadenhead's Authentic Collection Strathisla-Glenlivet Aged 19 Years** Bourbon Hogshead, dist 87, bott Spet 06 **(89) n**22 stunning esters; not a million miles from a Long Pond rum; **t**23 lush, continuing the rummy theme with a golden sugar edge to both the oak and barley; **f**22 continues its lengthy tale with more of the same and a gradual build up of drier vanilla; **b**22 a strange and delicious beast for rum lovers. **59.5%**. *264 bottles.*

**Cask Strength Strathisla 1985** bott 4 Jul 05 **(94) n**24 gorgeously floral with a touch of African violet. Honeyed and a tad spicy, too. Shimmering and fabulous; **t**23 wonderfully layered, there is a touch of rich copper adding lustre to the barley and honey. The intensity defies belief, but it is the layering that makes this so special; just so clean, too; **f**23 long, barley-sugar dotted again with acacia honey and that intense copper-effect; **b**24 absolutely everything you can ask for from this great distillery, and a little more besides. **62.8%**. *G&M USA* .

**Coopers Choice Strathisla 1969 Aged 36 Years** Single Cask Range, bott 05 **(95) n**25 a perfection of unblemished sherry, spiced apple tart, scalded raisins, molassed-sweet malt (even slightly Demerara rummy to that effect) and ripe, crushed sultanas. Nose for at least 10-15 minutes before drinking...; **t**23 big, pounding, sweet malt all wrapped in drying hickory and cocoa; **f**23 the enormity of the body continues but in pulsing waves of spice and other nuances of beautiful oak; **b**24 quite awesome: if you want to see what a sherry used to be able to do to whisky, exactly what perfection from Jerez means, then here is a malt that is both a stunning experience and an education to the uninitiated. This is one the likes of which we are unlikely ever to see again. And a primer as to why I often mark modern sherry butts so low. Easily one of the whiskies of the year. **55%**. *Vintage Malt Whisky Co.*

**D&M Aficionados' Club Bottling Strathisla Aged 30 Years** cask no. 4215, dist May 76 **(78) n**21 **t**19 **f**19 **b**19. Sound nose, but once on the palate starts wheezing a bit and has a furry finish. **43%**. **nc ncf.** *US by Angus Dundee.*

**Duncan Taylor Strathisla 1967** cask no.1881, dist Mar 67, bott 15 Mar 06 **(91) n**24 wonderful bourbon depth; leather armchairs, dates and walnuts topped by honeycomb: the way an old malt should be; **t**22 oak shapes the attack, first gently and then permitting toasty barley; drier towards the middle with roast malt. The secret, though, is the gentle honey background; **f**22 maintains its class despite the big oak thanks to a drizzle of maple syrup; **b**23 a glorious old 'un that has gone as far as it can and kept its charisma. A serious must have for bourbon lovers, too! **48.8%**

⋅⋅⋅ **Duncan Taylor Collection Strathisla 1967** Cask no. 1894 **(89) n**22 pure bourbon... **t**23 myriad dark sugars, mostly of the molassed variety, gather to make a juicy statement; **f**22 red liquorice, butterscotch on toast; the vaguest honey balancing out vanilla; **b**22 Yesiree, Bob... they darn tootin' know how to make great whisky in Kentucky. Errr... I mean, Speyside, ken. **48.8%**

**Gordon & MacPhail Distillery Label Strathisla 1960** bott 12.08.05 **(83) n**19 **t**23 **f**20 **b**21. The nose suggests a procession of splinters should follow but the grand old distillery retains a surprise smoke package which for about 45 glorious seconds lifts the malt into a glorious wrinkly world. The finish is dry and oak infested, but just hang on to those few glorious moments when you are transported back nearly 40 years and softly peated Speyside barley reigns supreme. **46%**. *US Market.*

**Kingsbury's New Celtic Strathisla 15 Years Old** dist 89 **(77) n**20 **t**19 **f**19 **b**19. Although sulphur has, sadly, got in among the grape, it must originally have been a supreme sherry butt *Japan Import System*

**Murray McDavid Mission Strathisla 1967** Bourbon/Grenache Banyuls **(85) n**22 **t**21 **f**21 **b**21. From the school of exotic fruit via bourbon college. Has just about controlled on the oak, but needed a few fruit salad/black Jack nails to help keep the lid on. **43.6%**. *300 btls.*

**Old Malt Cask Strathisla Aged 10 Years** Refill hogshead no.1497, dist Nov 93, bott Oct 04 **(86) n**22 **t**22 **f**21 **b**21. No complications here: just decent malt with a lovely barley richness. **50%. nc ncf.** *Douglas Laing.*

**Old Malt Cask Strathisla Aged 28 Years** dist Nov 75, bott Dec 03 **(79) n**18 **t**23 **f**19 **b**19. A summer or two too many for this one. Still sparkles with the fabulous mock bourbon on the fruity mouth arrival and offers a glorious mouthful. But the nose and tail show some cracks. **50%. nc ncf sc.** *Douglas Laing.*

**Private Collection Strathisla 1955 (84) n**23 coffee iced biscuit; thick, sweetish sherry and biting spice: classic ye-olde sherry butt and one, in its day, of the very highest order; **t**23 hold on to your seat: the spice latches on to your throat and tastebuds and refuse to let go; the sherry really is heavyweight stuff that is brilliantly balanced between sweet toffee and bitter pear-drops; **f**18 pretty shattered: an oak-exhausted bitterness softened by liquorice; **b**20 full tasting notes because this old timer deserves it. **59.2%.** *G & M*

⋅⋅⋅ **Provenance Strathisla Aged 11 Years** dist Winter 95, bott Winter 06 **(84) n**21 **t**22 **f**20 **b**21. Wow!. A syrupy little blighter. Lovely, but hard to find the second dimension. **46%**

**Provenance Strathisla 12 Years Old** dist 4 Jun 92, bott 15 Mar 05 **(80) n**19 **t**21 **f**20 **b**20. Malty but disappointingly flat and tired. **46%.** *Douglas Laing & Co.*

⋅⋅⋅ **Scotch Malt Whisky Society Cask 58.12 Aged 33 Years** Sherry Hogshead, dist Apr 73 **(93) n**25 a gem of a sherry butt from the golden (quite literally) age of when the Chivas distilleries were sent the finest casks in living memory from Jerez. This is typical: coral-reef clarity visually and on the nose with near perfect integration between oak and grape. Fabulous and faultless.... **t**23 some oaky traces on impact but the Dundee cake is both rich and a tad dry; **f**22 nougat and raisins; sawdusty towards the death **b**23 doesn't quite go along with the nose, but it would take a quite exceptional whisky to do that. Isn't that right, Doris...? **51.3%**

⋅⋅⋅ **Whisky-Doris Strathisla Aged 35 Years** Sherry cask no. 2516, dist 15 May 69, bott 11 Feb 05 **(97) n**25 A quite perfect sherry butt. The nutty, oloroso influence is not only faultlessly clean and perfectly defined but just osmotic enough to allow on board the barley and oak balance that a great whisky demands. Something that can be nosed for hours on end... **t**24 warming and intense, for a while the sherry holds complete control, but further analysis shows this is not just sherry, but melted into it is the barley, juicy enough to lighten the grapey intensity; then a wave of natural toffees gleaned from the oak and a drizzle of mocha for bliss; **f**23 the first hint of bitterness as the oak rumbles in, as it has every right to do after 35 years but the mocha continues; **b**25 May 1969: I was scoring the first run ever in the history of the newly opened Ruskin Junior School, far too young to drink whisky (though by then I had!!), and 500 miles away someone was filling new make into a butt blessed by angels. A dram of sighs... **56.3%.** *Germany*

# STRATHMILL
### Speyside, 1891. Diageo. Working.
**Strathmill Aged 12 Years** db **(79) n**21 **t**21 **f**18 **b**19. A big malt for a normally light,

delicate Speysider. Brilliant spice and rich mouthfeel but fatally let down by caramel-toffee. Strathmill, but not as God intended. **43%**. *Flora and Fauna range.*

**Cadenhead's Authentic Collection Strathmill Aged 12 Years** dist 92, bott Feb 05 **(77)** n19 t21 f19 b18. Off-balance and hot (and that has nothing to do with the strength). There is a wall of early malt, but it's just not up to this distillery's usual excellent standards. **63.9%**. *216 bottles.*

**Chieftain's Choice Strathmill Aged 11 Years** Refill sherry no. 226, dist Mar 94, bott Apr 05 **(75)** n18 t19 f19 b19. Even this great distillery can't win against a sulphur-nipped cask. **43%**. *Ian Macleod. 702 bottles.*

**Dewar Rattray Individual Cask Bottling Strathmill 1989 Aged 15 Years** cask no. 10303, dist Oct 89, bott Nov 04 **(94)** n23 wonderful spice buzz tries to disrupt the precision of the barley which in equal measures dishes out cut grass and honey on toast. Fascinating and fun; t24 the best body I have seen away from a French beech; the light oils help build the astonishing intensity to the barley. The tastebuds almost swoon under the attack; f23 sandalwood and demerara sugar unite for a long and delightful finale; b24 how long have I argued that this is an undiscovered jewel? Grab a bottle of this and see what I mean. **63.5%**. *407 bottles.*

**Duncan Taylor Strathmill 1975 Aged 28 Years** cask 1891 **(79)** n18 t21 f20 b20. Some lovely nougat-honey moments, but also hot and ungainly: the make is too delicate to take the weight. **48.7%**

⸭ **Norse Cask Selection Strathmill 1992 Aged 13 Years** **(87)** n20 heavier and relatively shapeless for this distillery at this age; a touch of bourbon; t22 stunning recovery as the crystal-clear barley punches through; f23 massive malt continues to shimmer despite having entirely consumed the soft oak; b22 quite an aggressive Strathmill with much greater weight to the barley than usual. **64%**. *WhiskyOwner.com, Denmark.*

**Old Malt Cask Strathmill Aged 40 Years** dist Apr 63, bott Aug 03 **(89)** n22 t23 f22 b22. On the edge of going over the top, we have almost nerveless brinkmanship here. Quite superb malt and rare to see such a light and delicate dram last the pace. **50%. nc ncf sc.** *Douglas Laing.*

⸭ **Old Malt Cask Strathmill Aged 45 Years** dist Apr 62, bott May 07 **(90)** n23 liquorice allsorts – especially the coffee ones. A hint of smoke on the oloroso; t22 brinkmanship oakiness early on but recovers as the black treacle leaches in; f22 molassed coffee and liquorice; again the vaguest echo of smoke b23 quite amazed that such a light malt – even sherry aided – could last this amount of time. One of the surprises of the year. **40.5%**. *Douglas Laing. 317 bottles.*

**Old Masters Strathmill 1992** bott 03 **(81)** n19 t22 f20 b20. Real highpropane, heavy-duty Speysider at its very maltiest. **64.2%. nc ncf.** *James MacArthur.*

⸭ **The Spirit Safe & Cask Strathmill 1988 Aged 16 Years** dist 1988, bott 2004 **(88)** n22 pulsing clean barley; t22 the oak has dampened down the barley sweetness but still the intensity is salivating and superb; f22 long, dry in parts and still very clean, some real old-fashioned J&B moments here; b22 Strathmill at its Strathmilliest... **43%. nc ncf.** *Celtic Whisky Compagnie.*

## TALISKER
### Highland (Island–Skye), 1832. Diageo. Working.

**Talisker Aged 10 Years** db **(93)** n23 Cumberland sausage and kipper side by side; t23 early wisps of smoke that develop into something a little spicier; lively barley that feels a little oak-dried but sweetens out wonderfully; f24 still not at full throttle with the signature ka-boom spice, but never less than enlivening. Some wonderful chocolate adds to the smoke; b23 it is wonderful to report that the deadening caramel that had crept into recent bottlings of the 10-y-o has retreated, and although that extraordinary, that wholly unique finale has still to be re-found in its unblemished, explosive entirety, this is much, much closer to the mark and a quite stupendous malt to be enjoyed at any time. But at night especially. **45.8%**

**Talisker Aged 18 Years** bott 21 Mar 05 db **(94)** n22 a curious delivery of soapy smoke and almost over-ripe nectarines; t23 wonderful, almost unbelievable softness to the arrival: the palate is met by a wall of brown-sugartinged malt and then a gradual build-up of smoke and spice; the middle is infiltrated by just enough oak to confirm its age;

**f**24 a gentle series of muffled explosions as the spice is almost, but thankfully not quite, contained by the richness of the fruit and malt; **b**25 you can forgive the odd old blemish on the nose: what happens in the palate is a masterful telling of the Talisker tale: all what should be is there and in perfect proportions. Exceptional. **45.8%**

**Talisker Aged 20 Years** db **(95) n**24 **t**24 **f**23 **b**24. I have been tasting Talisker for 28 years. This is the best bottling ever. Miss this and your life will be incomplete. **62%**

**Talisker 20 Years Old** db bott 03 **(93) n**21 **t**24 **f**24 **b**24. This is major whisky for most the demanding of palates. Absolutely no signs of weakness for its age. **58.8%**

∴ **Talisker 25 Years Old** Special Releases 2006 db **(95) n**24 as volcanic as the rocks surrounding the distillery, except there's nothing extinct here, despite the age…spices batter the nose and smoke keeps to grips with the oak; **t**24 Krakatoa on the tastebuds as the spices let rip from the first nanosecond, then a bedazzling array of smoke and malt and for a few seconds only some exotic fruit suggests the oak has aged too far – then disappears… **f**23 spicy aftershocks… **b**24 No 25-year-old has the right to be this feisty and fit. An amazing whisky experience where the spiced-up peat is indelibly tattooed on your tastebuds… **56.9%**

**Talisker 25 Years Old** db **(94) n**21 for all its strength, relatively docile and shy with sweet vanilla to the fore and some peek-a-boo smoke and a strand of honey; **t**24 sweet malt with more than a hint of exotic fruit, and then the most wonderful multiplying of smoke towards the middle, starting off as a suggestion and ending as a statement; oak also arrives in the first nanosecond but is controlled and adds structure; **f**25 fizzing, buzzing spices on a bed of Old Jamaica fruit chocolate. Soft oils help ensure this is the most faultless of finales…; **b**24 the nose lulls you into thinking this will be a dull affair. My God! It is anything but! Magical and enchanting. **57.8%**

∴ **Talisker 30 Years Old** Special Releases 2006 db **(91) n**22 the smoke has drifted off over time to leave soft fruits; **t**24 but the spices have stayed behind…and some!! A shattering attack of peppers while elsewhere the barley displays a lovely gloss and latent sweetness; **f**22 as everything else dies the spices remain and get warmer still; **b**23 this was the first distillery I ever visited – way back in 1975. When this malt was a glint in the stillman's eye. It was a distillery which changed my life. Taste this at 30…and you can see why. **51.9%**

**Talisker 175 Anniversary** db **(88) n**23 subtle and restrained by Talisker standards, with plenty of orange peel to complement the unusually even peats. There is a lovely Talisker buzz, though, if not particularly loud; **t**22 a toffeed, gentle sweetness accompanies the smoke and though some of the trademark peppers and spices escape the creamy clutches, it's all pretty restrained stuff; **f**21 a return of the marmalade but it's a relatively dull affair; **b**22 very good whisky? Yes. Great Talisker? No. Someone told me that a prominent website in France gave this 19/20. They could be right: everyone's opinion is valid. (Well, with the exception of one or two self-appointed duds I could name). But I'd happily wager £1,000 to charity that most people taking that lofty score to heart will be greatly disappointed. **45.8%**

**Old Malt Cask Director's Tactical Selection 1982 Aged 23 Years** Sherry dist 21 Jan 82, bott 31 Jan 05 **(79) n**20 **t**21 **f**19 **b**19. The kind of sherry cask which, for me, is just too in your face and over the top. The distillery character has entirely vanished under the grape. **50%**

**Old Malt Cask Director's Tactical Selection 1982 Aged 23 Years** dist 1 Apr 82, bott 14 Apr 05 **(84) n**20 **t**21 **f**22 **b**21. Beautifully intense malt, although the oak is a bit too indulgent. **50%**. *Douglas Laing.*

∴ **Old Malt Cask Tactical Aged 18 Years** dist Apr 85, bott Jan 07 **(94) n**23 butterscotch with some telling smoke; **t**24 honey-ginger delivery escorted by soft smoke; the trademark spices arrive on about the sixth flavour wave and build in beautiful intensity; **f**23 the spices hold sway as the smoked-honey retreats; **b**24 I'm amazed: even after 18 years the spices are there in force to dazzle in a glorious expression. **50%**. *327 bottles.*

∴ **Old Malt Cask Tactical Aged 25 Years Sherry Finish** dist Dec 80, bott Oct 06 **(78) n**20 **t**20 **f**19 **b**19. The spice tries to see off the unwelcome yellow intruder… **50%**.*418 btls.*

∴ **Secret Stills Isle of Skye 1955** Distillery No. 1 Release No. 1, bott 05 **(95) n**25 from the mahogany colour, I could have written the nosing notes even before I sniffed it. And it was exactly as expected: nutty, sweetly spiced but the body of the aroma held by absolutely unspoiled, rich old oloroso. This is OAP: Old Age Perfection… **t**23 dissolves on the palate on touchdown with the concentrated sultanas throwing a sweet blanket over any encroaching oak. This, being Talisker, just has to spice itself up, which it does, gloriously; **f23** some understandable tiredness to the oak, but it never comes close to threatening the unravelling of the Demerara- sweetened coffee and peppered oloroso finale; **b24** Once, G&M would have bottled this at 40% and a lot of the magic would have been lost. Here, we taste a malt that is immeasurably better than it has any right to be and simply reinforces exactly why tasting truly great whisky is as much an honour as it is a pleasure. **45%**. *Gordon & MacPhail. 573 bottles.*

**The Whisky Fair Artist Edition Talimburg Aged 20 Years** Bourbon Hogshead, dist May 86, bott June 06 **(86)** **n24 t22 f20 b20**. Breathtaking nose and start, but the cask hadn't read the script. **43.8%**. *Germany. 240 bottles.*

**The Whisky Fair Talimburg 23 Years Old** Bourbon Hogshead, dist May 82 **(92)** **n23** a right old duff up between some vicious peats and bruising oak. Sit back, close the eyes and sense the spectacle...!!; **t23** some real fire with the peat ripping into the tastebuds with trademark brio; the sweetness feathers perfectly with the developing smoke; **f23** an oilier than usual finale for this distillery with grist and citrus seeing off the vanilla; **b23** sheer, undiluted quality ...! **49.5%**. *Germany. 222 bottles.*

## TAMDHU
### Speyside, 1897. Edrington. Working.

**Tamdhu** db **(87)** **n23** grassy, fresh, juicy, youthful, boiled fruit candy, coke smoke: pure Speyside in a sniff; **t22** very light malt, extremely clean, newly cut grass, deliciously chewy; **f21** perhaps a hint of toffee but the malty show rumbles on with good weight and late burst of non-peated smoke; **b21** nothing like as oily as of old; charmingly refreshing, non-threatening and enjoyable. **40%**

**Tamdhu 25 Years Old** db **(88)** **n22** citrus showing now a more orangey based style to the lemon of its youth; **t22** typically fat and intense; the barley eventually escapes the gravitational pull of the oils to offer a wonderful barley sweetness; **f21** dried dates vanilla; **b23** radiates quality. **43%**

**Adelphi Tamdhu 1982 Aged 22 Years** cask no. 2453, dist 82, bott 05 **(88)** **n22 t23 f21 b22**. One of those drams that have theoretically gone OTT, but work rather beautifully. **55.2%**. *212 btls.*

**Chieftain's Tamdhu 12 Years Old Sherry Finish** **(80)** **n18 t22 f20 b20**. The sherry offers a pleasant, fruity weightiness and spice but the natural oiliness of the spirit limits the scope of complexity. **43%**. *Ian Macleod.*

**Dun Bheagan Tamdhu 12 Years Old Rum Finish** **(87)** **n22** the most distant hint of coal smoke anchors the grist and sprinkled sugar; **t22** an unusual and level sweetness rounds the barley's natural juiciness; **f21** soft, slightly sweetened vanilla and barley; **b22** much crisper than the standard Tamdhu, with a vague, brittle sugariness driving the style: complex and needs some patience. **43%**.

**Dun Bheagan Tamdhu Aged 15 Years** Port Finish **(84)** **n22 t20 f22 b20**. Enormously winy and a bit sticky around the gills; the malt has lost the space to breath. Conjures some lovely moments, though. **43%**. *Ian Macleod.*

**Harris Whisky Co. Tamdhu Aged 14 Years** cask no. 14085, dist Dec 91, bott Jan 06 **(86)** **n23 t22 f20 b21**. Another desirable malt from this excellent new company, but would have been at optimum ripeness for picking three or four summers earlier. **58.5%. nc ncf.**

⠿ **MacPhail's Collection Tamdhu 1962** Ref 1877 **(87)** **n20** a dash of creosote to complement the plums and toffee apple; **t23** enormous delivery with the spice hitting the tape alongside the medium roast Java. A teaspoonful of Demerara helps it along. Big... **f22** long, with plenty of coffee and liquorice amid the splinters; **b21** has withstood the years better than some individuals of this vintage I know. Been helped along the way by a pretty sound sherry butt. A long way from perfect, but a grand old timer nonetheless. **43%**

⠿ **MacPhail's Collection Tamdhu 1966** Ref 1879 **(77)** **n19 t19 f20 b19**. The odd decent bit of fruit and saving sweetness here and there, but bottled about a decade too late. **43%**

⠿ **Milroy's of Soho Tamdhu 1990** Hogshead, cask no. 10140, dist 20 Jun 90, bott 18 Aug 06 **(82)** **n19 t21 f21 b21**. Pleasant, malty and well spiced. **46%**. *373 bottles.*

**Old Malt Cask Tamdhu Aged 10 Years** Refill Hogshead no. 1925, dist Nov 94, bott Oct 05 **(93)** **n23** very delicate peat enhances the clarity of the barley: genuinely classy; **t23** the landing would barely cause a ripple on a pond: again the smoke shows early and acts as a buffer for the oily, mouth-watering barley; **f23** mocha and Demerara offer countless juicy waves in the very long finale; **b24** this malt in its natural blending colours

– and age – knocks the crap out of the majority of fancy finishes. A lesson to be learned? **50%. nc ncf.** *Douglas Laing.*

**Old Malt Cask Tamdhu 29 Years Old** dist Feb 77, bott Jan 06 **(89) n21** pretty ripe mango and calvados; **t23** luxuriant fruit again, especially bitter marmalade, but this time weighed down with a dash of peat and mocha; **f22** the chocolaty theme continues and even some barley reveals itself for a juicy burst at the death; **b23** first impression on the nose suggest a spent force; it's performance on the palate is a revelation! **50%. 211 bottles.**

**Provenance Tamdhu Aged 10 Years** dist Nov 94, bott Sept 05 **(77) n20 t19 f19 b19.** Oily and clean. But my God it's dull. **46%.** *McGibbon's.*

## TAMNAVULIN
**Speyside. 1966. Whyte and Mackay.**

**Tamnavulin 12 Years Old** db **(79) n19 t20 f21 b19.** Quite weighty for a Speysider with a deliciously massive malty kick. But missing out on complexity somewhat. **40%**

⋅:⋅ **Tamnavulin 1966 Aged 35 Years** Cream Sherry Butt db **(91) n24** cleanest sherry imaginable: thick, glutinous nose with cream soda and toffee; **t22** enormous delivery of oak and toffee raisin; **f23** thins out to allow complexity to evolve, which it does with a fudgy chewiness; **b22** for those who love great old sherry, this is an absolute. Perhaps too much sherry to ever make it a true great, but there is no denying such quality. **52.6%**

**Cadenhead's Authentic Collection Tamnavulin-Glenlivet Aged 14 Years** Bourbon Hogshead, dist 92, bott Sept 06 **(87) n21** unusual, clipped European style. Hints of tobacco and fruity barley; **t22** spice kick to the marauding, mouth-watering barley; **f22** long, leafy and lingering; the freshness of the barley is a constant; **b22** has the curious tobacco edge found in some mainland European malts. Entertaining. **58.2%. 258 bottles.**

**Cadenhead's Authentic Collection Tamdhu-Glenlivet Aged 15 Years** Bourbon Hogshead, dist 91, bott Sept 06 **(79) n20 t21 f19 b19.** Barley emphatic but unusually oil-less and coarse. **58.9%. 318 bottles.**

**Connoisseurs Choice Tamnavulin 1989 (82) n20 t21 f20 b21.** Delicate and retiring despite the intense malt holding court. For those with a penchant for egg custard. **43%**

⋅:⋅ **Master of Malt Tamnavulin 14 Years Old (74) n18 t19 f18 b19.** Decidedly below par. **46%.** *Master of Malt, UK.*

**Old Malt Cask Tamnavulin 14 Years Old** dist 31 May 91, bott Jul 05 **(91) n22** Marigolds growing from a bed of grist..??? A mixture of something astonishingly floral and the Porteus; **t23** a sensational ebullience to the ultra refreshing barley; liquidized grist; **f23** a tiny speck of smoke and spices make for an amazingly long, chewy finale with not a hint of bitterness or oaky over-excitement. Just lovely...! **b23** now this is simple and, quite simply, great malt. **50%.** *Douglas Laing. 328 bottles.*

**Provenance Tamnavulin 10 Years Old** dist 9 Dec 94, bott 23 Feb 05 **(88) n23 t21 f22 b22.** Clean, hard, yet entertaining and stylish. **46%.** *Douglas Laing.*

⋅:⋅ **Provenance Tamnavulin Aged 12 Years** dist Winter 94, bott Winter 07 **(83) n19 t22 f21 b21.** Wow! If you like your malt green, grassy and salivating then, at last, the dram of your dreams. **46%.** *Douglas Laing.*

## TEANINICH
**Highland (Northern), 1817. Diageo. Working.**

**Teaninich Aged 10 Years** bott 18 Feb 05 db **(84) n21 t21 f21 b21.** A very even, ultra-malty, outwardly light dram with some pleasantly lurking spice. **43%.**

**The Bottlers Teaninich 1982 Aged 21 Years** cask 7202 **(96) n24 t24 f24 b24.** Near faultless malt from the type of sherry butt that deserves worshipping. A genuine masterpiece bottled at an age that encompasses the brilliance of both the malt and the cask: one to remember for the rest of your life. **62.3%.** *Raeborn*

**Cadenhead's Authentic Collection Teaninich Aged 12 Years** Bourbon Hogshead, dist 93, bott Sept 06 **(88) n21** a curious grape and citrus freshness slightly out of sync; **t23** beautiful construction to the intensity of the barley and also those unusual fruit edges; **f22** thins out slightly to allow attractive oak dryness; **b22** juicy and attractive throughout. **58.3%. 282 bottles.**

**Cadenhead's Authentic Collection Teninich Aged 22 Years** dist 83, bott May 05 **(71) n18 t18 f17 b18.** Less than perfect sherry influence. **55.3%. 252 bottles.**

**Connoisseurs Choice Teaninich 1991 (83) n**21 t21 f21 b20. A basic, pretty simple banana and custard affair. **46%.** *Gordon & MacPhail.*

**Dewar Rattray Individual Cask Bottling Teaninich 1975 Aged 30 Years** cask no. 9419, dist Aug 75, bott May 06 **(86) n**23 t22 f20 b21. Too old, frankly. But there are some really excellent, highly complex moments to savour. **60.8%.** *486 bottles.*

**Lombard Brands Teaninich 12 Years Old Single Malt (85) n**21 t22 f21 b21. An agreeable, chewy malt with some good barley sugar. But it feels as though someone left the hand brake on... 43%. *Lombards Brands.*

**Part Nan Angelen Teaninich 25 years Old (83) n**21 t22 f19 b21. Softly smoked and floral nose, well supported by the early freshness of the banana and malt mouth arrival; very dry, tired finish. **43%**

⇌ **The Queen of the Moorlands Rare Cask Teaninich 1993 Edition XIX (93) n**23 so complex! Everything geared on the herby/spicy side of the spectrum... **t**24 a real touch of the 'Morangies about this one, showing much of its neighbourly trait of massive complexity with the odd orangey fleck that turns up now and again **f**23 very long, extremely delicate and goes back over the finer points of the taste but in almost minute detail; **b**23 anyone putting forward an argument that there is a Black Isle style of whisky will use this in evidence alongside a standard 10-y-o Glenmorangie. Sometimes the similarities are startling. Truly great whisky. **51.5%. nc ncf.** *Available at The Wine Shop, Leek.*

# TOBERMORY
**Highland (Island—Mull), 1795. Burn Stewart. Working.**

**Ledaig** db **(83) n**18 t22 f22 b21. A tad feinty (especially on the nose), though the extra oils help spread the dense peat. Interesting at this central European strength. **42%**

**Ledaig Aged 7 Years** db **(81) n**19 t21 f21 b20. Young, off balance, off key, though the salty nose might get those more red-blooded bulls among us purring...if you get my drift, lads! Enormously sweet, a hint of feint but quite a lip smacking experience, so to speak. 81/100 for a Ledaig. 181/100 if it's Miltonduff you're after... Meeeoww!! **43%**

⇌ **Ledaig Aged 10 Years** db **(76) n**18 t20 f19 b19. Smoky. But no prizes for great whisky-making in this bottling. **43%**

**Ledaig Sherry Finish** db **(79) n**19 t22 f19 b19. Sherry fails to master the feints. **42%**

**Ledaig Vintage 1972** Oloroso Sherry Cask Finished, cask filled 21 Dec 72, bott 08 Sep 04 db **(92) n**23 where worlds collide: massive sherry goes head first into solid peat; **t**24 wonderful: as good an arrival as any sherry cask in the last 12 months, with faultless oloroso caressing the vast expanse of smoky barley; **f**22 a bit thinner at the death but long and crisp; **b**23 like a smoky Macallan, but with some extra salt added. **48.5%. ncf.** *1,000 bottles.*

**Tobermory Aged 10 Years** db **(90) n**21 less floral than last year's bottling, a tad more youth but the salt still straps itself to the barley; **t**22 refreshing malt cleanses the palate; but now much heavier with some substantial oils bubbling up and, again, some youthfulness apparent; **f**24 the late middle and early finish offers a mind-blowing display of honey, helping cement the lush personality; **b**23 a slightly different character to previous bottlings with big honey through the middle making up for some under-developed areas. But the whole remains genuinely a great experience. **40%**

⇌ **Berry's Own Selection Tobermorey 1995** Casks no. 486/487, bott 07 **(86) n**19 t22 f23 b22. Marzipan and cherry kernel You'll go nuts for it once your palate acclimatizes... **51.8%**

**Berrys' Own Selection Tobermory 1995 Aged 11 Years (89) n**21 ordinary and unassuming; **t**23 young at first followed by gorgeous honey-salt delivery and then complex waves of bitter-sweet barley; **f**23 long, with a magnificent saline tail. The vanilla arrives late, but the salt still tenderly dominates; **b**22 busy, demanding malt full of riches: one that needs three or four mouthfuls before the enormity begins to bite. Seriously scrummy. **46%.**

**Blackadder Raw Cask Ledaig 13 Year Old** cask no. 123, dist 5 May 92, bott May 05 **(94) n**23 t23 f24 b24. What the hell is this freakish whisky?? Whatever it is, I want a full bottle, not this useless 10cl sample. Magnificent! **46.1%.** *Only 30 bottles.*

**Cadenhead's Authentic Collection Ledaig Aged 14 Years** Bourbon Hogshead, dist 92, bott May 06 **(91) n**21 crazy, confused nose: a hint of smoke, but it is swamped in an oaky-god-knows-what; **t**23 a pause on arrival and then a shuddering delivery of sharp intense barley and spice. Again the smoke struggles to find its place; **f**23 much better once it has calmed and some peat relaxes into the rich vein of barley and then rich, dry cocoa; **b**24 somewhat anarchic and enormous, this does not follow any pattern. The result, though, is wonderful: it is so diverse, so multi-layered, it is has many of the attributes of a fine blend! **59.6%.** *294 bottles.*

⋅⋅⋅⋅ **Chieftain's Ledaig 1973 Aged 32 Years** Hogshead, dist June 73 **(95) n**24 delicate smoke, honey and orange blossom: even though oak is apparent, it's just in the right quantities. A little charmer; **t**24 wonderful honey-smoke core puts paid to an oaky intent; the balance is stunning as is the degree of soft oil. A malt with near perfect weight... **f**23 incredibly light on its feet as it nimbly moves from smoke to cocoa to barley; **b**24 magnificent whisky that is as well balanced as absolutely no whisky of this age has any right to be! Unquestionably one of the bottlings of the year. **45%. nc ncf.** *Ian Macleod.*

⋅⋅⋅⋅ **Chieftain's Ledaig 1973 Aged 32 Years** Hogshead, dist June 73 **(86) n**22 **t**22 **f**21 **b**21. Just not in the same league as its twin. The smoke has been suppressed by something fruity giving the oak a chance to spoil the balance. Enjoyable, but as far as the oak goes, it's on the wrong side of the tracks. **45.9%. nc ncf.** *Ian Macleod.*

⋅⋅⋅⋅ **Connoisseurs Choice Ledaig 1990 (85) n**21 **t**21 **f**22 **b**21. The smoke is deceptive: there is less than there appears to be. Good honey, though. **43%.** *Gordon & MacPhail.*

**Murray McDavid Tobermory Aged 9 Years** cask MM0420, dist 95, bott 04 **(79) n**19 **t**21 **f**20 **b**19. Lacking cohesion, but the marzipan's a treat. **46%. nc ncf.**

⋅⋅⋅⋅ **Murray McDavid Tobermory 1994 Aged 12 Years** Bourbon/Madeira **(72) n**17 **t**19 **f**18 **b**18. Either a very average Madeira cask. Or poor distillate. Most likely both. **46%**

**Old Malt Cask Tobermory 10 Years Old** dist Apr 96 bott Jan 06 **(79) n**18 **t**21 **f**20 **b**20. Fresh and recovers with stimulating barley from a so-so nose. **50%.** *359 bottles.*

**Provenance Ledaig Aged 8 Years (86) n**21 **t**23 **f**21 **b**21. Thundering peat but new-makey and a tad feinty. An early juice-fest, though. **46%.**

**Signatory Ledaig 1974 Aged 30 Years** cask 3223, dist 25 Jun 74, bott 11 Mar 05 **(83) n**21 **t**22 **f**20 **b**20. Lots of toffee apple and spice ... and oak. **48.7%.**

⋅⋅⋅⋅ **The Single Malts of Scotland Tobermory 1995 Aged 10 Years** Small batch **(73) n**18 **t**19 **f**18 **b**18. Feinty. Off-key. **56.9%. cs.** *Speciality Drinks, UK.*

⋅⋅⋅⋅ **Whisky-Doris Tobermory Aged 34 Years** Sherry cask, dist Dec 72, bott Feb 07 **(90) n**23 a dripping nose...of pure, unruined, old time sherry... **t**22 spicy kick on entry then an outrageous, nutty grape attack with every soldier from Jerez; **f**23 much better when settled with a toffee apple fade; **b**22 I'm sure that once upon-a-time I used not to like this kind of whisky. Now, after so few chances to be merry thanks to poor sherry, I'm beginning to love even the odd OTT classic. **49.5%. ncf.** *Germany. 96 bottles.*

**The Whisky Shop Ledaig 8 Years Old (88) n**21 **t**22 **f**23 **b**22. Young yet confident, there are no significant feints: the distillery is deliciously back on track! **40%.** *(bottled in store) Scotland.*

**Wilson & Morgan Barrel Selection Tobermory 1995 Sherry Wood** dist 95, bott 06 **(84) n**20 **t**21 **f**22 **b**21. Some honey on the salty sherry. **46%.**

# TOMATIN
### Speyside, 1897. Working.

**Tomatin 12 Years Old** db **(79) n**21 **t**20 **f**19 **b**19. A much happier and better proportioned dram than of old, having eschewed its sherry weirdness for something a lot more mouthwateringly malty and vibrant. **40%**

⋅⋅⋅⋅ **Tomatin Aged 18 Years** db **(85) n**22 **t**21 **f**21 **b**21. I have always held a torch for this distillery and it is good to see some of the official older stuff being released. This one has some serious zing to it, leaving your tastebuds to pucker up - especially as the oak hits. **40%**

**Tomatin Malt 25 Years Old** bott 05 db **(88) n**22 pleasant citrus sharpens the straw and sawdust; **t**21 a beautiful, fresh fruit delivery....then goes flat. Revives after a few seconds to sweeten; **f**23 spicy cocoa balances the sweet barley marvellously; **b**22 a worrying fade to this dram and you think it's going to die on you. But fear not: loads of life in this gentle and lucid old timer! **43%**

⋅⋅⋅⋅ **Tomatin 1962** db **(86) n**22 barley sugar, cough drops and sweet pipe tobacco: something of an old-fashioned candy store here; **t**23 over-ripe greengages vie with the liquorice and malt for top dog: it's a hard call; **f**19 the oak finally gains control; **b**22 over-tired on the finish, maybe. But there is no shortage of class and character on the nose and delivery. **40%**

⫶ Tomatin 1974 db **(87)** n21 dusty but some fruit wafts in from somewhere to offer a certain richness; t23 salivating first with malt, but as the oak mounts up the fruit returns; a delicate delivery with a pleasing coating of soft oil; f21 mildly overdone toast but the malt hangs about; b22 just manages to keep the oak enough at bay to make this a decent light night treat. **40%**

Cadenhead's Authentic Collection Tomatin Aged 17 Years Bourbon Hogshead, dist 89, bott Sept 06 **(84)** n20 t22 f20 b22. Competent and enjoyable malt though the bitter ill-at-ease finale no way reflects the mouth-watering, tangy barley with a barley sugar theme. **56.4%. 294 bottles.**

⫶ Chieftain's Tomatin 1992 Aged 14 Years Muscatel Finish dist 92 **(84)** n23 t19 f22 **b**20. Superb, confident and busy nose with a dense suety, grapey character which feels just a little confused on the palate until it relaxes for a quite excellent finale. Extremely different, interesting...and challenging **43%. nc ncf.** Ian Macleod.

Connoisseurs Choice Tomatin 1988 **(83)** n20 t21 f22 b20. Docile, simplistic malt but with an unusual yeasty nose. **43%.** Gordon & MacPhail.

Duncan Taylor Collection Tomatin 1965 Aged 40 Years cask no.1903, dist Jan 65, bott Jan 05 **(85)** n22 t22 f20 b21. Either my tastebuds have gone deaf or this is one of the quietest 40-year-olds for a long time. **47.6%**

Duncan Taylor Collection Tomatin 1965 cask no. 1904, dist Jan 65, bott Mar 06 **(77)** n18 t19 f20 b20. Hangs on in there thanks to a surprising injection of Demerara and barley sugar. But it's a close call. **45.9%. 181 bottles.**

⫶ Duncan Taylor Collection Tomatin 1977 Cask no. 1901 **(84)** n22 t21 f20 b21. Plenty of bourbon notes here from nose to finish though the hickory does make for a tight finale. A pleasing experience all the same. **43.3%.** Duncan Taylor.

Norse Cask Selection Tomatin 1989 Aged 15 Years **(85)** n21 t21 f22 b21. Exceptionally oily and creamy with massive chewiness to both barley and fruit. Big stuff. **57.7%.** Quality World, Denmark.

Norse Cask Selection Tomatin 1996 Aged 7 Years **(79)** n20 t21 f19 b19. I must be one of the biggest advocates for young malt going. But this narrowly misses the mark, perhaps by being, despite the obvious youth on the nose, a tad too advanced for its years. The big malt thrust on arrival is wonderful, but it is far flatter than one might otherwise expect. Curious. **50%.** Quality World, Denmark.

⫶ Old & Rare Tomatin Aged 31 Years Rioja Finish dist 1975, bott 07 **(86)** n21 t22 f21 b22. Rioja and Tomatin are not usual bed-fellows. But this one appears to work: this isn't a distillery with a track record for excellence at old age, but here the lively fruit really does give a welcome crutch to the big barley. Good stuff!! **55.6%.** Douglas Laing. 252 bottles.

⫶ Scotch Malt Whisky Society Cask 11.28 Aged 16 Years Refill Hogshead, dist May 90 **(82)** n21 t22 f19 b20. Delicious early tangy citrus; fluffy, uncomfortable fade. **55.6%**

⫶ The Spirit Safe & Cask Tomatin 1989 Aged 17 Years dist 1989, bott 07 **(91)** n23 find yourself a quiet corner of the house, a spare half hour and indulge: intense barley, but on just how many levels..? t23 a tsunami of honeycomb barley sweeps over the tastebuds bringing in its wake no shortage of oak. But its all wonderfully integrated, giving a toasty effect to the honey; f22 beautiful soft coffee, mainly Mysore; b23 if all 17-y-o Speysiders were like this, the world would be a happier place... **58.6%. nc ncf.** Celtic Whisky Compagnie.

# TOMINTOUL
**Speyside, 1965. Angus Dundee. Working.**

Tomintoul Aged 10 Years db **(79)** n20 t21 f19 b19. A fresh, clean, malty dram but leading to toffee fudge simplicity. **40%**

Tomintoul Aged 16 Years db **(88)** n22 a sharper, zestier aroma than before with diced apple where there was once raisins; t22 crisp, juicy barley to start and a wonderfully impressive array of sweet notes, becoming heavier and more demerara and toffee in style as it wears on; f22 much more bitter yet still within range of those deft sweet notes; some very late, lethargic spice; b22 it is always interesting to see a whisky change its shape slightly. No better or worse than before in quality, the emphasis has moved slightly away from the old soothing delivery to something a bit sharper and more pronounced. Yet at times still has all the grace of Peter Osgood in his prime. **40%**

**Tomintoul Aged 27 Years** db **(86) n**21 **t**23 **f**20 **b**22. An accomplished malt that shows few cracks despite the obvious great age for a Speysider. **40%**

**Adelphi Tomintoul 1967 Aged 38 Years** Bourbon Hogshead cask no. 4485, dist 67, bott Jun 06 **(79) n**21 **t**19 **f**19 **b**20. A real pity: one of those vaguely exotic fruity whiskies that has gone a couple of summers too long in the cask. Perhaps four or five years ago this would have been a minor classic dripping in honeycomb. Still, here's one for Chelsea supporters: the distillery is owned by a lifelong Chelsea season ticket holder, the Blues between 1924-28 had a full back called Alphonse Adelphi (23 appearances, 0 goals), the club were FA Cup Finalist in '67 under Tommy Docherty (who has been to one of my tastings) and won the Premiership in 2006. When put like that, what's a few splinters...? (Actually, I made one of those facts up. But which one?). **49.2%.** *Adelphi Distillery. 196 bottles.*

⬥ **D&M Aficionados' Club Bottling Tomintoul Aged 25 Years** Cask no. 5964, dist Oct 81 **(89) n**21 mild sawdust and butterscotch tart; **t**23 seriously delicious barley that gets the saliva gushing: no mean feat for something this ancient; something of the caramelised biscuit, too; **f**22 excellent touch of medium roast Java helped along with some mollassed oils; **b**23 a quarter centenarian that holds its head high without a single wrinkle to its character. **43%. nc ncf.** *US by Angus Dundee Distillers.*

⬥ **The Dram Tomintoul Vintage 1989** bott **(80) n**22 **t**21 **f**18 **b**19. Disappointingly dull finish defies the promise on nose and early mouth arrival. **43%. nc ncf.** *Whisky-Doris, Germany. 120 btls.*

**Mackillop's Choice Tomintoul 1966** cask no. 5259, dist Sep 66 **(92) n**24 a gentle salt and spice seasoning stirs up the sleepy oak and honey-tinged barley; impressively adroit – in a sluggish kind of way; **t**23 beautiful and dignified mouth arrival with almost malt concentrate heading off the mild hint of fruitcake topped with marzipan: as graceful as you could expect of so ancient a malt; **f**22 a little bit of oak and marmalade bitterness creeps in, but it's all rather oncepaced; **b**23 lethargic, though showing remarkably few wrinkles until the end; leave it in the glass to breathe for half an hour to unleash a lurking degree of sophistication. About as close as you'll ever come to feeling like a tortoise making love.... **43%.** *Angus Dundee.*

**Murray McDavid Tomintoul 1973 Mission IV Aged 31 Years (94) n**23 a fruity scent: melons, passion fruit and papaya, sprinkled with honied malt. Alas, no figs...; **t**24 melts in the mouth, licks around the tastebuds with a demure spice and soft barley sugar; **f**23 gentle spasms of soft oak embedded in a malty frame; **b**24 aaahhhh...oh,yes! At the end of a long tasting day – week, come to that – this is exactly the kind of dram you need before heading to bed: soothing, gentle, with perfectly understated curves and showing that touch of class, breeding and energy that serves you well under the covers and until the next morning...and just the right age, too.... **46%**

**The Peated Malt Old Ballantruan Speyside Glenlivet (88) n**21 young, a tad feinty, but with bubbling peat complementing the barley/fruity fudge; **t**22 some serious oils where the cut has been so wide. The peat has little coastal quality but instead imparts a delightful sweetness which clamps itself to every corner of the palate; **f**23 pretty long, skimping slightly on complexity but the developing spices dovetail sexily with the light muscovado-tinted malt; **b**22 I had tasted the new make smoked Tomintoul, but this was my first look at it as the finished article. A Speyside Young Ardbeg, I have heard some day. Hmmm, I think not. The soft feints are still there, as though the stillman has tried to extract every last drop out of the still, but this is malt that ultimately succeeds on its gifts rather than the fortitude of its failings. Worth an investigation. **50%. ncf.**

**Scott's Selection Tomintoul 1989** bott 05 **(78) n**20 **t**20 **f**19 **b**19. Despite the rich malt start, this is otherwise hot and Spartan. Older whisky lovers will remember Glen Scotia being almost identical in taste and style many years ago. **56.9%**

**Vom Fass Tomintoul 8 Years Old (78) n**19 **t**19 **f**21 **b**19. Pleasant but frustratingly light and non-committal. **40%.** *Austria.*

**The Whisky Castle Tomintoul 1992** cask 3085, dist 20 May 92 **(87) n**23 **t**22 **f**21 **b**21. Sound, confident malt. **63.5%.** *The Whisky Castle.*

# TORMORE
**Speyside, 1960. Chivas. Working.**

**Tormore 12 Year Old** db **(79)** n19 t21 f20 b19. The influence of then distillery manager John Black is showing: this is now a tolerable malt with a clean, well-defined malty backbone. **40%** ☉

⁙ **Tormore Aged 15 Years "Special Distillery Bottling"** db **(71)** n17 t18 f19 b17. even a supposed pick of choice casks can't save this from its fiery fate. **46%**

**Cadenhead's Authentic Collection Tormore Aged 20 Years** dist 84, bott Feb 05 **(76)** n18 t21 f18 b19. Harsh, brittle, slightly hot and unforgiving; there is also an attractive sub-stratum of candy and oak which lessens the pain. **60.4%.** 258 bottles.

⁙ **Cask Strength Tormore 1994 (68)** n18 t17 f16 b17. Better nip down to the hospital to see if any of my torched tastebuds can be saved... **59.9%.** G & M.

⁙ **The Clydesdale Tormore 16 Years Old** Cask 0149/1966, dist Feb 90, bott Sept 06 **(72)** n17 t18 f20 b17. Perfect for those wanting barley welded to their tastebuds with a blowtorch, or who just can't spit that pesky ink stain out of their expensive, double-cuffed shirts. **65.9%.** Blackadder.

⁙ **Connoisseurs Choice Tormore 1996 (78)** n20 t20 f19 b19. Malty, clean but house-style thin. **43%.** Gordon & MacPhail.

**Signatory Vintage Single Malt Scotch Whisky Tormore Aged 11 Years** Refill sherry butt no. 920260, dist 11.5.89, bott 20.2.01 **(81)** n19 t21 f20 b21. Rich, dense and biscuity by Tormore standards. **43%**

# TULLIBARDINE
**Highland (Perthshire), 1949. Tullibardine Ltd. Working.**

**Tullibardine 1964** dist 64, bott 04 db **(78)** n21 t20 f18 b19. Fruity, buttery nose but it's seen a few summers too many: the finish in particular shows its oaky gums. **44.6%**

**Tullibardine 1965 Best Procurable** Hogshead cask no. 949, dist 65, bott 05 db **(79)** n21 t20 f18 b20. A light and fruity offering for a sherry butt with good countering spice. Rather tired, though. **48.3%. nc ncf sc.** 225 bottles.

**Tullibardine 1966** Ex sherry butt cask no. 1112, bott 06 db **(90)** n23 a delightful, mildly rummy, experience; t23 beautiful delivery of sherry-soaked barley, then a confused presentation of over-aged oak and dark cherries; f21 burnt fudge and cocoa at first, then the toffee really piles in; b23 the natural caramels have taken hold and, with the sherry, make for an enjoyable experience but lacking a few features. But if that sounds picky, I have been spoiled by the World Cup edition. In on its own right, this is a wonderful stuff. **49.8%**

**Tullibardine 1966 World Cup Edition** Ex sherry butt cask no. 2132, bott 06 db **(96)** n24 one of those gold nugget, pure magic casks with the marks of Hurst and Moore upon it. Forty years on and the sherry is still lashing it out with rich toffee apple, soft natural caramels and moist fruitcake. Not even the hint of an off note to be had; t24 mouth-watering barley...after all this time!! And then layer upon layer of sherry of varying viscosity and intensity. Lush, lithe and latently spicy; the oak is naturally deep but never gets caught out of position and knows exactly when to pass; f24 still developing as a touch of Jaffa cake sweetens the vanilla and coating of dark chocolate. After an almost world record number of taste waves for a non-peated cask, very late on even lighter, fresher fruits. There's some peaches running on to the palate. They think it's all over: it is now...; b24 this cannot be in any way confused with England's bid to win the 2006 World Cup. Because this has style, charisma, shape, purpose, the ability to attack, plenty in reserve and the unmistakable pedigree and aura of something that can not only match just about anything else in the world, but beat it. Ironically, the label says Butt – which sums up to the English France's World Cup comeuppance. And WC, which nutshells to the French (and everyone else) England's quality of management and play...This is one of the great single cask malts of our lifetime. Sven, being a Caol Ila man, would have no idea how to change tactics to understand this. But the rest of us can see what a World Cup winner this is... **48%**

**Tullibardine 1973** db **(91)** n22 no shortage of tangerines, which lifts the groaning oak; t23 the fruit influence develops from the first moment with that sublime citrussy freshness forming a wonderful counter-balance to the sawdusty oak; just a hint of spice works well with the dull, dry marzipan sweetness; f23 a hint of custard with a sprinkling of cinnamon; **b**23 never quite kicks its shoes off and relaxes like the 47.5% version, but the complexity rises as it works all the harder to hurdle the bigger oak. **49.2%**

**Tullibardine 1973** Ex sherry butt cask no. 4138, bott 05 db **(77) n**19 **t**21 **f**18 **b**19. Snatched moments of fruit/barley deliciousness, but feeling the oaky strain. **50.2%**

**Tullibardine 1973** cask no. 2518, bott May 05 db **(91) n**23 a lovely fruitiness: kiwi/passion fruit; **t**23 big barley delivery then quickly into silky fruit; **f**22 playful vanilla; **b**23 big age but very few wrinkles. Quite a treat. **45.7%. ncf.** 239 bottles.

⠿ **Tullibardine 1975** Hogshead cask no. 1009, bott Mar 07 db **(85) n**22 **t**20 **f**22 **b**21. Begins life as a garibaldi biscuit, suddenly overwhelmed by a forest of uncompromising oak and finishes life as a high quality Java/Blue Mountain mix latte. **52.7%**

**Tullibardine 1986 John Black Selection** Ex sherry Hogshead cask no. 697 db **(95) n**25 blackberries, freshly-made fudge, lichen-covered rocks, fresh grape, mildly burnt raisin. It is all there...and so much more. Some 500 whiskies into the 2007 edition and this is the best nose of the year so far; **t**24 dark, intense and slightly foreboding on arrival it lightens with a firm injection of toasted toffee and sweetening, intense barley; **f**22 sherry dulls things down but spices form and crème brulee sees us to the end; **b**24 there is good reason why John Black has long been one of the most respected distillers in Scotland. Here is liquid, 92 proof why...And though he may not have made it, there's now no doubt he knows what a stunning whisky should nose and taste like. **46%. nc ncf sc.** 255 bottles.

**Tullibardine 1987** db **(82) n**21 **t**21 **f**20 **b**20. Good, solid, ultra-malty and oily dram that just fails to go up that extra gear. **46%**

**Tullibardine 1988** db **(88) n**20 **t**22 **f**24 **b**22. In the great Tulli tradition, the complexity and subtlety demand that you take several good looks before making your mind up about this one. And each re-visit rewards you handsomely. This is big stuff! **46%. ncf.**

**Tullibardine 1991** db **(89) n**22 the seasoning oak does just enough to dry out the vivid malt; **t**20 again the dry oak is very upfront, suppressing the exuberance of malt; **f**24 settles down beautifully at last for a teasing interplay between cocoa and barley with a thin sugar and salt-coated veneer. Silence while you listen to sophisticated manoeuvring of the subtle bitter-sweet balance; **b**23 so delicate, you are frightened it might shatter. **46%**

**Tullibardine 1992** H/H & ex bourbon barrel vatting, bott 06 db **(89) n**22 young, citrussy and light but with just a glimmer of pre-pubescent bourbon; **t**23 undercooked, but as delicious as a doughy Maryland cookie..and with some of its attributes; **f**22 soft vanilla and crisp barley...for a long time; **b**22 spookily like the original Glenfiddich no age statement bottlings of a decade ago. For those who miss that little gem, this is a must. **46%. nc ncf.**

**Tullibardine 1992** cask 1871 (1st fill Bourbon barrel) db **(93) n**24 how do you measure such complexity? Despite the cask type, fruits abound: over-aged apple and simmering citrus plus grassy barley and sultana cake; **t**22 light, dusting the palate with barley and gentle vanilla; **f**24 gets more into its stride with some raspberry jam playing with the late, mouth-watering barley and drier cocoa. Brilliant; **b**23 there are first fill bourbons and first fill bourbons...this one probably came from a cask that held a bourbon for a dozen years or more, so measured is the oaky influence. The nose is whisky heaven. **46%. nc ncf sc.** 270 bottles.

**Tullibardine 1993 Port Wood Finish** db **(91) n**22 spicy tomato, pork (or should that be port?) scratchings; all very salty and savoury; **t**23 initially dry liftoff, then a warming spread of sweeter malt, followed by a third layer of something fruitier, softer and more estery; **f**22 very long and silky with a late vanilla-malt surge; **b**24 not sure about this one at first, but as your palate acclimatises you realise that the complexity and balance here are of rare depth. **46%**

**Tullibardine 1993** (H/H & ex bourbon barrel vatting) dist 93, bott 05 db **(85) n**21 **t**22 **f**21 **b**21. Putty-nosed, the delivery is sensuous and gossamer light if a little under-developed. **40%. nc.**

⠿ **Tullibardine 1993** bott Dec 06 db **(86) n**21 **t**22 **f**21 **b**22. An improvement on previous bottling thanks to much better defined barley. Charming. **40%**

⠿ **Tullibardine 1993 Rum Finish** Cask no. 15016, bott Mar 07 db **(81) n**21 **t**20 **f**20 **b**20 Thin and miserly on development. Crisp barley, though. **46%**

⠿ **Tullibardine 1993 Sauterne Finish** Cask no. 15014, bott Dec 06 db **(87) n**22 pulped sultana **t**22 sweet grape; **f**22 sweet grape; **b**21 sweet and grapey.... **46%**

**Tullibardine 1993 Marsala Wood Finish** H/H cask db **(89)** n22 a sharp fruitiness: sultanas and under-ripe pears; t22 a mouthwatering and quite vivid fruit kick adorned with spice; f22 lush finale with some extra cocoa to the spice; b23 sophisticated, with enough complexity to keep you quiet for quite a few minutes. **46%. nc ncf.**

**Tullibardine 1993 Muscatel Wood Finish** H/H cask db **(91)** n23 distinctly grapey in that double-edged Muscat style that seems simultaneously both sweet and dry; t22 dry and mouth filling with some pounding barley that has somehow had the sweetness removed: strange but very attractive; f23 remains bone dry and now some lovely spice begins to tingle the roof of the mouth; b23 seriously classy whisky which really does exploit a wine finish to the nth degree. And very different. **46%. nc ncf.**

**Tullibardine 1993 Port Wood Finish** Portpipe cask no. 15012, bott 06 db **(86)** n20 t21 f23 b22. A bit like a concert orchestra tuning up before four minutes of Beethovian bliss. **46%**

**Tullibardine 1993 Sherry Wood Finish** Ex oloroso butt cask no. 15004, bott 06 db **(94)** n25 stunning oloroso: one of the best butts I've come across in an age. Resplendent in toffee apple and ripe barley; and if that isn't enough there is also the most sublime bourbon edge. It is hard to ask for or expect more; t23 succulent fruit/barley mix, some early vanilla and cream toffee; f22 dried dates, busy spices and extra-dry vanilla; b24 forget about spitting this one out. A sherry-kissed wet dream. We are getting to the stage where Tullibardine is now becoming one of the true great single malts of Scotland. Even the younger vintages are showing a degree of brilliance some thought impossible. **46%**

**Tullibardine 1994** H/H cask no. 677, dist 94 db **(88)** n23 relaxed and floral. Citrus undertones cranks up the complexity; t22 evenly weighted barley with a delicate flourish; f21 thins out slightly complexity-wise, perhaps because of the lethargic sherry; b22 such a fragile thing for something that has spent time in a sherry hogshead. **46%. nc ncf sc.** 352 bottles.

**Dewar Rattray Individual Cask Bottling Tullibardine 1972 Aged 33 Years** cask no. 2597, dist Dec 72, bott Jan 06 **(84)** n20 t23 f21 b20. Stylish, especially on the silky fruit/barley delivery, but there is marked fade on nose and balance. Still, an unforgettable dram: a few minutes after tasting this I met for the first time unquestionably the most naturally beautiful English girl I have encountered in over a decade...and also, as fate would dictate, a 1972 vintage. Sadly (for me), Georgia (97) n24 t24 f24 b25 is freshly married to one of the most relentlessly decent guys I've ever known. So I'll have to make do with this. Sigh... **43.1%.** 141 bottles.

**Old Malt Cask Tullibardine Aged 14 Years** dist Jun 89, bott Jan 04 **(90)** n23 steaming suet pudding with freshly mashed barley malt; clean and sharp; t24 astonishingly clean and refined barley of the very top order; the mouth waters as the malt and then sensual spices play havoc with the tastebuds; f21 a cross between European bitters and pungent marmalade; b22 a refreshing and at times explosive concoction. **50%. nc ncf sc.** Douglas Laing. 360 bottles.

**The Queen of the Moorlands Rare Cask Tullibardine 1994 Edition XV** Hogshead no. 676 **(89)** n23 different from the Tulli of 20 years ago: a heathery job, this, crisper than the norm and excellent oak involvement; t21 chaotic barley and oak battle for a foothold; f23 beautiful simmering of busy barley and earthy oak. The slow cocoa crescendo is a joy; b22 pretty wild, and it has nothing to do with the strength. The delivery is scrambled but finds a rhythm late on and genuinely impresses. **57.7%.** The Wine Shop Leek and Congleton, UK.

**Scotch Malt Whisky Society Cask 28.15 Aged 16 Years** Refill Hogshead, dist Jun 90 **(89)** n22 pure tun room; t23 strangely gristy, oddly worty, distinct traces of new make...magnificently malty; f22 becomes hot and spiced; b22 weirdly idiosyncratic: it is if you are nosing and tasting the distillery itself. A real tasty freak. **54.7%**

**Scott's Selection Tullibardine 1989** bott 05 **(88)** n21 fighting juice, with some real sharp edges to the barley; t22 pulsing barley simutaneously heavy and refreshing. Big spice kick towards the middle; f23 oils add a lustre to the fizzing malt; the fade is long and classy, offering a delicious dose of Horlicks; b22 classically oily Tully: a bit rough and ready, but good slap and tickle. **55.1%**

## UNSPECIFIED SINGLE MALTS (Campbeltown)

**Cadenhead's Campbeltown Malt (92)** n22 a touch of cordite to the barley; t24 as explosive as the nose suggests as the taste bud-ripping barley produces a pyrotechnic display. Gung-ho spices kick in with the advancing oak; f23 long, enormous depth to the spices while eye-watering orange rind completes the complexity; **b**23 on their home turf you'd expect them to get it right...and, my word, so they do!! **59.5%**

**Cadenhead's Classic Campbeltown (92) n**23 balance at a premium but, my word, the salty liveliness to the malt is worth a few extra minutes to enjoy; **t**24 you can drown in your own saliva, so mouth-watering is the barley; a touch of salt accentuates the enormity; **f**22 pretty mainstream by comparison, with boring ole salty vanilla tucking in; **b**23 what a dram! Must be what they gave Lazarus... **50%**

## UNSPECIFIED SINGLE MALTS (Highland)

**Adelphi Breath of the Highlands 1985 Aged 20 Years** cask no. 1065, dist 85, bott Jun 06 **(86) n**22 **t**21 **f**22 **b**21. Loses way in middle but sprightly for its age. **54.8%**. *Adelphi Distillery. 176 bottles.*

**"As We Get It" Highland 8 Years Old (92) n**22 way beyond its years with massive oak, but the richness of the malt keeps it young; very bourbony in style except for a clever, lantern dryness; **t**24 genuinely astounding in its malt richness, there is a tantalising, mouth-puckering, copper-rich quality; **f**23 long, custard and butterscotch tart sweetness with molten Demerara sugar for topping; **b**23 macho to start, but really one for the ladies. **57.2%. nc ncf.** *Ian Macleod.*

**Asda Single Malt** (*see* Douglas MacNiven)

**Auld Edinburgh Highland 10 Years Old** cask AE 003 **(83) n**22 **t**22 **f**19 **b**20. The wonderful marzipan on the nose and enriching malt on arrival is let down slightly by the dull, natural caramel towards the finish. **43%**. *Blackadder.*

∵ **Breath of the Highlands Aged 20 Years** Cask no. 1065, dist 1985, bott 06 **(90) n**22 some mildly soapy exotic fruit; **t**24 beautiful delivery of perfectly weighted barley: just the right amounts of salt to season the malt to imply age and countering sweetness thanks to stunning rays of honey and spice towards the middle **f**22 back to a light soapiness and medium roast Blue Mountain; **b**22 at times hanging on for grim death so as not be overwhelmed by the oak – lost a few fingernails in the process, but it's survived and with aplomb!! **55.1%**. *Adelphi Distillery Ltd. 176 bottles*

**Cadenhead's Classic Highland (82) n**19 **t**22 **f**21 **b**20. The trace of fusel oil on the nose guarantees a big delivery. Highly malty! **50%**

**Cadenhead's Highland Malt (90) n**22 malt concentrate; **t**23 ditto for the delivery; soft oaks and apple develop countering complexity; **f**22 hard, fresh barley, vanilla and malt milk-shake all the way; **b**23 does barley come any more pure or intense than this...? **60.2%**

**Celtique Connexion 1993 Coteaux du Layon Finish 13 Years Old** dist Mar 93, bott May 06 **(78) n**18 **t**21 **f**19 **b**20. Highly unusual style: gives the impression of wanting to burst out but seems tied down. The nose is particularly off key. **46%**. *Celtic Whisky Compagnie. Distilled and aged in Scotland, and then, maturation being completed in Brittany, sold, as their right, as "Produit de France".*

**Celtique Connexion 1994 Quarts de Chaume Finish 11 Years Old** dist Apr 94, bott Mar 06 **(86) n**23 **t**23 **f**19 **b**21. A brilliant whisky at first, frustratingly halted in its tracks by caramel. **46%. nc ncf.** *Celtic Whisky Compagnie. Distilled and aged in Scotland, and then, maturation being completed in Brittany, sold, as their right, as "Produit de France".*

∵ **Celtique Connexion Highland Single Malt Aged 13 Years Monbazillac Finish** dist Mar 93, bott Apr 06 **(92) n**23 thick, coated-on grape: clean, sultana concentrate with a warm tanging; **t**23 sweet, apple and grape juice again with no shortage of spicy seasoning – the barley hobbles through towards the middle; **f**23 cotton-dry vanilla with raisins again keeping the balance. But only after that grape has gone almost the full distance; **b**23 it's so amazing what a lack of sulphur can do! Pretty memorable stuff. **46%. nc ncf.** *Celtic Whisky Compagnie.*

∵ **Celtique Connexion Highland Single Malt Aged 14 Years Vin de paille du Jura Finish** dist Oct 92, bott Jan 07 **(93) n**25 one of the noses of the year: the diffusion of bourbon notes with kumquat, peppery-cinnamon and grape juice is quite divine...; **t**23 juicy, barley-topped marriage of green, under-ripe fruits, including Kiwi Fruit – unbelievably salivating; **f**22 a much drier prospect thanks to the oak; **b**23 fruity, busy...and very different. **46%. nc ncf.** *Celtic Whisky Compagnie*

**Douglas MacNiven Highland Single Malt 12 Years Old (84) n**20 **t**22 **f**21 **b**21. Firm and bold throughout with chewy vanilla amid the malt. **40%**. *Asda UK.*

**Glenalmond Highland Malt** dist 96, bott 06 **(91) n**23 wonderful soft fruit and sugar crystals speckled with grist; **t**23 the sweetness remains, as does the gristy quality; beautifully refreshing and injecting just the right amount of oak when required; **f**22 blood oranges help break up the malt dominances; **b**23 I confess: I have no idea what this is...other than absolutely bloody excellent. **40%.** *The Vintage Malt Whisky Co.*

**Glen Andrew Single Highland Malt 1983** bott 04 **(84) n**20 **t**22 **f**21 **b**21. Just enough body to the sweet malt to see off the encroaching oak. **46%.** *The Highlands & Islands Scotch Whisky Co.*

**Glen Andrew Single Highland Malt 1988** bott 04 **(86) n**19 **t**23 **f**22 **b**22. The rich, honied palate makes a nonsense of the poor nose. **46%.**

**Glen Andrew Single Highland Malt 1991** bott 04 **(83) n**23 **t**20 **f**20 **b**20. Really great nose, this is simple but deliciously refreshing throughout. **43%.**

**Glen Burn Single Highland Malt (81) n**20 **t**20 **f**21 **b**20. Pleasant, gentle if simplistic pub fodder. **40%.** *Glen Burn Distillers*

**Glenfinnan Highland Scotch Single Malt Over 12 Years Old (84) n**22 **t**23 **f**19 **b**20. Starts beautifully with citrus and rose petals among other delights. But then stops dead just as you pass the middle. Damn!! **40%.** *Celtic Whisky Compagnie, France.*

**Glen Torran Highland Single Malt 8 Years Old (75) n**17 **t**21 **f**18 **b**19. Sparkles briefly on arrival, helped along the way by lovely spice. But the caramel on the nose and finish does it in. **40%.** *Roderick & Henderson for London & Scottish International.*

**Glen Turner Single Highland Malt Aged 12 Years** L616656B **(84) n**22 **t**23 **f**19 **b**20. There's a really lovely malt trying to escape there, but its wings are clipped by some over hefty caramel on the finish. But the nose and delivery sing beautifully and are joyously mouth-watering. I feel a Bible-thumping trip to France coming on....they must realize that because Cognac has spent the last few decades using caramel as a crutch for its own lack-lustre spirit, it doesn't mean to say that Scotch needs it. Absolutely the contrary! Right, down from my soapbox. **40%.** *Glen Turner Distillery for La Martiniquaise, France.*

**Glen Turner Single Highland Malt Aged 18 Years** L532556A **(87) n**21 **t**23  **f**21 **b**22. A wonderfully clean and characterful malt that lays it on thick with the barley but, again, could do with keeping the caramel at bay. **40%.** *Glen Turner Distillery for La Martiniquaise, France.*

**Ian MacLeod's "As We Get It"** (*see* As We Get It)

**Inverey Single Highland Malt Aged 12 Years (73) n**17 **t**19 **f**20 **b**17. A complete change in style, and nothing like the "light bodied" whisky described on the label. This is vaguely smoked but is wayward and off-balance, especially on the nose. **40%.** *Burn Stewart for Marks and Spencer, UK.*

**Inverey Single Highland Malt Aged 12 Years (82) n**22 **t**21 **f**19 **b**20. OK, forget about last year's smoky., Tobermory-esque wacko. This one's worth getting for the curious yeasty/penicillin/orange blossom nose alone. **40%.** *Burn Stewart for Marks & Spencer.* ☉☉

**The Lord Balliol Single Aged 20 Years** (*see* Glenfarclas)

⫶ **Matisse Aged 15 Years Highland Single Malt (87) n**21 toffee-nougat amid oaky barley **t**22 firm malt radiating barley and spice in equal measures; **f**22 toffeed yet dies as the oak drives home; **b**22 an impressive malt which appears to suffer slightly from some colour adjustment. Even so, superbly weighted and with busy spices and soft oak washing over the barley. Sound. **40%.** *The Matisse Spirits Co.*

**McClelland's Highland Single Malt (80) n**21 **t**20 **f**19 **b**20. Easy going − until the bitter finish kicks in. **40%** ☉☉

**McClelland's Highland Single Malt 16 Years Old (79) n**20 **t**21 **f**19 **b**19. A rich dram with lots of chewability. **40%.** *Morrison Bowmore.*

**MacLeod's Highland Aged 8 Years** ( *see* Glen Moray)

**Wm Morrison Highland Single Malt Aged 10 Years (73) n**18 **t**20 **f**17 **b**18. A much duller, less integrated dram from Morrisons than once was. And, worse still, some bright spark has just upped the caramel by a couple of notches. Not worth standing an hour in the queue for this.... **40%** ☉☉

**Sainsbury's Sherry Cask Malt Whisky 8 Years Old (69) n**16 **t**18 **f**17 **b**18. Why oh why do they do it? Why must they insist on pratting around with sherry butts? Hasn't anyone got the message yet? It's like playing Russian roulette these days. Sulphur-tainted and less than pleasant. What a surprise.... **40%**

Sainsbury's Single Highland Malt Aged 12 Years **(84) n**21 **t**23 **f**19 **b**21. An impressively tempered dram allowing full vent to a complex range of malty-vanilla tones. Cut the finish-deadening caramel and it would be right up there. **40%.** UK.

Stronachie Single Highland Malt Aged 12 Years **(83) n**19 **t**21 **f**22 **b**21. A very different profile from the first bottling and has moved even further away from how the long- defunct Stronachie distillery would have once made their malt, with this being exceptionally light and now entirely peat-free. Although 12-years-old there is evidence of some third-fill casks in use here as the nose is virtually embryonic and the citrus powers through early on. A very even malt and a pretty decent, face-slappingly refreshing glass to return home to. **43%.** Dewar Rattray. ☉ ☉

Tesco Highland Single Malt 12 Years Old **(87) n**22 **t**22 **f**21 **b**22. A quite lovely malt displaying no shortage of character and charm. **40%.** Tesco, UK.

Waitrose Pure Highland Malt **(84) n**21 **t**23 **f**19 **b**21. Well weighted with an impressive honey-marmalade thread running through it: wonderful improvement. **40%.**

Waitrose Highland Aged 12 Years bott code L6 206 **(84) n**20 **t**21 **f**22 **b**21. "Contains maize" says the label. Interesting....for a single malt whisky! Treads a slightly different path from the old bottling, this one being a softer, fruitier type than of yore. **40%** ☉ ☉

## UNSPECIFIED SINGLE MALTS (Island)

Auld Edinburgh Island 10 Years Old cask AE 005 **(84) n**19 **t**23 **f**21 **b**21. Firm and sturdy, the arrival and deployment of mouthwatering malt on the palate is a joy. **43%.** Blackadder.

Berrys' Own Selection Best Orkney 14 Years Old **(89) n**23 complex: a tad smoky but the strands of honey invigorate the malt; **t**23 soft and sensual, there is the most wonderful sharpness to the malt; **f**21 quietens with the spiced oak; **b**22 Orkney honey throughout; seriously high quality. **43%.**

⠿ Dun Bheagan Island Single Malt Aged 8 Years **(93) n**23 superb honey-smoke combo; **t**24 that wonderful promise on the nose is fulfilled twice over: the peat is even bigger than threatened but a rich seam of honey bores deep into it; **f**23 the finish demands smoky embers and chocolate and that's just what it gets...in spade-loads; **b**23 as beautiful as a Scottish isle. **43%.** Ian Macleod Distillers.

Majestic Wine Warehouses Island Single Malt 8 Years Old **(88) n**24 a nigh-faultless, clean, crisp peat aroma dovetails some youngish oaky notes: really fabulous; **t**22 complex interplay between fresh but mature sweet peat and first-class oak; **f**20 dies slightly and becomes a little bitter as complexity is lost; **b**22 although delivered to my tasting lab in May 2003, the bottler's date suggests early November 1999. Surely a malt as deliciously good as this hasn't been hanging around on the shelves that long? **40%.** Majestic Wine Warehouses Secret Stills Isle if Skye 1955 (see Talisker).

Waitrose Island 10 Year Old **(92) n**23 ravishing malt wrapped in diaphanous peat; **t**24 Highland Park, surely, at its most heather-honied. The tastebuds can only purr at the silky caress; **f**22 flattens slightly but some late citrus tones work well with gathering spice; **b**23 easily one of the best superstore malts around, and that thanks to a superstar distillery. One very odd thing: the label says, "Allergens: contains maize." How can a single malt whisky contain maize, one wonders? Not changing filters between blends and malts at the bottling hall? Or just legal covering of the backside gone completely "allergens nuts"? **40%.**

## UNSPECIFIED SINGLE MALTS (Islay)

As We Get It 8 Years Old Islay **(85) n**22 **t**21 **f**21 **b**21. A teasing malt lacking the peat some might buy it for, but showing fresh, lively barley throughout. **57.9%. nc ncf.** Ian Macleod.

Auld Edinburgh Islay 10 Years Old cask AE 004 **(88) n**22 **t**22 **f**22 **b**22. Not one for the peat-heads. But should you ever get cramp.... **43%.** Blackadder.

Auld Reekie Islay 12 Year Old **(82) n**21 **t**21 **f**19 **b**21. For its 12 years remains as raw as the wind that rips down Caol Ila on a January night. Oily and a fraction flat. **46%.** Duncan Taylor.

Auld Reekie Islay Malt **(95) n**24 a near-perfect nose with indecipherable complexity, though salt and peat are at the nucleus; **t**24 breathtakingly scrummy: bitter-sweetness – perfect; peat-levels – perfect; degree of oak weight – perfect; spice injection – perfect. Perhaps could just do with an addition of a surprise element for true perfection;

f23 long, chewy; Fisherman's Friends dipped in Camp Coffee and hickory; **b**24 my last whisky of the day and a dram I shall be tasting all the way to when I clean my teeth. On second thoughts...I'll do them in the morning. Only kidding. But this is a must have dram for Islayphiles: true genius. **46%**. *Duncan Taylor.*

**Berrys' Own Selection Best Islay 8 Years Old (82) n**21 **t**21 **f**20 **b**20. Slick and smoky. Look for effect rather than complexity. **43%**. *Berry Bros & Rudd.*

⁖ **Blackadder Peat Reek (88) n**23 dying embers of a peat fire: dry peat soot; **t**22 refreshing early on, then dries slightly though a gristy theme plays on; **f**21 soft with a touch of jammy fruit; **b**22 a clean, very gentle giant. **46%**. *Blackadder International.*

**Blackadder Smoking Islay** cask 2004/2 **(91) n**24 citrus amid the weighty smoke; softly oiled, but not overly so, and still pretty malt; **t**23 fabulous delivery of fresh malt thumping into the tastebuds with the weight of smoke behind it; **f**22 vanilla inlaid into persistently mouthwatering barley; **b**22 a peaty, perky cherub. **55%. nc ncf.**

**Blackadder Smoking Islay** cask 2004/4 **(83) n**21 **t**22 **f**20 **b**20. Entertaining, but the salt and oak can't find the right balance together. **55%. nc ncf.**

**Blackadder Smoking Islay** cask 2005/5 **(80) n**20 **t**21 **f**19 **b**20. Thin, for all the peat, and so sharp and dry your eyes water. **55%. nc ncf.**

⁖ **Breath of Islay Aged 14 Years** Cask no. 5347, dist 1992, bott 07 **(86) n**21 **t**23 **f**22 **b**20 Oddly enough, in some respects, is less Islay-ish than its sister "Breath of the Isles". So much oil on this one the peat, though big, is kept from delivering its full smoky message and complexity really is at a minimum. Extremely Caol Ila-ish in style. Pretty delicious, though! **56.5%.** *Adelphi Distillery Ltd. 278 bottles.*

**Cadenhead's Classic Islay (91) n**23 young, light and revealing viperish clarity. The smoky grist is such a delight; **t**23 gentle oils and lumbering smoke; the sweetness intensifies and displays a liquorice honeycomb quality; **f**22 soft and delicate with gentle smoky brush-strokes; perhaps a tad too bitter for its own good; **b**23 I admit: totally baffled by this one. Just can't read the distillery at all: a completely different take on any of them: kind of Ardbegian, but a Lahphraogish blast and a hint of Caol Ila's oils. Yet it is all, yet none of them. Oddly enough, it reminds of Port Ellen when about eight years old. But, obviously, can't be. Classic, indeed! **50%**

**Cadenhead's Islay Malt (84) n**22 **t**21 **f**20 **b**21. Fat, well enough peated but lacks ambition and complexity. **58%.**

**Classic of Islay** cask nos. 3910/3911, bott 05 **(93) n**23 brooding peat; dank and salty; **t**24 puckering sharpness to the malt; the dry oakiness meets the lemon-lime citrus with a puffed out chest. The peats play happily meanwhile; **f**23 continues to confuse slightly with the big salty blast and limp sweetness. Soft oils and thick peat abounds; **b**23 there really is only one place on earth this could come from...this is major whisky! **58%.** *The Vintage Malt Whisky Co.*

**Finlaggan Islay Single Malt 10 Years Old (82) n**21 **t**21 **f**20 **b**20. Beautiful citrus notes mildly tempered with smoke: an enormous improvement from the caramel-ruined previous "Lightly Peated" bottlings. **40%.** *The Vintage Malt Whisky Co.*

⁖ **House Malt** Cask no. 8638-8645, dist Oct 97, bott July 06 **(79) n**22 **t**20 **f**18 **b**19. Beautiful, fully smoked nose, but dulls significantly on the palate. **43%.** *Wilson & Morgan, Limited Edition.*

**The Ileach Peaty Islay Single Malt (94) n**24 a thick chunk of peat has been dissolved in my glass; **t**24 the oil-peat-barley balance is spot on, as is the bitter-sweet tone: just stunning; **f**23 the peat dissipates slowly to leave a slightly bitterish, oaky influence. But the spices compensate; **b**23 Fabulous stuff, a bottle of which should sit in every household cabinet. A wonder dram. **40%**. *The Highlands & Islands Scotch Whisky Co.*

⁖ **The Ileach Single Islay Malt Cask Strength (97) n**24 **t**25 **f**24 **b**24. Amazingly, my tasting notes for the original weaker version are exactly the same as for this sea-facing monster. Except here the enormity has risen by a significant factor, as has the intensity of each vital cog in its make-up. Perhaps the only change is the honey-thread to the sweetness that pervades throughout. Otherwise, identical. A wondrous, take-it-with-you-when-you-die malt that is easily a contender for whisky of the year. **58%.**

**Islay Storm (76) n**19 **t**20 **f**19 **b**18. More of a drizzle. **40%**. *C.S. James & Sons.*

**Islay Storm 12 Years Old (81) n**20 **t**21 **f**20 **b**20. Some lovely spice emphasis the seaweed kick. Decent oak weight, too. **40%**. *C.S. James & Sons.*

**MacLeod's Islay 8-y-o** (*see* Lagavulin)

**Majestic Wine Warehouses Islay Malt Whisky 8 Years Old** ("this whisky was aged in oak casks at the distillery") **(85)** n21 t22 f21 b21. This bottling from 2004 and still doing the rounds, apparently, just doesn't have the sheen of the previous one. Quite Bowmore-ish in style. **40%.**

**Marks and Spencer Islay Single Malt Aged 10 Years (90)** n23 buttered kippers with a side plate of smoked Alpine cheese...all lightly salted; t23 just one of those malts which just sings to your tastebuds with a sweet, if smoky, voice; the peat is multilayered and offers many variations of intensity over the course of just a minute or two; f22 dries for the perfect counterpunch with chalky oak; **b**22 a grand improvement on the old bottling and although this is from Burn Stewart, Bunnahabhein in style this is simply not!! **40%.** *UK.* ☉

**McClelland's Islay Single Malt (88)** n22 delicate yet confident smoke; t22 light at first then livens as the smoke kicks in; f22 beautifully long and clean with tapering Fisherman's Friend; **b**22 no mistaking which distillery this little beaut is from: Bowmore anyone? **40%** ☉ ☉

**Wm Morrison Islay Single Malt Aged 10 Years (84)** n21 t22 f21 b20. A uniform Islay which, though pleasant and initially sweet, fails to trouble the imagination or pulse. **40%.** *Wm Morrison Wines & Spirits Merchant.* ☉

**The Queen of the Hebrides Islay Single Malt Whisky (85)** n22 t22 f20 b21. Big, rolling fat peats: any fatter and it'd be declared obese. **40%.** *Available at The Wine Shop, Leek, and The Islay Whisky Shop.*

**Secret Stills Islay 1989** (*see* Bowmore)

**Smokehead Islay** db **(92)** n24 even iodine doesn't come more iodiney than this. Also salty, youngish and bracing; t23 sweet grist at first, moves into sharp citrus and back into malt; f22 the complex peats begin to fade as vanilla and caramel kick on; **b**23 this company does this kind of whisky so well. A little gem. **43%.** *Ian Macleod.*

⫶⫶⫶ **The Spirit Safe & Cask Islay Single Malt Vintage 1998 Aged 8 Years** Hogshead cask no. 52, dist 1998, bott 07 **(91)** n23 wonderful mixture of heavily peated grist and a cold distillery kiln... t22 a licentious delivery, with the peat pawing each taste bud with wanton abandon; f23 calms down for a hint of Bowmore-style cough medicine, but heads back to the mill for sweet grist; **b**23 for those of us who spent too many years of their adulthood hanging around the south-east coast of Islay, there shouldn't be too many problems spotting this guy. Great to see it so youthful. **58.8%. nc ncf.** *Celtic Whisky Compagnie. 305 bottles.*

**Tamifroyg Islay Single Malt Scotch Whisky: The Vaccine to Bird Flu (91)** n23 Few Islays so largely depend on dense citrus for the lead note, though the underlying peat possibly stretches back to the ice age. Big, but subtle...sort of; t23 remains fruity, but massive oils dredge up some serious oak and praline; f23 succulent oils sweetened by weakened mollased sugar and decent natural caramels; a slight raspberry jam sharpness titillates the tastebuds in the mid of this profound heaviness; **b**22 from the guys who brought you the original Papal Ardbeg, another enormous Islay that could – and if not, should - have been named after one of the people most seriously dear to my heart, the Islayphile extraordinaire Tammy Secor (please, darling, say yes to marrying me in my next life). This, very sensibly, has been brought out to ward off bird flu, though several glasses of this would probably mean that you would neither know – or indeed care – if you had it or not. Curiously, after I wrote these notes I was pointed in the direction of the website of the Lindores Whisky Society: a conclave of 12 noble souls in northern Belgium, I think, who have embraced the Jim Murray scoring system with a zeal demanding official blessing. I'm proud to report that they, like me, scored 91, though they have given 23-23-22-23 (as opposed to 23-23-23-22). However, they have spotted on the nose; "sqaushed (sic) strawberries...fine horsemeat..horseleather." Boys, it is nearly 25 years since I lived with a French girl, so I will bow to your Continental in-knowledge. But compared to you, and the amassed genii of Regensburger Whisky Club, I am not worthy... **49%.** *Regensburger Whisky Club. 26 bottles.*

**Tesco Islay Single Malt 12 Years Old (89)** n23 mottled peat vying with a salty, tangy barley and dryish toffee; t23 sumptuous and mouth coating, the sweetness threatens to overload but holds back. Some toffee notes dig in; f21 varying degrees of smoke, happily embracing the gathering oak; **b**22 timeless whisky: this is like going back 25 years and onto the island when the peat was thick and caramel was thicker!! Had this been at natural colour, I think we'd have a malt closer to about 92: this has come from some wonderful casks. **40%**. *UK.*

**Waitrose Islay Aged 10 Years** bott code P011467 **(82)** n21 t22 f19 b20. Big peat in part, but something has dulled the complexity and fireworks here. Some suspicious toffee might be a clue... **40%** ☺ ☺

## UNSPECIFIED SINGLE MALTS (Lowland)

**Auld Edinburgh Lowland 10 Years Old** cask AE 001 **(79)** n18 t22 f19 b20. The nose never quite settles but the body is clean, intensely malty and washes over you. **43%**. *Blackadder.*

**Berrys' Own Selection Best Lowland 12 Year Old (85)** n23 t22 f19 b21. Easy drinking stuff. **43%**. *Berry Bros & Rudd.*

**Cadenhead's Classic Lowland** Bourbon wood **(82)** n19 t21 f21 b21. Much juicier and fortified with rich barley than the nose suggests. **50%**

**Cadenhead's Lowland Malt (90)** n22 delightful division between bourbon and citrus; t23 again the citrus rattles the taste buds with grassy alt not far behind; f22 soft waves of tidy vanilla sprinkled with demerara; b23 one of the best lowlanders around. Fabulously fresh! **56.4%**

⠃⠃ **Master of Malt Secret Bottlings Lowland 12 Years Old Collection (83)** n20 t22 f20 b21 The nose may be from the sweaty armpit fraternity of casks, but there is enough honey around on the early delivery to compensate. **40%**. *Master of Malt, UK.*

**McClelland's Lowland Single Malt (75)** n17 t20 f19 b19. Off the pace – hopefully a blip from the normal tasty bottling. **40%** ☺ ☺

**MacLeod's Lowland Single Malt Aged 8 Years** (*see* Auchentoshan)

**Secret Stills Lowland 1989** (*see* Auchentoshan)

## UNSPECIFIED SINGLE MALTS (Speyside)

⠃⠃ **Apples & Pears Speyside Vintage 1991 Single Malt** bott Jan 07 **(71)** n16 t19 f18 b18 How about matchsticks and Rotarua? **46%**. *Wemyss Vintage Malts.*

**Asda Speyside Single Malt 12 Years Old (77)** n20 t20 f18 b19. While tasting this, some young thug has just tried to kick down the door of my office, smashed the glass of a neighbouring building, injuring a bystander, and I've dialled the police. The alleged perps have been caught red-handed. Literally, as they were bleeding. I identified handcuffed suspects. Oh, if only the whisky was as exciting as this.... **40%**. *Glenmorangie for Asda.* ☺ ☺

**Asda Speyside Single Malt 12 Years Old (81)** n19 t21 f20 b21. A vast improvement on previous years though the aroma hints at some casks whose next stop are flower pots; good verve to the beautifully balanced barley, though. **40%**. *Douglas MacNiven for.*

**Ben Bracken 12 Years Old (79)** n20 t20 f19 b20. Engagingly light with a real malty fizz. A tobacco hint amid the spice and cocoa. **40%**. *Clydesdale Scotch Whisky Co.*

**Celtique Connexion** (*see* Unspecified Single Malts (General))

**Celtique Connexion 14 Years Old 1990 Speyside Cadillac Finish** dist May 90, bott Oct 04 **(76)** n21 t19 f17 b19. A shrug of the shoulders here, guys. Pardon! But for me there is just too much oak dominance. **43%**. *ncf. Distilled and aged in Scotland, and then, maturation being completed in Brittany, sold, as is their right, as "Produit de France".*

**Celtique Connexion 1990 Armagnac Finish 15 Years Old** dist May 90, bott June 05 **(85)** n20 t22 f21 b22. I don't know for certain if these guys use caramel or not. But three out of three of their malts have witch's tit finales, though this one does retain some late pulse. Frustrating, especially if avoidable. Especially in this case where the mouth-watering delivery and early spices are superb! **54.4%. nc ncf.** *Celtic Whisky Compagnie. Distilled and aged in Scotland, and then, maturation being completed in Brittany, sold, as their right, as "Produit de France".*

⠃⠃ **Celtique Connexion Speyside Single Malt Aged 14 Years Sauternes Finish** dist Apr 91, bott Mar 06 **(89)** n20 messy, heavy-handed grape; t22 fruity, clean and hotly spiced; begins to harmonise towards the middle; f24 soft, integrated and the genuine subtlety on the fruit is amazing; b23 the sweet sub plot and sizzling spice make for a memorable and unusual dram. **50%.nc ncf.** *Celtic Whisky Compagnie.*

⸭⸱ **Celtique Connexion Speyside Single Malt Aged 16 Years Sauternes Finish** dist May 90, bott Oct 06 **(86) n**20 **t**20 **f**24 **b**22. Juicy, pleasantly spiced and no shortage of Demerara-sweetened Java on the astonishing finish. If you like to salivate, you won't be disappointed! **46%. nc ncf.** *Celtic Whisky Compagnie.*

⸭⸱ **Chocolate Heaven Speyside Vintage 1991 Single Malt** bott Jan 07 **(86) n**22 **t**21 **f**22 **b**21. Lovely gristy stuff at first, then a touch of chocolate sponge. **46%.** *Wemyss Vintage Malts.*

⸭⸱ **Coconut Cream Speyside Vintage 1990 Single Malt** bott Jan 07 **(87) n**22 does what it says on the label... **t**22 beautifully oiled allowing the barley to stick convincingly around the palate; some dried banana towards the middle; **f**21 soft vanilla as this gentle malt slowly dries **b**22 another good cask choice from Wemyss. **46%.** *Wemyss Vintage Malts.*

⸭⸱ **Glace Fruits Speyside Vintage 1994 Single Malt** bott Jan 07 **(93) n**23 fabulous nose with all kinds of fresh, juicy intent under a vanilla layer; **t**23 after barley-rich cloudburst rich, faultless malt floods the taste buds; **f**23 the clean barley intensity shows little sign of abating though deft spices and oak make their appearances as the name of good balance and whisky demands; **b**24 perfection for those looking for death by barley. **46%.** *Wemyss Vintage Malts.*

**Glen Darbach Single Speyside Malt Aged 12 Years (79) n**21 **t**20 **f**19 **b**19. Regressed from a very decent malt to something on the skimpy side. **40%.** *Burn Stewart for Marks & Spencer, UK.* ☺ ☺

**Glen Marnoch Aged 12 Years (77) n**20 **t**20 **f**18 **b**19. Pleasant, but the over indulgence in caramel limits its scope badly. **40%.** *Alistair Graham for Aldi Store, UK.*

**Glen Parker** (*see* GlenParker)

**GlenParker Speyside Single Malt (72) n**18 **t**19 **f**17 **b**18. Oh dear. Has lost some of its old charm: this is an adolescent whose voice is breaking – entirely off key and mildly irritating. The liberal dose of caramel exacerbates matters. **40%.** *Angus Dundee.*

**Jenners Speyside Aged 10 Years** bott lott 03/10013 **(92) n**22 big bourbon influence with acacia honey on slightly singed toast; **t**23 sublime mouthfeel to the sweet, confident, blemish-free malt; a touch of muscovado sugar sweetens the early vanilla; **f**23 long, with a touch of friendly spice to balance the continuing gristy sweetness. More toast on the finale and this time with some marmalade; **b**24 an excellent and massively impressive Speysider that keeps its shape and richness throughout. Complex and wonderfully structured. Yet another reason to visit Edinburgh.... **40%.** *Jenners, Edinburgh.*

**McClelland's Speyside (76) n**19 **t**19 **f**19 **b**19. A distinct improvement on the last bottling of this I came across. But the charisma bypass was still a complete success. **40%.** *Morrison Bowmore.* ☺

**MacLeod's Speyside Aged 8 Years** (*see* Glenfarclas)

⸭⸱ **Morrisons The Best Speyside Malt 15 Years Old** bott code L6 349 **(79) n**19 **t**22 **f**19 **b**19. Ever been at a dinner party and had someone sitting next to you who is awfully pleasant but a tad dull? Well, if that person was to come back in life as a whisky, it'd probably be as this. The explanation may lie in the colour: "matured in ex-bourbon casks" says the label. Only in Kentucky, and in virgin oak, do you get this depth of bronze. The oppressive hand of caramel can be felt in every mouthful. Shame, because a few moments after the initial entry this has all the hallmarks of a honeyed stunner. **40%**

**The Queen of the Moorlands Aged 12 Years (89) n**23 toffee apple and multiple layers of molassed malt; **t**23 just so big and chewy; again with this, tasteful layers of brown sugar coating the malt; **f**21 spices and developing oak; **b**22 what a lovely whisky for a small shop to have as their own label. Some serious quality here. **40%.** *The Wine Shop, Leek, UK.*

**Wm Morrison Speyside Single Malt Aged 10 Years** bott code L6 341 **(79) n**19 **t**22 **f**19 **b**19. Bit of a feinty beast, but the oils compensate and big up the barley. **40%** ☺ ☺

**Pebble Beach 12 Years Old (78) n**19 **t**20 **f**20 **b**19. The malt fits with the allusion to something rounded and smooth. But I also presume it's a beach to fall asleep on while sucking a toffee... **43%.** *Lombard Brands.*

⸭⸱ **Secret Stills Speyside 1966** Distillery No. 2, Release No. 2, Sherry hogshead casks no. 1204, dist 23 Apr 66, 1449 & 1452, dist 21 May 66, bott June 06 **(92) n**24 aromas don't come more refined than this: soft, vaguely citrus fruit combined with midnight floral, balanced perfectly with a lightly honey bourbon trait. Astonishing when wet in the glass, stunning when left to dry... t23 genteel oils, lovely barley sugar and oak that impacts gently; f22 light brush of softly oiled cocoa; b23 shows little sign of decay expected for this great age and fruit flies have driven themselves into this malt for a classy death in significant numbers. **45%**. Gordon & MacPhail. 600 bottles.

Tesco Speyside Single Malt 12 Years Old **(88)** n21 some stressed oak is becalmed by subtle smoke and firm barley; t22 outstanding delivery with a sheen to the barley as it glides over the palate; the spices mass as the oak concentrates; f22 a gentle return of smoke sits comfortably with the cocoa and barley; b23 no shrinking violet here: a Speysider with a touch of attitude – and class. **40%**. Tesco, UK.

Waitrose Speyside Aged 12 Years **(76)** n19 t20 f18 b19. Another Waitrose single malt that, according to the matter-of-fact label, "Contains maize" – rather than the more precautionary "May contain maize". More intriguing than the whisky, frankly. Because despite some pleasant passages this is just not a heart-stopper. Unless you are allergic to maize, of course.... **40%**

## UNSPECIFIED SINGLE MALTS (General)

⁘ Breath of the Isles Aged 13 Years Cask no. 3201, dist 1992, bott 06 **(91)** n23 earthy, peaty, sharp, salty and invigorating; t22 no shortage of smoke, stoked up on an oily fire; f23 some charming vanillas push through and some shades of grist and citrus crank up the complexity further; b23 well, maybe it isn't an Islay but when you close your eyes and taste this the Paps of Jura and squadrons of midges inexorably spring to mind. **52.6%**. Adelphi Distillery Ltd. 299 bottles.

Cu Dhu (see Speyside Distillery)

Fiskavaig 1977 Vintage 27 Year Old **(90)** n23 sharp, grassy, and lingering peat; t22 smoky, yet with plenty of young malt that defies the age statement completely; f22 two left jabs and peaty uppercut leave you floored; b23 what the hell is this stuff? From Islay almost certainly. But the intensity of the pure cocoa (75% at least) leaves you gasping. **51.3%**. The Whisky Shop.

Stonefield Castle Hotel Single Malt Whisky **(84)** n21 t22 f20 b21. A very pleasant, undemanding, gently-spoken dram that offers the most surprising prune-stone, fruit-spirit quality. **40%**. Tarbert, Argyll.

Wilson & Morgan Barrel Selection House Malt cask nos. 8586-8589 **(92)** n24 beautifully salted and coastal peats with enough youth to remain refreshing and profound; t22 lime juice lightens the smoke; f23 returns to a more gristy sweetness and depth; b23 a high quality (presumably) Islay of distinctive, compelling clarity. **43%**

# Scottish Vatted Malts
# (also Pure Malts/Blended Malt Scotch)

100 Pipers Aged 8 Years Blended Malt **(74)** n19 t20 f17 b18. A better nose, perhaps, and some spice on arrival. But when you consider the Speysiders at their disposal, all those mouth-wateringly grassy possibilities, it is such a shame to find something as bland as this. **40%** ☺ ☺

Anchor Bay Pure Malt Scotch Whisky **(81)** n20 t22 f19 b20. A significantly improved brand with much fresher, more stark barley....though I wish they'd do something about that furry finish. **40%**. Lombards Brands.

Asda Islay Pure Malt 10 Years Old **(82)** n21 t22 f19 b20. Sweet, chewy, excellent mouth arrival and fresh. Can simply do with losing the toffee at the death. **40%**. Douglas MacNiven for Asda. ☺

Ballantine's Pure Malt 12 Years Old **(88)** n22 as before, sans spice and smoke: so quite different, really...; t23 attractively lush with beautiful honey thread weaving through the barley; f21 much thinner than of yore with all emphasis on chalky oak; b22 has surrendered the delicate peat which gave it that vital extra oomph. **40%**. Chivas Brothers. ☺ ☺

⁘ Barrogill North Highland Blended Malt Mey Selections bott code PO12630 **(79)** n18 t21 f20 b20. Recovers attractively – helped by a mighty dose of concentrated maltiness - from the disappointing nose. **40%**. Inver House Distillers for North Highland.

Bell's Special Reserve Pure Malt **(87)** n22 t23 f20 b22. Absolutely excellent vatting, let down only by the pointless caramel denuding the gold leaf from the edges. Another example of this style of whisky coming out of the doldrums with some very careful and skilful mixing. Shame about the caramel, though. **40%**

**Berrys' Best Islay Vatted Malt Aged 8 Years (82)** n20 t21 f20 b21. Smoky, raw, sweet, clean and massive fun! **43%**. *Berry Bros & Rudd*.

**Berrys' Own Selection 25 Year Old Blue Hanger Second Limited Release (90)** n24 gooseberries and apricot on a butterscotch tart; t23 busy, spicy arrival with some chuntering oak trying to outdo the malt. Mildly estery and oily weight with a lighter, playful thread of honey; f21 vanilla and manuca honey; b22 a majestic and seamless transformation from blend to vatted malt. **45.6%. nc ncf.**

**The Big Smoke 40 Islay Malt (83)** n20 t21 f21 b21. Keeps it sweet, simple...and very smoky! **40%**. *Duncan Taylor*.

**The Big Smoke 60 Islay Malt (86)** n20 t23; f22 b21. Big and bolshy, the peats remorselessly thump anything in their path **60%**. *Duncan Taylor*.

**Black Ribbon 10 Years Old Lowland, Highlands and Islay (78)** n20 t21 f18 b19. The promising mouthwatering malt vanishes under a welter of caramel blows. **40%**

**Black Ribbon 21 Years Old Highlands and Islay (83)** n22 t22 f19 b20. Starts with a brilliantly chewy, deliciously spiced sweetness, but fades fast. **43%**

**Blairmhor 8 Years Old (84)** n22 t22 f20 b20. Reconstituted and a wonderful improvement. Some lovely smoke on the nose and excellent weight to mouth arrival, but the caramel flattens it latterly. **40%**. *Inver House*.

⋯ **Clan Campbell 8 Years Old Pure Malt (82)** n20 t22 f20 b20. Enjoyable, extremely safe whisky that tries to offend nobody. The star quality is all on the complex delivery, then it's toffee. **40%**. *Chivas Brothers*.

**Clan Denny** (Bowmore, Bunnahabhain, Caol Ila and Laphroaig) **(94)** n24 mildly awesome: a mixing of varying grists – peaty, but on so many planes...; t23 still on the grist blitz with a powdery smokiness working well with a veiled honey theme; f23 dries out at first but a smoky butterscotch balances things out; b24 a very different take on Islay with the heavy peats somehow having a floating quality. Unique. **40%**. *Douglas Laing*.

⋯ **Clan Denny Speyside (87)** n22 big, big malt: exceptionally clean and soft. Oily, too; t22 a charming sweetness to the barley helps counter the more bitter aspects of the approaching oak; delicate oils help make for an exceptionally soft delivery f21 no shortage of vanilla as it bitters out; b22 a Tamdhu-esque oiliness pervades here and slightly detracts from the complexity. That said, the early freshness is rather lovely. **46%**. *Douglas Laing*.

**Compass Box Eleuthera Marriage** Married for nine months in an American oak Hogshead **(86)** n22 t22 f20 b22. I'm not sure if it's the name that gets me on edge here, but as big and robust as it is I still can't help feeling that the oak has bitten too deep. Any chance of a Compass Box Divorce...? **49.2%**. *Compass Box for La Maison du Whisky in commemoration of their 50th Anniversary*.

⋯ **Compass Box Flaming Heart** bott 06 **(93)** n23 arousing and rich, the smoke rumbles below the curious theme of liquorice and lychee: deep and different; t24 hard to pin-point the leader: is it that throbbing peat or something more ethereal and honeyed? Either way it's a sublime experience; f22 some age apparent at the death with the toasty oaks having a surprisingly big say; b24 an astounding combination of peat and honey, like Highland Park on steroids. Another true masterpiece from Compass Box. **48.9%**. *2,100 bottles*.

**Compass Box Juveniles** Lot Code L5021 **(93)** n23 fresh, grassy and salivating. There is a touch of soap, but in almost attractive proportions, which adds to a subtle, scented fruitiness; t24 just so light – almost flimsy – in body, yet with oily malt sturdy enough to bless it with a sweet charm; a touch of passion-fruit adds lustre; f23 soft, playful spices arrive quite early and intensify, and then layers of rich cocoa; b23 so subtle you won't get the full picture until the fourth of fifth mouthful. Less honied than the last bottling and with more stealthy weight towards the finish. But just fabulous all the same...! **43%. nc ncf.**

**Compass Box Magic Cask Limited Edition** bott Oct 06 **(89)** n20 confused, jaded and just a bit top-heavy with fruit; t24 almost liqueur-like in body: more silk than a High Court Judge riffling through a Madame's underwear draw; distinctly intense malt but the juicy, grapey fruits are such a treat; f23 magically buzzing spices kick in and add layers to the sultana; b22 disappointing nose, but beyond that you enter a world of unbridled, peatless enormity with a distinct sma' still richness. What a glassful!! **46%**. *480 bottles for the LCBO, Canada.*

**Compass Box Oak Cross Malt Scotch Whisky** bott 06 **(94) n**23 the spiced French oak has been cleverly tamed thanks to an understated lustre to the barley; **t**24 such delicate fruit, not entirely unlike Payne's Raisin Poppets, then an oak surge towards the middle; throughout subtle spices pop and tickle around the palate. The oak/spice/barley/fruit ratio is just about perfect; **f**23 some wonderful semi-dry marzipan at the death is cloaked in cocoa; **b**24 a vatting of exceptionally high class malts which have embraced the oak without ever yielding to it. Superb! Ignore entirely the instructions on the back to add ice, water or whatever: this is genius whisky that must be drunk exactly as nature intended. **43%. nc ncf.**

**Compass Box The Peat Monster** Lot Code L4337 **(88) n**22 **t**22 **f**22 **b**22. This ain't no monster...it's pure pussy! **46%. nc ncf.** ☉

**Compass Box The Spice Tree Inaugural Batch (93) n**23 a thick nose, almost offering the botanicals of gin but without the juniper. Oak influence is all-consuming, the barley acting as a thinning agent for the pungent spices and vanilla; **t**23 immediately warming yet almost syrupy-sweet; the accent is on spiced orange (I think I can see where they are coming from cinnamon-wise, but not cloves); **f**23 such is the intensity and enormity, it is hard to pick out individual flavour: we have a marriage of styles in which the key is beautiful, bitter-sweet integration; **b**24 the map for flavour distribution had to be drawn for the first time here: an entirely different whisky in shape and flavour emphasis. And it is a map that takes a long time to draw... **46%.** *4150 bottles.*

**Compass Box The Spice Tree** 2nd release, Apr 06 **(94) n**22 lighter, more citrussy gathering of complex aromas; barley is refreshing and grassy; **t**24 astonishing dexterity to the sweetness and though well oiled, not quite as thick in body as the first bottling. But this allows the honeyed elements to flourish. And with aplomb...; **f**24 spicy, but not as fizzing as the inaugural bottling with a roasty honeycomb flourish; **b**24 I think this probably wins it over the first bottling, but only on account of the better finish helped along by slightly more sympathetic oak. Either way, make the most of either or both of them. They have been outlawed as illegal Scotch by the industry's association because of the use of oak staves. How dare you produce whisky like this, Compass Box? You are a disgrace to whisky: what were you thinking of? You should have darkened and flavoured it with caramel, instead. Or even a sherry butt humming with sulphur. **46%**

**Co-operative Group (CWS) Blended Malt Aged 8 Years (82) n**19 **t**22 **f**21 **b**20. With its intense syrup thrust, one of the sweetest malts on the market: a touch of spice and vanilla add welcome relief. Book your visit to the dentist after this one...! **40%.** *Watson & Middleton for Co-operative Group (CWS).* ☉

**Driftwood Highland Pure Malt Scotch Whisky (82) n**20 **t**22 **f**19 **b**21. Just like driftwood, this is hard to get a fix on. One minute you think you have it, then it disappears for a bit. Certainly a better mixing than two or three years back, with a curiously smoky edge to some shimmering honey. The finish, though, is duller than it should be. That said, it is something to hold on to... **40%.** *Lombard Brands.*

**Duncan Taylor Regional Malt Collection Highland 10 Years Old** dist 1995, bott 05 **(78) n**20 **t**21 **f**18 **b**19. Must be the region that's in the middle of the road. **40%.** *920 bottles.*

**Duncan Taylor Regional Malt Collection Islay 10 Years Old (81) n**21 **t**22 **f**19 **b**19. Soft citrus cleanses the palate, while gentle peats muddies it up again. **40%.** *888 bottles.*

**Duncan Taylor Regional Malt Collection Speyside 10 Years Old** dist 1995, bott 05 **(79) n**19 **t**22 **f**19 **b**19. Decent enough, but irritatingly non-committal and Tandhu-ish oily on the finish. Come on guys: you are in the heart of Speyside – give us something to get our pulses racing!! **40%.** *838 bottles.*

**The Famous Grouse Malt (79) n**19 **t**21 **f**19 **b**20. Very sweet, intense malt, but a slight but noticeable blemish spoils the party. **40%.** *Taiwan.*

**The Famous Grouse 10 Years Old Malt (77) n**19 **t**20 **f**19 **b**19. The nose and finish headed south in the last winter and landed in the sulphur marshes of Jerez. **00%.** *Edrington Group.* ☉ ☉

**The Famous Grouse 12 Years Old Malt (87) n**21 the kumquats have stayed the course but a little duller than of old; **t**23 fabulous, fighting spices offer an almost gin-like juniper edge; **f**21 a little sweetness evolves as the malts do battle with the cocoa-oak; **b**22 under a different plumage from when I last tasted this, being heavier, spicier and a little more aggressive on the palate as if to make up for the sluggish nose. **40%.** *Edrington Group.* ☉ ☉

The Famous Grouse 15 Years Old Malt **(86)** **n**19 **t**24 **f**22 **b**21. There had been a hint of the "s" word on the nose, but it got away with it. Now it has crossed that fine – and fatal – line where the petulance of the sulphur has thrown all else slightly out of kilter. All, that is, apart from the delivery which is a pure symphony of fruit and spice deserving a far better introduction and final movement. Some moving, beautiful moments. Flawed genius or what…? **40%.** *Edrington Group.* ☉ ☉

The Famous Grouse 18 Years Old Malt **(84)** **n**19 **t**23 **f**21 **b**21. Mildly flawed sherry, but the honied melt-in-the-mouth malt on the palate is such a treat. **43%.** *Taiwan.* ☉

The Famous Grouse Malt 21 Years Old **(91)** **n**22 candy jar spices, green apple and crisp barley. **t**24 spot on oak offers a platform for the myriad rich malty notes and now, in the latest bottlings, enlivened further with an injection of exploding spice… wow! **f**22 flattens slightly but muscovado sugar keeps it light and sprightly; **b**23 a very dangerous dram: the sort where the third or fourth would slip down without noticing. Wonderful scotch! And an object lesson in how vatted malt whisky should be. **43%.** *Edrington Group.* ☉ ☉

The Famous Grouse 30 Years Old Malt **(94)** **n**25 the level of complexity here rockets off the scales: swirling, distant peat-reek, acacia honey, pipe smoke, French toast…it simply goes on and on – flawless and fabulous; **t**23 lush, honey-enriched barley weighted down with a smokiness almost too delicate to register; **f**23 it's all about the oak, yet again the molten honey sweetens any possible excess; **b**23 I have been trying hard to think of any whisky quite so delicate – and failed. Blending at its most sublime. **43%.** *Taiwan.* ☉

Glencoe Aged 8 Years ( *see* MacDonald's Glencoe)

Glen Martin Pure Highland Malt 5 Years Old **(76)** **n**18 **t**20 **f**19 **b**19. A slightly feinty nose underscores the obvious youth here. Not as well balanced as before but the puckering maltiness delights. **40%.** *James Martin for Sainsbury's, UK.*

Glen Nicol **(80)** **n**20 **t**20 **f**20 **b**20. An honest Joe of a malt: lots of lively character and straight as a die. **40%.** *Inver House.* ☉

Glen Turner Pure Malt Aged 8 Years L525956A **(84)** **n**20 **t**22 **f**22 **b**20. A lush and lively vatting annoyingly over dependent on thick toffee but simply brimming with fabulously mouth-watering barley and over-ripe blood oranges. To those who bottle this, I say: let me into your lab. I can help you bring out something sublime!! **40%.** *Glen Turner Distillery for La Martiniquaise, France.*

Grand Macnish Vatted Malt Scotch Whisky **(82)** **n**19 **t**24 **f**19 **b**20. A real shame: a vatting which offered so much has been done to death with caramel. The mouth-watering ultra-intense and beautifully sweet malt which just makes the heart pound on delivery deserves so much more. **40%.** *MacDuff International. Taiwan.*

Grand Macnish 12 Years Old Vatted Malt Scotch Whisky **(78)** **n**18 **t**23 **f**18 **b**19. The oak and caramel carry out a nifty pincer movement on the barley. Dull. **40%.** *MacDuff International. Taiwan.*

Grand Macnish 21 Years Old Vatted Malt Scotch Whisky **(86)** **n**21 **t**23 **f**21 **b**21. After the velvety landing  remains firm throughout but a persistent touch of class is there to see. **40%.** *MacDuff International. Taiwan.*

Glen Orrin Six Year Old **(88)** **n**22 a bit sweaty but the oranges delight. Some delicate background smoke is a surprising complement; **t**23 big, chewy and rugged with outstanding soft-oiled lushness which helps to dissipate the youthfulness; **f**21 delicate spice and arousing coffee-cocoa: a bigger age signature than you might expect **b**22 a vatting that has improved in the short time it has been around, now displaying some lovely orangey notes on the nose and a genuinely lushness to the body and spice on the finish. You can almost forgive the caramel, this being such a well balanced, full-bodied ride. A quality show for the price. **40%.** *Alistair Graham for Aldi Stores, UK.* ☉ ☉

Golden Harvest **(75)** **n**19 **t**20 **f**18 **b**18.  The rich early barley-fest apart, still seems a little flat to me. **40%.** *Lombard Brands.*

Hammer Village No.12 Hammerby F.C. **(87)** **n**21 **t**23 **f**22 **b**21. This is a special bottling for the supporters of the Swedish football side Hammerby FC. Made from the turf, on this evidence...!! **43%**. *Blackadder*.

❖ **Harris Whisky Co. Islay Aged 12 Years** dist 93, bott Aug 06 **(82)** n20 t21 f21 b20 A jarring whisky: at times flat, then very sharp. Jerks around the palate without finding a rhythm. The odd moment, though, when it comes together superbly. **57.3%. nc ncf**.

❖ **Hedges and Butler Special Pure Malt (83)** n20 t21 f22 b21 Just so laid back: nosed and tasted blind I'd swear this was a blend (you know, a real blend with grains and stuff) because of the biting lightness and youth. Just love the citrus theme and, err...graininess....!! **40%**. *Ian Macleod Distillers*.

**Inverarity Islay 10 Years Old (85)** n22 t21 f21 b21. A teasing dram, so soft the flavours barely make it round the mouth. Delightfully different. **40%**

**Islay Connection Scotch Vatted Malt Over 10 Years Old (86)** n22 t21 f22 b21 Hullo..! The peat's back. Last year it went missing. This time has returned carrying more than its fair share of Bowmore-esque Fisherman's Friend but also a gristy character more in keeping with somewhere much further south-east on the island. **40%**. *Celtic Whisky Compagnie*. ☉ ☉

**Islay Trilogy 1969** (Bruichladdich 1966, Bunnahabhain 1968, Bowmore 1969) Bourbon/Sherry **(91)** n23 sooty embers in a hearth; kiwi fruit and peaches offer sweetness; t23 pure silk that melts and moulds into the tastebuds, with the best bit coming about ten seconds in as creamy cocoa tries to usurp the barley-sugar and fruits. And fails...; f22 much drier with chalky, salty vanilla and the weakest hint of peat imaginable; b23 decided to mark the 700th tasting for the 2007 edition with this highly unusual vatting. And no bad choice. The smoke is as elusive as the Paps of Jura on a dark November morning, but the silky fruits and salty tang tells a story as good as anything you'll hear by a peat fire. Take your time...the whiskies have. **40.3%**. *Murray McDavid. 1,200 bottles*.

**J & B Exception Aged 12 Years (80)** n20 t23 f18 b19. Very pleasant in so many ways. A charming sweetness develops quickly, with excellent soft honeycomb. But the nose and finish are just so...so...dull...!! For the last 30 years J&B has meant, to me, (and probably within that old company) exceptionally clean, fresh Speysiders offering a crisp, mouth-watering treat. I feel this is off target. **40%**. *Diageo/ Justerini & Brooks*.

**J & B Nox (89)** n23 classy Speyside thrust, youthful and crisp with a wonderful strand of honey. Gentle oak balances pleasingly; t23 the nose in liquid form: exactly the same characteristics with some extra, gently peppered toast towards the middle; f21 dries just a little too much as the barley tires; b22 a teasing, pleasing little number that is unmistakably from the J&B stable. **40%**. *Diageo*.

**Johnnie Walker Green Label 15 Years Old (92)** n24 this is one of the best vatted noses on the market: superb complexity, relatively peatless but still boasting big weight amid some fresher Speyside notes; t23 bingo! Serious flavour explosion which leans towards malty sweetness with a gradual fade-in of drier oak; f22 now some oils arrive, plus a little mint suggesting good age; b23 this is easily one of the best vatted malts in the market, pretty sweet, too. **43%**

**Jon, Mark and Robbo's The Rich Spicy One (89)** n22 a real fruitcake nose; clean and complete with spices and cooked, pithy fruits; t23 pretty rich, again with a raisiny fruit density and excellent bitter-sweet balance; f22 half-hearted spices tag along with the vanilla; b22 so much better without the dodgy casks: a real late night dram of distinction though the spice is perhaps a little on the subtle side... **40%**. *Edrington*.

**Jon, Mark and Robbo's The Smoky Peaty One (92)** n23 a faultlessly clean aroma where the reek enjoys a distinctive salty, coastal rock-pool edge; t22 again the peat is delicate yet coastal with a build-up of intense barley; f23 beautiful honey tones accompany the peat like a high phenol Highland Park; b24 genuinely high-class whisky where the peat is full-on yet allows impressive complexity and malt development. A malt for those who appreciate the better, more elegant things in life. **40%**. *Edrington*.

**Label 5 Pure Highland Malt Aged 12 Years** L534956A **(78)** n19 t20 f20 b19. Crushed by caramel, this never quite gets off the ground despite some promising moments. Won a Gold medal at the International Spirit Competition. I am mystified. **40%**. *The First Blending Co for La Martiniquaise, France*.

⫶⫶⫶ **Lapbeg 75/25 Aged 8 Years Pure Peated Islay Malt Scotch Whisky** Butt no. 2, dist 98, bott 06 **(95) n25** takes me back to lying by a cliff overlooking an Islay distillery, with the peat-reek wafting over me and caught in a fresh sea-weedy breeze; just a touch of anthracite to this, too, with a sharp volley of something citrussy; **t24** dry, intense and a little flaky with the bipolar peats offering both weight and something very delicate; some oak apparent early on; no shortage of coffee-cocoa towards the middle and just a brush of something oily; **f22** a fraction bitter towards the finale, but again you cannot but chew at the varying degrees and styles of peat, all topped off by a mild hint of hickory; **b24** once upon a time in the misty Hebridean past, the distillers of Islay, especially those on the south-east coast where Ardbeg and Laphroaig stand, insisted that their whiskies were at their very best on reaching eight years. To mark their 10th anniversary, the Danish whisky importers Mac Y launched this one-off vatted malt consisting of Laphroaig and Ardbeg at those now relatively tender ages. It is, frankly, as near perfection as you might pray for, a malt which takes me back to the first-ever Islays I consumed: or should I say consumed me. Here we have a marriage in heaven of freshness and intensity; a lesson in vitality and complexity. Whether it can ever be repeated, I have no idea. So if you are an Ardbeg or Laphroaig fan, or even brand new to whisky, try and grab a bottle. It will be both an experience and an honour. And for some, the moment when they actually twigged what I have been saying about age and natural colour. **48%. nc, ncf.** *Mac Y, Denmark. 900 bottles.*

**The Living Cask Anniversary Offering (79) n20 t21 f20 b18.** Not a happy bunny, this. Intense and chewy but never finds its rhythm or the usual degree of charm. **59%.** *Loch Fyne Whiskies.*

**Loch Fyne Whiskies Living Cask Volume XXIV** bott 26 June 06 **(92) n22 t24 f23 b23.** Another snapshot from this wonderful, ever-evolving cask at Loch Fyne. No point doing full notes, as it'll be quite different when you get there. But this one comes alive on the palate with the most wonderful marriage of great age and something young enough to salivate yourself to death with. Always a highlight of the year when I get a sample! **57.5%.** *Loch Fyne Whiskies.*

**Lochinvar Pure Malt (83) n18 t22 f22 b21.** The careless nose is more than made up for by the scrambled delivery on the palate. There is no rhythm to this whisky and absolutely no plot. It feels like a bunch of casks slung together at random...but the result, though confused, has some deliciously spicy and barley-rich moments. A fun dram. **40%.** *Roscow Greig & Co for Somerfield, UK.*

**MacDonalds Glencoe Aged 8 Years (81) n19 t22 f19 b21.** Invigorating and enjoyable if slightly out of sync. Much more honeycomb than before and a tad oilier. **58%. nc.** *Ben Nevis Distillery.*

⫶⫶⫶ **Matisse Aged 21 Years (79) n17 t21 f20 b21.** Not sure if some finishing or re-casking has been going on here to liven it up. Has some genuine buzz on the palate, but intriguing weirdness, too. Don't bother nosing this one. **40%.** *The Matisse Spirits Co.*

**Monkey Shoulder (93) n23** busy, complex and wonderfully weighted: the theme is orangey-citrus softened by vanilla. Excellent malt-oak ratio; **t24** soft mouth arrival and then a steady increase in malt intensity; shards of Demerara sweetness help counter the vanilla; some firm grain early on also guarantees a degree of mouthwatering freshness and bite to balance against the creamy softness; **f22** enormous length with layer upon layer of gently oiled malt slowly diminishing in sweetness; **b24** outstanding vatting here by David Stewart, who clearly has the malts in the palm of his hands. Pity a freak accident in a bottling hall should deprive him of a Bible award! A joy. **40%.** *William Grant & Sons.*

⫶⫶⫶ **Norse Cask Selection Vatted Islay 1995 Aged 10 Years** Hogshead no. AR04000008, dist 95, bott 06 **(86) n22 t23 f20 b21** A spicy beast, this. The oak really does get stuck in just taking the edge off the interplay between the varied malts. Some lovely smoky phases, though and the sweetness helps. **59.4%. nc ncf.** *WhiskyOwner.com, Denmark. 318 bottles.*

**Norse Cask Selection Vatted Islay 1991 Aged 12 Years (89) n24** stonking peat. The barley must have been grown on a peat bed and then dried over a peat fire for about three years. Bloody hell's-peaty-bells...; **t23** no prizes for guessing what's first to show, but a massive spice kick is not far behind; **f21** sweetens out towards a toasty-gristiness;

**b**21 fabulous, but not much going in the way of complexity. But if you're a peat freak, I don't think you either notice...or much care...!! **59.5%**. *Quality World, Denmark.*

**Old Master's Islay Pure Malt 1991 12 Year Old** bott May 04 **(93) n**22 **f**24 **t**23 **b**24. Some very clever vatting makes for a diamond of a bottling. **59.3%**

**Old Masters Islay Pure Malt Aged 14 Years** dist 91, bott 05 **(86) n**22 **t**22 **f**20 **b**22. I'd hazard that there's a cask of Caol Ila in there somewhere, and it's a bit too much for the better Islays in this bipolar mix. **58.3%**. *James MacArthur.*

⋰ **Old Masters The Trinity II Islay Pure Malt** dist 00, bott 06 **(84) n**21 **t**20 **f**22 **b**21 Sweet peat and plenty of Bowmore-style cough tablet. As wild and unruly as an early summer storm hitting the Oa. And as strangely enjoyable. **61%**. *James MacArthur for Japan only.*

**Poit Dhubh 8 Bliadhna (83) n**22 **t**22 **f**19 **b**20. Generously peated and rich in the middle but foiled by very un-Gaelic toffee. **43%**. *Praban Na Linne. Conduct their business, whenever possible, in Gaelic: bliadhna means "years old".*

**Poit Dhubh 12 Bliadhna (82) n**20 **t**22 **f**20 **b**20. The bitterness of old has been eradicated, though the deliciously mouth-watering start comes to grief on caramel. **43%. ncf**. *Praban na Linne.* ⊙

**Poit Dhubh 21 Bliadhna (84) n**21 **t**21 **f**21 **b**21. A couple of years back you might have spotted me drinking this once seriously complex dram in a Scottish bar. Now it has lost a degree of its buzz and heart with the removal of all the old peat; the attractively fruity remains are still enjoyable, though toffeed. **43%. ncf**.

**The Pot Still Scotch Vatted Malt Over 8 Years Old (90) n**22 excellent oak sub plot to the ballsy barley; **t**24 goes down with all the seductive powers of long fingernails down a chest: the wonderful honey and barley richness is stunning and so beautifully weighted; **f**22 a lazier finale, allowing the chalky oaky notes to make folly of those tender years; **b**22 such sophistication: the Charlotte Rampling of Scotch. **43.5%. ncf**. *Celtic Whisky Compagnie, France.*

**Pride of Speyside (91) n**22 **t**23 **f**23 **b**23. This is a one-off whisky vatted by David Urquhart in aid of charity. As part of his recuperation after undergoing emergency major heart surgery he, quite amazingly, cycled some 150 miles to all 44 working distilleries in his beloved Speyside, collecting samples of their malt from each of them. He then vatted the whiskies together to produce a very limited number of bottles which will eventually be auctioned off for worthy causes including the Moray Cardiac Project. This really is a nuggety little fighter brimming with character and style – and the same can be said about the whisky.... **57.6%**. *Gordon & MacPhail.*

⋰ **Prime Blue Pure Malt (83) n**21 **t**21 **f**21 **b**20 Steady, with a real chewy toffee middle. Friendly stuff. **40%**

⋰ **Prime Blue 12 Years Old Pure Malt (78) n**20 **t**20 **f**19 **b**19 A touch of fruit but tart in places. **40%**

⋰ **Prime Blue 17 Years Old Pure Malt (88) n**23 clever weight and a touch of something fruity and exotic, too; **t**21 thick malt concentrate; **f**22 takes a deliciously latte-style route and would be even better but for the toffee; excellent spicing; **b**22 lovely, lively vatting: something to get your teeth into! **40%**

⋰ **Prime Blue 21 Years Old Pure Malt (77) n**21 **t**20 **f**18 **b**18 After the teasing, bourbony nose the remainder disappoints with a caramel-rich flatness. The reprise of a style of whisky I thought had vanished about four of five years ago **40%**

**Sainsbury's Malt Whisky Finished in Sherry Casks (72) n**19 **t**19 **f**17 **b**17. Never the best, this still remains somewhat cloying with over-indulgent sweetness and an aggressive bitterness. The finish remains a mess. **40%**. *Sainsbury's, UK.*

**Sainsbury's Pure Islay Malt Aged 10 Years** bott code L7 073 **(91) n**23 the iodine reeks from the glass: there is a wonderful balance between oily, soft smoke and something altogether more punchy and complex; **t**24 a change of shape here to the last bottling; after the initial gristy sweetness: much drier, less barley gloss and the oils have vanished: even so, this cotton-dry number oozes quality; **f**22 a shorter finish than last year with more vanilla amid the dry embers; **b**22 another fabulous bottling from Sainsbury, though this time it's all about the mouth arrival; the nose and finish have just been shortened slightly. Still value-for-money whisky of the very top order and a must have for the home collection. **40%**. *Sainsbury's, UK.* ⊙ ⊙

**Scottish Leader Imperial Blended Malt (77)** n20 t20 f18 b19. Now don't be confused here: this isn't Imperial malt from Speyside. And although it says Blended, it is 100% malt. What is clear, though, is that this is pretty average stuff. **40%**. *Burn Stewart.*

**Scottish Leader Aged 14 Years (80)** n21 t21 f19 b19. A cleaner, less peaty version than the no-age statement vatting, but still fails to entirely ignite the tastebuds **40%**. *Burn Stewart.*

**Serendipity (96)** n23 do giant noses come any more gentle than this? The peat is thumping, wide-ranging and of the style unique to when Ardbeg was cut from its own peat bogs; but this peat is harnessed by layers of sweet, soothing malt; t25 I have tried. Believe me, I have tried, but I cannot find a single fault, a single crack on the palate. It is perfect: just like the nose, the peat arrives with a fanfare, it caresses with great might, but never leaves a mark. The intensity of the maltiness and the opaqueness of the peat are the only things that can control the enormity of the oak. Yet control it they do. And with something to spare; f23 much drier, the oak begins to get away slightly from the malt, but it remains in check and delivers the most exquisitely complex sensations imaginable; b25 the story behind this whisky beggars belief. If you made it up no-one would believe you. But it was an accident – a major one in whisky terms. Standard common or garden Glen Moray 12 years old is mixed by accident in the bottling hall with genuinely antique Ardbeg: yes, we are talking some of the rarest, most priceless whisky in the world. It works out at just 20% Glen Moray, but it is still vatted whisky and Ardbeg lovers are deprived of casks of the most sought-after malt this universe has ever seen. The result is this. Something, by sheer chance, that borders perfection. The blender in me wants to weep. Whatever you have to do, do it. Just get a bottle. **40%**. *Glenmorangie.*

**Smoking Ember (81)** n22 t20 f20 b19. The nose is glorious, fresh, straight from the malt kiln. But the full follow-through fails to materialise. **40%**. *Lombard Brands.*

**Tidal Ebb Islay Distillation Area (83)** n21 t22 f20 b20. Some lovely peaty tones softened by light muscovado sugar. **40%**. *Lombard Brands.*

**Wemyss Vintage Malt The Peat Chimney Hand Crafted Blended Malt Whisky (80)** n19 t22 f20 b19. The balance is askew here, especially on the bone-dry wallpapery finish. Does have some excellent spicy/coffee notes, though. **43%**. *Wemyss Vintage Malts.*

**Wemyss Vintage Malt The Smooth Gentleman Hand Crafted Blended Malt Whisky (83)** n19 t22 f21 b21. Not sure about the nose: curiously fishy (very gently smoked). But the malts tuck into the tastebuds with aplomb showing some sticky barley sugar along the way. **43%**. *Wemyss Vintage Malts.*

**Wemyss Vintage Malt The Spice King Hand Crafted Blended Malt Whisky (84)** n22 t22 f20 b20. Funnily enough, I've not a great fan of the word "smooth" when it comes to whisky. But the introduction of oily Caol Ila-style peat here makes it a more of a smooth gentleman than the "Smooth Gentleman." Excellent spices very late on. **43%**. *Wemyss Vintage Malts.*

**Whisky Galore Pure Malt Aged 10 Years** dist 95, bott 05 **(89)** n22 gristy, grassy and classy; t22 mouth-watering but there is weight to the mildly honeyed barley; f23 real complexity as soft citrus and vanilla rye with the malt. A superb mid-day dram; b22 talk about the Power of the Whisky Bible. When I first reviewed this brand, it marked up a staggering 60 points....and was lucky to get that. It was a dram scuppered by the OTT use of caramel which left it flatter than an East Anglian pancake. My comments brought shockwaves to Huntley, and the town's drains filled with discarded pots of caramel. (Not really, but you get the drift...) Here is a direct result. Not a whisky that you would jump off a rushing train to retrieve (mind you, thinking about it, the company's owner is about as Scottish as you can get) but one unspoiled that you can genuinely enjoy. **40%**. *Duncan Taylor. 120 bottles.*

**Wild Scotsman Aged 15 Years Vatted Malt (95)** n23 a seriously attractive marriage between gentle oaky vanilla and preening barley; diluted honey and spiced apple abound; t24 you really can't ask for more from a malt delivery than this. Soft and vaguely lush, the taste buds are overrun by an enchanting Danish-style moist marzipan in dark chocolate. It is impossible to fault the intensity and beauty of the early barley charge; f24 settles down to drier marzipan and pistachio oil. The interplay between barley and oak is exceptional and even proffers some very late and welcome spices. One of the longest finishes in the business; b24 if anyone wants an object lesson as to why you don't screw your whisky with caramel, here it is. Jeff Topping can feel a justifiable sense of pride in his new whisky: for its age, it is an unreconstituted masterpiece... **46% (92 proof). nc ncf.** *USA.*

**Wm Morrison Islay Pure Malt Aged 10 Years (84) n**20 **t**22 **f**21 **b**21. A very delicate and well-structured Islay for reflective moments. Doesn't paint the peat with a tar brush.; maybe an extra layer than previous years. **40%**

**Wm Morrisons Pure Malt Aged 8 Years (77) n**20 **t**22 **f**17 **b**18. Starts with a shock wave of stunning young grassy malt, but then a curtain of caramel descends and life in the glass is extinguished. What a shame. What a waste. **40%**

## MYSTERY MALTS

**Blackadder Raw Cask Blairfindy** (*see* Glenfarclas)

**Chieftain's Limited Edition Aged 40 Years** Hogshead **(78) n**22 **t**22 **f**16 **b**18. Oak-ravaged and predictably bitter on the death (those of you who enjoy Continental bitters might go for this..!). But the lead up does offer a short, though sublime and intense honey kick. The finish, though... **48.5%.** *Ian Macleod.*

**Inverarity 10 Years Old** (*see* Aultmore)

**Inverarity Ancestral 14 Years Old** (*see* Balmenach)

# Scottish Grain

**I**t's a bit weird, really. Many whisky lovers stay clear of blended Scotch, preferring instead single malts. The reason, I am often told, is that the grain included in a blend makes it rough and ready.

Yet I wish I had a twenty pound note for each time I have been told in the last year how much someone enjoys a single grain.

The ones that the connoisseurs die for are the older versions, usually special independent bottlings displaying great age and more often than not brandishing a lavish Canadian or bourbon style.

Like single malts, grain distilleries produce whisky bearing their own style and signature. And, also, some display characteristics and a richness that can surprise and delight. Most of the grains available in (usually specialist) whisky outlets are pretty elderly. Being made from maize and wheat helps give them either that Canadian or, depending on the freshness of the cask, an unmistakable bourbony style. So older grains display far greater body than is commonly anticipated.

Light whiskies, including some Speysiders, tend to adopt this north American stance when the spirit has absorbed so much oak that the balance has been tipped. So overtly Kentuckian can they be, I once playfully introduced an old single grain Scotch whisky into a bourbon tasting I was conducting and nobody spotted that it was the cuckoo in the nest ... until I revealed all at the end of the evening. And even had to display the bottle to satisfy the disbelievers.

Younger grains may give a hint of oncoming bourbon-ness. But, rather, they tend to celebrate either a softness in taste or, in the case of North British, a certain rigidity. Where many malts have a tendency to pulverise the taste-buds and announce their intent and character at the top of their voice, younger grains are content to stroke and whisper.

Scotch whisky companies have so far had a relaxed attitude to marketing their grains. William Grant has made some inroads with Black Barrel, though with nothing like the enthusiasm they unleash upon us with their blends and malts. And Diageo are apparently content to see their Cameron Brig sell no further than its traditional hunting grounds, just north of Edinburgh, where the locals tend to prefer single grain to any other whisky. And the latest news from that most enormous of distilleries...it is getting bigger. Not only are Diageo planning to up their malt content by building a new Speyside distillery, but Cameronbridge, never a retiring place since the days of the Haigs in the 1820s is set for even grander expansion. Having, with Port Dundas, absorbed the closure of a number of grain distilleries over the last 30 years something had to be done to give it a fighting chance of taking on the expansion into China, Russia and now, most probably, India.

The news for grain lovers had not been good lately with the demolition of Dumbarton. I hope Chivas, as a mark of respect for the lost and, for my money, best grain distiller to operate out of Scotland following the closure of Cambus, each year launch a special vintage of this crisp grain. As a distillery that distilled from both wheat and corn, it would make a fascinating addition for whisky lovers to be able to try and spot the difference in style from the same age.

The tastings notes here for grains – both single and vatted – cover only a few pages, due to their scarcity. However, it is a whisky style growing in stature, helped along the way by Compass Box's recent launching of a vatted grain. And we can even see an organic grain on the market, distilled at the unfashionable Loch Lomond Distillery.

At last the message is getting through that the reaction of this relatively lightweight spirit - and please don't for one moment regard it as neutral, for it is most certainly anything but - to oak can throw up some fascinating and sometimes delicious possibilities. Blenders have known that for a long time. Now public interest is growing. And people are willing to admit that they can enjoy an ancient Cambus, Caledonian or Dumbarton in very much the way they might celebrate a single malt. Even if it does go against the grain...

# Single Grain Scotch
## ALLOA (see North of Scotland)

## CALEDONIAN

**Cadenhead's Caledonian Aged 31 Years** dist Jan 63, bott Feb 94 **(88) n**22 **t**23 **f**21 **b**22. The last hurrah of a grain that obviously put a metal backbone into many a blend. **48.7%**

⠿ **Clan Denny Caledonian Aged 40 Years** dist 65 **(90) n**23 sublime intermingling of ripe apricot and custardy-vanilla. The weight is perfect; **t**22 glorious grains hit the spot immediately with the sugars hitting the tannins head on; **f**23 long, with evidence of Demerara and hickory: not entirely unbourbony **b**22 classy act from a dead distillery that lives on through this stunning bottling. **43.7%. ncf** *Douglas Laing.*

**Clan Denny Grain Caledonian 40 Years Old** dist Aug 75, bott Aug 05 **(94) n**25 does the aroma of grain get better than this? No, I don't think it does. What we have here is bourbon at its most honeycombed, leather armchaired and toffee-appled. But the oak hasn't even remotely gone OTT. It was for this that nature gave us a nose…It even makes you forget about drinking the stuff…; **t**23 soft and lush, the corn gives up a wonderful Demerara sheen to the oak-controlled sweetness; again soft honey flitters about. Not a jagged edge, the tastebuds have rarely been so tenderly caressed; **f**22 fades more quickly than one might expect from a 40-year-old, but that is because the oak is controlled and doesn't offer a shred of bitterness; instead, delicate vanillins abound as do the well manicured sugars; **b**24 Grain is an inferior type of whisky…? Yeah, right…!! **47.4%.** *Douglas Laing.*

## CAMBUS

**Cadenhead's Cambus Aged 31 Years** dist 63, bott 94 **(87) n**21 **t**23 **f**21 **b**22. An impressive grain that has taken the years in its stride and remained upbeat and full of character. **53.2%**

## CAMERONBRIDGE

**Cameron Brig** bott code L6355CS000 01313297 db **(69) n**18 **t**18 **f**16 **b**17 Bland beyond belief. **40%** ☺ ☺

⠿ **Duncan Taylor Collection Cameronbridge 1979** Cask no. 3582 **(85) n**20 **t**23 **f**21 **b**21 Almost pure Canadian in style but with the oak perhaps making too many inroads. There is a superb richness to the grain which dovetails wonderfully with the sweetened spices. **52.4%**

**Duncan Taylor Cameronbridge 1979** cask 3523, dist Feb 79, bott Jan 05 **(83) n**21 **t**22 **f**19 **b**21. Few whiskies in the world can boast quite so much natural caramel. **59.9%**

**Duncan Taylor Cameronbridge 1979** dist 79, bott 3 Mar 06 **(94) n**23 wonderfully firm nose with soft muscovado sugar and playful oak spices; **t**24 blind-tasted, this could be exceptionally fine Canadian with the oaky-grain inter-play being a picture of harmony. The soft-firm delivery is also exceptional; **f**23 long, with soft oils fanning out the coffee and corn; **b**24 a wonderful, stylized grain of the highest quality. This bottling is unmistakably from this distillery, so true to type is it. Sensational. **59.5%**

## CARSEBRIDGE

⠿ **Chieftain's Carsebridge 42 Years Old** Oloroso Sherry, dist Feb 60 **(94) n**24 faultless oloroso of a type now sadly lost to us. Note the entire lack of sulphur and the grapey density: this is just about an extinct race of butts. **t**23 almost pompous in its spicy nuttiness, the oloroso is heard loud and clear and fends off heckling from oak with contemptuous ease; **f**24 long, lithe and loaded with sherry. Loads of burnt raisin and burnt fudge; **b**23 I remember stumbling across this cask in a warehouse about five years ago. I couldn't resist having a good sniff as it slept and it was more verbose then with greater spice and a sharper bite and wit. Now it is something of Nigel Bruce's Watson to Sherlock Holmes, doddering around with an old world charm and genial simplicity. A whisky you should buy if you see, for it is highly unlikely you will see its like again. **41.6%. ncf.** *Ian Macleod Distillers.*

⠿ **Duncan Taylor Collection Carsebridge 1979** Cask no. 32902 **(92) n**22 butterscotch tart of the highest order with a dollop of cream and vanilla; **t**23 busy yet clean start with oak and grains battling out for early supremacy; stage two sees the palate filled with lush, almost barley-sugar-esque notes dried by an excellent sprinkling of mocha; all through these battles a lively spice bristles playfully f23 long, with a fruity, mildly sugary edge clinging to the fading oak; b24 exceptionally well balanced grain getting the emphasis between the spices and bitter-sweet texture absolutely spot on. Fabulous! **60%**. *Duncan Taylor.*

**Duncan Taylor Collection Carsebridge 1979 Aged 25 Years** cask no. 32901, dist Mar 79, bott Jan 05 **(90)** n22 subtle spices and crushed pine nuts; t24 exceptional arrival with wonderfully weighted corn enriched in its own sweet oil; f22 soft vanilla and corn; b22 never understood why this was not bottled more often. Well done to Duncan Taylor for helping to show what we have been missing... and shall continue to miss. **56.4%**

## DUMBARTON

**Cadenhead's Dumbarton Aged 32 Years** dist Feb 62, bott Feb 94 **(85)** n21 t22 f21 b21. Amazingly firm grain with a lovely fruity edge. **49.9%**

**Clan Denny Grain Dumbarton 40 Years Old** dist Dec 64, bott Nov 05 **(90)** n22 if you adore sticking your nose in an over-ripe mango, then this is the one for you...some orangey-bourboney notes also bubble up as it oxidizes; t23 mouth-watering and fresh to start, the soft delivery is fruit accented and a near perfect sweetness; f22 the corn offers enough oil to accept the growing, drier oak; b23 a proud grain with no buckling at the knees to oak and a luxurious lift off. **44.1%**. *Douglas Laing.*

## GIRVAN

⠿ **Berry's Own Selection Girvan 1989** Bott 07 **(91)** n22 freshly polished wooden floors, gentle bourbon, spiced vanilla; t23 silky and not entirely un-Canadian in its delivery; the sweetness doesn't entirely camouflage the cleverness of the soft-hard duality of the body f23 long, surprisingly well oiled and showing something of a late corn (as opposed to wheated) character; fabulous depth as the soft oaks grow b23 a Steady-Eddie and eventually beautiful grain with no blemishes or fault-lines giving a good insight into why this make is so popular among blenders. **46%**. *Berry Bros & Rudd.*

**Berrys' Own Selection Girvan 1989 Aged 17 Years (87)** n21 creamy vanilla; t23 skydivers landing in a lake of blancmange wouldn't get a softer touchdown than this; the oak-grain interplay is impressive; f22 lashings of vanilla and a touch of spice; b21 pure silk: beautifully soft and a must for Canadian whisky lovers. **46%**. *Berry Bros & Rudd.*

**Black Barrel** db **(82)** n20 t20 f22 b20. Dangerously drinkable, moreish grain oasting a soft, Canadian-style oakiness. Light, spicy fizz on the long finish. **40%**

**Girvan 1964** casks filled 30/4/64, bott 10/10/01 db **(88)** n22 beautiful, rich corn notes: sweet, deep, yet clean and crystal clear despite age; t23 sweet, oily, bourbony, sensual. Brilliant mouthfeel; f21 lots of liquorice, oak and subtle vanilla; b22 a luscious, classical well-aged grain straight from the top drawer. **48%**. *1200 bottles.*

**Old Master's Girvan (87)** n21 t23 f22 b22. Standard, high quality Girvan at its sexiest. **60.4%**. *James MacArthur*

**Old Masters Girvan Aged 16 Years** cask no. 110632, dist 89, bott 06 **(89)** n22 untypically Girvan-esque tough cop-soft cop approach. But, overall, fresh and seriously tender; t23 beautifully, intense, sweet grains softly oiled and alluring; f22 bitters down as the oak takes hold. Good length and poise; b22 Quality whisky: Girvan at its most forthright. **58%**. *James MacArthur.*

## INVERGORDON

**Invergordon Single Grain** db **(84)** n20 t21 f22 b21. High-quality, sweet, velvety grain: a fine representative of medium-aged stock from this distillery. **40%**

**Dewar Rattray Individual Cask Bottling Invergordon Aged 40 Years** cask no. 57633, dist 14.8.64, bott 29.6.05 **(91)** n23 you can almost hear the pack ice cracking on Lake Winnipeg. Nosed blind, it's pure Canadian; t23 startling, lush and mouth-watering corn laced with maple syrup; perfect vanilla undercurrent; f22 relatively short and docile but the honey remains intact; b23 more Canadian in style than a Film Board. **48.1%**. *270 bottles.*

**Duncan Taylor Collection Invergordon 1965 Aged 39 Years** cask no. 15504, dist Dec 65, bott Dec 04 **(87)** n21 t22 f23 b21. It's as though the corn and oak have cancelled each other out to give a highly enjoyable but relatively featureless experience. **49.6%**

**Duncan Taylor Collection Invergordon 1965** cask no. 15508, dist Dec 65, bott Feb 06 **(86) n**21 **t**22 **f**22 **b**21. Needs a good prod to show it's still alive but when it does wake up the spices excel. **50.3%.** *243 bottles.*

⁘ **Duncan Taylor Collection Invergordon 1965** Cask no. 15514 **(86) n**19 **t**23 **f**22 **b**22 Lovely old grain that gets over the flat-ish, faltering, somewhat gluey nose to let loose with a superb display of spices on the otherwise soft and corn-rich arrival. Excellent fade as the oaks integrate with grace. Entirely charming whisky. **50.3%.** *Duncan Taylor.*

**The Whisky Fair Invergordon Aged 39 Years** dist Dec 65, bott Feb 05 **(89) n**22 floral, even a touch herbal; **t**24 massive and complex arrival of firm oak and even firmer corn with the bitter-sweet complexity of epic proportions; weirdly estery for a grain – almost like a rum; **f**21 slightly tired and vanilla-rich; **b**22 a bit of a spent force by the finish, but the early delivery is stupendous. **49.8%. nc ncf.** *90 bottles.*

## LOCH LOMOND

**Da Mhile Organic (88) n**21 **t**23 **f**22 **b**22. A calm, genteel grain up to the usual very high Loch Lomond standards and always exuding a certain, effortless touch of class. **46%.** *Da Mhile.* 1000 bottles.

**Dà Mhile Loch Lomond Organic** dist July 00, bott Mar 06 **(90) n**23 gentle sweetness that sits well with vanilla; curiously firm yet soft at same time; **t**23 beautifully chewy with teasing, subtle vanilla and butter tones; **f**21 pretty short but refuses to lose balance; **b**23 great to get a chance to see Loch Lomond's high class and complexly bodied grain – organic or not. **46%. nc ncf.** *6500 miniatures bottles.*

⁘ **Loch Lomond Cask No. 37697 Single Organic Grain Distillery Select** Organic French Oak, dist 24 July 00, bott 27 Apr 07 db **(76) n**18 **t**21 **f**18 **b**19 I wonder if the sulphur is organic.... **45%.** *475 bottles.*

**Loch Lomond Organic Single Grain in Organic wine Hogshead** cask no. 37700, dist 24 July 00, bott 27 July 05 db **(86) n**21 **t**22 **f**21 **b**22. Astonishing for a 5-year-old whisky. Amazing for a grain. And is one of the "must experience" whiskies of the year. But it can be even better when not rounded off...believe me! **45%.** *402 bottles.*

## LOCHSIDE

**Clan Denny Grain Lochside Aged 42 Years** dist Nov 63, bott Nov 05 **(89) n**23 I'm in deepest Kentucky and just opened up a 17-year-old barrel: it's tired and groaning but the hickory and muscovado sugar are such a treat; nice chestnuts, too; **t**23 silky, mesmerising oak with splinters in every direction; lovely heavy roast Java coffee at the very centre; **f**21 fades and becomes mildly bitter and tired with the coffee-bourbon theme continuing; **b**22 a bit like clapped out bourbon on the nose and even more clapped out bourbon on the finish. My researcher put this under single malts, but as soon as I tasted it, I smelt (and tasted!) a rat. Proof positive that old grain Scotch can produce vintage bourbon!! **44.1%.** *Douglas Laing.*

## NORTH BRITISH

**Adelphi North British 13 Years Old** cask 52640, dist 90, bott 03 **(87) n**22 **t**22 **f**21 **b**22. Faultlessly rich and chewy grain: fascinating that when compared with previous bottlings the scores are almost identical – 100/100 for consistency!! **63.5%**

**Adelphi North British 13 Years Old** cask 52640 **(87) n**21 soft, Canadian style corn and oak: enticing; **t**21 delicious fat toffee with growing oak offering soft spice. Some fruit hangs around, too; **f**23 long, chewy with a hint of cocoa and increasing sweetness: stunning; **b**22 exemplary. **63.5%**

**Clan Denny Grain North of Scotland 39 Years Old** dist Jun 66, bott Nov 05 **(76) n**21 **t**20 **f**17 **b**18. Curious, farm-yardy nose and early grain arrival, but then the off-key development is startling; almost like some experimental rye whiskies I have seen in Europe go slightly wrong. Odd. **44.4%.** *Douglas Laing.*

⁘ **Duncan Taylor Collection North British 1978** Cask no. 239966 **(88) n**21 curious aroma of cured ham amid the butter biscuits; **t**23 wonderfully firm grains branch out into something vaguely spicy and a little orangey. A sub stratum of gentle oils delights; **f**22 much drier and some pronounced oak in part, but the oil and sweetness just about remains intact; **b**22 pretty complex and always beautifully balanced. **51.6%.** *Duncan Taylor.*

Scott's Selection North British 1974 bott 05 (86) n22 t23 f20 b21. Attractive, but lacking in complexity towards the end. 43.6%. *Speyside Distillers.*

## NORTH OF SCOTLAND

⫶⫶⫶ Clan Denny North of Scotland Aged 39 Years dist June 66 (85) n20 t22 f22 b21 If I didn't know better I'd say this was a chunky old grain beefed further up in a sherry butt: tell me it's not true...!! 44.4%. nc ncf. *Douglas Laing.*

Hart Brothers Alloa 1964 cask 30296, dist Jul 64, bott Feb 05 (89) n24 toasted marshmallows, natural vanilla and sweet Muscovado sugar all in a Canadian coating; t23 silky; begins in a bourbon sweetness, then dries more towards very old Canadian: the mildly spicy corn is paramount and rich; f20 although feeling a bit tired there is enough custardy vanilla to see it through; b22 better in bottled form than the sampler I received last year, it's like being transported to the lakes of Winnipeg or Manitoba: outstanding quality and very Canadian in style. An absolute quality straight grain of the highest magnitude. Alloa grain was made at the North of Scotland distillery but tankered and filled into cask at their Dillichip Bond. Very rare stuff. 44.1%. *Hart Brothers Ltd.*

⫶⫶⫶ Private Cellar North of Scotland 1970 bott 07 (92) n24 stunning mixture of honey and stem ginger; t23 lush, lusty corn with some amazing notches of honey marked on the softest of oak; f22 long, vanilla-clad, gently drying, a touch of the Canadians; b23 this is the way old grain should be: slightly off the wall but radiating charm and class. 43%.

Private Cellars Selecton North of Scotland 1970 bott 03 (91) n23 t23 f22 b23. One of those great old grains that are a class apart. 43%. *Speyside Distillers.*

⫶⫶⫶ Private Cellars Selection North of Scotland 1973 bott 05 (85) n21 t22 f21 b21 A sweet core, but otherwise a safe bottling with lots of naturajl caramel dependence. 43%. *Speyside Distillers.*

Scott's Selection North of Scotland 1964 bott 03 (90) n22 buttery, sweet corn: slightly bourbony with a dash of Canadian; t23 extraordinary early sweetness that maintains balance and corn richness: the oak is a distant rumble; f22 Demerara sugar abounds, a touch of liquorice but the corn still blossoms even at the death; b23 is this really almost 40 years old? One hell of a cask for one hell of a whisky ... 43.6%

Scott's Selection North of Scotland 1971 bott 02 (81) n21 t21 f19 b20. Soft, sweet Canadian/bourbon notes are overpowered on the finale by a persistent off-key bitterness. 49.9%

Scott's Selection North of Scotland 1973 bott 05 (90) n22 firm grain and soft vanilla; t22 mouthwatering with a real juicy edge; f23 long, cornlaced and sweetening; b23 mouthwatering, fresh and relaxed. About as entertaining as they come: yet another classic from this lost distillery. 45%. *Speyside Distillers.*

## PORT DUNDAS

⫶⫶⫶ Duncan Taylor Collection Port Dundas 1973 Cask no. 128317 (96) n24 Christ!!! It's rum!!!! From Demerara. What the bloody hell is going on..? Let me have a look at the bottle. No, it's grain...from Port Dundas. Ah, right the stills...there you go!! Entirely different from any other whisky in the market place. And this is whisky..right? The natural caramelisation from the oak is not dissimilar to the pre-caramelisation in Demerara rum...another confusing point; t24 makes all the right noises for a supreme corn grain whisky, especially that big corny oiliness. Yet so many aspects of this display a Demerara rum-like sweetness and texture, only with the brilliance of subtlety achieved normally only by corn...my mind, like my tastebuds, is exploding...; f24 a bitter-sweet balance that you attain normally in your dreams: absolutely zero bitterness or off notes from the cask; the oiliness persists, as does the corn, as does the rum, as do gentle spices b24 never have I seen a better example of a Coffey still in action: before I actually knew what I was nosing I had, in my mind, been transported back to Guyana and was nosing some Coffey still rum from there: the similarity is extraordinary!! And, believe me, this is one whisky I don't spit whilst working on this book!! A landmark whisky in my long experience. And an award winner of some type. 57.9%

**Duncan Taylor Collection Port Dundas 1973 Aged 32 Years** cask no. 128316, dist Jan 73, bott Feb 05 **(87) n**23 t19 f23 **b**22. I've experienced some strange whiskies in my time, but this almost takes the fruity biscuit. Pass me a straightjacket.... **59.3%**

**STRATHCLYDE**

**Duncan Taylor Strathclyde 1973 Aged 31 Years** cask no. 74061, dist Nov 73, bott Jan 05 **(80) n**20 t21 f19 **b**20. Lots of peaches and tropical fruit, but the shape and balance are all over the shop. **62.8%**

⋅⋅⋅ **Duncan Taylor Collection Strathclyde 1973** Cask no. 74062 **(78) n**20 t21 f18 **b**19 Exactly two years after its twin cask was bottled...and just about identical results, except for extra bitters on the finish..!! **56.5%**

**Duncan Taylor Strathclyde 1980 Aged 24 Years** cask no. 1462, dist Aug 80 , bott Jan 05 **(75) n**18 t19 f19 **b**19. Harsh and puckering. **62.6%**

⋅⋅⋅ **Duncan Taylor Collection Strathclyde 1980** Cask no. 1496 **(79) n**20 t21 f18 **b**20 Like an out-of-sorts old Canadian – but with an early, viperish bite. **58.2%**

# Vatted Grain

**Clan Denny Speyside** (Mortlach; Glendullan; Linkwood and Dufftown) **(84) n**22 t21 f20 **b**21. When I saw Mortlach and Dufftown in there I feared the worst. But a genuine Speyside grassy nose is backed up with a malty charge on the palate. **40%.** *Douglas Laing.*

**Compass Box Hedonism** bott 04 (bottle identification L4097) **(89) n**22 soft, circular vanilla with a spec of honey; t22 soft landing but enough chew in there to make it entertaining; f23 good length and spice; **b**22 grain again shown to its advantage. **43%**

**Compass Box Hedonism Vatted Grain** (second bottling, small central illustration, described as "Vatted Grain") **(87) n**21 t22 f22 **b**22. Really mouthfilling and intense. Canadian style. **43%. nc ncf.**

**Compass Box Hedonism Vatted Grain** (third bottling, same label as second bottling, but laser jet bottling code number L3 136) **(89) n**22 t22 f22 **b**23. This is the other side of the same Hedonism coin: really classy, but in this case light and spicy rather than the overtly sweeter, oilier, more velvety texture of the previous bottling. This one, though, wins hands down for eye-closing, contemplative complexity. **40%**

**Compass Box Hedonism** bott lot no L5035 **(88) n**22 t22 f21 **b**23. A drier version of Hedonism, but the gentle complexity is a treat. **43%**

**Jon, Mark and Robbo's The Fresh Fruity One (84) n**21 t22 f20 **b**21. Lovely to see vatted grains coming into vogue after years of campaigning for distillers to take such a course. Enjoyable drinking. But Fresh and Fruity? Well, a touch too much oak for this ever to be fresh and not estery enough to be fruity. Doesn't do what it says on the tin. **40%.** *The Easy Drinking Whisky Company.*

# Scottish Blends

**W**ith a Scottish blend last year for the very first time being named Jim Murray's Whisky Bible's Whisky of the Year, the time surely has come for re-evaluating this most misunderstood and undervalued of whiskies. For it really is quite extraordinary how people the world over, with refined palates and a good knowledge of single malts, are so willing to dismiss blends out of hand. Certainly, from the amount of publicity the news received around the world, and some of the shock, horror reactions to it - especially when interviewed by journalists or cornered by malt fundamentalists - it was as if the end of the whisky world was nigh.

Perhaps it is a form of malt snobbery: if you don't drink malts, then you are not a serious Scotch whisky connoisseur ... or so some people think. Perhaps it is the fact that something like 94 out of every 100 bottles of Scotch consumed is a blend that has brought about this rather too common cold-shouldering. Well, not in my books. In fact, perhaps the opposite is true. Until you get to grips with blends you may well be entitled to regard yourself knowledgeable in single malts, but not in Scotch as a whole. Blends should be the best that Scotland can offer, because with a blend you have the ability to create any degree of complexity. And surely balance and complexity are the cornerstones of any great whisky, irrespective of type.

Of course there are some pretty awful blends created simply as a commodity with little thought going into their structure – just young whiskies, sometimes consisting of stock that is of dubious quality and then coloured up to give some impression of age. Yes, you are more likely to find that among blends than malts and for this reason the poorest blends can be pretty nasty. And, yes, they contain grain. Too often, though, grain is regarded as a kind of whisky leper – not to be touched under any circumstances. Some writers dismiss grain as "neutral" and "cheap", thus putting into the minds of the uninitiated the perception of inferiority.

But there really is nothing inferior about blends. In fact, whilst researching The Bible, I have to say that my heart missed more than one beat usually when I received a sample of a blend I had never found before. Why? Well, with single malts each distillery produces a style that can be found within known parameters. With a blend, anything is possible. There are many dozens of styles of malts to choose from and they will react slightly differently with certain grains.

For that reason, perhaps, I have marked blends a little more strictly and tighter than I have single malts. Because blends, by definition, should offer more.

And they do not have to be of any great age to achieve greatness. Look at the brilliance of the likes of Johnnie Walker Gold, Royal Silk, Black Bottle, Bailie Nicol Jarvie, Grant's and, of course, the all-conquering Old Parr Superior. Look, also, at the diversity of style from crisp and light to peat dominant and myriad styles between. Then you get others where age has also played an astonishing role, not least a 50-years-old, such as Royal Salute.

Just like malts, blends change in character from time to time. In the case of blends it often has much to do with the running availability of certain malts and grains. The most unforgivable reason is because the marketing guys reckon it needs a bit of extra colour and precious high notes are lost to caramel or sherry. Subtlety and character are the keys for any great blend without fail.

The most exciting blends, like White Horse 12 (why, oh, why is that, like Old Parr 18, restricted mainly to Japan?) and Grant's show bite, character and attitude. Silk and charm are to be appreciated. But after a long, hard day is there anything better than a blend that is young and confident enough to nip and nibble at your throat on its way down and then throw up an array of flavours and shapes to get your taste-buds round? Certainly, I have always found blends ultimately more satisfying than malts. Especially when the balance simply caresses your soul.

With Blended Scotch the range and possibilities are limitless. All it takes is for the drinker not just to use his or her nose and taste-buds. But also an open mind.

## Scottish Blends

**100 Pipers (67) n**17 **t**17 **f**16 **b**17. 100 Pipers: zero harmony. Young, less than pleasant grain and now lashings of caramel on top. Was called 100 Pipers, then re-named Black Watch – now appears to be 100 Pipers again, though there is still a Black Watch. They keep changing the name but the same bloody awful whisky keeps appearing. **40%.** *Chivas.*

**100 Pipers** Batch no. 391, bott Dec 05 **(81) n**20 **t**21 **f**20 **b**20. Now this is pretty good: excellent citrussy grain and the odd wave of Speysidey freshness. Now I know where to get some decent 100 Pipers... **42.8%.** *Chivas Bros./Seagram Distilleries India.*

**Aberdour Piper (83) n**21 **t**21 **f**20 **b**21. For an economy bar whisky, this offers unusual depth with satisfyingly lucid crunchy grain, excellent bite and just the right addition of smoke. A real clean mouthful and an attractive and cleverly blended one at that. **40%.** *Haymon Distillers.*

**Acing Superior (76) n**18 **t**22 **f**18 **b**18. A really enjoyable and impressive 5-y-o-style blend with decent malt and sparkling grain, but let down for the purists by the colouring. **40%**

**Adelphi Ben Nevis Blend 1970 Aged 24 Years** cask no. 4640, dist 70, bott 05 **(92) n**24 hypnotic malt and oak intensity: wonderful age and harmonisation here, together with stunning (kiwi?) fruit lightness; **t**23 lush body again, with the barley and oak absolutely at one; some strands of fruit here but entirely [OK?] non-specific; **f**22 much drier with the malt offering required sweetness; **b**23 what the hell is this stuff? I'd better consult The Bible...oh, hang on...this is The Bible! It turned up after I had been away for a month – haven't had the official word. But it feels like something that has been married in oak for a long, long time. Can't spot any discernible grain here at all. **50.3%.** *186 bottles.*

⠐⠂ **Adelphi Private Stock Loyal Old Mature (88) n**21 big grain overture; **t**23 golden syrup notes and bound tightly by firm grain; **f**22 delightful coffee with just the perfect degree of bite; **b**22 a very attractive number, especially for those with a slightly sweet tooth. **40%.** *Adelphi Distillery Ltd.*

**Aged Blend** (*see* Duncan Taylor Aged Blend)

**Aisla Craig Blend (84) n**19 **t**23 **f**21 **b**21 Once a notoriously anarchic number with plenty of rumbling smoke, this guy wears a different mask now. Still at times wondrously haphazard in its malt-grain delivery and still something of a happy accident rather than a structured blend, it has benefitted from reducing the early smoke impact slightly and giving a louder voice to the barley. Much more of a chew and never less than a thumping, fascinating dram as the peat claws back ground. **40%.** *Dewar Rattray.* ☺ ☺

**Alistair Graham Scotch Whisky (71) n**17 **t**19 **f**18 **b**17. Spot the malt contest. Decent enough grain, though. **40%.** *For Sainsbury's, UK.*

**Ancient Clan (75) n**17 **t**20 **f**19 **b**19. Furry on the plate and, despite a lovely clean-malt purple patch in the middle, suffers from a rough periphery. **40%.** *Tomatin Distillery Co.*

**The Andrew Usher Memorial Blend (92) n**23 beautifully firm grain which seems attached to succulent fruit. The malts are busy and spicy: a real blender's blend; **t**24 explosive, mouth-enveloping stuff. The malts go hand-inhand with the grain to create complex patterns all around the palate while the fruit ensures softness reigns; **f**22 much lighter with toffee-vanilla gentleness against the foraging spice; **b**23 one for the Andrew Usher hall of fame. The old man would have been proud of a blend that has it all. **49%.** *Kyndal.*

**The Antiquary 12 Years Old (92) n**23 a stunning Speyside top note reflects perfectly off the crisp, clean grain; **t**24 mouthwatering, sweet grain refreshes and re-ignites the tastebuds. Just so salivating and delightful with the grain crackling around the palate; **f**22 long, with the malt-grain interplay sending continuous shock waves; **b**23 enormously improved in recent years with a growling, purring interplay between grain and quite stunning malt. The caramel has been ditched and it's a delight! This is just how I see many blends before they are ruined in  the bottling hall when colour is added. **40%.** *J & W Hardie Ltd.*

**Antiquary 21 Years Old** bott 05 **(95) n**25 some lovely honey interlaced with pure barley and crisp grain; and where before there was an off-key note, now we have something almost too harmonious for words. A wonderful injection of bourbon-laden grain offers supreme depth to counter the light fruitiness; **t**23 big, booming malt with honey at its centrefold and succulent white grape juice in the wings; **f**23 just layers of interwoven acacia honey and grape with barley hunkering down with the vanilla; the grain offers a firm background for the malts to rebound from with interest; **b**24 probably the most improved blend of the year: nigh on faultless. This is erotic whisky: dab it behind the ears of the one you love. Viagra has a rival. **43%.** *The Tomatin Distillery.*

**Asda Blended Scotch (83) n**21 **t**21 **f**20 **b**21. Sound, honest, whisky with excellent grain bite adding steel to the softer Speyside malt: all you could ask and more from a standard own label. **40%.** *Glenmorangie for Asda.* ⊙

∴ **Asda Extra Special 12 Years Old (78) n**19 **t**21 **f**19 **b**19. Pleasantish but dragged down by the dreaded S word. **40%.** *Glenmorangie for Asda.*

**Asda Finest Old Scotch Aged 8 Years (79) n**19 **t**22 **f**19 **b**19. A more than competent supermarket blend that positively shimmers on the tastebuds with a wondrous delivery of fresh, mouthwatering malt aided and abetted by crisp yet well aged grain. A slightly bitter finish, though. **40%**

**Asyla** (*see* Compass Box)

**Avonside (74) n**17 **t**20 **f**19 **b**18. Pleasant, but a little flat. **40%.** *Gordon & MacPhail.*

**Avonside 8-years-old (82) n**20 **t**21 **f**22 **b**19. Pleasant, a degree flattish but at least the nose has been sorted somewhat. **57%.** *Gordon & MacPhail.* ⊙ ⊙

**The Bailie Nicol Jarvie (B.N.J). (89) n**22 decidedly Speysidey with caressing grain; **t**23 where the malt and grain rebounded and sparred off each other, we now have two distinct cultures trying to harmonise and bringing in the faintest smoke to help. Delicious, but...; **f**22 the extra oak flattens out the blend further and adds a degree of bitterness; **b**22 lovely blending still but the crisp, shrapnel-sharp edge to the grain and malt has blurred to become something softer and less heart-pounding. Just too damned civilised! All armchairs slippers and pipes  hen you are looking for juicy action. **40%.** *Glenmorangie.*

**Ballantine's Aged 12 Years (87) n**21 **t**22 **f**21 **b**23. The kind of old-fashioned, mildly moody blend Colonel Farquharson-Smythe (retired) might have recognised when relaxing at the 19th hole back in the early 50s. Too good for a squirt of Soda, mind. **40%** *Allied.*

**Ballantine's Gold Seal 12 Years Old (88) n**23 **t**21 **f**22 **b**22. Very complex and alluring. **40%.** *Allied.*

**Ballantine's Royal Blue 12 Years Old (90) n**23 fabulous chalky-oak and big malt presence; **t**22 mouthwatering, fat, some dazzling citrus notes and then cocoa/coffee towards the spiced, complex middle; **f**22 sweetens with both malt and soft brown sugar The texture remains lush without ever being oily; **b**23 this blend has improved beyond recognition since I last tasted it: my hats off to the blender. This is for the Japanese market and, had I tasted this blind, I would have marked it down as a Japanese blend of the top order... which is some compliment. **43%.** *Allied.*

**Ballantine's 17 Years Old (96) n**24 a floral lavender-mint combination balance with aplomb with the most intrinsic peat and grain: beguiling and wonderfully sexy. Only a coating of ultra-clean sherry deviates from earlier bottlings; **t**25 this is it: balance, charm, guile, charisma ... the entire works in one voluptuous mouthful. First a sweet sheen coats the mouth then some grassy notes get you salivating before soft smoke provides the weight. Enormous with wave upon wave of intense barley sugar and peat but never heavy enough to snap a twig. This is masterful blending; **f**23 some oaks finally settle like sediment. Raisins and walnut complete the rich picture and spices add that extra dimension ... as if it was needed; **b**24 it's amazing that out of one lab comes two blends that give masterclass performances: Ballantine's 17 and Teachers. Both are outwardly weighty but reveal so much more that is gentle and complex. The point about this whisky is that you feel you never quite get to the bottom layer: labyrinthine liquid genius. **43%.** *Allied.*

**Ballantine's 21 Year Old (93) n**22 suet pudding laced with gentle oloroso and molasses, with a few fresh figs to freshen things up a little; **t**24 silky arrival on palate as the charming grain magnifies the rich barley presence; the bittersweet theme is glórious; **f**23 pulsating oaky vanilla soothed by the firming cocoalaced grain and developing spices; **b**24 an entirely different animal to before, sensual and supremely balanced: top draw blending. **43%.** *Allied.*

**Ballantine's 30 Year Old (84)** n21 t21 f22 b20. Changed dramatically from of old, with sterner, more dominating, drier oak and an overall much crisper, less embracing character. Lovely malty, Horlicky finish, though. **43%**. *Allied*.

**Ballantine's Black (85)** n22 t23 f20 b20. Could be so much more elegant and complete if that early smoke-wafting malt stretched a bit further. **40%**. *Allied*.

**Ballantine's Finest (87)** n22 t22 f20 b23. Always a classy, classic act, this has softened and become a little smokier, fuller bodied and significantly more complex in recent times. **40%**. *Allied*.

**Ballantine's Limited (89)** n22 excellent clarity of fruit and barley; t24 early grain and then a slow, complex delivery of malt surrounded by soft grape and the lightest coating of muscovado sugar; f21 dryer with some bitter-almond and cocoa on the oak; b22 a quality newcomer that is beautifully textured, fabulously constructed and an almost teasing rum-like quality. **43%**. *Allied*.

**Ballantine's Master's (82)** n21 t22 f19 b20. Excellent lively grain and chewy malt, but the always suspect, grain-drizzled finish has become even more nondescript in recent bottlings. **40%**. *Allied*.

**Ballantine's Original Character (94)** n22 chunky, almost thick in its heady malt richness; the grain chips in with deft oak; t24 near perfect mouth arrival with an explosion of spices that sends sweet malt to all parts of the palate. The grain comfortably criss-crosses the malt to lighten the load on the tastebuds; f24 more grain involvement now, but the burnt caramel/mild roast Java coffee effect adds another degree of glorious complexity. The finale is near endless with some Demerara digging of further depth; b24 this is big, bold blending from the old school that really rattles the tastebuds.A stunner. **47%**. *Allied*.

**Bell's Aged 8 Years (83)** n19 t22 f21 b21. The soapiness on the nose and late finish are compensated for by a surprisingly rich malt, biscuity backbone. **40%**. *Diageo/Arthur Bell & Sons*.

**Bell's Extra Special (75)** n19 t19 f18 b19. A faded dram that shows overdependence on a nondescript fruitiness. **40%**. *Diageo/Arthur Bell & Sons*.

**Bell's 12 Years Old (90)** n22 new leather and a hint of honey; t23 both grains and malts arrive in just about equal measures for very busy, complex start. Silky mouthfeel and some wonderful gently smoked spices; f22 long and clean with vanilla dominating; b23 absolutely quality blending, and pretty remarkable considering the mass scale on which it is achieved. No one style dominates, though it would be fair to say this is on the light side of medium in weight. **40%**. *Diageo/Arthur Bell & Sons*.

**Bell's Islander (82)** n21 t21 f20 b20. A blend that has been discontinued a little while, though in 2003 I have spotted it in bars as far apart as Copenhagen and Oxfordshire. These later bottlings were softer than the first run with the added Talisker not showing to great effect. Chewy, but a little toffeed. **40%**

**Ben Aigen (68)** n17 t18 f16 b17. Sweet caramel; bland and dusty. **40%**. *G&M*.

**Ben Alder (89)** n22 firm, well- structured grain embraces a host of livewire Speysiders; t23 an absolute avalanche of complex fruit and barley flavours, stretched out by silky grain; f22 the toffee has made its excuses thanks to less caramel input and instead we are left marvelling at the grain/barley interplay b22 a dram that has gone up a notch with a cleaner, more refined zing from nose to finale. A quite excellent little blend: absolutely love it! **40%**. *Gordon & MacPhail*. ⊙ ⊙

**Beneagles (67)** n17 t18 f16 b16. Flat and lifeless. **40%**

**Benmore (74)** n19 t19 f18 b18. Underwhelming to the point of being nondescript. **40%**. *Diageo*.

**Ben Nevis "Blended at Birth" 40 Years Old** Matured in sherry cask, dist 1962, bott 2002 **(91)** n22 what an intriguing overture: coal smoke and apricots add weight and softness to the ultra-firm grain. A very soft waft of bourbon adds to the mix; t24 this is where it hits top gear: the stunning arrival on palate and immediate impact. The gristy malt sweetness radiates in all directions taking with it a gooseberry-like fruitiness. The grain, though cumbersome, then strikes home bringing with it oak and spice; f22 delicate cocoa at first, then bitters; b23 the Ben Nevis distillery manager sent me another bottle of this, as he was a bit miffed I wasn't too impressed by this blend when I first tasted it in 2002. Oddly, I can't find any previous reference in the Bible, so gave it another shot. And am I glad I did. This would have been better called "Married at Birth" because the Ben Nevis grain and Ben Nevis malt were blended as new make and then allowed to mature for 40 years in sherry butts. There is nothing else like it on the market, and there are still some of these to be had at the distillery. **40%.** *Ben Nevis Distillery.*

**Ben Roland Five Years Old (81) n**19 **t**21 **f**20 **b**21. Caramel led, sweet, spicy and quietly complex. **40%.** *For Unwins, UK.*

**Berrys' Blue Hanger 30 Years Old (88) n**22 curiously, a touch of the Blue Mouse distillery in Germany about this one, such is the way the bitter-ish oak is grabbed in. Attractive with a tantalizing degree of exotic fruit, but distinctly curious for a blended Scotch; **t**22 an unusual, bitter start, despite the near perfect body; then a starburst of malt and kiwi fruit and then back to some oily oak; hard to spot the grain: it must be here somewhere; **f**22 an attractive fall out of vanilla and dusty barley; **b**22 just a shade too oily for it to blossom to its full potential, perhaps. Stunningly beautiful in part but is it good enough to bear the Blue Hanger badge of brilliance? You decide. **45.6%.** *Berry Bros & Rudd.*

**The Best 8 Years Old Scotch Whisky** (*see* Morrison's The Best)

**The Big Ben Special Reserve (83) n**20 **t**22 **f**20 **b**21. Bong: big caramel. Bong: rock hard and irresistible grain fortified by Speysidey malts. Bong: fabulous bite. Bong: the most outrageous bottle on the market moulded as the famous London landmark. Bong: if you've seen an old black and white film of the place, this is just the kind of whisky they would have been drinking – as this is a style recognizable 50 or 60 years ago. Bong: who needs a clock? This should live on the mantelpiece and every home should have one. **40%.** *Angus Dundee.*

**Big "T" (77) n**19 **t**20 **f**19 **b**19. Not long ago I would drink this with anyone, anywhere. Something drastic has happened and some pretty poor standard whisky has crept into this to disrupt the pristine elements that can still be spotted. Still has its moments, but would the real Big T please come forward.... **40%.** *Tomatin Distillery.*

**Black & White (88) n**24 **t**22 **f**20 **b**22. Such is the enormous jump in quality from a couple of years back, I had to taste this one three times. Just wonderful blended whisky, not only of the old school but of a style I remember from this brand 20 years ago and I feared lost for ever. The return of a minor classic. **40%.** *Diageo/James Buchanan & Co.*

**Black Bottle (91) n**22 some gnawing grains make the teasingly smoked malt work hard for its money; **t**23 a battling fizz reveals some youngsters having fun in there. Like the nose, the grain really does fight its corner and the fault line where it meets the malt is marked by a spicy, smoky sweetness; **f**23 the buzz continues and there is a touch of demerara sweetness and coffee to the chewy smokiness; **b**23 it has taken me a bit of time to get used to this slight change in style for this persistently brilliant blend. This one's been reduced in smoke and roughed up a little: the intervening grain which restrained the battling malts has now become a bit of a bruiser in its own right. Ignore the nonsensical claim of "Original Blend" on the label: this is a very old brand that has gone through many changes in its lifetime and will be unrecognizable from the modest whisky concocted over a century ago in an Aberdeen pub. And there are any number of us who are so glad it is nothing like the seething firewater it was 20-30 years ago. But it has kept true-ish to its re-birth under Allied when they turned it into a peaty beast and is probably closer to that in style that Highland's subsequent, lush re-working of it. **40%.** *Burn Stewart/Gordon Graham & Co.*

**Black Bottle 10 Years Old (89) n**22 so age-weightedly peaty it could be almost a single malt: the grains make little discernible impact; **t**23 soft, deft malt and firmer grain. The peat arrives after a short interval; **f**22 more vanilla and other oaky tones; **b**22 a stupendous malt of weight and poise, but possessing little of the all-round steaming, rampaging sexuality of the younger version ... and like the younger version showing a degree less peat: here perhaps even two. Not, I hope, the start of a new trend under the new owners. **40%.** *Burn Stewart/Gordon Graham's.*

**Black Cock (78) n**19 **t**20 **f**19 **b**20. Overtly grainy but a surprisingly malty mouthwatering quality makes for a half-decent blend. **40%**

**Black Dog 12 Years Old** Batch no. 015, bott Nov 05 **(92) n**21 distinctly nutty – especially walnuts – with no more than a hint of citrus lightening the deep vanilla and toffee. Gentle and attractively layered; **t**23 soft grains delve gently into the tastebuds offering light oak and a distinct toastiness. The barley sweetness is relaxed and clean; f24 traces of soft honey and a strand of marmalade welcome the visiting spices which cling to the subtle oils clamped to the roof of the mouth. Almost a near perfect finish for a blend this age. Stunning!; **b**24 an altogether thinner style than Century but offering genuine sophistication and élan. This minor classic will probably require two or three glass-fulls before you take the bait... **42.8%.** *United Distillers India Ltd.*

**Black Dog Century (89) n**21 a big nose displaying grainy teeth at first but chunky fudge and dried dates weigh in impressively; **t**23 mouth-filling and distinctly viscous, chocolate fudge clamps itself to the roof of the mouth allowing a lighter, teasingly spicy pulse to do its work around the back of the tongue. A well-mannered sweetness lurks around every corner ensuring the oak is on its best behaviour. Big and no shortage of complexity; **f**23 brilliantly long and chewy with the chocolate fudge **b**22 I adore this style of no-nonsense, full bodied bruising blend which amid the muscle offers exemplary dexterity and finesse. What entertainment in every glass!! **42.8%.** *McDowell & Co Ltd, India. Blended in Scotland/ Bottled in India.*

**Black Douglas (83) n**20 **t**20 **f**22 **b**21. Big, chewy, well weighted and fat. Pretty long, decently smoked nose and finale. **40%.** *Australia.*

⠿ **The Black Douglas** bott code 340/06/183 **(84) n**19 **t**20 **f**23 **b**22 Don't expect raptures of mind-bending complexity. But on the other hand, enough chewability and spice buzz here to make for a genuinely decent whisky, especially on the excellent finish. Not dissimilar to a bunch of blends you might have found in the 1950s **40%.** *Foster's Group, Australia.*

⠿ **The Black Douglas Aged 8 Years** bott code 348/06/187 **(79) n**20 **t**21 **f**19 **b**19 Slightly lacking for an 8-y-o: probably duller than its non-age-statement brother because of an extra dollop of caramel. **40%.** *Foster's Group, Australia.*

⠿ **The Black Douglas Aged 12 Years "The Black Reserve"** bott code 347/06/188 **(87) n**21 weighty and a bit of sweat from the interesting areas, if you know what I mean....nice touch of smoke, as well; **t**21 thick, soupy-caramel delivery with excellent early grain softness and a slow flowering of barley; **f**23 comes into its own for a massive finish with burnt honeycomb and spice making this way above the norm finale. A real treat...; **b**22 the toffee does its best to wreck the show – but there are simply too many good things going on to succeed. The slight smoke to the nose delights and the honeycomb middle really does star. **40%.** *Foster's Group, Australia.*

⠿ **Black Grouse (94) n**23 outwardly a hefty nose, but patience is rewarded with a glorious Demerara edge to the malt and oak: superb, understated stature; **t**24 again the smoke appears to be at the fore, but it's not. Rather, a silky sweet delivery also covers excellent cocoa and spice **f**23 so gentle, with waves of smoke and oak lapping on an oaky shore. Brilliant... **b**24 a superb return to a peaty blend for Edrington for the first time since they sold Black Bottle. Not entirely different from that brand, either, from the Highland Distillers days with the smokiness being superbly couched by sweet malts. A real treasure. **40%.** *Edrington Group.*

**Blackpool (73) n**18 **t**19 **f**18 **b**18. Grain and sweet toffee. Easy going but never hits the bright lights. **40%.** *Invergordon.*

**Black Prince (68) n**16 **t**19 **f**17 **b**16. One rich flourish apart, way off target. **40%.** *Burn Stewart.*

**Black Prince 12 Years Old (80) n**19 **t**22 **f**19 **b**20. Soft and silky, there is good fruit and crisp grain. A spicy but toffeed finish. **43%** *Burn Stewart. A discontinued blend now: a collector's item if you see it.*

⠿ **Black Ram Aged 12 Years (85) n**21 **t**23 **f**21 **b**20. An upfront blend that gives its all in the chewy delivery. Some major oak in there but it's all ultra soft toffee and molasses towards the finish. **40%.** *Vinprom Peshtera, Bulgaria.*

**Black Top Finest De Luxe (77) n**19 **t**21 **f**18 **b**19. Silky, sweet and rich, but a touch too much caramel dulls the complexity. **40%.** *Aberfoyle & Knight.*

**Black Watch** *(for tasting notes see* 100 Pipers*)*

**Blue Hanger 25 Years Old** bott 03 **(93) n**23 a silky sheen makes for the softest of nasal impacts; ripe grape and mango to the fore with a barley-sugar sub plot. Real fruit cake fodder; **t**24 lush arrival and then a slow unravelling of subtle spices; the fruitiness clings to the roof of the mouth as an obviously high malt percentage makes its mark; **f**22 some grain and oak are visible at last as a gradual thinning out of flavours begins; **b**24 an exceptional blend that offers a subtle bite to balance perfectly the lush intensity. The biter-sweet balance is exemplary. Brilliant. **45.6%. nc ncf.** *Berry Bros & Rudd.*

**Blue Hanger 30 Years Old** (*see* Berry's Blue Hanger)

**Bruce and Company Scotch Whisky (79)** n19 t21 f20 **b**19. The minimalist label – "Scotch Whisky" in black on white – somehow perfectly summarises a minimalist dram. This, for all intents and purposes, is young slate whisky with a dash of malt – and I do mean a dash. And topped up with some colouring. Yet, it's sweet, has a rich mouthfeel, there are no off-notes and perfectly enjoyable – providing you are not on the hunt for complexity. **40%.** *Exclusive to Tesco UK.*

**Buchanan's De Luxe Aged 12 Years (91)** n23 freshly-squeezed grape and profound clean barley. Excellent; **t**23 luxurious and lucid with a wonderful development of classy Speysidey-malt weighed down by a burst of peat and cocoa; **f**22 the grains move in offering vanilla and a drying shelter from the mouth-watering malts; **b**23 a significantly improved blend over recent years and some time since I've come across the duff sherry that used to mar it. Genuine elegance and now back up there with the world's classier blends. **40%.** *Diageo Venezuela/James Buchanan & Co.*

**Buchanan's Red Seal (90)** n22 clean with almost equal portions of grain, malt and oak; **t**23 wonderful malt clarity guarantees a rare charm; the grains are crisp and amplify the barley sweetness; **f**22 lovely sweet vanilla complements the persistent barley; **b**23 exceptionally good, no-frills blend whose apparent simplicity paradoxically celebrates its complexity. **40%.** *Diageo.*

**Buchanan's Special Reserve Aged 18 Years (86)** n22 t22 f21 **b**21. Has flattened out slightly in recent years and become somewhat dull. **40%.** *Diageo*

**Budgens Scotch Whisky Finely Blended (84)** n20 t21 f22 **b**21. A quite dramatically improved blend from the old grain and caramel fest it once was. Stirring a decent amount of peat into the mix has helped the cause no end. **40%.** *Budgens, UK.*

**C & J Fine Old (89)** n22 the soft grains help further the marmalade and malt; **t**23 absolutely spot-on malt integration: sparkling and fresh on the palate with delicate oak notes popping in; **f**22 vanilla and more citrus; **b**22 I didn't get where I am today without spotting a surprisingly spacious, excellently blended, high quality dram when I see one. Super. Great. And I raise my sample glass to toast: Happy 70th Birthday, David Nobbs! And, also, Henry Pratt! **43%.** *Diageo.*

**Campbeltown Loch (90)** n22 sparkling barley; **t**23 clean, crisp grain helps accentuate the mouthwatering malt; **f**22 lightens with vanilla; **b**23 restored to its former classical grace and beauty. A blend-lover's delight. **40%.** *Springbank.*

**Campbeltown Loch 21 Years Old (91)** n24 stunning depth here: the oak seems to be part of the barley, which in turn folds neatly into the silky grain. A gentleman; **t**22 the light grains show first, and then the malt arrives to offer soft waves of more complex but restrained substance; **f**23 fabulous fade: long with a development of fruit and very mild smoke; **b**22 there's 60% malt in this one. And, my word, it shows...!! **40%**

**Catto's Deluxe 12 Years Old (81)** n19 t22 f20 **b**20. Appears to have changed shape considerably: the nose has a sulphury catch and after a delicious sparkle to the palate settles down slightly **40%.** *Inver House.*

**Catto's Rare Old Scottish Highland (89)** n22 fresh, sensual. The grains are brilliantly chosen to allow full malt impact; **t**22 adorable formation of sweet Speysidey malts just melt in with the lush grain; **f**23 long and spicy and a touch of chalky oak adds to the balance; **b**22 silky and rich, this is delicious everyday fare of considerable charm. A truly classic, crisp young malt that is way above its station. For confirmation, smell the honey on the empty glass. **43%.** *Inver House.*

**The Charles House (73)** n18 t19 f18 **b**18. Sweet and sticky. **40%**

**Chequers De Luxe** bott lott L5108 **(76)** n19 t20 f18 **b**19. Standard, uncomplicated fare for Venezuelans with big grain lead and toffee finish. **40%.** *Diageo/John McEwan & Co.*

**Chivas Brothers 1801 (92)** n23 t24 f22 **b**23. The kind of dram you just can't say no to. Quality. **50%.** *This, tragically, has now been lost to us and has evolved into Chivas "Revolve".*

**Chivas Brothers Oldest and Finest (94)** n24 beguiling stuff of most untypical Chivas style: smoke and peat blending in with the fruit, nutmeg and allspice. The sherry influence is sublime; **t**24 just flows on from where the nose left off. The sherry is clean and weighty and beautiful spices arrive to flit around the palate. The malt is big with a degree of smoke and the grains do what grains should do best: polish the malts and marry the styles. Absolutely breathtaking; **f22** long with smoke and a sound structure. The spices continue to sparkle and the fruit also gathers intensity; **b24** it breaks my heart to announce that the blend has been discontinued, though a search through specialist outlets should reveal the odd bottle or two lurking about. Make no mistake: this is testimony to the art of brilliant, sympathetic and intuitive blending. What we have here is a masterpiece. **43%**

**Chivas Regal 12 Year Old (82) n**19 **t**20 **f**23 **b**20. A great improvement on recent years. But 30 years ago this used to be my house whisky and I still expect a lot more from it than this. The nose is much repaired, with a distinct Speyside thread now visible through the grain, but after a muddled, slightly dull arrival on the palate it is the finish that stars, and that owing mainly to some decent oak (offering stunning mocha and praline) and malt. The grain remains a headache and the whisky staggers around unbalanced for the most part. Still, at least it is heading in the right direction, though a bottle I tasted earlier this year, a few months before this sample, was a bit of a horror show. Let's pray it is heading in the right direction because this does have one or two truly classy moments. **40%**. *Chivas.*

**Chivas Regal 18 Year Old (77) n**20 **t**20 **f**18 **b**19. The 12 may have picked up, but this has regressed badly. Good fruit on the nose, but it is hard to escape from the bitter grain and caramel. A massive disappointment. **40%**. *Chivas.*

**Chivas Revolve (79) n**18 **t**22 **f**19 **b**20. Although tasting significantly better than it noses (some pretty tired casks have made it into this one), this brand is going backwards. **40%**. *Chivas Brothers.*

**Clan Campbell (84) n**20 **t**22 **f**21 **b**21. Genuinely enjoyable whisky, but much too dependent on the caramel. The puckering, mouthwatering Speyside and spice of yore have been seen off by an altogether silkier dram. **40%**. *Chivas.*

**Clan Campbell Legendary Aged 18 Years (89) n**22 accomplished oloroso notes are thinned by attractive grain-led vanilla: stylish stuff; **t**23 superb: a real outbreak of all things complex with soft grain at the centre but fruit heading from one malt to another and a very subtle smokiness from elsewhere; **f**22 more simple but the gentle vanilla and distant echo of spice is a tease; **b**22 greatly improved on recent years and now a dram of unquestionable distinction. **40%**

**Clan MacGregor (92) n**22 superb grains allow the lemon-fruity malt to ping around: clean, crisp and refreshing; **t**24 as mouthwatering as the nose suggests with first clean grain than a succession of fruity and increasingly sweet malty notes. A brilliant mouthful a tad oilier and spicier than of old; **f**23 yielding grain; and now, joy of joys, an extra dollop of spice to jolly it along; **b**23 just gets better and better. Now a true classic and getting up there with Grants. **43%**. *William Grant & Sons.*

**Clan MacGregor 12 Years Old (84) n**21 **t**20 **f**22 **b**21. The suspicion is that the grains are a lot older than 12: there is a lot of bourbon-oaky character on the nose and on the mouth arrival. Great finish, but lacking the all-round fresh-faced charisma of the young MacGregor. *Wm Grant's US.*

**Clan Murray Rare Old (84) n**18 **t**23 **f**21 **b**22. The wonderful malt delivery on the palate is totally incongruous with the weak, nondescript nose. Glorious, mouth-watering complexity on the arrival, though. Maybe it needs a Murray to bring to perfection... **40%**. *Benriach Distillery.*

**Clan Roy (87) n**20 gritty and grainy, still too much caramel here; **t**22 the peaty influence of Bowmore takes a little time to arrive and takes second place to some pretty attractive grassy malt and firm grain; **f**23 wonderfully long and perfectly spiced. A lingering sweetness allows the finish to continue in its soft and silky vain; **b**22 a vastly improved, chunky and now hugely enjoyable blend showing big malt on the palate despite the grainy nose. Terrific session whisky. **40%**. *Morrison Bowmore.*

**The Claymore (76) n**17 **t**20 **f**19 **b**20. A much more tastebud-friendly blend than the old cut-and-thrust number of yore. Still can't say the nose does much for me but the developing fruitiness on the middle and finish is silky and complex. **40%**.

**Cluny (85) n**20 **t**21 **f**22 **b**22. I adore this kind of slightly rough-edged blend: every time you take a mouthful something slightly different happens. If I were to find fault, a touch too much caramel is evident at the very death. **40%**. .

**Compass Box Asyla** (second bottling (2003) – small picture, fluted bottle 40% abv) **(93)** n23 t23 f23 b24. So sexy, you could almost make love to it. Unquestionably one of the best light blends on the market. **nc ncf.**

**Compass Box Asyla** bottle identification L4097 **(92)** n22 like a trifle ... but without the sherry; t23 very clever strands of sugar-honey intertwine with both grassy malt and clean grain; f23 long and laid-back with no weight whatsoever but an erogenous caressing of the tastebuds with an almost covert flavour attack; b24 subliminal whisky that may wash over you unnoticed for the first two or three mouthfuls but then you wake up to what is happening to you: and that is pretty sexy stuff, believe me ... **40%**

**Compass Box Asyla Marriage** Married for nine months in an American oak barrel **(88)** n22 a soup of a nose, though slightly over oaked for perfect harmony; t23 a big, sweet cherry tart kick off with custard and spices galooped on top; f21 warming, spiced vanilla; b22 a lovely blend, but can't help feeling that this was one marriage that lasted too long. **43.6%.** Compass Box Whisky for La Maison du Whisky in commemoration of their 50th Anniversary.

**Compass Box The Double Single (83)** n21 t22 f20 b20. This is a lively blend consisting of a single cask of malt and a single cask of grain. For all the brightness, doesn't entirely work because of the nose prickle, early hotness and slightly ungainly finish. But refreshing and chewy all the same. **46%.** Compass Box for The Craigellachie Hotel, Speyside.

**Co-operative Group (CWS) Scotch Whisky (86)** n20 t23 f21 b22. Always great to see a standard blend going up in quality – in this case dramatically. A beautifully clean Scotch (and would be a real pale stunner if they ditched the caramel), refreshing, salivating and bursting with excellent grain and Speyside-style malt. Has every right to stand by the big boys in the family cupboard. **40%.** ⊙

**Co-operative Group (CWS) Premium Scotch Whisky Five Years Old (78)** n19 t21 f19 b19 Much improved and with a real chew to the delivery. But still a bit of a sweaty armpit aroma and way too caramel dependent. **40%** ⊙ ⊙

**Corney & Barrow No. 1 Scotch Whisky 12 Years Old (85)** n20 t23 f20 b22. Attractive and beautifully structured, this would be a real classy stunner but for the overuse of caramel. **40%.**

**Corney & Barrow No. 6 Scotch Whisky (76)** n18 t20 f19 b19. A raw, viperish blend that strikes immediately but sooths with an overly sweet, oily fade. **40%**

**Covent Garden 10 Years Old (88)** n22 the style is classical and one of crystal clarity; t23 the marriage between those crisp, clean Speyside malts and refreshing grain is one of harmony and bliss: seems younger than its 10 years thanks to minimal oak interference; f21 which arrives towards the finish and dumbs down the rampaging complexity; b22 what an outstanding blend this is: pity – though no surprise – that the Cadenhead's shop in Covent Garden that sells it runs out so quickly. **40%** Cadenhead's.UK.

**Craigellachie Hotel Quaich Bar Range (81)** n20 t21 f20 b20. A delightful malt delivery early on, but doesn't push on with complexity as perhaps it might. **40%**

**Crawford's (79)** n19 t21 f19 b20. An attractive, delicate little creature until the caramel takes hold. **40%.** Whyte and Mackay Ltd.

**Crawford's 3 Star (87)** n22 t21 f22 b22. An honest, complex and characterful dram that's worth a shout. **40%.** Diageo.

**Crown Whisky Co. Very Rare Highland Special Reserve (74)** n18 t19 f18 b19. A competent grainy blend with a hint of oak. **40%.** Denmark only.

**Custer's Imported Scotch Whisky (81)** n19 t21 f20 b21. For an ultra cheapy there is surprising dexterity to this caramel-rich but otherwise clean and attractive dram. **40%.** Pierre Charles, Europe.

**Cutty Sark (88)** n23 light and floral with firm grain accentuating the malt; t22 big grain surge then a slow build-up of Speyside maltiness. Grassy and sharp throughout with a lovely Tamdhu-esque oiliness; f21 lots of vanilla and a thread of cocoa on the finale; b22 always been light, but virtually all peatiness has vanished of late. Even so, a real cracker of crispy grain. **40%**

**Cutty Sark Aged 12 Years (82)** n18 t22 f21 b21. A blemish on the nose, but an otherwise lovely, fresh blend showing more sherry than of old and excellent spices throughout. **40%**

**Cutty Sark Aged 15 Years (78)** n19 t20 f19 b20. Drinkable and at times charming, but an off sherry butt has upset the delicacy and rhythm somewhat. **40%.**

**Cutty Sark Aged 18 Years (93)** n24 outstanding clean sherry influence, softly smoked and good oak, almost bourbony, input. Beautiful; t23 big, spicy and immensely chewy; f22 lots of cream toffee, and a hint of tiring oak, but the grain is really high quality and delicious; b24 absolutely stunning. The clever use of the grain is simply breathtaking. **43%**

**Cutty Sark Aged 25 Years (90)** n23 massive acacia honey and vanilla sing sweetly; t23 as intense as an old pot-still demerara with absolutely stunning mouthfeel and fruity richness; f22 long, with gathering spices and a hint of smoke. The grains are minute but exemplary and chocolate-coated; b22 heavy and honeyed, chewy and charming, the oak has a fraction too big a say but still quite delicious! **45.7%**

**Cutty Sark Discovery** (*see* Cutty Sark Aged 18 Years)

**Cutty Sark Emerald** (*see* Cutty Sark Aged 12 Years)

**D Steven & Son (Wick) Ltd Finest 8 Years Old (80)** n20 t21 f19 b20. A solid, firm blend with satisfying smoke, bite and spice. Big grain finish. **40%**

**Da Mhile Organic Blended Scotch (89)** n21 the grain is typically Loch Lomond-ish in its embracing style, wrapping soft arms around the flintier, more energetic malt; not exactly perfect harmony but an endearing overture nonetheless; t23 now the blend comes together with the malt – sharp, mouthwatering, grassy and fresh – battling for independence from the enveloping grain but failing. Lots of complexity and character; f22 waves of soft vanilla and spice sit comfortably with the enduring malt; b23 a delicious blend against the odds: the grain and malts were mixed together from what was available from an organic point of view and make for a light, singular but highly attractive style. By no means perfect but it has worked, perhaps helped by liberal use of Springbank, making this probably the only blend made from organic Springbank malt you are ever likely to come across! **46%.** *Da Mhile. 1000 bottles.*

⋰ **Demijohn's Finest Blended Scotch Whisky (88)** n21 strange, out of shape, but soft; t22 salivating delivery with a wonderful firmness to the grain; the malts eventually mould into the style; t23 remains tangy to the end, even with a touch of marmalade thrown in; b22 a fun, characterful blend that appears to have above the norm malt. Enjoy. **40%.** *Adelphi for Demijohn Ltd, UK.*

**Dewar's White Label (83)** n21 t22 f19 b21. A decent, punchy, mildly biting blend where the grains are proud to show themselves and the malt makes enjoyable, soothing and sweetening noises. The toffee dims the sparkle somewhat, though. **40%.** *Curiously, White Label is now the possessor of a pale yellow one...*

**Dewar's Ancestor Aged 12 Years** db **(77)** n18 t20 f19 b20. Usually this was, as old man Dewar might have said, a Ramble Round the Gob. This strange animal, though, a weird mix of enchanting complexity and several freshly struck sulphur matches, graphically underlines that nowadays using sherry butts can be tantamount to playing cricket with hand-grenades. **43.5%**

**Dewar's Special Reserve Aged 12 Years** batch 0403 db **(91)** n23 exceptionally well designed with the heavier smoke and fruit notes adding only a background noise to the slightly more three-dimensional grain and soft honey-malt; t23 big and mouthwatering with spices developing fast. Beautiful integration of the harder grains and a developing oakiness; f21 way too much toffee undoes some of the intricate complexity. The spices carry on unabated, though; b24 an unashamedly old-fashioned type of blended Scotch and closest to the traditional Dewar's style of pre-Second World War days. A seriously delicious transportation back in time to the days when blends were cherished. **43%**

**Dewar's 18 Years Old** db **(93)** n22 the oak from the grain leads the way on this with some soft malt and citrus fruit playing catch-up; surprisingly light and elegant for the colour; t24 the Dewar's signature of rigid complexity strikes from the off; a rock-hard wall of grain at first seems impenetrable then a fizzing, breathtaking and quite glittering array of malty-oaky tones of varying degrees of sweetness batter the grain into submission. Again some citrus bares its teeth in the middle; f23 there is a delicate cocoa dustiness to the malt that at last has broken free of the grain and fruit; b24 like all better blends, this is a whisky that needs re-visiting and listening to to get the best results. Handsome, distinguished and displaying almost immeasurable complexity. **43%**

**Dewar's Signature** bott code A 13122 **(95) n**23 distinctive and lucid despite some obvious age around. Very firm, almost crisp apples with sweeter malt softening the sharpness. The most subtle hint of something smoky ensures weight to the elegant, flighty complexity. One to take your time over and get to know; **t**24 an adorable attitude and edge to this one: the tastebuds are immediately pounded by jagged, busy spices; the grain is hard as nails with fabulous nip and bite and allows the truly mouthwatering malts to ricochet around the palate. Lusty and luscious, this is great stuff which gets even better as the cocoa-smoky middle emerges; **f**24 again the grains are confident enough to have their say, offering, amid clarity, a firm, cocoa-dusted hand that points to some serious age; the finale is at first slightly estery but at last unusually clean and clear; **b**24 a blend-drinker's blend that is uncompromising and not stinting on old-fashioned sophistication. Just love that spice kick and the biting boldness of the grains that hold their own amid some mouthwatering malt. This is serious whisky, of a style easily identified in the East by connoisseurs of Suntory's freshest and finest. An outstanding addition to the highest echelons of the blended Scotch and in recent bottlings has remained true to type but added an extra dimension of juicy exotic fruit which reveals itself randomly, as though there are now older whiskies being used. The result is a greatly improved and much longer finale that even shows some delicate peat. To keep its mind-boggling complexity and integrity, the age profile should go no higher. And to drink, there is now only one way: do not sip, take a large mouthful and keep it on the palate for about 12-15 seconds and then swallow whole. Welcome to the world of superblends!! **43%**. *John Dewar & Sons*.

**Dewar's Signature** Batch 0403 db **(93) n**23 **t**24 **f**22 **b**24. As above, except for the most subtle, barely perceptible replacement of some smoke with top-notch, clean-as-a-whistle sherry. **40%**

**Dew of Ben Nevis (76) n**18 **t**19 **f**20 **b**19. Heavy duty stuff with a sweet finish. **40%**. *Ben Nevis Distillery.*

**Dew of Ben Nevis Hector's Nectar** (*see* Hector's Nectar)

**Dew of Ben Nevis Special Reserve (81) n**19 **t**20 **f**22 **b**20. Very firm malt, sweet, full-bodied and punchy grain – even a hint of honey on the spicy finale. **40%**.

**Dew of Ben Nevis Aged 12 Years (86) n**21 **t**22 **f**22 **b**21. An enormous improvement: a richer, roastier, all-round more delicious blend. **40%**. *Ben Nevis Distillery.*

**Dew of Ben Nevis Aged 21 Years (90) n**23 citrus 'n' salt; **t**23 fabulous complexity wth illuminating malt showing sweetness to a salty depth and toasty oak; **f**21 thins out towards vanilla and milky coffee, but with a little orange to lighten the load; **b**23 a really lovely aged blend where the complexity is mindblowing. Go get...!! **43%**. *Ben Nevis Distillery.*

**Dew of Ben Nevis Blue Label (82) n**19 **t**22 **f**20 **b**21. A busier, lighter blend than the old Millennium one it replaced. The odd off-key note is handsomely outnumbered by deliciously complex, mocha tones with a touch of demerara. Ditch the caramel and you'd have a sizzler! **40%**. *Ben Nevis Distillery. Replacement for Dew of Ben Nevis Millennium Blend.*

**Dew of Ben Nevis Supreme Selection (77) n**18 **t**20 **f**20 **b**19. Some lovely raspberry jam swiss roll moments here. But the grain could be friendlier, especially on the nose. **40%**. *Ben Nevis Distillery.*

**Dimple 12 Years Old (83) n**21 **t**20 **f**21 **b**21. A puff of smoke adds a touch of clout to an otherwise light yet gently spiced and deliciously grained blend. **43%**

**Dimple Years 15 Old (79) n**18 **t**20 **f**21 **b**20. A sturdier dram than before, but over-sweet and still fails to get my pulse racing. **40%**. *Diageo.*

**Diners Deluxe Old Scotch 12 Years Old (85) n**21 **t**22 **f**21 **b**21. Genuinely classy stuff with attitude. **43%**. *Douglas Denham for Diners Club.*

**Diners Supreme Old Scotch 21 Years Old (82) n**20 **t**21 **f**21 **b**20. A massive blend with no little bourbony-oaky style. **43%**. *Douglas Denham for Diners Club.*

**The Dowans Hotel (88) n**22 **t**22 **f**22 **b**22. A marginally lighter (in character), fruitier version of The Inverarity (see below). Not quite so smoky as previous bottlings but remains a stylish treat. **40%**. *Inverarity Vaults for The Dowans Hotel, Aberlour.*

**Duggans (76)** n17 t20 f19 b20. A young, high-grained blend which enjoys a short malty, spicy blast early on before settling for grainier, safer ground. **40%.** *Morrison Bowmore.*

**Duncan Taylor Aged Blend 35 Years Old** (Bourbon) **(81)** n18 t22 f20 b21. Worn and weary but just enough honeyed touches to keep it impressive. **46%.**

**Duncan Taylor Aged Blend 35 Years Old** (Sherry) **(83)** n20 t19 f23 b21. Exceptional chocolate honeycomb on the fruity finish. **43%.**

**Duncan Taylor Auld Blended Aged 35 Years** dist Pre 1970 **(93)** n23 a knife and fork nose appears too oaked but time in the glass allows some excellent marmalade and marzipan to appear; t24 glorious delivery: amazing silk, lots of gentle, natural caramel but topped with honeycomb; f22 chocolate malt and burnt toast; b24 only a handful of companies could come up with something like this. An infinitely better dram than previous bottlings, due mainly to the fact that the dangers of old oak appear to have been compensated for. **46%.** *131 bottles.*

**Duncan Taylor Auld Aged Blend 38 Years Old** dist 68, bott Mar 06 **(86)** n22 t22 f21 b21. Incredibly soft for all those years, but not a patch of the 35-y-o. **40%.** *623 bottles.*

⋄ **Duncan Taylor Collection Rarest of the Rare Deluxe Blend 33 Years Old (94)** n24 a heady fusion of rich bourbon and old Canadian characteristics beefed up further with diced exotic fruit and a dash of ancient Demerara rum Uitvlught to be precise; t24 the bourbon hits the track running, closely followed by some silky barley couched in velvet grain; invariably some spices pitch in to ramp up the complexity even further; f22 no great length, but no off notes, either. Instead the oak adds an unsweetened custardy grace; b23 outstanding and astounding blended whisky. An absolute must for blend lovers....especially those with a bourbony bent. **43.4%**

**The Dundee (78)** n19 t21 f19 b19. A slight improvement on previous years but the caramel still undoes slightly the deliciousness of the bright, grainy arrival. Not a bad dram, though, with the excellent spice and bite doing a grand job. **40%.** *Angus Dundee.*

**Dunfife (75)** n18 t20 f19 b18. Refreshing and chewy. **40%.** *William Maxwell.*

**EH10 (86)** n22 t23 f20 b21. From the same charm school as Bailie Nicol Jarvie, but lacks finish. Otherwise delicious. **40%.** *Sainsbury UK (from Glenmorangie).*

**The Famous Grouse (87)** n21 brusque, flinty grain which anchors the flighty malt; t23 comes into its own here with a fabulous heather-honey malt arrival which is at once soft but with a rod of steel through its spice with Speysiders bouncing off the grain. A flutter of busy spices help see off any early caramel involvement; f21 a touch sweeter and maltier than of late; at the death back to being much drier and Spartan; b22 remains sexy, elegant and refined with a stunning opening on the palate. The balance has improved of late with some extra, subtle spices, punching through the threatening caramel making for an altogether busier blend. **40%**

**The Famous Grouse Cask Strength (87)** n22 amazingly big, fresh clean sherry for a light blend: the grains cut into the fruit with precision and no little grace; t22 seriously fruity at first then a wave of malt and toffee. The grain reforms towards the middle; f21 quite soft with lots of toffee and vanilla; b22 a chewy, stylish dram that absorbs the strength easily. Again the toffee is a bit on the heavy side but the overall grain-malt balance is deft and delicious. **59.4%**

**The Famous Grouse Gold Reserve Aged 12 Years (85)** n19 t23 f21 b22. A much more honeyed, richer and improved dram than of old. But the caramel could be cut considerably. **43%**

**The Famous Grouse Islay Cask Finish (88)** n21 beautifully weighted with kippery tones amid nipping grains; t22 a real chewy mouthful: sweet with lots of obvious malt; f23 more grain presence with vanilla drying out the sweeter barley. Remains smoky and very long; b22 if ever you wondered what a peaty Grouse would be like, here you go. What makes it work is the alluring softness of the smoke. Genuinely graceful for all its weight. **40%**

**The Famous Grouse Port Wood Finish (75)** n20 t20 f17 b18. A surprising hint of smoke, but otherwise fruity and flat. **40%**

**The Famous Grouse Scottish Oak Finish** bott Nov 05 **(95)** n23 not dissimilar to the European oak of Czech whiskies, but better control. This seems to accentuate the smoke slightly and the grain is lost in a fusion of malt and butter. Really lovely – and very different: in fact unique to any blend I've come across; **t24** wow, wow, wow, wow, wow...!!! The mouth arrival is memorable and truly orgasmic: just wave upon wave of something beautiful, seamless and spicy. A kind of half-sweet honeycomb – all roast and chewiness – stars with the grains at last making themselves heard with a string of vanilla thrusts. Those spices pound the sides of the tongue and the roof of the mouth and the bitter-sweet balance is sensational. Just to make things better still, there is just the right degree of bite one desires in a blend; **f23** long, with mounting signs of oak dominance, but those glorious toasted-barley waves, now topped with muscovado sugar keep the blend honest. The final embers offer a surprising hint of juniper. Is that the oak...or the bottling hall?; **b25** what a stunner! What a one off....!!! Sadly, this is a limited edition blend...and once those 7,092 bottles have been drunk, that's it! I sincerely hope they are already planting new Caledonian oak to make this a fixture on the whisky shelves for future generations! **44.5%**.

**Findlater's Finest (69)** n17 t18 f17 b17. A furry, sticky palate; mildly rubbery. **40%**.

**Findlater's Deluxe 15 Years Old (81)** n21 t20 f20 b20. The fruity nose is followed by a chunky arrival on the palate where the malt is thick and chewy. Some coffee on the finale. Takes time to acclimatise to this style of blend, but worth every second. **40%**.

**Findlater's Deluxe 18 Years Old (91)** n22 a hint of dry Lübeck chocolate marzipan; **t23** decent soft malt sprinkled with light muscovado sugar; **f22** back to bitter almonds and bourbon amid the lush grain; **b24** the cleanest, lightest yet most comfortably weighted of the Findlater clan by some margin; supremely balanced with a lush texture and lilting complexity. Some serious blending went into this one. **40%**. *Kyndal*.

**Findlater's Deluxe 21 Years Old (89)** n22 subtle sherry, clean with simmering spice just below the surface; **t23** lazy and demure for a blend of such age: the malt does possess a certain countering brittleness to the softer grain; **f21** vanilla and a hint of sultana and toffee fudge; **b23** dreamy, end-of-day blend when you want your tastebuds featherdusted before retiring. **40%**.

**The Formidable Jock of Bennachie (82)** n19 t22 f21 b20. "Scotland's best kept secret" claims the label. Hardly. But the silky delivery on the palate is worth investigating. Impressive roastiness to the malt and oak, but the caramel needs thinning.   **40%**. *Bennachie Scotch Whisky*.

**Fortnum & Mason Choice 5 Year Old (83)** n20 t21 f22 b20. Good, solid grain helps propel a decent percentage of malt to rich, gently spicy deeds. An impressive 5-y-o by any standards. **40%**. *UK*.

**Frasers Supreme (77)** n19 t19 f20 b19. A dash of smoke helps add weight. **40%**.

**"Frisky Whisky" Macho 60% (81)** n19 t20 f20 b21. Big, grainy caramel: a standard, mildly smoky blend apart from the warehouse strength delivery and excellent finish. Possibly the best label on the market, though. **60%**. *John Milroy*.

**Gibson Glengarry (68)** n16 t18 f17 b17. Tough going. **40%**

**Glen Alba (76)** n20 t18 f20 b18. Changed shape slightly of late, with heaps of toffee. **40%**. *Duncan Taylor*.

**Glenalmond "Everyday" Pure Highland Malt (73)** n18 t19 f18 b18 What happened to the charming Glenalmond I last tasted? Syrupy and off key. Usually sound whisky: hopefully a one off.  **40%**. *The Vintage Malt Whisky Co.* ☉ ☉

**Glen Calder (76)** n19 t20 f18 b19 much improved, with the sweetness usurped by spice. The telling caramel drops it down a few points, though. **40%**. *Gordon & MacPhail*. ☉ ☉

**Glen Catrine De Luxe (77)** n17 t22 f19 b19. A dusty nose, but recovers for a rich, softly honeyed middle before caramel intervenes on the finish. **40%**. *Glen Catrine*.

**Glen Crinan (72)** n17 t19 f18 b18. Oily; full in places. **40%**. *Edrington France*.

**Glen Crinan 12 Years Old (75)** n17 t20 f19 b19. Maybe I'm being fanciful, but I'm sure I'm detecting Glenturret's hand in there somewhere. A little soapy at first, honey and spice later. **40%**. *Edrington*.

**Glen Clova (70)** n18 t18 f17 b17. Grain and caramel all the way. I'm sure there must be some malt in there somewhere, but the grain is clean and decent quality, at least. *Ewen & Co for Oddbins UK*.

**Glendarroch Finest 15 Years Old (91)** n21 very firm grain surrounded on all sides by peaty ancient malt and bourbony oak; **t24** impressive mouthfeel and early spice arrival, then a glorious expansion of quite stunning malt of a richness that needs tasting for comprehension. You can lose yourself in this one for some time; f23 the grains bite back and are quite welcome to rescue you from a malty trance: you will appreciate it more if you wallow in the bourbony afterglow; b23 this is exceptionally high-quality blending and a marriage of malts and grains that were meant for each other. **43%**. *William Gillies & Co.*

**Glen Dowan (79) n**18 **t**21 **f**21 **b**19. Does Scotch whisky come any sweeter than this? **40%**

**Glen Dowan 21 Years Old (89) n**21 fresh, coastal and lively; **t**22 a real live wire around the palate with big malt presence; **f**23 lovely spices and exceptional oak control: truly brilliant; **b**23 big, bold and a little salty. Delicious, especially the finale. Out of this world bitter-sweet balance. **43%**. *J&G Grant Taiwan/Jap/Asia.*

**Glengarry** (*see* Gibson Glengarry)

**Glen Grigg (71) n**16 **t**19 **f**18 **b**18. Heavy; subtlety at a premium. **40%**. *Spar UK.*

**Glen Heather (90) n**22 hard, unyielding and grain-heavy it may be but the ginger nut bite is engaging. Enticing, confident stuff with the faintest touch of peat; **t**23 fresh, young and mouthfilling. The grains remain brittle and reflect perfectly the Speysidey malts which ensure maximum salivation. Some really excellent spice. Exceptionally clean and crisply defined; **f**22 pretty long with a slight sweetening and softening towards the finale. Some late evidence of age; **b**23 a quite lovely and lively blend from the old school. Clean and distinctive with a marauding spiciness, this is a blend that takes me back 25 years in style. The colour suggests caramel should be lurking somewhere and it does show very briefly and causing virtually no damage at the death. But as a whole this is a throwback, a minor classic blend worthy of discovery. **40%**. *SH Jones at their shops in Banbury and elsewhere in the heart of England.*

**Glen Lyon (78) n**20 **t**19 **f**20 **b**19. Light, clean and non-committal except, perhaps, for the hint of juniper on the nose. **43%**. *Diageo.*

**Glenmonarch (63) n**16 **t**17 **f**15 **b**15. Grim nose despite a inconclusive hint of peat; untidy mouth arrival while grain sweetens and then embitters for an awful finish. If there is malt in there I can't spot it other than possibly on the nose. And is it Scotch for sure? Doesn't say so on the label and although it is heavily implied, I'd be surprised if it is. All horribly synthetic. **40%**. *Belarus Bottling Co.*

**Glen Niven (79) n**20 **t**19 **f**20 **b**20. Way above average supermarket stuff: the nose shows superb grain qualities while the decent malt reveals itself in the finish. Overall, silky and complex. Rip out the OTT caramel and you would have a quality blend here. *Douglas MacNiven (Asda) UK.*

**Glen Osprey (71) n**17 **t**18 **f**18 **b**18. A pageant of young grain that is generally pleasant enough, especially towards the finish. Beware, though. Another I tasted earlier in the year was off-key and seriously awful. **40%**. *Duncan MacBeth & Co.*

**Glen Rosa (74) n**19 **t**18 **f**19 **b**18. Disappointing, oversweet and banal. Still room for improvement. **40%**. *Isle of Arran Distillers.*

**Glen Rossie (68) n**18 **t**18 **f**15 **b**17. A marked deterioration with lower-grade grain and heightened superficiality. Massively disappointing: the significantly increased caramel cannot make up for the dramatic extraction of character while the finish is abysmal. I mourn the passing of a once good whisky. **40%**. *Quality Spirits International for Thresher Group, UK.*

**Glen Shira (79) n**20 **t**21 **f**19 **b**19. A young blend that shows delicious citrusfruit qualities. **40%**. *Burn Stewart.*

**Glenshire (71) n**18 **t**18 **f**17 **b**18 Solid early grain, better bite but still disappears under caramel. **40%**. *Ian Macleod Distillers.* ☺ ☺

**Glen Stuart (79) n**18 **t**20 **f**21 **b**20. Honest whisky despite the caramel with an excellent grain lead: good session stuff. **40%**. *For Unwins, UK.*

**Glen Urquhart (82) n**20 **t**21 **f**20 **b**21. Gentle and mouthwatering with a touch of spice. **40%**. *Gordon & MacPhail.*

**Glinne Parras (85) n**23 **t**23 **f**19 **b**20. Brilliant nose and oily-coated malt mouth-start: the real enjoyment is all upfront. The finish could do with some attention. *Eaux de Vie.*

**Glob Kitty (77) n**17 **t**20 **f**19 **b**21. Clean, firm-grained, light and biting. Good standard whisky. **40%**. *Lehar Aus.*

**Golden Blend (88) n**21 a teasing aroma, one minute heavy the next of a fleeting grainy lightness: intriguing and attractive; **t**22 honeyed and complex, major chewy sweet malt against melting grain; **f**22 enters overdrive here, as the softness of the grain is stupendous. The malt has every chance to form a complex liaison with the gentle oak; **b**23 a sound, sophisticated blend of excellent weight and evenness. At no time either bitter or sweet. **40%.** *Kyndal.*

**Golden Dew (78) n**20 **t**20 **f**19 **b**19. High apparent grain and caramel. But pretty decent grain, it must be said. **40%.** *Burn Stewart.*

**Gordon Graham's Black Bottle** (see Black Bottle)

**The Gordon Highlanders (85) n**21 **t**22 **f**21 **b**21. A seemingly light whisky but with a weighty middle of some aplomb. The arrival on the palate is almost brain-exploding: in many ways one of the most complex drams on the market. But I suspect a big caramel presence prevents this from being a genuine classic. Glorious, creamy, sweet and lip-smacking stuff. **40%.** *Wm Grant.*

**The Grand Bark (84) n**22 **t**22 **f**20 **b**20. The nose and malty-spicy arrival on the palate are to die for. *Symposium International.*

**The Grand Bark 21 Year Old (74) n**18 **t**20 **f**18 **b**18. The malt and grain just don't get on. **40%.** *Symposium International.*

**Grand Old Parr Aged 12 Years** batch no. L33P00063748 **(90) n**21 the sherry notes help cover a slight soapiness. The addition of the black pepper, though, is a masterstroke; **t**22 succulent mouth arrival: almost an Oregonian Pinot Noir in its burst of mouthwatering fresh fruit that is tempered by firm grain and gently spiced malt; **f**23 the spices continue as the vanilla arrives with a wonderful sunset of cocoa-imbued grain; **b**23 just such a massive improvement on the unwieldy mess that was Old Parr a couple of years back. Much more refined and dignified. **43%.** *Diageo.*

**Grant's** (see William Grant)

**Green Plaid (90) n**22 soft strains of Bowmore-style young peat; **t**23 remains youthful, and the smoke is still there, but the overall complexity as the crisp grains enter is worth a fanfare; **f**22 more kindergarten smoke while the barley remains fresh and mouthwatering; **b**23 has kept true to style but is now one of the best young blends around; very old-fashioned and a real cracker. **40%.** *Inver House.*

**Green Plaid 12 Year Old (87) n**22 **t**21 **f**22 **b**22. Very subtle, almost whispering whisky. **40%.** *Inver House.*

**Haig Gold Label (86) n**21 **t**22 **f**21 **b**22. A much lusher blend than of old, with nothing vague regarding its quality. **40%.** *Diageo/John Haig & Co.*

**Hamashkeh (79) n**21 **t**21 **f**18 **b**19. A good old-fashioned blend with a delightful grain bite. Love it, but could do with dropping the caramel slightly for a crisper flavour. The only blended Scotch kosher whisky on the market. **40%.** *The Hamashkeh Co. (VDB Spirits Ltd). Specially prepared whisky, ensuring that the entire system is sherry-free, with barrels and even the bungs being thoroughly cleaned for use.*

**Hankey Bannister (87) n**21 **t**23 **f**21 **b**22. From an ordinary Joe to damned fine blend in the space of two years. You get the feeling that Inver House are reaping the rewards of some inspired distillery buying. **40%.** *Inver House.*

**Hankey Bannister Aged 12 Years (82) n**20 **t**22 **f**19 **b**21. The best bottling of this for a while: much cleaner and slightly cavalier on the palate with Speyside-style malts given much better support by the grain. Still needs to get the finish sorted, but a decent mouthful. **40%.** *Inver House Distillers.*

**Hankey Bannister 21 Year Old (91) n**21 fruity, clean and lush but a hint of sap; **t**24 mouthwatering and improbably soft for its age, with the grain showing no claws whatsoever: you get the feeling this has been married for some time; **f**23 minimum oak fuss as the fruit continues for a very long finish; **b**23 for those who prefer their blends to purr rather than hiss and scratch. Quite magnificent. **43%.**

⟜ **Hankey Bannister 40 Years Old (89) n**22 evidence of high malt levels here: pungent, nippy and lively. No shortage of over-ripe oranges, either. **t**23 juicy, salivating delivery with a silky texture to the grain bringing out the best of the intense, sweet malt; the fruitiness is mixed, rich and blunted only by the toasty oaks; **f**22 pretty oak spattered with the grains continuing their soft theme. Enough barley remains to add another cushion against the age; **b**22 "This is some of the last whisky produced before England won the

World Cup in 1966," Gareth Stanley of Inverhouse gleefully tells me. Yes, Gareth. Thanks for reminding me. But at least I can look Alex Salmond and his brothers straight in the eye and tell him: "Well, at least we once won the bloody thing..." This blend, though, has been put together to mark the 250th anniversary of the forging of the business relations between Messrs. Hankey and Bannister. And although the oak creaks like a ship of its day, there is enough verve and viscosity to ensure a rather delicious toast to the gentlemen. Love it! **44%** *Inverhouse*

**Harrods Finest Blended Aged 5 Years (83) n**21 **t**21 **f**21 **b**20. Gives an impression of something older and wiser than five years in this one. Silky and old-fashioned in style, the grains have the leading edge and jag around the palate impressively. Too much toffee for this age, though: cut the caramel and you'd have something better still. Love it. **40%**

**Hector's Nectar (84) n**19 **t**22 **f**22 **b**21. A giant of a blend that takes no prisoners: young and pretty generous with the malt thrust, leaving complex grains for the biting finish. A good, rich, sweet session dram to be chewed and then the empty glass thrown in the fire!. **40%**. *Ben Nevis Distillery.*

**Hedges & Butler Royal (75) n**18 **t**20 **f**18 **b**19. Mouthwatering and crisp. **40%**

**Hedges & Butler Royal 15 Years Old (87) n**21 heavy and fruity with real grainy bite; **t**22 no less weight: again the grain bites deep but there is a lot of viscous fruit to soften the impact; **f**22 long and chewy, delicious bitter-sweet finish; **b**22 bit of a throwback: not an uncommon style of blend before the Second World War. **43%**

**Hedges & Butler 21 Years Old (91) n**24 gently smoked and generously honeyed, this is an essay in subtlety and complexity; **t**23 mouth-filling, rich and lush, the grains then begin biting and nipping; **f**22 shows some silky ageing, offering a hint of top-order bourbon with lots of butter-toffee but also some caramel; **b**22 As a taster, just about impossible to spit out! Absolutely classic stuff. You cannot ask for more than an aged blend. Except the strength to be at 46% and to be non-filtered or coloured. **40%**. *Ian MacLeod.*

**Henry Mason Scotch Whisky (72) n**17 **t**19 **f**18 **b**18. Dusty; overly sweet. **40%**

**High Commissioner** bott May 07 **(88) n**20 weighty but so much cleaner than before: you can even spot the malt. This is High Commissioner...???? **t**21 chewy with the yielding, melt-in-the-mouth grain offering up just the right amount of sweetness; **f**24 now hits top gear with a wonderful smattering of spices helping to pin together the dried dates and vanilla; big and chewy, thanks to late smoke involvement, yet not entirely without a degree of refinement: genuine complexity here; **b**23 a spectacularly improved blend: the days of hiding the label under a napkin have gone. Much, much cleaner than before: the rubbery character has been almost entirely replaced by something still full bodied and lush but with layers of malt amid the rich grain and clever spices. You get the feeling that the blender who has revamped this blend is something of a genius...or a guru, even...!!! **40%**. *Loch Lomond Distillery.* ⊙ ⊙

**Highland Bird (79) n**19 **t**20 **f**21 **b**19. An entirely competent whisky with a soft, malty strand amid the clean grains. Enjoyable. **40%**. *Robert McKie Neil Co.*

**Highland Black 8 Years Old Special Reserve (81) n**18 **t**22 **f**20 **b**21. Dramatically changed direction in the last year or two, offering increased spice to cut through the caramel and far better balance and chewability. Clean the nose, cut the caramel and you would have a glint up in the healthy 80s. **40%**. *Alistair Graham for Aldi.* ⊙

**Highland Choice (74) n**17 **t**19 **f**20 **b**18. Soft, silky grain, sweet and attractive. **40%**. *Alistair Graham Ltd (Aldi Stores).*

**Highland Cross (89) n**21 a very comfortable grain firmness; **t**22 mouthwatering malts arrive early and make a soft landing for the gathering grain; **f**22 there is a rich Speyside thread amid the oily grain; **b**24 This is a wonderful blend: deceptively complex and always refreshing. Love it! **40%**. *Edrington Group.*

**Highland Dream 18 Years Old (87) n**21 busy with the grain lively and enlivening; **t**23 brawny at first then a wonderful pell-mell of malty tones of varying intensity. Soft spice add further illustration; **f**21 a little toffee on the big grain-vanilla finale; **b**22 a handsome blend of the old school: my kind of relaxed session stuff. **43%**. *J & G Grant.*

**Highland Earl (82) n**19 **t**22 **f**20 **b**21 A blend hewn from a different stone; softer than of old with a touch of extra sweetness. Still a joy. **40%**. *Aldi Stores* ⊙ ⊙

**Highland Gathering Blended Scotch Whisky (78) n**19 **t**20 **f**19 **b**20. Attractive, juicy stuff, though caramel wins in the end. **40%**. *Lombards Brands.*

**Highland Gold (80) n**20 **t**19 **f**21 **b**20. A very clean if slightly oversweet blend boasting soft, yielding grain and even a hint of peat and age. Not at all bad. **40%**. *Australia.*

**Highland Harvest Organic Scotch Whisky (76) n**18 **t**21 **f**19 **b**18. A very interesting blend. Great try, but a little bit of a lost opportunity here as I don't think the balance is quite right. But at least I now know what organic caramel tastes like... **40%**. *London & Scottish International.*

⠿ **Highland Piper (79) n**20 **t**20 **f**19 **b**20 Good quaffing blend – if sweet - of sticky toffee and dates. Some gin on the nose – and finish. **40%**.

**Highland Poacher (81) n**18 **t**20 **f**22 **b**21. Young, grainy, mouthwatering. The nose and early arrival are odd, the development, though, is excellent and displaying early hints of smoke and delicious cocoa on finale. **40%**.

**Highland Queen (81) n**20 **t**22 **f**19 **b**20. A clean, grassy, Speyside-led young blend, the crispness clipped by caramel and perhaps a shade more emphasis on the grain. **43%**. *MacDonald & Muir.* ☉☉

**Highland Reserve (78) n**20 **t**21 **f**18 **b**19. Simplistic, untaxing, clean, sweet, over-dependent on caramel at the death....and thoroughly enjoyable! **40%**. *Quality Spirits International.*

**Highland Rose (83) n**20 **t**22 **f**21 **b**20. Firm, high-quality blend with superb grains. Nothing withered about this one. I adore this style of whisky for everyday dramming. **40%**

**Highland Stag (74) n**17 **t**19 **f**20 **b**18. Grainy, biting, raw... but fun. **40%**. *R.N MacDonald. US.*

**Highland Way (83) n**20 **t**21 **f**22 **b**20. A lush, clean dram with a rich middle and brilliantly spiced finish. For a duty free blend, you can't go wrong. **40%**. *Highland Way Whisky Co.*

**Highland Wolf (83) n**19 **t**21 **f**22 **b**21. Firm to crisp grain with impressive bite and spice. Good weight and late arrival of malt on finale. Well blended but let down a little by caramel. **40%** *Longman Distillers*

**House of Campbell Finest (73) n**18 **t**18 **f**19 **b**18. Very grainy and hard. **40%**.

**House of MacDuff Gold Rush Scotch Whisky (81) n**20 **t**20 **f**21 **b**20. Clean, grain-laden and slight caramel. An acceptable and enjoyable blend, but is it whisky? This blend actually has tiny slivers of gold added and, strictly speaking, to be called whisky nothing outside caramel can be added ... time to pour yourself a glass and have a 24 carat debate. **40%**

**House of Peers (88) n**21 a soft wave of peat is the perfect go-between as grain and malt collide; **t**21 the marriage between delicious, biting grain and sweet malt is harmonious; **f**23 really goes into overdrive as that gentle smoke returns. Additional tingling grain helps make this a long, classical finish; **b**23 delicate smoke gives this attractive dram something extra to chew on. A really excellent example of how to make an outwardly light blend go a long way. **43%**. *Douglas Laing.*

**Ian MacLeod's Isle of Skye** (*see* Isle of Skye)

**Immortal Memory (69) n**17 **t**18 **f**17 **b**17. Easily forgotten. **40%**. *G&M.*

**Imperial Classic 12 Years Old (83) n**20 **t**22 **f**21 **b**20. A two-toned dram that is hard as nails on one hand and yielding and succulent on another. Tasty stuff on both levels. **40%**. *Chivas.*

**Imperial 17 Years Old db (82) n**19 **t**21 **f**21 **b**21. Seems lethargic at first, but it's so complex in the middle it's difficult to say where the middle ends and the end starts ... a real mouth-pleaser. **40%**. *Chivas. Korea only.*

**The Inverarity (90) n**22 pungent and waspish, there is a welcome degree of peat to overcome the grains; **t**22 mouth filling and chewy, the malt has much to say and dominates the weight and shape. Thrilling throughout; **f**23 the grains return but no balance is lost as the tangy barley and subtle smoke fight to the last; **b**23 truly wonderful complexity swamps the palate offering a vaguely orange-citrus theme to be replaced by something smokier: what a true classic this could be without the caramel dumbing things down slightly just as it promises so much. A real old-fashioned blend and a vast improvement on the last bottling I encountered. **40%**. *Inverarity Vaults.*

**Iona Royale 25 Years Old (89) n**22 the rigid grain nails the malt to the glass. Yet there is something attractively of the dank forest about this; **t**23 hold on to something tight: several tidal waves of oak-spattered malt crash about the palate; a second wave of barley remains fresh and salivating before drying with the warming grain; **f**21 lots of burnt fudge and vanilla softened by an evasive sweetness; **b**23 a massively malt-rich blend that piles on the complexity early on. **43%. J&G Grant.**

**Islay Hallmark 8 Years Old (76) n**19 **t**20 **f**19 **b**18. Pleasant whisky that's just a bit too subtle with the Islay for it's own good. **40%.** *Morrison Bowmore.*

**Islay Legend (86) n**22 **t**22 **f**21 **b**21. Threatens to go on the rampage, but behaves itself perfectly thanks to the most velvety grain imaginable. **40%.**

**Islay Mist Aged 8 Years (85) n**19 **t**22 **f**22 **b**22. Excellent weight and peaty freshness. Despite the youth, there is big character. **40%.** *MacDuff International.*

⁃⁞⁃ **Islay Mist 12 Years Old (90) n**22 Bowmore-style cough sweet dominates over the most gentle of grains; **t**23 decent smoke drive, intense at first then feathering out; remains sweet to the house style **f**22 long, back to cough sweet and a long fade of gristy, muscovado sugar; **b**23 adore it: classic bad cop - good cop stuff with an apparent (taste-wise) high malt content. **40%.** *MacDuff International.*

**Islay Mist 17 Years Old (89) n**21 soft smoke with a curious egg yolk and doughy mix; **t**23 caresses the palate as it delivers silk-like bourbon-tinged grain with a series of fruity, sultana-style juices; **f**22 just a very light echo of smoke, otherwise sugared almond all the way; **b**23 Every time I taste this it changes shape. This is much lighter than before. I'd suggest they return to 43% to help maximise intensity, though it has to be said that this is one of the silkiest blends on the market. **40%.** *MacDuff International.* ☺☺

**Islay Mist Deluxe (82) n**19 **t**22 **f**21 **b**20. For a blend, the grain is barely in evidence – texture apart – massacred under the weight of the fresh, young-ish peaty malt. Sweet, mildly citrussy chewy and lush. Great fun. **40%.** *MacDuff International.*

**Isle of Skye 8 Years Old (94) n**23 layers of peat dovetail with barley and solid grain while a wisp of honey sweetens things; **t**23 stunning. Magnificent fresh, oily peat pings round the palate, but leaves a smoky, toasty, oaky trail with a hint of marmalade fruitiness; **f**24 ridiculously long, remaining sweet and viscous with no shortage of oak and malt to bring the curtain down – eventually; **b**24 A textbook blend and an absolute must for any Islay-philes out there – in fact, a must for everybody! Your tastebuds are beaten up and caressed simultaneously. One of the most enormous yet brilliantly balanced whiskies in the world. **40%.** *Ian Macleod & Co.* ☺☺

**Isle of Skye 12 Years Old (92) n**23 buttered kippers, big malt presence – even a hint of bourbon; **t**22 firm grain holds together the deft peat and intense vanilla; **f**24 one of the great blend finishes: smoky but allowing both oak and grain to shine for a sweetening finale; **b**23 This is a simmering blend of the very highest order: there is so much more beyond the peat. A real classic. **40%.** *Ian Macleod.* ☺☺

⁃⁞⁃ **Isle of Skye 50 Years Old (82) n**22 **t**21 **f**19 **b**20 A 50-year-old blend...wow!! And how apposite that it should be released in 2007, the year I celebrate my 50th birthday. The bad news is that this, for all its honey-oaked splendour, appears to be laid low by a hint of sulphur. Now there wouldn't have been sulphured casks around in 1957 and before, so my guess is that some whisky has been finished in newer sherried casks to take out some oaky cobwebs – hence the slight problem. I may be completely wrong but, even so, something has crept in. A superb delivery, though, as the grain slides like silk over the tonsils. For all its fault lines, still has much going for it. **50%.** *Ian Macleod Distillers.*

**The Jacobite (76) n**19 **t**20 **f**19 **b**18. A young, clean, no-nonsense, enjoyable blend with a big grain presence that puts the "bite" in Jacobite. **40%.** *Malt House Vintners.*

**James King 12 Years Old (81) n**19 **t**23 **f**19 **b**20. Caramel dulls the nose and finish. But for some time a quite beautiful blend soars about the taste buds offering exemplary complexity and weight. **40%.** *Quality Spirits International.*

**James King 15 Years Old (87) n**21 attractive amalgam of sawdust, crisp grain, grassy malts and a vague smoky toffee; **t**23 stunningly lush with fabulous weight attached to the malt, which just pings of the firm grains; **f**21 vanilla and toffee; **b**22 An impressive blend. **40%.** *Quality Spirits International.*

**James Martin's 20 Years Old (76) n**20 **t**19 **f**18 **b**19. A bucking bronco of a blend: wild, feisty and never properly tamed. **43%.** *Glenmorangie Co.*

**Jas Gordon Choice Highland Blend (77) n**19 t20 f19 b19. Beautiful grains from an eight-year-old. **40%**. *Gordon & MacPhail.*

**J&B –6C (87) n**23 t23 f19 **b**22. Quite a bizarre whisky because even youngsters often show more oak than this: it has been entirely deforested. A whisky that has been cleaned maniacally, yet there is still enough beautiful freshness within the barley to make this delightfully mouthwatering. I have to say this, though: give me this little belter any day over a blend lost in caramel. A dram I have become fond of (and would be fonder if they could sort the finish out) – even slightly chilled! **40%**.

**J&B Jet (88) n**21 good, firm grain with a light Speyside shadow; t23 sublime mouth arrival with mouthwatering Speyside-esque malt leaping around the palate with enormous freshness, youth and energy; f21 mildly disappointing as some vague toffee notes dull the complexity, though gentle grainy-spice brightens the finale; **b**23 very much in the traditional J&B mould with some livewire malt and grain keeping the tastebuds on their toes. **40%**. *Diageo.*

**J&B Rare (90) n**21 firm grain with a gentle Speyside edge; t22 mouthwatering and brittle, light yet stupendously rich as the malts fan out in all directions – other than a peaty one; f24 this is getting serious: the vanilla is spot on while shards of sharp malt and flinty grain rattle around the tastebuds; **b**23 for a while directly after the merger/takeover this blend went flat on us and I thought one of the great blends had been lost for good. Good news, folks, it's back! That wonderfully crisp Speyside freshness has been re-established and the blend is just like the old days. This is precious stuff: a bit of whisky heritage. Don't lose it again!!! **43%**. *Diageo/Justerini & Brooks.*

**J & B Reserve Aged 15 Years (78) n**23 t19 f18 **b**18. What a crying shame. The sophisticated and demure nose is just so wonderfully seductive but what follows is an open-eyed, passionless embrace. Coarsely grain-dominant and unbalanced, this is frustrating beyond words and not worthy to be mentioned in the same breath as the old, original J&B 15 which, by vivid contrast, was a malty, salivating fruit-fest and minor classic. **40%**. *Diageo/Justerini & Brooks.*

**John Barr (74) n**18 t20 f17 **b**19. Attractive, mouthfilling start, but marred by a bitter finale. **40%**. *Whyte and Mackay.*

**Johnnie Walker Black Label 12 Years (89) n**23 the fingerprint smoke has returned, yet the grains are making a bigger impression than of old; still the fruit offers further body, with citrus and apple to the fore; t23 mouthfilling and chewy, deftly peated and boasting more lush grain; f21 more than normal fruit around, a bit on the sherry-ish side; **b**22 a hugely complex blend that has struggled to find its old cocksure form in recent years but is beginning to show signs of its former, stunning self. The peat is better dispersed, but still some fruity flatter notes refuse to allow it to quite reach its once classic status. Tastebud seducing stuff all the same. **40%**

**Johnnie Walker Blue Label (88) n**21 the old, cleverly peated nose has been lost to us and now the accent falls on fruit though this is hardly as cleanly endearing as it might be; t24 but the magnificence of the mouth arrival is back with a bang with the most sumptuous marriage of over-ripe figs, voluminous malt and lightly sprinkled peat all bound together and then expanded by a brilliant use of firm and soft old grain. Spices also sparkle tease. Magnificent...; f21 oh, so disappointing again, with the plot played out on the arrival and there being insufficient reserve to see off the broodier elements of the slightly bitter oak; **b**22 what a frustrating blend. Just so close to brilliance but the nose and finish just being slightly out of kilter. Worth the experience of the mouth arrival alone. **43%**. *Diageo/John Walker & Sons.*

**Johnnie Walker Gold Label (90) n**23 strands of honey hold together some clean, firm grain and Speysidey grassiness and the most distant toll of peat: meticulous and refined; t23 spicy and sweet malt arrival on the palate with some much harder grains following up close behind; f21 relatively thin and bitter with the grains dominating to an unfair degree, though some peat smoke rumbles on to ensure weight and balance; **b**23 I have tasted any number of these since the very first bottling, and this is the first time it has out-scored Black Label – not least because it is so crisp, clean and beautifully defined. Also just slightly more peaty than most expressions which has guaranteed a superb balance. A blend connoisseur's blend. **40%**

**Johnnie Walker Gold Label The Centenary Blend 18 Years Old (96) n**24 at first it seems a level nose with little happening. But look again...deeper. Stirring in the glass are diced apples and moist raisins, a squirt of something peaty, and a honey and golden syrup mix. Sweet yet weighty with just enough smoke and oak to anchor; **t**24 the silky arrival magnifies the smoky edge to this: some Caol Ila here, I guess, doing what Caol Ila does best – buck up blends. But also that hallmark honey thread is there to savour, linking beautifully with soft grains carrying vanilla and fudge; meanwhile playful spices...play!; **f**23 a beautiful denouement in which the vanilla-edged oak refuses to hide, but smoke and barley dovetail in wonderful counterbalance; **b**25 at the moment I would say that the blending lab at Diageo is going through a kind of legendary period. In years to come people will look back at it fondly and with a healthy degree of awe and ask: "do you remember when?"; or they will point to this era and say: "that's when it all started." White Horse 12, Old Parr and Johnnie Walker Gold: three blends where the gauntlet has been laid down to all: blenders and drinkers alike. And also where I say to Scotch lovers: well, you might love malts, but just how many can match these for brain-exploding complexity? This is another astonishing whisky which just has to be included in people's must have lists. Some of you I was talking to at a tasting in San Francisco, I think, will remember when I answered a question about age and blends: how I said that Walker's Gold appears to have older whiskies than when it was launched. Well this is because it slipped my radar that it was now a 18-year-old, rather than the original 15. Sorry about that. Age, as I have often argued, is as likely to do a whisky down as improve it. Certainly, though, not in this case... **40%**. *Diageo/John Walker & Sons.*

⸬ **Johnnie Walker King George V** db **(88) n**23 delicate smoke and honey with green tea. Unusual, but it works; **t**22 good weight and spice buzz on delivery; melting grains help lighten the oak; **f**21 gets lost in toffee. Pity... **b**22 One assumes that King George V is no relation to King George IV. This has genuine style and breeding, if a tad too much caramel. **43%**

**Johnnie Walker Premier (89) n**22 leathery and waxy with distant hints of honey and peat; **t**23 big age on the malt, chewy nutty-toffee and quiet spices; **f**22 more peppery now with excellent oak amid the grain with toffee returning with some sweet coffee; **b**22 a luxurious blend with firm grain and big weight. A dram to take your time over. **43%**

**Johnnie Walker Red Label (84) n**20 **t**21 **f**22 **b**21. The Striding Man has taken enormous steps in the last year or so to compensate for the caramel with some voluptuous fruity notes and more comfortable smoke. The clarity of the grain on the finish is excellent. **43%**. *Diageo/Johnnie Walker.*

**Johnnie Walker Swing (79) n**19 **t**22 **f**18 **b**20. Grainy, biting and explosive, this blend sets itself apart from the other JW brands but is ultimately too well toffeed for its own good. **43%**

**John Player Special (89) n**23 plenty of grassy fresh malt softens the grain. Genuinely wonderful and unfettered; **t**22 beautiful thirst-quenching fresh malt is lightened by good quality, clean grain; **f**22 clean, long, very soft vanilla but impressive malt; **b**22 Why can't more young blends be like this? Refreshing and mouthwatering, it positively basks in its youth. Of its type, utterly superb. **40%**. *Douglas Laing.*

**John Player Special 12 Years Old (81) n**20 **t**21 **f**20 **b**20. Solid and quite weighty, there are some teasing spices to go with the chewy malt. **43%**.

**John Scott's Superior Blended Aged 35 Years** bott 03 **(87) n**22 **t**22 **f**20 **b**23. Works incredibly well considering the big oak presence. Just enough smoke and honey to make this one to find and savour. **43%**. *675 bottles (two Highland Park quarter casks from 1965 and three more from '68, with a cask of 37-y-o Invergordon thrown in).*

**Kenmore Special Reserve (75) n**18 **t**21 **f**18 **b**18 Lost its balance, rather. And now the caramel has really taken hold. **40%**. *Burn Stewart for Marks & Spencer, UK.* ☉ ☉

**Kenmore Gold Special Reserve Deluxe Aged 10 Years (79) n**18 **t**21 **f**20 **b**20. Rich, well malted with a little spice and grain-cocoa on the finish. Done down by too much caramel, though. **40%**. *Marks & Spencer UK.*

**King George IV (70) n**18 **t**18 **f**17 **b**17. Sweet but caramel dominated. **40%**. *Diageo/John McEwan & Co.*

**King of Scots (84) n**20 **t**21 **f**21 **b**22. This is pretty raw whisky in places but what makes it a top-notch youngster is the superb balance. The grains dominate, but the malts really do make their weighty mark. Some good oiliness acts as a rich and tasty buffer. Great fun. **43%**. *Douglas Laing.*

**King of Scots 12 Years Old (80) n**19 t22 f19 b20. Some lovely oak involvement as well as rich malt and spice. But some toffee in there flattens the party somewhat. **43%**. *Douglas Laing.*

**King of Scots 25 Years Old (90) n**22 bourbon territory – age has given the nose a rare sheen: fruity and malty, too; **t**23 really excellent use of oak: acts as a counter to the sweet, silky grain enveloping the grapey malt; **f**23 long and richly textured with some bitter oaky tones but again the grain is absolutely outstanding; **b**22 supremely structured whisky with a most judicious and enterprising use of grain. The malts are clean and mouthwatering. A stunner. **40%**. *Douglas Laing.*

⋯ **King Robert II (77) n**19 t19 f20 b19. A bustier, more bruising batch than the last 40 per cent version. Handles the OTT caramel much better. Enjoyable, agreeably weighty slugging whisky. **43%**. *Ian MacLeod.*

**King Robert II (71) n**17 t20 f17 b17. An otherwise honest, decent and mouthwatering blend spoiled somewhat by caramel. **40%**. *Ian MacLeod & Co.* ⊙

**King's Crest Scotch Whisky 25 Years Old (83) n**22 t22 f19 b20. A silky middle weight. The toffee-flat finish needs some attention because the softly estered nose and delivery is a honey-rich treat and deserves better. **40%**. *Speyside Distillers.*

**King's Pride (85) n**20 t23 f20 b22. Take away some of the toffee effect and you have a chewy, old-fashioned complex blend. **43%**. *Morrison Bowmore.*

**Kings Scotch (71) n**18 t19 f17 b17. Thin, with few surprises. **40%**. *The High Spirits Co.*

**Kuchh Nai (81) n**19 t22 f20 b20. Big, bold, spicy and immensely enjoyable. **40%**. *Kuchh Nai Marketing.*

**Label 5 Classic Black** L617456A **(75) n**18 t20 f18 b19. The off-key nose needs some serious re-working. Drop the caramel, though, and you would have a lot more character. Needs some buffing. **40%**. *The First Blending for La Martiniquaise, France.*

**Label Five Aged 18 Years** L606133A **(87) n**22 compare the nose with a fruit smoothie and try and spot the difference....! Some wonderful bourbony notes accentuate the age; **t**22 the oils could not have been better placed and the integration of the soft grain and the slowly pulsing malt is a joy: simple but sumptuous; **f**21 just loses its sure footedness with an overdose of flattening caramel; **b**22 a lovely little blend with a genuinely first-rate mouthfeel. **43%**. *The First Blending for La Martiniquaise, France.*

**Lancelot 12 Years Old (81) n**19 t22 f20 b20. A more succulent blend than of old. **40%**. *Edrington Group.*

**Lancelot 17 Years Old (77) n**19 t21 f18 b19. The old honey has been lost, but better grain balance. A slight fruity bitterness (perhaps from a sulphured cask) warps the finish. **40%**. *Edrington Group.*

**Langs Supreme (89) n**22 a big change to the nose with the thrust now on the grain rather than varied fruit of yore. That said there is still enough complexity to tease, though now more biscuity and barley-rich; **t**24 sensational delivery for a young blend with a distinctive malt theme, the firm and soft grains intertwining superbly; clean early on and crisp; **f**21 the grains return for a comfortable finale, though again the malts still have much to say. However, there is a slight toffee-dullness though some spices pep it up cleverly; **b**22 a changed blend with those fruits lost. But there is a very deft use of grain styles here allowing the clean malt extra élan. Remains a thoroughbred blend. **40%**. *Ian Macleod Distillers.* ⊙ ⊙

**Langs Select 12 Years Old (88) n**21 glimpses of a whisky of a certain age here with exotic fruit abounding. The grains used are of the sumptuous type; **t**23 a carpet of silk laid for the procession of sweet malts; the grains shimmer alongside showing a delectable softness **f**22 multi-layered vanilla and a coating of toffee; **b**22 entirely unrecognisable from the old bottling, with this one brimming with fruit and fizz. You get the distinct impression that something a lot older than 12 has made its way into this one. **40%**. *Ian Macleod Distillers.* ⊙ ⊙

**Lauder's Blended Scotch Whisky (74) n**18 t21 f17 b18. Standard, caramel-rich fare. Delicious if shortlived mouth arrival, though. **40%**. *Macduff International.*

**Lauder's 12 Year Old (85) n**21 t21 f22 b21. A really beautifully constructed blend offering finesse. **40%**. *MacDuff International.*

**Lauder's 15 Year Old (86) n**21 **t**23 **f**21 **b**21. Oddly enough it needs the grain to inject complexity into a blend that is otherwise seamless. **43%.**

**Little Frog (84) n**21 **t**22 **f**20 **b**21. A big, succulent Speysidey number with considerable charm. France only. **43%.** *William Maxwell for Société Dugas France.*

**The Loch Fyne (85) n**21 **t**22 **f**21 **b**21. Any peat about is now covertly operating within the spice. A good session dram, a little lighter than it once was. **40%.** *Loch Fyne Whiskies, Inverary, UK.*

**Loch Lomond Single Blend (85) n**21 **t**22 **f**21 **b**21. A real heavyweight with a massive punch. A blend of malts and grains from the Loch Lomond distillery, including some crisp peaty stuff. Not exactly an exhibition of finesse, but real fun all the way. **40%**

**Loch Lomond Single Highland Blended** bott May 07 **(86) n**20 **t**22 **f**22 **b**22 A more precise and attractively integrated blend than the wham-bam-thank-you-dram it originally was. Still something of a work in progress and hindered by the caramel but finesse is definitely in the agenda here and the soft, rather unusual, barley preserve finale is a treat. **40%.** *Loch Lomond Distillery.* ☺☺

**Loch Ranza** (two words, old all blue label) **(83) n**19 **t**22 **f**21 **b**21. A good, solid chewy blend of some panache. But a tad more bitter and toffeed than the present new bottling. **40%.** *Isle of Arran Distillers. Still found in miniatures.*

**Lochranza** (all one word, cream and blue label) **(78) n**20 **t**19 **f**20 **b**19. Has dived a bit over the last year or two, with the malt far harder to fathom. **40%.** *Isle of Arran.*

**Logan (83) n**22 **t**22 **f**20 **b**19. Great nose and mouth arrival but vanishes towards the end, though it is not without a certain complexity. It seems like it's the end of Logan's run. It's been discontinued, I understand. Worth adding to a collection, though. **40%**

**Lombard's Gold Label (88) n**22 chunky with a good malt depth; **t**22 silky and mouth-filling with the malts weaving beautifully into the grains; honeycomb towards the middle; **f**22 delicate spice and toffee-nut; **b**22 excellently weighted with some wonderful honeycomb and spice making their mark. **40%.** *Lombards Brands.*

**Long John (72) n**17 **t**20 **f**18 **b**17. Grainy, fruity, lush but throat-gripping. **40%.** *Allied.*

**McAndrews (66) n**17 **t**18 **f**15 **b**16. The old rum effect has gone on this. Now it's just a rum whisky. Dirty and cluttered around the palate. Seriously grim. **40%.** *Malt House Vintners.*

**McArthurs (77) n**18 **t**21 **f**19 **b**19. A decent touch or two, but basic. **40%.** *Inver House.*

**McArthurs 12 Year Old (79) n**19 **t**21 **f**19 **b**20. A decent touch or two, but dull. **40%.** *Inver House.*

**McCallum's Perfection (80) n**20 **t**21 **f**18 **b**21. Pretty competent and clean of no great age. Lovely malty sweetness combining with soft smoke for a fullbodied start and then finishing with firm grain. **40%.** *D & J Wallum, Australia.*

**McDonalds (74) n**18 **t**19 **f**18 **b**19. Any thinner and it would be on a drip. **43%.** *Diageo.*

**McGibbons (79) n**19 **t**19 **f**21 **b**20. A pretty fat yet medium weighted blend that gathers momentum as the complexity builds. Good spicy finale. **43%.** *McGibbons.*

**Mackinlay's** (*see* Original Mackinlay)

**MacLeod's Isle Of Skye** (*see* Isle of Skye)

**Mac Na Mara (88) n**21 salt and soft fruits; **t**22 changed shape with softer, more yielding grains and malts now but still attractively assembled; **f**22 remains malty and complex; **b**23 a very impressive blend which I adore for its mildly rugged, macho character and superb complexity. **40%.** *Praban na Linne.*

**Mac Na Mara Rum Finish (93) n**22 as is often the case, the rum has hardened the aroma; **t**24 beautifully crisp with fragile malts clashing with equally crisp barley; the touch of golden syrup works wonders; **f**23 serious depth to the malt; the grains soften out with vanilla; **b**24 this is high quality blending, and the usage of the rum appears to have retained the old Mac Na Mara style. Sublime. **40%.** *Praban na Linne.*

**Majestic Wine Fine Oak Cask Matured Scotch (78) n**20 **t**20 **f**19 **b**19. Youthful, biting grain forms the backbone and much of the meat of this pretty tasty and easily drinkable dram. **40%.** *Majestic Wine UK.*

**Major Parka (76) n**16 **t**20 **f**21 **b**19. Poor nose, but refreshing grain on the palate. A light but solid and enjoyable blend. **40%.** *Lehar Austria.*

**Marshal (72) n**17 **t**19 **f**18 **b**18. Very decently spiced. The nose has enough caramel to be a rum. **40%.** *Wm Maxwell Ltd.*

**Martins VVO (76)** n19 t20 f18 b19. Pleasant, sweet, non-committal. **40%.**

**Martins 20 Years Old (87)** n22 clean, intricate and lightly spiced; t23 massive malt presence for a blend; the grain offers a brick wall hardness from which some Speyside reflects beautifully; some superb slap and prickle; f20 short and quite dull; b22 such an improvement on the sherry-ruined previous bottling, this has great charm but the finish needs attention. **43%**. *Glenmorangie*.

**Martins 30 Years Old (87)** n22 clean, ripe sherry, grains very soft, mildly spiced; t22 silky, melt-in-the-mouth grain gives way to some sherry and sweet ginger; f22 soft vanilla and spices; b21 it's unlikely many drams are quite as laidback as this. What it misses in complexity (where the 20-y-o wins hands down) it makes up for in succulent, sherried sloth. **43%** *MacDonald & Muir*.

**Matisse 12 Years Old (89)** n22 distinctly fruity with diced orange peel and hints of Lubec's finest marzipan. Subtle and increased complexity with clean and both soft and firm grains: very clever; t23 big grain statement from earliest mouth arrival; good age and intensity of chewy malt towards the now tantalisingly spicy middle; f23 stunning array of beautifully composed grain guarantees the most vivid bitter-sweet cocoa finale. Excellent length with very slow and equal fade; b22 distinct improvement on the old-style, lumbering, heavyweight Matisse, with a wonderfully oldfashioned, ultra-traditional grain bite that accentuates the crispy-malt middle. A quietly classy dram. **40%**. *Glenmorangie for UIES, Taiwan.* ☉ ☉

**Matisse 21 Year Old (92)** n24 stunningly complex citrus notes link wonderfully with the gentle oak and grains. Sheer seduction...; t23 the oak arrives first but lays a sawdusty platform for trilling malt and more lethargic grain. Again, this just works the palate so beautifully; f22 some coffee notes and spice offer a deft finale; b23 wonderful blending: quality here is never an issue. Worth a trip to Taiwan just to find! **40%**. *Angus Dundee for UIES, Taiwan.*

**Matisse Old (83)** n20 t22 f20 b21 A blend that has made an interesting change of direction of late with the (now softer) grain big on nose and finish and the juicy malt arriving much earlier. Remains refreshing. **40%**. *The Matisse Spirits Co.* ☉ ☉

**Matisse Royal (86)** n20 t22 f22 b22 The big grain nose gives no warning of the massive spice buzz which engulfs the palate. Just so lush and chewy, to boot. A thumping dram for those whose palates aren't stuck in neutral. **40%**. *The Matisse Spirits Co.* ☉ ☉

**Mitchell's 12 Years Old (93)** n23 pounding sea-spray of Springbank offset by hard grain: oaky, clean yet brilliantly complex; t23 vigorous, juicy malt and quite stunning bitter-sweet banter; f23 too long to be true. Some oak drifts in but can't dislodge the salty grain. Softer yet older than before: stunning! b24 almost too complex and beautiful to be true. Magnificent. An already great malt has got even better. **43%**. *Springbank*.

**Monster's Choice (69)** n18 t19 f16 b16. Lots of liquorice and grain. **40%**. *G&M*.

**Morrisons The Best 8 Years Old** bott code L6Q 6995 **(87)** n21 a clumsier aroma than last year with the toast, grain and caramel still to the fore, but the vital honey and soft smoke now at a premium. Decent, but no longer great; t23 weighty stuff with the grains showing a touch of class but the malt really fighting to battle through the toffee; the spices are superb, though f22 long, pretty thick and chewy in places and at last some hints of oak amid the burnt fudge; some bitter notes where last year there had been none; b21 I could almost weep: last year this was a blend to delight and win over converts. It was the whisky I was telling everyone to go out and get. This year, some of the traces of its excellence are still there, it remains highly drinkable, but that greatness has been lost in a tide of caramel. Yes, there was caramel used last year, but it had not crossed that fine line: here it was and paid the price and all the high notes have been ruthlessly flattened. When, oh when, are people going to understand that you can't just tip this stuff into whisky to up the colour – even minimally as in the case here - without causing a detrimental effect on the product? Is anybody listening? Does anyone care??? Someone has gone to great lengths to create a sublime blend – to see it wasted. Natural colour and this'd be an experience to die for. 40% ☉ ☉

**Muirheads (83)** n19 t22 f23 b21 A beautifully compartmentalised dram that integrates superbly, if that makes sense. In other words, the nose is crisp grain but the flavours display big Speyside malt – mouthwatering and lush. With the aid of a fatty mouthfeel, the two meet on the finish, which now has greater weight, length, dexterity and class. Old fashioned and delicious. **40%**. *MacDonald & Muir.* ☉ ☉

**Northern Scot (68) n**16 **t**18 **f**17 **b**17. Heading South bigtime. **40%**. *Bruce and Co. for Tesco UK.*

**Old Crofter Special Old Scotch Whisky (83) n**18 **t**22 **f**21 **b**22. A very decent blend, much better than the nose suggests thanks to some outstanding, velvety grain and wonderfully controlled sweetness. **40%**. *Smith & Henderson for London & Scottish International.*

**Old Glen (81) n**20 **t**21 **f**20 **b**20. The grain stars despite the 60% malt content. *V&S Sweden.*

**Old Glenn (78) n**20 **t**20 **f**19 **b**19. Young, clean, refreshing house whisky. **40%**

**Old Inverness (71) n**17 **t**18 **f**19 **b**17. Annoyingly cloying and heavy-handed in parts, but the spice on the finish does offer relief. **40%**. *J G Thompson & Co.*

**Old Masters Deluxe (78) n**17 **t**22 **f**19 **b**20. The odd blemish here and there doesn't detract from the rich-textured malt-rich sweetness that charms. **40%**. *James MacArthur.*

⋰⋰ **Old Masters "Freemason Whisky" (92) n**24 the perfect nose to experience blindfolded (how else...?) as the depth of the fruit and grain – and their happy intermingling – is astonishing. A few under-ripe gooseberries here; **t**23 light, graceful arrival with the early emphasis on a Speyside malt theme before some grain and oak kicks in; **f**22 pretty long with touches of cocoa though the fresh malt lingers; **b**23 a high quality blend that doesn't stint on the malt. The nose, in particular, is sublime. **40%**. *Supplied online. Lombard Brands Ltd, UK.*

**Old Mull (83) n**22 **t**21 **f**20 **b**20. The nose offers fight and bite, but the body is lush and yielding. A real contradictory dram. **40%**. *Kyndal.*

**Old Orkney "OO" 8 Years Old (79) n**19 **t**21 **f**19 **b**20. A great improvemnet on the old "OO", with intense, delicious malt bouncing off the grain. Too much caramel, though. **40%**. *Gordon & MacPhail.*

**Old Parr Aged 15 Years (84) n**19 **t**22 **f**21 **b**22. Absolutely massive sherry input here. Some of it is of the highest order. The nose, reveals, however, that some isn't... **43%**. *Diageo/MacDonald Greenlees.*

**Old Parr Superior 18 Years Old** Batch no. L5171 **(97) n**25 here's a nose with just about a touch of everything: especially clever smoke which gives weight but allows apples and bourbon to filter through at will. Perfect weight and harmony while the complexity goes off the scales; **t**25 voluptuous body, at times silky but the grains offer enough jagged edges for a degree of bite and bourbon; mouthwatering and spicey with the peats remaining on a slow burner. Toasty and so, so chewey; **f**23 the vanilla is gentle and a counter to the firmness of the combined oak and grain. A flinty, almost reedy finish with spices and cocoa very much in evidence; **b**24 year in, year out, this blend just gets better and better. This bottling struck me as a possible Whisky of the Year, but perhaps only an outsider. Familiarity, though, bred anything but contempt and over the passing months I have tried to get to the bottom of this truly great whisky. Blended whisky has long needed a champion. This grand old man looks just the chap. This is a worthy, if unexpected (even to me), Jim Murray' Whisky Bible 2007 World Whisky of the Year. **43%**. *Diageo/MacDonald Greenlees.*

**Old Parr Classic 18 Year Old** bott 11 Apr 05 **(86) n**22 **t**23 **f**20 **b**21. A strange whisky that promises so much but while always interesting fails to live up to its early glory. **46%**. *Diageo.*

**Old St Andrews 5 Years Old (77) n**19 **t**21 **f**19 **b**18. Very soft, sweet, safe and friendly. Good middle with expansive texture. Caramel bowed. **40%**

**Old St Andrews 8 Years Old (69) n**16 **t**19 **f**17 **b**17. A flat, lifeless blend being phased out of existence. **40%**

**Old St Andrews 12 Years Old (88) n**21 fresh for age, clean, big malt and fine, clipped grain, distant hint of smoke; **t**23 outstanding Speyside-style clarity of malt, rich but never too sweet; **f**22 tapering finale with excellent vanilla; **b**22 an impressive newcomer for 2003. Loads of malt character thanks, ironically, to some excellent grain selection. Superb. **40%**. *Old St Andrews Japan.*

**Old St Andrews Clubhouse (90) n**22 clean as a whistle: both malts and grains are young but proudly so. A Speyside influence comes through loud and clear: mouthwatering; **t**23 the early arrival is identical to the nose: clear as the morning dew on the first green and no less grassy; **f**22 long with some grain gaining hold but bringing with it some soft vanillas; **b**23 a fair way to start any day. How I love young blends: fresh and lacking any sort of pretensions. It has quality enough. **43%**.

**Old St Andrews Golf Ball Miniatures** (*see* Old St Andrews Clubhouse)

**Old Smuggler (79) n**18 **t**21 **f**20 **b**20. Remains enjoyable fare, but much more emphasis now on the caramel softness than the old cutlass hardness and sharpness that I once so loved. **40%**. *Allied*.

**Old Spencer (73) n**18 **t**19 **f**18 **b**18. Attractive and clean but ultimately rather too sweet for its own good. **40%**. *Australia*.

**The Original Mackinlay (76) n**19 **t**20 **f**18 **b**19. Toffee, anyone? Some thought Fettercairn was in this. The talentless know-nothings... **40%**. *Whyte and Mackay*.

**The Original Mackinlay 12 Years Old (80) n**19 **t**21 **f**20 **b**20. Quite hefty with a spicy buzz and lingering complexity. **40%**. *Kyndal*.

**Parkers (78) n**17 **t**22 **f**20 **b**19. The nose has regressed, disappearing into ever more caramel, yet the mouth-watering lushness on the palate remains and the finish now holds greater complexity and interest. **40%**. *Angus Dundee*.

**Parkers 12 Years Old (81) n**18 **t**19 **f**24 **b**20. Don't expect a mass market sop. Real bite to this, and for what it lacks in grace it makes up for with a finish of pure roast Brazilian coffee. Some real demerara rum style in there. **40%**. *Angus Dundee*.

**Passport (82) n**21 **t**21 **f**20 **b**20. Much tidied up since I last tasted it. But when will it ever return to the virtually non-coloured Speyside-sharp work of art that I used to worship as a regular dram all those years back? **40%**. *Chivas*.

**Peaty Craig** (*see* Tanner's Peaty Craig.)

**Peter Dawson (74) n**18 **t**19 **f**19 **b**18. Toffee, anyone? **43%**. *Diageo*.

**Pig's Nose Aged 5 Years (79) n**20 **t**22 **f**18 **b**19. A big, sweet, chunky, gawky, grain-lashed but hugely enjoyable blend which needs a little tweaking at the finish. Lots of caramel gives this little piggy a strange, overly dark complexion for its age. Hopefully the new owners will tidy this up. **40%**. *Spencerfield Spirit Co*.

**Pinwinnie Royale (83) n**19 **t**23 **f**20 **b**21. An absolutely classic, fresh young blend with crisp, rock-hard grain forming the frame on which the clean, mouthwatering malt hangs. Then a slow gathering of complex spices for good measure. Only a tad of caramel on the finish can be detected that lessens the allround complexity and charm. **40%**. *Inver House*.

**Pinwinnie Royale 12 Years Old (85) n**20 **t**22 **f**21 **b**22. Finely-textured and attractive throughout with greatr spice finale. **40%**. *Inver House*.

**Potters** (aged 36 months) **(64) n**15 **t**17 **f**16 **b**16. Awful. **40%**

**Prince Charlie Special Reserve (73) n**17 **t**20 **f**18 **b**18. Thankfully not as cloyingly sweet as of old, but remains pretty basic. **40%**. *Somerfield, UK*.

**Prince Charlie Special Reserve 8 Years Old (81) n**18 **t**20 **f**22 **b**21. A lumbering bruiser of a dram; keeps its trademark shapelessness but the spices and lush malt ensure an enjoyable experience. **40%**. *Somerfield, UK*.

**Prince Consort (78) n**19 **t**20 **f**20 **b**19. Enjoyably honest, clean and pleasant if a little conservative. **40%**

**Queen Elizabeth (78) n**20 **t**20 **f**18 **b**20. Pleasant, grainy, toffeed and easy-going. **43%**.

**The Queen's Seal (73) n**18 **t**19 **f**18 **b**18. Mildly dusty but decent Speyside input. **40%**.

**Real Mackenzie Extra Smooth (81) n**18 dull; **t**22 a silk landing with crystal clear grains for a second or two, then the honied malt really takes off, and with it some peppers. A wonderful battle ensues; **f**20. Where the battle once played out, the malt and grain become friends and smooch under a toffee umbrella; **b**21 once, the only time the terms "Real Mackenzie" and "Extra Smooth" were ever uttered in the same sentence was if someone was talking about the barman. Now it is a genuine descriptor. Which is odd, because when Diageo sent me a sample of their blend last year it was a snarling beast ripping at the leash. This, by contrast, is a whimpering sop. "Killer? Where are you...???" **40%**. *Diageo*.

**Real Mackenzie (80) n**17 **t**21 **f**20 **b**22. Gets off to a flyer on the palate with fabulous grain helping the young malts to go for it. Never the gentlest of drams; great to see it maintaining its raucous spirit. **40%**. *Whyte and Mackay*.

**Red Seal 12 Years Old (82)** n19 t22 f20 b21. A mouthwatering blend that starts with a lovely grain kick. Overall balance is charming, but toffee numbs it down towards the finish. Still, a pretty good pub blend. **40%.** *Charles Wells UK.*

**Reliance PL (83)** n20 t20 f22 b21. Some really lovely spices complement the green apple fruitiness. Juicy and never less than charming. **43%.** *Diageo.*

**Rob Roy (88)** n21 t23 f22 b22. A profound whisky with big malt character and impressive complexity. A real no-nonsense, blend-drinker's dram. **40%.**

**Robbie Dhu 12 Years Old (83)** n21 t21 f20 b21. Maintains its hallmark fruitiness but the usual soft peat is much reduced and silkiness has replaced complexity. This brand some years ago replaced the old Grant's 12-y-o. **40%.** *Wm Grant's.*

**Robert Burns (78)** n19 t20 f19 b20. If Burns were alive today perhaps his tasting notes might be something like this. Ode to a blend: Och, wee shimmering noblest blen', tha most braken heart ye men', and this'n sets oot with grain so soft, til malt an' spice are heild aloft. **40%.** *Isle of Arran.*

**Robert Burns Superior 12 Years Old (88)** n21 excellent, refreshing, tingling, early clarity to both grain and malt; t23 mouth-tingling complexity is well weighted behind some very decent malts; no little fruit either; f22 the oak on the grain wrestles with the malt but never gains the upper hand; b22 a teasing blend that needs a second glass before it comes alive. **43%.** *Isle of Arran.*

**Robert Burns Superior 17 Years Old (73)** n18 t19 f18 b18. An awkward, lumbering dram that lost its compass. **43%.** *Isle of Arran.*

**Robert Burns Superior 21 Years Old (87)** n23 thick cut marmalade on salt-buttered, slightly singed toast; distant peat smoke binds in almost imperceptibly; t22 excellent richness and little stinting on the honey; a lovely buzz; f21 high coppery-malt presence; a delicious sheen rounds off the charm and some late grain bites wonderfully; b21 out of a very similar, impressive, pod to the 12-y-o. **43%.**

**Robertson's of Pitlochry Rare Old Blended (83)** n21 t20 f21 b21. Handsome grain bite with a late malty flourish. Classic light blend available only from Pitlochry's landmark whisky shop. **40%** ⊙ ⊙

**The Royal & Ancient** bott code L19.12.06 **(87)** n20 dull toffee; t23 fat mouthfeel with a beautiful burnished honey follow-through; no shortage of burnt fudge and biting spice; f22 toffee has replaced the usual Demerara; the grain remains firm and friendly; b22 just a shade of carelessness with the caramel has shaved off the finer points. Last year a staggeringly good blend; this year simply very good, indeed!! **40%.** *Cockburn & Campbell.* ⊙ ⊙

**The Royal & Ancient 28 Years** malt content 50% **(95)** n24 enormously rich, floral, softly peated with stunning oak: a few molecules from perfection; t24 big malt arrival that just swamps the mouth with the enormity of its richness. Intense bitter-sweet barley along with something smoky, but honeyed enough to keep fabulous harmony; f23 signs of tiring oak, but forgivable. The malt is toasty, roasty, lightly peated and chewy. The grains, firm yet light, begin to glow as all else fades; b24 an incredible blend. The mouthfeel is spot on: the whole is a sheer masterpiece! **40%.** *Cockburn & Campbell.* ⊙

**Royal Castle (51)** n15 t14 f10 b12. Mustiness and caramel: genuinely unappealing. **40%.** *Arcus Norway.*

**Royal Household (88)** n22 a natural harmony between crisp grain and crisper malt, wonderfully refreshing and refined; t23 the translation onto the palate is spot on with a Speyside-style maltiness clipping alongside the rock-hard grain and a swirl of peat just about noticeable in the far distance; f21 taken down a peg by the late caramel; b22 this is a wonderfully sophisticated blend, far too delicate and high class to be able to support something as trade door as caramel. **43%.** *Diageo.*

**Royal Salute 21 Years Old (91)** n23 where there was once smoke there is now extra fruit, but this remains sensual and glorious; t24 your tastebuds are caressed by grains that give themselves entirely to your desires, the malts provide the background music while vanilla-rich oak expresses maturity; f22 a simplistic, light landing, with a rich vanilla balancing well against the malt and lightening grains; b22 not as smoky or full-bodied as it once was, but kind of reminds me of a Canadian whisky from the same stable, Seagram's Crown Royal, of about 20- 25 years ago, in the way that a soft caramel touch is imbued in the rich complexity of the grains. Just a tiny shift in caramel (either natural or added) could ruin this balance, but just now it works wonderfully. **40%**. *Chivas*.

**Royal Salute Destiny 38 Years Old (92) n**22 some sappy, soapy, oaky grumbling, but this is overwhelmed eventually by the playful barley; **t**24 fabulous delivery of ripe dates and thick maltshake. Chew this for hours! **f**23 the oak returns here but actually slightly lightens the loads with some gentle vanilla; **b**23 an enormous blend that is half drink, half meal.... **40%**. *Chivas*.

**Royal Salute 50 Years Old** distilled before 1953 **(95) n**24 **t**24 **f**22 **b**25. A decade ago I tasted the Royal Salute 40 Years Old. It was probably the finest blend I had ever tasted. Now they have the 50-year-old. And it has ripped up and laughed at every rule in the book: finish apart, it has just got better and better. The most extraordinary thing here is the oak involvement. At 50 years you should be picking it out of your teeth. Not here. Instead, after its appearance on the wonderful nose, it all but vanished. Instead we are left to deal with an essay in balance. This is going for £6,000 a bottle. In reality a blended whisky showing this degree of balance and élan is truly priceless. **40%** *Chivas. 255 bottles.*

**Royal Salute The Hundred Cask Selection (92) n**23 some serious age here but attractively tempered by sober herbal-floral tones. Busy, complex and lightly spiced with just a dash of something tart and vaguely marmalady to add extra life; **t**23 fabulous weight as the malt-grain combination arrives hand-in-hand. The sweetness is initially propelled by very precise, clean malt and counters effortlessly the early oak. Some white chocolate heralds the spicier bourbon cask influence while the late middle enjoys a degree of fruitiness; **f**22 long, velvety textures with gentle hints of some bourbon-oaky tones from the grain and lingering more mouthwatering freshness from the malt. Some oaky-cocoa bitterness at the tapering finish; **b**24 knife-edge whisky: serious brinkmanship. The oak so often threatens to dominate, but the diffusion of Speysidey clean malt and sharper fruitiness guarantees a stunning experience. Almost a novel of a blend, with you rapidly turning the pages trying to unravel the mystery of what's going on and what's going to happen next: the way blended whisky should be. And because this is an addition to the lofty Royal Salute stable, I've tried to be hypercritical. But this is worthy of the great name. **40%**. *Chivas.* ☉

⁖ **Royal Salute The Hundred Cask Selection Limited Reserve No. 3 (90) n**22 honey, chocolate, a touch soapy but lovely wine gum fruits, too; **t**23 soft barley lift off, melting bourbony tones and weak golden syrup; excellent understated spices towards the middle; **f**22 clean, humble vanilla and spice; **b**23 can a blend be too charming and well behaved? Elegance, or what? **40%**. *Chivas Brothers.*

**Royal Silk Reserve (93) n**22 classically light yet richly bodied under the clear, crisp ethereal grains. The freshly-cut-grass maltiness balances perfectly; **t**24 crystal clear grains dovetail with intense, mouthwatering and refreshingly sweet malt to create a perfect pitch while the middle is heavier and livelier than you might expect with the very faintest echo of peat; **f**24 delicate oils and wonderful grainy-vanilla ensures improbable length for something so light. Beautiful spices and traces of cocoa offer the last hurrah. Sheer bliss; **b**23 I named this the best newcomer of 2001 and it hasn't let me down. A session blend for any time of the day, this just proves that you don't need piles of peat to create a blend of genuine stature. A must have. **40%**. *International Whisky Company.*

**Sainsbury's Scotch Whisky (82) n**19 **t**21 **f**20 **b**22. Thinned out significantly over the last year allowing a pleasing degree of complexity amid the agreeable chewability. A great improvement: pretty good, indeed! **40%**. *Sainsbury's, UK.*

**Sainsbury's Finest Old Matured Aged 5 Years (72) n**19 **t**19 **f**17 **b**17. A comfortable dram until the caramel kicks in. **40%**

⁖ **Sainsbury's Finest Old Matured Aged 8 Years** bott code L7 109 **(83) n**20 **t**21 **f**21 **b**21 Reasonable fare with firm grain and a juicy depth. Lots of toffee. **40%**

**Sainsbury's Finest Old Matured Aged 12 Years (84) n**20 **t**22 **f**21 **b**21. Great stuff: once past the caramel the honey blossoms in all directions. A hint of smoke does no harm, either. No shame in having this around the house. **40%**. *UK.*

**Sandy Mac (76) n**18 **t**20 **f**19 **b**19. Basic, decent blend that's chunky and raw. **40%**.

**Savoy Blended Scotch (75)** n18 t20 f18 b19. A pleasant young malt lift in the early middle palate. **40%**. *Savoy Hotel UK.*

**Scoresby Very Rare** (aged 36 months) **(69)** n17 t19 f16 b17. Furs the teeth. **40%**

**Scotch Brothers (70)** n17 t19 f17 b17. Grainy, hard, biting and young. **40%**. *Russia.*

**Scotch Blue 17 Years Old (78)** n21 t20 f18 b19. Salty and biting complexity makes for impressive blend, but a little too sappy and caramelised. **40%**. *Korea.*

**Scotch Blue Aged 21 Years (80)** n21 t20 f19 b20. A pleasingly spiced, rich blend with agreeable chewability. **40%**. *Korea.*

**Scots Club (72)** n17 t19 f18 b18. Young, pleasant, basic fare. **40%**. *Kyndal.*

**Scots Earl (83)** n19 t22 f21 b21. A characterful, mildly disharmonised blend that is so full of mouth-bulging character that you cannot fail to be entertained. Love it! **40%**. *Loch Lomond Distillers.*

**Scots Grey De Luxe (83)** n19 t22 f21 b21 The toffeed nose is less than promising but the quality of their grain is outstanding with very impressive malt infusion. Chewy and desirable, despite the so-so aroma. **40%**

**Scottish Collie (74)** n19 t20 f17 b18. A frustrating blend because to seasoned campaigners, you just know when there is a little beaut dying to get out. What could have been a really lovely number appears to have been sacrificed on the altar of caramel. **40%**. *Quality Spirits International, UK.* ☉ ☉

**Scottish Collie 12 Years Old (85)** n22 t22 f20 b21. On the cusp of a really classy blend here but the bitterness on the finish loses serious Brownie points. **40%**. *Quality Spirits International, UK.* ☉ ☉

☼ **Scottish Collie 18 Years Old (92)** n24 the most gentle honey-ginger theme delights; aided and abetted by evidence of some very old grain which radiates succulent, over-ripe exotic fruit amid the drier oaks and gathering spices: a real, rounded charmer; t23 those sweeter notes apparent on the nose are at the vanguard of a sublime procession of silk-edged barley; myriad sugar-coated notes ranging from acacia honey to maple syrup and brilliantly balanced by the slow march of drier oakier tones; f22 remains soft and free from the usual Scottish Collie bitterness, though the toffee apparent sits comfortably with the toasty oak; b23 this, honey-led beaut would be a winner even at Crufts: an absolute master class of how an old, yet light and unpeated blend should be. No discord whatsoever between the major elements and not a single hint of over-aging. Superb. **40%**. *Quality Spirits International, UK.*

**Scottish Glory** dist 02, bott 05 **(85)** n21 t21 f22 b21. An improved blend now bursting with vitality. The ability of the grain to lift the barley is very pleasing. **40%**. *Duncan Taylor. 960 bottles.*

**Scottish Leader (77)** n19 t21 f18 b19. Formerly the "Supreme". Revamped both inside and out, this has much more vitality than recent bottlings but is brought down by too heavy-handed use of caramel for a dull finish. The new label with its "Deanston Estd 1785" is somewhat misleading: the buildings may date from then but it became a distillery only in 1966. **40%**. *Burn Stewart.*

**Scottish Leader 12 Year Old (77)** n19 t22 f18 b18. Fruity nose and lovely, complex mouth arrival but falters latterly. **40%**. *Burn Stewart.*

**Scottish Leader 15 Year Old (87)** n22 fabulous, supreme mixture of deep fruity tones, soft oak, rich barley and a wisp of smoke; t22 brilliant texture: sweet with malt and plummy fruit and natural oak-caramel; f21 long, oily, chewy with lots of vanilla; b22 this is big stuff, sweet and yet gentle with it. **40%**. *Burn Stewart.*

**Scottish Leader 22 Years Old (86)** n23 t22 f21 b20. This is a lovely dram, but would be better if it wasn't quite so sweet. Much of its complexity is hidden. **40%**. *Burn Stewart.*

**Scottish Leader Aged Over 25 Years (91)** n24 charismatic peat offers the most sublime aroma you could imagine for a blend of this age. No off-notes whatsoever: what little grain can be detected stands firm and clean; t22 chewy, massively intense malt framed by succulent grain; f23 the peat returns, dovetailing with vanilla and lingering sweet barley; b22 a changed character from a few years back: heavier and fuller yet refusing to let age dim its innumerable qualities. A real belter of a blend. **40%**. *Burn Stewart.*

**Scottish Leader Blue Seal (82)** n21 t22 f19 b20. Impressive grain bite on the nose softened by rich malt. A fine dram by any standards. **40%.** *Burn Stewart.*

**Scottish Leader Platinum (73)** n19 t19 f18 b17. Rather bland. **40%.**

**Scottish Leader Supreme (80)** n21 t21 f18 b20. Lush and delicious on the nose and mouth arrival, but the hoped-for big finale is flattened by some outrageous use of caramel. Pity, as there is so much to get your teeth into early on. Enjoyable when all's said and done. **40%.** *Burn Stewart. Gold label for export, especially Japan.*

⠒⠒ **Scottish Piper (80)** n20 t20 f20 b20 A light, mildly- raw, sweet blend with lovely late vanilla intonation. **40%.**

**Scottish Prince Aged 19 Years (86)** n22 t22 f21 b21. Not a single off-note: nothing like as foppish as the Prince on the label. **40%.** *Forbes Ross & Co Ltd.*

**Scottish Prince Aged 21 Years (86)** n20 t22 f23 b21. If I was a gambling man, I'd say there was a decent amount of ancient grain. No matter: this is stunning entertainment for the tastebuds. **43%.** *Forbes Ross and Co Ltd.*

**Shieldaig The Classic Uisge Beatha (66)** n15 t19 f16 b16. Thin and grainy. **40%.** *William Maxwell and Son (Ian Macleod).*

**Shieldaig Collection Finest Old Uisge Beatha** (*see* Shieldaig The Classic). *William Maxwell and Son France.*

**Silver Barley (84)** n20 t22 f21 b21. Pre-pubescent even to the point of a slight new-makish quality. A blend, but no sign of the grain: just lots of invigorating, mouthwatering barley. Forget about mixers, one to start the day with. **40%.** *John Milroy.*

**Something Special (84)** n21 t22 f20 b21. Changed shape, yet still about the same quality as before. Much lighter, friendlier nose now and the grains are real fun. But lacks that degree of extra complexity. Enjoyable and worth drinking for all that. **40%.** *Chivas.*

**Something Special Premium Aged 15 Years (89)** n22 a vague, distant smokiness sits prettily with some fruity caramel; t23 boisterous delivery with unshackled malt adding a wonderful, zesty spiciness amid much more mouth-watering Speyside-style fresh grass; the grain offers the desired cut-glass firmness; f21 lots of vanilla and too much caramel, but remains busy and entertaining; b23 a hugely enjoyable, fun whisky which pops around the palate like a crackerjack. Fabulous malt thread and some curious raisiny/sultana fruitiness, too. A blend-lover's blend. **40%.** *Chivas/ Hill Thompson, Venezuela.*

**Spar Finest (80)** t20 t21 f19 b20. A standard blend, but of a superblybalanced style I adore. The exquisite clean grains show nip and attitude – as they should – but there is sufficient malt for depth. Love to see the toffee effect go, though, and have it raw and refreshing. **40%.** *UK.*

**The Spey Cast 12 Years Old (81)** n18 t22 f21 b20. Lovely, complex, fruity dram. **40%.** *Gordon & MacPhail.* ⊙

**Spey Royal (76)** n18 t20 f19 b19. Quite a young blend with a big toffee effect but not without a delicious and lush early malt-grain explosion. **40%.** *Diageo Thailand.*

**SS Politician Finest (89)** n21 pretty sharp grains softened by first-class crisp malt: light and flighty; t22 really excellent used of clean young malt – probably the most of it Speyside - to refresh the tastebuds and make for a lip-smacking middle; f23 excellent complexity here as the malt and grain battle it out. It's, literally, clean fun all the way; b23 this is a terrific young blend. With its obvious reference to my favourite film of all time, Whisky Galore, it needed to be good – even go down well, if you pardon the pun – and hasn't disappointed in the slightest way. Stand up that blender and take a bow! **40%.** *Duncan Taylor.*

**Standard Selection Aged 5 Years (92)** n22 the rock-hard grain deflects the delicate malt: uncompromising and enticing; t23 fabulous collection of fruity tones, balanced by an ever-increasing malt presence, brilliantly subtle with honey-barley; f23 the oak seems more than five years and softens the smoke; b24 a brilliant blend that appears a lot older than its five years: a stupendously stylish interpretation of peat with sweet barley. **40%.** *V&S Stockholm.*

**Stewarts Cream Of The Barley (74)** n19 t20 f17 b18. A dram that's improved a lot since its grimmer days, with passable early malt delivery. But the grain remains unwieldy and stand-offish. **40%.** *Allied.*

**Stewart's Finest (75) n**17 **t**20 **f**19 **b**19. Raw nose; body sweet, curvaceous, toffeed and chewy. Annoyingly and dangerously drinkable. **40%.** *Kyndal.*

**Sullivan's Cove Premium Blend Scotch Whisky (69) n**16 **t**18 **f**17 **b**18. Sweet and fat on the palate with caramel and late grain bite. Shame about the nose. **40%.** *Tasmania Distillery Pty. Australia only.*

**Swords (78) n**20 **t**21 **f**18 **b**19. Beefed up somewhat with some early smoke thrusting through and rapier grains to follow. **40%.** *Morrison Bowmore.*

**The Talisman (81) n**20 **t**22 **f**19 **b**20. Good grain and Speyside early delivery, but a lot of the sparkle has vanished from this, and the caramel, once a bit-part player, now dominates. **40%.** *J & W Hardie Ltd.*

**Tam Touler's Dram (79) n**19 **t**21 **f**19 **b**20. A shade too much caramel and grain, but the immediate, malty arrival on the palate does sing. **40%.** *The Whisky Castle, Tomintoul.*

**Tanner's Peaty Creag Aged 8 Years (94) n**23 Lordy me! Just such an astonishing delivery of heavyweight aromas from molten liquorice to top-rate peat; **t**24 sensational arrival of intense, thick malt with both the gristy barley and peat on full display; the grain offers a welcoming thinning but it's all amazingly integrated; **f**23 one of the few blends that has enough smoky, malty clout to carry the caramel with it and land wave after wave of peaty punches. Superb! **b**24 if I lived in the Shrewsbury/Hereford area of the UK this would be a daily tipple for me. Instead I'll have to make do with the closely related Isle of Skye. **40%.** *Tanners Wine Merchants, Shrewsbury & Hereford* ☉

**Teacher's Highland Cream (90) n**23 firm, flinty grain; a tad fruity with gently smoked malt-ensuring weight; **t**23 mouth-filling with a tender sweetness; the grains seem softer than the nose suggests; **f**22 toffee and lazy smoke; **b**22 not yet back to its best but a massive improvement on the 2005 bottlings. So harder grains to accentuate the malt will bring it closer to the classic of old. **40%.** *Fortune Brands.*

**Teacher's Highland Cream** Batch no. T073, bott Nov 05 **(88) n**22 busy with limited harmonization but attractive weight; **t**21 excellent delivery but the sweetness and grains run amok; **f**23 finally finds its range and now we have super-charged complexity: wonderful spice buzz as the peats begin to kick on; **b**22 the finish entirely outclasses the British version. If they could get a marriage of the two styles: what a blend...!! **42.8%.** *Allied Domecq Spirits, India.*

**Te Bheag (84) n**19 **t**22 **f**21 **b**22. Well balanced with good spice bite. **40%.**

**Te Bheag Connoisseurs' Blend (87) n**21 coastal and salty; **t**22 more oily textured than of late with the accent on the malt and toffee; **f**22 beautifully coastal finally, but fat and sweet; **b**22 an attractive, relaxing dram, but not a patch on what it was. It as if the peat has been surgically removed. **40%.** *Praban na Linne.*

**Tesco Special Reserve (80) n**16 **t**22 **f**21 **b**21. The sweaty armpit nose is relieved by the massively improved, rich, chewey and silky body. **40%.** *Tesco UK.*

**Tesco Scotch Whisky Finest Reserve Aged 12 Years (80) n**19 **t**21 **f**20 **b**20. A thumping, thudding blend as hard as the granite rocks over which the waters ran to the Speyside distilleries used in the recipe. Value-for-money-wise, not a bad blend at all but for all the charm and mouth-watering properties of the malt, the grains are seismic. **40%.**

⠿ **Tesco Value Scotch Whisky (83) n**19 **t**21 **f**22 **b**21 Young and genuinely refreshing whisky. Without the caramel this really would be a little darling. **40%**

**Ubique (82) n**20 **t**22 **f**21 **b**19. Fresh, juicy, Speysidey, classy. **40%**

**Upper Ten (68) n**17 **t**18 **f**17 **b**16. Makes a point of peat on the label, but fails to deliver balance. **40%.** *Arcus Norway.*

**Ushers Green Stripe (83) n**20 **t**21 **f**21 **b**21. Light, mouthwatering and with more than a hint of Speyside controlling its style. **43%.** *Diageo.*

**VAT 69 (86) n**20 **t**22 **f**21 **b**23. Exemplary young blend: fresh, clean and mouthwatering. This, to me, offers the kind of balance and style that encapsulates a light blend. No problems with water and even ice on the hottest days. **43%.** *Wm Sanderson/Diageo.*

**Waiting Thirty Three Years** (*see* The Whisky House)

**Waitrose Scotch Three Years Old (76) n**17 **t**21 **f**19 **b**19. A dirty nose, which makes the clarity on the palate all the more remarkable. **40%**

**Walker and Scott Finest (82) n**20 **t**21 **f**20 **b**21. Rock-hard and brittle grain gives a clean shape for the malts to develop around. High grain content, but a Speysidey grassiness is quite delicious as is the mildly citrussy nose; marks docked only for late toffee. Impressive and old-fashioned. **40%**. *Sam Smith's UK.*

**The Watsonian Club Whisky (77)** n19 t20 f19 b19. A soft, sweet, clean blend with a dry finish. **40%**

**The Whisky House 33 Years Old 1969 (92)** n23 some serious age here, but the integrity of the malt never wavers. The grain is barely discernible except maybe that bourbony background; t24 a series of explosions, controlled and uncontrolled, offer pace and thrust to the mouth arrival: the delivery and diversity of flavours is fast and complex. Again there is a slick bourbony edge, not to mention some very distant smoke amid the Demerera sweetness; f22 more spices as the vanilla bites deep; b23 a very unusual blend of no little antiquity. Perfect for bourbon-loving Scotch drinkers. Its overall finesse, however, is unambiguous. **50.5%**. *The Whisky House, Belgium.*

**White Horse (92)** n23 beautifully smoky: big weight with the grains shrinking by comparison; t24 magnificently rounded at first then wave upon wave of varying characteristics ranging from clean, fresh malt to heavier, smoky notes with even room for a little vanilla and sultana; f22 long, vanilla-rich with some light peat still drifting around; b23 this is one of the greatest young blends on the market: only the oiliness presented by, probably, Caol Ila, takes it out of a mark in the mid-90s. When Lagavulin was used there was a cleaner, crisper feel. But I am nit-picking: it is not entirely unknown for me to have a less than harmonious reltionship with some of the world's bigger distillers. But if I were Holmes, I would doff my deerstalker to this masterpiece of a blend, as it is one even he would fail to fathom and one that proves that greatness is not achieved by the age of the whisky but the understanding and feel for how the elements combine and interact. Proof, were it needed, that even among the big boys there are still quality blenders around who know how to make a pulse race. **43%**. *Diageo.*

**White Horse Aged 12 Years (94)** n23 chunky, heather-honied and smoky. A few staves of oak visible, too; t23 big malt content apparent here and the liquorice-led honey show an age greater than the stated 12. Multi-layered, with the firm grain making a belated and complex introduction; f24 incredibly long, with the smoke re-establishing itself, though very subtly. The vanilla has a wonderfully gentle honey glow to it; b24 brilliant blending from the highest echelons. A masterful balance of great age and something a little younger, and one of the most deft uses of peat in the business. A real thoroughbred. **40%**. *Diageo.*

**Whyte and Mackay (86)** n21 t23 f20 b21 while the odd bottling can be pretty bland fare, overall this is a very subtly changed and much improved blend. This last bottling, though, was distinctly on the dull side. **40%**

**Whyte and MacKay 12 Years Old (84)** n21 t21 f20 b22. Beautifully wallowing grain offers little shelter to some rollicking malty notes: curiously light yet weighty – totally intriguing. **40%**. *Kyndal.*

**Whyte & Mackay 15 Years Old Select Reserve (86)** n21 t23 f21 b21. A really neat blend with slightly more toffee effect than the old version. **40%**

**Whyte & Mackay 18 Years Old (89)** n22 dried dates moistened by sultanas: the malt hangs firm; t23 voluptuous and silky, sweet grain and malt marriage made in heaven; f22 simplifies and reverts back to the dates again; b22 a stylish, tamed brute of a blend. A whisky as expansive as its creator. But a whole lot sexier. **40%**. *Kyndal.*

**Whyte & Mackay 21 Years Old (85)** n20 t22 f21 b22. A blend so well married it wears slippers and smokes a pipe. **43%**. *Kyndal.*

**Whyte & MacKay 30 Years Old (93)** n24 flawless fruit, amazingly intense clean malt and the softest of vanilla-laden grain, all entwined with a waft of light smoke; t22 a very fresh sherry feel dominates at first, then behind that arrives a procession of muted malty notes; f23 so soft and gentle you could wash a baby in it. Probably the result of W&M's marrying process, the subtlety is quite astonishing. Some treacle toffee on the very finish is still outflanked by some gathering spice; b24 there is no evidence of a tired cask here at all: the tastebuds are entirely engulfed by something enormous and deeply satisfying. **40%**. *Kyndal.*

**Whyte & Mackay High Strength (87)** n18 rubbery, the weak link; t22 beautifully sweet with lashings of lightly molassed sugar forming the bridge between the soft grain and harder, more rigid malts; f24 long and caressing, massively intense with hints of liquorice and malt concentrate. One of the best finishes of any blend on the market: positively sensual; b23 only the poor nose prevents this from being one of the greatest blends of them all. It has enormous character and confidence and flavours attack the tastebuds from all angles. Damn it: forget the nose, just go for it and enjoy something a little special. **52.5%.** *Kyndal.*

⋯∵ **Whyte & Mackay Original Aged Blended 40 Years Old (93) n**23 anyone remember fruit fudge? Well, this is it in its toasted form; with burnt raisin and a Melton Hunt Cake. So yummy...!! **t**24 appears to have some Fettercairn in there: nonsense malt when young, but when older opens up and delivers the kind of sublime, intense juicy dates to chew on here; also the grains begin to show a gossamer touch and, finally, a soft pastel-shaded barley sweetens the proceedings as the oak arrives; **f**22 ultra-light and melt-in-the mouth **b**24 I admit, when I nosed and tasted this at room temp, not a lot happened. Pretty, but closed. But once warmed in the hand up to full body temperature, it was obvious that Richard Paterson had created a quite wonderful monster of a blend offering so many avenues to explore that the mind almost explodes. Well done RP for creating something that further proves, and in such magnitude, just how warmth can make an apparently ordinary whisky something bordering genius. **45%**

**William Grant's 100 US Proof Superior Strength (92) n**23 sublime chocolate lime nose, decent oak; **t**24 big mouth arrival, lush and fruity with the excellent extra grain bite you might expect at this strength, just an extra degree of spice takes it into even higher orbit than before; **f**22 back to chocolate again with a soft fruit fade; **b**23 a fruitier drop now than it was in previous years but no less supremely constructed. **50% (100 US proof).**

**William Grant's Ale Cask Reserve (89) n**21 old, peculiar aroma of spilt beer: pretty malty to say the least at this strength; but now with some vivid grain poking through; **t**23 enormous complexity with myriad malt notes varying from sweet and chewy to bitter and biting; **f**22 quite long with some toffee and hops(??) Yes, I really think so; **b**23 a real fun blend that is just jam-packed with jagged malty notes. The hops were around more on earlier bottlings, but watch out for them. Nothing pint-sized about this: this is a big blend and very true in flavour/shape to the original with just a delicious shading of grain to really up the complexity. **40%.** *William Grant & Sons.*

**William Grant's 12 Years Old Bourbon Cask Reserve (89) n**22 a hard nose until warmed, then the malts blossom with sweeter balance; **t**23 delicate wafer dissolving in the mouth; the oak arrives quite early but behaves impeccably; padded out further by teasing smoke; **f**22 only towards the finish can the grain really be picked out, being one of a number of chewy layers; lovely cup cake death; **b**22 clever weight, but not one for the crash, bang, wallop merchants. **40%**

**Grant's Cask Selection Over 15 Years Old (90) n**23 firm, dry oak balances well against the fresher, fruity elements; delicate and distinguished; **t**23 very good grain on the arrival and middle with a distinct evenness throughout; **f**22 lots of chocolate character as the oak and grain gang together; **b**22 wonderful blending, as one might expect from this stable, but perhaps the finishing in sherry has just flattened slightly any pulse-quickening peaks that that may have been there. Even so, sheer quality. **40%.** *William Grant & Sons.*

**William Grant's 15 Years Old (85) n**21 **t**23 **f**20 **b**21. The grain and, later, caramel dominates but the initial delivery reveals the odd moment of sheer genius and complexity on max revs. **43%.** *William Grant & Sons.*

**William Grant's 18 Years Old Port Cask Reserve (86) n**22 (apologies in advance, but ...) bluebells in a dank, earthy, north-facing garden enlivened by beautifully fresh fruit; **t**23 it would probably not be possible to make the landing on the palate any softer: a mixture of firm and soft grain play their part in keeping the complexity going; **f**20 lengthy, but flattened rather by a prolonged toffee effect; **b**21 doesn't quite unravel the way you might wish or expect. **40%**

**William Grant's Classic Reserve 18 Years Old (93) n**24 salty, aroma of crashing waves on a beach, seaweed, yet no more than a hint of peat. Grains are crisp and biting but the malt blunts them: sensational; **t**23 big fruit kick-off followed by wave upon wave of breaking malt. The grain bites now and again. The complexity, especially with the arrival of the peat, is nothing short of mindboggling; **f**23 long, fruity and still softly peated. The grains offer gentle oak and a drifting sweetness; **b**23 few whiskies maintain such high levels of complexity from nose to finish. A true classic. **40%**

**William Grant's 25 Years Old (95) n**23 some serious oak, but chaperoned by top quality oloroso, itself thinned by firm and graceful grain; **t**24 sheer quality: complexity by the shovel-load as juicy fruits interact with darting, crisp barley; again the grain shows elegance both sharpening increasingly mouth-watering malt and softening the oak; **f**24 medium length, but not a single sign of fatigue: the sweet barley runs and runs and some jammy fruits charm. Just to cap it all, some wonderful spices dazzle and a touch of low roast Java enriches; **b**24 absolutely top-rank blending that appears to maximize every last degree of complexity. Most astonishing, though, is its sprightly countenance: even Scottish footballing genius Ally MacLeod struggled to send out Ayr Utd. sides with this kind of brio. And that's saying something! A gem. **43%**. *William Grant & Sons.*

**William Grant's Family Reserve (94) n**25 this, to me, is the perfect nose to any blend: harmonious and faultless. There is absolutely everything here in just-so proportions: a bit of snap and bite from the grain, teasing sweet malts, the faintest hint of peat for medium weight, strands of oak for dryness, fruit for lustre. Even Ardbeg doesn't pluck my strings like this glass of genius can; **t**23 exceptionally firm grain helps balance the rich, multi-layered malty tones. The sub-plot of burnt raisins and peek-a-boo peat adds further to the intrigue and complexity (if it doesn't bubble and nip around the mouth you have a rare sub-standard bottling); **f**22 a hint of caramel can be detected amid returning grains and soft cocoa tones: just so clean and complex; **b**24 there are those puzzled by my obvious love affair with blended whisky – both Scotch and Japanese – at a time when malts are all the rage. But take a glass of this and carefully nurture and savour it for the best part of half an hour and you may begin to see why I believe this to be the finest art form of whisky. For my money, this brand – brilliantly kept in tip-top shape by probably the world's most naturally gifted blender – is the closest thing to the blends of old and, considering it is pretty ubiquitous, it defies the odds for quality. It is a dram with which you can start the day and end it: one to keep you going at low points in between, or to celebrate the victories. It is the daily dram that has everything. **40%**

**William Grant's Sherry Cask Reserve (82) n**20 **t**22 **f**20 **b**20. Raspberry jam and cream from time to time. Very attractive, but a somewhat plodding dram that's content in second gear. **40%**. *William Grant & Sons.*

**William Lawson's Finest (83) n**19 **t**21 **f**21 **b**22. Not only has the label become more colourful, but so, too, has the whisky. However that has not interfered with the joyous old-fashioned grainy bite. A complex and busy blend from the old charm school. **40%**

**William Lawson's Scottish Gold Aged 12 Years (88) n**22 **t**23 **f**22 **b**21. For years Lawson's 12 was the best example of the combined wizardry of clean grain, unpeated barley and good bourbon cask that you could find anywhere in the world: a last-request dram before the firing squad. Today it is still excellent, but just another sherried blend. What's that saying about if it's not being broke...? **40%**

**William Lawson's 21 Years Old (90) n**23 soft apple-cinnamon overture with deft malt; **t**24 the grain arrives early and is clean and precise; the malt forms an alliance with softer grains while the crisper ones cuts like a knife through the palate; **f**21 the malt falls away quickly leaving clean grain; **b**22 the stunningly complex nose and first minute on the palate is a hard act to follow – too hard for the finale. Only a small tinker away from being an absolute must-have-at-allcosts classic. **40%**

**William Lawson's Founder's Reserve Aged 18 Years (96) n**24 just so gloriously intricate and with teasing aromas; never less than spellbinding....etc etc; **t**25 {remove "yes, its Lawson's....am stunned} {after "caressed with honeytoasted malt" add} The subtlety has been cranked up beyond belief, almost beyond scale, by the most enormously skilful use of dissolving peat. Best taken as a pretty decent mouthful and open the mouth to let in the air; **f**23 long vanilla notes with soft, smoky spice: the finish is short-ish ... probably all the excitement; **b**24 sensual and seductive, this quite extraordinary dram was just what I needed after the relative disappointment of Lawson's 12. Such is the sheer élan, the brilliance of the whisky and the blending behind it, a bottle of this sits in my living-room as an everyday, tangible, drinkable reminder that in a world that can often be so crushingly average and crass, we are still capable at times of genius and the creation of beauty. And hopefully the ability to appreciate it. **40%**

**William Peel Founder's Premium Aged 7 Years (77) n**18 **t**20 **f**20 **b**19. A decent, solid blend. **40%**. *France*.

**Windsor Aged 12 Years Premier (84) n**20 **t**22 **f**21 **b**21. A sweet, jam-tart of a blend that offers silk and grace but also a tad too much blandness. **40%**. *Diageo*.

**Windsor Aged 17 Years Super Premium (89) n**23 a fabulous aroma which bombards the nose with both luxurious grain and a hint of something smoky above the butter-honey theme; **t**22 sweet, as is the house style, with a Demerara coating to the crisp malt and gathering vanilla; silky and voluptuous throughout; **f**22 a gentle, soft-textured landing with an echo of spice; **b**22 still a little on the safe side for all its charm and quality. An extra dose of complexity would lift this onto another level altogether. **40%**. *Diageo*.

**Windsor 21 Years Old (90) n**20 fruity and weighty but something a bit lactic and lethargic from some old bourbon casks has crept in; **t**23 excellent oils surround the silk to help amplify the intensity of the fruit and drifting smoke; **f**24 some spiciness that shows towards the middle really takes off now as drying vanilla counters the sweet grains; **b**23 recovers fabulously from the broken nose and envelopes the palate with a silky-sweet style unique to the Windsor scotch brand. Excellent. **40%**. *Diageo*.

**Wm Morrisons Finest Scotch (71) n**18 **t**18 **f**17 **b**18. A lot of the old caramel this was caked in has been stripped away. What it reveals, though, isn't too pretty!! Supermarket fodder. **40%**

**Ye Monks** bot lot L5110 **(83) n**21 **t**20 **f**21 **b**21. "A Curious Old Whisky," claims the front label. Not really, unless you regard finding such a decently complex yet light blend in Venezuela a curiosity. Just enough fruit and malt plus cocoa on the finale to demand a refill at the bar. **40%**. *Diageo/Donald Fisher*.

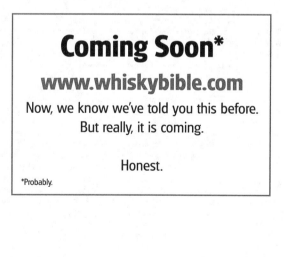

# Irish Whiskey

**A**s is the way with Empires, they grow then blossom and, finally, fall. And so it is now in Ireland.

Until the advent of the Cooley distillery in the late '80s, all Ireland's whiskey was made under the umbrella of Irish Distillers. And for a short period in the '90s it looked like it would be so again when ID tried to consume Cooley whole. But they choked on it and had to spit out when the Irish Government ruled against the move in the interests of competition. Cooley continues to this day as a maverick distiller helping forge new interest and markets in Irish whiskey.

That left Irish Distillers' owners, Pernod Ricard, with Ireland's two other distilleries. In the south they held Midleton, near Cork, where their stupendous pot still whiskey is made. And in the north, just two miles from the cliffs of Antrim, the malt distillery of Old Bushmills dating all the way back to 1784. That was until last year. Then, as part of Great Whisky Merry-Go-Round following Pernod's acquisition of Allied and all the resultant sell-ons, Diageo parted with the stunning sum of £200 million and in return got The Old Bushmills Distillery (Established 1874) and all its satelite blends and brands.

For a year or so Irish Distillers' blender Billy Leighton has been travelling to Midleton and back to Bushmills in a dual role as blender for both companies, though of course being an Irish Distillers man through and through but helping Diageo create their own blending team. His work is just about complete and soon he will be letting go of the ties that have held him to Bushmills most of his professional life. Though his imput at Midleton has already seen some interesting developments, with an apparent improvement in Midleton Very Rare and his putting together of the stunning Redbreast 15, I cannot believe that there will not be a major tweak in Billy's big heart when he says goodbye at Bushmills for the last time. And just to prove it, even now in July 2007 he still has an office there - but no official position. That might be because the new blender at Bushmills no sooner got her feat under her new desk than she was off on maternity leave. A first, it is believed, in Irish whiskey-making history.

Without doubt Redbreast 15 is the most significant development in Irish whiskey for the last few years. Long have I wailed and gnashed my teeth that more was not done with their pot still stocks, as relatively low as I know they are. For 15 years I have been pearching myself on the shoulder of every Irish Distillers executive I can find asking them to bring out pot still (that type of whiskey made from a mixture of malted and unmalted barley unique to Ireland - and now Midleton distillery in particular) as something above the usual Irish Distillers norm of 40abv and at a variation of ages. Yes, I was told. Great idea. It would happen one day, I was reassured. Just needed the stock. And the market.

They have at last responded, I am told, to a request from by Le Maison du Whisky in Paris who required something similar to sell. The result is Jim Murray's Whisky Bible 2007 Irish Whiskey of the Year. And a lot of interest from drinkers who before rarely gave Irish a second glance. Or chance. Now, if I can get a result for my constant beseeching them to tone down - and one day remove - colouring from Midleton Very Rare and Powers in particular....

But after all the palaver surrounding Irish Distillers and Diageo, it's great to see Cooley now grabbing the headlines and for all the right reasons. In March 2007 one of the most beautiful whisk(e)y sites in the world, Locke's Distillery at Kilbeggan, changed from being a sealed-in-aspic museum to a working one. A 2,000 litre still has been installed there and is now contentedly making spirit from low wines produced at Cooley's original distillery up north. With Irish Distillers moving from their offices at the old Jameson Distillery in Dublin and Mitchell's of Green Spot fame this year quitting their famous shop in Kildare Street, this was a shot in the arm Irish whiskey history needed very badly.

And just to round things off for them, Colley have picked up their first-ever Jim Murray's Whisky Bible Irish Whiskey of the Year with their sophisticated Madeira Fishish Tyrconnell. How long before Kilbeggan Distillery picks up it's first award...?

Key
- ● **Major Town or City**
- ⛰ Distillery

## Pure Pot Still
### MIDLETON (old distillery)

**Midleton 25-y-o Pot Still** db **(92) n**24 **t**24 **f**21 **b**23. A really enormous whiskey that is in the truest classic Irish style. The un-malted barley really does make the tastebuds hum and the oak has added fabulous depth. Interesting when tasted against an American rye – the closeness of the character is there to be experienced, but also the differences. A subtle mature whiskey of unquestionable quality. Superb. **43%**

**Midleton 30-y-o Pot Still** db **(85) n**19 **t**22 **f**22 **b**22 a typically brittle, crunchy Irish pot still where the un-malted grains have a telling say. The oak has travelled as far as it can without having an adverse effect. A chewy whiskey which revels in its bitter-sweet balance. An impressively tasty and fascinating insight into yesteryear. **45%**

**Midleton 1973 Pure Pot Still** db **(95) n**24 **t**24 **f**23 **b**24 the enormous character of true Irish pot still whiskey (a mixture of malted and unmalted barley) appears to absorb age better than most other grain spirits. This one is in its element. But drink at full strength and at body temp (it is pretty closed when cool) for the most startling – and memorable effects. I have no idea how much this costs. But if you can find one and afford it ... then buy it!!

### MIDLETON (new distillery)

**Green Spot (93) t**23 mouthwatering and fresh on one level, honey and menthol on another; **t**24 crisp, mouthwatering with a fabulous honey burst, alarmingly sensuous; **f**23 faint coffee intertwines with the pot still. The thumbprint thread of honey remains but a touch more caramel than yore; **b**23 this honeyed state has remained a few years, and its shar ness has now been regained. Complex throughout. Unquestionably one of the world's greatest branded whiskies. **40%.** *Irish Distillers for Mitchell & Son, Dublin.*

**Green Spot 10 Year Old Single Pot Still** dist 93 **(92) n**23 firm barley and orangey fruit with gentle hints of early bourbon: some serious ageing effect on this; **t**22 mouthwatering and firm, then a gradual increase in the barley input and spices; f24 shafts of honey throws a sweetening light on the bitter marmalade; b23 launched to celebrate the 200th anniversary of this wonderful Dublin landmark, this is bottled from three mixed bourbon casks of Irish Pot Still. The extra age has detracted slightly from the usual vitality of the standard Green Spot (an 8-y-o) but its quality still must be experienced. **40%**. *Mitchell & Son. 1000 bottles.*

**Green Spot 12 Year Old Single Pot Still** dist 91 **(93) n**24 spices and zesty oranges abound, even a distant trace of coriander; uncompromising barley sugar and heather; **t**24 a stunningly wonderful arrival: layers of sweet malt at first, but that takes a battering from much sharper, more prickly grains and spices. An enormous, vigorous mouthful; **f**24 a degree of bourbon-style liquorice, vanilla and caramel; **b**23 a single cask restricted to exactly 200 bottles to mark the 200th anniversary of the grand old man of Kildare Street, this is the first Middleton pot still I have seen at this strength outside of a lab. A one-off in every sense. **58%**.

**Redbreast 12 Years Old (90) n**23 unhurried display of ripe fruits which, together with the sharpness of the pot still, reminds me of a firm, pure rye, only this is a tad spicier; **t**23 more lazy spice, though not before the shock waves of complex, juicy barley notes on a field of clean sherry; **f**22 lingering fruity toffee-sherry; **b**22 remains an all-Ireland institution: one of the few pure pot-still whiskeys still around. Amazing to think this was a dead duck until my book Jim Murray's Irish Whiskey Almanac was released in 1994 when the brand was due to be withdrawn. The only change over those passing dozen years is that the sherry now is a tad lighter, the heavy effect once being similar to that found in the equally glorious Jameson 1780. Not to be confused with the rare blend Redbreast Blend (see Irish Blends) **40%**. *Irish Distillers.*

**Redbreast 15 Years Old** db **(94) n**23 seductive soft fruit wrapped in a hard barley shell. A slight soapy blemish, but minor; **t**24 such enormity and depth fair takes the breath away; soft hints of citrus amid the pulsing grain. Stunning clarity and delicate spice. Extraordinary; **f**23 multi-layered, panning out with barley-edged cocoa; **b**24 for years I have been pleading for Irish Distillers to launch a pot still at 46%, natural colour and unchillfiltered. Well, I've got two out of three wishes. And what we have here is a truly great Irish whiskey and my pulse races in the certain knowledge it can get better still... **46%. ncf.** *France.*

## OLD COMBER

**Old Comber 30 Years Old Pure Pot Still (88) n**23 **t**24 **f**20 **b**21. A classic example of a whiskey spending a few summers too many in wood: increasing age doesn't equal excellence. That said, always very drinkable and early on positively sparkles with a stunning mouthfeel. Out of respect for the old I have made the markings for taste cover the first seven or eight seconds ... **40%**

## TULLAMORE

**Knappogue Castle 1951** bott 87 **(93) n**23 heady mix of over-ripe – almost black – banana and big oak. Molasses and demerara sugar mixed with honey, ripe greengages and pepper ... almost rum-like; **t**24 big, booming. Rich start, attractively oily and juicy. The unmalted barley and even oats show well while the middle provides plenty of estery Jamaican pot-still rum; **f**22 long, hard and brittle – as to be expected from an Irish of this genre. Bourbon-style vanilla with chewy liquorice. An estery, vaguely honeyed finale; **b**24 highly individualistic. Another year in cask might have tipped this over the edge. We are talking brinkmanship here with a truly awesome display of flavour profile here ranging from traditional Irish pot to bourbon via Jamaican pot-still rum. A whiskey of mind-boggling duplicity, tricking the tastebuds into one sensation and then meandering off on a different tangent altogether. About as complex and beguiling as a straight Irish whiskey ever gets. **40%**. *Great Spirits.*

## Single Malt
### COOLEY

**Connemara** bott code L5045 db **(85) n**22 **t**20 **f**22 **b**21 better, but still not quite at its best as it finds balance hard to come by. **40%**. *Cooley.*

**Connemara Cask Strength** db **(94) n**23 a mixture of turf smoke and bonfires; **t**23 unbelievably sweet at first despite the close attention of drying oak, but the smoke chimes in with an outrageously spicy attack; f24 burnt toast and liquorice; a mixture of medium and heavy Java coffee, lightly sweetened with Demerara sugar, makes for one giant finale; **b**24 at first it is hard to see the direction this malt is taking. Give it a while, and on about the third tasting you realise there is more to the madness than meets the eye. Superb, so it is!! **58.9%**

**Connemara Aged Twelve Years** bott code L5044 db **(91)** n23 youthful, with myriad citrus notes trying to outdazzle the gathering peat; shows great subtlety and fun; t22 refreshing, with the barley insisting on behaving half the age it actually is. The smoke appears lethargic but grows into a spicy crescendo; f22 lots of vanilla amid the dusty malt; lots of coffee fudge to balance the smoke; **b**24 the best bottling yet with complexity a byword here. **40%**. *Cooley.*

**The Tyrconnell** db **(89)** n22 oranges and cedar, clean malt and courteous oak; t23 blemish free, so clean and mouthwatering but with a hint of something almost salty; f21 pretty long with the malt continuing to buzz around the palate. The vanilla also begins to show well; **b**23 this is easily the best Tyrconnell yet. The quality of The Tyrconnell has been maintained impressively over the last couple of years and the score might rise higher should they manage to lose that caramel flatness towards the middle and finish. **40%**

◦◦ **The Tyrconnell Aged 10 Years Port Finish** db **(93)** n23 puckering fruit with a hint of spicy menace; t23 firm body at first – to the point of shattering; oils out rather beautifully with a touch of raspberry preserve before going all solid again; f24 very soft spices and lots of fruity cocoa; **b**24 Cooley has excelled with its first serious foray into cask finishing. I didn't think this could be topped – until I came across the Madeira version. This, though, is like a fruit and nut chocolate bar – without the nuts. Wonderful. **46%**

◦◦ **The Tyrconnell Aged 10 Years Madeira Finish** db **(95)** n24 apricots jelly, marzipan and orange-mango hybrid: just about unique; t24 supreme balance of oil to barley with intense malt spinning around the tastebuds, kept in company by an astonishingly thick oaky-fruity-milkycocoa backdrop; f23 banana milkshake and vanilla; **b**24 this has to be one of the finest Madeira finishes I've ever come across. The balance defies belief while the higher notes make one purr. I am quite astonished. **46%**

◦◦ **The Tyrconnell Aged 14 Years** Cask no. 3179, rotation K92/25 db **(93)** n23 apple blossom (no, honestly!), cedar wood and still remnants of ultra clean barley; t23 refreshingly rich barley offering a shard of golden syrup to its perfectly lush delivery; f23 long, soft vanilla, a touch of tannin and those continuing gentle oils....sigh, what bliss!! **b**24 By rotation, K92 means it was distilled in 1992. Which just proves this distillery really has come of age, because, make no mistake, this is a belter.... **46%**

**The Tyrconnell (Limited Edition)** db **(84)** n19 t21 f22 **b**22. Lovely citrus on nose and palate, but goes curiously flat at point of entry. Even so, lots of charm and sophistication, especially on the finish. **40%**. *Cooley. 5000 bottles. Confusingly, the label says "Single Malt" and "Pure Pot Still".*

**Avoca (76)** n19 t20 f18 **b**19. Chewy and sweet at first but turns bitter as the grain and oak bite. **40%**. *Cooley for Aldi.*

**Cadenhead's Cooley Aged 13 Years** bott 05 **(93)** n24 attractively smoked: orange and mango juice with the kippers; t23 multi-shaded smoke fighting on varying levels with an influx of natural oaky-caramel and unusual oils; f23 prickly spices and then a rerun to a semi-gristy sweetness; **b**23 absolutely top-rate peaty Irish. **60.6%**. *228 bottles.*

**Cadenhead's Cooley Aged 14 Years** bott May 06 **(80)** n20 t21 f19 **b**20. Slightly hot and perhaps not from the best bourbon barrel to visit Ireland. **58.7%**. *222 btls.*

**Cadenhead's World Whiskies Cooley Peated Single Malt Individual Cask Aged 12 Years** bott Feb 05 **(93)** n23 bonfires and grist. Just so attractive! t24 the sweet smoke laps around the tastebuds with some wonderful fresh barley and oranges lightening things up; f23 long, spicy waves of oak and barley. Relaxed and completely in tune with itself; **b**23 an exceptionally fine cask of very well made whiskey. **59.7%**. *216 bottles.*

◦◦ **Cadenhead's World Whiskies Cooley Aged 15 Years** Bourbon Barrel, bott May 07 **(94)** n23 perhaps as nonchalant a peat delivery as you are likely to find – kilny yet so clean! t24 soft and silky oils carrying the most sensual, sweet and mildly gristy peat imaginable: sublime.. f23 long fade with again those perfectly-weighted oily peats callings all the shots... **b**24 perhaps the oldest Irish peated single barrel malt to hit the market for over a century, this is nigh on faultless and a revelation... **58.6%.** *222 bottles.*

**Clonmel (78) n**19 **t**22 **f**18 **b**19. Starts beautifully, brightly but dies under a welter of toffee blows. Won a Gold Medal in Brussels, apparently ... amazing: shows you what a lifetime of drinking Cognac does to some people ... Claims to be "Pure Pot Still". It isn't (in Irish terms): it's malt. **40%.** *Celtic Whisky Co.*

**Clonmel Peated Aged 8 Years (86) n**22 **t**23 **f**20 **b**21. Take the toffee away and you would have one hell of an Irish. Claims to be "Pure Pot Still". It isn't (in Irish terms): it's malt. **40%.** *Celtic Whisky Compagnie.*

⸭ **Craoi na Mona Irish Malt Whiskey (68) n**16 **t**18 **f**17 **b**17 I'm afraid my Gaelic is slipping these days: I assume Craoi na Mona means "Feinty, badly made smoky malt"... (that's the end of my tasting for the day...) **40%**

**Glen Dimplex (88) n**23 solid malt with a hint of honey; charming, blemish-free; **t**22 gentle development of the malts over simple dusty vanilla; **f**21 quite dry, spiced and a little toffeed; **b**22 overall, clean and classically Cooley. **40%.**

**Jon, Mark and Robbo's The Smooth Sweeter One Irish Malt (89) n**22 a dry, oak-rich vanilla aroma with barley, dried pine nuts and distant honeybourbon to balance; **t**23 much more fresh and mouthwatering than the nose suggests with a thick dollop of honey for the main theme: pretty young, almost embryonic, whiskey; **f**22 decent spice, nut oils and then more vanilla and late cocoa-caramel; **b**22 seriously enjoyable whiskey for all its youth, especially for those with a sweet tooth. **40%.** *Easy Drinking Whisky Co.*

**Knappogue Castle 1990 (91) n**22 **t**23 **f**22 **b**24. For a light whiskey this shows enormous complexity and depth. Genuine balance from nose to finish; refreshing and dangerously more-ish. Entirely from bourbon cask and personally selected and vatted by a certain Jim Murray. **40%. nc.** *Great Spirits.*

**Knappogue Castle 1991 (90) n**22 **t**23 **f**22 **b**23. Offers rare complexity for such a youthful malt especially in the subtle battles that rage on the palate between sweet and dry, malt and oak and so on. The spiciness is a great foil for the malt. Each cask picked and vatted by the author. **40%. nc.** *Great Spirits.*

**Knappogue Castle 1992 (94) n**23 **t**23 **f**24 **b**24 a different Knappogue altogether from the delicate, ultra-refined type. This expression positively revels in its handsome ruggedness and muscular body: a surprisingly bruising yet complex malt that always remains balanced and fresh – the alter-ego of the '90 and '91 vintages. I mean, as the guy who put this whiskey together, what do you expect? But it's not bad if I say so myself and was voted the USA's No. 1 Spirit. Virtually all vanished, but worth getting a bottle if you can find it (I don't receive a penny – I was paid as a consultant!). **40%. nc.** *Great Spirits.*

**Knappogue Castle 1993** (*see* under Bushmills)

**Knappogue Castle 1994** (*see* under Bushmills)

**Locke's Aged 8 Years Crock (92) n**23 pounding, intense, grassy-sweet barley; **t**24 excellent mouth arrival and almost immediately a honey-rich delivery of lush, slightly oily malt: wonderful, wonderful stuff! **f**22 soft oak tempers the barley and a degree of toffee digs in and flattens the .....; **b**23 much, much better cask selection than of old: some real honey casks here. A crock of gold...! **40%.**

**Magilligan Cooley Pure Pot Still Single Malt (91) n**22 slightly waxy and honeyed; **t**22 beautiful arrival of highly intense, spotlessly clean malt. The sweetness level is near perfect; **f**24 spiceless – unlike the previous bottling. Now just the longest fade-out of malt concentrate in Irish whiskey...and with a touch of honey for good measure; **b**23 ...or maybe not..!! **43%.** *Ian MacLeod.* ⊙ ⊙

**Magilligan Irish Whiskey Peated Malt 8 Years Old (89) n**21 old, blackening banana and peat; **t**23 lush, sweet barley, wonderfully oiled with the softest injection of smoke; **f**22 long, long fade with those oils working wonders. The smoke gathers in intensity considerably before dispersing; **b**23 such a different animal from the docile creature that formally passed as Magilligan peated. Quite lovely...and very classy. **43%.** *Ian Macleod Distillers.* ⊙ ⊙

**Magilligan Vintage 1991 Sherry Finish (79) n**22 **t**19 **f**19 **b**19. The rare experience of a Cooley in sherry butt. But one doesn't quite hang together. **46%**

**Merry's Single Malt (83) n**20 **t**22 **f**20 **b**21. Ultra-clean barley rich nose is found on the early palate. The finish is flat, though. **40%**

⸬ **Michael Collins Irish Whiskey Single Malt db (76) n**20 **t**19 **f**19 **b**18. The sooner some people in this industry realize that Cooley is far too good and delicate a malt to withstand this insane degree of caramel, the better off everyone will be. **40%** *(80 proof)*.

⸬ **Michael Collins Irish Whiskey Single Malt db (68) n**17 **t**18 **f**17 **b**16. Bloody hell, I thought. Didn't anyone get my message from last year? Apparently not – and it's our fault as the tasting notes above were accidentally edited out before they went in. Sorry. But the caramel in the latest bottling has been upped to take the whisky from deep gold to bronze. Making this among the most over-coloured single malt I have tasted in years. Please guys. For the love of whiskey. Please let us taste exactly what a great malt this could be. **40%** *(80 proof)*.

⸬ **Milroy's of Soho Cooley 1999** First fill Bourbon, cask lot K99/20, dist 13 Jun 99, bott 27 Mar 06 **(85) n**21 **t**22 **f**21 **b**21 You can rest assured that with the exception of Cooley blender Noel Sweeney no other living person has tasted as many different Cooleys from the cask as I have. And I have never yet found a cask like this one: showing the exotic fruit one normally associates with a half clapped-out barrel; the body is oil on silk. I am quite bemused and tasted blind wouldn't have marked this down as a Cooley in about 1,000 million years - give or take the odd 200,000 decades.... Weirdo Whisky of the Year, without doubt. **46%**. *289 bottles.*

**Sainsbury's Single Malt Irish Whiskey (84) n**21 **t**22 **f**20 **b**21. A decent spice buzz to the lively malt and coal smoke. **40%**

**Shanagarry (76) n**19 **t**20 **f**18 **b**19. Pleasant, but lacks depth. **40%**. *For Intermarche France. Note: Label says "Pure Pot Still". But it is single malt.*

**Shannahan's (92) n**23 beautifully young, fresh and zesty: this distillery's best style; **t**22 refreshing, clean barley that tries to be little else; **f**24 excellent late complexity as some first-class soft vanilla appears; more citrus cleans the palate; **b**23 Cooley natural and unplugged: quite adorable. **40%**

**Slieve na gcloc Single Peated Malt (84) n**21 **t**20 **f**22 **b**21. No, I wasn't drunk when I typed the name. And I was sober enough to detect a slight feinty note that reappears towards the death. Until then, curiously thin. A pleasant cocoa and peat malt, but one not quite gelling as it perhaps might. **40%**. *For Oddbins.*

**The Spirit Safe & Cask Selection Cooley 1991 12 Years Old** dist Sept 91, bott Oct 03 **(89) n**22 **t**23 **f**22 **b**22 struggles to find a rhythm but the acacia honey holds it together. **43%. nc ncf.** *Celtique Connexion.*

**Vom Fass Cooley 4 Years Old (82) n**22 **t**21 **f**19 **b**20. Wonderfully clean; for a Cooley, actually has extra sheen and copper richness. Just fades towards the finish and lacks depth. **40%**. *Austria.*

**Vom Fass Cooley Peated 8 Years Old (89) n**22 gently smoked; lightly cured bacon; **t**23 sweet delivery with a wonderful honey shadow to the smoke; **f**22 oily liquorice and vanilla; **b**22 much more recognisable. This is a treat from an above average cask, though the peating is subtle and subdued. **40%**. *Austria.*

**Waitrose Irish Single Malt (83) n**20 **t**22 **f**20 **b**21. Pulsating sweet malt: clean as an Irish whistle and beautifully mouthwatering. Really impressive. With the slightly flat finale I suspect it has caramel: without it, it would be better still. **40%**. *UK.*

## OLD BUSHMILLS

**Bushmills 10 Years Old** Matured in Two Woods db **(82) n**22 **t**21 **f**19 **b**20. A beefed-up, sherried number compared to a few years back; attractive but in need of finding some complexity from somewhere. **40%**. *Irish Distillers*

**Bushmills 12 Years Old Distillery Reserve** db **(87) n**22 a near sneezeinducing black pepper bite to the rolling citrus and malt; **t**23 intense, marmaladesharp malt and big spice; **f**21 vanilla and caramel; **b**21 improved in recent years with a distinct fruitiness now to the middle. **40%**

**Bushmills Select Casks Aged 12 Years** Married with Caribbean Rum cask db **(95) n**23 unusual moist rum and raisin cake effect: effective and just enough spice to deliver extra complexity. Just the very slightest hint of bourbon, too; **t**24 adorable malt richness; biscuity and stupendously seasoned yet always remains fresh and mouthwatering. The sweetness is very cleverly controlled; f24 there are just so many layers to this: the oak is a growing force, but restricts itself to a vanilla topping; b24 one of the most complex Bushmills in living memory, and probably since it was established in 1784. **40%**

**Bushmills Aged 16 Years** Matured in Three Woods db **(88)** n20 a touch of sulphur detracts somewhat from the fresh fruit delivery. Still get pomegranates, though! t24 seismic waves of spicy fruit, juicy and salivating in effect; f21 that haunting of poor sherry just takes the edge off the fun; b23 until the advent of the wonderful Bushmills Select Casks 12 and the extraordinary improvement in the awesome Bushmills 21 this was leader of the distillery tribe. Would have been overthrown irrespective of the sulphur, which is hardly the norm for this distillery whose sherry casks are usually the finest in the world's whisky businesss. **40%**

**Bushmills Rare Aged 21** Years Matured in Three Woods Madeira Finish, bott 04 db **(96)** n25 it doesn't come much better than this as a variable but unbelievably clean grape intensity flickers like twinkling lights. Yet for all this the malt still has much to say and the oak butts in with some teasing mocha and spice; t24 amazing! After three mouthfuls or so, it's still impossible to pinpoint what is happening exactly. What I do get is a chocolate effect, like the chocolate the ice-cream man pours on your whipped ice-cream. There are also sultanas in there and walnuts and drier Madeira-induced coffee notes, which then sweeten to give the effect of iced coffee-flavoured biscuits. To complete the harmony youwould need spice...and it turns up on cue; f23 after further layers of grape and spice, becomes much more serene with oakiness taking a slight chalky effect; b24 it looks as though the early gremlins that got into the first bottlings of this expression have been overcome. The harmony here defies description, let alone belief, especially in a golden period about ten seconds after it hits the mouth through to the early part of the finish. Is this a one-off vatting that has hit heights hitherto thought impossible: a one-off freak? Or will the 2005 bottling somehow capture this improbable brilliance? I wouldn't take the chance: if you can find this bottling now, get a case!! **40%**

**The Old Bushmills Single Cask 1989 Bourbon Barrel** cask 7986 **(88)** n22 big vanilla thrust; t23 quite an outstanding intensity to the buttery malt with the sweetness almost on a precise curve upwards; some oak offers countering dryness; f21 surprising toffee late on; b22 perhaps a better malt than the early nose suggests, but very unusual in style for this distillery and would mark higher but for the debilitating toffee. **56.5%. ncf.** *Specially selected for Canada.*

**The Old Bushmills Distillery Single Cask Bourbon Barrel 1989** db cask 8139 **(88)** n21 fruity, but otherwise languid, with some dry, solid age apparent; t23 juicy malt that really allows the barley to shine; f22 long and revelling in its fresh barley richness; some very late, papery and dry oak at the death; b22 Old Bushmills really springing a surprise with its depth for the age. **56.5%. USA.**

**The Old Bushmills Distillery Single Cask Bourbon Barrel 1989** db cask no 8140 **(84)** n20 t22 f21 b21. Quite a fiery number, closed early on but with excellent cocoa finale. **56.5%. USA.**

**The Old Bushmills Distillery Single Cask Bourbon Barrel 1989** db cask no 8141 **(88)** n20 dry; soft barley; t23 pure Bushmills in all its chalky yet oaky barley richness: distinctive and delightful with a bit of a nip; f23 seriously impressive on the barley front with better balanced cocoa; b22 the only one of the three bourbon casks to scream "Old Bushmills" at you for its unique style. **56.5%. USA.**

**The Old Bushmills Distillery Single Cask Rum Barrel 1989** cask no 7110 db **(81)** n21 t20 f20 b20. Big, biting and hot but some serious malt. **53.7%. USA.**

**The Old Bushmills Distillery Single Cask Rum Barrel 1989** cask no 7112 db **(84)** n20 t21 f22 b21. Sweet and attractively simple with excellent late malt. **53.7%. USA.**

**The Old Bushmills Single Cask 1989 Rum Barrel** cask no. 7115 **(93)** n22 delicate coating of sugar over malt; t24 a uniquely complex series of wonderful, prickly, banana-essence, liquorice-hinting waves of malt and spice: labyrinthine hardly does it justice; f23 the honied, mildly toffeed richness of the malt seems to multiply in intensity, as does the gentle hint of bourbon: a finish from near the top echelon; b24 some in Canada may have seen me taste this for the first time with the country's most effortlessly beautiful and charming tv presenter Nancy Sinclair. I said then I thought we had a great malt on our hands, and a later tasting of it under more controlled – and private – conditions confirmed those initial suspicions. A real honey: elegant, deeply desirable, lip-smacking, memorable and something to get your tongue round and experience slowly at least once in your lifetime. And the whiskey's not bad, either.... **53.7%. ncf.** *Canada.*

**The Old Bushmills Distillery Single Cask Rum Barrel 1989** db cask no 7122 **(77)** n18 t19 f21 **b**19. Hot and refuses to hang together although the finale is a late delight. **53.7%.** *USA.*

**The Old Bushmills Distillery Single Cask Sherry Butt 1989** db cask no 7428 **(79)** n19 t20 f20 **b**20. Rich and malty in parts but hot and just not quite gelling. **53.7%**

**The Old Bushmills Distillery Single Cask Sherry Butt 1989** db cask no 7429 **(90)** n22 passion fruit among the citrus. Sensual and gentle; t22 gets into a malty stride from go then a slow burning sherry fuse; f23 delightful finish that is long, vanilla-rich but with the most subtle interwoven fruit and barley and natural caramel; **b**23 charismatic, charming, self-confident and supremely elegant. **53.7%.** *USA.*

**The Old Bushmills Distillery Single Cask Sherry Butt 1989** db cask no 7430 **(91)** n21 slightly sweaty armpit but a good malt recovery t23 sweet, enormously malty for a sherry-influenced dram f24 mildly salty, with many layers of sweet malt and spice that go on almost endlessly **b**23 this is a massively complex and striking Bushmills well worth finding: casks 7429 and 7430 could be almost twins...!! **53.7%.** *USA.*

**The Old Bushmills Single Cask 1989 Sherry Hogshead** cask no. 7431 **(78)** n20 t20 f19 **b**19. Wake me up when something happens: a real dullard. **53.7%. ncf.**

**Clontarf Single Malt (94)** n22 intense barley but clipped slightly; t24 mouth-watering, young, fresh and wonderfully busy. Outstanding blood orange clinging to the sharp barley edges; soft spices buzz and the juiciness intensifies; f24 long with myriad waves of fruity barley of varying intensity, sometimes bringing with them cocoa and mocha; **b**24 young, steady as a rock yet wonderfully perky: just so great to taste Bushmills at this sexily tender yet ripe age. Irish most excellent! **40%**

⋇ **The Irishman Single Malt** bottle no. E2496 **(83)** n20 t21 f21 **b**21 Highly pleasant malt but the coffee and toffee on the finish underline a caramel-style whiskey which may, potentially, offer so much more. **40%.** *Hot Irishman Ltd.*

**Knappogue Castle 1990** (*see* Cooley)
**Knappogue Castle 1991** (*see* Cooley)
**Knappogue Castle 1992** (*see* Cooley)

**Knappogue Castle 1993 (91)** n22 b22 f23 b24. A malt of exceptional character and charisma. Almost squeaky clean but proudly contains enormous depth and intensity. The chocolate finish is an absolute delight. Quite different and darker than any previous Knappogue but not dwarfed in stature to any of the previous three vintages. Created by yours truly. **40%. nc.** *Great Spirits.*

**Knappogue Castle 1994 (95)** n24 teasingly delicate and complex: first with a mouthwatering intertwining of fresh cut grass enlivened by hints of zesty lemon, then a mild floral tone. The sharpness is not blunted even by soft oaky vanilla. The whole is crisp, clean and vivid: a Bushmills nose that will leave you gasping; t24 soft, malty arrival at first which is delicately sweet, then an on-rush of lively barley notes flood around the tastebuds. The oak ties in with the natural zestiness to help form a wonderful bitter-sweet feel to the proceedings; f23 barley and oak remain in harmony as soft spices add extra warmth; unbelievably clean despite the subtle cocoa notes indicating advancing years. A shy oiliness keeps the sweeter notes locked to the roof of the mouth. Some late natural toffee/butterscotch dulls the brittleness of the barley; **b**24 the blender, I can tell you with uncanny insight, aimed at re-creating the delicate, complex feel of the K92 and this has been achieved with something to spare. Now the big question for him is: how the bloody hell does he improve on this? Perhaps by plugging the small gap between vatting and bottling where the extra time in the cask saw a minor degree of toffee develop, docking the brand by a point. But this remains the most sophisticated Knappogue of them all not least because of the extra depth. And the one of which I am most proud as there are 150 ex-bourbon casks here and not a single peep of an off-note. **40%.** *Castle Brands.*

**Knappogue Castle 1994** Lot no. L6 **(89)** n23 clean, pleasantly crisp barley; soft vanillas dance with the fresh grass; t24 beautifully weighted, multi-layered delivery where the clarity of barley is almost eye watering. Stunning...; **f**20 remains salivating at first, then goes slightly wrong as an annoyed oakiness dries things too fast and injects an off-key bitterness; **b**22 a wonderful whiskey in the Knappogue tradition, although this one was not done by its creator. That said, it does have an Achilles heel: the finish. This is the most important bit to get right, especially as this is the oldest Knappogue yet. But not enough attention has been paid to getting rid of the oak-induced bitterness. **40%.**

## Single Grain
### COOLEY

**Greenore 8 Years Old** db **(89) n**23 soft, sweet corn, delicious hints of bourbon; **t**22 rich, soft oils, melt-in-the-mouth grain and just a hint of barley for good measure; **f**22 crisps up as the oak returns; **b**22 just a lovely grain whiskey from one of the world's finest grain distilleries. **40%.**

## Blends

**Asda Finest Irish Whiskey (79) n**21 **t**20 **f**19 **b**19. Sweet, chunky, chewy: not unlike a chocolate toffee. Minimal complexity except for some lovely citrus on the nose. **40%.** *Cooley for Asda.*

**Ballygeary (80) n**20 **t**21 **f**20 **b**19. Fresh and mouthwatering with an impressive malty thrust. Decent oak, too. **40%.** *Cooley for Malt House Vintners.*

**Black Bush** (see Bushmills Black Bush)

**Brennan's** bott code L5033 **(86) n**21 **t**22 **f**21 **b**22. A very well put together blend with impressive malt magnitude. **40%.** *Cooley for Shaw Ross USA.*

**The Buena Vista** bott code L5051 **(84) n**20 **t**21 **f**22 **b**21. A much lighter, brighter, more integrated whiskey with attractive malt bite linking to the softer grain. Very decent blending for San Franciscans. Mr Delapre would have been proud. **40%.** *USA.*

**Bushmills Black Bush (91) n**24 amazingly spicy – a bit like the old 1608! – with clean but lively sherry and freshish malt. This is one crackerjack nose; **t**23 stunning: the sweetness is exemplary as it sits snugly between the enormity of the fruit and the clarity of the malt. Somewhere in there is a raisiny sheen; **f**21 dropped points for a toffee-caramel finale, which undermines some of the complexity. Even so, the sherry remains lip-smacking and the spices behave themselves; **b**23 the quality of the sherry used boggles the mind. Remains a true classic. My word, though, what I would do to see a 46% non-coloured, non-chill filtered version. **40%.** *Diageo.*

**Bushmills** (formerly Original) **(79) n**19 **t**20 **f**19 **b**21. A light blend that has improved dramatically in recent years. The aroma is of Fox's Biscuits Party Rings, as is the finish topped with some toffee and chocolate. **40%.** *Diageo.*

**Bushmills 1608 (88) n**22 massive surge of fruit and malt, intermingling with light spices with hardly any grain evidence; **t**23 pure silk: sherry holds the foreground allowing spices to build up from the rear; **f**22 at last a little grain appears, accentuating the sherry; **b**21 beautiful Irish that on the evidence of this bottling has turned away from big'n'spicy to a more velvety sherry number. **40%**

**Cassidy's Distillers Reserve (87) n**22 genuine balance and harmony between soft grain and even softer, fresher barley; caramel weighs it down: without that it would be a rare treat; **t**22 brilliant interaction between stunning grain and top quality malt is evident early on; **f**21 lush, sweeter than of old with a bit extra grain bite than of old; **b**22 some lilting, fresh complexity on nose and mouth arrival and even the toffee on the finish can't tellingly detract from a very high grade Cooley blend. **40%.** *Marks & Spencer, UK.* ☉ ☉

**Castelgy Gold Shield (81) n**20 **t**20 **f**20 **b**21. Strange name, familiar blend style from Cooley. This one does have a little extra fruit from somewhere on the nose and excellent young malt grip on the finish. **40%.** *Cooley for Lidl.*

**Clancey's** bott code L5037 **(87) n**22 really lovely grain firmness with a soft oaky, floral interjection; **t**22 deft and as soft as the nose; **f**21 just an extra shade of oaky bitterness at the death; **b**22 the excellent grain nose sets it up well and the rest is honest and very enjoyable. **40%.** *Cooley for Wm Morrison UK.*

**Clontarf Classic Blend (86) n**18 **t**23 **f**23 **b**22. This has to be treated as a new whiskey. Many moons back I created this as a 100% grain from Cooley, a velvet-soft job of real subtlety. These days, with me having no involvement, the whiskies are from Irish Distillers. This is no longer all grain, though the malt content is no more than fractional. And it really underscores the difference in style between Midleton and Cooley grain. For every degree Colley is soft and yielding, Midleton is unremittingly rigid. The nose (though not the taste) is recognizable to devotees of White Bush and Paddy. Which means aroma-wise, with the caramel, it's pretty austere stuff. But you cannot fault the delivery which is crisp, salivating and offering surprising sweetness and big citrus. Not bad once you adapt: in fact, seriously entertaining. **40%**. *Clontarf Irish Whiskey Co.*

**Clontarf Reserve (84)** n19 t22 f21 b22. Frighteningly similar to the Classic Blend with the rock-solid grain gouging into the tastebuds. Some extra, softening oil helps soften the blows. In fact, the palate doesn't have quite the same all-round charisma and snarling attitude. **40%**. *Clontarf Irish Whiskey Co.*

**Coleraine (74)** n18 t21 f18 b17. Another improved offering than compared to recent years: less firebrand and more sweet and sultry. Still lacks any real complexity although the mouth arrival is much, much more fulfilling than it once was. **40%**. *Irish Distillers.*

**Crested Ten** (see Jameson Crested Ten)

**Dunphys (68)** n16 t18 f17 b17. Hard-as-nails blend: rigid grain allows little other development. At least what appears a little pot still does give an Irish feel to it. **40%**. *Irish Distillers IR.*

**Delaney's Special Reserve** bott code L5036 **(89)** n23 the oak offers a surprising degree of floral subtlety, with pansies slightly outweighing the distant citrus: genuinely sophisticated; t22 silky early malt arrival but the malt gathers fast: quite sweet and lush; f22 subtlety the name of the game here, with the gentle oak adding a dusty finale; b22 vast, almost immeasurable improvement in this blend, with the grain showing beautifully and the malt really sharp and precise. In fact, this is really charming and a little classy. **40%**. ⊙

**Dundalgan Irish Gold Shield (80)** n20 t20 f19 b21. Light and refreshing. **40%**.

**Feckin Irish Whiskey (81)** n20 t21 f20 b20. Tastes just about exactly the feckin same as the Feckin Strangford Gold... **40%**. *The Feckin Drinks Co.*

**Finnegan (75)** n19 t19 f18 b19. A simple blend with good malt showing. **40%**

**Golden Irish (93)** n24 firm yet deeply complex with fabulous malt/grain texture. Text-book stuff; t22 voluptuous, silky, ultra malty and fresh; f23 long, with gathering grains and sublime vanilla; b24 a stunning, brilliantly balanced blend that groans with mouthwatering complexity. **40%**. *Cooley Distillers for Dunne's Stores IR.*

**Hewitts (87)** n22 big, intense, heavy malt-rich with some clean fruity-grapey notes in the background. Dark cherries and chocolate complete the mix; t22 intriguingly deep, packed with even more grapey fruitiness. The malt clings to the mouth in tandem with crisp grain, though the body is curiously oily and full; f20 custard creams and dry, thinner grain with just a late hint of malt; b23 a lovely blend that somehow manages to be light, medium and heavy at various stages. **40%** *Irish Distillers. The only blend from Midleton using exclusively malt and grain and no pot still (mixture of malted and unmalted barley).*

**Inishowen** bott code L7004 **(93)** n24 perhaps the most subtle aroma of any Irish blend; caressing lime and playful peat offer an immaculately clean and teasing nose; t23 the peats are still gentle but more telling than some recent bottlings, thanks to the crispness of the barley and clarity of the grain; f23 medium length soft vanilla and citrus with a gentle peaty underscore; b23 my smoky son...you have returned to your loving family...!!! **40%**. *Cooley.*

⋯ **The Irishman Superior Irish Whiskey** bott code L6299L059 **(93)** n23 chunky caramel perhaps, but the apple is green and inviting; even an inclusion of soft manuka honey and ginger – most un-Irish; t23 lush, with a distinct malt charge before the caramel and oaky spice arrive; f23 those spices really tick, accentuated by the contrasting molasses and more honey but doused in vanilla; b24 what a quite wonderful blend: not of the norm for those that have recently come onto the market and there is much more of the Irish Distillers about this than most. Forget about the smoke promised in the tasting notes on the label...it gives you everything else but. And that is one hell of a lot!! **40%**. *Hot Irishman Ltd.*

**Jameson (95) n**23 crisp pot still bounces off some firm and clean grain. Fresh sherry offers a softer dimension; **t**24 melt-in-the-mouth sherry is the prelude to brilliant pot-still sharpness. A real mouthful that you can suck and chew at the same time with some real bite in there; **f**24 vanilla, fruit and some prickly spice; **b**24 from a pretty boring bit-of-a-nothing whiskey to a sheer classic in the space of a decade: not bad going. The inclusion of extra pot still is one thing; getting the balance as fine as this is something else. Truly magnificent: this is the current Irish masterpiece. As classically Irish as someone called Seamus O'Crimmins. **40%.** ☉

**Jameson 12 Years Old (88) n**22 dusty, dry, soft grain; **t**23 superb delivery of mouth-watering malt and grape. The pot still, though about, is harder to locate, making for a softer middle; **f**21 gentle vanillas and muscovado sugar; **b**22 a softer, more grainy animal than it recently was with both the pot still and sherry in retreat. Beautiful, but not quite so uncompromisingly Irish. And a good distance away from the old 1780 version. **40%.** *Irish Distillers.* ☉ ☉

**Jameson 18 Years Old Third Batch ||**18-3 db **(89) n**21 **t**23 **f**22 **b**23. This is big Irish with attitude. Much closer to the first bottling, it cuts down on the honey slightly and offers a more bourbony character. That said, the pot still guarantees this as uniquely Irish. The spices amaze. Beautiful stuff. **40%**

**Jameson 18 Years Old Fourth Batch (83) n**21 **t**21 **f**20 **b**21. Very pleasant but limited degree of sparkle: the age is evident, as is the toffee. **40%.** *Irish Distillers.*

**Jameson 18 Years Old Fifth Batch (89) n**22 some enlivening pot still moments; very deep and fruity; **t**23 really delightful meeting between friendly pot still, oaky spice and fruit; **f**22 some toffee seeps in but the slight liquorice depth compensates slightly as the age really begins to sing ballads of yesteryear; **b**22 great to see this charming blend back on track; understated to the point of shyness. **40%.** *Irish Distillers.*

**Jameson 1780 Matured 12 Years (94) n**23 lush and confident, spicy and warming: there is a prevailing oloroso undercurrent head on against some sharp pot still; **t**24 a whiskey that fills the mouth with thick, bitter-sweet sherry, then the unmistakable delights of old pot still coupled with a short but effective flypast of spice. The pot still dominates – towards the middle after the early sherry lead; **f**23 pretty long with neither pot still nor sherry showing any signs of wanting to leave; **b**24 now discontinued and if you should see one hanging around an old off licence grab it with both hands. The 12-y-o that has taken its place appears to be using as much sherry, but it appears to be a lighter style, as is the pot still. The 1780 was the last commercial link with the old Irish whiskies I fell in love with in the early 70s. A colossus of an Irish, of a sherry type now entirely lost which couldn't come from any other country in the world. **40%**

**Jameson Crested Ten (88) n**23 the enormity of the pot still is awesome: lovely sherry-ginger balance; **t**23 amazingly clean sherry then traces of malt and vanilla; **f**19 too much toffee but some decent spice helps compensate; **b**23 a beautifully balanced whiskey let down only by the weak finish. **40%.** *Irish Distillers.*

**Jameson Distillery Reserve** (available at Jameson, Dublin) **(74) n**20 **t**20 **f**17 **b**17. Starts well but becomes flatter than the Irish Midlands. Nothing like as good as previous bottlings I have tasted. Just a one-off, I am sure. **40%.** *Irish Distillers.*

**Jameson Distillery Reserve** (*available at Midleton. See Midleton Distillery Reserve*)

**Jameson Gold (94) n**24 layered elements of soft honey and subtle, mildly bourbony oak criss-crossing the crisp pot still; **t**24 honey and barley all the way, wonderfully rich and silky, cocoa shows early too with a fruit chocolate character; **f**22 some age apparent towards the bitter-sweet finale, as is butterscotch; **b**24 if you don't enjoy this, then you just don't get what Irish whiskey is all about. Vattings vary from bottling to bottling, but this is quite representative and falls comfortably within its colourful spectrum. **40%.** *Irish Distillers.* ☉

**Kilbeggan** bott code L5054 **(80) n**19 **t**20 **f**21 **b**20. An improvement on recent years, though the nose is a bit dodgy. Just love the malt thrust half-way through the proceedings. **40%.** *Cooley, John Locke & Co. Ltd.*

**Kilgeary** bott code L4168 **(78) n**20 **t**21 **f**18 **b**19. Pleasant, especially the fleeting delicate grain on arrival, but this is way too feeble-bodied a blend to withstand the caramel onslaught. **40%.** *Cooley.*

**Locke's bott code L5039 (72)** n18 t19 f17 b18. Does a job of sorts, but never quite finds its character and finishes poorly. **40%**. *Cooley, John Locke & Co.*

**Merry's Special Reserve (75)** n20 t19 f18 b18. Dull. **40%**

**Michael Collins A Blend (77)** n19 t20 f19 b19. Michael Collins was known as the "big fellow". This pleasant, impressively spiced dram, might have enjoyed the same epithet had it not surrendered to and then been strangled by caramel on the finish. **40% (80 proof)**. *Cooley Distillery.* ⊙ ⊙

**Midleton Distillery Reserve (85)** n22 t22 f20 b21. A whiskey which, for all its muscovado sweetness offers some memorable barley moments. **40%**. *Irish Distillers Midleton Distillery only. Was once bottled as Jameson Distillery Reserve exclusive to Midleton. Changes character slightly with each new vatting. This one is some departure.*

**Midleton Very Rare 1984 (70)** n19 t18 f17 b16. Disappointing with little backbone or balance. **40%**. *Irish Distillers.*

**Midleton Very Rare 1985 (77)** n20 t20 f18 b19. Medium-bodied and oily, this is a big improvement on the initial vintage. **40%**. *Irish Distillers.*

**Midleton Very Rare 1986 (79)** n21 t20 f18 b20. A very malty Midleton richer in character than previous vintages. **40%**. *Irish Distillers.*

**Midleton Very Rare 1987 (77)** n20 t19 f19 b19. Quite oaky at first until a late surge of excellent pot still. **40%**. *Irish Distillers.*

**Midleton Very Rare 1988 (86)** n23 t21 f21 b21. A landmark MVR as it is the first vintage to celebrate the Irish pot-still style. **40%**

**Midleton Very Rare 1989 (87)** n22 citrussy and spicy, the malt is hardchiselled into the overall chararacter: some formidable pot still, too; t22 very vivid pot still which follows the firm grain; f22 the hard, brittle unmalted barley makes itself heard: you could break your teeth on it; b21 a real mouthful but has lost balance to achieve the effect. **40%**. *Irish Distillers.*

**Midleton Very Rare 1990 (93)** n23 carrying on from where the '89 left off. The pot still doesn't drill itself so far into your sinuses, perhaps: more of a firm massage; t23 solid pot still again. There is a pattern now: pot still first, sweeter, maltier notes second, pleasant grains third and somewhere, imperceptibly, warming spices fill in the gaps; f24 long and Redbreast-like in character. Spices seep from the bourbon casks; b23 astounding whiskey: one of the vintages every true Irish whiskey lover should hunt for. **40%**. *Irish Distillers.*

**Midleton Very Rare 1991 (76)** n19 t20 f19 b18. After the Lord Mayor's Show, relatively dull and uninspiring. **40%**. *Irish Distillers.*

**Midleton Very Rare 1992 (84)** n20 t20 f23 b21. Superb finish with outstanding use of feisty grain. **40%**. *Irish Distillers.*

**Midleton Very Rare 1993 (88)** n21 pot still with sub plots of honey and pepper; t22 the pot still makes use of the dry hardness of the grain; f23 beautiful elevation of the pot still towards something more complex and sharp balancing superbly with malt and bourboy-oak texture; b22 big, brash and beautiful – the perfect way to celebrate the 10th-ever bottling of MVR. **40%**. *Irish Distillers.*

**Midleton Very Rare 1994 (87)** n22 pot-still characteristics not unlike the '93 but with extra honey and ginger; t22 the honeyed theme continues with malt arriving in a lush sweetness; f21 oily and a spurt of sharper, harder pot still; b22 another different style of MVR, one of amazing lushness. **40%**. *Irish Distillers.*

**Midleton Very Rare 1995 (90)** n23 big pot still with fleeting honey; t24 enormous! Bitter, sweet and tart all together for a chewable battle of apple and barley. Brilliant; b21 some caramel calms proceedings, but Java coffee goes a little way to restoring complexity; b22 they don't come much bigger than this. Prepare a knife and fork to battle through this one. Fabulous. **40%**. *Irish Distillers.*

**Midleton Very Rare 1996 (82)** n21 t22 f19 b20. The grains lead a soft course, hardened by subtle pot still. Just missing a beat on the finish, though. **40%**

**Midleton Very Rare 1997 (83)** n22 t21 f19 b21. The piercing pot still fruitiness of the nose is met by a countering grain of rare softness on the palate. Just dies on the finish when you want it to make a little speech. Very drinkable. **40%**. *Irish Distillers.*

**Midleton Very Rare 1999 (89)** n21 malt and toffee: as sleepy as a nighttime drink; t23 stupendous grain, soft enough to absorb some pounding malt; f22 spices arrive as the blend hardens and some pot still finally battles its way through the swampy grain; **b**23 one of the maltiest Midletons of all time: a superb blend. **40%.** *Irish Distillers.*

**Midleton Very Rare 2000 (85) n**22 **t**21 **f**21 **b**21. An extraordinary departure even by Midleton's eclectic standards. The pot still is like a distant church spire in an hypnotic Fen landscape. **40%.** *Irish Distillers.*

**Midleton Very Rare 2001 (79) n**21 **t**20 **f**18 **b**20. Extremely light but the finish is slightly on the bitter side. **40%.** *Irish Distillers.*

**Midleton Very Rare 2002 (79) n**20 **t**22 **f**18 **b**19. The nose is rather subdued and the finish is likewise toffee-quiet and shy. There are some fabulous middle moments, some of flashing genius, when the pot still and grain combine for a spicy kick, but the finish really is lacklustre and disappointing. **40%.** *Irish Distillers*

**Midleton Very Rare 2003 (84) n**22 **t**22 **f**19 **b**21. Beautifully fruity on both nose and palate (even some orange blossom on aroma). But the delicious spicy richness that is in mid launch on the tastebuds is cut short by caramel on the middle and finish. A crying shame, but the best Midleton for a year or two. **40%.**

**Midleton Very Rare 2004 (82) n**21 **t**21 **f**19 **b**21. Yet again caramel is the dominant feature, though some quite wonderful citrus and spice escape the toffeed blitz. **40%.**

**Midleton Very Rare 2005 (??) n**23 **t**24 **f**22 **b**23. OK, you can take this one only as a rough translation. The sample I have worked from here is from the Irish Distillers blending lab, reduced to 40% in mine but without caramel added. And, as Midleton Very Rares always are at this stage, it's an absolute treat. Never has such a great blend suffered so in the hands of colouring and here the chirpiness of the pot still and élan of the honey (very Jameson Gold Label in part) show just what could be on offer given half the chance. Has wonderful natural colour and surely it is a matter of time before we see this great whiskey in its natural state. **40%**

**Midleton Very Rare 2006 (92) n**22 real punch to the grain, which is there in force and offering a bourbony match for the pot still; **t**24 stupendously crisp, then a welter of spices nip and sting ferociously around the palate; the oaky coffee arrives early and with clarity while the barley helps solidify the rock-hard barley; **f**23 usually by now caramel intervenes and spoils, but not this time and again it's the grain which really stars; **b**23 the best Midleton for some time: as raw as a Dublin rough-house and for once not overly swamped with caramel. An uncut diamond. **40%.** *Irish Distillers.*

**Millars Special Reserve** bott code L5047 **(80) n**20 **t**21 **f**18 **b**21. A big, grainkicking blend which has lost some of its old spicy perzazz and suffers from a harsh finale. Some odd juniper notes here and there. **40%.** *A. Millar & Co. Ltd.*

**Wm Morrison** (*see* Clancey's)

**O'Briens** bott code L4118 **(78) n**19 **t**20 **f**19 **b**20. Fractionally cleaner than of old; very firm and crisp. **40%.** *Cooley for P.J. O'Brien & Sons.*

**O'Hara** bott code L5043 **(74) n**19 **t**19 **f**17 **b**19. Caramel dominated and showing all the subtlety of Graham Norton. **40%.** *Cooley for Millar Products Ltd.*

**Old Dublin (73) n**17 **t**20 **f**17 **b**19. A clean blend that rarely troubles the inner tastebuds. Sweet with no pretensions of grandeur whatsoever. **40%.** *Irish Distillers.*

**Old Kilkenny (86) n**21 **t**22 **f**21 **b**22. A real shock to the system. Traditional pot still character in an own-label product, and real quality stuff to boot. However, gather up as many of the labels as you can that tell you it's triple distilled. Cooley are likely to take over the blend from Irish Distillers later in 2003 so the biting barley character will be lost for a softer malt-based blend. In this form a collectable one for Irish whiskey lovers worldwide. **40%.** *Asda UK.*

**Old Midleton Distillery Blended Whiskey 1967 35 Years Old (92) n**24 **t**23 **f**22 **b**23. This is a real one-off bottling of a quite unique Irish whiskey (actually coming from the old Midleton distillery, surely that should be "whisky"?). Apparently this one cask was filled in 1967 from a mixture of Midleton pure pot still and Midleton grain. After all this time, no-one knows why. But it was rescued by enthusiasts David Radcliffe and Sukhinder Singh and bottled for their respective businesses. I'm delighted to report (unlike Sukhinder's soon-to-become legendary Dunglass) that this is a little stunner. **41.1%.** *www.potstill.com*

**Paddy (68) n**16 **t**19 **f**16 **b**17. Good old Paddy: I knew it wouldn't let me down. While other lesser Irish whiskies have improved, Paddy has steadfastly refused to budge: dusty, cloyingly sweet and shapeless. Like an ugly duckling, I'm almost becoming fond of it. Hang on a minute, I'll ha[ve] anot[h]er taste: no, actually I'm not. Unclassically Irish. **40%.** *Irish Distillers.*

**Powers (91)** n23 rugged pot still a[nd] beefed up by some pretty nip by grain; t24 brilliant mouth arrival, one of th[e best] in all Ireland: the pot still shrieks and attacks every available tastebud; f22 pu[ll]ing s[p]ices and mouthwatering, rock-hard pot still. The sweetness is a bit unusual [...] you can just chew that barley; b22 is it any coincidence that in this bottling the influence of the caramel has been significantly reduced and the whiskey is getting back to its old, brilliant self? I think not. Classic stuff. **40%.** *Irish Distillers.*

**Powers Aged 12 Years Special Reserve Gold Label (79)** n21 t20 f19 b19. Seriously underpowered, remains one of the most disappointing blends in the Irish Distillers armoury. Still can't quite work out what they are trying to do **40%.** *Irish Distillers.* ☉ ☉

**Redbreast Blend (88)** n23 some genuinely telling pot-still hardness sparks like a flint off the no less unyielding grain. Just love this; t23 very sweet and soft, the grain carrying a massive amount of vanilla. Barley offers some riches, as does spice; f20 a climbdown from the confrontational beginnings, but pretty delicious all the same; b22 really impressed with this one-off bottling for Dillons the Irish wine merchants. Must try and get another bottle before they all vanish. **40%.** *Irish Distillers for Dillone IR (not to be confused with Redbreast 12-y-o Pure Pot Still).* ☉

**Sainsbury's Blended Irish Whiskey (79)** n19 t21 f19 b20. A lush, mouthwatering charge of malt towards the very middle. **40%**

**Shamrock (78)** n19 t21 f19 b19. A standard Cooley blend, but the promising complexity is lost under a welter of caramel. **40%.** *Cooley.*

**Strangford Gold (81)** n20 t21 f20 b20. A simplistic, exceptionally easy drinking blend with high quality grain offering silk to the countering spice but caramel flattens any malt involvement. **40%.** *The Feckin Drinks Co.*

**Tesco Special Reserve Irish Whiskey bott code L5053 (87)** n21 belligerent malt, young but well directed, spices the more docile grain; t23 the malts are stupendously juicy and have no problems punching their way entirely through the rich, clean grain; f21 really it's the grains that have the day here, but such is their superb quality, no problem; b22 underlines the fact that Cooley produces one of the world's best grain whiskies and a very sharp, decent malt. **40%.**

**Tir No Nog (78)** n20 t21 f18 b19. Lots of overactive toffee. **40%.** *Cooley.*

**Tullamore Dew (75)** n18 t20 f18 b19. Less than inspiring, maybe. But it has picked up on the pot still in recent years. Less throat-ripping, more balance. There is hope yet. **40%.** *Irish Distillers for Campbell and Cochrane.*

**Tullamore Dew 12 Years Old (81)** n21 t21 f20 b19. Enjoyable citrussy, pot-still tones criss-cross from the nose to the toffeed, Canadian finale. **40%.** *Irish Distillers for Campbell & Cochrane.*

**Tullamore Dew Heritage (79)** n20 t22 f19 b18. Fat and lush, the mouthwatering action is upfront on the tastebuds before the long toffeed, mildly spiced finale. **40%.** *Irish Distillers for Campbell & Cochrane.*

**Waitrose Irish Whiskey (77)** n20 t19 f20 b18. Very sweet but the grain is stupendous. **40%.** *UK.*

**Walker & Scott Irish Whiskey "Copper Pot Distilled" (83)** n20 t22 f20 b21. A collectors' item. This charming, if slightly fudgy-finished blend was made by Cooley as the house Irish for one of Britain's finest breweries. Sadly, someone put "Copper Pot Distilled" on the label, which, as it's a blend, can hardly be the case. And even if it wasn't a blend, would still be confusing in terms of Irish whiskey, there not being any traditional Irish Pot Still, that mixture of malted and unmalted barley. So Sam's, being one of the most traditional brewers in Britain, with the next bottling changed the label by dropping all mention of pot still. Top marks, chaps! The next bottling can be seen below. **40%.** *Sam Smith's.*

**Walker & Scott Irish Whiskey (85)** n21 t22 f21 b21. Oddly, sharper grain has helped give his some extra edge through the toffee. A very decent blend. **40%.**

**The Wild Geese (79)** n20 t22 f18 b19. Easy drinking and pleasant late spice but not enough gravity for the caramel. **40%.** *Cooley for Avalon.*

# American Whiskey

**N**ot that long ago American whiskey meant Bourbon. Or perhaps a very close relation called Tennessee. And sometimes it meant rye. Though nothing like often as it did prior to prohibition. Very, very rarely, though, did it ever get called single malt, because virtually none was made on the entire North American continent. That was a specialist – and very expensive - type left to the Scots and, to a lesser extent, the Irish. Or even the Japanese if a soldier or businessman was flying back from Tokyo.

I say "virtually" none was made because, actually, there was the odd batch of malt produced in America and, in my library, I still have some distilled at a rye distillery in Maryland in the early 1970s. But it was hardly a serious commercial concern and the American public were never made greatly aware of it.

Just how many know about the malt whiskey revolution presently hitting the States is open to debate, but I guess very few. Those I have spoken to about it seem surprised when I tell them the standard of the quality is exceptionally high. I'm not too convinced they believe me.

But the healthy state of malt whiskey making was brought home to me just as I was completing the previous Bible, when a bottle of Strahan's Colorado Whiskey arrived in my sample room. This is America's latest distillery to bottle and these Denver guys were using, like their Kentucky colleagues, virgin oak casks in which to mature their spirit. So although only two years old the wood impact with the barley was profound: indeed, there were more bourbony notes than barley. But yet again I have been left almost speechless by the sheer excellence of the malt I poured. It may not have eclipsed the stupendous Clear Creek of Oregon – last year's Whiskey Bible's Best Small Batch Distillery Whisky of the Year - but it certainly helped underline that the USA has a malt whiskey industry that, though tiny, has now to be taken seriously in terms of quality alone. Because of this, I have begun making plans to spend part of 2007 and 2008 investigating these wonderful new frontiers of the malt whisky revolution.

I will also be back in Kentucky for while, hopefully to do some work on my house, but also to wake up some of the distillers there. My word, it has been quiet. Yes, they have been busy distilling, but compared to the intrigue in the rest of the whisky world, Kentucky has gone back to its sleepy old ways. Which is how most distillers there I know prefer it.

Buffalo Trace have been busy installing a new still over the last few weeks, but it is unlikely the public will ever get to taste its fruits. The still, based on a German style of pot and rectifier, is destined for a secret life of experimentation away from the main plant. The idea is for the distilling and blending team to create new styles of whiskey without interfering with their precious main stills.

The best news of the year regarding American whiskey happened in Lawrenceburg, Indiana, where the Pernod Ricard Seagram Distillery, an enormous operation that, from the outside, looks to be able to cure America's bourbon shortage single handed, has been saved from closure. Gin distilling will certainly continue and one can only pray that whiskey production remains intact, too. Not least because their sublime bourbon, Cougar, a mainstay of Australian bourbon enjoyment, has picked up an award in this year's Bible - even though it is bottled at 37% alcohol by volume. As the ink on the agreement has yet to dry, I don't know for sure where the distillery's whisky future lies. Or even whether it has yet been re-named. For this year it shall stay on the map as Pernod Ricard.

The Lawrenceburg distillery is also famous for its hugely flavoured traditional rye. But once again this year it was the latest idiosyncratic offering from Anchor which won the grand prize in this year's Jim Murray's Whiskey Bible. Just like last year's bottling, the rye boasts an extraordinary botanical element to the usual rich rye mayhem which makes tasting a glass of this slow the book-writing process down by several hours! Absolutely amazing stuff!

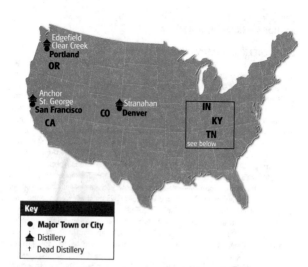

## Key

- ● **Major Town or City**
- ▲ Distillery
- † Dead Distillery

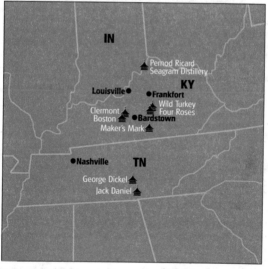

**Bardstown**
- ▲ Heaven Hill†
- ▲ Barton

**Frankfort**
- ▲ Buffalo Trace

- ▲ Woodford Reserve

**Louisville**
- ▲ Early Times
- ▲ Bernheim
- ▲ Stitzel Weller

# American Single Malt
## ANCHOR DISTILLERY (see Rye)

### CLEAR CREEK DISTILLERY (Portland, Oregon)

**McCarthy's Aged 3 Years** bott 05 **(96) n**24 the deepest, most toe-curling peat-reek outside Islay. And better, even, than one or two distilleries on the island...; **t**24 is it the demerara-molassed sweetness or that stunning gristy barley that hits the palate first and stops you in your tracks? It is impossible to determine, though the smoke, which starts as a whisper, builds up to something profound and beautiful; **f**24 the works: demerara sugared Jamaican coffee; dry cocoa and , of course, that distinctly iodiney, gristy peatiness. And a touch of late vanilla; **b**24 it's a straight shoot out between this and a Tasmanian single malt for the best small distiller of the year. I thought the Taz guys had it...until I tasted this. But how can you fault the near faultless....??? **40% (80 proof).**

**McCarthy's Oregon Single Malt Aged 3 Years (92) n**24 smoked kippers, very lightly oiled; old-fashioned Ardbeg; **t**23 very sweet initial arrival that dampens down with a surge of soft oak then sparks again as pressed-cane juice carries with it a rip-tide of peat; **f**22 soft, gentle, pulsating malt and light spice; **b**23 another excellent effort from McCarthy, but the sweetness and oil have just taken a fraction from the normal brilliance. I'm looking forward to when the distillery do finally start batch-marking their bottles, which they will do by the time of the 2007 edition. **40% (80 proof).**

**McCarthy's Oregon Single Malt Aged 3 Years (95) n**23 kippery but also soft grist and spices and a hint of slightly overdone brown toast; **t**24 jackpot hit as the sweetness is controlled and instead we have lush waves of ultra-clean smoke; the oiliness is there but defused enough to allow only a perfect coating of the palate; **f**24 not far off the perfect finale. The oak adds a drier element but really it is the Port Ellen-style fresh gristiness that keeps your tongue working overtime as the finish refuses to fade; **b**24 this is, unquestionably, the finest bottled whiskey I have tasted anywhere in the world from a small-batch distiller. Only Islay's very finest can out-complex this not so little chap. **40% (80 proof).**

### EDGEFIELD DISTILLERY (Portland, Oregon)

**Edgefield Distillery Hogshead** db bott 4 Sep 03 **(93) n**24 **t**24 **f**22 **b**23. It really takes some believing that a distillery, at its third attempt, has come up with something quite this brilliant. I'm not sure where the caramel is coming from: either natural or added, but without it, it would be phenomenal. **46% (92 proof).**

**Edgefield Hogshead (89) n**22 big, big malt and ripe banana; **t**23 silky, tastebud soothing yet intense. The clarity of the barley and total lack of smoke allow the vanilla of the oak full early entry; **f**21 sweetish, with the oak juices mingling happily with the intense barley. Very attractively spiced; **b**23 there have been no fewer than six bottlings of this small-batch malt since the 2005 edition was written. Unfortunately the bottles aren't batch-marked, so the public are denied the fun of comparing differences. Here I went to the distillery in Oregon to try their latest, from 21 March 05. **46%**

### ST GEORGE DISTILLERY (San Francisco, California)

**St George Single Malt Aged 3 Years** db **(75) n**17 **t**19 **f**20 **b**19. Without doubt the fruitiest whisk(e)y I have tasted in nearly 30 years of sampling the stuff. The nose in particular is some kind of raspberry or similar fruit, more eau de vie than whiskey. That said, this is beautifully distilled and clean with a wonderful bite near the finish: it is just that the malt has been lost along the way. **43%**

**St George Single Malt Aged 3 Years Lot 2** db **(82) n**19 **t**21 **f**21 **b**21. Much better. The fruit still clings to the nose, but this time malt rings loud and clear round the tastebuds and there is superb interaction with the oak. Once more, supremely made and, once that fruit is lost, we will have an absolutely toprank malt on our hands. **43%**

**St George Lot 3** db **(82) n**20 **t**20 **f**21 **b**21. Another fruitfest from St George that again shows excellent clarity, but has wandered off the malty path. Quite pithy in places and always enjoyable. **43%**

**St George Lot 4** db **(87) n**23 for some reason there is a beguiling drift of rye, apple and cinnamon, but – at last!!! – it is the richness of the malt that really takes off; **t**20 drier than any

other St George, with a slow evolution of malt against some flakey, oaky tones; **f**22 remains dry but the slight bitterness is perfectly received by barley and busy spices; **b**22 Eureka! Them thar pesky Californians have gone and struck themselves malt. Not fool's malt, but the pure stuff, yessiree!!! Just took four years of copper panning. **43%**

## STRANAHAN DISTILLERY (Denver, Colorado)

Stranahan's Colorado Whiskey Batch No 5 dist 9 Sep 04 **(90) n**23 pretty bourbony as manuka honey and soft liquorice pulse their way through the firm, gently spiced oak. Big stuff!; **t**24 wonderful, bourbon-style honey-sweetness to the delivery and the spice promised on the nose arrives in droves; superb texture and weight and rounded beautifully with touch of oil; **f**21 perhaps slightly over-oaked and thins quickly; **b**22 if the Rockies is where east meets west, then this first-ever Colorado whiskey is where bourbon meets single malt. The quality of the distilling is beyond reproach and this 3,608th, and final, whiskey to go into this 2007 Bible really is the perfect way to end six months' solid tasting. But if the whiskey does has a fault it is the enormity of the oak: for a two-year-old only  Indian malt whisky matures faster. My instincts tell me that distillers Jake and Jess will benefit in future years from using a mixture of virgin and used casks to maximise the complexity lurking in the obvious riches found in this gold strike. But hey, this is Colorado. Where you don't mess with a man's woman...or his whiskey... **47% (94 proof).**

# Bourbon Distilleries

Bourbon confuses people. Often they don't even realise it is a whiskey, a situation not helped by leading British pub chains, such as Wetherspoon, whose bar menus list "whiskey" and "bourbon" in separate sections. And if I see the liqueur Southern Comfort listed as a bourbon one more time I may not be responsible for my actions.

Bourbon is a whiskey. It is made from grain and matured in oak, so really it can't be much else. To be legally called bourbon it must have been made with a minimum of 51% corn and matured in virgin oak casks for at least two years. Oh, and no colouring can be added other than that which comes naturally from the barrel.

Where it does differ, from, say Scotch, is that the straight whiskey from the distillery may be called by something other than that distillery name. Indeed, the distillery may change its name which has happened to two this year already and two others in the last three or four. So, to make things easy and reference as quick as possible, I shall list the Kentucky-based distilleries first and then their products in alphabetical order along with their owners and operational status.

## BARTON

Bardstown. Barton Brands. Operating.

## BUFFALO TRACE

Leestown, Frankfort. Sazerac. Operating.

## BROWN-FORMAN

Shively, Louisville. Brown-Forman. Operating.

## FOUR ROSES

Lawrenceburg. Kirin. Operating

## HEAVEN HILL BERNHEIM DISTILLERY

Louisville. Heaven Hill Distillers. Operating.

## JIM BEAM

Boston and Clermont. Fortune Brands. Operating.

## WOODFORD RESERVE (formely Labrot & Graham)

Near Millville. Brown-Forman. Operating.

## MAKER'S MARK

Loretto. Fortune Brands. Operating.

## WILD TURKEY

Lawrenceburg. Pernod Ricard. Operating.

## Bourbon

**1492 Bourbon** (see Heaven Hill 80 Proof)

**A H Hirsch Reserve 16 Years Old (91) n**23 waxy honeycomb embedded in marzipan and dark chocolate; **t**24 again the honey is at the centre of things with a soft, corny development; more Lubek marzipan, this time with a soft, sweet lemon centre. The mouth-feel is exceptional; **f**21 smaller grains here and developing firmer, drier oak; **b**23 not until November did I discover that this bourbon, the last surviving to be made in Pennsylvania, was still doing the rounds. The distillery closed way back in 1988 and much of its maturing stock was destroyed by court order. I last tasted the 16-y-o back in the 90s and in Jim Murray's Complete Book of Whisky (1997) I described it as "big, confident, highclass whiskey". Says it all. Michter's Distillery, Pennsylvania.

**American Star (86) n**21 **t**22 **f**21 **b**22. A seriously good rye-recipe bourbon with enormous full-bodied and fruity character. Sweet and lingering. **40% (80 proof).** Bernkasteler Germany.

**Ancient Age (75) n**18 **t**19 **f**19 **b**19. Light, pleasant but half cooked. **40% (80 proof).**

**Ancient Ancient Age 10 Star (89) n**22 lavender and soft rye amid the rich corn; **t**23 complex small grain, centring around the rye, but also slightly nutty with some raisiny fruits; **f**22 oak comes steaming in to gently dry the broadening corn. Spices begin to bite; **b**22 what we have here is a bourbon that knows how to offer complexity: a thinking man's bourbon. Much better than it once was. **45% (90 proof).** Buffalo Trace.

**Ancient Ancient Age 10 Years Old (81) n**20 **t**20 **f**21 **b**20. Drat and blast! One of my favourite whiskeys way off form, here showing its normal complexity only in patches and, by its own massive standards, just all round too plain and flat. **43% (86 proof).** Buffalo Trace.

**Ancient Age Preferred (76) n**17 **t**19 **f**20 **b**20. Sweet, thin but with excellent spice build-up. **40% (80 proof).** Buffalo Trace.

**Anderson Club** (see Heaven Hill Aged 6 Years 90 Proof)

**Aristocrat** (see Heaven Hill 80 Proof)

**Austin Nichols Wild Turkey** (see Wild Turkey)

**Baker's Aged 7 Years** batch B-90-001 **(85) n**21 **t**22 **f**21 **b**21. Not quite in the same league as the bigger batch 85, but pretty timeless, enjoyable stuff. **53.5%.** Jim Beam.

**Barclay's Bourbon (79) n**20 **t**21 **f**18 **b**20. Economical in development, there is still enough rye and nutty oiliness to keep the tastebuds amused. Little sparkle on the finish. **40% (80 proof)**

**Basil Hayden's (77) n**21 **t**19 **f**18 **b**19. Some attractive rye riches, but overall disappointingly thin and lacking in depth. **40% (80 proof).** Jim Beam.

**Benchmark** (see McAfee's Benchmark)

**Black Jack (86) n**23 **t**22 **f**20 **b**21. What starts as a ryefest loses power dramatically, though the outcome remains tasty. **37%.** Australia.

**Blanton's Gold Edition** barrel no 12 w/house H rick 35 dumped 16 Oct 03 **(91) n**22 a fraction closed for Blanton's but spice enough to show it's ticking; **t**24 a velvety coating of sweetcorn with a tingling layer of rye and leathery liquorice; the elan is spellbinding; **f**22 remains sweet with lashings of natural toffee; **b**23 seamless. **51.5% (103 proof).** Buffalo Trace.

**Blanton's Single Barrel Green Label** barrel 139 dumped 10-1-05 **(89) n**23 kumquats and blood orange abound; **t**23 a big rye presence on delivery which shows some delicate touches amid the odd punch; **f**21 drier vanilla; **b**22 deliciously fruity and rye proud. **40%**

**Blanton's Red (91) n**24 an essay in delicate form and complexity; **t**22 your tastebuds are kissed by soft tannins; **f**22 blackberries and cocoa; **b**23 the nose is simply to buy for...this is one of the most delicate Blanton's of all time. **40%**

**Blanton's Silver Edition** barrel no 118 w/house H rick 27 dumped 12 Jun 03 **(83) n**20 **t**22 **f**20 **b**21. Genteel and refined with the accent on corn and some waspish rye spice. **49% (98 proof).** Buffalo Trace.

**Blanton's Single Barrel 7 Years Old (86) n**22 **t**22 **f**21 **b**21. Enjoyable, but not exactly what I expected. The bourbon and oak haven't quite gelled: a teen beauty with a few unsightly spots. **51.5%.** Buffalo Trace. This is one of the single barrels used to make up 1500 bottles for readers of the Suddeutsche Zeitung Magazin, Germany.

**Blanton's Single Barrel** barrel no 69 w/house H rick 55 dumped 19 Jan 04 **(91)** n23 a riot of small grains with distant marmalade; sweet ripe plums, too; t22 simmering bittersweet corn-rye battle with rich banana and custard middle; f23 quite intense with a liquorice, bitter coffee surge; b23 goes down a treat: one to swallow and never spit. **46.5% (93 proof).** Buffalo Trace.

**Blanton's Uncut/Unfiltered (84)** n21 t22 f20 b21. For all its strength this one proves to be on the light, enormously sweet and shy side. **65.9% (131.8 proof).**

**Blue Grass State (77)** n19 t19 f20 b19. Clean, good toast and vanilla. **40% (80 proof).** Somerfield UK.

**Bowman's Bourbon (81)** n20 t20 f21 b20. A very decent, well-balanced, softly spiced and rich young-to-medium-age bourbon originating from Heaven Hill. A fine everyday shot. **40% (80 proof).** A Smith Bowman.

**Booker's 8 Years 8 Months** batch no. C87-D-21 **(86)** n22 t23 f20 b21. A rich bourbon that varies in style from batch to batch. This one has a better than average middle with no shortage of rye, but is let down in the final stages. **62.45% (124.9 proof).** Jim Beam.

**Bourbon Falls** (see Heaven Hill 86 Proof)

**Bourbon Royal** (see Heaven Hill 80 Proof)

**Buffalo Trace (94)** n24 sharp rye screams above the complex corn, citrus and oak: seriously absorbing; t23 stupendous, softly oiled mouthfeel with the corn absorbing some prickly rye and spice; f23 sweet, remains oily with some cream toffee. The small grains re-emerge for a last battle with the corn; b24 I simply adore this whiskey: the weight is just about perfect as is the corn-oak, bittersweet harmony. The small grains add great colour and complexity. A whiskey gem of the world. **45%. (90 proof).**

**Buffalo Trace Experimental Collection Fire Pot Barrel Aged 10 Years** dist 6 Feb 96, bott 24 Feb 06 **(92)** n24 an essay in subtlety with caressing fingers of vanilla and kumquat plus gently molassed, Jamaica Blue Mountain light roast; t23 gentle oils help mould liquorice and heavy roast raisin to the roof of the mouth; f22 long, remaining on that roasty theme; b23 the great thing about experiments in bourbon is that the whisky is not under threat from hideous sulphur-stained casks or dreadful European wines. This experiment is a success. **45% (90 proof).**

**Buffalo Trace Experimental Collection French Oak Aged 10 Years** dist 6 Apr 95, bott 24 Feb 06 **(86)** n23 t23 f19 b21. Unusual, polarized whiskey that is seriously bitter-sweet and though a great experience, it is possible to spot the odd flaw. **45%**

**Buffalo Trace Experimental Collection Twice Barrelled** dist 4 Apr 93, bott 24 Feb 06 **(96)** n24 big, big age yet an astonishing, fruity freshness piles on the citrus, rye and spice. Just gets better as it sits in the glass and the complexity bedazzles; t25 talk about a gentle giant: this really does radiate enormous depth yet without becoming too stuffed on sweet sugars or thumping oak. There is a laid-back, acceptance of pure brilliance in the natural harmonization here that I cannot remember finding in any other bourbon I have ever tasted: and we are talking thousands!! All the usual leathery, liquoricy, honeycombed suspects are there, but the restraint and control is awesome; f23 long with a gradual increase in vanillas and caramels and a small touch of sugar to ward off encroaching, more bitter oak; b24 perhaps the ultimate bourbon. Would prefer to have seen this at 50.5 and unchillfiltered – but that's being greedy... **45% (90 proof).**

**Bulleit Bourbon Frontier Whiskey (88)** n22 light and teasing: mallows roasting on an open fire plus pine nuts and vanilla. Honest, folks; t22 the faintest dry oak start vanishes within seconds for a rich follow-through of sweet chestnut, a busy complexity of malted barley and rye and then spice; f22 mildly oily, softly honeycombed and chocolatey for a chewy, bitter-sweet finale. Like all that's gone before, exceptionally well balanced and satisfying; b22 absolutely excellent from first to last, an essay in balance and control: I doubt if any frontier whiskey of Boone's day was half as good as this. **45% (90 proof).**

**Cabin Hill** (see Heaven Hill 80 Proof)

**Cadenhead's Heaven Hill Aged 8 Years** bott Feb-05 **(88)** n21 some polite liquorice and hints of rye; t22 the corn comes out to play with a sweet, oily rush; f23 much more complexity here as the small grains and oak really go head to head; some zesty tartness completes a busy finale; b22 big, complex whiskey. **62%.**

**Cadenhead's Heaven Hill Aged 14 Years** bott May 06 **(89)** n23 polished leather, oranges...the whole nine yards; t23 glossy coffee-sugar and liquorice; searing spices keep the vanillins in check; **f**21 deft mollassed vanillas; **b**22 a wonderful bourbon, but just on the way down with the oak showing big control. Still a corker, though. **56.9%**

⠿ **Cadenhead's World Whisky Heaven Hill Aged 10 Years** Bourbon barrel, bott Feb 07 **(94) n**23 pure leather with some kumquats crushed into it for good measure; the rye is mountainous; **t**24 rye delivery offering a fruitiness beginning with blood orange and kumquats and moving out towards crushed violets and Demerara; **f**23 still the rye hangs around with a custardy sub-plot; too fruity and clean to be true; **b**24 not from the original, torched HH distillery, but in the unbelievably high rye style likely to be associated with the Early Times distillery. Classic one-off stuff. **62.2%**. *Cadenhead's. 168 bottles.*

**Champion** (*see* Heaven Hill 80 Proof)

**Chapin & Gore** (*see* Heaven Hill 80 Proof)

**Chapin & Gore 86 Proof** (*see* Heaven Hill 86 Proof)

**Chesapeake** (*see* Heaven Hill 80 Proof)

**Chillie Gone Crazy** (*see* Heaven Hill 80 Proof)

**Colonel Lee (69) n**17 **t**17 **f**18 **b**17 Should be shot at dawn. **40%**. *Barton.*

**Colonel's Pride** (*see* Heaven Hill 80 Proof)

**Corner Creek Reserve Aged 8 Years (93) n**24 one of the fruitiest and frankly most attractive noses on the bourbon shelves: massive orangey citrus lead, wonderful small grain follow-on; **t**24 hits a hollow on entry and a few seconds later erupts into a fruity free-for-all with the rye really packing a punch; **f**22 a bitter marmalade tartness to the sour dough finale; **b**23 hard to find but the unique tune played on this is so worth searching for. **44% (88 proof)**. *Corner Creek Distilling Co., Bardstown.*

**Cougar (93) n**24 biting, rip-roaring, rabid rye offering astonishing crispness and finesse on the corn. One of the all-time great rye-rich bourbon aromas; **t**23 massive rye makes for a crisp, fruity and mouth-watering arrival. The corn eventually softens the impact and ensures sweetness; **f**23 much more well-behaved with vanilla and corn now leading the way but the rye just continues to salivate the palate; **b**23 one of the most characterful, purposeful bourbons you could imagine. This Illinois cracker is one of the best-kept secrets in the bourbon world. **37%**. *Australia.*

⠿ **Cougar Bourbon Aged 5 Years** bott code 038/07/13 **(95) n**25 light, fruity rye offers an aroma I have only ever encountered in an Alpine meadow with myriad flowers popping up through the earthy moss; this is probably the best rye in the world diffused to perfection; **t**24 soft, sweet delivery with again the rye taking central command, directing fruity, rooty elements in all directions; **f**23 dries agreeably with vanilla subduing the fruity freshness **b**23 if Karl Kennedy of Neighbours really is the whisky buff he reckons he is, I want to see a bottle of this in his home next to Dahl. By the way: where is Dahl these days...? (And by the way, Karl, the guy who married you and Susan in London is a fan of mine. So you had better listen up...!) **37% (74 proof)**. *Foster's Group, Australia.*

**Daniel Stewart Aged 8 Years (88) n**22 rich, leathery and pipe-tobacco sweet but underneath a second stratum of young grain: unusual; **t**22 brilliantly spiced yet sweet corn forms an oily-textured middle; **f**22 lots of blistering small grain and spice; **b**22 very sweet yet complex bourbon of light-to-medium weight. **45%** *Heaven Hill.*

**Daniel Stewart Aged 12 Years (95) n**24 floral, honey and outstanding clean oak and corn: a classy act; **t**24 heather, honey, hints of citrus and then some serious oak, but always sweetened by the rich corn. The rye offers a spicy and even more complex background; **f**23 such a delicate fade: the sweetness falls over aeons, the oak gathering density at the same rate. But the rye continues its merry tune; **b**24 it is pretty obvious that the original old Heaven Hill peaks at 12: it always has in the time I have known it. Awesome, spellbinding bottlings like this place it amongst the world's elite. **53.5% (107 proof)**. *Heaven Hill.*

**Dierberg's** (*see* Heaven Hill 80 Proof)

**Distiller's Pride** (*see* Heaven Hill 80 Proof)

**Don & Ben's** (*see* Evan Williams Aged 7 Years 86 Proof)

**Dowling De Luxe 8 Years Old 100 Proof (93) n**23 salty, big-oaked, atouch minty but enough small grain to see it through; **t**23 big burnt oak arrival then the middle is awash with ultra-ripe fruit, especially dates and even over-ripe banana; **f**23 calms down for more oaky strands on which the small grains and soft spices flourish; **b**24 this wasn't a whiskey you would always associate with complexity – until now. Forget the age statement. A very similar proposition to the stunning Virgin 7, but with a little extra fruit. **50% (100 proof).** Heaven Hill.

**Eagle Rare Aged 10 Years Single Barrel Mac Y 10th Anniversary (93)** n23 unmistakable Buffalo Trace whiskey with the vanilla revealed in so many textured layers; **t**23 surging oaks on delivery. Then a backing off to allow a more measured, mildly molassed sweetness to interlink with some orangey citrus; **f**23 slow spice arrival, a brushing of hickory and some developing rye fruitiness; **b**24 beautiful bourbon from the school of complex shades and inferences. **45%.** Denmark.

**Eagle Rare Single Barrel Bourbon 10 Years (94)** n23 leathery and honied; astonishingly soft and delicate; **t**23 at first sweet-corn, then a gradual build-up of spices, though the sweetness refuses to fade while a vague murmer of fruit can be found; **f**24 long, lots of vanilla threading through, while the small grains and late rye are a treasure; **b**24 just one of those effortlessly brilliant whiskeys that seem to get it right without trying. The best ERSBB I've come across as yet. **45%.**

**Eagle Rare Kentucky Straight Bourbon 17 Years Old 90 Proof** bott Fall 06 **(93)** n23 maple syrup; rye-liquorice mix; **t**23 sweet and delicate arrival; the silky delivery intensifies as the natural oak sugars begin to take hold; **f**24 long, burnt fudge and mocha. Just so beautifully weighted and elegant; **b**23 one of the steadiest ships on the bourbon shelves. **45% (90 Proof).** Buffalo Trace.

**Early Times Kentucky Straight Bourbon (brown label) (80)** n21 t20 f19 b20. Not quite as fruity a profile but the clarity is unblemished. Very corny. **40% (80 proof).**

**Early Times (yellow label) (83)** n20 t21 f21 b21. A heavier, more vanillarich bourbon that offers a consistent, delicate, sweet theme throughout with butterscotch on the finish. **40% (80 proof).**

Echo Spring (see Heaven Hill 80 Proof)

**Elijah Craig 12 Years Old (96)** n24 honey-roast nuts with the usual HH kumquaty citrus character. Quite smoky with wonderful bitter-sweet alignment; **t**23 deft, articulate oak offers sweet vanilla and distant honeycomb; fruity with figs and raisin; **f**24 eternally mouthwatering despite the gathering of drier vanilla-oak and spices. Take an evening out to wait for this to end; **b**25 you cannot but sit on the chair, chew on near perfection and be simply amazed. And a couple of bottlings I tried this year were, if anything a tad richer. Grab now: with the loss of the origianl HH distillery, soon they will be gone forever. **47% (94 proof).**

**Elijah Craig Aged 18 Years Single Barrel** barrel no. 1226, barrelled on 8 Sep 81 **(93)** n23 concentrated tangerine on the turn, but when mixed with rye like this works well. Like disappearing into an old Gentlemen's club leather armchair on which pipes have been smoked. Massive esters. Massive full stop; **t**24 hold on to your armchairs: just so confrontational with screeching rye and malt smashing head-first into the citrussy oak without stopping in time. A collision of flavours and styles that leaves you reeling; **f**22 big tangerine finale with spice and rye: the fade is even and almost infinitely long; **b**24 give anyone who regards bourbon as an inferior species a dose of this and they will be cured: astonishing and truly beautiful. **45% (90 proof).**

**Elmer T Lee Single Barrel (88)** n22 distinct citrus and light corn-rich notes; **t**23 sweet corn again with hints of banana and rye; **f**21 a very settled, toffeed finale with a hint of spicy rebellion; **b**22 a more delicate and less rye-infested bottling than some. Really delicious. **45% (90 proof).** Buffalo Trace.

**Elmer T Lee (85)** n22 t22 f20 b21. A tad muted and not quite up to the usual ETL brilliance. **43%**

Evan Williams (see Heaven Hill 80 Proof)

Evan Williams 100 Proof (see Heaven Hill 100 Proof)

**Evan Williams Aged 7 Years (83)** n22 t21 f20 b20. Sweet, corn-rich with caramel on the middle and a dry, oaky finish. **43% (86 proof).** Heaven Hill.

**Evan Williams 10 Years Old (84)** n22 t22 f19 b21. Fabulous start but loses map towards the finish. **43% (86 proof).**

**Evan Williams 12 Years (96)** n24 how can something so big be so well-mannered and controlled? Expensive suede prickled by rye and small grain. A hint of hickory smoke; **t**24 busy spices attack the tongue from the off, then waves of liquorice and gentle rye wash against the tastebuds. The sweetness is unbelievably exact and refined, balancing against the chunkier roasty notes; **f**24 more corn oil here than other HH oldies, but as well as upping the sweetness exactly when it's needed, it also helps paint broad rye and creosotey stripes across the palate. The very finish has an exotic fruit salad, mainly of the papaya variety – not unknown to this distillery; **b**24 it must be some ten years ago I first came across this in Japan and fell under its spell. This is the first time I have officially tasted it for the Bible, having somehow failed to get up-to-date bottlings. The quality hasn't dropped one iota. Quite simply: one of the greatest whiskey experiences you will ever have. **50.5% (101 proof).**

**Evan Williams 15 Years (95) n**24 rye-induced lavender, black peppers, jack fruit and sweet liquorice: just so busy; **t**24 surprising sweetness to the arrival with corn up front followed by big rye and fruit procession; a wonderful unripened fruit sharpness offers supreme balance; **f**23 recedes so slowly you can barely notice: just enough sweetened spice to see off any oaky counter at this good age; an unusual papaya bitterness at the death completes the exotic festival; **b**24 just such brilliantly balanced and entertaining bourbon that loses out to its younger brother only on account of subtlety. **50.5% (101 proof).**

**Evan Williams 23 Years Old (91) n**23 one of the spiciest noses in all Kentucky! Allow to oxodise after 23 years in barrel and you will see sharp rhubarb battling it out against the oaky polished floors. Just this side of oblivion...; **t**23 the spices leave you spellbound and gasping; bitter yet somehow controlled, with the oak staying the right side of the white line as a burnt Demerara sugar, hickory and toasted raisins assault the tastebuds. No shortage of sweetness as rye and marzipan balance the books; **f**23 little can follow the big assault other than intense vanilla and burnt custard...and bitter marmalade; **b**23 a far greater event than the previous EW23 simply because the oak has never taken control and the complexity refuses to surrender. One for the collection. **53.5% (107 proof).**

Evan Williams 1783 (*see* Heaven Hill 10 Years 86 Proof)

Evan Williams Old (*see* Heaven Hill 100 Proof)

**Evan Williams Single Barrel 1997** Barrel no. 1, barreled 20 Feb 97, bott 10 Oct 06 **(87) n**22 dense, mildy syrupy but not rye-edged as is the old house style; **t**24 beautifully exotic with massive delivery of varying sugars, mostly brown and molassed. The flavours all arrive in a fury with a burnt liquorice also having a big say. The tastebuds are almost run over in the rush. but what a way to go; **f**20 a surge of oaky bitterness controls the shape: short, thin and limited by EW standards; **b**21 all the wondrous sugary, toasty notes arrive early on, leaving behind a thinner, more bitter finish. For those of you wondering why this is so removed from the usual EW Single barrel we have come to know and love over the last decade, the answer, of course, is that it was made at a different distillery following the Great Heaven Hill fire of 1996: in this case the Clermont Distillery of Jim Beam. The recipe may be identical. But the difference is in the glass for all to taste. **43.3%**

**Evan Williams Single Barrel Vintage 1996** Barrel no. 1, bott 4 Oct 05 db **(92) n**24 classic nose full of usual fruitcake but beefed up by additional liquorice and molasses; **t**23 drier than the norm as the oak gets in early but maple syrup and a dash of rye do the biz; **f**22 lots of natural caramels leached from the oak; **b**23 up to the usual superb standards. **43.3% (86.6 proof).**

**Evan Williams Vintage 1993 Single Barrel (89) n**22 busy citrus battling with fresh and fruity rye; **t**22 delicate small grains dominate at first, then a wave of oak followed by sweet corn; **f**22 pretty long and quite dry with some chalky oak enlivened by returning rye and liquorice; **b**23 a steady, sexy, delicate bourbon that is a lot more complex than it initially seems. **43.3% (86.6 proof).**

**Evan Williams Vintage 1994 Single Barrel Vintage** barrelled on 28 Oct 94, barrel no. 394, bott 8.12.04 **(89) n**23 carrot cake, red liquorice and honey; **t**22 enormously sweet: an outpouring of sugar-cane juice and corn; **f**22 some tingling oak add chocolatey dryness; **b**22 a shade too sweet for perfection, but one for the ladies. **43.3% (86.6 proof).**

**Evan Williams Vintage 1995 Single Barrel Vintage** barrelled on 1 May 95, barrel no. 308. bott 5 May 05 **(94) n**23 exceptional balance between honeycomb and liquorice; **t**23 that honey and honeycomb thread is insistent through the brilliance of the vanilla-rye domination; **f**23 wonderful spices play out as a soft apple and custard sweetness is topped with vanilla; **b**24 the back label is a must to find: brilliant and just about flawless. **43.3% (86.6 proof).**

**Evan Williams Vintage 1995 Single Barrel Vintage** barrelled on 18 Aug 95, barrel no. 01, bott 13 Oct.04 **(92) n**23 deep cinnamon and fruitcake; **t**24 sublime oak scaffolding on which the corn and late, fruity rye hang; **f**22 wonderful small grain spices gain ground; **b**23 beautifully complex and well weighted. **43.3% (86.6 proof).**

**Ezra Brooks (79) n**19 **t**20 **f**20 **b**20. A light-to-medium weight bourbon with a standard nose but offering good sweet liquorice on the rich finish. **45%**

**Fighting Cock Aged 6 Years (84) n**22 **t**22 **f**20 **b**20. Brilliant nose of old, waxy wooden floors and a really battling palate arrival of almost fruity corn. Quite hot. **51.5% (103 proof).** *Heaven Hill.*

**Four Roses (84) n**22 **t**21 **f**20 **b**21. A sweet and charming bourbon that is light and sophisticated but always pulls up short of being a world beater. Now that the distillery is on its own I expect this perennial under-achiever to go through the roof quality-wise. The stocks are there, as the single-barrel expressions illustrate, and as I have seen over the years when inspecting the warehouses. Keep your eyes peeled and tastebuds at the ready. Four Roses is likely to become a thorn in their competitors' sides. **40% (80 proof).**

**Four Roses Black Label (89) n**21 lazy at first, but gentle handwarming encourages an oaky confrontation with soft rye; **t**22 thicker, weightier, more intense than the standard bottling, it again leans on the rye to do battle with the tastebuds; sweetening corn adds fine balance; **f**23 drier, sharper, with a touch of late honeycomb; **b**23 takes time to get started, but once rolling won't stop. **40% (80 proof).**

**Four Roses Platinum (87) n**24 burnt caramel fudge with diced nuts and dried dates: one of the most integrated and classy little FR noses I've ever come across, especially when the rye delivers a fruity edge; **t**23 serious weight and early spice to this: only a big influx of sweet-corn and flat caramel buries the gathering complexity; **f**20 a degree of rye-induced bitterness and spice, but the leaden corn and caramel really is powering; **b**20 something odd here: you think you have a world-beater on your hands but an avalanche of caramel arrests all further development. A bit of tinkering here and you might have something extra special. **43% (86 proof).**

⸬ **Four Roses Single Barrel** Warehouse no. CS, barrel no. 48-6C **(92) n**24 absolutely in your face honey, liquorice and spice: much more confident than your average Four Roses; **t**23 sharp, puckering rye notes deliver a fruity retort to the tastebuds; driers vanillins follow behind; **f**22 blackberries in full cry, as are the mottled honey and butterscotch oaky notes; **b**23 I was there the day master distiller Jim Rutledge took aver as manager of this understated little peach of a distillery. That was a very long time ago and I must say he now certainly knows his way around the warehouses. The nose is among the top three I have ever come across from here: this is the type of bourbon that will win converts the world over. You have no idea how long I've been waiting for Four Roses to make this kind of statement of intent.... Wonderful! **50%.** *Four Roses Distillery.*

**Four Roses Single Barrel (90) n**22 unusual port cask-style fruitiness as rye-spices nip at the nose; **t**23 really fresh, full, clean and fruity. Just so mouthwatering; **f**22 the trademark caramel digs in, but some spices keep it alive; **b**23 faultless, refreshing bourbon that underlines this distillery's latent excellence. **43% (86 proof).** *Four Roses Distillery.*

**Four Roses Single Barrel** warehouse no. AS, barrel no. 23-5A **(83) n**23 **t**21 **f**19 **b**20. Great nose of formidable complexity, but what follows is on the dull side with too much sweet-corn and caramel. **50% (100 proof).** *Four Roses Distillery.*

⸬ **Four Roses Small Batch (93) n**24 a quiet aroma of cinnamon, allspice and red liquorice: soothing, if it wasn't so irresistibly drinkable... **t**22 sweet, with some telling rye fruitiness; **f**23 long, a degree of oils and juicy, fruity notes; **b**24 pure Four Roses. Nosing and tasting this was so in keeping with its style that it took me back to a journey I once made on the Kentucky River when golden Baltimore Oriols and fireflies danced by the riverbank...and Four Roses was the perfect companion. I need a break at my old Kentucky home... **45% (90 proof).** *Four Roses Distillery.*

**Four Roses Super Premium (83)** n22 t21 f20 b20. Corn oil dominates, caramel hovers, lazy spices buzz: business as usual. **43% (86 proof).** *Four Roses Distillery.*

**Gentleman Earl** (*see* Heaven Hill 80 Proof)

**George T. Stagg (94)** n23 vanillin dominates slightly over the small grain, which is unusual, and although there are some citric segments the oak dominates; t24 back on course with wondrous verve and vigour, fruity rye tones leading the way followed by big liquorice; f23 toasty, hints of hickory; b24 another thundering glass of genius and so complex despite the massive strength. Perhaps a shade oakier, though, than some of its predecessors. **70.6% (141.2 proof).** *Buffalo Trace.*

**George T Stagg (97)** n24 for all its enormity in strength, this is a pussycat on the nose with playful yet elegant brushstrokes of cough sweet (Fishermen's Friends!), dried dates and camp coffee. Busy and beautiful; t24 wonderful delivery of confident tannins, bolstered by a double whammy of fruit and corn which dissolve in the mouth to quite stunning effect. Enormous, yet so wonderful: perhaps this is what sex is like for masochists; f25 again, the alcoholic strength is defied by the deftness of the lapping flavours that break upon the tastebuds: more coffee and also cocoa notes with slightly sweetened citrus zest; b24 whisky of the year? Probably has to be. The tasting of whiskies for this year's Bible has been so difficult because the quality has jumped so high. But nothing has quite reached these heights.... **64.5% (129 proof).**

**George T Stagg (97)** n25 t24 f23 b25. I have tried this with water at varying strengths, but to get the best out of this bourbon you must be brave. Take at full strength, but only in very small amounts. Such is the enormity of this whiskey it will soon spread around the palate offering its full service. Along with a certain Ardbeg, this George T Stagg is without any shadow of a doubt one of the two   best whiskies it has ever been my luck and privilege to taste in nearly 30 years. **68.8% (137.6 proof).** *Buffalo Trace.*

**George T. Stagg (96)** n25 can something this delicate really be 140 proof?? An aroma that drifts like butterflies with no shortage of nectar to feed on; the strands of honey are both deft and deep and balance well with the honeycomb; dulcet rye tones soar on the spirity thermals and oak offers a soft, vanilla-rich cladding. Simply the stuff of whiskey dreams...; t22 begins sweet but nosedives into something surprisingly dry, mildly compromising the balance for a while until it rediscovers its equilibrium with a wave or ten of Belgian chocolate; f25 returns to its brilliance once more with those cocoa notes now harmonising with the returning rye; just so long and the late arrival of an orangey, citrus thread doesn't hurt at all; in fact the finish is near perfection; b24 just one moment or two's madness, where the plot is lost may have cost this one World Whisky of the Year. Another staggering Stagg, a serious improvement on the previous bottling and a collector's must-have. **70.3% (140.6 Proof). ncf.**

**George T. Stagg Spring 2005 Release (92)** n22 lazy, depending on heaps of natural caramel; t24 big, blustery start and then a massive delivery of spice on top of the coffee-tannin; lashings of sweet corn; f23 a long finish, as can be expected, but much more corn than usual and less complexity; b23 truly great whiskey, but slightly lacking in style by Stagg's almost unseemly high standards. **65.5% (130.9 proof).** *Buffalo Trace.*

**George T Stagg Spring 2005 Release (97)** n24 pulsing corn and rye; more small grain involvement than usual – fabulous complexity and grace; t24 the rye delivers the first bite, then come several waves of rich tannin; lots of Demerara richness in there, too; f24 long, gradually sweetening, soft waxiness helps the burnt honeycomb stick to the roof of the mouth and keep the fun lasting longer; with the Fishermen's Friends cough sweets (on the nose of the 129 version) appearing at the death here; b25 just what is it about George T Stagg? Three bottlings in the last year, and two are in the short-list of six for Whisky of the Year. The quality defies belief...!! **65.9% (131.8 proof).** *Buffalo Trace.*

**Gold Country Aged 8 Years (88)** n22 marzipan and marmalade; t22 the most teasing criss-crossing soft, sweet vanilla and firmer grains; never more than a gentle caress; f21 soft as a marshmallow and as roasted at the end as a toasted one; b23 exceptionally delicate for its age and colour. Take your time to discover this most subtle of bourbons. **40% (80 proof).** *France, Denmark.*

**Gold Label** (*see* Heaven Hill 80 Proof)

**Hancock's Reserve Single Barrel (83)** n21 t22 f20 b20. Cream caramel... with a dose of rye to liven things up. **44.45% (88.9 proof).** *Buffalo Trace.*

**Heaven Hill Old Style Bourbon (77)** n18 t20 f19 b20. Young, yet a sweeter, weightier, mildly oilier expression than a couple of years back, with better balance and depth to finish. **40%**

**Heaven Hill 86 Proof (83)** n20 t22 f20 b21. Probably the maltiest bourbon I have tasted in 29 years of savouring the stuff: barley springs out at you from all directions. Fresh, juicy and mouthwatering: delicious and a real surprise package. **43% (86 proof).**

**Heaven Hill 100 Proof (78)** n19 t20 f19 b20. Lots of rye and toffee. **50%**

**Heaven Hill 6 Years Old (83)** n19 t21 f22 b2. Quite a change from previous bottlings, with more youth here, less evident rye domination but lashings of mouthwatering grains nonetheless. Some late liquorice hinting age at the finish. **40% (80 proof).**

**Heaven Hill Old Style Bourbon 6 Years Old 90 Proof (85)** n20 t21 f22 b22. Very well made whiskey on permanant cruise control. **45% (90 proof).**

**Heaven Hill Old Style Bourbon 6 Years Old 100 Proof (93)** n23 big rye fizz nibbles at the nose while some orangey oakiness adds brilliant balance; t23 massive arrival of small grains, perfectly presented. Demerara sugar gently coats the thickening oak and the spiced fruitiness really takes off as the rye dominates; f23 long, with those soft sugars still keeping the oak under control. The spices pulsate and some deliciously bitter, tangy marmalade completes the mind-blowing complexity; b24 I've been drinking HH at six years for a long, long time. And this is easily the best expression I ever happened across. A firecracker! **50% (100 proof).**

**Heaven Hill Aged 10 Years 86 Proof (86)** n21 t21 f22 b22. Takes a little time to get going but a sophisticated number in some ways showing greater age than expected with the whole being better than the parts. **43% (86 proof).**

**Heaven Hill Ultra Deluxe (89)** n22 no shortage of pounding rye lessens an oaky grip; t22 again the rye wants to lead the way, but a custardy, corny sweetness keeps it in check; f22 wonderful small grain interplay lightens the developing big oak liquorice; b23 no age statement on label, so presumably a 4-y-o. The thing is, it's taken off from the old standard bottling which was once the same recipe and age, leaving it standing. Much sturdier, oakier and and just so deliciously bourbony!! Just great stuff and one of the biggest improvements on the Kentucky stage. **40% (80 proof).**

**Heaven Hill Ultra Deluxe 5 Years (76)** n20 t19 f18 b19. In a bit of a toffeed trough here, halfway between the juicy, lively 4-y-o and the more, smallgrain pounding, oak-heavy 6-y-o. **40% (80 proof).**

**Heaven Hill Ultra DeLuxe 6 Years** (*see* Heaven Hill Aged 6 Years 90 Proof)

**Henry McKenna** (*see* Heaven Hill Aged 6 Years 80 Proof)

**Henry McKenna Single Barrel Aged 10 Years** barrel 278, barrelled on 21 Jun 94 **(86)** n20 t23 f21 b22. This guy looks as though he's lived most his life in the rafters. Great stuff, but the more complex notes are lost under the oak. **50% (100 proof).**

**Henry Mason Bourbon (83)** n19 t21 f22 b21. Light and playful with a delicious citrus edge to the liquorice. **40% (80 proof).**

**Jacob's Well** batch B-0230-JW459 **(84)** n22 t20 f21 b21. Still seen around from time to time (though pretty rarely), this small-batch bourbon concentrates on a lavender delicacy and subtle sweetness. **42% (84 proof).** *Jim Beam.*

**Jefferson's Reserve 15 Year Old** batch no. 2 **(94)** n24 this is to die for: gently oiled, which means the rye and corn stick to the nose, the sweetness and sharp fruit in equal measure; t24 brilliant corn/rye entry on the palate then a shimmering honey. Great age, but always elegant and refined while the complexity dazzles; f22 very soft landing with vanilla and rye to the fore. The complexity remains superb; b24 a great whiskey: simple as that. **45.1% (90.2 proof).**

**Jim Beam (85)** n21 t21 f22 b21. This whiskey has improved enormously in recent years. Still light and easy going, there appears to be an element of extra age, weight and complexity. **40%**

**Jim Beam Black (91)** n23 big and bruising, there is weighty oil and liquorice; t23 beautifully sweet, manuka honey and then liquorice, candy and rich rye; f22 soft vanilla and liquorice; b23 I just so love this bourbon. The closest in style to a Jack Daniel's because of a mildly lumbering gait. Any time, any day whiskey of the very top order. **43% (86 proof).**

**Jim Beam Premium Aged 7 Seven Years Old** (White Label) db **(82)** n21 t21 f20 b20. Hard, uncompromising and showing little of what is to come with a stunning 8-years-old. Young in character even to the point of the Old Taylor from the same stable entirely outflanking this for complexity and riches. That said, good crispness and a lovely – and unexpectedly – malty tail- off in middle. Decent but disappointing. **40% (80 proof).**

**Jim Beam's Choice Aged 5 Years (86)** n21 t21 f22 b22. Soft and impressive in places with the emphasis on natural caramel. A slightly different Beam style. **40% (80 proof).**

**Jim Porter** (see Heaven Hill 80 Proof)

**John Hamilton** (see Heaven Hill 80 Proof)

**J T S Brown** (see Heaven Hill 80 Proof)

**J T S Brown 86 Proof** (see Heaven Hill 86 Proof)

**J T S Brown 100 Proof** (see Heaven Hill 100 Proof)

**J T S Brown 6 Years 80 Proof** (see Heaven Hill Aged 6 Years 80 Proof)

**J T S Brown 6 Years 100 Proof** (see Heaven Hill Aged 6 Years 100 Proof)

**J T S Brown 8 Years** (see Old Heaven Hill Very Rare Aged 8 Years 86 Proof)

**J T S Brown 10 Years** (see Heaven Hill 10 Years 86 Proof)

**J W Dant 80 proof** (see Heaven Hill 80 Proof)

**J W Dant 100 proof** (see Heaven Hill 100 Proof)

**J W Kent** (see Heaven Hill 80 Proof)

**Kentucky Beau** (see Heaven Hill 80 Proof)

**Kentucky Crown Aged 8 Years (88)** n22 pipe-tobacco-sweet, sensual; t22 there is a layer of oily, sweet corn before spices arrive; f22 sweet vanilla and corn; b22 a charmingly sweet yet spicy bourbon. **45% (90 proof).** Germany.

**Kentucky Crown Very Rare Aged 16 Years (87)** n22 distinct kumquat and over-ripe pears, really excellent oak; t23 sweet, oily corn followed by liquorice and citrus: big, threatening yet mouthwatering; f20 levels out with a tad too much natural caramel; b22 a mildly abrupt toffeed end just when it was getting good. **53.5% (107 proof).** Germany.

**Kentucky deLuxe** (see Heaven Hill 80 Proof)

**Kentucky deLuxe 86 Proof** (see Heaven Hill 86 Proof)

**Kentucky Gentleman (89)** n23 improbable small-grains complexity for a whiskey so young; t23 lots of rye charging around the palate and malt adds something sweet and weighty. The corn imposes itself gently; f21 quietens and becomes a little bitter; b22 this was always a little belter for its age, but this is the best I have tasted yet. The small-grain quality is unimpeachable. Delicious. **40% (80 proof).** Barton.

**Kentucky Gold** (see Heaven Hill 80 Proof)

**Kentucky Spirit Single Barrel** (see Wild Turkey)

**Kentucky Supreme Aged 8 Years (78)** n20 t21 f18 b19. Flinty, a little rawer, more awkward and younger than it should be for its age, and has changed track from the Old Heaven Hill 8-y-o it used to tread. **40%.** Heaven Hill.

**Kentucky Tavern (86)** n22 t22 f21 b21. Typical fare from Barton distillery: for Scotch drinkers, their whiskey is the equivalent of young Speyside malt, refreshing and mouthwatering. This is no exception. **40% (80 proof).** Barton.

**Knob Creek Aged 9 Years (90)** n24 marmalade on slightly burnt toast, beautiful, sweet fruit, mainly pears, and then a dash of soft rye and an edge of saltiness, some honey as a side-dish; t22 softly spiced, oaky, busy start; then a powerful delivery of natural toffee. A playfully biting, tastebud-nipping character tries to add momentum; f22 chocolate toffee balances out the vanilla and ensures a dry, slightly oily and long finish; b22 the best aroma from the JBB Small Batch selection; softer on the tastebuds than previous bottlings, but still a power player. **50% (100 proof).** Jim Beam.

**Labrot & Graham Woodford Reserve** (see Woodford Reserve)

**Lone Oak Aged 12 Long Years (89)** n23 t24 f20 b22. The short, simple finish is a bit of a surprise package in one of the silkiest bourbons on the market shelf. **50.5% (101 proof).** Germany.

**McAfee's Benchmark (79)** n20 t21 f19 b19. Light, young, corn-rich with big caramel. **40% (80 proof).** Buffalo Trace.

**McAfee's Benchmark 8 Years Old (83)** n21 t21 f20 b21. Fruity, mouthwatering and refreshing. **40% (80 proof).** Buffalo Trace.

**McScrooge's** (see Heaven Hill 80 Proof)

**Maker's Mark (Black Wax Seal)** (gold on black label) **(93)** n23 thick, charred notes, deep, mildly waxy, hints of cordite; t24 oily and immediately mouthfilling with a quite stupendous soft honey, grainy sweetness that balances almost to perfection with the toasty, liquorice-caramel, burnt sugar deeper tones. A pepperiness is on a wavelength almost too subtle to be heard. This is cerebral drinking; **f**22 much less taxing on the tastebuds with a more toffeed departure. Vanilla and other well-ordered oaky tones are also present and correct; **b**24 simply outstanding bourbon with the most clever weight ratio. A whiskey that demands solitude and the ability to listen. The story it tells is worth hearing again and again. **47.5% (95 proof).**

**Makers Mark (Gold Wax) Limited Edition (89) n**22 distinctly fruity, nutty and dense; **t**23 full-bodied and full-throttle corn carrying a lovely liquorice sweetness; **f**21 thins out to allow a waxy oakiness to develop; quite flinty at the death; **b**22 majestic and a meal in itself. **50.5% (101 proof).**

**Maker's Mark (Red Wax Seal)** (black on buff label) **(89) n**23 wispy aroma with delightful strands of exotic fruit and honey. The old fruitcake is still there, but these days the complexity and balance are nothing short of stunning. Beguiling oak adds to the overall feeling of class; **t**23 lush, pleasingly deep and quite malty. A firm nuttiness adds extra oily, chewability to the toffee and liquorice; **f**21 perhaps drier than of old with signs of a little extra age. Caramel toffee continues its interplay with the oak to guarantee a bitter-sweet edge; **b**22 an old faithful of a bourbon. Never lets you down and being from the wheaty school always shows good oak balance. **45% (90 proof).** *Fortune Brands.*

**Mark Twain** (*see* Heaven Hill 80 Proof)

**Mark Twain Aged 12 Years 100 Proof (88) n**22 the obvious oak remains light and corny; **t**22 hard rye and fruity, the sweetness is well camouflaged; **f**22 slightly burnt toast, very roasty; **b**22 a well-disciplined bourbon that looks at one point as though the oak has taken too firm a grip but the complexity never ends. **50% (100 proof).** *Heaven Hill.*

**Martin Mills** (*see* Heaven Hill 80 Proof)

**Mattingly & Moore** (*see* Heaven Hill 80 Proof)

**May's** (*see* Heaven Hill 80 Proof)

**Medley (85) n**18 **t**23 **f**22 **b**22. Intimate small grains make this an unusual and sophisticated experience. **40% (80 proof).**

**Mellow Bourbon** (*see* Heaven Hill 80 Proof)

**Military Special** (*see* Heaven Hill 80 Proof)

**Mound City** (*see* Heaven Hill 80 Proof)

**Noah's Mill** batch 02-71, dist 2 Jul 87, bott 1 Nov 02 **(91) n**23 **t**23 **f**21 **b**24. This is one of Kentucky's most complex whiskies by far. Small grains, big heart. **57.15% (114.3 proof).**

**No Face** (*see* Heaven Hill 80 Proof)

**No Face 86 Proof** (*see* Heaven Hill 86 Proof)

**Old 1889** (*see* Heaven Hill 80 Proof)

**Old 1889 Aged 10 Years 86 Proof (85) n**22 **t**20 **f**22 **b**21. Really quite different HH from what I usually see. This is much more light and delicate with less of the usual richness those old big copper stills guaranteed. A real one-off. **43% (86 proof).** *Heaven Hill.*

**Old 1889 Royal Aged 12 Years (79) n**22 **t**20 **f**18 **b**19. Like a heavier, older version of Sam Clay 12 with a unique style based on small grain, but the balance isn't quite there. **43% (46 proof).** *Heaven Hill.*

**Old Bardstown Aged 6 Years (83) n**19 **t**21 **f**22 **b**21. A thin nose compensated for by decent rye-based small grain on entertaining finale. **40% (80 proof).**

**Old Bardstown Aged 10 Years Estate Bottled (95) n**24 syrup; heavyduty molten liquoricel lovely rye sub-strata with even a hint of lavender. Some kumquats and burnt raisin complete the dreamy ultra-complex intro; **t**24 sit down and take a thumping: like chewing chocolate fudge except each and every tasebud is caked in a beautifully oiled, all-consuming liquor from heaven (hill?); **f**23 lighter oils allow the small grains to display their soft, surprisingly mouthwatering charms; some surprising late oranges; **b**24 this is what great bourbon is all about. An absolute masterpiece from the old school and, tragically, also probably from a now lost distillery. Go get!! **50.5% (101 proof).**

**Old Charter 8 Years Old (77) n**19 **t**19 **f**20 **b**19. A simple, sweet, toffeed bourbon with limited complexity. On this evidence, not quite what it once was. **40% (80 proof).**

**Old Charter 10 Years Old (93) n**24 busy, beautifully balanced and ball-busting. Brilliant! **t**23 so much zipping spice from the off, it's like Talisker has come to Kentucky; **f**22 sweetens out to its old corn-fest...eventually. Chewy and lip-smacking, being mouthwatering from first to last; **b**24 whoa! What's happened here? A real candy Charter that has eschewed its old plodding style for something, for all its sweetness, that exudes a touch of dynamite. **43% (86 proof).** *Buffalo Trace.*

**Old Charter 12 Years Old (87) n**22 some dazzling oak but always enough room for the small grains to flourish; **t**23 small-grain arrival on palate; genuinely complex with a spicy kick all the way; **f**20 surprising amount of natural toffee flattens it a little; **b**22 until that toffee arrives this is a deliciously complex dram. Well worth an investigation. **45% (90 proof).**

**Old Charter Proprietor Reserve 13 Years Old (89) n**23 kumquats and lemon peel, marmalade on light toast; **t**22 fruity from the word go then a wave of corn and very soft rye; **f**21 gentle vanillas; **b**23 what an enormously delicate bourbon for such great age. Graceful and charming. **45% (90 proof).**

**Old Crow (79) n**19 **t**20 **f**21 **b**19. Young, sweet, oddly minty, reasonably chewy, and with recent bottlings improving deliciously on some flat offerings of a year or two back. Pretty impressive for a self-declared 3-y-o. **40% (80 proof)**. *Jim Beam.*

**Old Fitzgerald (79) n**18 **t**20 **f**21 **b**20. One of the sweetest bourbons around: the nose does it no favours but a chewy toffee fightback. **43% (86 proof).**

**Old Fitzgerald Very Special 12 Years Old (80) n**18 **t**23 **f**20 **b**19. Warming spice paves the way for a crashing wave of corn and oak. But that excellent middle apart, something is curiously lacking. **45% (90 proof).**

**Old Fitzgerald's 1849 8 Years (90) n**21 ethereal corn and wheat; **t**23 lush and sweet arrival with a mixture of sugar and honey on the corn: the wheat fizzes around the roof of the mouth; **f**23 remains sweet with a late citrus surge and then drier vanilla tones; **b**23 light yet big. The sweetness is enormous but avoids going OTT thanks to excellent oak balance. A delight and the best of the Old Fitz range by a country mile. **45% (90 proof).**

**Old Forester (89) n**22 an explosion of small grains pepper the nose, hints of marmalade; **t**23 chunky and deep with liquorice-toffee but it's the softly spiced apple and pear juiciness that wins the day; **f**22 the liqorice factor increases as oak makes a stand; **b**22 if anyone asks me to show them a classic rye-rich bourbon where the small grains really count, as often as not I'll show them this. **43%**

**Old Forester Birthday Bourbon Vintage 1990 (90) n**23 **t**23 **f**22 **b**22. Seriously delicate and sophisticated bourbon. **44.5% (89 proof).** *Brown-Forman.*

**Old Forester Birthday Bourbon Vintage 1990 95 Proof (91) n**22 **t**23 **f**23 **b**23. Not for the squeamish: there is enormous complexity, but laid on with a trowel. **47.5%**

**Old Forester Birthday Bourbon Distilled Spring 1993 Bottled 2005 (94) n**24 intense, almost concentrated form of a bury-fruited rye-rich Forester. Absolutely massive, yet strokes the nose rather than biffs it; **t**23 silky from the moment of delivery on the tastebuds to the final fade, that intensity encountered on the nose is no less complete here. There is rye enough to make you swoon, packaged in an oaky cloak; **f**23 first, great corn oil seeps through the oak-rye dominance to offer a sweeter edge and the most gentle of landings; **b**24 one of the most rye-studded stars in the bourbon firmament and wholly in keeping with the fabulous quality for which this brand has now become a byword. **40%**

**Old Forester Birthday Bourbon 1995** dist Fall 95, bott 04 **(94) n**23 ultra-ripe apples and sultanas, a sprinkling of black pepper and a firm rye skeleton on which for it to hold; **t**24 the corn is friendly and yielding, the oak is controlled yet profound with some toasty, burnt raisiny qualities; **f**23 sultry, juicy fruits and then a blossoming of gingery spice; **b**24 just so wonderfully fruity and full: the stuff of traditional British fruitcake. Yet it doesn't come more American than this.... **47% (94 proof).** *Brown-Forman.*

**Old Forester 100 Proof (89) n**23 beautifully weighted clementine, hickory and coffee: a real nose full; **t**22 cream toffee sweetens out with fat corn and a sprinkling of molassed sugar. The rye thuds in alongside some glittering spice; **f**22 the spice just continues its tingling journey around the palate, soft toffee and vanilla offering a softer finish than predicted; **b**22 as ever, very high quality bourbon from one of Kentucky's most consistent distilleries. **50% (100 proof).**

**Old Grand-Dad 100 Proof (89) n**23 excellent hickory and charcoal signature. Excellent weight and gentle fruit input; **t**23 rugged silky; bites as rye hits home; **f**21 just loses it here slightly as the oak seems to caramelise out the fun; **b**22 still has beef and guts, packs a punch and delights. But even so, just not in the same league as the original masterpiece from the lost Frankfort distillery. **50%**

**Old Heaven Hill** (*see* Heaven Hill 80 Proof)

**Old Heaven Hill 100 Proof** (*see* Heaven Hill 100 Proof)

**Old Heaven Hill Very Rare Aged 8 Years 80 Proof (82) n**20 **t**21 **f**21 **b**20. Unusually citrussy for this distillery: lemon and lime knitting with green corn. Amazingly youthful for its age. **40% (80 proof).**

**Old Heaven Hill Very Rare Aged 8 Years 86 Proof (86) n**21 **t**22 **f**21 **b**21. Intriguing bourbon with greater maturity than the 80 proof version: delightful in its own right, but just on the edge of something significant, you feel. **43%**

**Old Heaven Hill Very Rare Old Aged 10 Years (86) n**22 **t**21 **f**21 **b**22. An improvement thanks to some subtle extra rye activity. **40% (80 proof).**

**Old Heaven Hill Very Rare Aged 10 Years 86 Proof** (*see* Heaven Hill 10 Years 86 Proof)

**Old Heaven Hill Very Rare Aged 10 Years 100 Proof (93) n**23 heavier and rich, fruitcake style. Really beautiful and subtle but telling rye involvement; **t**24 weighty and just so spectacularly rich. Really is prize-winning heavy British fruitcake with raisins and cherries to chew on before a lovely walnut oiliness arrives, followed by corn concentrate; **f**23 the lull after the storm, but the birds sing sweetly because the rye re-appears for a gentle but wonderfully complex finale; **b**23 this is astonishing bourbon, the type that makes you glad to be in the know. Brilliant. **50% (100 proof).**

**Old Heaven Hill Aged 15 Years 100 Proof (86) n**21 **t**22 **f**22 **b**21. For all the whiskey's colour, this doesn't have much of a 15-years-old's normal belligerent attitude. This is sweet and flighty and a little oily, too. Most un-Heaven Hill. **50%**

**Old Joe Aged 12 Years Bottled in Bond** (distilled at DSP KY 39) **(91) n**21 perhaps sluggish at first but some biting corn and oak make amends before the rye really takes off; **t**24 beautiful radiance of sweet, rich corn backed by deep rye. Lots of copper influence here: amazingly rich yet firm and solid; **f**23 still bites deep but the rye/oak/coffee/burnt raisin union is strong and long; **b**24 an absolutely top-notch bourbon, beyond the nose, of the very old school that just exudes class and charisma. **50% (100 proof).**

**Old Kentucky Amber Aged 10 Years (87) n**22 **t**21 **f**22 **b**22. A chilled-out, relaxed bourbon at first finally gets the rye to talk. **45% (90 proof).** *Germany.*

**Old Kentucky No. 88 Brand Aged 13 Years (92) n**22 **t**24 **f**23 **b**23. Stunning: classic proportions: hard to find, but grab a bottle if you can. **47%** *Germany.*

**Old Rip 12 Years Old (93) n**22 heavily molassed, kumquats and grapes; **t**24 shimmering over-ripe tomatoes with red liquorice candy; lots of rye spice prickles about; **f**23 much more sensual now with sweet corn mash fading out with some vanilla and bitter-sweet chocolate; **b**24 for a 12-y-o the colour is sensationally dark: must have spent a lifetime in the highest ricks: textbook bittersweet balance. **52.5% (105 proof).**

**Old Rip Van Winkle Bourbon Aged 10 Years (91) n**23 bigger than its ten years: must have lived in a warehouse roof. German-style caramelized biscuit and hint of molasses; **t**22 honeycomb from the off, drying towards middle; again a touch of molasses and rye-rich fruitiness; **f**23 big, long, slightly fat and some lovely and lively liquorice and Java/Kenya blend medium roast coffee at the very death; **b**23 big stuff: a bourbon not for the faint hearted. **53.3%.** *Buffalo Trace.*

**Old Rip Van Winkle 10 Years Old 90 Proof (88) n**23 chocolate marzipan and corn; **t**22 sweet, slightly oily and demerara sugar; **f**21 spicy vanilla; **b**22 really well balanced and weighty whiskey. **45% (90 proof).**

**Old Rip Van Winkle 10 Years Old (92) n**22 tangerine and oak dust; **t**24 improbable oak arrival for a 10-y-o offset by the mouth luxurious delivery of wonderful rye and asociated fruitiness. The depth of sweetness for balance has been calculated to the nth degree; **f**22 calms towards vanilla; **b**24 some 10-y-o! Must have come from the top of the warehouse or thereabouts. A real big mouthful of chunky excellence. **53.5% (107 proof).** *Buffalo Trace.*

**Old Rip Van Winkle 12 Years Old (89) n**21 light and fruity, figs and distant liquorice; **t**23 juicy, a hint of malt at first, grass and grapes and then harder rye and soft corn: deliciously complex; **f**22 liquorice and some gritty rye; **b**23 wonderful balance and drive to this bourbon: for something so outwardly light, the flavours just keep on coming. **45.2% (90.4 proof).**

**Old Rip Van Winkle Bourbon Aged 13 Years (87) n**22 so astonishingly spiced and big, this could easily be read as a Swedish aquavit; **t**22 yes, I must be in Stockholm: those extraordinary battles between soft sugars and spice; **f**21 chewy vanilla and caramel; some major age at the death; **b**22 very different: in fact I have never seen a Buffalo Trace whiskey like it. There are restaurants in Stockholm's Old Town whose owners would offer major favours to have a house aquavit like this. **53.3%.** Buffalo Trace.

**Old Rip Van Winkle 15 Years Old (95) n**24 intense honey-nut and corn, like breakfast cereal in which you could happily bury your nose; **t**24 biting corn forms the bitter-sweet, slightly oily background with some oak arriving early, but adds only depth and something else to chew on; **f**23 enormously complex: again the corn leads the way but the honey returns with some cocoa and a bit of mouth prickle keeps the tastebuds occupied further; **b**24 this is a cracker. It always was and it appears to have gone up a notch in intensity all along the line. For weight, texture and complexity, this is a superstar whiskey. **53.5% (107 proof).** Buffalo Trace.

**Old Taylor Aged 6 Years** (present bottling) **(89) n**23 marzipan and Seville orange offer a delightful lightness of touch and teasing complexity; **t**23 almost a hint of single malt about the lightness of touch to the honey here; the arrival is sweet and busy with just enough oaky depth to add ballast; **f**21 almost vanishes off the palate though the rye and spice stick around to impress; **b**22 the curiously thin finish is in telling contrast to the superbly honeyed middle that simple dances with small-grain charm. So much lighter than the original Old Taylor (see below) of McCracken Pike. But certainly has enough weight and fruit punch to make this better than the cheap brand it is perceived to be. **40%**

**Old Taylor Aged 6 Years** (old bottling) **(94) n**24 there is a beautiful affinity between the deep vanilla and the orange and rye fruitiness. Textbook harmonization and bourbon, though I suspect whiskeys old than six are in this; **t**23 comforting oils help propel that distinct rye note to deep areas of the palate; rich and mildly mollassed; **f**23 long, lots more vanilla but you can't escape the twist of rye and a soft honeycomb and spice flourish; **b**24 just a mile from my home in Kentucky stands, or perhaps I should say stood, the Old Taylor distillery. It may not still be there because the widow of my close and dearly missed friend, Cecil Withrow, finally sold it and the old place where Cecil once worked and, until his untimely death, harboured dreams of distilling again, faces the almost certain prospect of the demolition ball. I thought it fitting, then, that for my 1,000th whiskey tasted from this 2007 edition of the Bible it should be an original Old Taylor six-years-old which I found this year in a back street liquor store in Verona, Italy. In fact there are still many bottles of this truly classic bourbon to be found in that country and if visiting Italy for its architecture and food isn't enticing enough, then here must be the ultimate reason. And just to put a strange and fitting twist to this tale, how about this: as I was tasting and writing these notes a delivery van turned up. Nothing unusual there: we get four or five deliveries of samples every day. This, though, was a special shipment from Peru: the very first copy of a special edition of the Whisky Bible I produced for the 2006 US Christmas market. And the book had been specially dedicated to... the memory of Cecil Withrow... **40%.** Old Taylor & Co.

**Old Virginia Aged 8 Years** L434401A **(85) n**22 **t**21 **f**21 **b**21. Vanilla-rich and never quite lives up to the bold nose. **40%.** La Martiniquaise, France.

**Old Weller Antique 107 7 Years in Wood (89) n**21 a bit of a young scrapper; **t**22 nitro on a bed of TNT with some unstable plutonium thrown in for good measure; **f**23 at last reveals some sanity as a soft corn base offers some sweet goodies. Long and just so soothing...; **b**22 to think I once called this lethargic...!! Bloody hell...!!! **52.5% (107 proof).** Buffalo Trace. See also Weller and WL Weller for other members of the same "family".

**Original Barrel Bourbon Aged 12 Years** (see Daniel Stewart Aged 12 Years)

**Pappy Van Winkle 20 Years Old (79) n**19 **t**22 **f**19 **b**19. Just so weird how this whiskey refuses to play ball at this age. It's won awards left, right and centre, got marks fom judges that leave you gasping...yet for me, as ever, it just falls all over the place with an over-sweet, total inability to find its story. That said, one or two wonderful phrases along the way and far less oak than before. **45.2% (90.4 proof).** Buffalo Trace.

**Pappy Van Winkle 23 Years Old (88) n**22 forests of oak somehow tempered by the likes of green peppers and sprawling rye; **t23** explosive arrival of salty, tangy, black peppered oak which dovetails with at first soft corn and then a bigger hickory smoke kick; **f21** the oak really bites at first, but there is a surprising small grain revival...and then burnt toast; **b22** where the 20-y-o fails, the 23-y-o somehow succeeds despite the big oak. Flawed, but defies logic and your tastebuds. **47.8% (95.6 proof)**. *Buffalo Trace.*

**Pennypacker (87) n22** rye-rich small grains bury themselves deeply into the fruit and oak; **t22** a firm, brittle mouthfeel, again with the rye showing brightly; **f21** lots of honeyed vanilla and hazelnuts amid the vanilla; **b22** the PR blurb from the importers that came with this bottle said the whiskey is three years old. It's a lot older than that, I can assure you. **40% (80 proof)**. *Borco Hamburg.*

**Real McCoy (82) n21 t20 f21 b20.** Some early rye and liquorice fails to give this oily bourbon the firm backbone it needs or a conclusive direction. Attractive and mildly spiced but a little frustrating. **37%.** *Australia.*

**Rebecca** (*see* Heaven Hill 10 Years 86 Proof)

**Rebel Yell (86) n22 t21 f21 b22.** My word: this brand has moved on some. The fiery, spicy peppery attack has vanished entirely and the citrus notes have been replaced by softer strawberries, but stays true to its fruity style. Lovely wheated stuff. **40% (80 proof).**

**Red Eye Aged 6 Years (86) n21 t22 f21 b22.** A bourbon of attractive complexity and weight. **45% (90 proof)**. *Bardstown.*

**Ridgemont Reserve 1792 (90) n22** small grains abound with rye and vanilla passionately embraced; a lovely waft of acacia honey offers the balance; **t23** subtle delivery of rich small grains again, this time on a bed of Muscovado sugar; **f22** a gathering of oaky spices with weighty honeycomb, liquorice and hickory confirming the age; **b23** quality bourbon from a distillery that rarely allows its spirit to age this far. The result is a sophisticated bourbon exuding a rye-rich charisma and the most subtle of sweet themes. **46.85% (93.7 proof)**. *Barton Brands.*

**Rock Hill Farms (89) n21** thin, but honeyed; **t22** slightly hot at first with developing sweet corn; **f24** slowly awakens and the small grains go wild: the rye kicks in to give a hard fruit edge, a hint of malt but the sweet corn and oak combining is superb; **b22** rock by name, rock by nature: a very hard whiskey which rewards patient study handsomely. **50% (100 proof)**. *Buffalo Trace.*

**Rowan's Creek** batch 02-72, dist 26 Feb 85, bott 5 Nov 02 **(78) n21 t20 f18 b19**. Loads of honey and liquorice, but way too heavily oaked. **50% (100 proof)**

**Russell's Reserve 10** (*see* Wild Turkey Russell's Reserve 10 Aged 10 Years)

**Sainsbury's Kentucky Bourbon Three Years Old (71) n18 t18 f17 b18.** Pleasant, sweet but too young to have gathered a personality. The bland, caramel finish is rather odd. **40% (80 proof)**. *Sainsbury's, UK.*

**Sam Clay** (*see* Heaven Hill Aged 6 Years 80 Proof)

**Sam Clay 8 Years** (*see* Old Heaven Hill Very Rare Aged 8 Years 80 Proof)

**Sam Clay Aged 12 Years (87) n24** it is all about small grain plus a carrot juice and vanilla flourish. Unique...; **t22** an uneven arrival of fruit and rye with the corn having varying depth: at once big and small; **f20** so light it almost flutters off without noticing, save for a gentle sugar juice layer; **b21** really don't know how to describe this, other than different. Suspect more than one distillery's bourbon has gone into this, because it refuses to follow any known route or style. **40% (80 proof).** *Heaven Hill.*

**Sam Sykes** (*see* Heaven Hill 80 Proof)

**Samuels 1844** (*see* Heaven Hill Aged 6 Years 101 Proof)

**Seven Hills** (*see* Evan Williams Aged 7 Years 86 Proof)

**Smokey Jim's (85) n21** excellent small-grain complexity; **t22** rich, full arrival on the palate; brilliant mouthfeel; **f21** back to a dark, juicy, fruity rye character towards the end; **b21** genuinely complex and satisfying everyday bourbon. Excellent. **40% (80 proof).**

**Stars & Stripes (79) n19 t20 f21 b19.** Curious whiskey: good colour yet seems young and unfulfilled in many ways. Competent and enjoyable. **40%**

**Ten High (70) n17 t18 f17 b18.** Light, clean and untaxing. Good for mixing. **40% (80 proof)**. *Barton.*

**Tesco Old Kentucky (78) n19 t20 f19 b20.** Young, sweet, very clean with a hint of hickory. **40% (80 proof).**

**Thedford Colonial Style** Batch No 001 **(93)** n24 whoa boy!!! Enormous and gratifying. Big age with coffee and vanilla thumping home, but kept in check by old orangey fruitiness. Immense; **t22** back to normality after the big alcohol bite, bringing in softer vanilla and small grains; **f24** feather-soft finish with lovely oils and deep, dark mocca; an absolute joy; **b23** not an easy whiskey to find, but find it you must. It is a tame monster. Last seen at The Vintage House, Soho, London. **46.3% (92.6 proof)**. *Josiah Thedford and Sons, Louisville.*

**Tom Moore (83)** n21 t20 f22 b20. The rye on the nose pops up at regular intervals on the palate, but overall this is a really deft, undemanding whiskey yet offering above-average complexity. **40% (80 proof)**. *Barton.*

**Tom Sims** (*see* Heaven Hill Aged 6 Years 80 Proof)

**T W Samuels** (*see* Heaven Hill 80, 86 and 100 Proof)

**T W Samuels 6 Years 90 Proof** (*see* Heaven Hill Aged 6 Years 90 Proof)

**Van Winkle Lot B 12 Years Old (80)** n18 t21 f20 b21. Competent, with required chewability, spice and sweetness, but loses out on a slightly suspect nose and too much natural caramel. **47.2% (94.4 proof)**. *Buffalo Trace.*

**Van Winkle Special Reserve (82)** n19 t22 f20 b21. Subdued nose, then a sweet, almost molassed explosion before a quick fade. Good early oak, though. **45.2% (90.4 proof)**.

**Very Old Barton Aged 6 Years (90)** n22 green and lively with the rye really getting in amongst the powering corn. Green tea is also about; **t22** brittle small grains melt into the sweetening corn: a touch oily and a tad spicier than of old **f24** the sharpness to the grain is stunningly accentuated in the late middle and the finish; ends like no other bourbon and offers a freshness that totally batters the tastebuds; **b22** it's a bit like sweetened green tea in alcohol with a strong rye kick-back. Unique as a style amongst bourbons and wholly enjoyable. More mouth-watering than any other bourbon known to mankind! **40% (80 proof)**. *Barton.*

**Virgin Bourbon 7 Years Old 101 Proof (92)** n23 pungent yet surprisingly deft oak, with chunky kumquats and hickory. Seven years old...?? **t23** terrific bittersweet arrival like honey and jam on burnt toast; slicks out surprisingly with corn oil. Soft rye noises are everywhere; **f22** foot of the gas to a degree, but the building of spice ends all hope of corn domination; **b24** if this is a 7-y-o, then every single barrel must have been drapped down from the top rick. [Allo Allo?] Deep amber and looking three times its stated age. Big stuff, as usual: in some ways even bigger than of old. **50.5% (101 proof)**. *Heaven Hill (Meadowlawn Distilling Co.).*

**Virgin Bourbon 15 Years Old 101 Proof (94)** n23 nutty, with small grains drifting in an oaky, saline sea; the nose doesn't quite prepare you for this Demerara-infested perfection of copper-topped small grain and the most mountainous and brilliantly balanced meltdown of oak and corn. A wizard has been at work here; **f23** calms slowly, with the oak always showing perfect manners. Traces of liquorice amid some flinty rye and that amazingly gentle corn; **b24** enjoy these last days of the original Heaven Hill, offering us almost heartbreaking vistas of what we are about to lose for ever. This is a classic bottling that has so improved on the last version. No lot number on this, sadly. It is unlikely you will ever forget the extraordinary bitter-sweet balance on this. A world heritage whiskey. **50.5% (101 proof)**. *Heaven Hill (Meadowlawn Distilling Co.).*

**Vom Fass Kentucky Straight Bourbon (83)** n20 t20 f22 b21. Young, sweet, unchallenging, well-made bourbon with a hint of Fisherman's Friend cough sweet. **40%**.

**Walker & Scott Bourbon (84)** n23 t20 f20 b21. A delightful pub bourbon of good age and impressive complexity. The nose in particular is an orgy of superb small grain. **40%**. *Samuel Smith UK.*

**Walker's DeLuxe 3 Years Old (86)** n22 t22 f21 b21 excellent by 3-y-o standards. **40% (80 proof)**.

**Weller Centennial 10 Years Old (90)** n23 soft fruit, citrus and freshly shelled peas: a delight; **t22** very dry start with a soft oak kick and spices: very warming; **f22** the small grains are now pounding at the tastebuds relentlessly; **b23** once a massive step upwards in a year or two. Once as gentle as a cruise on the Kentucky, now more a bungee off Natural Bridge. **50%**. *Buffalo Trace.*

**Weller 12 Years Old (90) n**23 oak is the star here, and at several levels, offering heavier liquorice notes and soft vanilla. Mint and apple also get in on the act; **t**23 sublime corn attack but the oak gives it a bitter edge: this is enormously intense stuff; **f**21 back to that toffee again: sweet and creamy and seeing off the oak; **b**23 immensely deep and satisfying with a magnificent chewability. **45%**

**W L Weller Special Reserve 7 Years Old (84) n**21 **t**22 **f**20 **b**21 A bigger whiskey than of old with lots of orangey tones on the nose and a lush, sweet and peppery body. **45% (90 proof)**. *For other members of the Weller "family" see also Old Weller and Weller.*

**Westridge** (*see* Heaven Hill 80 Proof)

**Wild Turkey 80 Proof (76) n**18 **t**19 **f**20 **b**19. Reverted to type with the corn not been quite happy either with itself or the half-cocked degree of oak penetration. Improves on palate, but shows little of the genius to follow in later ages. **40% (80 proof)**.

**Wild Turkey 86.8 Proof (87) n**20 attractive traces of walnut oil amid the soft corn and firmer rye; **t**22 an immediate impact of massive, oak-laden, liquoriced corn and firmer, more mouthwatering grains; **f**22 sweetens with a slight stirring of honey; **b**23 it's not just the extra strength that takes this into a different class from the 80 proof. Much better barrel selection, underlined by some surprising liquorice notes. Easily the best non-age-stated standard Wild Turkey I've ever come across. **43.4% (86.8 proof)**.

**Wild Turkey 101 Proof (85) n**19 **t**21 **f**23 **b**22 needs a bit of a kick start and then clucks and gobbles along beautifully. **50.5% (101 proof)**.

**Wild Turkey 8 Years Old (88) n**22 bingo! The real Wild Turkey is standing up with extra spices on the orange field; **t**22 massive spice infusion from the start with the sweet, oily corn softening things down slightly; **f**22 more rye to be seen
and the oak really does make a gracious exit; **b**22 quality whiskey showing effortless grace and deceptive weight. **50.5% (101 proof)**.

**Wild Turkey Russell's Reserve Aged 10 Years 101 Proof (96) n**23 stunning rye-citrus combo pans out to reveal a mint and oak-encrusted, leathery corn sweetness; **t**24 seriously mega for its age, not so much in the firm cocoa-oak but the utter enormity of the small-grain depth. Once more all paths lead to clean and chewy corn; **f**24 gentle, minty spices cool the mouth; **b**25 this is dream-time whiskey, entirely befitting the name of my close friend and mentor Jimmy Russell. This is a controlled explosion of complexity, the constant light sweetness overseeing those darker, brooding passages. Only Yoichi in Japan offers a stated 10-y-o whisky which can stand shoulder to shoulder with this, though not always. Entirely flawless whiskey. **50.5% (101 proof)**.

**Wild Turkey Russell's Reserve Aged 10 Years 90 proof (91) n**23 citrussy orange and kumquats play beautifully with the prominent rye; **t**24 brilliantly subtle and silky mouth arrival with a sweet-corn and acacia honey counter to the darker rye and oak tones; **f**21 trails off much faster than you might expect for an aged Wild Turkey, allowing the oak-caramel just a little too much depth, though the citrus returns as a pleasant afterthought; **b**23 I knew there was something quite different here from last year's Russell's Reserve, to which I gave the 10 and Under Bourbon of the Year award: that was élan, real Kentucky dynamite. Don't get me wrong. Remains brilliant to the last drop, but has lost that all-conquering controlled enormity, that touch of genius, that's helping convert people to bourbon the world over. Then I spotted the strength. To my astonishment it has been dumbed down from a 101 to a 90. Bizarre. Absolutely mind-boggling. Especially when you consider that Jimmy Russell himself has told me for the last decade and more that he knows Wild Turkey is at its very best as a 101. This makes it, with no little irony, the weakest of Wild Turkey's top agerange bourbons. Someone has goofed here. Big time. Just keep hunting the original bottling until this is re-instated as one of the absolute world-class top 20 whiskies, as it so recently was. **45%**

**Wild Turkey Aged 12 Years (90) n**22 peaches and cream, topped with demerara sugar, beautiful nutty fruitcake; **t**22 pretty sweet on the uptake with that sugary quality bursting forward, and estery like an old Jamaican rum; **f**23 liquorice and corn interweave beautifully; **b**23 this is great whiskey, perhaps not the most complex from this stable but the effect is uplifting. **50.5% (101 proof)**.

**Wild Turkey Kentucky Spirit Single Barrel** bott 1 Mar 05, barrel 15, warehouse E, rick no. 25 **(89) n**23 crushed black pepper over well-oiled corn and the usual penetrating rye; soft fruits in there, too; **t**23 goes in rye first, with lovely mouthwatering, tingling riches and liquorice. Chewy and very true to the distillery; **f21** flattens out surprisingly as the caramel takes hold; **b22** doesn't quite live up to the nose and mouth arrival, but I defy you to say no to a second. **50.5%**.

**Wild Turkey Rare Breed** batch no. WT-03RB **(95) n25** mesmeric and almost too complex for human analysis. The degree and ratio of honey, mixed spices, vanilla-wielding oak, tart stewed apple (probably from the rye) and softening corn are the stuff of legend and an hour of anyone's time; there is something of the fermenting vessel about this. It is whiskey in all its Kentucky guises; **t24** the translation on to the palate is close if incomplete. Liquorice-coated Demerarah honeycomb trailblazes and then a bickering feud follows between the rye and corn; the oak is always around and adds a slightly drier, sawdusty element; **f22** only medium length but with a cola-style sharpness and groaning, mildly bitter rye. The corn and oak semed pretty wrapped up and cancel each other out; **b24** bourbon at its most complex, and this reminds me very much of some of the very first expresions of this stunning whiskey. An absolute must have. **54.1% (108.2 proof)**.

**William Larue Weller (92) n22** doughy, spiced but a tad lazy; **t23** hard as nails delivery with as much liquoricey oak as there is small grain; slowly the middle conjures up a much richer backbone and a touch of oil to soften things up. Spices offer a delicate detour; **f24** now goes into overdrive as the right degree of sweetness balances the oak; shades of Demerara here though the threatening spice avalanche never arrive; **b23** lovely and quite different whiskey here – takes about four or five mouthfuls before you start getting the picture -  with a clever build up of sugars. Relatively spiceless for a wheated bourbon but its all about structure and form. Even straight, the strength never overwhelms. **60.95%. (121.9 proof). nf**

**William Larue Weller Kentucky Straight Bourbon Barrel Proof Limited Edition (91) n22** the usual wheated traditional of over-emphasizing the oak and spice. And it is big...; **t22** too much oak to begin, splinters all over the tongue; a soft-oiled compensation of gathering liquorice and hickory strides down the middle; **f24** goes into super-complexity mode as the full gamut of coffee, hickory and cocoa goes on for ever and a day. Magnificent; **b23** it always takes time to adjust to wheated whiskey. And outside of a warehouse it's pretty rare to encounter one such as this. But take your time; don't judge on first tasting and only on your fourth of fifth glass should you begin truly to appreciate all that is on offer. And, for interest, compare the two Larue tasting notes up to the end of the last sentence: sampled about a month apart and without the other's notes to hand. Strikingly similar, or what? **64.95% (129.9 Proof). ncf.** *Second Bottling 2006. Buffalo Trace.*

**Woodford Reserve Distiller's Select** batch 19 **(88) n23** pure Forester with the soft molasses oak pitted by firm, fruity rye; **t22** the rye again is at the vanguard followed by some dry, nipping oak; **f21** relatively silent with layers of vanilla; **b22** big, at times broody, but also a bit of a mouse. **45.2%.** *Brown-Forman.*

**Woodford Reserve Distiller's Select** batch 20 **(87) n22** burnt raisin, nuts and caramel; **t23** wonderful acceleration of Demerara and spice that simply exudes harmony and class; **f20** dry dates and caramel: falls a bit flat; **b22** the finish is a disappointment but the mouth arrival is a treat. **45.2%.** *Brown- Forman.*

**Woodford Reserve Master's Collection Four Grain (95) n24** highly unusual with a different nose from any other bourbon I know: very light liquorice, kind of Old Forester but with souped up intensity, and extraordinary floral tones; **t24** big and rambling with a quite massive flavour and spice explosion. The small grains are working overtime to provide a deep spicy-fruit texture to the oak. The liquorice comes through, but so does the rye by the spadeful and much softer, oily corn notes. Sensational; **f23** calms down, though it takes its time: very rarely have I experienced the small grains in a bourbon working with such complexity; the oak drives up the intensity as the story unfolds; **b24** Sod's law would have it that the moment we removed this from the 2006 Bible, having appeared in the previous two editions without it ever making the shelves, it should at last be belatedly released. But a whiskey worth waiting for, or what? The tasting notes are not a million miles from the original. But this is better bourbon, one that appears to have received a significant polish in the intervening years. Nothing short of magnificent. **46.2%**

**Wm Morrison Old Kentucky Special No. 1 Brand (76) n**18 **t**20 **f**19 **b**19. A very decent cooking bourbon with some weight, spice and natural toffee. A genuine chewing bourbon. **40% (80 proof)**. *Wm Morrison UK. Ignore the back label nattering on about three years and blended and all that rubbish. This is a straight bourbon.*

**Woodstock (86) n**23 **t**22 **f**21 **b**20. A lazy bourbon towards the very end that does its best not to impress despite the early sharp rye presence. Still a charmer, though. **37%.** *Australia.*

**Yellow Rose of Texas** (*see* Heaven Hill 80 Proof)

**Yellow Rose of Texas 8 Years** (*see* Old Heaven Hill Very Rare 8 Years 86 proof)

# Tennessee Whiskey
## GEORGE DICKEL

**George Dickel Superior No 12 Brand (90) n**21 so floral and perfumy that I actually sneezed! Otherwise a bit lazy and over-relaxed; **t**22 varying intensity throughout; sweetened by a barley-sugar richness unusual in American whiskey. However, resonating rye refreshes the palate and steers it back on course; **f**24 goes into overdrive with astonishing length and stupendous oak: the complexity has earned its corn, so to speak, with the drying oak offering a get-out clause for the developing sugars; **b**23 like watching a sea eagle take to flight after catching a larger fish than anticipated: a lumbering take off that at times looks doomed to failure but finally lift off is achieved with spell-binding grace and beauty. Welcome back to a great whisky after years in the doldrums! **45%**

## JACK DANIEL

**Gentleman Jack Rare Tennessee Whiskey (79) n**19 **t**21 **f**20 **b**19. One of America's cleanest whiskeys, sweet and improbably light. An affront to hardened Jack drinkers, a blessing for those with a sweet tooth. **40%.** *Brown-Forman.*

**Jack Daniel's (Green Label) (84) n**20 **t**21 **f**22 **b**21. A light but lively little gem of a whiskey. Starts as a shrinking violet, finishes as a roaring lion with nimble spices ripping into the developing liquorice. A superb session whiskey. **40% (80 proof)**. .

**Jack Daniel's Old No. 7 Brand (Black Label) (87) n**21 thick, oily, smoky, dense, corn syrupy ... it's Jack Daniel; **t**23 sweet, fat, chewy, various types of burnt notes: tofffee, toast etc. etc; **f**21 quite a sweet, fat and toffeed finale; **b**22 a quite unique whiskey at which many American whiskey connoisseurs turn up their noses. I always think it's worth the occasional visit; you can't beat roughing it a little. **40% (80 proof)**. *Brown-Forman.*

**Jack Daniel's Single Barrel (88) n**22 more fruit on this than most Jacks, still plenty of liquorice and burnt toast; **t**22 spicy and immediately warming: some real kick to this with the blows softened by the sweetness of the corn and the surrounding thick oils; **f**22 very consistent with the sweetness fading, despite some rye input, then oak starting to make a stand; **b**22 a characterful, rich whiskey, with plenty of corn sweetness and some excellent spice. **40% (80 proof)**. *Brown-Forman.*

**Jack Daniel's Single Barrel (90) n**22 JD in concentrate: oily, full, phenolic and a touch sweet; **t**23 wonderful delivery with the intense corn oil making the liquoricey oak rock. Great depth and harmony and with relatively subdued spices; **f**22 trails off with a hint of Demerara; **b**23 just from time to time a real honey pops up with these single barrels, and this sample is one of those. **47% (94 proof).**

## VIRGINIA BOURBON

**Virginia Gentleman 80** (cream, sepia and red label) **(84) n**20 **t**22 **f**21 **b**21. A very light bourbon with a distinctive, easy-going sweet corn effect then spicy, mildly bitter oak and cocoa. **40% (80 proof)**. *A Smith Bowman.*

**Virginia Gentleman 90** (coloured label) **(89) n**21 the leathery oak has much more to say than the corn, but it's all done in whispers; **t**23 charming entry onto the palate with, first, chewy oak then more teasing rye and a dash of honey here and there; **f**22 the small grains really come out to play, accompanied by spices, superb mouthfeel with excellent drying towards the very end; **b**23 you know, forget about this being the only Virginia whiskey. Romance apart, this is one hell of a whiskey where complexity is the foundation stone. Marvellous stuff. **45% (90 proof)**. *A Smith Bowman.*

## Corn Whiskey

**Dixie Dew Kentucky Straight Corn Whiskey (89) n**22 Very decent oak and vanilla adds to dryish corn; complex by corn whiskey standards; **t**22 wonderfully balanced, starting dry and oaky then the corn building up with the sweetness; **f**22 long with even a dash of spice – much improved than in recent years; **b**23 brilliant whiskey that should have a far wider market. **50%** Heaven Hill.

**Georgia Moon Corn Whiskey** Aged less than thirty days **(84) n**20 **t**22 **f**21 **b**21. Agreeable, sweet, mildly syrupy white dog. Would love to see this at full strength. **40%.** Heaven Hill.

**J W Corn 100 Straight Corn Whiskey (87) n**21 oily and rich with some much drier oak present; **t**22 thumping early oak offsets the sweet corn which fails to quite take off; **f**22 really spicy and big; **b**22 this has the biggest oak character on the market at the moment, which means a drier style and no shortage of spice. **50% (100 proof)**. Heaven Hill.

**Mellow Corn (85) n**21 **t**22 **f**21 **b**21. I first drank this brand back in 1974 and I can safely say that I've never encountered it, or any other whisk(e)y, with an oilier texture: if you don't like the whiskey, you could always fry your eggs in it. Seriously delicious, though! **50%** Medley Company. (Heaven Hill).

## Single Malt Rye
### ANCHOR DISTILLERY

**Old Potrero 18th Century Style Whiskey Essay 10-RW-ARM-3-C (90) n**20 distinctly 18th century with a cut the size of the Grand Canyon. Or should that be the San Andreas fault....?; **t**23 Good grief...!!! Where do I start? I won't even bother. Find about an hour and a very quiet room. Don't sip. Take a serious mouthful. Tilt the head back. Chew, allowing every cell in your mouth to be washed by this rye. Then swallow. There are all kinds of oils that should have been re-distilled. But they weren't, so make the most of them, because, frankly, they are fabulous and may never be seen again...; **f**24 the purists' nightmare continues as praline bites deep into the ultra-rich rye; it's oily tsunamis all the way; **b**23 always remember something about wide cuts. The nose will be off beam. But the flavours hitting the tastebuds will be off the Richter scale. After tasting this I need to lie down somewhere and rest. Because so few whiskeys in the world are half as big as this, or more fun. Forget descriptors: this one writes its own book... **62.55% (125.1 proof).**

**Old Potrero Single Malt Hotaling's Whiskey Aged 11 Years Essay MCMVI-MMVI (96) n**24 aged Geneva with juniper latching onto the rock-hard rye; **t**25 San Francisco meets Belgium: again that Geneva kick-start with juniper, spices and orange peel. But, like Geneva, there is a rye base and that begins to completely dominate – until the oak-led top quality cocoa arrives as domination is never allowed in greatness. We just weren't given enough tastebuds for this one...; **f**23 despite some soft oils, thins out quicker than expected with vanilla and rye vying for top dog. The spices also play a quiet but rather beautiful tune; **b**24 this may sound coarse (and I apologise, but it is relevant), but I belched (twice) whilst tasting this. Oddly enough, that never happens when I taste whisky...only gin...And I was spitting. I think gin lovers will be converted and whiskey drinkers truly amazed. Let's make no bones here: this is one of the world's true great whiskies, which just shows the quality of Ritttenhouse barrel 28. Even so, rarely have I encountered complexity like it. I admit rye whiskey is my favourite genre. And no rye in the world offers anything like this. A must have bottling: there is nothing even close in style. **50% (100 proof).**

⁖ **Old Potrero Single Malt Hotaling's Whiskey Aged 12 Years Essay MCMVI-MMVII (96) n**24 **t**25 **f**23 **b**24 I have tasted this Essay against the previous one, and whilst there are the odd subtle differences, this is the closest in style I have ever found two Potreroes to be: their likeness, in general terms, is uncanny. This one has perhaps the slightly drier finish but on the complexity front there is nothing to compare in the whisky world. I am not, remotely, an advocate of whisky and food. But I could murder a beautifully marbled T bone at my third favourite steak joint in the world, Harris's of San Francisco (still has a little way to go to match the incomparable The Ring in Portland and, at a shorter distance, Barbarian's in Toronto), and follow after a delicate pause with a glass of this local super whisky. Life rarely, if ever, gets better than that. **50%** (100 proof).

**Old Potrero Single Malt Straight Rye** Whiskey Aged Three Years Essay 5 - **RW-ARM-2-A (93) n**24 textbook stuff: liquorice-embossed rye, hard as nails, but caresses the senses. You beauty! **t**24 big, uncompromising, both angry and fruity. Just so sweet with hints of honey and demerara, but the firmness of the rye is a spine to it all and cocoa provides a perfect counterweight; **f**22 slightly toffeed with rich oaky-vanilla but all the time the rye peppers the tastebuds; **b**23 this is what makes rye whiskey, for me, the most enjoyable style in the world. Brazen and bedazzling. **62.6% (125.2 proof)**. *1880 bottles.*

**Old Potrero Single Malt Straight Rye** Essay 10-SRW-ARM-A db **(93) n**22 despite the lower strength there is no shortage of he-man aromas; the slight feintiness takes a tad longer to burn off but it's a harmless, earthy flaw compensated by a bewildering array of overmatured fruity notes seasoned by soft linseed, a vague herbal note and a dollop of manuka honey. One of the heaviest OP noses yet; **t**24 you need about five minutes to sort your way through this one: the rye is the first note apparent and then it breaks off into three or four different directions, each with a varied flavour code: part of the rye contains cocoa and is dry and deliciously chocolaty while another faction takes the route to Demerara with a softly estered rum beat to it. As a compliment to this a rye and honeyed thread weaves its way around the palate. Finally the rye also links up with a sawdusty vanilla effect, which passes for oak; **f**23 impossible to tell where the middle ends and the finish starts: this is top shelf whiskey for adults and ones who know how to make the most of the finish of their mouthful: just sit back, eyes closed and listen to spellbinding, bitter-sweet tales of rye and honey; **b**24 I know some of you will be beating your breasts and wailing: OP's down from teeth dissolving barrel proof to a sissified 45% abv. The reason, I have been told, is that barmen have a big problem when trying to mix at cask strength. I understand the problem, but it is one easily overcome: drink it straight … **45%**

**Old Potrero Single Malt Straight Rye** Whiskey Essay 10-SRW-ARM-E **(94) n**24 roasting chestnuts and salted yam; all closely bound by essence of kumquat and rye. Give this time and oxygen and it will undergo countless, giddy transformations. Unique and astonishing...; **t**23 exceptionally fruity and salivating from the off; the rye starts slow and builds up a chewy head of steam; **f**24 delicate spice, layers of bitter-sweet cocoa. Oh..and rye...; **b**23 the whiskey from this distillery never fails to amaze. **45% (90 proof).**

# Straight Rye

∷ **Cougar Rye (95) n**25 OK. I have died. I have gone to heaven...what next...? **t**24 the nose, an impossible jumble of fruity, spicy elements, is nearly perfectly translated onto the palate with the added extra of burnt toast and impressively cindered fruitcake; **f**23 the spices prevail as does a liquorice and vanilla dryness; **b**23 if I gave World Whisky of the Year to a rye that's 37% I'd be taken out by Malt Extremists who'd have issued a fatwa on me. It's bloody tempting mind... had it been at full strength of about 50% abv, I don't think there would have been much debate. And to think this is from yet another distillery (Lawrenceburg, Indiana) that has been closed and is no more, I'd cry had not my tears run dry for the countless others. **37%**. *Foster's Group, Australia. To be launched in Australia later this year.*

**Fleischmann's Straight Rye (93) n**23 a wonderful confusion of rock hard rye and softer, fruitier notes: uncluttered by too great age, it is unambiguously rye; **t**24 clean arrival, soft fruits and then gradual scaling up of the firmness of the rye: just so magically mouth watering and warming at the same time; **f**22 hard, chunky rye softened by vanilla and orange marmalade; **b**24 it is hard to believe that a whisky as classically simple and elegant as this, and so true to its genre, comes in a plastic bottle. You don't have to pay through the nose for magnificent whisky. **40%**. *Fleischmann Distilling Co (Barton).*

**Jim Beam Rye (93) n**24 lemon zest, mint and lavender: a stunning bag of tricks; **t**24 early rye broadside followed by some tender fruit and oak. This battle between rock-hard rigidity and gentle fruit is astonishing; **f**22 long and flinty with cocoa rounding things off; **b**23 almost certainly the most entertaining and consistent whiskey in the entire Jim Beam armoury. A classic without doubt. How much longer will it be before they start releasing this worldwide? **40%**

**Old Overholt Four Years Old (86) n**23 **t**21 **f**21 **b**21. A very decent score for a decent whiskey. But it used to be so much more in your face and full of character. Maybe just a blip. **40% (80 proof)**. *Jim Beam.*

**Old Rip Van Winkle 12 Years Old** Time Rye (90) n23 t23 f22 b22. A profound, fruity, refreshing and old-fashioned rye that's hard to find. 45% (90 proof).

**Old Rip Van Winkle 15 Years Old** (985) Family Reserve Rye (91) n22 t23 f23 b23. A supremely improbable rye that has managed to retain a zesty freshness over 15 summers. Brilliant. 50% (100 proof).

**Pikesville Supreme Straight Rye** (87) t23 a curious and delicious mixture of traditional British scrumpy cider and new car interior: this is straight rye at its freshest and fruitiest; t21 much lighter arrival than nose suggests, even a hint of corn in there. The fruit slowly starts to return, but only after a sprinkling of brown sugar then a thumping measure of rye; f21 that usual Heaven Hill rye bitterness on the ending plus some caramel-vanilla to sweeten things a little; b22 not quite as in your face with the rye as was once the case. 40% (80 proof). Heaven Hill.

**Rittenhouse Straight Rye** (85) n21 t21 f21 b22. This is the only rye in America I'm aware of spelt "Whisky" rather than "whiskey." And has always been the least rye-pronounced. But this bottling makes a virtue of it. 40% (80 proof). Heaven Hill.

**Rittenhouse Straight Rye 100 Proof Bottled in Bond** (86) n21 t22 f21 b22. A weighty guy. 50% (100 proof). Heaven Hill.

**Rittenhouse Very Rare Single Barrel 21 Years Old** (91) n25 Incredible. Intriguing. Unique. Such is the punch to the super-ripe fruit, so intense is the oak that has fused into it, that it takes literally hours to try and make sense of what is happening here. There is no other aroma in the whisky or whiskey world that matches, the closest relation being ancient pot still whiskey from Ireland for reasons I will explain later. It perhaps needs a whisky lover with the mind of an archaeologist to understand this one, because the nose is a series of layers built up over time. The key is to dig deeper than the surface spices and burnt honeycomb. In there, in varying strata, are diffused mint and lemon zest and a fruity intensity on the rye grain normally found only when malted. Astonishing and almost too beautiful for words; t23 impatient oak rampages through the early, oily arrival of rye concentrate. Then waves of spice, of steadily increasing intensity crash lip-smackingly into the tastebuds. But such is the magnitude of the rye it absorbs the oak without too much early damage and only towards the middle does it begin to lose the battle; f21 a dry finale as the come-of-age oak demands the last say; b22 I may be wrong, but I would wager quite a large amount that no-one living has tasted more rye from around the world than I. So trust me when I tell you this is different, a genuine one-off in style. By rights such telling oak involvement should have killed the whisky stone dead: this is like someone being struck by lightning and then walking off slightly singed and with a limp, but otherwise OK. The closest style of whisky to rye is Irish pot still, a unique type where unmalted barley is used. And the closest whiskey I have tasted to this has been 35 to 50-year-old pot still Irish. What they have in common is a massive fruit base, so big that it can absorb and adapt to the oak input over many years. This has not escaped unscathed. But it has to be said that the nose alone makes this worthy of discovery, as does the glory of the rye as it first melts into the tastebuds. The term flawed genius could have been coined for this whisky alone. Yet, for all its excellence, I can so easily imagine someone, somewhere, claiming to be an expert on whiskey, bleating about the price tag of $150 a bottle. If they do, ignore them. Because, frankly, rye has been sold far too cheaply for far too long and that very cheapness has sculpted a false perception in people's minds about the quality and standing of the spirit. Well, 21 years in Kentucky equates to about 40 years in Scotland. And you try and find a 40-year-old Scotch for £75. If anything, they are giving this stuff away. The quality of the whiskey does vary from barrel to barrel and therefore bottle to bottle. So below I have given a summary of each individual bottling (averaging (91.1). The two with the highest scores show the least oak interference...yet are quite different in style. That's great whiskey for you. 50% (100 proof). ncf. Heaven Hill.

Barrel no. 1 (91) n25 t23 f21 b22. As above. 50%
Barrel no. 2 (89) n24 t23 f20 b22. Dryer, oakier. 50%
Barrel no. 3 (91) n24 t23 f22 b22. Fruity, soft. 50%
Barrel no. 4 (90) n25 t22 f21 b22. Enormous. 50%
Barrel no. 5 (93) n25 t23 f22 b23. Early rye surge. 50%
Barrel no. 6 (87) n23 t22 f20 b22. Juicy, vanilla. 50%
Barrel no. 7 (90) n23 t23 f22 b22. Even, soft, honeyed. 50%

**Barrel no. 8 (95) n**25 t24 f23 **b**23. The works: massive rye. **50%**
**Barrel no. 9 (91) n**24 t23 f22 **b**22. Sharp rye, salivating. **50%**
**Barrel no.10 (93) n**25 t24 f22 **b**22. Complex, sweet. **50%**
**Barrel no.11 (93) n**24 t24 f22 **b**23. Rich, juicy, spicy. **50%**
**Barrel no.12 (91) n**25 t23 f21 **b**22. Near identical to no.1. **50%**
**Barrel no.13 (91) n**24 t24 f21 **b**22. Citrus and toasty. **50%**
**Barrel no.14 (94) n**25 t24 f22 **b**23. Big rye and marzipan. **50%**
**Barrel no.15 (88) n**23 t22 f21 **b**22. Major oak influence. **50%**
**Barrel no.16 (90) n**24 t23 f21 **b**22. Spicy and toffeed. **50%**
**Barrel no.17 (90) n**23 t23 f22 **b**22. Flinty, firm, late rye kick. **50%**
**Barrel no.18 (91) n**24 t24 f21 **b**22. Big rye delivery. **50%**
**Barrel no.19 (87) n**23 t22 f21 **b**21. Major coffee input. **50%**
**Barrel no.20 (91) n**23 t24 f22 **b**22. Spicy sugar candy. **50%**
**Barrel no.21 (94) n**24 t23 f24 **b**23. Subtle, fruity. **50%**
**Barrel no.22 (89) n**23 t22 f22 **b**22. Mollased rye. **50%**
**Barrel no.23 (94) n**24 t23 f24 **b**23. Soft fruit, massive rye. **50%**
**Barrel no.24 (88) n**23 t22 f21 **b**22. Intense oak and caramel. **50%**
**Barrel no.25 (93) n**25 t22 f23 **b**23. Heavy rye and spice. **50%**
**Barrel no.26 (92) n**23 t23 f23 **b**23. Subtle, delicate rye. **50%**
**Barrel no.27 (94) n**25 t23 f23 **b**23. Delicate rye throughout. **50%**
**Barrel no.28 (96) n**25 t24 f23 **b**24. Salivating, roasty, major. **50%**
**Barrel no.29 (88) n**23 t22 f21 **b**22. Hot, fruity. **50%**
**Barrel no.30 (91) n**24 t23 f22 **b**22. Warming cough sweets. **50%**
**Barrel no.31 (90) n**25 t22 f21 **b**22. Aggressive rye. **50%**

**Sazerac Rye 6 Years Old (91) n**24 the rye is firm, gripping and clean; the fruitiness never diminishes thanks to a low oak profile; **t**22 clean, fresh rye with a toffee-apple fruitiness; **f**22 only as the oak arrives does the grain really begin to gather momentum and display complexity; **b**23 a fascinating rye which seems to change pace and intensity at different points. Great stuff! **45% (90 proof)**.

**Sazerac 6 Years Old (95) n**24 just hold your arms up and surrender to this granite-soft beast; **t**23 the clarity of the rye could not be sharper: the fruitiness is matched only by the sweetness; **f**24 the length of the finish leaves you salivating. Just so wonderfully structured and succinct in part, then so unbelievably expansive; **b**24 this appears to have a very big rye percentage and the freshness of the fruit and grain is spellbinding. Even I suggest the odd drop of water with this one...eventually...!!! **65.4% (130.8 proof)**. *Buffalo Trace.*

**Sazerac Kentucky Straight Rye 18 Years Old 90 Proof** bott Fall 06 **(94) n**24 the fruit theme of the rye simply pulses from the glass with some countering toasty dryness. It's the honey-demerara with a smidgen of mint that stars, though; **t**23 as ever, an astonishingly soft façade to something so blisteringly firm as the rye; fruity and so salivating; **f**24 long, and now firms up entirely with wonderful shafts of oak being drilled into sweeter fruity-rye; **b**23 one of those whiskeys with a truly unique signature: nothing else like it and the quality entirely uncompromised. Terrific stuff! **45% (90 Proof)**. *Buffalo Trace.*

**Sazerac Rye 18 Years Old Rye** Autumn 2004 release **(96) n**25 trad straight rye doesn't come more complex, confident or clean than this: there's a hard grainy edge, softened by over-ripe juicy cherry and blackberries. Subtle and sophisticated; **t**24 the brittle quality of the rye shows to full effect here, but there is a yield – a tad oily – which also beguiles. Fruity and improbably flavoursome: close your eyes and wallow; **f**23 takes a little rest as the toffee makes a mark, but such is the intensity of the rye and oak that waves of spices and fruit continue to break against the tastebuds; **b**24 I remember being given my first sample of this: it was in the lab at Buffalo Trace before it went into bottle and a legendary brand was born. I wondered what it would be like to sample away from the romance of the beautiful distillery where the casks were laying ... well, now you know. I was presented with the first-ever bottle of Sazerac Rye as a token of thanks for my help in identifying its qualities and (some hope) weaknesses. I trust the person who stole it out of my bag while I was giving a tasting in New York appreciated. If he/she still has it, I would be grateful if it is returned, no questions asked. And for those who prefer to look at their whiskeys Sideways, the joint hardness and mouth-dousing fruitiness – plus the overall scarcity – makes this the Pinot Noir of the rye world. **45%** *Buffalo Trace.*

**Thomas H. Handy Sazerac Straight Rye Barrel Proof Limited Edition (93) n**24 boiled fruit candy. Just so mouth-wateringly firm and sexy; **t**21 takes its time to find a rhythm as neither the oak nor rye are sure whether to lead. Settles towards the middle as the salivating rye takes control; a few hickory notes add further depth; **f**25 faultless and mesmeric. The tongue is left to wander the mouth involuntarily investigating myriad flavour trails. Early doubts are erased by the majesty of small grain and the perfection of the bittersweet harmony which unravels. Even the late-arriving spices deliver something almost too teasing to be true. One of the greatest finishes in world whiskey, and no mistake; **b**23 what a box of tricks! Early on it's as mad a bag of snakes but the finish is something to inspire you to get in the chimney sweep, clean out the hearth and get the ol' log fire going for the first time in 20 years. A fabulous addition to the ever-growing rye family. **66.35% (132.7 Proof). ncf.** *First-ever bottling.*

➤ **Van Winkle Family Reserve Rye 13 Years Old (91) n**23 big and belligerent, the rye forms a fruity, rock-hard crust; **t**24 vroom ... !! Off she goes on a massive ryefest. Brilliant bitter-sweet grain stomps with hob-nailed boots around the palate, both fresh yet well aged. Everything is a contradiction – so complex; **f**21 quietens down alarmingly as the caramel kicks in which sweetens it a little while some bitter coffee/rye notes still chatter in the background; **b**23 an alarmingly complex whiskey that seems to make the rules up as it goes along. Anarchic and adorable. **47.8% (95.6 proof).**

**Wild Turkey Real Kentucky Straight Rye (88) n**23 the firmest, fruitiest WT rye nose I've come across in bottled form: clean and compelling; **t**23 fabulous micro explosions of juicy, fruity rye; **f**20 unusual softening and blunting by caramel. Little of the old spice kick; **b**22 still continues to change character from previous bottlings, in some ways for the better, in others worse. But you can't help thinking that this has another gear or two to use. **50.5% (101 proof).**

## MICHTERS DISTILLERY

**Overholt "1810" Sour Mash Straight Rye Whiskey (91) n**23 allow a minute or two to oxidize then breath in sweet rye, primroses and ginger bread, and a fair chunk of oak, too; **t**23 just fabulously explosive: the oak is pretty big but cannot undermine the intensity of the rye. The spice sizzles and spits at you like a Cumberland sausage; **f**22 very hard rye chisels at the taste buds; some cocoa for good, bitter yet balanced effect; **b**23 I have been hearing reports that this truly classic Old Timer, complete in 4/5 quart bottles, can still be dug up in back-wood liquor stores. This, the very last of the true Pennsylvanian rye, is Klondike stuff. **46.5% abv (93 proof).** *A Overholt & Co, Pennsylvania.*

# Straight Wheat Whiskey

**Bernheim Original Straight Wheat Whiskey (90) n**23 biscuity and crisp, yet sweet, grainy and a little spicy: exceptionally clean and carrying the freshness of newly bound straw; **t**23 outstanding mouth arrival with a sharp, salty tang that coats the roof and teases the tastebuds; then melts into a full, slightly oily body, and again the biscuity quality appears. The spices, though, are controlled and even refuse to disappear. Salivating and juicy throughout; **f**21 soft vanilla against rock-hard grain. The lightness of the wheat doesn't allow for enormous depth, but the bitterness is seen off by a delicious delivery of sugar cane juice; **b**23 great stuff: a superb addition to the American whiskey lexicon. Firm, consumer friendly yet at times fluffy. The complexity comes in broad, sweeping waves rather than small grain intricacy, but the spicy undercurrent guarantees a healthy degree of busy playfulness. A must for those with a sweet tooth, this new style takes until about the third tasting before you begin to fully understand its charm and refreshing richness. An immediate classic. **45% (90 proof).** *Heaven Hill.*

# Kentucky Whiskey

**Early Times Kentucky Whisky (74) n**19 **t**19 **f**18 **b**18. Slightly improved with some extra beefing up, but still light and over sweet. **40% (80 proof).** *Brown-Forman*

⋯ **Medley's Kentucky Whiskey** bott code L6114 **(81) n**21 **t**21 **f**19 **b**20 Very tight grains. Pleasant, but limited complexity. **40%.** *Berentzen Distillers.*

# American/Kentucky Whiskey Blends

**Beam's Eight Star Kentucky Whiskey A Blend** 75% grain neutral spirits 25% straight whiskey **(67)** n16 t17 f17 b17. Just the odd wisp of something chewable. **40% (80 proof)**.

**Broker's Reserve American Blended Whiskey 36 Months Old** 80% grain spirits **(61)** n14 t16 f16 b15. A fruity, spicy, synthetic, entirely avoidable little non-whiskey-more-brandy-type number. **40% (80 proof)**.

**Monarch Kentucky Bourbon Whiskey A Blend (69)** n18 t17 f17 b17. Half-decent body with touches of oak and spice. **40% (80 proof)**.

**Potter's Whiskey** 20% straight whiskey 80 grain neutral spirits **(64)** n15 t18 f16 b15. Sweet, clean, caramelised at finish and entirely featureless. **40%**

**Seagram's 7 Crown (89)** n23 rich with heavy vanilla and rye; t22 complex grain and oak battle: the softness of the neutral grain acts as the perfect foil for the crisper rye; f22 silky, sweet, soft corn and vanilla; b22 this is beautiful whiskey, but on this evidence not a patch on the rye-infested giant it has been for the last couple of decades. The rye level seems to have been reduced and I trust that this is just a rogue batch. Still a little mouthwatering stunner for sure, but it was much better the way it was: semi-wild and flavour-explosive. Like that it was an American institution — something too rare and precious to be tampered with ... **40% (80 proof)**.

# Other American Whiskey

⋰ **Buffalo Trace Experimental Collection Chardonnay After 6 Years Old** dist May 92, bott Feb 07 **(77)** n21 t19 f18 b19 A less demanding ride than the 10-y-o and, thanks to the lesser time in Chardonnay, the tastebuds are not so violently pulped by the oak intrusion. Some pleasant chocolate-y notes bring reward and soften the blow. **45% (90 Proof)**.

⋰ **Buffalo Trace Experimental Collection Chardonnay After 10 Years Old** dist Apr 88, bott Feb 07 **(76)** n23 t20 f16 b17 The stunning nose is a Siren as the taste buds are massacred by the unrelenting sharpness of the grape. Further proof if it were needed that great whisky is great whisky and great wine is great wine. But never shall the two twins meet. Seeing how Buffalo Trace is unquestionably one of the best three distilleries in the world with lesser stocks than their greatness demands, one wonders why their priceless lifeblood is so wasted. **45% (90 Proof)**.

**Jackpot (81)** n18 t22 f21 b20. For a label with all four card suits displayed, it's fitting that the nose is a pair of deuces. However, a powering and impressively complex bourbon thrust on mouth arrival comes up trumps. **40%**

**Old Virginia Extra Rare American Whiskey Aged 12 Years** L530133A **(90)** n22 molten honeycomb and dark chocolate; almost a Jamaican rummy ester sweetness; t23 imagine a nubile body contouring a silk gown: that's the shape and texture here as excellent vanillas integrate with honey; f22 back to the honeycomb again with marmalade as a delightful bitterness creeps in; b23 Good grief: this is damn good stuff. The most honeyed and high-class non-bourbon on the market. **40%**. *La Martiniquaise, France.*

**Wild Turkey Sherry Signature** "Made with 10 Years Old Kentucky Straight Bourbon Whiskey finished in sherry casks enhanced with Oloroso Sherry" **(81)** n19 t21 f20 b21. They kind of don't get much stranger than this: bourbon meets Speyside meets Canadian...I suppose the adding of pure oloroso to the mix precludes this from being whiskey at all, but it seems a bit churlish not to have it in the Bible, seeing how the Canadians can add 9.09% of anything and the remainder of the world add caramel. To treat it at face value, an enjoyable, pleasantly honied experience where the oloroso gets out of control, momentarily, only towards the finale. Otherwise, a silky, quite skilfully steered ride. **43%**

# Canadian Whisky

**I**t is becoming hard to believe that Canadian was once a giant among the world whisky nations. Dotted all over its enormous land large distilleries pumped out thousands upon thousands of gallons of spirit that after years in barrel became a clean, gentle whisky.

It was cool to be seen drinking Canadian in cocktail bars on both sides of the pond. Now, sadly, Canadian whisky barely raises a beat on the pulse of the average whisky lover. It would not be beyond argument to now call Canadian the forgotten whisky empire with column inches devoted to it measured now in millimetres. It is an entirely sad, almost heartbreaking, state of affairs though hopefully not an irreversible one. The finest Canadian, for me, is still whisky to be cherished and admired. But outside North America it can be painfully hard to find.

Especially seeing how whiskies containing the permitted 9.09% of non-Canadian whisky (or whisky at all) had been barred from the European market. So just to ensure Jim Murray's Whisky Bible is on the ball I spent time in Canada tasting every Canadian whisky I could find on the market. The result was illuminating. In the two years since I last blitzed Canadian there was now a clear divergence of styles between

BRITISH
COLUMBIA

ALBERTA

MANITOBA

●Vancouver

🔺Alberta
Calgary

Winchester
Cellars

🔺Okanagan

🔺Palliser

Gimli🔺

**Key**

● **Major Town or City**

🔺 Distillery

+ Dead Distillery

tradionalist whisky like Alberta Premium and a more creamy textured, fruit-enhanced product once confined to the USA but now found in Canada itself. It has made for a re-evaluation of Canadian and a few surprises. I have returned many times since, not only to continue my search for Canadian but to spend more time with some of the people who make it, blend it, sell it. And, no less vitally, perhaps, drink it.

There is no doubt that we are seeing a change in the perception of Canadian by drinkers who had previously confined themselves to top quality Scotch malt. Following my award of Jim Murray's Whisky Bible Canadian Whisky of the Year 2006 to Alberta Premium, I had the chance to spend time in televison and radio stations around the country talking about the exceptionally high quality of top Canadian whiskies. It has led to a string of emails from readers telling me they had since tasted Alberta and been somewhat shocked to find a world classic whisky lurking so unobtrusively - and cheaply - on their shelves. For many, this had led to further exploring of Canadian, and uncovering of further gems. The 2008 award goes to Alberta again, the third time running, this time for their newly launched 25-year-old. It makes the heart pound to see the industry take such confidence in their own whisky, though perhaps they could have been a bit more confident with the price: Canadians have been handed the best bargain in world whisky right now!

And Canadian whisky moved up a further notch in quality during 2007 with the arrival on the market of the super-illusive Crown Royal XR Extra Rare. This rye-rich gem includes some of the last barrels from one or two of Seagram's long lost distilleries and there is always the argument that perhaps they should have been bottled in their own right as one-off single casks, so people could enjoy them the same way they sample the fading lights of Port Ellen and Brora in Scotland. Get a first-hand taste of some true Canadian whisky heritage. This 2008 edition of the Whisky Bible includes only the first bottling of the two so far: I thought I had both but they turned out to be from the same first expression and there wasn't time enough to bring in a replacement.

So, with Glenora winning their battle against the mighty Scotch Whisky Association for the right to market their Glen Breton single malt, and confident they will see off their appeal against the decision, this has not been too bad a year. There is an entire nation, indeed world, waiting for Canada to show what it can do: in 20 years I have never known such interest. Now I look forward to other Canadian distillers moving away from fruit juice thinking and putting the rye back into good old Canadian Rye.

QUEBEC
ONTARIO
Glenora
NOVA SCOTIA
Valleyfield
●Quebec
●Montreal
Canada Mist ● Toronto
Kittling Ridge
Walkerville

# Canadian Single Malt
## GLENORA

**Glen Breton** db **(81) n**19 **t**21 **f**20 **b**21. Enormously sweet malt, in almost concentrated form with a tantalising whiff of smoke hanging around; mildly spiced and slightly oily, soapy finale. **43%**

**Glen Breton Rare** db **(73) n**14 **t**21 **f**19 **b**19. This is a version – probably a very early one – I had not seen and it makes for exceptionally grim nosing. However, after that very unpleasant, feinty experience, it comes back to life on the palate with remarkable honey and copper input. A right mixed bag. **40%**

**Glen Breton Rare** db **(80) n**18 **t**21 **f**20 **b**21. Caramel nose a bit soapy but the buttery, sweet malt, with its vanilla fizz, makes for a pleasant experience. **43%**

**Glenora 1990 Aged 14 Years Single Cask** db **(89) n**22 firm malt but with a distinctive bourbony (or very old Canadian) weight and some attractive natural toffee; **t**23 massive malt arrival on the palate buoyed with that dense fudge-caramel; **f**22 the oak is distinctive and almost Kentuckian; the malt is profound and the chewy weight is excellent; **b**22 by far and away the best Glenora yet bottled. And good to see the distillery use its actual name. **43%**

## OKANAGAN

**Long Wood 8 Years Old Malt** db **(74) n**19 **t**20 **f**17 **b**18. There are no discernable off notes and a pleasant liquorice-spice prevails. But the true life has been strangled out if it by caramel. A tragedy, in whisky terms, as this is very rare malt from a lost distillery. **40%**. *Germany.*

# Canadian Grain Single Barrel

**Century Reserve 13 Years Old Single Cask Unblended (92) n**22 massive vanilla and toffee but delicately handled and delivered; some very soft prickle helps balance the sweetening grain; **t**23 big corn kick from the start with an immediate movement towards sweetness that is stopped in its tracks by developing oak; just so silky despite the natural oak bite; **f**23 long, lush in part, with the corn really getting stuck into the oak; **b**24 surely "Bush Pilot" by any other name. Those with an affinity with old Scottish grain would recognise this style of corn-led whisky. Very tasty. **40%**. *Century Distilling Co.*

**Century Reserve 15 Years Old 1985 Limited Edition (89) n**20 dry oak; mildly burnt toast and red liquorice; **t**23 a delicious corn-oil lushness helps keep at bay some bourbony overtures; the degree of Demerara sweetness against the oak is exemplary; **f**23 cream toffee that you can chew and chew until subtle spices arrive; **b**23 the nose ("smoky, reminiscent of single malt", according to cask selector Nick Bennett; "oaky, reminiscent of Okanagan grain", according to Jim Murray...) reveals little of the joys that are to follow. **40%**. *Century Distilling Co.*
*Century Reserve 21 Years Old (see Blended Canadian)*

**Forty Creek Single Barrel (93) n**23 clean, uncluttered sherry and cherry; **t**23 more cherry flanked by gentle spice and silky, mildly oily grain: genuinely complex and classy; **f**24 loses balance towards the end, although the sweetness, combined with the bitter cocoa finale, is not entirely unlike a Belgium cherry chocolate; **b**23 there are so many things about this whisky that infuriate me...yet I adore it. Perhaps I am a sucker for premier quality liquor chocolates; maybe I get turned on by very clean yet complex distillate. So much of this goes against the purists' grain. Yet it has to be said: this is bloody delicious whisky of the highest magnitude!! **40%**. *Kittling Ridge.*

# Canadian Blended Whisky

**Alberta Premium (95) n**24 remains as hard and impenetrable as the Rockies that overlook the distillery from afar; the rye is brittle and rigid, but just gracious enough to allow a sweet fruitiness to develop: classic stuff; **t**25 one of the great deliveries of world whisky: the rye is both intense and yielding, enveloping and rigidly distant; lovely rye-oriented fruit and then an intrusion of irritating toffee; **f**22 just a fraction too caramel-rich but a distant spice does try to break it up a bit; some late oak also present; **b**24 one of the great, most wonderfully consistent whiskies of the world that is genuinely a Canadian rye and a must have for those searching for the real thing. **40%**. *Alberta Distillers.*

**Alberta Premium 25 Years Old (95) n**24 a fabulously weighted nose: diamond couched in silk. It is the vivid hardness which is first to show, with the firmness the rye can muster. Then that softness makes itself felt; a rolling, juicy fruitiness (not dissimilar to an almost lost form of most exquisite Cognac) that has dissolved into it a drier vaguely bourbon-esque oakiness. For complexity few, if any, Canadians are this subtle or sublime. Masterful; **t**23 again we have a bipolar story. On one hand the rye takes a rigid course as a hard edge cuts through all else to dominate. Then it fails as it is swamped by that same soft fruit as on the nose and also a crescendo of cocoa. Soft-hard. Sweet-dry. Velvety caresses-playful nips. Whatever you concentrate on dominates: put the tastebuds into neutral and you have a wonderful battle, not fought by fist but wit; **f**23 my word: if you are into chocolate you'll love this. Gently sweetened cocoa spreads around the palate, first as a hint then as a full-blown plain chocolate dessert sweetened only by a sprinkling of muscovado. Very long. Improbably gentle; **b**25 faultless. Absolutely nothing dominates. Yet every aspect has its moment of conquest and glory. It is neither bitter nor sweet, yet both. It is neither soft nor hard on the palate yet both elements are there. Because of the 100% rye used, this is an entirely new style of whisky to hit the market. No Canadian I know has ever had this uncompromising brilliance, this trueness to style and form. And, frightening to think, it could be improved further by bottling at least 46% and un-chillfiltered. For any whisky lover who ever thought Canadian was incapable of hitting the heights  among the world's greats, I have previously recommended Alberta Premium. I still do. But if they want to taste something that will amaze then they can do worse than this. The question will now rage: which is the better of the two? For me, perhaps the Premium, because it also has bite as well as guile and slakes thirsts as well as outrageously entertains. Having made love to a young vixen this, though, is perhaps closer to spending a night in the arms of a sultry lady of greater experience. Passion or elegance? We are back to whisky being a mood thing. And if this doesn't get you in the mood, nothing will. **40%**. *Alberta Distillers.*

**Alberta Springs Aged 10 Years** bott lot no. 04327 **(89) n**24 absolute classic delivery of both intense rye and oak: crisp, weighty and wonderful; **t**23 massive rye again on early delivery, then a succession of waves of vanilla, each reducing the grain input; the delicate Demerara sweetness is a charming constant; **f**20 very short for its age and not helped by a toffee caramel trail-off; **b**22 compared to the way many Canadian whiskies are shaping these days, this, along with Alberta Premium, is becoming something of a port in a storm. Wonderfully traditional in style, this is Canadian at its most rip-ryeing and definitely a degree better than when I last tasted it a couple of years back. Fabulous stuff. **40%**. *Alberta Distillers.*

**Barton's Canadian 36 Months Old (78) n**19 **t**20 **f**19 **b**20. Sweet, toffeed, easy-going. **40%**. *Barton.*

**Black Velvet (80) n**20 **t**20 **f**20 **b**20. Consistent, clean, toffeed Canadian with rich body and decent fizz on the finish. **40%**. *Hiram Walker.*

**Canadian Club Premium (78) n**19 **t**20 **f**19 **b**20. Lovely nip and pinch on the nose and some bite on the finish. Enlivening and, in parts, lush. The most visible Canadian whisky in the world, and pretty consistent, too. **40%**. *Hiram Walker.*

**Canadian Club Sherry Cask Aged Eight Years (76) n**22 **t**17 **f**19 **b**18. The problem with putting Canadian whisky into what here appears to be a very high-quality sherry fresh-fill cask or two is that the spirit is naturally too light to withstand the grapey onslaught. The result is less whisky but more high-proof sherry. I admire the effort; the nose is quite lovely and the late finish also has some delightful fruit-spice moments. But the middle is just too one-dimensional. I'd keep the faith, but some tinkering is needed here. If you don't like it first time round, give it a year and see what happens. **41.3%**. *Hiram Walker.*

**Canadian Club Reserve 10 Years of Age (93) n**23 fizzing, busy grain weaves into and thins a distinctively clean, grapey heart; cinnamon and apples complete the gentle fruit theme; **t**23 soft grains, especially lush corn, surrounded by rich, oily vanilla; **f**24 comes into its own with a return of the fruit and spice; a big, juicy grape impact with a sublime bitter-sweet backbone; some late medium roast Java helps get oak back into circulation; distant honeycomb helps with the bitter-sweet balance; **b**23 what a stunning whisky this has developed into over recent years. More sherry involvement, which can so often result in a disastrous finish. Here the opposite is true: the complexity appears to know no bounds. Quality blending, and remains an everyday whisky of distinction. **40%**. *Hiram Walker.*

**Canadian Club Classic Aged 12 Years (79) n**21 **t**21 **f**18 **b**19. Pleasant at first, but has crossed that fine line where the fruit and caramel interfere to the detriment of the blend. Good spice, though. **40%**. *Hiram Walker.*

**Canadian Club 100 Proof (89) n**21 an odd biryani note gives an exotic feel to the firm grains which course through this; **t**23 one of the sweetest Canadians around with a light Demerara lilt to the intense corn; massive grain assault; **f**22 fruit dives in to break up the cornfest; **b**23 if you are expecting this to be a high-octane version of the standard CC Premium, you'll be in for a shock. This is a much fruitier dram with an oilier body to absorb the extra strength. An entertaining blend. **50%**. *Hiram Walker.*

**Canadian Host (74) n**19 **t**18 **f**19 **b**18. Sweet, light, weirdly fruity. **40%**. *Barton.*

**Canadian Mist (74) n**19 **t**18 **f**19 **b**18. One of those helium-light blends with lots of sweet fruitiness. Lots of vanilla. **40%**. *Brown-Forman.*

**Canadian Pure Gold (81) n**20 **t**20 **f**21 **b**20. Well-made, tastebudattacking whisky full of lush, rich fruit – especially raisins. Molten fruitcake. **40%**. *Kittling Ridge.*

**Canadian Spirit (78) n**20 **t**20 **f**19 **b**19. A real toffee-fest with a touch of hard grain around the edges. **40%**. *Carrington Distillers (Alberta Distillers).*

**Canadian Supreme (74) n**18 **t**19 **f**19 **b**18. A light, banana-ry blend that is young but extremely fruity. **40%**

**Centennial 10 Years Limited Edition (84) n**20 **t**22 **f**21 **b**21. One of the cleanest, most non-committal noses in Canada, save for the caramel and cherries; the mouth arrival is excellent with caramel and a honied grain thread running through it. But then you are left with one of the cleanest, most noncommittal finishes in Canada...save for the caramel and cherries. Very drinkable and one to appeal to those whose preferred tipple is brandy or fruit spirit. But for corn lovers, not one to wheat your appetite... **40%**. *Highwood Distillers.*

**Century Reserve 8 Years Old Premium (82) n**20 **t**21 **f**20 **b**21. Clean vanilla and caramel. **40%**. *Century Distillery.*

**Century Reserve 15 Years Old** (*see* Canadian Grain Single Barrel)

**Century Reserve 21 Years Old** (*see* Canadian Grain Single Barrel)

**Century Reserve 21 Years Old (83) n**21 **t**21 **f**20 **b**21. Refreshing, fruity and sweet, it somehow refuses to be its age. Highly drinkable. **40%**. *Century Distilling Co.*

**Corby's Canadian 36 Months Old (85) n**20 subtlevariance of vanilla; **t**21 sweetcorn to start, oils up and then fills the mouth; **f**22 develops into something almost sawdusty. Impressive complexity for one so young; **b**22 always attractive with fine bitter-sweet balance and I love the late spice kick-back. **40%**. *Barton. Interesting label: as a keen ornithologist, I had no idea there were parrots in Canada. Must be related to the Norwegian Blue.*

**Crown Royal** bottling lot no. L4110 (Crown Royal on back label printed in red) **(93) n**23 seriously big rye offers a hard and fruity edge to the soft corn and oak; **t**24 rock-hard and crisp mouth arrival thanks to the early rye, softens for the corn and then the rye sends some fruity shockwaves around the palate; **f**22 bitter and booming: big controlled oak finale on gentle oil; **b**24 this has definitely changed in the last seven or eight years, as all blends must. It has a slightly larger rye dependency than of old but the mouthwatering effect is sublime. An international great. **40%**

**Crown Royal** bottling lot no. L4307 (Crown Royal on back label printed in royal blue) **(88) n**23 **t**21 **f**22 **b**22. Still plenty of rye to go around, with the complexity really taking off towards the finish, but lacking the overall depth of L4110 and with fruit at a minimum. **40%**

**Crown Royal** bottling lot no. L5035 (Crown Royal on back label printed in royal blue) **(83) n**19 waiting for the trademark rye – it's not there! Instead a light, papery dustiness settles over flattening grape; **t**23 fresh fruitiness, with an attractive intermingling of clean corn and juicy, grapey apple; **f**20 spices dance around to help lighten the developing oaky dryness, but it's all disappointingly and irritatingly flat and overly sweet; **b**21 this is one of my regular drinking whiskies, and I thought I had spotted a massive sea change in recent months. So whilst in Vancouver in May, with the help of my dear friend Mike Smith, I was able to compare this once hallmark whisky with three previously unopened Crown Royals: a wonderful (and par for course) 2004 bottling, a corn-laced, beautifully balanced 1979 vintage, and one from 1968 (youngest whisky 10, oldest 30), an absolute stunner of rye-infused complexity that would have given it a 96 in this Bible had it been on the market today...and very close to how I first tasted it in 1974. The results were staggering, and confirmed my suspicions: someone has decided to up the colour and do away with rye. "The Legendary Whisky" says, rightly, the back label. But not like this was it made legendary: whatever agent is being used to increase the colour (and it isn't age), please drop it and reinstate the rye. This, so recently one of the great whiskies of the world, has followed the fruity trend sweeping Canadian whisky and has become an also ran. So bloody frustrating, considering the marked improvements in its sister blends of Limited Edition and Special Reserve. Oi! Mister!! Please can we have our Crown Royal back...!!! **40%**

**Crown Royal Limited Edition** bott lot no L4315 **(95) n**24 floral tones to the fore as the rye shows its hand with a wonderful and perfectly matched hint of citrus, too; **t**24 thumping rye makes for a mouthwatering, crisp, slightly stark arrival, all this on an oily bed of corn. Some glazed cherries dive in for a sweetening edge; **f**23 layer upon layer of alternating corn and rye; the cherry effect still hangs in there; **b**24 the complexity is awesome with the rye offering a delicate fruitiness and disarming charm to the more succulent cherry and softening corn. This has not so much overtaken Crown Royal, as lapped it...!! **40%**

**Crown Royal Special Reserve** bott lot no: L4350 **(93) n**23 great subtlety: various small grains – you could swear barley was in there somewhere – gang together to offer a nose worth five minutes of anyone's time; **t**23 firm rye impact and then a rich development of sweet corn; **f**23 the fruitiness of the rye positively pulsates with some hickory and vanilla, helping to add some oaky age to the event. Fabulous! **b**24 "re-introduce some life back into the finish and you'd have a classic on your hands," I wrote in last year's Bible. Ladies and gentleman, we have a classic on our hands.... **40%**

⊹ **Crown Royal XR Extra Rare** bott lot no. L6239 NA2A db **(93) n**24 some serious and very varied rye notes; orange peel and bourbon battle it out with marauding vanillas for the sweet-sour supremacy. It's a tie... **t**23 those ryes deliver first and do so as part of a breathtaking soft-hard balance. The ryes are hard, the corn and vanilla offer the silky cushion; silver sugar is sprinkled over the mounting vanillins; **f**22 medium length, runs out of puff as regards the rye; toffee takes care of the finale; **b**24 pretty damn good stuff. This first version of this hen's-teeth bottling may be on the sweet side but makes complexity and balance its be-all and end-all. Wonderful, and another leg up to get people to realise just how good whisky from this country can be. An instant classic. **40%.**

**Forty Creek Barrel Select (84) n**22 **t**21 **f**22 **b**19. A prime example of where less would be so much more. Of all the world's distillers, there are few I hold in higher esteem than KR's John Hall. But if he reduced the percentage involvement of the sherry here, we would have one of Canada's finest on our hands. Instead he has a really velvety, massively fruited Canadian that would be one basking in its own brilliance...but balance is never achieved, despite the stupendous nose and mouthwatering edges. Because of the massively high quality of the distillate I really think we have a classic whisky in the making...but only if the sherry is tamed in future bottlings: watch this space.... **40%.** *Kittling Ridge.*

**Forty Creek Three Grain (89) n**21 a real, massive amalgam of ripe fruit, including figs, dates and blueberry and grape juice; **t**22 big fruit arrival from the start: slightly bitter and dry, then a rich and unusual delivery of plums and rye; **f**23 drier finale as some small grain complexity make spicy overtures but are overwhelmed by the late dominance of greengages and soft liquorice; **b**23 I am confused: this is fabulous whisky, real late night, dim lights, crackling log fire stuff that improves on the palate with time and perception. Yet, with all that said, why call this Three Grain? The grains are, for the most part, entirely lost under the charming delights of massive fruit. This should surely be called something else entirely, while a whisky made to such extraordinarily high standards in which small grains are blended with maize should be a bourbon-barrel, fruit-free classic in its own right. **40%.** *Kittling Ridge.*

**Gibson's Finest Canadian Whisky Bourbon Cask Rare Reserve (89) n**23 beautiful bourbon, fruity, kick; **t**21 toasty, corn, and light honeyed sugars; **f**23 wonderfully long with more golden honey sticking to the corn-rich thread; **b**22 a much better version than the first bottling I found, the depth this time being massively greater. **40%** ☉ ☉

**Gibson's Finest Aged 12 Years (93) n**24 enormously busy with fresh fruit, but it's very light, leaving oak, corn and a touch of rye in the ascendency: in many ways, Canadian whisky nutshelled; **t**23 mouthwatering, fat without being oily, with a lovely Demerara sugar coating to the corn without being particularly sweet; **f**22 oak spices dig in to bolster the already big and chewy finish. Excellent shape and curvature to this, even at the death; **b**24 great to see a wonderful whisky back on tip-top form after a year or two in the doldrums. Great Canadian whisky that balances out with rare depth. **40%.**

**Gibson's Finest Rare Aged 18 Years (92) n**23 bold oak, soft white peppers and befriending corn; **t**23 just such a yielding delivery with hints of ripe banana and raisin amid the melting corn; **f**22 soft vanilla, lazy spice, a hint of fruit and very, very late honey; **b**24 just wonderful whisky in which you can lose yourself. Not quite as honied as before, or as rye-rich as some of the earlier bottlings. But remains a true beaut, though the 12-y-o currently has the greater finesse. Interestingly the back label claims the whisky will "add a new dimension to your drinking enjoyment". While the Bible for the last couple of years has been telling you: "It takes Canadian whisky into a new dimension." Where's my agent when I need her.... **40%** ☉

**Gibson's Finest Sterling Edition (79) n**21 **t**20 **f**19 **b**19. Big disappointment here: this has softened up, gone fruity and lost so much shape. Drinkable in a crowd, but nothing like up to the great Gibson name. **40%**

**Gibson's New Oak (88) n**22 decent smattering of spice interrupts the sweet fanfare; **t**21 this would be one sensationally lush, almost syrupy, Canadian were it not for sub-strata of light grain and gathering oak; **f**23 this is where that new oak does its business with the casks ensuring a delicious counter dryness and spice; **b**22 distinctly different from any other Canadian doing the rounds: the oak influence makes a wonderful and clever impact. **40%**

**Golden Wedding** (*see* Schenley Golden Wedding)

**Gooderham & Worts Ltd (90) n**23 excellent trilogy of fresh corn, soft rye and something fruity; **t**23 a supremely weighted and deliciously sweet start bursts from the off. Not as much rye as I remember, though, as I was involved in the blending development of this brand; **f**22 lots of rich corn and deep oaky vanilla. Pure Canadian on a golden platter; **b**22 sensational Canadian, though on this bottling the rye input has been taken down a peg or two, which is a shame. Even so, a real stunner for its genre. **45%**

**Hamilton (77) n**18 **t**20 **f**20 **b**19. Young grains are kept on the leash to offer very sweet toffee. Very well made and easy-going. **40%**

**Highwood Pure Canadian (73) n**20 **t**19 **f**17 **b**17. When they say "Pure" Canadian they're not joking: the cleanest nose in Canada, from a wheated distillate brought to the edge of pure alcohol. The rest, I'm afraid, is a tale of caramel. **40%**

**Hiram Walker Special Old (92) n**22 rock-solid nose that is hard as nails yet reveals a soft belly on which corn gently floats and citrus notes flutter; **t**23 brittle, flinty mouth arrival that hints at dryness and then is outmanoeuvred by stunning, well controlled sweet-corn and rye; **f**24 complex, long, with fabulous grain structure and only an echo of caramel as a tangerine, citrus note cuts through any developing weight. Absolutely brilliant rye and oak involvement and the faintest wisps of honey and cocoa complete a brilliant experience; **b**23 anyone wanting to taste good, honest, old-fashioned Canadian at its most understated and complex should give this one a shot. It's always been one I've enjoyed, but in the last couple of years it has really taken on an extra degree of panache. Almost has a touch of the Irish pot still about it. **40%**

**Lot No. 40 (93)** n24 one of the most magnificent and rarest noses in the world: malted rye. Hints of spearmint chewing gum, kumquats, boiled sugar candy, all enveloped in that unique rye fruitiness; t24 brittle and hard at first, then soft rye-powered fruit arrives, slightly peppery towards the middle, heavy roast cocoa and soft rye oil; f23 decent oak presence and some straggling fruity rye notes; b23 this is great whisky, irrespective of whichever country it came from. As for a Canadian, this is true rye whisky, one with which I was very proud to be associated in the early blending days. Elegant stuff. And these notes brought back to you by popular demand!! **43%**

**McGuinness Silk Tassell (79)** n21 t20 f19 b19. Silk by name and nature: softer and silkier than of old, but way too caramel dependent and needs a rye injection. **40%**. *Corby.*

**McMaster's (80)** n19 t20 f21 b20. Velvet-textured and buttered sweet corn. Dangerously easy-to-drink session whisky. **40%**. *Barton.*

**Monarch Canadian Aged Thirty-six Months (84)** n20 t22 f20 b22. An attractive, entirely refreshing Canadian that goes surprisingly easy on the caramel. Sweet and with good grain-oak ratio. Really good fun for the cut-price sector. **40%**. *Monarch Import Company.*

**Mountain Rock (89)** n22 soft grains and gentle, reserved fruits in the bourbony toffee; t22 beautifully mouth-enveloping; faintly lush and never less than juicy; f23 simmers down into a more complex, finely-layered beauty and wonderfully deft oak on the long finish; b22 an oxymoron of a whisky: for a Mountain Rock, it's just a big - and beautiful - softie! **40%**. *Kittling Ridge.*

**Wm Morrison Imported Canadian Rye (89)** n23 there is actually a touch of rye on the nose here (unusual in Canadian these days) and the fruity depth is compelling; t23 more mouthwatering grains with an excellent oaky balance; f21 leans too heavily on caramel; b22 a top-notch Canadian for a supermarket brand. **40%**

**Northern Light (82)** n20 t21 f20 b21. A young, natural, unpretentious Canadian grain blend with a good, clean character and first-class bite. Very attractive. **40%**.

**Pendleton Let'er Buck Aged 10 Years (81)** n21 t22 f19 b19. A sweet, corny romp. Brought in from Canada. Probably the caramel as well. **40%**.

**Pike Creek** finished in port barrels **(87)** n21 curious amalgam of corn and fresh wine; t23 soft, silky mouthfeel and then a whoosh of sweetness; f21 some spices prosper as the port makes a stand, genuinely fruity at first then becoming a little more bitter as the oak arrives; b22 much more complexity now than from the first bottlings. A Canadian of genuine style and character. **40%**. *Allied.*

**Potter's Crown (70)** n19 t18 f16 b17. Ferociously fruity and showing little backbone. Pleasant in part. **40%**. *Potter Brands, San José.*

**Potter's Special Old (90)** n22 the clarity of the grain is profound and unambiguous: this is Canadian whisky! t23 a natural translation on to the palate with a delicate toffee input, possibly from caramel, but the corn can be heard loud and clear, and those with a penchant for a walnut whip will understand why I find an oily, candy link...; f22 chewy with decent oaky vanilla; b23 after the strangulation of Canadian whisky in recent times by fruit, have you any idea how refreshing and heart-warming it is to come across such a wonderfully honest and traditional whisky as this? Very limited fruit input, high quality grain all the way. It may come in a plastic bottle. It may be cheap. But it's Canadian whisky as it has been known for the last 100 years and the mark reflects that fact. **40%**

**Pure Gold** (*see* Canadian Pure Gold)

**Royal Reserve (85)** n21 t21 f22 b21. A lovely Canadian which doesn't suffer from too much fruit interference and actually appears to have some discernible rye in the blend. **40%**. *Corby.*

**Sam Barton Aged 5 Years** L617802A **(83)** n20 t21 f21 b21. Entirely acceptable and mildly juicy Canadian with an attractive honey and vanilla strand. **40%**. *La Martiniquaise, France.*

**Seagram's 83 Canadian Whisky (68) n**18 t17 f16 b17. Caramel-dominated these days. **40%**. *The "83" refers to 1883, not a 1983 vintage, and certainly not its rating...*

**Seagram's Five Star (75) n**18 t20 f18 b19. Doesn't make you physically shudder like the "83" but hasn't improved in time. The middle does still show some admirable graininess despite the cloying sweetness. **40%**

**Seagram's VO** bottling lot no. L5054 **(85) n**20 lots of dull corn and toffee; **t**23 delicious sweet-corn with a slow but profound vanilla build-up; **f**21 oily, soft and sweet; the finale is pleasnt without anything like the usual compelxity and near genius; **b**21 for all its early charm on the palate, another 2005 bottling of a Canadian great that has lost both its distinctive rye character and its claim to greatness. Is this the start of an extremely worrying trend, or just a one-off blip...? What is going on? **40%**

**Schenley Golden Wedding** bottling lot no. L5018 **(83) n**20 t21 f21 b21. Beautifully silky textured and rich. Great distillate used here which is both prickly and luxurious. Lovely stuff. **40%.**

**Schenley OFC Aged 8 Years (93) n**24 brilliant nose: awesome complexity here as the grains tease around the vanilla. Perfectly weighted; **t**23 again, outstanding balance on the sweetness as you chew at the grain and lick at the thin sugary coating; **f**23 soft spices, vanilla and traces of late honey; **b**23 some re-writing of history here: the label says "Original Fine Canadian" under OFC. Actually, I'm pretty convinced it originally meant Old Fire Copper. I can think of other things OFC stand for, perhaps not suitable for this book, but I will settle instead for Outstandingly Flavoured Creation, for this remains one of Canada's top three finest traditional blends, one which comes back at you with each mouthful with greater and greater complexity. **40%**

**Silk Tassel** (*see* McGuinness Silk Tassel)

**Tangle Ridge Aged 10 Years (67) n**17 t17 f16 b17. One of the worst Canadians I have tasted in years: something sweet and unpleasant has been added. The mouthfeel and effect are dreadful, the nose isn't much better. Considering this is based on rye whisky, you could almost cry. Still see it in specialist outlets from time to time: one to avoid. **40%**

**Tesco Canadian Whisky (75) n**18 t18 f20 b19. A reasonable sweet, clean if uninspiring Canadian. **40%**. *UK.*

**Windsor (91) n**21 kind of typical Canadian – its atypicality packed full of bizarre little nuances that don't quite fit, yet work: perhaps eclectic is the best term here; **t**24 wonderful, and entirely unexpected rye arrival really sets the tastebuds at fever pitch; very clean and grainy all the way; **f**22 some soft fruit and caramel drop in to say farewell; **b**24 an inexpensive, charming, honest and true Canadian that is worth discovering. **40%**

**Wiser's 10 Years Old** (*see* Wiser's De Luxe)

**Wiser's 18 Years Old (88) n**23 of all Canada's whiskies this probably has the most deceptive and delicate nose. There is gentle toffee, but lurking below that apples, leather, oloroso sherry and black pepper; **t**23 some blending brinkmanship going on here, with the oak and corn being pushed to the limit by fruit. The underlying crispness of the grain punches through to plant the Canadian flag; **f**20 here it loses control after taking one bend too many. Crashes into the fruit and oak and comes to a bitter end; **b**22 I spent a couple of days tasting and deliberating over this one, as it is quite an odd fish, and on the first run marked it low. My initial thoughts were that the caramel had perhaps taken too many prisoners and the fruit was out of sync. But over time I found greater shape and complexity. If you fancy yourself as a doctor of whisky, here's one to give a thorough examination to...and then a second opinion! **40%**. *Hiram Walker.*

**Wiser's De Luxe (89) n**23 beefy with sharpening touches of rye and other slightly fruity, citrus notes; **t**23 very busy mouth arrival with a complex array of corn on the cob and then much cleaner, small grain notes. Good weight to the oiliness which never goes OTT; a brief spice fly-past and an early vanilla-oak attack. Absolutely superb! **f**20 a mark or two dropped for the uncharacteristically bitter finale, though not of a rye-based character; slightly more toffee and fruit character, yet against all this soft corn sifts through pleasantly on the unbelievably silky fade-out; **b**23 this is mysterious and magical stuff. They tell me at Hiram Walker that nothing has changed. Yet I have been drinking Wiser's regularly for a decade and I can assure you it has. Far more non-specific fruit now, with the subtle grainy complexity overshadowed by a heavier, richer backdrop. Still genuinely attractive, chewy and fabulously complex whisky, but it seems to have darkened up both in looks and character. This is marketed as Wiser's 10 outside Canada. And remains a classic, if a slightly different one.... **40%**. *Hiram Walker.*

**Wiser's Reserve (90) n**22 rock-firm and almost austere; **t**23 the slow build-up of intensity is almost mesmerising: like watching a train coming at you from a distance. The sweetness is controlled superbly with oaky-spice darting in and adding balancing dryness; **f**22 excellent oak with a really grainy sunset radiating late but weak sweetness, but it's those spices that really make an imprint; **b**23 just a little bit of attitude here goes a long, long way. Impressive. **43%**

**Wiser's Special Blend (76) n**17 **t**21 **f**19 **b**19. A marginally improved, far more silky blend, but still never quite gets over the over-enthusiastic fruit nose or toffeed finish. Still, the middle does have a new shape with the spice kick and firm grain. By no means unpleasant. **40%**. *Hiram Walker.*

# Japanese Whisky

**S**adly, if you want to discover Japanese whisky you must still go to Japan. Of the 200 Japanese whiskies I have tasted for this year's Whisky Bible, only a handful are available in markets outside the nation in which they were distilled or blended. This is very frustrating when you see that many of the distilleries are nowhere near on full production and some are either silent or closed.

Part of the problem has been the Japanese custom of refusing to trade with their rivals. Therefore a Japanese whisky, if not made completely from home-distilled spirit, will instead contain a percentage of Scotch rather than whisky from fellow Japanese distillers.

This, ultimately, is doing the industry no favours at all. The practice is partly down to the traditional work ethics of company loyalty and an inherent, and these days false, belief that Scotch whisky is automatically better than Japanese. Back in the late 1990s I planted the first seeds in trying to get rival distillers to discuss with each other the possibility of exchanging whiskies to ensure that their distilleries worked more economically.

In the meantime word is getting round that Japanese whisky is worth finding. Indeed, there is so much interest in these little-known brands (outside Japan that is) that I have even given an all-Japanese whisky tasting in Holland.

Two leading lights are getting whisky drinkers switched on to just what oriental delights we are missing: the malts of Yoichi and Hakushu. Both make whiskies that rank unquestionably among the very finest in the world, though Yoichi – the brilliance of which I'm proud to have first brought to the world's attention in 1997 – these days has to be a little more careful with their use of sherry. Less than a handful of Scotch distilleries, though, can match their and Hakushu's supremely complex makes.

As if stirred by the recent success and fame of Yoichi, other distillers in Japan have begun bringing out vintage single cask bottlings. So slowly, as if by degree, interest in Japanese whiskies is being raised. One place this can clearly be seen is at whsiky festivals. Five or six years ago years ago a bottle or two on Japanese on a table full of scotch would last a long time. Now it is often the first to go. And what is more, if attending these events I am now asked by whisky enthusiasts if I can tell them anyone who has any Japanese on display or , preferably, to taste.

Word, then, is clearly getting around that Japanese whiskies, in whatever form, are worth finding. And that word gets ever larger and louder spoken when relatively unknown distilleries like Hanyu can produce bottlings of the magnitude King of Diamonds which has scooped Jim Murray's Whisky Bible 2008 Japanese Whisky of the Year. This is not just good whisky: it is great whisky on the world stage and must give confidence for Japanese distillers to take on markets they had previously thought the domain of Scotch and bourbon.

The arrival of the Hanyu malts into my lab is further proof that, for the very first time, there is now both a Japanese whisky industry which believes it might just have a product worth the effort of selling around the world and importers keen to get their hands on it and take the plunge. If Japanese whisky is to make a success of it around the world, it will take a lot more time, hard work and inner belief. Surely, though, it cannot any longer be be a case of if. With the whisky-loving public taking notice, it now has to be a matter of when.

## Single Malts
### CHICHIBU

**Golden Horse Chichibu** db **(80) n**19 **t**21 **f**20 **b**20. Light, toasty and delicate yet the oak is prominent throughout. Good balancing sweet malt, though. **43%**. *Toa*.

**Golden Horse Chichibu 10 Years Old Single Malt** db **(82) n**19 **t**22 **f**21 **b**20. Developing citrus notes lighten the weight as the oak and sweet malt go head to head. **43%**. *Toa*.

**Chichibu 14 Years Old Single Malt** db **(89) n**20 tangerine peel and rice: two years older than the 12-y-o, that hint of bourbon has now become a statement; **t**23 brilliantly eclectic arrival on the palate with no organisation at all to the flurry of malt and bourbony oak and tangerine-fruity spices that are whizzing around; **f**23 pretty long with firm vanilla and a distinctive oiliness. Something approaching a whiff of smoke adds some extra ballast to the oak; **b**23 we are talking mega, in-your-face taste explosions here. A malt with a bourbony attitude that is unquestionably superb. **57%**. *Toa*.

### FUJI GOTEMBA, 1973. Kirin Distillers.

**The Fuji Gotemba 15 Years Old** db **(92) n**21 diced nuts, especially pistachio with vanilla and a sprinkling of sugar; **t**23 mouth watering from the start with a sensational development of sweet malt; **f**24 plateaus out with textbook spices binding sweet malt and dry oak. The length is exemplary; **b**24 quality malt of great poise. **43%**. *Kirin*.

**The Fuji Gotemba 18 Years Old** db **(81) n**20 **t**19 **f**21 **b**21. Jelly-baby fruitiness, complete with powdered sugar. Big, big age apparent. **43%**. *Kirin*.

**Fuji Gotemba 20th Anniversary Pure Malt** db **(84) n**21 **t**20 **f**22 **b**21. The nose is a lovely mixture of fruit and mixed oak; the body has a delightful sheen and more fruit with the malt. Handsome stuff. **40%**. *Kirin*.

### HAKUSHU, 1973. Suntory.

**The Hakushu Single Malt Whisky Aged 10 Years** db **(89) n**23 exemplary grassiness, fresh malt: mouthwatering and refreshes the senses; **t**24 spot-on, top-of-the-range malt. The freshness and integrity of the barley is beyond belief: thirst-quenching whisky of the highest order; **f**20 becomes rather toffeed and less well defined. A subtle display of spice compensates; **b**22 beautifully crafted whisky that's fresh and rewarding. **40%**. ⊙ ⊙

**The Hakushu Single Malt Whisky Aged 12 Years** db **(92) n**23 one of the most intricate peat noses around, made all the lighter by the citrus touch... **t**23 ...and no less delicate on arrival. Every strand of oak and smoke feels as though it could snap at any moment; **f**22 some soft oils and liquorice ensure a weightier finale; **b**24 sheer smoky elegance. **43%** ⊙ ⊙

⠿ **Hakushu Single Malt Aged 12 Years** db **(91) n**22 revitalising barley with smoke as distant as a cloud over Fuji; **t**23 multi-layered barley with so many levels of sweetness; the very faintest hint of smoke on the middle; **f**23 long with the accent now on vanilla and soft, developing oil and spice; **b**23 an even more lightly- peated version of the 40%, with the distillery's fabulous depth on full show. **43.3%**.

**The Hakushu Single Malt Whisky Aged 15 Years Cask Strength** db **(95) n**24 pure, unmistakable Hakushu: intense, powering, yet clean and refined. Loads of citrus to lighten matters but the local oak ensures enormity; **t**23 big, initially oak-threatened but the barley comes flooding back with light oils helping to soften the early scratchiness; first mouthful is dry, the second shows a much truer picture; **f**24 now goes into complexity overdrive as all those fruity-barley-oaky- elements continue to jostle for supremacy, only for late spices and gorgeous milky mocha to come in and steal the thunder; **b**24 last time round I lamented the disappointing nose. This time perhaps only a degree of over eagerness from the oak has robbed this as a serious Whisky of the Year contender. No matter how you look at it, though, brilliant!! **56%** ⊙ ⊙

**The Hakushu Single Malt Whisky Aged 18 Years** db **(93) n**23 not dissimilar to medium ester Jamaican pot still rum with a squeeze of lemon and a bowl of barley juice thrown in for good measure; **t**23 delicate, ultra-clean barley which intensifies by the second into gristy sweetness; **f**23 toasted vanilla and mallows; then a burst of malt-(milk)chocolate candy; **b**24 this distillery never fails to delight me. The high grade malt is no shock: I realised just how extraordinary their whisky was on my last trip there. Another is overdue. The depth to the intensity of the malt reaches new peaks for this, or probably any other distillery I can think of. A whisky for Malteser lovers the world over... **43%** ⊙

**Hakushu 1984** db **(95) n**22 delicate banana and malt with a gentle fly-past of peat. The oak is unbowed but sympathetic; **t**25 staggeringly beautiful: wave upon wave of astonishing complexity crashes against the tastebuds. The malt is intense but there is plenty of room for oak in varying guises to arrive, make eloquent speeches and retire. The intensity of spice is spot on – perfect; **f**24 long, more spice and greater malt intensity as the oak fades. Only the softest hints of smoke; mouthwatering to the last as mild coffee appears; **b**24 a masterpiece malt of quite sublime complexity and balance. The sort of experience that gives a meaning to life, the universe and everything ... **61%**

**Hakushu 1988** db **(92) n**21 overtly peaty and dense, pleasant but lacking usual Hakushu complexity; **t**24 mouthwatering start with massively lively malt and fresh peating hanging on to its coat-tails. Some amazing heather–honey moments that have no right to be there; the peat intensifies then lightens; **f**23 lots of rich peat and then intense vanilla; crisp and abrupt at the finale with late bitter chocolate; **b**24 like all great whiskies this is one that gangs up on you in a way you are not expecting: the limited complexity on the nose is more than compensated for elsewhere. Superb. If this were an Islay malt the world would be drooling over it. **61%**

**Hakushu Vintage Malt 1990** db **(89) n**22 firm barley and firmer oak; **t**23 serious intensity on delivery, this time with all the action being enjoyed by the concentrated, grassy barley; **f**22 layers of vanilla add balance to the fade; **b**22 warming in places with the tastebuds never getting a single moment's peace. **56%**. *Suntory*.

**Hakushu Vintage Malt 1981** bott 04 **(90) n**22 biting sherry gnaws at the nosebuds; **t**22 mouthwatering despite the sherry influence and a wonderful chocolate-barley interlude ensures complexity; **f**23 spices that arrive at the middle continue their course towards the finale where more fruit arrives in the form of sultanas and cherries; **b**23 a beautifully clean sherried malt but, fabulous as it may be, the gap between this and the '89 Cask of Hakushu is never less than a chasm. **56%**. *Suntory*.

**Hakushu Vintage Malt 1985** bott 04 **(88) n**21 egg yolk; vanilla omelette; **t**22 perky malt edges towards a grassy theme; **f**23 excellent layers of oak and barley with a late fruity development; **b**22 clean, bourbon-matured malt that is younger than normal Japanese whisky of this age and reveals delightful deftness of touch. **56%**. *Suntory*.

**The Cask of Hakushu 1989** Sherry Butt cask 9W50004, dist Nov 89, bott Apr 05 **(96) n**25 where the hell can you begin?? OK, in no particular order: high roast Java with whipped cream; a mixing of pot and column still Dememara rum (of at least 8 years matured in Guyana); cocoa oil; liquorice-stained ryerecipe 12-y-o bourbon; some corn-stained 10-y-o rye; playful barley with a dash of very distant smoke. Oh, and some Oloroso sherry. The greatest Japanese nose of all time? Very possibly; **t**23 extraordinary eruption of spices and then a delightful delivery of Walnut Whip, strawberry jam and juicy barley; **f**24 the oloroso returns with myriad layers of oak and barley that pan out towards a cherry pie fruitiness and so much else. The spice continues to nip and bite; the sherry kisses and caresses; **b**24 f*** me!!! I needed about five to ten minutes to recover from this...Now, I don't often mention colour. But this is like an ancient Tawny Port and looks either wonderful or terrifying – because so often sulphur can be detected. Here, there is not a single trace of a trace. This is from an extraordinary butt, the purest imaginable, most probably the best I have seen the in the last decade. In the same league as (if not better than) those great Chivas Speyside casks of the mid to late 70s. What we have here is a whisky that catapults Japan on to the superstar map. Yoichi has done it for years, and Hakushu has given close support, but any whisky lover not yet convinced that Japanese is worth the effort must find a bottle of this. It will change their perception – even their lives – for ever.... **63%**. *Suntory*.

**The Cask of Hakushu 1994** Bourbon cask 4E05405, dist May 94, bott Apr 05 **(92) n**24 a wonderful, unbelievable, soft aroma offering hazelnut oil, and barley against very dry oak: absolute harmony; **t**23 sweeter than nose with an early honied, orangey development; **f**22 dries towards vanilla but still the intense barley holds ground; very late spice adds a fighting spirit; **b**23 a wonderful cask that is bursting at the seems with depth and committal but somehow remains in harness. **58%**. *Suntory*.

Suntory Pure Malt Hakushu Aged 20 Years db **(94)** n23 fresh, mildly grapey fruit combined with subtle waves of peat; t24 the peat is now less subtle: wave upon wave of it bringing with it flotsam of drifting oak and then a very sharp malt tang; f23 long, sweet spice but the oak forms a chunky alliance with the firm peat. The bitter-sweet compexity almost defies belief; b24 a hard-to-find malt, but find it you must. Yet another huge nail in the coffin of those who purport Japanese whisky to be automatically inferior to Scotch. **56%**

## HANYU

⁘ **Ace of Spades 1985** Cask no. 9308, dist 85, bott 06 db **(88)** n22 big sherry fanfare; t22 grapey, juicy, spicy; f22 dries on one hand then bursts out with more fruit on another; spices prevail; b22 a decent sherry cask with the spices helping to give an extra lift. **55.7%.** *Ichiro's Malt Card Series.*

⁘ **Jack of Clubs 1991** Cask no. 9001, dist 91, bott 06 db **(87)** n22 sweet bourbon-esque notes, except the oak is more European in style; t22 mouth-watering barley sugar with that diffused and powerful oak leading the way; f21 thins out; b21 an enjoyable malt just missing out on complexity. **56.8%.** *Ichiro's Malt Card Series.*

⁘ **King of Diamonds 1988** Cask no. 9003, dist 88, bott 06 db **(96)** n25 the most subtle, electrically stimulating peat on any nose on any whisky this year. The smoke caresses the nasal orifice like the nails of a temptress on your back; the sweetness is controlled and faultless...I'm getting goose bumps every time I stick my proboscis in the glass.. t23 soft slivers of fruit help gently ease the oak and barley into its comfortable smoky suit; f24 long, delicate, the smoke every bit as teasing and playful as on the nose; rum and raisin cake topped by a dollop of chocolate mousse; b24 this is what whisky should be all about: subtlety and class. And this King of Diamonds has it in Spades.... **56%.** *Ichiro's Malt Card Series.*

⁘ **King of Spades 1986** Cask no. 9418, dist 86, bott 07 db **(91)** n22 various layers of oak – including some from the deepest parts of the stave – embellish the fruity lead; t23 big barley-fruit delivery; sharp, eye watering, grassy style. Very clean and precise for age; f23 no less salivating on the finish with some spicier notes now throbbing through and the trademark cocoa trait to tie things off; b23 another little belter from this excellent distillery showing confidence at this age to the point of arrogance. **57%.** *Ichiro's Malt Card Series.*

⁘ **Two of Clubs 2000** Cask no. 9500, dist 00, bott 07 db **(92)** n22 fruity; what appears a local/European oak hybrid embraces clean barley; t24 exceptional delivery with outstanding fruity intensity to the barley which is almost too clean and concentrated to be true...wonderful! f23 simplistic fade, but nothing wrong with luxurious, lightly oiled malt still pulsing a semi-sweet barley residue; b23 beautifully made and full of malty gusto. A genuine treat – especially for a malt so young. Two of Clubs, maybe. A Full House in anyone's books, though. **57%.** *Ichiro's Malt Card Series*

## KARUIZAWA, 1955. Mercian.

**Karuizawa 1972 Aged 31 Years** cask 5530 db **(78)** n19 t18 f21 b20. Oaky and hot with just a bit too much age.

**Karuizawa 1973 Aged 30 Years** cask 6249 db **(84)** n20 t21 f22 b21. Sweet barley and very silky oaky vanilla. Plucked from the cask just in time.

**Karuizawa 1974 Aged 29 Years** cask 6115 db **(91)** n23 brilliant complexity: juicy dates and figs wrapped around a theme of richly oaked barley; t22 much sweeter arrival on the nose with burnt fudge and toast arriving for the middle; f23 slightly salty, the barley seems both sweet and roasty. Soft liquorice makes this one you can chew for hours; b23 an exhibition of bitter-sweet enormity.

**Karuizawa 1975 Aged 28 Years** cask 4066 db **(85)** n20 t21 f23. Much more relaxed late middle and finish with they honey thread soothing the singed taste buds; b21 loud at first, it sings sweet lullabies at the death. Always complex.

**Karuizawa 1976 Aged 27 Years** cask 6949 db **(83)** n19 t20 f23 b21. Big, mouthfilling but just a touch too much oak among the honey.

**Karuizawa 1977 Aged 26 Years** cask 7614 db **(74)** n17 t20 f19 b18. Some decent sweetness but doesn't quite work.

**Karuizawa 1978 Aged 25 Years** cask 2368 db **(87)** n21 seaweedy and shoreline, but without the peat; t20 almost violent arrival of searing sherry and vicious oak: hang on to your chair; f23 calms down stupendously with soft smoky peat to be found in the many strata of clean fruit and barley; b23 extra dry sherry, biting, salty and with a big coastal tang.

**Karuizawa 1979 Aged 24 Years** cask 8835 db **(94)** n23 much more fruit than is usual for this distillery with apples and fresh pear; lots of barley survives despite the age; t23 the barley is drinking in gentle honey and cocoa-enriched oak; f24 marvellously long with teasing, toasted caramelised oak adding a glorious repost to the rich, Demerara-sweetened barley; b24 one of those rare casks that appears to have had a magic wand waved at it and stardust sprinkled liberally.

**Karuizawa 1980 Aged 23 Years** cask 7614 db **(89)** n22 solid age but the softness of the toffee-apple and barley sugar is first class; attractive bourbony notes develop; t21 gripping, wild and hot at first, then a series of soothing waves of malt and liquorice; f24 peppery and estery; the honey-malt mouthfeel is long, lush and fabulous; b22 a classy Japanese malt that relishes the battle against advancing oak.

**Karuizawa 1981 Aged 22 Years** cask 8280 db **(73)** n17 t19 f19 b18. Sharp redcurrants but too obvious off-notes abound.

**Karuizawa 1982 Aged 21 Years** cask 8527 db **(85)** n21 a forest full of honey bees; t21 deep honey and toasted fudge; the middle erupts with strangely enjoyable sap; f22 gentle malt with a pinch of moscavado sugar and liquorice; b21 a mature whisky showing some sag but just hanging onto its sexy, alluring figure.

**Karuizawa 1983 Aged 20 Years** cask 8609 db **(88)** n20 slightly estery; chocolate honeycomb and a slice of pine; t24 estery, rich enormous copper presence; f22 medium length with elegant wisps of honey and toffee; b22 tasted blind you would bet your own grandmother that this was pot still Jamaican rum. And one probably older than your gran.

**Karuizawa 1984 Aged 19 Years** cask 2563 db **(78)** n17 t20 f21 b20. Some quality touches of grape against smoky grist, and the mild peat is a redeeming and unexpected surprise, but what a shame that minor sulphury blemish.

**Karuizawa 1985 Aged 18 Years** cask 6885 db **(90)** n22 honey as a side dish on butterscotch tart; t22 mouth filling, oilier than usual with sumptuous malt and oak; f23 wonderful tones of butterscotch sweetened over the broadening oak. Just a slight sprinkling of cocoa; b23 whisky that celebrates its middle age with a show of complex intensity.

**Karuizawa 1986 Aged 17 Years** cask 8170 db **(94)** n23 full-frontal, naked sherry. And spicy, too; t23 massive, almost uncontrollable sherry-malt explosion; dried dates and vanilla concentrate form an unlikely but delicious alliance; f24 long, fruity with hidden spices; the malt ducks in and out playfully; b24 find a faultless sherry butt and place in it a whisky of the very finest quality and complexity. This is the result.

**Karuizawa 1987 Aged 16 Years** cask 8694 db **(93)** n23 amazingly soft malt with just a touch of far-away, background smoke; t23 brilliant malt arrival: the barley sings from every direction; f24 surprising lack of development as the oak remains shy and the barley rules unhindered; just the faintest wisp of smoke here and there; b23 almost like a malt-shake in its barley intensity. No complaints here, though.

**Karuizawa 1988 Aged 15 Years** cask 691 db **(88)** n20 malty banana and custard; t22 drying oak at first and then the most teasing build-up of honey imaginable; f23 this creeping effect continues with a crescendo of acacia honey and green-grassy barley in total control of the oak; b23 quite fabulous whisky that exudes confidence and charisma.

⋅∴⋅ **Karuizawa 1988 Single Cask No. 3397** dist 88, bott 07 db **(90)** n21 red liquorice and grist; a soft smokiness helps control some oaky off-notes; t23 magical delivery with a golden syrup/molassed malt sweetness going head to head with much aggressive oak; f23 fabulous, pin-pricky spices lengthen the sweet finish; b23 technically a slightly flawed dram. But there is no denying its drama. **59.8%**

**Karuizawa 1989 Aged 14 Years** cask 2941 db **(91)** n22 soaring fruity notes interlock beautifully with soft bourbon; t23 hard, metallic arrival at first then a fabulous deployment of sugared fruits on a bed of chewy oak; f23 big vanilla, subtle spices and a very late waft of smoke; **b**23 there would be quite a number of Scottish distilleries who would pray to produce a malt this simplistically stylish.

**Karuizawa 1990 Aged 13 Years** cask 7905 db **(85) n**19 **t**21 **f**23 **b**22. Deliciously mouth-watering yet firm and unyielding barley is stand-offish towards the oak. The finish is awesomely rich. The texture is excellent.

**Karuizawa 1991 Aged 12 Years** cask 8294 db **(87) n**22 beautifully fresh and gristy; **t**22 big delivery of clean malt which sweetens; **f**22 a simple barley vanilla tail with some soft brown sugar; **b**21 charming, well proportioned but not overly taxing.

**Karuizawa Pure Malt 15 Years (76) n**17 **t**21 **f**20 **b**18. Some vague sulphur notes on the sherry do no favours for what appears to be an otherwise top-quality malt. (Earlier bottlings have been around the 87–88 mark, with the fruit, though clean, not being quite in balance but made up for by an astonishing silkiness with roast chestnut puree and malt). **40%**

**Karuizawa Pure Malt Aged 17 Years (90) n**20 bourbony, big oak and pounding fruit; **t**24 enormous stuff: the link between malt and fruit is almost without definition; **f**23 amazingly long and silky. Natural vanilla melts in with the almost concentrated malt; **b**23 brilliant whisky beautifully made and majestically matured. Neither sweetness nor dryness dominates, always the mark of a quality dram. **40%**

## KOMAGATAKE

**Komagatake 10 Years Old Single Malt** db **(78) n**19 **t**20 **f**19 **b**20. A very simple, malty whisky that's chewy and clean with a slight hint of toffee. **40%**. *Mars.*

## MIYAGIKYO (see Sendai)

### SENDAI, 1969. Nikka.

**Miyagikyo 10 Years Old** batch 18C10D db **(88) n**22 **t**20 **f**23 **b**23.0 By far and away the most deftly smoked and complex Sendai seen on the market. **45%**

**Miyagikyou 10 Years Old** Batch 20C44D db **(85) n**19 **t**22 **f**22 **b**22. The nose offers little to encourage, but the sweetened softness of delivery is delicious; there is even a swirl of smoke on the finish to add weight. **45%**

**Miyagikyou 10 Years Old** Batch 08F20C db **(83) n**20 **t**21 **f**21 **b**21. Light and amazingly even throughout with the accent very much on the barley. **45%**

**Miyagikyou 12 Years Old** Batch 12F30C db **(88) n**22 gooseberries, oak and barley; **t**21 some Japanese oak bites hard and kicks the big barley off balance; **f**23 recovers sensationally, with soft oils allowing the fruit-barley complexity to really take hold; **b**22 classy and complex. **45%**

**Miyagikyou 12 Years Old** Batch 24C38A db **(78) n**21 **t**19 **f**19 **b**19. Some pleasant barley-rich moments, but doesn't quite come together. **45%**

**Miyagikyou 15 Years Old** Batch 02F60B db **(92) n**22 a fruitcake density (and a distant sulphurous something) but big barley, too; **t**24 spiced and lush, a marmalade sharpness bites playfully; amid the sublime integration marzipan offers sweetness; **f**23 long oaky strands of liquorice and vanilla cut through the re-grouping barley; **b**23 the fruit/spice influence has "sherry" written all over it. And, if you are being picky, the odd fault can be found with it. But taking the thing as a whole: wow!!! **45%**

**Miyagikyou 1990** cask no. 27216, dist 8 Nov 90, bott 26 July 06 db **(91) n**22 pear drops, apples: light and fruity; **t**24 barley sugar melts into the delicate oak. Delicious intensity; **f**22 clean and elegant; **b**23 a mouth-watering, high quality experience. This distillery has definitely improved in recent years. **54%**. *France.*

**Miyagiko Single Malt 12 Years Old 70th Anniversary (93) n**23 any hint of sulphur is extinguished by light smoke and intense barley amid the crushed raisin; **t**24 mouthwatering, mouth-shattering barley that is so brittle that it fragments in a thousand pieces. Gathering spice sits well with the soft honey and liquorice; **f**23 continuous layers of molassed barley and burnt oak. You need teeth to get through this one...; **b**23 Amazing stuff: if it was an earthquake it would fly off the Richter scale. This is big and body-rocking. **58%**. *Nikka.*

**Miyagiko Key Malt Aged 12 Years "Fruity & Rich"** db **(90) n**22 fruit biscuits with burnt raisin and sugar; **t**23 wonderful lift-off of sultana and burnt raisin on a sea of chewy barley. Towards the middle, a brief expression of oak and then much sweeter – and oilier – barley. Fruity; **f**22 rich! **b**23 a very comfortable whisky, much at home with itself. **55%**. *Nikka*.

**Miyagiko Key Malt Aged 12 Years "Soft & Dry"** db **(85)** **n**22 **t**21 **f**21 **b**21. Perhaps needs a degree of sweetness.... **55%**. *Nikka*.

**Miyagikyou 15 Years Old** batch 20C44C db **(84)** **n**20 **t**21 **f**22 **b**21. Very typically Sendai: light body and limited weight even with all the fruit. Clean and gathers in overall enjoyability, though. **45%**

**Sendai 12 Years Old** (code 06C40C) db **(83)** **n**17 **t**22 **f**23 **b**21. To put it politely, the nose is pretty ordinary; but what goes on afterwards is relative bliss with a wonderful, oily, fruity resonance. For those thinking in Scotch terms, this is very Speysidey with the malt intense and chewy. **45%**. *Nikka*.

**Sendai Miyagikyou Nikka Single Cask Malt Whisky 1986** dist 16 May 86 bott, 5 Dec 03 db **(88)** **n**22 stewed prunes and oranges; the first rumbles of bourbon and smoke wafting around for extra weight; **t**20 big fruit kick but a little out of sync; **f**24 a super nova of a kick back with peat appearing as if from nowhere and the big, booming, bourbony notes and sweetness at the end offering dozens of waves of complexity. A touch of cocoa rounds it off magnificently; **b**22 little to do with balance, everything about effect. **63.2%**

**Sendai Miyagikyou Nikka Single Cask Malt Whisky 1992** dist 22 Apr 92, bott 5 Dec 03 db **(84)** **n**19 **t**20 **f**24 **b**21. Very strange whisky: I would never have recognised this as Sendai. I don't know if they have used local oak on this but the fruity, off-balance nose and early taste is compensated by an orgy of mouth-watering, softly smoked barley that sends the taste buds into ecstasy. A distinct, at times erratic, whisky that may horrify the purists but really has some perzaz and simply cannot be ignored. **55.3%**

## SHIRAKAWA

**Shirakawa 32 Years Old Single Malt (94)** **n**23 ripe mango meets a riper, rye-encrusted bourbon. We are talking a major aroma here; **t**24 the most intense malt you'll ever find explodes and drools all over your tastebuds. To make the flavour bigger still, the oak adds a punchy bourbon quality. Beautiful oils coat the roof of the mouth to amplify the performance; **f**23 long, sweet and malty. Some fruitiness does arrive but it is the oak-malt combination that just knocks you out; **b**24 just how big can an unpeated malt whisky get? The kind of malt that leaves you in awe, even when you thought you had seen and tasted them all. **55%**. *Takara*.

## YAMAZAKI, 1923. Suntory.

**Yamazaki Vintage 1979** db **(78)** **n**20 **t**21 **f**18 **b**19. Spicy and thick malt. But this has plenty of wrinkles and a stoop, too. **56%**. *Suntory*.

**Yamazaki Vintage Malt 1980** db **(75)** **n**19 **t**19 **f**18 **b**19. Some lovely blood oranges, but no whisky can survive this amount of oak unscathed. **56%**

**Yamazaki Vintage 1982** db **(84)** **n**20 **t**22 **f**21 **b**21. Big, muscly malt with some sexy spices. **56%**. *Suntory*.

**Yamazaki Sherry Wood Vintage 1986** db **(93)** **n**24 a sherry butt found in heaven: clean, absolutely dripping in grapejuice yet light enough to allow further complexity from bright malt and a touch of smoke; **t**23 mouthwatering fruit clings, thanks to the estery malt, to every crevice in the mouth; **f**23 exceptionally long fade with a chocolate and sultana finale, topped with a puff of smoke; **b**23 something here for everyone; one of the most outstanding "new" sherry casks of the year. **45%**. *Suntory Whisky*.

**Yamazaki Vintage 1991** db **(88)** **n**23 a curious mixture of peat reek and Golden Graham breakfast cereal; **t**23 soft smoke at first and then the grain hardens and takes a stranglehold; **f**21 honied yet remaining firm; **b**21 hard and tough as nails towards the finish: a surprising conclusion after such a yielding start. **56%**. *Suntory*.

**Yamazaki 1991** db **(88)** **n**21 bourbony and light with a substratum of soft malt; **t**23 astonishing unfurling of mouthwatering malt tones that spreads over the mouth revealing a subtle hint of smoke and beautifully graceful oak; **f**22 long, lashings of cocoa powder and again soft barley hand-in-hand with gentle oak; **b**22 closed when cold, improves dramatically when warmed on the hand. But the mouth arrival really does deserve a medal. **61%**

**Yamazaki 1993** db **(87) n**23 smoky and clean; gristy and Port Ellen-ish with a bit of extra exotic oak; **t**23 sweet, spicy, vaguely Islay-ish start with the peats developing but not at the expense of dense malt. The oak is refined and there is something unusually coastal for a non-Scottish peated malt; **f**20 rather hard, closed and brittle. Metallic malt scrapes against rock-like peat; **b**21 a real surprise package. At times quite Islay-ish in style – Port Ellen in particular – but the finish is more realistic. A really delicious experience nonetheless.

**Yamazaki Vintage 1994** db **(91) n**23 butterscotch and cedarwood; **t**24 intense, ultra-clean malt and honey; soft oak and spice add balance; **f**22 drier, toasty with residual malt; **b**22 very high quality whisky without a single blemish. **56%**. *Suntory.*

**Yamazaki Vintage Malt 1983** bott 04 db **(89) n**20 the malt is tired and oak is threatening to pounce despite a hint of smoke; **t**21 uncompromisingly warming and a little thin; **f**25 whoomph!!! Earth to Tokyo...we have whisky!!! Having taken off like a rocket, it now circles the tastebuds sending back unbelievable messages. The first is one of unruined barley, that is both refreshing and refined; next comes a spicy subtext with a Demerara sweetness lightening things. The finale is fabulous, with succulent fruits including greengages and dried dates teaming up with the persisting massive malt; **b**23 slightly hot at first but then goes into overdrive: the finish is something to be etched on to the memory for life. **56%**. *Suntory.*

**Yamazaki Vintage Malt 1989** bott 04 db **(90) n**22 seasoned oak with the saltiness adding a piquancy to the malt, too; **t**23 big, unremitting malt with that salty tang transferring to the taste; **f**22 sweetened vanilla and dry cocoa enlivened by a dose of Lukec's finest! **b**23 this is quite enormous whisky that may not seem like too much at first, but on second or third mouthful leaves you in no doubt about its stupendous depth. **56%**. *Suntory.*

**Yamazaki Vintage Malt 1992** bott 04 db **(85) n**19 dry parchment; distilled nut kernel; oak; **t**23 gushing, concentrated malt makes for a salivating experience, especially with the fruit of barley juiciness; **f**22 long, well layered malt with some developing cocoa; **b**21 fruity and fractionally fundamental. **56%**. *Suntory.*

**The Yamazaki Single Malt Whisky Aged 10 Years** db **(89) n**22 subtle vanilla; clean, grassy barley – for those into Speyside style malts; **t**23 mouth-watering and wonderful display of barley offering a golden syrup counter to the drier oaks; **f**22 more strands of syrup but never over the top as the vanilla pods crank up the intensity **b**22 a beautifully improved, charismatic malt displaying a voluptuousness and understanding between clean barley and drier oak that had been previously lacking. Not anything like so fruity and a very charming experience. **40%** ⊙ ⊙

⋰ **The Yamazaki Single Malt Whisky Aged 12 Years** db **(83) n**21 **t**21 **f**20 **b**21 The flattest Yamazaki 12 I have ever tasted. Partly due, I'd say, to an increase in oak and caramel levels, as the toffee is a driving force. Also, perhaps to a degree of extra oil. Some butterscotch around, but it's an uphill battle. **43%**

**The Yamazaki Single Malt Whisky Aged 15 Years Cask Strength** db **(94) n**23 just a hint that its gone OTT oak-wise, but there is a wisp of smoke to this, too. All in all, wonderful brinkmanship that pays off; **t**24 stunning: a massive injection of bourbon-style liquorice and honeycomb plays perfectly against the softer malts. The most controlled of malty explosions... **f**23 long, lascivious, the tastebuds are debauched by ingots of honeycomb, molasses and dark sugary notes balanced by the drier oaks; **b**24 an extraordinary bottling that far exceeds any previous version I have encountered. Stunning. **56%** ⊙ ⊙

**The Yamazaki Single Malt Whisky Aged 18 Years** db **(79) n**18 **t**21 **f**20 **b**20 Evidence of sulphur-tainted sherry has wounded what is normally one of Japan's finest. Some decent moments but... **43%** ⊙ ⊙

**The Cask of Yamazaki 1990** Hogshead cask 0W70223, dist Nov 90, bott Apr 05 **(89) n**21 dried fruits and dry in general; **t**23 a thousand battles for supremacy between insurgent oak and the controlling barley: the barley holds the fort; **f**22 the oak begins to win more and more of the skirmishes and a waft of smoke hangs over the battle scene; some lovely roast Santos completes the job; **b**23 not too many elements involved here, but the effect on the tastebuds is wonderful: pure sophistication...for warriors! **55%**. *Suntory.*

**The Cask of Yamazaki 1993** Hogshead cask 3P70277, dist Apr 93, bott Apr 05 **(91)** n24 attractive, light smoke and citrus; the oak well developed yet adding only a required dryness; t22 mouthwatering malt and then a relaxed development of something smoky; f23 wonderful waves of spice and thickening peat balanced perfectly to fresh barley. The oak, again, adds just the right amount of dryness; b22 a fascinating bottling showing Yamazaki at its most stylishly demure despite all the peat. **54%**. *Suntory*.

**The Yamazaki Single Malt Whisky Aged 25 Years** db **(87)** n23 no sulphur here – just sherry...and more sherry....!! Once you get below the grapey surface the degree of complexity is bewitching, with the bitter-sweet spices and bourbons really going to town; t22 good grief; the tastebuds are flattened by the oak and sherry-weighted steamroller; f20 pretty bitter as what seems like highly aged oloroso and extremely old oak kick in with a vengeance; b22 it has taken me over an hour to taste this. And still I don't know if I have marked it too high. You'll either love it or hate it – but you'll find nothing else like it..!! **43%** ⊙ ⊙

**Suntory Pure Malt Yamazaki 25 Years Old** db **(91)** n23 quite intoxicating marriage between grapey fruitiness and rich oak: supremely spiced and balanced with a wave of pure bourbon following through; t23 big, big oloroso character then an entrancing molassed, burnt raisin, malty richness; f22 subtle spices, poppy seed with some late bitter oak; b23 being matured in Japan, the 25 years doesn't have quite the same value as Scotland. So perhaps in some ways this can lay claim to be one of the most enormously aged, oak-laden whiskies that has somehow kept its grace and star quality. **43%**

⋰⋱ **Suntory Single Malt Yamazaki Aged 12 Years** db **(87)** n22 delicate, chalky vanilla with a squeeze of kiwifruit and butterscotch; t23 a wonderfully light touch with fresh house-style mouth-watering barley and transparent fruit setting up the busy middle spice; f20 pretty dry with oak and toffee; b22 this was the 2006 bottling which somehow missed entry into the Bible, although tasted. A fruity little babe. **43%**

# YOICHI, 1934. Nikka.

**Hokkaido 12 Years Old** db **(87)** n23 t22 f21 b21. Full-flavoured malt with absolutely zero yield. Just ricochets around the palate. **43%**. *Nikka*.

**Yoichi 10 Years Old** batch 14116A db **(75)** n19 t19 f18 b19. Proof that sulphur can detract even from a great like Yoichi. **45%**

**Yoichi 10 Years Old** (code 14B22 new "Yoichi" distillery label) db **(88)** n18 t23 f23 b24. Typical Yoichi. Even when it shows a flaw it recovers to an unbelievable degree: like a champion ice skater who falls at the first leap and then dances on as if nothing happened. Keeps you guessing to the very last about what is to happen next. Fabulous verve and complexity. **45%**. *Nikka*.

**Yoichi Single Malt 10 Years Old** Batch 12F04C db **(89)** n21 vague echo of oak sappiness rescued by top-notch, weighty barley; t24 the tongue is forced to inspect the roof of the mouth countless times as wave upon wave of complex barley-honey notes rocket around the palate; f21 long with a tangy, coppery richness that counters perfectly the barley, golden syrup and toffee; b23 mildly dodgy nose, overly toffeed finish... and still it's a lightweight treat! **45%**

**Yoichi 10 Years Old** (code 12I32 old Hokkaido "Yoichi" distillery label) db **(91)** n22 the peat brushes the nose like a feather over skin: just so delicate; t23 immediate flinty malt, amazingly hard and tooth-cracking then softened slowly by a salty, peaty edge; f23 peaty, delicate and now as soft, thanks to vanilla, as it was previously uncompromisingly hard. Some toffee and coffee aid the finale. **43%**. *Nikka*.

**Yoichi 10 Years Old** (code 14H62A old Hokkaido "Yoichi" distillery label) db **(91)** n23 big malt but it is the delicate quality of the peat that is most remarkable. Oak is present, but this is almost too clean to be true; t23 sweet and soft, then that Yoichi trademark gradual build-up of peat; f22 hard and brittle despite the softness of the peat, long and chewy with a hint of liquorice and honey; b23 the crispness and bite of this whisky makes it almost blend-like in style – which goes to underline the complexity. **43%**. *Nikka*.

**Yoichi 10 Years Old** (code 14H62B old Hokkaido "Yoichi" distillery label) db **(89)** n23 t21 f22 b23. Soft and delicate with beautifully chewy peat throughout. **43%**. *Nikka*.

**Yoichi 10 Years Old** (code 24G48C old Hokkaido "Yoichi" distillery label) db **(93) n**23 for an aroma carrying smoke this is almost austere: but this is an illusion. Some crisp malty, softly peated notes give it a delicate depth and massive sophistication; **t**23 enormous malt, absolutely brimming with lusty barley. Refreshing and mouthwatering, yet all the time that soft peat present; **f**24 a quite brilliant marriage between rich barley and soft oak. No more than the slightest hint of very distant smoke; **b**23 a Yoichi in its "Old Speyside" phase, with just a waft of peat-reek to add some ballast to the enormous, clean malt. The fade is nothing short of fabulous. A Japanese version of Ardmore: whisky for grown-ups. **43%.** *Nikka.*

**Yoichi 10 Years Old** (code 24H18C old Hokkaido "Yoichi" distillery label) db **(89) n**20 **t**23 **f**23 **b**23. Another bottle of understated genius. **43%.** *Nikka.*

**Yoichi 12 Years Old** (code 06C14 new Yoichi label with distillery drawing) db **(91) n**21 spicy fresh oloroso; **t**24 big, clean sultana-fruit with a gathering intensity of ripe dates and sweet, gently smoked malt; **f**22 the dates remain, as does the smoke. The oak kicks in with a late bitter finale; **b**24 absolutely magnificent malt with a no-holds-barred intensity of fruit and malt. **45%.** *Nikka.*

**Yoichi Single Malt 12 Years Old** Batch 14F36A db **(91) n**22 soft smoke and under-ripe fruit; **t**23 profound, chewy barley; lots of small still coppery sharpness and then a gentle awakening of peat; **f**23 sweet peats dusted with demerara; it takes some time for the chalky oak to finally have a say; **b**23 best when left in the glass for 10-15 minutes: only then does the true story emerge. **45%**

**Yoichi 12 Years Old** (code 16J32 new Yoichi label with distillery drawing) db **(87) n**20 **t**22 **f**23 **b**22. A pretty light Yoichi almost devoid of peat. After getting over a toffee-led lull the malt comes to life with impressive results. **45%.** *Yoichi.*

**Yoichi Key Malt Aged 12 Years "Peaty & Salty"** lott 12D50B db **(95) n**23 the peat rumbles like distant thunder, difficult to pinpoint but letting you know that it is there. The oaky tones suggest a mixing of Kentucky and something local; soft fruits make an almost apologetic appearance; **t**25 there is perfect distribution of peat. It rumbles around the palate offering bitter-sweet depth, and a salty, coastal tang emphasises the richness of the malt; **f**23 waves of vanilla begin to outflank the soft peat: the finish is long and there is no victor between the sweet malt and the more bitter, salty oak; **b**24 of all the peated whiskies of the world, only Ardbeg can stand shoulder to shoulder with Yoichi when it comes to sheer complexity. Here is an astonishing example of why I rate Yoichi in the best five whiskies in the world. Forget the odd sulphur-tarnished bottling. Get Yoichi in its natural state with perfect balance between oak and malt and it delivers something approaching perfection. And this is just such a bottling. **55%.** *Nikka.*

**Yoichi Key Malt Aged 12 Years "Sherry & Sweet"** lott 12D48C db **(80) n**19 **t**22 **f**19 **b**20. Sad to report that this should be called "Very Slight Sulphur and Sweet". A real pity because it is obvious that had the Spaniards not molested these butts, they would have been absolutely top-of-the-range. And probably would have scored in the low to mid 90s. I could weap. **55%.** *Nikka.*

**Yoichi Key Malt Aged 12 Years "Woody & Vanillic"** lott 12D50C db **(83) n**21 **t**22 **f**20 **b**20. Pretty decent whisky. Not sure about creating one that sets out to be woody: that means balance has been sacrificed to concentrate on a particular essence to the whisky that should be used only as a component of complexity. Still, there is enough sweet malt on arrival to make this a dram to be enjoyed. **55%**

**Yoichi 12 Years Old 70th Anniversary** db **(96) n**24 what a tease! The most gentle of smokes creeps around playfully but adding telling, near perfect weight to the lighter, orange-flecked malt. Again, showing extraordinary balance, the fruit-oak harmonisation is practically faultless. Meanwhile the earthiness is not entirely like the animal house at the zoo. Sounds awful: it's not. It's wonderful. Wow!! **t**24 salivating young barley offers an unusual gristy feel, and then the smoke arrives, keeping in check the drier, slightly bitter-chocolate oak; **f**24 long, with wave upon wave of smoky oak. A late tangerine tartness lightens the load. But then it would, wouldn't it? **b**25 just incredible. Had they chosen this selection of casks but from two or three years earlier, so the oak was not quite such a force, I think the record books regarding the Bible would have to be re-written. Confirmation, not that it is ever needed, that Yoichi can offer something that just about no other distillery can. **58%.** *Nikka.*

**Yoichi Single Malt 15 Years Old** Batch 04F44D db **(86) n**22 **t**22 **f**20 **b**22. Zesty and tangy; most peculiar by Yoichi standards. But still big, rich and lip-smacking. **45%**

**Yoichi 15 Years Old** (code 10J44 old green back label) db **(94) n**23 roast chestnuts plus salty, soft peat and dried dates: awesome complexity; **t**24 the dates have moistened, the peat positively glows, having been seasoned with salt, the fruitiness is full but in perfect proportion; **f**23 for the enormity of the nose and mouth arrival, the soft peated spices offer a charming sophistication to the intense barley. The fruit remains yielding and the oak no less soft and accommodating; **b**24 the kind of whisky that propels a distillery into super league status. A classic. **45%**. *Nikka.*

**Yoichi 15 Years Old** (code 06C10 new buff-coloured back label) db **(90) n**22 nutty, intense clean malt with just a light dusting of peat. The fruits are light and plummy; **t**22 very clean malt, almost gristy in its delicate nature. The peat no more than tickles the tastebuds. A weak grapejuice sweetness offers further complexity; **f**23 amazingly delicate, a beautiful combination of barley and vanilla. The peat remains playful and wonderfully balanced; **b**23 this is a succulent malt of enormous complexity. Typical Yoichi. **45%**. *Nikka.*

**Yoichi 20 Years Old** db **(95) n**23 magnificently intense oloroso (a tiny fleck of sulphur burns off in about 10 minutes when warmed), the background malt oak-laden; **t**23 again it's oloroso that leads the way, apparently too intensely at first but quickly settling to allow some stupendous spices to unravel and create balance. Fabulous bitter-sweet harmony; **f**25 Okay, guys, help me out here. Spot the fault. I can't. The fruit is now spotlessly clean and displaying a grapey complexity, the spices are warming but not entirely engulfing, the oak is firm and adds no more than a hint of dryness and at last the malt comes into full play to offer both mouthwatering barley and something slightly smoky. If you can pick a defect, let me know; **b**24 I don't know how much they charge for this stuff but either alone or with mates get some for one hell of an experience. What makes it all the more remarkable is that there is a slight sulphury note on the nose: once you taste the stuff that becomes of little consequence. **52%**. *Nikka.*

**Yoichi 1987** cask no. 113200, dist 19.7.87, bott 27 Jul 06 db **(87) n**20 heavy duty, orangey but slightly flawed sherry; **t**24 juicy grape, concentrated barley then, slowly, the peat delivers by degree; **f**21 dries significantly as the sulphur takes a grip; **b**22 dense and desirable at times: just so easily could have been a great dram but undone by a poor butt. **63%**. *France.*

**Yoichi Single Cask 1987** No. 3 dist 27 Apr 87, bott 1 Feb 05 db **(87) n**22 throbbing oak; marmalade on toast; **t**23 the malt is just so intense, offering at first a charismatic, mouthwatering depth and then something more deeply oaky; **f**20 dry, tannin heavy and chewy; **b**22 hints here of old age and over-exposure to oak. But the overall thrust remains delightfully rich. **52%**. *Nikka.*

**Yoichi Single Cask 1988** No. 29 dist 7 May 88, bott 3 Feb 05 db **(89) n**21 a distinct bourbony style to this, with citrus abounding; **t**23 light and bourbony at first, then intensifies as a fruity maltiness digs deep into the tastebuds; **f**22 spices and vanilla; **b**23 effortless to the point of arrogantly beautiful. **60%**. *Nikka.*

**Yoichi Nikka Single Cask Malt Whisky 1990** db dist 4 Aug 90, bott 17 Oct 03 **(84) n**21 **t**20 **f**22 **b**21. Most probably a dry sherry cask set the tone for this: astringent by Yoichi standards and although the finish offers a complex vanilla and liquorice counter, this isn't an Hokkaido great. **60.8%**

**Yoichi Nikka Single Cask Malt Whisky 1991** db dist 25 Feb 91, bott 12 Dec 03 **(95) n**24 **t**24 **f**23 **b**24. It was because I managed to taste many casks like this while tramping through Yoichi's warehouses over the years that I declared the distillery in the world's top six. Taste this, then e-mail me to disagree. **64.5%**

⋰∵ **Nikka Whisky Yoichi (78) n**18 **t**20 **f**21 **b**19 Not often I'm lost for words...but this one left me stunned. Nothing like I expected. Not least because it seems either very young. Or not remotely short of feints. Or both. And the whole thing is propped up by caramel. The best bit is the late spice attack....but this is like nothing I would have expected from one of the top five distilleries in the world. As my one time Japanese girlfriend would have said: " I am shocked..." **43%**

⋰∵ **Nikka Whisky Yoichi 1986 20 Years Old (94) n**23 age, the salty sea air of Hokkaido and sweet oak have accounted for the more excessive possibilities of the peat:

weighty but restrained; **t**24 no holding back here, though, as the delivery is one first of juicy fruit and then silky waves of peat; chunky heavy-duty stuff which, for some reason, appears to float about the palate; the spices shoot on sight; **f**23 a sweeter, more sober finale with liquorice and molasses joining forces with the salty oakiness to keep the lid on the smoke; **b**24 now this is unambiguous Yoichi :exactly how I have come to know and adore this distillery. **55.0%**

⁙ **Scotch Malt Whisky Society Cask 116.10 Aged 18 Years** Refill Hogshead, dist Apr 87 **(93) n**23 almost a Bowmore-style cough candy bite to this, then it becomes more saline and moves towards Arbroath smokies; **t**23 quite wonderful delivery with the tongue thrown into automatic investigation mode by the unbelievable number of smoke layers integrated with the gently oiled barley; the (American?) oak is very well behaved; **f**23 long, a tad lush and those smoky waves keep on rolling in; **b**24 beautiful, but one of the most Islay-style Yoichies I have ever come across. And as for an 18-y-o, I am agog...!! **52.2%**

## Unspecified Malts

**"Hokuto" Suntory Pure Malt Aged 12 Years (93) n**22 trademark delicate lightness; fleeting barley chased by soft vanilla; **t**24 melt-in-the-mouth malt arrival; hints of honey work well with the loftier barley and earthier oak; **f**23 honey on toast with just a little toffee; **b**24 another example of Suntory at its most feminine: just so seductive and beautiful. Although a malt, think Lawson's 12-y-o of a decade ago and you have the picture. **40%**

**Nikka Whisky From the Barrel (89) n**20 carries some weight; good age and subtle malty sugars; **t**23 exemplary mouthfeel: delightful oils and nipping spices but the malt remains clean and very sweet; **f**22 some dryer oakiness but the malt keeps its balancing sweetness; **b**24 a whisky that requires a bit of time and concentration to get the best out of. You will discover something big and exceptionally well balanced. **51.4%**. *Nikka.*

**Nikka Whisky From the Barrel** Batch 02F26A **(82) n**20 **t**22 **f**20 **b**20. Some attractive honey notes and caramel, but a bit laboured. **51.4%**

**Nikka Whisky From the Barrel** Batch 12F32C db **(91) n**22 date and brazil cake; **t**24 monumental delivery with soft smoke melting into the most glorious honeycomb known to man; tingly spices and toffee-apple, too; **f**22 caramel kicks in slightly but some butterscotch rounds it off wonderfully; **b**23 truly great whisky that mostly overcomes the present Japanese curse of big caramel finishes. **51.4%**

## Vatted Malts

**All Malt (86) n**22 **t**21 **f**21 **b**22. The best example by a mile of an almost unique style of vatted whisky: both malt and "grain" are distilled from entirely malted barley, identical to Kasauli malt whisky in India. Stupendous grace and balance. **40%**. *Nikka.*

**All Malt "Pure & Rich" (89) n**22 honeycomb and liquorice with some thumping oak; **t**24 beautifully mouthfilling, and "rich" is an understatement. Barley sugar and molten brown sugar combine and then there is a soft gristiness. Big...; **f**21 vanilla and caramel with some residual malt; **b**22 my word, this has changed! Not unlike some bottlings of Highland Park with its emphasis on honey. If they could tone down the caramel it'd really be up there. **40%**. *Nikka.* ⊙

**All Malt Pure & Rich** Batch 14F24A **(77) n**19 **t**20 **f**19 **b**19. My former long term Japanese girlfriend, Makie (hope you enjoyed your 30th birthday in April, by the way), used to have a favourite saying, namely: "I am shocked!" Well, I am shocked by this whisky because it is much blander than the previous bottling (04E16D), with all that ultra-delicate and complex honeycomb lost and lovely gristiness removed. For me, one of the biggest surprises – and disappointments - of the 2007 Bible. But proof that, when using something so potentially dangerous as caramel, it is too easy to accidentally cross that fine line between brilliance and blandness. Because, had they gone the other way, we might have had a challenger for World Whisky of the Year. **40%**. *Nikka.*

**Hokuto Pure Malt Aged 12 Years (86) n**20 **t**22 **f**22 **b**22. An oaky threat never materialises: excellent mixing. **40%**. *Suntory.*

**Malt Club "Pure & Clear" (83) n**21 **t**22 **f**20 **b**20. Another improved vatting, much heavier and older than before with bigger spice. **40%.** *Nikka.*

**Mars Maltage Pure Malt 8 Years Old (84)** n20 t21 f21 b22. A very level, intense, clean malt with no peaks or troughs, just a steady variance in the degree of sweetness and oak input. Impossible not to have a second glass of. **43%**. *Mars.*

**Nikka Malt 100 The Anniversary Aged 12 Years (73)** n18 t19 f18 b18. The depressing and deadly fingerprint of sulphur is all over this. Shame, as the spices excel. **40%**

**Pure Malt Black** batch 02C58A **(95)** n24 an exquisitely crafted nose: studied peat in luxuriant yet deft proportions nestling amid some honeyed malt and oak. The balance between sweet and dry is faultless. There is neither a single off-note nor a ripple of disharmony. The kind of nose you can sink your head into and simply disappear; t23 for all the evident peat, this is medium-weighted, the subtlety encased in a gentle cloak of oil; f23 long, silky, fabulously weighted peat running a sweet course through some surging malt and liquorice tones with a bit of salt in there for zip; b25 well, if anyone can show me a better-balanced whisky than this you know where to get hold of me. You open a bottle of this at your peril: best to do so in the company of friends. Either way, it will be empty before the night is over. **43%**. *Nikka.*

**Pure Malt Black** Batch 06F54B **(92)** n24 great balance to the nose with a careful sprinkling of barley, honey, peat and oak – but never too much of any; t24 massive, ultra-intense sweet malt with a delicate sub-stratum of smoke; a spiced fruitiness also cranks up the weight and depth; f21 vanilla kicks in as it thins surprisingly fast; b23 not the finish of old, but everything else is present and correct for a cracker! **43%**. *Nikka.*

**Pure Malt Red** batch 02C30B **(86)** n21 t21 f22 b22. A light malt that appears heavier than it actually is with an almost imperceptible oiliness. **43%**. *Nikka.*

**Pure Malt Red** Batch 06F54C **(84)** n21 t22 f20 b21. Oak is the pathfinder here, but the oily vanilla-clad barley is light and mouth-watering. **43%**. *Nikka.*

**Pure Malt White** batch 02C30C **(92)** n23 massive, Islay-style peat with a fresh sea kick thanks to brine amid the barley; t24 again, the peat-reek hangs firmly on the tastebuds from the word go, the sweetness of the barley tempered by some drying oaky notes suggesting reasonable age. Lots of subtle oils bind the complexity; f22 liquorice and salt combine to create a powerful malty-oak combo. An oily, kippery smokiness continues to the very end; b23 a big peaty number displaying the most subtle of hands. **43%**. *Nikka.*

**Pure Malt White** batch 06J26 **(91)** n22 soft peat interrupted by gentle oak; t23 biting, nippy malt offering a degree of orangey-citrus fruit amid the building smoke; f22 sweet vanilla and light smoke that dries towards a salty, tangy, liquorice finish; b24 a sweet malt, but one with such deft use of peat and oak that one never really notices. Real class. **43%**. *Nikka.*

**Pure Malt White** Batch 10F46C **(90)** n23 the quality of the delicate peat is beyond reproach; some attractive kumquat juices it up nicely; t23 wonderful balance between silky-soft and nail-hard malts with some tasty local oak getting in on the act; f22 the smoke lessens to allow vanilla and toffee dominance; a sawdusty dryness brings down the curtain; b22 there is a peculiarly Japanese feel to this delicately peated delight. **43%**

**Southern Alps Pure Malt (93)** n24 bananas and freshly peeled lemon skin: one of the world's most refreshing and exhilarating whisky noses; t23 crisp youngish malts, as one might suspect from the nose, mouthwatering and as a clean as an Alpine stream; f22 some vanilla development and a late slightly creamy flourish but finished with a substantial and startling malty rally boasting a very discreet sweetness; b24 this is a bottle I have only to look at to start salivating. Sadly, though, I drink sparingly from it as it is a hard whisky to find, even in Japan. Fresh, clean and totally stunning, the term "pure malt" could not be more apposite. Fabulous whisky: a very personal favourite. **40%**. *Suntory.*

**Super Nikka Vatted Pure Malt (76)** n20 t19 f19 b18. Decent and chewy but something doesn't quite click with this one. **55.5%**. *Nikka.*

**Taketsuru Pure Malt 12 Years Old (80)** n19 t22 f19 b20. For its age, heavier than a sumo wrestler. But perhaps a little more agile over the tastebuds. Lovely silkiness impresses, but lots of toffee. **40%**. *Nikka.*

**Taketsuru Pure Malt 17 Years Old (89)** n21 firm oak, but compromises sufficiently to allow several layers of malt to battle through with a touch of peat-coffee; t22 massive: a toasted, honeyed front gives way to really intense and complex malt notes; **f**23 superb. Some late marmalade arrives from somewhere: the toast is slightly burnt but the waves of malty complexity are endless; **b**23 not a whisky for the squeamish. This is big stuff – about as big as it gets without peat or rye. No bar shelf or whisky club should be without one. **43%.** *Nikka.*

**Taketsuru Pure Malt 21 Years Old (88) n**22 middle-aged bourbon with a heavy, vaguely honeyed malt presence; **t**21 the oak remains quite fresh and chewy. Again, the malt is massive; **f**22 sweet, oily and more honey arrives; **b**23 a much more civilised and gracious offering than the 17-y-o: there is certainly nothing linear about the character development from Taketsuru 12 to 21 inclusive. Serious whisky for the serious whisky drinker. **43%.** *Nikka.*

**Zen (84) n**19 **t**22 **f**22 **b**21. Sweet, gristy malt; light and clean. **40%.** *Suntory.* ☉

## Japanese Single Grain

**Nikka Single Cask Coffey Grain Whisky Aged 12 Years "Woody & Mellow" (93) n**22 delicate vanalins and tannins; **t**24 sweet and yielding (probably corn) with layers of drying spices. Stupendous; **f**23 long, with subtle oils lengthening the grain effect and spice; more vanilla at the very death...eventually. Vague bourbony tones towards the finale; **b**24 exceptional grain whisky by any standards – and helps explain why Japanese blends are so damn good!! **55%.** *Nikka.*

**Nikka Single Cask Coffey Grain 12 Years Old 70th Anniversary (85) n**20 biting, nose, tingling oak; **t**22 massive oak delivery sweetened and soothed by the rich grain; lush and brilliantly weighted throughout; **f**22 long liquorice and cocoa tones are met by some bitter, zesty, oaky notes; **b**21 more woody than the "woody and mellow". **58%.** *Nikka.*

**Nikka Single Cask Coffey Grain Aged Over 13 Years** Batch 20 116399, dist 31.1.92, bott 30.5.05 db **(85) n**22 **t**23 **f**20 **b**20. Distinctly subdued by this brand's normal high standards, though the early bourbon riches are mesmerizing. The finish, though attractive, is too simplistic. **62%. sc.**

**Nikka Single Cask Coffey Grain Whisky 1991** dist 1 Oct 91, bott 12 May 03 db **(93) n**22 **t**24 **f**23 **b**24. I have tasted much Japanese straight grain over the years but this is the first time in bottled form for public consumption. And Nikka have exceeded themselves. Forget the word "grain" and its inferior connotations. This is a monster whisky from the bourbon family you are unlikely ever to forget. Use the first couple of mouthfuls for a marker: once you get the idea, life will never quite be the same again. Track down...and be consumed. **61.9%**

**Nikka Single Cask Coffey Grain 1992** dist 31.2.92, bott 25.7.06 db **(95) n**24 a curious mixture with hints of Japanese oak (from the cask heads?) and a bourbony, hickory edge. Rich and rousing; **t**24 sweet, flushed with maize and a silky body, almost verging on demerara. Honeyed and revelling in its bourbon theme; **f**23 vanilla layers, again with a deep, delicious touch of molasses; **b**24 make no mistake: this grain is as entertaining as any malt. Those loving high-class bourbon will be thrilled. **57%.** *France.*

## Blends

**Ajiwai Kakubin** (*see* Kakubin Ajiwai)

**Amber (75) n**18 **t**20 **f**18 **b**19. Similar in style to "Old" but with more toffee caramel. A silky experience. **40%.** *Mars.*

**Black Nikka (72) n**17 **t**20 **f**17 **b**18. Big grain presence and decent middle; carries a caramel tang. **37%.** *Nikka.*

**Black Nikka Special (70) n**16 **t**20 **f**17 **b**17. Simliar to ordinary Black Nikka, except weighed down by extra caramel **42%.** *Nikka.*

**Black Nikka Aged 8 Years (82) n**20 **t**21 **f**21 **b**20. Beautifully bourbony, especially on the nose. Lush, silky and great fun. Love it! **40%.** *Nikka.*

**The Blend of Nikka (90) n**21 a dry, oaky buzz infiltrates some firm grain and sweeter malt; **t**23 brilliant! Absolutely outstanding explosion of clean grassy malts thudding into the tastebuds with confidence and precision: mouthwatering and breath-catching; **f**22 delightful grain bite to follow the malt; **b**24 an adorable blend that makes you sit up and take notice of every enormous mouthful. Classy, complex, charismatic and brilliantly balanced. **45%.** *Nikka.*

**Boston Club** (Brown Label) **(73)** n17 t20 f18 b18. "More Boston Strangler than Boston Club", I wrote somewhere on tasting this some years back. They have sorted out the dreadful finish on the old bottling. Pleasant enough, but devoid of any challenge thanks possibly to caramel although the spice does. **40%**. *Kirin.*

**Boston Club (70)** n16 t19 f18 b17. Less opaque than the Brown Label, lighter in body with a fraction less toffee-caramel **37%**. *Kirin.*

**Crescent (82)** n19 t22 f20 b21. Fresh, grassy, lightweight malt dominates. A spot of the old caramel toffee, perhaps? Without it, this would be a stunner. **43%**. *Kirin.*

**Diamond Whisky (73)** n17 t20 f18 b18. Another blend where complexity takes second place to caramel though it does have some sweet, attractive moments. **43%**. *Nikka.*

**Emblem (76)** n18 t20 f18 b20. Richly textured bend with a deliciously clean and salivating malt character. **40%**. *Kirin.*

**Evermore (90)** n22 big age, salt and outstanding malt riches to counter the oak; t23 more massive oak wrapped in a bourbony sweetness with glorious malts and a salty, spicy tang; f22 long, sweet malt and tangy grains: plenty to chew on and savour; b23 top-grade, well-aged blended whisky with fabulous depth and complexity that never loses its sweet edge despite the oak. **40%**. *Kirin.*

**Gold & Gold (83)** n21 t22 f20 b20. Some lovely, crisp malty moments set against firm grain and softened by honey. Something to get your teeth into, but perhaps a touch too much toffee. **43%**. *Nikka.*

**Golden Horse Bosyuu (80)** n20 t21 f19 b20. Soft grain melts beautifully in the mouth. **40%**. *Toa.*

**Golden Horse Busyuu Deluxe (93)** n22 some decent signs of age with some classy oak alongside smoke: sexy stuff; t24 enormous flavour profile simply because it is so fresh: massive malt presence, some of it peaty, bananas and under-ripe grapes; f23 clean malt and some sharpish grain with a touch of bite, continuing to tantalise the tastebuds for a long time; b24 whoever blended this has a genuine feel for whisky: a classic in its own right and one of astonishing complexity and textbook balance. **43%**. *Toa. To celebrate the year 2000.*

**Golden Horse Grand (78)** n19 t21 f19 b19. Decent malt, sweet and a little chalky. **39%**.

**Hibiki (82)** n20 t19 f23 b20. The grains here are fresh, forceful and merciless, the malts bouncing off them meekly. Lovely cocoa finale. A blend that brings a tear to the eye. Hard stuff – perfect after a hard day! Love it! **43%**. *Suntory.*

**Hibiki 17 Years Old (81)** n20 t22 f19 b20 A vast improvement on previous bottlings, though the amount of caramel added detracts from the higher notes you can tell the malts are trying to reach. Bland. **43%**. *Suntory.* ☉☉

**Hibiki 50.5 Non Chillfiltered 17 Years Old (84)** n22 t22 f20 b20 Pleasant enough in its own right. But against what this particular expression so recently was, hugely disappointing. Last year I lamented the extra use of caramel. This year it has gone through the roof, taking with it all the fineness of complexity that made this blend exceptional. Time for the blending lab to start talking to the bottling hall and sort this out. I want one of the great whiskies back...!! **50.5%**. *Suntory.* ☉☉

**Hibiki 21 Years Old (93)** n24 fruitier notes of cherry and sherry with a triumphal triumvirate of intense malt, the subtlest of peat smoke and leathery oak combining for maximum, stupendous complexity, also a dash of kumquats; t22 fat and oily, like the nose hinting slightly at bourbon but the grains thin the middle out sufficiently to let the malt, mildly peaty and otherwise, through; f23 long and intense with more lightly orchestrated smoke and lashings of late, grapey fruit and a build-up of, first, sweet malts, then a drier, spicier oak; b24 when people refer to Yoichi as the exception that proves the rule about Japanese whisky, I tend to point them in the direction of this. If I close my eyes and taste this, cherry blossom really does form in my mind's eye. **43%**. *Suntory.* ☉

**Hibiki 30 Years Old (88)** n21 less smoky than before, a touch of soap and no shortage of bourbon honeycomb; t22 sweet delivery with that Kentuckian drawl to the middle; f22 long, with some extra molasses to the finale; a few extra splinters of oak, too; b23 still remains a very different animal from most other whiskies you might find: the smoke may have vanished somewhat but the sweet oakiness continues to draw its own unique map. **43%**. *Suntory.* ☉☉

**Hibiki 30 Years Old (87) n**21 curious mix of peat and bourbon; **t**22 sweet, fat oak: bourbon all the way; **f**22 the glorious rich-textured sweetness continues forever; **b**22 Kentuckians would really go for this one: the smoke might confuse them a little, though. Pretty unique the world over. **43%**. *Suntory.*

**Hi Nikka Whisky (68) n**16 **t**18 **f**17 **b**17. Very light but lots of caramel character. A good mixer. **39%**. *Nikka.*

**Hokuto (86) n**22 **t**24 **f**19 **b**21 a bemusing blend. At its peak, this is quite superb, cleverly blended whisky. The finish, though, suggests a big caramel input. If the caramel is natural, it should be tempered. If it is added for colouring purposes, then I don't see the point of having the whisky non-chillfiltered in the first place. **50.5%. ncf.** *Suntory.*

**Imperial (81) n**20 **t**22 **f**19 **b**20. Flinty, hard grain softened by malt and vanilla but toffee dulled. **43%**. *Suntory.*

**Kakubin (92) n**23 lemon zest and refreshing grain: wonderful; **t**23 light, mouthwatering, ultra-juicy with soft barley sub-strata; true melt-in-the-mouth stuff; **f**22 long, with charming vanilla but touched by toffee; **b**24 absolutely brilliant blend of stunningly refreshing and complex character. One of the most improved brands in the world. **40%**. *Suntory.* ☉ ☉

**Kakubin Ajiwai (82) n**20 **t**21 **f**20 **b**21. Usual Kakubin hard grain and mouthwatering malt, with this time a hint of warming stem ginger. **40%**. *Suntory.*

⁂ **Kakubin Kuro 43° (89) n**22 a confusing but sexy mix of what appear to be old oak and burnt toffee; **t**23 fabulous weight on arrival with again the oak in the vanguard but controlled by a malty, chewy-toffee arm; **f**22 long with soft vanillins and toffee; **b**22 big, chewy whisky with ample evidence of old age but such is the intrusion of caramel it's hard to be entirely sure. **43%**. *Suntory.*

**Kakubin New (90) n**21 gritty grain with very hard malt to accompany it; **t**24 stunning mouth arrival with heaps of mouthwatering young malt and then soft grain and oil. Brilliant stuff; **f**21 some beautiful cocoa notes round off the blend perfectly; **b**24 seriously divine blending: a refreshing dram of the top order. **40%**. *Suntory.*

**Kingsland (81) n**21 **t**22 **f**17 **b**21. An ultra-lively and mouthwatering blend with a short, dry finish. Overall, quite impressive, refreshing and moreish. *Nikka.*

**Master's Blend Aged 10 Years (87) n**21 **t**23 **f**22 **b**21 chewy, big and satisfying. **40%**. *Mercian/Karuizawa.*

**New Kakubin Suntory** (*see* Kakubin New)

**New Shirokaku (74) n**18 **t**19 **f**19 **b**18. Grain-heavy, hard and toffeed. **40%**. *Suntory.*

**Nikka Master Blend Blended Whisky 12 Years Old 70th Anniversary (94) n**24 nothing shy or retiring here: big oak, big sherry. A little nervousness with the smoke, maybe; **t**23 lush, silky grain arrives and then carries intensely sweet malt and weightier grape; **f**24 dries as the oak takes centre stage. But the peripheral fruit malt, gentle smoke and grain combine to offer something not dissimilar to fruit and nut chocolate; **b**23 an awesome blend swimming in top quality sherry. Perhaps a fraction too much sweetness on the arrival, but I am nit-picking. A blend for those who like their whiskies to have something to say. And this one just won't shut up. **58%**. *Nikka.*

**The Nikka Whisky Aged 34 Years** blended and bottled in 99 **(93) n**23 **t**23 **f**24 **b**23. A Japanese whisky of antiquity that has not only survived many passing years, but has actually achieved something of stature and sophistication. Over time I have come to appreciate this whisky immensely. It is among the world's greatest blends, no question. **43%**. *Nikka.*

⁂ **Nikka Whisky Tsuru Aged 17 Years (94) n**23 the usual fruity suspects one associates with a Tsuru blend, especially the apple and oranges. But the grains are now making a bourbony impact, too; **t**24 advanced level textbook delivery here because the marriage between fruit, grain and oak is about as well integrated as you might wish for; simperingly soft yet enough rigidity for the malts to really count and the palate to fully appreciate all the complexities offered; **f**23 brushed with cocoa, a touch of sultana and some gripping spices, too; only the caramel detracts; **b**24 unmistakingly Tsuru in character, very much in line, profile-wise, with the original bottling and if the caramel was cut this could challenge as a world whisky of the year. **43%**

**Oak Master (78) n**19 **t**20 **f**19 **b**20. Foraging malts on nose and palate counter big grain surge. Silky whisky, if a little on the bitter side. **37%**. *Mercian.*

**Ocean Luckey (70)** n17 t18 f17 b18. Grainy, chalky, weightless. **37%** *Merc.*

**Ocean Whisky Special Old (83)** n20 t21 f21 b21. Deliciously rich malt is absorbed effortlessly into melt-in-the-mouth grain. Good blending. **40%**

**Old (77)** n18 t20 f20 b19. Sweet, chewy, clean session whisky. **43%**. *Mars.*

**Old Halley (71)** n18 t19 f17 b17. Flat, pleasant but toffee-reliant. **37%**. Toa

**Red (79)** n19 t20 f20 b20. On the thin side: the grains are to the fore and aft but there is good late spicy bite amid the toffee but unquestionably improved of late. **39%**. *Suntory.* ⊙⊙

**Robert Brown (74)** n19 t20 f17 b18. What a pity! Too much toffee has overshadowed some lovely spice. **40%**. *Kirin.*

**Royal 12 Years Old (91)** n23 chalky and dry, but malt and oranges – and now some extra juicy grape - add character; just a soupcon of smoke adds the perfect weight; t23 fabulously complex arrival on the palate with some grainy nip countered by sparkling malt and where once there was smoke there is now ultra clean sherry; f22 the grains and oak carry on as the spice builds; b23 a splendidly blended whisky with complexity being the main theme. Beautiful stuff that appears recently to have, nose apart, traded smoke for grape. **43%**. *Suntory.* ⊙⊙

**Royal Aged 15 Years (95)** n25 soft ribbons of smoke tie themselves to a kumquat and sherry flag; supremely well weighted and balanced with the grains and malts united by invisible strands; t24 few whiskies achieve such a beautifully soft and rounded delivery: there is no dominance on arrival as the tastebuds are confronted by a silky marriage of all that is found on the nose, aided and abetted by luxurious grain; f22 a degree of toffee slightly hinders the fade but the lightness of touch is spellbinding; b24 unquestionably one of the great blends of the world that can be improved only by a reduction of toffee input. Sensual blending that every true whisky lover must experience: a kind of Japanese Old Parr 18. **43%**. *Suntory.* ⊙⊙

⋰∴ **Shirokaku (79)** n19 t21 f20 b19 Some over-zealous toffee puts a cap on complexity. Good spices, though. **40%**. *Suntory.*

**Special Reserve 10 Years Old (94)** n23 magnificent approach of rich fruit buttressed by firm, clear grain. Some further fruity spices reveal some age is evident; t24 complex from the off with a tidal tsunami of malt crashing over the tastebuds. The grain holds firm and supports some budding fruit; f23 a touch of something peaty and pliable begins to take shape with some wonderful malty spices coating the mouth; b24 a beguiling whisky of near faultless complexity. Blending at its peak. **43%**. *Suntory.*

**Special Reserve Aged 12 Years (89)** n21 peaches and cream with a dollop of caramel; t24 luxurious delivery of perfect weight and softness to body; the barley sweetness works beautifully with the buzz of oak and yielding grains; f21 caramel-coffee crème from a box of chocs; b23 a tactile, voluptuous malt that wraps itself like a sated lover around the tastebuds, though the complexity is compromised very slightly by bigger caramel than the 10-y-o. **40%**. *Suntory.* ⊙

**Suntory Old (87)** n21 dusty and fruity. Attractive nip and balance; t24 mouthwatering from the off with a rich array of chewy, clean fresh malt: textbook standard, complete with bite; f20 thins out far quicker than it once did leaving the vanilla to battle it out with toffee; b22 a delicate and comfortable blend that just appears to have over-simplified itself on the finale. Delicious, but can be much better than this. **40%** ⊙⊙

**Suntory Old Mild and Smooth (84)** n19 t22 f21 b22. Chirpy and lively around the palate, the grains soften the crisp malts wonderfully. **40%**

**Suntory Old Rich and Mellow (91)** n22 very lightly smoked with healthy mal* iness; an extra touch of older oaks in the most recent bottling helps the balance and works wonders; t23 complex, fat and chewy, no shortage of deep malty tones, including a touch of smoke; f23 sweeter malts see off the grain, excellent spices; b23 a pretty malt-rich blend with the grains offering a fat base. Impressive blending. **43%** ⊙⊙

**Super Nikka (93)** n23 excellent crisp, grassy malt base bounces off firm grain. A distant hint of peat, maybe, offers a little weighty extra; t23 an immediate starburst of rich, mouthwatering and entirely uncompromising malt that almost over-runs the tastebuds; f23 soft, fabulously intrinsic peaty notes from the Yoichi School give brilliant length and depth. But the cocoa notes from the oak-wrapped grain also offer untold riches; b24 a very, very fine blend which makes no apology whatsoever for the peaty complexity of Yoichi malt.

Now, with less caramel, it's pretty classy stuff. However, Nikka being Nikka you might find the occasional bottling that is entirely devoid of peat, more honeyed and lighter in style (21-22-23-23 Total 89 – no less a quality turn, obviously). Either way, an absolutely brilliant day-to-day, anytime, any place dram. One of the true 24-carat, super nova commonplace blends not just in Japan, but in the world. **43%**. *Nikka.*

**Torys (76) n**18 **t**19 **f**20 **b**19. Lots of toffee in the middle and at the end of this one. The grain used is top class and chewy. **37%.** *Suntory.* ☉☉

**Torys Whisky Square (80) n**19 **t**20 **f**21 **b**20. At first glance very similar to Torys, but very close scrutiny reveals slightly more "new loaf" nose and a better, spicier and less toffeed finale. **37%.** *Suntory.*

**Tsuru (93) n**23 apples, cedar, crushed pine nuts, blood oranges and soft malt, all rather chalky and soft – and unusually peatless for Nikka; **t**24 fantastic grain bite bringing with it a mouthwateringly clean and fresh attack of sweet and lip-smacking malt; **f**22 a continuation of untaxing soft malts and gathering oak, a slight "Malteser" candy quality to it, and then some late sultana fruitiness; **b**24 gentle and beautifully structured, genuinely mouthwatering, more-ish and effortlessly noble. If they had the confidence to cut the caramel, this would be even higher up the charts as one of the great blends of the world. As it is, in my house we pass the ceramic Tsuru bottle as one does the ship's decanter. And it empties very quickly. **43%.** *Nikka.*

**The Whisky (88) n**22 **t**22 **f**21 **b**23. A really rich, confident and well-balanced dram. **43%** *Suntory.*

**White (80) n**19 **t**21 **f**20 **b**20. Boring nose but explodes on the palate for a fresh, mouthwatering classic blend bite. **40%.** *Suntory.* ☉☉

**Za (79) n**19 **t**21 **f**19 **b**20. Some lively boisterous grain offers a suet-pudding chewiness. A little bitter on the finish. **40%.** *Suntory.*

# European Whisky

**E**urope is getting bigger and more diverse ... and I don't just mean thanks to the recent enlargement of the EU. In whisky terms distilling has not only expanded and embraced new cultures, but to a degree has become a little more refined. It is a continent where distillers appear impressed by single malt and other whisky traditions, but are determined to go about things in their own, idiosyncratic way.

In previous Bibles I have told you about the quite brilliant, and entirely unique oat whisky from Austria's Oswald Weidenauer; from France Eddu Silver, a massively flavoured dram made from buckwheat – or Black Wheat as they call it there.; from Germany Hessicher whisky made from 56% corn and the remainder split equally between barley and rye; in Switzerland Eddie Pierri has been perfecting the making of malt whisky in stills on wheels. Each year I wonder what was coming next. Previously it was a wheat whisky. Whilst Heaven Hill were launching theirs with a fanfare, back in Austria the ever resourceful Oswald Weidenauer was quietly unleashing the world's first Spelt whisky - another form of wheat distillate.

Now it is Swedish. Last year's launching of the malts from Mackmyra was the highlight on the world's new whisky front simply because we have a distillery determined to make no "me too" malt. Mackmyra's is as individualistic as they come. The fact that they saw off the Swiss to land Jim Murray's Whisky Bible 2007 European Whisky of the Year reveals that quality plays a part every bit as important as style. The big question was: could Sweden's finest keep up the quality for a second successive year? The answer was an emphatic yes. To the point that they have again walked away with the top European prize for Jim Murray's Whisky Bible 2008. Absolutely no fluke. Big whiskies making a big statement.

Naturally, the biggest Eurosceptics come from the UK, where I have listened to arguments among people in the trade there that these whiskies are a poor relation to Scotch. And certain critics' marks I have seen given for these whiskies tend also to treat them as if by the same rules as, say, a Speyside malt.

Of course they could not be any more different. It is like comparing Pure Irish Pot Still to an Irish single malt or straight rye to a straight bourbon. Comparisons are pointless: they are a different species of whisky and should be enjoyed and treated that way. Therefore, in the marks I give the points are dropped only if they are poorly made or matured, or suffer by comparison to previous bottlings from the same distillery or region, or if vital balance is lacking. It is not because they don't taste like Scotch ... In the same way, it would be pointless comparing a Buffalo Trace against the Hessicher Whisky from Germany.

Again Switzerland, as a nation, have provided the best quality malts when spread as an average amongst their distilleries. Topping the bill yet again was Eddie Pierri's Swissky who was pipped to a gong only by Mackmyra's bravery and star quality, though I am increasingly finding myself drawn to Swissky as an every day drinking malt: there are very few where the barley plays such a convincing role. Castle Hill's new bottling also took this intense barley route and it was wonderful to see the husband and wife team at Zurcher prove their one previous bottling of some years back was not beginners' luck.

The Welsh whisky of Penderyn has continued to blaze the most impressive international marketing trail, finding itself being sold extensively in North America and has kept up its early high quality and promise. Other European malts, with much smaller stills, will have to settle for now to sell to their own localised markets and whisky clubs.

And last year I tasted the promising new make of a brand new distillery in Denmark while distilling has begun at the first purpose-built distillery in England for over a century. European whisky is not just getting better in quality year by year, it is expanding at a heart-warming rate. Continue to watch this space...!!

# AUSTRIA
## HAIDER (see Waldviertler Roggenhof)

## REISETBAUER
**Reisetbauer Single Malt Whisky 7 Years** db **(76)** n18 t19 f20 b19. No great nose, but the nuttiness on the palate is attractive. **43%**

**Reisetbauer Single Malt Whisky 1996 Destilliert** db **(71)** n16 t18 f18 b18. Some sound maltiness, but the stale tobacco and nuttiness are a problem **56%**

**Reisetbauer Single Malt Whisky 1997 Destilliert** db **(73)** n17 t19 f18 b19. Some mouthwatering malt, but struggles with a belligerent degree of feintiness. **56%**

## WALDVIERTLER ROGGENHOF
### Roggenraith. Working.

## Single Malt
**J H Gersten-Malzwhisky L10/99** db **(80)** n19 t21 f19 b21. Slightly chalky with a tad more oak interference than it needs. That said, the malt is gristy, chewy and clean with a slight buzz of spice. Impressive. **41%**

**J H Gersten-Malzwhisky L10/99 Fassstärke** db **(83)** n20 t21 f21 b21. Holds together better on the nose at a fuller strength plus an extra hint of honey on the finish. More compact and not far off delicious. **54%**

**J H Gersten-Malzwhisky Karamell L66/98** db **(74)** n16 t19 f20 b19. An off-beam nose – well it was a very early barrel – is rescued to a degree by a sweet malt surge towards the death. **41%**

**J H Gersten-Malzwhisky Karamell L66/98 Fassstärke** db **(77)** n16 t21 f20 b20. Much more early intense malt offers a sugared coating at the start and a hint of liquorice on the finale. A big difference. **55%**

**J H Gersten-Malzwhisky Nougat L3/99 Fassstärke** db **(78)** n17 t20 f21 b20. The rye sparkles much more here than at the lower strength, especially on the long finish. **50%**

**Waldviertler Gersten-Malzwhisky Fassstärke** (single malt) L10/99 db **(90)** n22 thick malt with equally weighty oak; t22 first the malt comes through loud and clear. Then liquorice kicks in as the oak really goes into overdrive. Lovely oils coat the palate; f23 huge finale with the emphasis very much on dark – though not bitter – chocolate; b23 this is right back up there with some of those great casks I nosed some years back. Massive and the stuff of stars. **54%**

**Waldviertler J H Single Malt** L18/00 db **(85)** n21 t22 f21 b21. Eminently drinkable stuff; the tobacco edge to the nose doesn't translate onto the thick, barley-sugared tinted delivery and follow through. Big stuff. **41%**

**Waldviertler J H Fassstärke Single Malt** L10/01 db **(91)** n23 chunky, intense with good oak distribution; t22 excellent early spice-barley fruit balance; a short burst of sweetness, mouth-watering and increasingly lush and oily; f23 settles for some serious complexity with layers of cocoa and it dries with supreme elegance; b23 a similar beauty to last year's bottling. If they can maintain this brand, it will become an Austrian institution. **54.5%**

**Waldviertler J H Single Malt Karamell** L22/00 db **(80)** n18 t19 f22 b21. Saved by the long chocolate-caramel (also powerful hints of chocolate Swiss roll) on the finish after a less than glorious opening. **41%**

## Pure Rye Malt
**J H Roggen-Malzwhisky Reserve Nougat L17/99** db **(75)** n18 t18 f20 b19. Sharp, hot and hard as nails. **43%**

**J H Roggen-Malzwhisky L20/98** db **(90)** n22 intense, sweet rye and clean, spicy, fruit; t23 outstanding clarity of crisp, hard rye that sweetens by the second, quite plummy and juicy; f22 the bitterness returns – and then some – and dry pounding oaky tones add a late chalkiness. Hints of honey lurk in the background; b23 simply excellent and quite classic rye whisky. Congratulations to all concerned for a delicious job well done. **41%**

**J H Roggen-Malzwhisky Fassstärke L6/98** db **(88)** n20 surprisingly closed nose; t25 high octane, faultlessly clean rye that completely hammers the palate with a welter of fruity, cherry-laden punches. Clean, chewy and breathtaking: man, this is rye whisky!!!! **f**21 just like the nose, flattens alarmingly; **b**22 if it could be like the arrival on the palate from nose to finish, we'd have a world classic! **55%**

J H Roggen-Malzwhisky Nougat L3/99 db **(74) n**17 **t**19 **f**19 **b**19. The rye has been flattened into submission. **41%**

Waldviertler J H Pure Rye Malt L3/01 db **(92) n**22 crunchingly hard rye; elements of the house tobacco diced with clove; **t**23 soft delivery, at first sweet and almost gristy; hardens as the rye takes command; **f**24 astonishingly long finish for its strength; the degree of complexity amazes as the vanillins begin to make their play; **b**23 just so delicate and elegant. **41%**

Waldviertler J H Pure Rye Malt Nougat L9/00 db **(77) n**17 **t**21 **f**19 **b**20. Still something of an acquired taste (or should that be nose?), though this has kinder and more complex elements than previous bottlings. New-found spices impress. **41%**

Waldviertler J H Roggen-Malzwhisky (pure rye malt) L6/99 db **(91) n**21 hard to get beyond the rye, though when fully warmed there is a hint of cloves; **t**24 absolutely hard as nails: the rye dominates and chisels and drills into the tastebuds like a demented dentist. Mouthwatering and sharp; **f**23 no yield or give at all: it's rye all the way, with the oak trying to get the odd word in but usually failing. Some very late honey does ease the tension; **b**23 this is uncompromising and wonderful whisky of a style so different from those other rye malt makers at Old Potrero. Here the flintiness is of a unique race. **41%**

## Rye

J H Feinster Roggenwhisky L4/00 db **(88) n**22 fabulously pungent in that unique Haider style: both floral and fruity at the same time and in equal measure with a dollop of manuka honey for extra kerpow; **t**23 soft mouth arrival, a quiet punch-up between spices and then an oily smattering of rye; **f**21 quite hard but always chewy rye and oak; **b**22 this is a highly unusual, in your face, whisky which takes some acclimatising to: once you get the picture it's fun all the way. **41%**

J H Feinster Roggenwhisky Fassstärke L4/99 db **(88) n**21 a distinctively herbal rye style with minimum fruit; **t**22 mouthfilling and sweetened by almost molassed rye; **f**23 the rye hangs round but only to keep the oak development under control; unrefined sugar softens the final blows; **b**22 something of a bruising whisky where the aggressive rye fist-fights all comers ... and wins. **54%**

J H Feinster Roggenwhisky L21/98 **(81) n**18 **t**20 **f**22 **b**21. Very sweet with excellent oak weight and even rye distribution. Lovely spice v demerara at the finale. **41%**

J H Feinster Roggenwhisky Fassstärke L42/97 **(91) n**20 sharp, hard and flinty. The grains really kick hard here; **t**24 brilliant weight on the mouth and then a series of slow spicy explosions, each unleashing clear, chewy rye on the palate: a pyrotechnical display of rye at near enough perfection; **f**24 superb chocolate adds sublime balance to the fruity rye and bitter oranges; **b**23 look at this from any angle and you have a minor masterpiece on your hands: quite sublime. **54%**

Waldviertler Feinster Roggenwhisky (rye whisky) L19/98 db **(83) n**19 **t**20 **f**23 **b**21. Slight tobacco on the nose, but the enormity of the rye cannot be suppressed, especially for the excellent finish. **41%**

Waldviertler J H Fassstärke Rye Whisky L11/01 db **(89) n**20 rye impeded by closed oak; **t**23 another story entirely as the rye first melts into the mouth, then explodes to colossal effect. Classic fruit and spice kick as you would expect; **f**23 a beautiful molassed sheen to the grain guarantees a stunning bitter-sweet play; not only big rye kick but cloves oil, too; **b**23 forget the nose. With this one it's all about what happens on the palate. And what happens is brilliance! **54.4%**

## WEIDENAUER DISTILLERY
### Kottes. Working.
## Oat whisky

Waldviertler Hafer Whisky 1998 db **(79) n**20 **t**21 **f**18 **b**20. An oily, assertive whisky that, while sweet, shows signs of a bitterness and imbalance despite the enormous fruitiness on the nose. That said, the oats do come through loud and clear and make quite a porridge, if a slightly salted one. **42%**

**Waldviertler Hafer Whisky 1999** db **(89) n**23 oat-crunchies breakfast cereal combined with soft honey and a sprinkling of sugar: amazingly clean yet so much going on; **t**21 initially hard on the palate then it softens as a grainy sweetness spreads across the roof of the mouth, excellent texture; **f**22 pure oats: just so pure and clean, you could almost chew it: remarkable; **b**23 this is unique whisky and as such deserves time in the glass to oxidise and warm. Once you become accustomed to the taste, the complexity is spellbinding. **42%**

**Waldviertler Hafer Whisky 2000** db **(94) n**23 some delicate spices link beautifully with oak 'n' oats; **t**24 sumptuous, just about perfectly weighted with the most sublime oil involvement, then that unique oaty quality that is sweetish, but softly so, yet with a drying mealiness; **f**24 long, really intense oat character which dries in the most delicious manner of any whisky I have ever encountered! **b**23 this was the best new whisky worldwide of 2002. Totally unique in character, flawless in distillation and awesome in subtlety. **42%**

**Waldviertler Hafer Whisky** (with 2004 silber medaille sticker on neck) db **(89) n**21 sharp and punchy nose; a salted porridge character; **t**23 so much sweeter than the nose with the most astonishing take-off of tart oat, with a countering subtle, milky sweetness that fills the palate; **f**22 still sharp and bitters slightly; a vaguely rye-like fruitiness hovers around a bit; **b**23 brilliant, though not quite the all-round grace of the last uniquely oaty bottling; but still your taste buds know they've been hafered. **42%**.

## Spelt whisky

**Waldviertler Dinkel-Whisky** (marked with 2005 golden label on neck) db **(88) n**21 a touch smoky, like very lightly cured bacon. A kind of feint overture, but never quite reaches the second bar; **t**23 big, mouthwatering grain notes that seem to gather in intensity; the mild muscovado sugar is a delightful touch making for very subtle complexity. Very big indeed; **f**22 big vanilla and more layered grain; **b**22 the distiller here has taken the widest cut he can and got away with it – just! The result is a throbbing, full-flavoured beast that keeps the tastebuds on maximum alert. **40%**

### WOLFRAM ORTNER DESTILLERIE

**Nock-Land Pure Malt 2000** db **(77) n**18 **t**20 **f**19 **b**20. Intense, sweet malt and spices combine with a mild tobacco effect for a curious, distinctive but decent dram. **48%**

## BELGIUM
### DISTILLERIE LAMBICOOL

**Belgium Pure Malt** db **(81) n**19 **t**19 **f**22 **b**21. This is a new make and therefore not strictly whisky. The distillers are marketing this in order to fund their whisky-making venture, a wise move not least because the rich, superbly textured finish overcomes the hesitant tobacco-smoke start for a rewarding and impressive finale; and there is even lavender on the nose of the empty glass. Well worth finding a bottle to help support a promising cause. **40%**

## BULGARIA

**12 Years Finest Bulgarian** db **(81) n**19 **t**21 **f**21 **b**20. Some whisky! Takes no prisoners with an onslaught of what appears to be fresh European oak: more like a 35–40-year-old Scotch. Chewy, sweet with a big liquorice finish. Some decent malt does makes it through and shows at the end. Beautifully textured, clean and obviously well made. Very drinkable whisky indeed, but not for the lilylivered. **43%**

## FRANCE
### Single Malt
### DISTILLERIE DES MENHIRS

**Eddu Gold (93) n**22 greater harmonization than the silver; still a hint of tobacco but now a richer, honeyed tone compensates and flourishes; **t**23 big, bulging arrival. There is a real pulse to the grain, a sturdiness which helps intensify the controlled Demerara sweetness. Big yet elegant; **f**24 now goes into overdrive as the oak adds further weight and spices. Yet the satin effect remains intact; **b**24 rarely do whiskies turn up in the glass so rich in character to the point of idiosyncrasy. Some purists will recoil from the more assertive elements. I simply rejoice. This is so proud to be different. And exceptionally good, to boot!! **43%**

**Eddu Grey Rock Special Blend (89) n**21 pleasantly grainy and clean, though flat and unprepossessing; **t**23 soft, lilting, melt-in-the-mouth with an enormous surge of juicy, grassy barley; **f**22 exceptionally clean, with little oak interfering with the grassy grains; **b**22 a classy, chic blend that sates the tastebuds. **40%**

**Eddu Silver** db **(91) n**21 slight tobacco yet clean enough to allow the grain a big fruity entrance; **t**24 an outstanding arrival of something sweet and simmering; a unique mouthwatering character appears half rye half barley yet something deliciously different again; the salivating sweetness that builds is surprising and has a distinct Demerara sugar feel to it; **f**22 quite a deep and lengthy finial chapter with the clean, boiled apple fruitiness balancing comfortably with subtle oak. Some bitterness digs in but is dealt with by pulsating grain; **b**24 once, the best whisky to come out of France by some considerable distance. This is distilled from Buckwheat, the kind of thing the Japanese are tempted to work with on their own indigenous spirits. The massive flavour profile will win appreciation from anyone who enjoys a no-holds-barred rye. **40%**

## DISTILLERIE GLANN AR MOR

**Taol Esa 1999** dist Dec 99, bott May 04 db **(94) n**24 perhaps the best marriage yet of malt and French wine: the high quality Bordeaux is so easy to detect (and even a touch of vinegar), but it's the effortless integration with the rich barley and resultant mildly salty, spicy complexity that really sets the pulses racing. It's the best of both worlds. Magnifique!; **t**24 salivating and sensuous, again we have complete harmony between the pulsing grape and the vivid, mildly honeyed barley. The trick, though, is that it never becomes too sweet or dry; **f**22 quite long and shows just a little too much bitter oak **b**24 Taol Esa means "The Essay" in traditional Breton language. And this really is an essay in finely distilled whisky matured in sympathetic casks. A genuine joy. And honour, due to its scarcity. Because not only are there just 99 bottles of this, the still with which it was made is now redundant. I sincerely hope they bring it back into service for one special distillation a year. **46%. nc ncf.** *99 bottles.*

## DISTILLERIE GUILLON

⋰⋱ **Guillon No. 1 Single Malt de la montagne de Reims** db **(87) n**22 slight tobacco kick from, presumably, the still. But the crushed (slightly jaded) orange works well with the malt; **t**21 lively malt, not entirely clean, has enough in fruity-doughy reserve genuinely to attract; **f**22 dry with a shortcake butteriness; the sugarless custard tart finish is excellent **b**22 right. I'm impressed. Not exactly faultless, but enough life here really to keep the tastebuds on full alert; By and large well made and truly enjoyable. Well done, Les Chaps! **46%**

## DISTILLERIE WARENGHEM

⋰⋱ **Armorik** db **(91) n**23 alluringly spicy and biting, the oak jabs with limited venom whilst the malt takes the blows with ease. Highly attractive and complex; **t**22 sweet, easily recognisable malt glides over the palate charmingly; some serious gristy notes develop early; **f**23 a long, exceptionally malty finish, again with the barley in the ascendancy and with few challengers; **b**23 I admit it; I blanched, when I first nosed this, so vivid was the memory of the last bottling. This, though ,was the most pleasant of surprises. Fabulous stuff: one of the most improved malts in the world. **40%**

**Armorik** db **(63) n**15 **t**18 **f**14 **b**16. Too feinty and what appears to be caramel dependent. Some of the fat, oiliness is pleasant for a while, but a long way to go on the learning curve here. **40%**

## DOMAINE MAVELA DISTILLERIE ARTISANALE

**P&M Pure Malt Whisky** bott 05 db **(91) n**23 an extraordinary injection of kumquats makes for a pleasing – and individualistic – aroma; **t**23 amazingly sharp and mouthwatering. There are flavours new to me here – and that doesn't happen often; f22 almost bitter at times; b23 an outstanding whisky which, being French, seems to offer a style that is entirely different from anything else around. I have been told there is chestnut within the grist which, strictly speaking, means this is not whisky as we know it. My French is not good enough to discover the truth of this. Between now and the 2008 Bible I shall travel to the distillery in Corsica to get to the bottom of this. In the meantime, though, I shall occasionally enjoy this delicious dram! **42%**

## Blends

**P&M Blend Supérieur (82) n**21 t21 f20 b20. Bitter and botanical, though no shortage of complexity. **40%.** *Mavela Distillerie.*

**P&M Whisky (89) n**22 light, lemony, mildly Canadian wheated in style; t23 beautiful, sharpish citrus ensures a salivating experience; f22 soft oak lowers the sweetness levels; b22 no mistaking this is from a fruit distillery. Still quite North American, though. **40%.** *Mavela Distillerie.*

**Whisky Breton (80) n**19 t20 f21 b20. An altogether better effort; malty and assertively drinkable with attractive, firm, chewy grains and a late, lingering sweetness. A lively, characterful and creditable blend. **40%**

## GERMANY
### BELLERHOF-BRENNEREI
### Owen. Working.

⠿ **Schwäbischer Whisky vom Bellerhof** db **(88) n**21 European-style Kentucky dry tobacco with a vaguely honeyed edge; t22 soft, entirely melt-in-the-mouth barley with dissolving brown sugars; f23 the most butterscotchy finish of all time with wonderful elements of the softest oak and honey imaginable; b22 easy drinking clean and deliciously sweet malt with that indelible touch of class. **43%**

⠿ **Schwäbischer Whisky vom Bellerhof** db **(88) n**23 subtle honey and vanilla: exceptionally clean; t22 more melt-in-the-mouth malt just as before; f21 dries until the oak bites; b22 an entirely different route to the same high quality whisky...! **47.4%**

### BLAUE MAUS
### Eggolsheim-Neuses. Working.

**Blaue Maus Single Malt** Fass Nr 2, dist 8/92, bott 3/04 db **(83) n**20 t21 f22 b20. The nose offers childhood memories of damp washing through a mangler. **40%**

**Blaue Maus Single Malt Whisky** Fassstärke 2, dist 8/93, bott 9/02 db **(84) n**19 t22 f21 b22. This is more of a man than a maus: big, oily, heavyweighted deep molassed sweetness. Lovely spices, too. Really well balanced and a better nose would catapult it into the top bracket. **40%**

**Blaue Maus Single Malt** Fass Nr 1, dist Jun 94, bott Apr 05 db **(85) n**22 t19 f23 b21. Bitter delivery apart, this is getting better and better. **40%**

**Blaue Maus Single Malt** Munhner Whiskyfestival 4-6 Februar 2005 Fass Nr 1, dist Jul 90 db **(93) n**23 minty, lavender, faintly herbal; t24 dry and toasty at first, there is a mad rush of malt before the soft liquorice, oaky notes begin to arrive in numbers, as does the deep honey; f22 cream toffee and wonderful honeycomb; b24 tasted blind this could so easily be mistaken for a bourbon. The oldest European mainland whisky I have ever come across. **40%**

**Gruner Hund Single Malt** Fass Nr 3, dist Sep 92, bott Apr 05, db **(84) n**22 t21 f20 b21. Chewy, silky, spicey: cream toffee has edged out usual complexity. **40%**

**Krottentaler Single Malt Whisky** Fassstärke 1, dist 6/94, bott 7/02 db **(77) n**16 t21 f21 b19. On the feinty side but, as ever, the result is a big whisky with chewy sweet oils and intense malt. Once over the nose, it is a lovely journey. **40%**

**Krottentaler Single Malt** Fass Nr 2 dist 7/94, bott 3/04 db **(87) n**21 freshbaked fruitcake; t23 quite an impressive arrival of legions of burnt raisins sweetened with toffee; f22 sweet with lingering oak and barley; b21 caramel cuts out some complexity but also the bitterness: a very big whisky. **40%**

**Krottentaler Single Malt** Fass Nr 1 dist Jul 95, bott Jan 05 db **(90) n**23 wonderfully confident honey with surging bourbony tones. Rich and beautiful; t21 the usual Blaue

Maus bitterness is calmed down here by silky, sweetening malt. Strands of liquorice continue the soft bourbon theme; **f**22 toasty and delicate with receding vanilla; **b**23 a little gem of a whisky. **40%**

**Mouse** db (**92**) **n**22 rich, big vanilla and thick malt: a touch of distant honey to a nose more akin to bourbon than malt; **t**24 sensational: the mouthfeel is near perfect with just the right amount of subtle sweetness leaking into the big oak; **f**23 more bitter as the tannins mount, roast Java coffee; **b**23 this is an outstanding whisky that any bourbon lover will cross a few countries for. And you will have to: this is malt kept in a small barrel at the distillery bar at Egolsheim/Neuses. You cannot get it anywhere else. *Strength unknown.*

**Piraten Pur Malt Whisky** Fass Nr 1 dist 8/95, bott 1/04 db (**84**) **n**20 **t**21 **f**22 **b**21. As chewy as a mouth of tobacco and Bristol-fashion on the superbly honeyed if somewhat toffeed finale. Whimsically, the first-ever whisky I know of to come with its own leather eye-patch: just as well you don't need your sight to enjoy this. Do ye all knock it back at once ... **40%**

**Schwarzer Pirat Single Malt** Fass Nr 1 dist 7/94, bott 3/04 db (**86**) **n**19 **t**22 **f**23  **b**22. Similar in many ways to Krottentaler (bott 04) except that there is less toffee and the complexity has risen accordingly. **40%**

**Schwarzer Pirat Single Malt Whisky** Fassstärke 3, dist 7/94, bott 9/02 db (**77**) **n**17 **t**20 **f**20 **b**20. Again the nose is hard going but this is compensated for by a sweet, spicy, charismatic malt on the palate. **40%**

**Schwarzer Pirat Single Malt** Fass Nr 2 dist Aug 95, bott May 05 (**87**) **n**21 bourbon and honeycomb; **t**22 sweet liquorice and toasted raisins; **f**22 excellent depth to the finish: like an of bourbon with leathery liquorice and burnt honeycomb; **b**22 delightfully complex and engaging. **40%**

**Spinnaker Single Malt** Fass nr 2 dist 7/93, bott 1/04 db (**85**) **n**19 **t**22 **f**22 **b**22. Seriously enjoyable, intense malt whisky. **40%**

**Spinnaker Single Malt Whisky** Fassstärke 3, dist 9/93, bott 9/02 db (**82**) **n**19 **t**22 **f**21 **b**20. Superbly made malt, delicate in its weight and possessing a light muscovado sugar sweetness the entire voyage. Just a little heavy on the nose to be a ship-shape great whisky, but I could drink this one any time any place. Especially Germany... **40%**

**Spinnaker Single Malt** Fass 1, dist May 92, bott May 05 db (**89**) **n**23 comfortable signs of age with the oak melting into a treacle cake and intense malt sweetness; **t**23 bitter coffee and then sweetening molasses; **f**21 tons of natural oak-stained caramel; **b**22 the consistency from this small distillery is getting impressive. **40%**

## GRUELS

**Schwabischer Whisky Single Grain** db (**80**) **n**19 **t**21 **f**19 **b**21. Full credit for an excellent first attempt. The nose is good if a tad off-key and the dying embers a little bitter. But the intense oily, rich, sweet, buttery middle is a delight. Familiarity breeds anything but contempt with this characterful whisky. **43%**

**Schwabischer Whisky Single Grain 1991** db dist Feb 91 (**84**) **n**20 **t**22 **f**21 **b**21. Nutty-toffee nose translates into a firm, mouth watering whisky of some finesse that loses out at the finish with that toffee again. **43%**

## BRENNEREI HOEHLER

**Hessicher Whiskey** db dist 17 Feb 01 bott 17 Feb 04 (**91**) **n**23 A diamond hard nose, the sparkle offered by a clever malt-oaky sweetness, the rigidity by the unforgiving rye: lovely stuff; **t**22 stunning arrival of rye that does a comprehensive hatchet job on the tastebuds as it gets into stride. The corn offers a more neutral sweetness; **f**23 remains hard at the core but there is a toffee sweetness lurking and some latent spice; **b**23 one of the real perks of the job is the sheer diversity: here we have a superbly made bourbon style German whiskey with roughly 56/22/22 recipe of corn/rye/malted barley. And it has been distilled to a very high standard. It doesn't taste exactly like bourbon, nor is it like malt. But it is entirely delicious. Go and find it. **42%**

## OBST-KORN BRENNERIE
### Köngen. Working.

**Schwäbischer Whisky** (**76**) **n**18 **t**20 **f**19 **b**19. Digestive biscuit and enormously intense malt. Sharp and slightly out of alignment. **40%**

## BRENNEREI RABEL

**Brennerei Rabel Single Grain (81) n**19 **t**21 **f**20 **b**21. Quite light and very gently oiled, but the integration with oak makes for an impressive depth. **40%**

## SLYRS

**Slyrs Bavarian Single Malt 1999** db **(84) n**20 **t**21 **f**22 **b**21. Competently made malt whisky that celebrates its clean simplicity. Nose is vanilla-bound but on the palate it takes off slowly, first clearing a soft oak hurdle and then really letting the malt go into overdrive. Thoroughly enjoyable, high-quality quaffing whisky that will need to be made in greater amounts if they keep up this standard. **43%**

**Slyrs Bavarian Single Malt 2001** db **(79) n**18 **t**19 **f**22 **b**20. Different fingerprints from previous bottlings with the nose offering curious bacon pizza and the palate shimmering with distant honey on the excellent malty finish. **43%**

**Slyrs Bavarian Single Malt 2002 (84) n**20 **t**21 **f**22 **b**21. The 1999 version may well have been a blip, as this is so much closer to the '99 in style (I have this very moment noticed that I have marked them identically!), though this one has a touch extra sweetness and attitude coursing through it. **43%**

**Slyrs Bavarian Single Malt 2003** L14413 **(88) n**21 docile honey and marzipan; **t**22 lush barley with a tiny dash of golden syrup; **f**23 now this is classy with fabulous length and glorious cocoa, complete with oils, to aid the dull barley throb; vaguely bourbony at times; **b**22 a distinct improvement on all previous bottlings: this young distillery is finding its feet with style. **43%**

## SONNEN SCHEIN

**Sonnen Schein Sherry Wood Finish 1989** db bott 00 **(57) n**14 **t**17 **f**12 **b**14. Oddly enough, the sherry appears to accentuate the dreadful tobacco smoke character to this. The finish really does hurt. **43%**

**Sonnen Schein Single Malt Whisky 1989** bott 00 db **(69) n**17 **t**17 **f**18 **b**17. Very unusual stale tobacco aroma and possibly (I am guessing as a lifelong non-smoker) taste. A whisky that tastes slightly better second time round, though not by much. Room for improvement here, I think. **43%**

## STEIGERWALD

**Whisky aus dem Steigerwald 1988 Single Grain 13 Years Old (88) n**21 just wonderful sugared vanilla; **t**23 the tastebuds are brushed with spices and golden syrup. Some of the oak is perhaps a little too old, but such is the delicate nature of the sugars present it works stupendously well; firm and probing throughout; **f**22 long, gentle vanilla with oak now tamed; **b**22 highly unusual malt that at times reminded me of OTT over-aged pot still Irish. But this has a deftness to the sweetness that makes for a lovely dram. **43%**.

## BRENNEREI VOLKER THEURER

**Black Horse Ammertal Whisky Malt & Grain (88) n**20 **t**23 **f**23 **b**23 a busy, beautifully punctuated whisky that gets past the indifferent nose to unleash a welter of complex tone poems. Hardly surprising, considering this 7-year-old is made up from 70% malted barley and 30% wheat and rye and has been aged in three different types of cask ranging from sherry refill to new German oak...whew!!! **40%**

**Black Horse Ammertal Whisky Malt & Grain** BL 2005 **(91) n**22 a shade cleaner perhaps; a touch of celery and bourbon to the nougat and nuts but it's the warm haystacks that star; **t**23 soft barley layers arrive early before a delivery of something more profound and tasty - the rye; **f**23 a wonderfully rich continuation on a theme, though now some Java coffee and demerara-sweetened cocoa have become embroiled with the juicier grains; **b**23 less immediate impact, mouth-watering or rye-rich. Or so it at first seems. Then the gradual realisation that the complexity levels have risen significantly, as have the distilling skills. Quite excellent. **40%**

## UNIVERSITÄT HOHENHEIM

**Hohenheim Universität Single Malt (82) n**21 **t**20 **f**20 **b**21. The aroma is atractively nutty, marzipan even, and clean; the taste offers gentle oak, adding some weight to an otherwise light, refreshing maltiness. Pleasant if unspectacular. **40%.** *Made at the university as an experiment. Later sold!*

# LATVIA

L B Lavijas Belzams **(83) n**20 **t**22 **f**20 **b**21. Soft and yielding on the palate, this is said to be made from Latvian rye, though of all the world's rye whiskies this really does have to be the softest and least fruity. I'll be astonished if there isn't a fair degree of thinning grain in there, too. **40%**

# POLAND
## LIEBONA GIORA

Dark Whisky **(77) n**19 **t**19 **f**20 **b**19. Lots of grain character with perhaps a tad too much toffee, but the texture is alluring and appealing and finishes well with decent oak and lustre. **40%**

# SPAIN
## Blends

DYC **(81) n**20 **t**21 **f**19 **b**21. Thin and grainy in parts but the bite is attractive and assertive while the malt comfortably holds its own. **40%**

# SWEDEN

Mackmyra Preludium 01 Svensk Single Malt Whisky bott 07 Feb 06 db **(91) n**23 gentle aniseed and Swedish oak combine for a weighty heralding to Sweden's first malt. The sweet malty edge ensures balance and helps cushion the impact. Once you acclimatise, it makes for gently honeyed, surprisingly soft nosing; **t**24 exceptional body weight and near perfect oil ratio. The barley purrs over the tastebuds, leaving a manuka honey trail in its wake; **f**21 slightly bitter as the oaks gain a foothold; spices I had expected to see earlier arrive with burnt toast; **b**23 So here it is: a new dawn (from a country that has far fewer than most), a new distillery, a new whisky, a new distilling nation. We'll draw a discreet veil over Mackmyra's claims that this is the first ever Scandinavian single malt (actually, chaps, you were beaten to it by a decade or two by the Finns and Danes) and instead concentrate on a whisky I have been watching mature since the end of the last century. Or was it the beginning of this one? Well, whenever, I was the first whisky guy to visit the place...and predicted stardom. So I have left this to last while writing The Bible 2007, as I regard this the most vital and exciting addition to the whisky world this year and wanted to leave on a high. Or low, depending on the final product. Well it is certainly different, something it always promised to be from the evidence of my past visits. The input of European oak (or should I say Scandinavian?) has been vital as it has shaped the nose in a direction some whisky lovers may find strange. But you will also find a similar tint to the aromas of whiskies made in Germany, Austria, the Czech Republic and elsewhere. This is one whisky I had to swallow: no matter how professional, there is nothing like a touch of romance to make you do things that perhaps you shouldn't...I can't say it's faultless: the finish might have been improved. But is it good whisky? Indubitably. Is it excellent whisky? Undoubtedly. Is it a true great? Not yet. But it unquestionably has the potential. **55.6%**

Mackmyra Preludium 02 Svensk Single Malt Whisky bott 14.7.06 db **(91) n**23 a dense, tight nose with better control of the oak and some welcome citrus to thin and integrate with the barley. Intriguingly, there is something of the Alpine meadow about this with a delightful floral lilt; **t**23 oily delivery with the citrus again digging deep into the oak; the barley is more shielded here and appears towards the very middle as some whacky vanillins also take position; **f**22 a curiously smoky finish – probably something local – but I wish they'd get a handle on that trailing bitterness; **b**23 a roller-coaster of a malt, at times superbly integrated, at others heading off in any direction at will. Oh, if only Sven had been this unpredictable and exciting... **54.2%**

Mackmyra Preludium 03 Svensk Single Malt Whisky bott 13 Oct 06 db **(95) n**24 Mackmyra!!! That unique half kipper, half smoky bacon, half Rupp (and there's nothing more unique than three halves) that comes from malting from local wood and peat. I've only ever found the style at this distillery, and couldn't wait until I saw it in bottle. I am not disappointed. Subtle? Superb? Not half...!!!; t24 for the first time it is the barley that really springs forward, sweet, gristy and young. As it should be. The oak has backed off allowing the malt full rein. There is also an unexpected fruity element to this, almost like powering Melton Hunt Cake, with a orange peel and sultana; f23 still evidence of that damn bitterness. But now there is so much to counter it, especially those long, glorious, silky waves of smoked barley; b24 this was the one I had been waiting for – especially the nose. If the first two bottlings was the distillery clearing its throat, here is the speech that clearly marks Mackmyra's intentions to be a complete one off. This is the Great Whisky I had been hoping for: full of unique aromas, flavours and shapes on the palate and more delicate than I could possibly have predicted.. Some of you, I suspect, will taste this and wonder what all the fuss is about. All I ask is that you forget Scotch, Japanese and all the other malts for a while. Clear your mind and start afresh. Others will already be booking tickets for Stockholm. Abba Dabba Doo...!! **52.2%**

⬩ **Mackmyra Preludium 04 Svensk Single Malt Whisky** bott 11 Apr 07 db **(91)** n22 heavy oils of the small pot but more of a Lubec marzipan to this guy, rather than the usual curious smoky aromas; t23 enormous body with the barley showing a thickness of character that requires a gently oiled oakiness to penetrate; the bitter-sweet ration is again spot on; f23 no shortage of cocoa oils and delicate maple syrup sweetness to the retreating barley; b23 most distilleries have a trademark character, but Mackmyra's is entirely unique. What is becoming clear now is a density to the malt matched nowhere else. I admit: I adore it...! **53.3%**

⬩ **Mackmyra Preludium 05 Svensk Single Malt Whisky** bott 08 Aug 07 db **(87)** n22 thick, mildly burnt honeycomb and chocolate and that peculiarly attractive Mackmyra oil; t21 very odd delivery, with those coppery oils just having too big a say, though the barley returns to restore parity with a deftly sweet touch; f22 much better, with the vanilla siding with the barley to up the complexity; b22 a thinner, more metallic beast but still an enormous mouthful that never seems to taste the same twice. **48.4%**

⬩ **Mackmyra Privus 01 Topp Tunnor** bott 06 Mar 07 db **(91)** n24 astonishing array of herbal and fruity tones: plum pudding and creamed rice but the complexity heightened by astonishing oaky-woody notes like no other whisky on earth; bitter-sweet ration: near perfection... t24 no less fantastic delivery, again with the controlled explosion of sweetness totally in sync with more aggressive,drier herbal tones; there is one enormous wave of oak which is met by countering soft oils; f21 just loses the balance slightly as the dryness takes control as those strange and varied herbal/woody tones take greater weight; b22 no other whisky on the planet matches this in style. It takes some getting used to....but it's worth it! **54.5%**

⬩ **Mackmyra Privus 02 Näsa För Sprit** bott 07 Mar 07 db **(94)** n23 nutty on several levels, from dry, barely sweetened marzipan to diced hazelnut; some of the famous Mackmyra oils are present but so is a dull malty sweetness; all balanced by an injection of orange peel; t24 mouth-filling and mouth-watering, this is simply a pantone book of delicate sugars, though the nutty ones are there in greater numbers; there is even a gristy streak to this; f23 a gentleman of a finale, dying by degrees over a long period with each sweet nutty note bidding its adieu.. b24 excellent balance from first to last, poise, charm and idiosyncrasy are there in equal measures. Quite simply makes my whisky tasting year complete to find something so unique – and astonishing. **54.5%**

⬩ **Mackmyra Privus 03 Rökning Tillåten** bott 08 Mar 07 db **(96)** n24 peat – Mackmyra style! That means both boldness and delicate tones moulded together – and something herbal just to offer a unique slant; t24 unusual dryness to the smoke; soft oils help spread the phenols and varied herbal oaky notes in equal measure; but there has to be balance and that comes in ample waves of manuka honey f24 remains dry and long with the smoke prevailing, a vaguely gristy barley providing sufficient sweetness for balance. Every single flavour wave offers something different from any other whisky's end: the marriage between oak and smoke has an organic bond matched nowhere else; b24 previously at Mackmyra: fruity, then nutty. Now this. Sensational. Because this is no "me too" whisky. It challenges, asks questions, makes statements. Every expression appears to further and expand my own experience and expectations of whisky, which really is saying something. **56%**

# SWITZERLAND
## HAGEN DISTILLERY
### Huettwilen. 1919. Working.

HR Distillery Lott no.10099, dist Dec 99, bott Jan 05 db (88) n21 clean, fine malt. Crisp with a degree of fruit, especially freshly bitten green apple. Some soft dough adds the extra depth; t23 mouthwatering and deft, this offers a butterfly delivery of sweet young malt backed again by that apple-fresh fruitiness; f22 lovely delivery of vanilla which balances just so well with the barley; b22 again we have an enormously impressive whisky from Switzerland. Here we have a classic case of a whisky that has matured for a few years side by side with fruit spirit (probably apple) and has breathed in some of those delicate elements. 42%

## BRAUEREI LOCHER
### Appenzell. Working.

Santis Swiss Highlander Single Malt db (86) n22 t22 f20 b22. Lovely stuff from a whisky that shows more than a degree of sophistication. Apparently the whisky has been matured in 60-year-old oak beer barrels and despite the age makes a telling and slightly unusual contribution. 40%

## BRENNEREI SCHWAB
### Oberwil. Working.

Buechibaegger Singelmalt db (84) n23 t21 f20 b20. The nose is immaculate with essence of praline running with the malt. But the intensity of the European oak just tips the balance away from the excellence the whisky threatens. Lovely whisky, but could do with a little extra youth, though the innate sweetness does enough to see off the oaky excesses. 42%

## MAISON LES VIGNETTES

Glen Vignettes "Abred" Peated Swhisky Pur Malt db (89) n22 delicate peat; beautifully gristy nose and the background noise is easily ignored; t23 awesome delivery with top-rate bittersweet edge as the peat yodels without an off-note in the background; f22 dryish vanilla and sweet peat; b22 fabulous whisky from a distillery that finds peat to its liking and suiting its style: no coastal notes here – hardly surprising ...! – but just great virtuosity with the smoke. 45%

Glen Vignettes "Annouim" Initial Swhisky Pur Malt db (85) n19 t22 f22 b22. The odd distilling anomaly cannot disguise a top-grade malt of easy drinking. 45%

Glen Vignettes "Gwenwed" Syrah Cask Swhisky Pur Malt db (74) n17 t20 f18 b19. A lush, big-impact malt weighed down by caramel and that distinctive celery-spicy distilling character. 45%

## WHISKY CASTLE
### Elfingen. Working.

8820 Whisky 1378 Tage im Fass (days in cask) db (87) n20 vaguely piny and herbal; t22 massive malt that sweetens with each crashing wave. The opening is typically European, threatens to turn nasty but in seconds changes direction and goes into malty overdrive; f23 fabulous oak interaction as vanilla and very dry walnut and date cake; b22 one of those whiskies that grow on you once you understand that it has a different viewpoint. Hugely entertaining. 55%. For Wadi Brau Wadenswil.

Castle Hill Whisky unfiltert Nummer1 1125 Tage im Fass (days in cask) db (84) n20 t21 f22 b21. Big, chewy malt. The oaky bitterness is easily matched by the sweet, grassy barley. 43%

Castle Hill Whisky Nummer 4, 1125 Tage im Fass (93) n22 big barley from a small still. There is a copperish element to this, plus a nutty intonation. Something to really get the nose into; t24 near perfect delivery: the full mouthfeel is stunning. Perfectly weighted, just the right degree of natural sweetness and the most glorious barley development; f23 a light finale yet the waves of sweet peat and vanilla are almost endless. Long, charming and a magic wand waved over the degree of gristy sweetness; b24 has someone moved Cardhu to Switzerland??? I am truly astonished.

I have missed out on nummers 2&3 (but I'm hunting!), but this is so far removed from nummer 1 that they are hardly worth comparison. One of the cleanest, most malt intense and unerringly delightful whiskies you will find in Europe and would be a title contender but for the slightly more elegant Swissky. Reaffirmation, that Switzerland is the finest producer of malt whisky on mainland Europe. **40%**

## BRENNEREI-ZENTRUM BAUERNHOF
### Zug. Working.

Swissky db (**91**) n23 young, clean, fresh malt which sparkles with a hint of apple: one of the best noses on the European scene; t23 stunningly clean arrival and then the most delicate of malty displays that all hinges around a juicy youth to the barley. The sweetness is controlled, refined and evenly distributed; a soft oiliness helps to lubricate the tastebuds; f22 no less soft and simple with the oak offering the kind of weight that can barely be detected; b23 while retaining a distinct character, this is the cleanest, most refreshing malt yet to come from mainland Europe. Hats off to Edi Bieri for this work of art. Moving stuff. **42%**

Swissky (label shows boxed drawing of pot still) db (**84**) n19 t22 f21 b22. Only the most distant hint of feintiness takes away from the beauty of this rich malt. The oils are sublime, as usual from this distillery, and the malt is sweet and chewy. If anything, I am marking down. **42%**

Swissky (label shows man working a pot still) db (**83**) n20 t21 f21 b21. A thinnish, clean malt at first with some decent oak depth to bolster the copper-rich finale. **42%**

Swissky Exklusiv Abfüllung db (**93**) n23 just so clean: absolutely flawless. Despite the clarity the malt has a Cardhueque richness and purpose that is spellbinding; t23 intensity of the malt is stupifying: again a Cardhu character except this probably has a bit of extra vanilla spice early on; f23 layers of ultraclean barley; b24 every year every new bottling of Eddie's just gets better and better. Only the sheer brilliance and depth of McCarthy's keeps this off small batch whisky of the year. But of the entirely non-peated or smoked variety this has no peer: there will many a distiller in Scotland who would wish their maturing spirit possessed such élan. Swiss it may be, but there is absolutely nothing neutral about this! **40%**

Swissky Exklusiv Abfüllung L3365 (**94**) n23 more intrinsic barley than previous years; the oak offers the perfect frame for the diced, slightly spiced apples and pears; t23 mouth-watering, beautifully clean barley in Swissky's classic style; f24 drier, vanilla-led but the waves of rich barley and delicate oak seem endless; b24 a supremely distilled whisky with the most subtle oak involvement yet. Year after year this distillery bottles truly great single malt, a benchmark for Europe's growing band of small whisky distillers. **40%**

## SPEZIALITÄTENBRENNEREI ZURCHER
### Port. Working.

Zurcher Single Lakeland Malt Whisky 3 Years Old (dist 10 Jul 00, bott 10 Sep 03. Not stated on bottle) db (**94**) n23 t24 f23 b24. A one-off bottling from a highly respected Swiss distiller. On this evidence whisky should be a regular part of their life: for first attempt nothing short of spectacular. Had I received it when launched, would have been a certain award winner. If you happen to be in Switzerland and see one in a shop somewhere, rip the seller's arm off.... **42%**

Zurcher Single Lakeland 3 Years Old dist Jul 03, bott Jul 06 db (**93**) n22 the house style of mesmerising intensity has been continued: less smoke, more spiced honey, but a hint of feints; t24 a real small pot still feel to this, with the richness of it all almost making you swoon; the stupendously spiced middle really does offer a fabulous counter to those sweeter, persistent honey tones and the vague fruity sub-text; the weight is sheer perfection; f23 the intensity dissipates slightly to allow a more relaxed vanilla-oak unfolding. The spices becoming ever more frenzied before suddenly vanishing; b24 the label claims smoke, but I can't find any though there's no shortage of spice. The distillery's second bottling: the first was sensational, this is Highland Park on steroids. A wonderful follow up, depite the extra width to the cut. And as for a three-year-old...well, even I'm agog...!!! Let's now hope that this will become an annual offering, rather than once every three years. We need more! **42%**

## TURKEY

**Ankara Turk Viskisi (80) n**20 **t**20 **f**19 **b**21. Soft and gentle despite the clear grain with soft delicate oak on the finish. Quite beautifully balanced: a genuinely charming whisky to be taken seriously. **43%**

## WALES

**Penderyn** cask nos 5–99 db **(91) n**23 raisins on the nose, light playful malt and then a backdrop of sweet wine; **t**23 absolutely staggering arrival on the palate of malt landing with almost snowflake delicateness. Immediately a second movement, this time of bitter-sweet fruit, blood orange included, sweeps down over the startled tastebuds. Astonishing stuff; **f**22 slightly bitter and tart towards the finish and two variants of oak begin to dive into the melee; **b**23 it was my pleasure and privilege to be the first person from outside the company to discuss and analyse the beauty of this whisky at its spectacular official launch on St David's Day 2004. I told them they were tasting not just an historic malt whisky, but one that deserved the highest praise in its own right. Re-tasting it again for the Bible, I stand by every word. **46%**

**Penderyn** bott code Nov 04 db **(89) n**21 unsalted butter on spotted dog; **t**24 fabulous combination of malt concentrate and fruitcake; **f**22 the oak hits back with a late bitter edge; **b**22 the mouth arrival is to Di [Dai?] for.... **46%. ncf.**

**Penderyn** bott code Dec 04 db **(83) n**19 **t**22 **f**22 **b**20. Assertive and warming, but struggles slightly against a big oak imbalance. **46%. ncf.**

**Penderyn** bott code Jan 05 db **(91) n**20 this really takes the biscuit: hints of crushed gingernuts amid the fruit shortbread and digestive; **t**24 mind-blowing malt delivery underpinned by a sensational wave of voluptuous grape: the balance could have been calculated with a slide rule; **f**23 first-rate spice adds extra length; **b**24 what a little jewel! The malt somehow finds the legs to pierce through the powerful Madeira shell. **46%. ncf.**

**Penderyn** bott code Feb 05 db **(82) n**18 **t**22 **f**21 **b**21. After the disappointingly soapy nose the fruit integrates with the malt superbly to save the day and deliver a decent malt. **46%. ncf.**

**Penderyn** bott code Jun 05, casks 55-165 db **(89) n**23 an impressive collision between candy store grape and thumping oak; **t**22 soft and sultana-led; **f**22 drier as the vanillas arrive, but tantalizing fruit to the last; **b**22 for those of you wondering what happened to the March, April and May 2005 bottlings, fear not: they don't exist. The whiskies which would have supplied them were instead harnessed to create the special "Grand Slam" edition, to celebrate the country's rare success in the Six Nations Rugby championship. But service is resumed as normal here with a delicately fruity number. **46%. ncf.**

**Penderyn** bott code July 05, casks 160-270 db **(91) n**23 molten vanilla ice-cream topped with breadfruit ad sultanas. Very different and curiously attractive; **t**22 mouth-watering barley, lots of oak buzz but calmed by lush fruit; **f**23 just so delicate and complex, with more of what went before except in tantalizing, shadowy form; **b**23 a complex, thinking man's whisky. **46%. ncf.**

**Penderyn** bott code Aug 05, casks 160-270 db **(79) n**21 **t**21 **f**18 **b**19. Mouth-watering and juicy as usual but a bitter bite to the finish has crept in. **46%. ncf.**

**Penderyn** bott code Sep 05 db **(87) n**22 loads of soft oaky vanillins of varying hues **t**22 big, clean barley kick-off and then becomes oily and little spiced; **f**21 crème caramel; **b**22 lots of natural caramels (and for those of you who write in to me, no, Penderyn doesn't add colouring to their whisky, though they don't yet state the fact) make this an charming and unusual ride. Oh, and the sharp-eyed collectors amongst you may, also, have noticed that there are no barrel references to this bottling. That is because they kind of lost track back in Wales (see the confusing numbers above)...and just gave up...!! **46%. ncf.**

**Penderyn** 750ml bottle USA batch db **(93) n**23 injection of extra oak, light hints of young bourbon and sultana pudding; **t**24 big oak-fruit statement from the off with spices abounding and some zesty, refreshing barley filling in elsewhere. A mouth-filler with no shortage of bourbon notes; **f**23 pretty lengthy with the accent on chalky vanilla; **b**23 quite weighty affair compared to other bottlings so far and the chewability goes off the scales:

the mouth arrival is classic. Or at least as classic as a distillery this young can get... **46% (92 proof). ncf.** *(bott 01 Sept 05 but not stated).*

**Penderyn** bott code Oct 05 db **(92) n**22 wonderful, half-praline/half-Lubeck-style dry marzipan wrapped in soft, European oak; **t**24 pure silk: the yielding grape carries with it in equal measures delicate barley and firm oak. A myriad of textures; **f**23 lovely spices tingle and sultanas and spotted dick make for a lovely finale; **b**23 sumptuous and highly complex, a malt that takes some time to unravel. And it's worth every second. **46%. ncf.**

**Penderyn** bott code Nov 05, casks 160-270 db **(84) n**20 **t**21 **f**22 **b**21. Nose suggests a bitter-ish, almost fruit-stone brandy style borne out by the early delivery. Gentle, fruity somewhat sweet and simplistic delivery. **46%. ncf.**

**Penderyn** bott code Dec 05 db **(88) n**21 dried grapeskin and vanilla; **t**23 lush, fat; some very serious Madeira influence; **f**22 creamy-textured vanilla and toasted raisin; **b**22 one of the fruitier expressions. **46%. ncf.**

**Penderyn** bott code B266 - Jan 06 db **(89) n**21 weak orangey-citrus, vanilla; **t**23 the tastebuds are nuked by big spice parade; **f**22 butterscotch and vanilla, late juicy barley; **b**23 wonderfully lively and bracing. **46% (92 proof). ncf.**

**Penderyn** bott code Feb 06 db **(92) n**22 spotted dog, sultanas and custard; **t**23 the spicy spearhead is swamped with some salivating grape and barley; **f**24 long, multi-layered and continues of the clean fruit theme. Perhaps the softest Penderyn landing yet; **b**23 starts off similarly to the Jan bottling, but then fruits out. **46%. ncf.**

**Penderyn** bott code Mar 06 db **(83) n**20 **t**21 **f**21 **b**21. Busy vanilla with some spicy oak and young bourbon notes. **46%. ncf.**

**Penderyn** bott code Apr 06 db **(85) n**20 **t**22 **f**22 **b**21. Soft, supple and opens out to offer a fruity sheen. **46%. ncf.**

**Penderyn** bott code May 06 db **(91) n**22 an unusual salty tang complements the barley; **t**23 soft delivery yet very busy with a mottled barley and oak effect; **f**23 the usual vanilla, but a lovely gristy cameo; **b**23 the first bottling for a couple of months to accentuate the barley. **46%. ncf.**

**Penderyn** bott code Jun 06 db **(88) n**21 in your face pubescent bourbon; **t**22 lovely early wine delivery, refreshing and vaguely tart. Soft vanilla and barley bring up the second act; **f**23 long and astonishingly well defined and cultured. The mildest spice buzz accentuates the oak and the fruit-barley core goes on forever; **b**22 in many ways, this is a pretty average Penderyn. Which says much... **46%.**

**Penderyn** bott code Jul 06 db **(90) n**21 slightly disproportionate oak; **t**23 pure silk as the plummy, greengagey fruits takes hold and mouth-watering barley makes a sweet counter attack; **f**23 back to the oak which is again heading down a honeycomb-bourbon path; **b**23 another big whisky from this small distillery. **46%. ncf.**

**Penderyn** bott code Aug 06 db **(88) n**20 hmmm, slightly sweaty armpit. Misbalance between fruit and some of the oak extract; **t**23 no problem here as the palate is swamped with a glorious marriage of astonishingly fit grape and ultra-intense barley. There is a teasing spice rift towards the middle; **f**23 more grapey glory on the finale which is long, warming and just so wonderfully delicate; **b**22 ignore the nose and just get on to the tasting bit! **46%. ncf.**

⠈⠶ **Penderyn** bott code Sep 06 db **(93) n**23 voluptuous, with all the fruity bits in the right places; **t**24 sizzling fruit offering sublime freshness and a welter of spicy punches; **f**23 returns to safer vanilla ground though that spice does hang on; **b**23 a cracker of a whisky. From a 75cl bottle – presumably for the US market. Lucky them. **46%. ncf.**

⠈⠶ **Penderyn** bott code Oct 06 db **(84) n**19 **t**22 **f**22 **b**21 After the Lord Mayor's Show: in itself a very decent malt. But thin by comparison and runs to a sharper, oakier theme. Some decent cocoa, though and the overall taste experience amply compensates for the disharmony on the nose. **46%. ncf.**

⠈⠶ **Penderyn** bott code Nov 06 db **(89) n**21 mildly perfumed, like a kindly old aunt from the early 60s; **t**23 crisp and beautifully clean malt delivery with juicy encore; **f**22 flattens a degree as the vanillins kick in; **b**23 intriguingly spiceless: a gentle ride all the way. **46%. ncf.**

⠈⠶ **Penderyn** bott code Dec 06 db **(92) n**23 apples and celery; **t**22 lazy delivery and then green shoots of fruit that grow alarmingly fast; **f**24 praline chocolate wafers; **b**24 wonderful oak interception so the malt just grows and grows **46%. ncf.**

:- **Penderyn** bott code Jan 07 db **(88)** n21 sharp, spiced citrus; t23 wow! The nose doesn't warn of the onrush of barley juice and fruit that hits the tastebuds like an avalanche; f22 soft mocha; b22 the flavour profile is all upfront. Quite charming, though. **46%. ncf.**

:- **Penderyn** bott code Feb 07 db **(89)** n22 punchy grape; sharp vanilla – the beginning of something bourbony; t22 soft barley sweetness, even gristy which is usual for this distillery; f22 big vanilla; fruit pith dryness; b23 elegant and understated all the way. **46%. ncf.**

:- **Penderyn** bott code Mar 07 db **(90)** n21 citrus and vanilla; t22 velvet delivery of barley and a slow move through the fruity gears; f24 a fantastic finale with ever intensifying cocoa oils; b23 high quality, softly spoken malt. **46%. ncf.**

:- **Penderyn** bott code Apr 07 db **(76)** n18 t21 f18 b19 Hmmm. Oily, a touch hot, bitter and even an unusual hint of feint. Hardly your classic Penderyn. **46%. ncf.**

:- **Penderyn** bott code May 07 db **(92)** n21 lively combo of kumquats and unripe gooseberry...gosh!! t23 wonderful, dissolving barley-fruit delivery with a real grape juiciness; f24 long, continues along its sweet, juicy course even when vanilla pods and warming spices and honey arrive...wonderful b24 normal, quite beautiful service has been resumed...! **46%. ncf.**

**Penderyn Cask Strength First Release** db **(86)** n21 t21 f22 b22. A very different Penderyn that should seduce the gin and tonic merchants: oddly delicious. **61.8%**

**Penderyn Grand Slam Edition 2005** Madeira finish db **(89)** n22 light grape, spiced oak; t23 soothing juicy fruit then a delivery of spice and chewy oak: very much the nose in liquid form, except more intense; f21 a movement toward bitterness is checked by honeycomb; b23 chunky and chewy: a good try, some Welsh might say... **46%. ncf.** *Limited Bottling.*

**The Penderyn Millenium Cask 2000** db **(90)** n22 delicate soft-bourbon oaky tones, which is not what you expect from a three-year-old whisky; the fruit is soft yet somehow champions the clean malt; t22 warming, massively malt at first and then big vanilla and a mouthwatering grape and lychee fruit cocktail; f23 just so long with loads of natural toffee vanilla perfectly at home with the concentrated malt and layered fruitiness; b23 this is one very complex whisky offering style and first-class integrity. A dilemma for those who own this historic whisky: luckily you can taste the miniature while keeping the full bottle for posterity. Or should that be the other way round? **61.6%**

**Penderyn Oloroso Edition** db **(76)** n17 t20 f21 b18. By no means showing Penderyn at its best: the nose is poor and imbalanced (it needs a good half-hour in the glass to find some clean fruit) but there is a degree of compensation on the sweet depth of the finish, especially once the influence of the grape has lessened. A reminder of what a delicate creature this Welsh whisky is and just how steep the learning curve can be.... **50%**

**Penderyn Peated Edition** db **(92)** n22 just so delicate and gristy: the smoke almost makes an apology on its aromatic arrival; t24 subtle, mouthwatering and quite stunningly crafted; the malt works on two levels in that the barley is clear and clean, yet the smoke gives much to chew on. The middle, in which some spicy oak interaction takes place, is almost the stuff of erotic dreams; f22 not too long, with a gentle, pulsing smokiness; b24 this low level of peating absolutely fits the shape of the whisky like a glove: inspired stuff! You would never in a million years believe its youth. **50%**

**Penderyn Welsh Rugby Union 125th Anniversary Edition** Madeira finish db **(95)** n23 dripping in lightly spiced grape, the vanilla-barley sub-plot adds just the right weight; t24 My word! There'll be a few people in Madeira surprised that their fortified wine can be quite this good...the spice-fruit balance is now the stuff of Welsh legend; f24 the accent falls on the oak but so many layers of grape and barley and black-peppered spice wash over it that you wonder if it will ever end. Even a tendency towards bitterness works in its favour as that honeycomb arrives to absorb it. Stunning; b24 lamb apart, the best thing from Wales I have ever got my lips round... (!) And I say that with full apologies to a young lady from Maesteg, but it's true, you see... **50%.** *1250 bottles.*

# World Whiskies

**I have long said that whisky can be made just about anywhere in the world; that it is not writ large in stone that it is the inalienable right for just Scotland, Ireland, Kentucky and Canada to have it all to themselves. And so, it seems, it is increasingly being proved. Perhaps only sandy deserts and fields of ironstone can prevent its make physically and Islam culturally, though even that has not been a barrier to malt whisky being distilled in both Pakistan and Turkey. While not even the world's highest mountains or jungle can prevent the spread of barley and copper pot.**

Outside of North America and Europe, whisky's traditional nesting sites, you can head in any direction and find it being made. South America may be well known for its rum, but in the south of Brazil, an area populated by Italian and German settlers many generations back, malt whisky is thriving. In even more lush and tropical climes it can now also be found, with Thailand leading the way.

Japan has long represented Asia with distinction and whisky-making there is in such an advanced state and to such a high standard Jim Murray's Whisky Bible has given it its own section. But while neighbouring South Korea has ended its malt distilling venture, further east, and at a very unlikely altitude, Nepal has forged a small industry to team up, geographically, with fellow malt distillers India and Pakistan. The one malt whisky from this region making inroads in world markets is India's Amrut single malt. The tasting notes included here are from the first bottling, but for the 2007 edition I included two extraordinary single casks, too. Both reveal that the quality really can raise eyebrows: this is a much better balanced affair, quite excellent in places, and it appears the distillers are beginning to learn to make the most of their fast-maturing stocks.

And Africa is also represented. There has long been a tradition of blending Scotch malt with South African grain but now there is single malt there, as well. Two malt distilleries, to be precise, with a second being opened this year at the Drayman's Brewery in Pretoria

One relatively new whisky-making region is due immediate study: Australia. From a distance of 12,000 miles, the waters around Australia's distilleries appear to be muddied. Quality appears to range from the very good to extremely poor. And during the back end of 2004 I managed to discover this first hand when I visited three Tasmanian distilleries and Bakery Hill in Melbourne which perhaps leads the way regarding quality malt whisky made south of the Equator.

Certainly green shoots are beginning to sprout at the Tasmania Distillery which has now moved its operation away from its Hobart harbour site to an out of town one close to the airport. The first bottlings of that had been so bad that it will take some time and convincing for those who have already tasted it to go back to it again. However, having been to the warehouse – and having tasted samples from every single cask they have on site – I reported in previous Bibles that it was only a matter of time before those first offerings would be little more than distant – though horrific – memories. Well, as predicted, it is now safe to put your head above the parapet. Their latest cask strength bottling for the 2008 Bible was a bloody beaut.

It may still be a year or two before Whisky Tasmania's malt is ripe enough for bottling, though they have now made some heavily peated spirit which will give them vatting options in three or four years time. Away from Tasmania there is malt distilling – and further plans to distil – all over Australia. On that has already made it into the shops is from Booie Range, which like Sullivan's Cove suffers from a frighteningly unattractive nose, but unlike early bottlings of the Hobart whisky regroups and recovers significantly on the palate. Meanwhile. the remaining casks of Wilson's malt from New Zealand are disappearing fast and when in New Zealand I discovered the stills from there were not just making rum in Fiji but whisky as well. We are all aware of the delights of island whisky ... just what a Pacific Island whisky will be like though? I can feel another journey coming on .... Which leaves Antarctica as the only continent not making whisky, though what some of those scientists get up to for months on end no one knows. Still, effluent might be a problem there, though it should make the perfect whisky with ice....

# ARGENTINA

**Breeders Choice (84) n**21 **t**22 **f**21 **b**20. A sweet blend using Scottish malt and, at the helm, an unusually lush Argentinian grain. **40%**

# AUSTRALIA
## BAKERY HILL DISTILLERY, 1999. Operating.

⟡ **Bakery Hill Classic Malt** Cask no. 2707 db **(84) n**19 **t**22 **f**21 **b**22 Bizarre. Just checked – and found I have given almost identical marks to last year's version – and the tasting notes remain spot on. **46%**

**Bakery Hill Classic Malt** barrel 2606, bott 06 db **(93) n**23 enough citrus to start a Vitamin C factory; beautifully refreshing with pulsing malts; **t**23 salivating and fresh with continuous waves of young, clean barley with not all the new make element completely lost; **f**24 major complexity here as the oak inches itself in with a vanilla sheen, but malt refuses to fade; **b**23 just so beautiful..!!! **46%. ncf.**

**Bakery Hill Classic Malt** db **(83) n**19 **t**22 **f**21 **b**21. Lots of serious attitude and gristy sweetness, but a tad feinty. **46%**

**Bakery Hill Classic Malt** cask no. 08, bott 04 db **(91) n**22 florid, highly intense malt with a speckle of feint and peat; **t**23 beautifully salivating and rich with the intensity of the sweet malt leaping off the scales; **f**23 mega cocoa, long and wonderfully structured wind-down; **b**23 this has moved on massively from the first test bottlings of a year ago. The slight feints burn off on the nose quickly and we are left with something copper and malt rich and very special from Australia's finest distillery. **46%**

⟡ **Bakery Hill Classic Malt Cask Strength** Cask no. 2707 db **(86) n**20 **t**22 **f**22 **b**22 A big malty march from delivery to finish aided by some enthusiastic oils that slightly undid the nose. **58%**

**Bakery Hill Classic Malt Cask Strength** db **(87) n**22 astonishingly clean with young gooseberries attached to the malt; **t**22 young malt rips through the tastebuds and settles comfortably with an oily landing; **f**22 big cocoa thrust seems to be the hallmark of the distillery; **b**21 relatively youthful and for all its malty razzmatazz would benefit with a touch more oak. **65%**

**Bakery Hill Classic Malt Cask Strength** barrel 2606, bott 06 db **(94) n**23 a distinct Speyside style with fresh grasses and citric fruits linking with delicate vanilla for a beaut of an aroma; **t**24 almost unbelievable barley intensity, but wonderful cocoa background (curiously cocoa can arrive as an effect of new make, slightly under-matured malt, or later from the oak: here it is possibly from all of these); **f**24 that wonderful cocoa theme continues but again the barley is spot on; **b**23 there are about 20 distilleries in Speyside that would die to be able to make a whisky this stunningly integrated. Young, barely pubescent but sheer, unadulterated, class... **60.1%**

**Bakery Hill Classic Malt Cask Strength** db **(86) n**20 **t**22 **f**23 **b**21. A shadow of something feinty, but nothing like the 46% version. The result, though, is about as big a whisky as you'll get for something theoretically unsmoked...! **60.1%**

⟡ **Bakery Hill Double Wood** Cask no. 2719 db **(92) n**22 some major citrus and grape makes inroads into the oaky malt; a wisp of smoke, or my imagination...? **t**23 more of the same with a fruitcakey feel now, complete with a slight doughyness to the malt; big, busy middle; **f**23 long, classy finish with some chocolate adding to the fruitcake and some smoke ensuring, with the delicate oils, depth, further length and weight; **b**24 high class whisky is high class whisky wherever its made. Get up to body temp – and marvel..! **46%**

**Bakery Hill Double Wood** cask no. 0508, bott 04, db **(80) n**19 **t**19 **f**21 **b**21. The introduction of the French oak serves only to add a certain fruity astringency to an otherwise clean and attractive dram. **46%**

**Bakery Hill Double Wood** db **(84) n**21 **t**22 **f**20 **b**21. Attractively chewy, juicy in places but ultimately heavy duty and a tad fey on the finish. **46%**

**Bakery Hill Double Wood** cask no. 2621, bott 06 db **(91) n**23 juicy; incredible clarity to the barley; **t**23 decent spice peppers the fruity barley; a lovely bitter-sweet tale; **f**22 long, lush and light; **b**23 does whisky come any more refreshing than this? **46%**

⟡ **Bakery Hill Peated Malt** Cask no. 1307 db **(90) n**22 half Bowmore-half Laphroaig-style kippery, Fisherman's Friend cough sweet element to this – the most Islay style from this distillery yet; **t**23 perfect weight on the oils ensure the delivery is soft and, at first malty. The smoke gathers density... **f**23 a sharp, citrus kick to the lightly-oiled finish – smoked marmalade on toast... **b**22 well made and simply lovely whisky. **46%**

**Bakery Hill Peated Malt** cask no. 12, bott 04 db **(90) n**22 soft peat harmonises with intense malt, deftly weighted and oozing class; **t**23 there is teasing gentleness to the smoke that borders on eroticism, the sweetness is refined and layered with oak piling in the riches; **f**22 thins out a little towards the dry finale; **b**23 for sureness of touch at such young age, this is quite an amazing malt. For those who prefer their peat brushed on rather than glued. **46%**

**Bakery Hill Peated Malt** cask n. 2006, bott 06 db **(93) n**23 "dry" iodine: nothing coastal, just a tangy, clean peatiness lightened by soft citrus; **t**23 sweet, fresh young and then a big bursting out of grassy barley amid the smoke and spices; **f**23 pretty long with lashings of late vanilla and butterscotch; remains salivating; **b**24 seriously well-made malt with genuine complexity. Textbook balance. **46%**

**Bakery Hill Peated Malt** db **(89) n**21 ultra delicate: the very lightest smoke and vanilla; **t**22 delightful barley sugar lead with peat tagging along as a faint shadow; **f**23 the peats begin to gather and some spices arrive; **b**23 restrained and delicate from first to last. **46%**

⠸ **Bakery Hill Peated Malt Cask Strength** Cask no. 1307 db **(93) n**23 **t**24 **f**23 **b**24 No surprise: it is just like the 40% version (being from the same cask), except the bigger notes are huge and there is just a greater degree of harmony to assist the overall balance. More absolutely outstanding distilling from that true master distiller, David Baker....someone so deserving of an overused and lately cheapened nomenclature. **59.8%**

**Bakery Hill Peated Malt Cask Strength** cask no. 14, bott 04 (aged 4 years) db **(94) n**24 kippery aroma with a dash of lemon on the side; **t**23 a real mouthful of subtle, pulsating peats which have to battle through the sweet malt; young but has such extraordinary depth and charisma; **f**24 goes into overdrive, fabulously long with layer upon layer of encrusted peat that clings limpet-like to the roof of the mouth; **b**23 show this to anyone and tell them it not an Islay: they will never believe you. The phenol levels here are quite stunning, but so too is the excellence of distillation. I found this cask in Bakery Hill's warehouse last year and swooned, even queried its origins – so distillery Dave Baker bottled it! The good news is that I have tasted a cask or two similar to this at the distillery: there is more of this kind of brilliance to come over the years! **65%**

**Bakery Hill Peated Malt Cask Strength** cask no. 2006, bott 06 db **(91) n**22 disorganised and wild; a three-day cold peat fire and citrus; **t**23 sma' still copperiness, a touch of honeycomb 'n' apple to the metallic sheen; **f**23 long, remaining on that coppery theme but now the peats gather for a rich finale; **b**23 you get the feeling that this is made in an ancient still. Lush and rich all the way. How long before we see it in the Scarlet Bar? **60.1%**

**Bakery Hill Peated Malt Cask Strength** db **(89) n**23 clean, the usual citrus house-style; the peats are a bit laid-back but charming; **t**23 stunningly refreshing with superb soft oils for the sweet peat to melt into; **f**21 a minor vanilla fest and some coppery sharpness; **b**22 another really lovely malt from this outstanding distillery. **60.1%**

## BOOIE RANGE DISTILLERY

**Booie Range Single Malt** db **(72) n**14 **t**20 **f**19 **b**19. Mounts the hurdle of the wildly off-key nose impressively with a distinct, mouth watering barley richness to the palate that really does blossom even on the finish. **40%**

## LARK DISTILLERY

⠸ **The Lark Distillery Single Malt Whisky** Cask LD48, bott Jan 07 db **(88) n**21 some slight feints quickly burn off to leave a bit of a fruity monster; **t**23 immediate spice prickles from the off; calms down for a fruit salad/blackjack candy combo; **f**22 the vanillins arrive for a custard and fruit finale; **b**22 knife and fork whisky – and a spoon wouldn't go amiss. **58%. sc.**

⠸ **The Lark Distillery Single Malt Whisky** Cask LD46, bott Apr 07 db **(86) n**20 **t**22 **f**22 **b**22 Some serious malty oomph to the middle and latter stages of this one with heaps of natural caramel. **40%. sc.**

**Lark Distillery Single Malt Single Cask Bottled April 01** db **(88) n**22 apples and cinnamon: other peppery spices dig in to the oily malt; **t**22 massively malty, clean and fruity with a powdery oak offering further complexity; oily and fat; **f**22 beautifully spiced and delicate with fluttering malty tones caressing the palate; **b**22 this is lovely whisky, superbly made and offering both guile and charisma. Congratulations: Australia has entered the ranks of serious whisky distilling nations. **40%**

**Lark Distillery Single Malt Single Cask Bottled Jan 03** db **(83) n**19 **t**21 **f**22 **b**21. Again big malt intensity but the body is thinner, the finish, as the malts begin to show their complexity, is brilliant. A superb dram with a slight nose blemish. **40%**

**Lark Distillery Single Malt Whisky** Sept 03 db **(79) n**18 **t**21 **f**20 **b**20 this has to be the Jekyll and Hyde of malt whisky. Taste it direct from the bottle and the feints trouble you. Allow it to breath in the glass for an hour and burn off the oils and you are left with a superbly peated malt of great character. Patience is certainly a virtue with this one. *(My marks are an average between the two).*

⋰ **The Lark Distillery Single Malt Whisky Distillers Selection** Cask LD51, bott May 07 db **(91) n**22 a juniper/gin-style aroma; **t**23 typical massive delivery, again with a juniper/botanical kick and lovely bitter-sweet fruit/barley/oak threesome; **f**23 so long your tongue licks grooves into the roof of your mouth; subtle spice **b**23 one very big malt that keeps your tastebuds guessing all the way. A treat of a whisky. **46%. sc.**

## SMALL CONCERN DISTILLERY

**Cradle Mountain Pure Tasmanian Malt (87) n**21 curiously vivid bourbon character; sweet vanilla with hints of tangerine and hazelnut. Really very, very attractive; **t**22 an almost perfect translation onto the palate: gloriously sweet and gently nutty. The mouthfeel and body is firm and oily at the same time, the barley sparkles as the oak fades. Exceptionally subtle, clean and well made; **f**21 pretty long with some cocoa offering a praline effect; **b**23 a knock-out malt from a sadly now lost distillery in Tasmania. Faultlessly clean stuff with lots of new oak character but sufficient body to guarantee complexity. **43%**

**Cadenhead's World Whiskies Cradle Mountain Aged 10 Years** Ex Cabernet Sauvignon barrel, bott Sep 06 **(71) n**14 **t**19 **f**20 **b**18. Entirely baffling whisky. The Cab Sauv cask is horrendous and not helped by some feints, but what happens next is bemusing: it has every hallmark of rum. Had this not been sent to me as a whisky, I'd have never guessed. That said, some decent notes beyond the nose. **57.9%.** *270 bottles.*

## TASMAN DISTILLERY

**Great Outback Rare Old Australian Single Malt (92) n**24 I could stick my nose in a glass of this all day. This is sensational: more a question of what we don't have here! The malt is clean, beautifully defined and dovetails with refined, orangey-citrus notes. The oak is near perfection adding only a degree of tempered weight. I don't detect peat, but there is some compensating Blue Mountain coffee; **t**24 just so beautifully textured with countless waves of clean, rich malt neither too sweet nor too dry. This is faultless distillate; **f**21 lightens considerably with the oak vanilla dominating; **b**23 What can you say? An Australian whisky distillery makes a malt to grace the world's stage. But you can't find it outside of Australia. This will have to be rectified. *Strength not known.*

## TASMANIA DISTILLERY

**Old Hobart** db **(69) n**16 **t**19 **f**17 **b**17. The nose still has some way to go before it can be accepted as a mainstream malt, though there is something more than a little coastal about it this time. However, the arrival on the palate is another matter and I must say I kind of enjoyed its big, oily and increasingly sweet maltiness and crushed sunflower seed nuttiness towards the end. Green (and yellow) shoots are growing. The whisky is unquestionably getting better. **60%**

**Old Hobart** db **(78) n**18 **t**20 **f**21 **b**19. Ground-breaking stuff. The first-ever truly drinkable whisky from the Tasmania Distillery. An impressive double whammy of virgin oak and fresh Australian port wood manages to overpower the usual ugly aroma that offers little more than ,a minor blemish. Some bite and spice on the finish guarantees complexity to a fruity procession. **60%.** *(2003 bottling).*

**Sullivan's Cove** db **(61) n**13 **t**15 **f**17 **b**16. Some malt but typically grim, oily and dirty; awesomely weird. **40%.** *(2003 bottling). Australia.*

⸪ **Sullivans Cove Cask Strength** Port Maturation, Barrel no. HH0548, dist 14 Nov 00, bott 14 Feb 07 db **(93)** n23 thick grape dipped in molasses; chunky oils; t24 absolutely off the scales delivery-wise: the tastebuds are caked in the almost glutinous fruit offering near perfect bitter-sweet charms, while the roof of the mouth is sprayed with chocolate mousse and raspberry jam; f23 massively long with more cocoa and cocoa oil; b23 nosed blind I might have mistaken this for a Demerara rum! Big and ballsy. **60%**. *427 bottles.*

**Sullivan's Cove Classic** (capped with a black seal) db **(64)** n15 t16 f17 b16. A feinty dram, off-key and in need of a good tidy-up, though much better and cleaner than the gold seal. As this is a distillery's first attempt, I would rather encourage than fire off shells at a soft target. My advice is always to buy a bottle and see how a new distillery evolves. Again, the whisky can be improved dramatically by heating the glass in your hand to burn off the excess oils. **40%**

**Sullivan's Cove Classic** (capped with a gold seal) db **(58)** n12 t15 f16 b15. Feinty with a weird aroma of rotting vegetables on top. Some malt gurgles through, but it's not a pleasant experience. The gold cap and seal at the top was used only by the founders of the distillery and therefore represents the first-ever bottlings from Sullivan's Cove. **40%**

⸪ **Sullivan's Cove Double Cask** Bourbon & Port Oak db **(87)** n20 off- key oils are rounded off by fruit with chocolate-y results; t22 excellent body and weight with a malty flourish; f23 excellent finale, most probably thanks to the oils that shouldn't be there adding chewiness to the fruit and malt. Long, as one might expect; b22 right: here's a bet – any money you like. Take a glass of this malt. Leave it by a fire/radiator and come back to it in about an hour. I am sure those off notes will have vanished and you'll have a malt in the 90s displaying the honey notes just dying to get out. Not had time to do it myself, but as soon as the Bible's complete... **40%**

**Sullivans Cove Single Malt Whisky 6 Years Old** Bourbon maturation cask no. HH0274 db **(95)** n23 rich and intense, there is a lovely jammy fruitiness attached to the big barley; t24 barley concentrate with a dab of golden syrup and raspberry jam towards the middle. The body and weight are nigh perfect. Sensational!!; f24 lovely strands of vanilla interplay with the barley and then cocoa to see out the lightly oiled finish; b24 great on these guys. This must be the biggest Australian comeback since Larwood and Voce taught them how to bowl. A distillery once understandably a byword for less than brilliant whisky has come up with something that is truly beautiful. When I was in their warehouse a few years back, I detected the odd cracking cask, so knew their future could be bright. But perhaps not quite this brilliant...! **60%**

**Sullivans Cove Single Malt Whisky 6 Years Old** Port maturation cask no. HH0571 db **(90)** n23 so much grape but enough room for lots of natural caramel and vanilla; t23 lush, grapey delivery, which is no surprise. Excellent spice burst in the middle; f22 those caramels begin to spread; b22 high quality whisky helped by some pretty top dog casks. **60%**

**Sullivans Cove Single Malt Whisky 6 Years Old** Matured in French Oak Port and American Oak Bourbon casks db **(88)** n22 butterscotch tart, grape juice and barley in just-so portions; t23 oak-led and dry with just enough clean barley to sweeten the edge; f21 vanilla and toast breeze through to the finish; b22 subtle and sensuous. A bit like your average Tasmanian... **40%**

## YALUMBA WINERY

⸪ **Smith's Angaston Whisky Vintage 1997 Aged 7 Years** db **(88)** n20 an attractive, if not entirely faultless, combination of barley and fruit sewn together by honey; t22 an almost implausible silkiness to this: the barley and honey tip-toe over the tastebuds using a touch of oil to help them glide as well; f23 now we have some serious complexity with the fruits showing a berry-like sharpness, but it's all very effete; b23 easily one of the most delicate whiskies of the year and one that puts Samuel Smith on the map. Perfect for the hipflask for a night at the ballet. **40%**

⸪ **Smith's Angaston Whisky Vintage 1998 Aged 8 Years** db **(86)** n20 t22 f22 b22 Perhaps conscious that their first offering, a genuine touch of culture that it was, wasn't quite Bruce enough to called Australian, this one's showing bit of aggression. And I mean a bit, as this is no tackle from Lucas Neil. Because after the delivery it's back to the girlie stuff with some admittedly delicious Swiss Roll filling fruitiness. Lovely malt from a distillery I'm going to have to keep my eyes on. **40%**

# BRAZIL
## HEUBLEIN DISTILLERY

**Durfee Hall Malt Whisky (81) n**18 **t**22 **f**20 **b**21. Superbly made whisky; the intensity of the malt is beautifully layered without ever becoming too sweet. Very light bodied and immaculately clean. Good whisky by any standards. **43%**

## UNION DISTILLERY

**Barrilete (72) n**18 **t**19 **f**18 **b**17. Nothing particularly wrong with it technically; it just lacks vitality. Thin but extremely malt intense. **39.1%**

## Blends

**Cockland Gold Blended Whisky (73) n**18 **t**18 **f**19 **b**18. Silky caramel. Traces of malt there, but never quite gets it up. **38%**. *Fante*.

**Green Valley Special Reserve** batch 07/01 **(70) n**16 **t**19 **f**17 **b**18. A softly oiled, gently bitter-sweet blend with a half meaty, half boiled sweet nose. An unusual whisky experience. **38.1%**. *Muraro & Cia*.

**Natu Nobilis** batch 277929A **(81) n**19 **t**21 **f**20 **b**21. The grain is sympathetic and soft; the malt is shy but makes telling, complex interceptions. Very easy and enjoyable dramming. **39%**. *Seagram do Brasil*.

**Malte Barrilete Blended Whisky** batch 001/03 **(76) n**18 **t**20 **f**19 **b**19. This brand has picked up a distinctive apple-fruitiness in recent years and some extra oak, too. **39.1%**. *Union Distillery*.

**O Monge** batch 02/02 **(69) n**17 **t**18 **f**17 **b**17. Poor nose but it recovers with a malty mouth arrival but the thinness of the grain does few favours. **38.5%**. *Union Distillery*.

**Old Eight (83) n**22 **t**20 **f**20 **b**21. A decent, very lightly peated blend with no shortage of grain. **39%**

**Pitt's (84) n**21 **t**20 **f**22 **b**21. The pits it certainly aint!! A beautifully malted blend where the barley tries to dominate the exceptionally flinty grain whenever possible. Due to be launched later in 2004, this will be the best Brazil has to offer – though some fine tuning can probably improve the nose and middle even further and up the complexity significantly. I hope, when I visit the distillery early in 2005, I will be able to persuade them to offer a single malt: on this evidence it should, like Pitt's, be an enjoyable experience and perfect company for any World Cup finals. **40%**. *Busnello Distillery*.

# INDIA
## AMRUT DISTILLERY

**Amrut Single Malt** B.No.01 25-2-04 db **(82) n**20 **t**22 **f**19 **b**21. A very decent quality single malt easilly mistaken for a Speysider at about 35 or 36 years. That, usually, isn't always good. However, the sweet richness of the malt on the palate is a joy, with a boundless energy that pulses through to the prickly, oaky finish. Solid, honest whisky (with a non-scotch flourish at the finish) that would, after a black coffee, follow the finest Chicken Korma. (If you want to know more about Indian whisky, find the chapter on the distilleries I visited there in Jim Murray's Complete Book of Whisky). **40%. ncf.**

**Amrut Cask Strength** dist 6 May 01, bott May 06 db **(94) n**24 vibrant blood oranges with a sugar-coated vanilla topping. Clean and classy; **t**23 early arrival of rich, bourbony oak offers a momentarily dry start but sweet barley is not far behind. Bitter-ish honeycomb which sweetens in layers until the middle: a sumptuous battle between oak and barley with no winners..or losers; **f**23 an essay in chewability: wave upon wave of contradictory sweet and dry notes forged by the enormous confidence of high quality oak and intense malt; **b**24 From the moment you take in the aroma, stunningly structured with the citrus overture teasingly overtaken by the near near-perfect harmonization of vanilla and barley, you know you are if for a rare treat. Certainly the best non-peated Indian single malt to hit the international market. **62.8%**

**Amrut Cask Strength** dist 6 May 02, bott May 06 db **(92) n**23 chunky, dry, forests of fresh oak – even an unmistakable, and delightful, degree of bourbon which provides the required sweetness. And with an additional touch of seaweed and sea salt we have India's first coastal aroma; t23 lush, slightly viscous with spices clutching the palate and punctuating the soft barley; f22 oak arrives, but at a slower rate than the nose suggests but retains balance at all stages with the sweet, rich barley; b24 it is impossible not to be impressed with a sub-continental showstopper like this. Broad brushes here rather than delicate pastels but the balance is awesome. **62.6%**

⋰∴ **Amrut Cask Strength** bott Dec 06 db **(87)** n23 bigger oak intake than previous bottlings, resulting in bourbony sweetness; t22 much more severe oak arrival than previous cask bottlings, making for a mildly bitter experience on the palate. That bourbony trait, plus a honeycomb middle, helps even things out; f20 dry, again with big oak statement; b22 so intense is the heat in India, so critical the maturation time, that just a matter of weeks, let alone months, can make a life and death difference between the brilliance of previous bottlings and the oaky near-disaster of this. Another couple of months and it would have been curtains: as it is, there is enough – especially on the nose – still to admire. **63.8%. ncf.**


## PONDA DISTILLERY

**Stillman's Dram Single Malt Whisky Limited Edition** Bourbon cask ref. 11186-90 **(94)** n23 beautifully soft peats fuse with lime-led citrus notes. At once delicate and enormous; t23 softly smoked malts dissolve into honeyed pools on the palate. Sexier and more relaxing than a Goan foot massage; f24 the way the delicate oak washes gently against the palate, the manner in which the soft peats build to a crescendo - and yet still refuse to overpower – the entrancing waves of muscovado-sweetened coffee, all make for a sublime finale; b24 well, I thought I had tasted it all with the Amrut cask strength. And then this arrived at my lab...!! I predicted many years back that India would dish out some top grade malt before too long. But I'd be stretching the truth if I said I thought it would ever be this good... **42.8%.** *McDowell & Co Ltd, India.*

# Blends

**Antiquity** Blend of Rare Scotch and matured Indian malts, bott 14.2.06 **(79)** n20 t21 f19 b19. Uncluttered but clever in places with a silky and distinctly malty delivery on the palate; the oak – not noticeable on the nose - dominates the finish intertwined with toffee-caramel. Attractive, but never quite works out which direction it is going. **42.8%.** *Shaw Wallace Distilleries, India. No added flavours.*

**Antiquity Blue** bott Oct 05 **(85)** n19 t23 f21 b22. A deliciously subtle smoky edge to this guarantees excellent weight and chewability throughout. Hugely enjoyable. **42.8%.** *Shaw Wallace Distilleries, India. No added flavours.*

**Blenders Pride** Blend of imported Scotch malts and select Indian grain spirits, bott Sept 05 **(74)** n19 t20 f17 b18. The rich mouth arrival descends into dullness: don't know too many blenders who would be proud of that! **42.8%.** *Seagram Distilleries, India.*

**Peter Scot Malt Whisky (84)** n20 t21 f22 b21. Enjoyable balance between sweetness and oak and entertainingly enlivened by what appears to be some young, juicy malt. **42.8%.** *Khoday India Limited.*

**Royal Challenge** A blend of rare Scotch and Matured Indian Malt Whiskies, batch no. 350, bott 29 Dec 05 **(78)** n21 t20 f18 b19. A clean, exceptionally firm blend that could do with a little lift on the finish. **42.8%.** *Shaw Wallace Distilleries, India.*

**Royal Stag** A blend of imported Scotch malts and select Indian grain spirits, batch no. 068, 27 Feb 06 **(90)** n20 firm, clean good oak and barley presence; t23 crisp, refreshing Speyside-style malt dominates early; f24 attractive drying cocoa and spice prickle; gathering sweetness and even a touch of something very vaguely smoky; b23 thoroughly attractive, well-balanced and rewarding whisky by any standards: the finish is fabulous. Average nose part, just love it! **42.8%.** *Seagram's/Gemini Distilleries, India.*

**Signature** Batch no. 01, bott Dec 05 **(87)** n20 very young, Bowmore-esque tint that needs an extra dimension; t23 superb mouth arrival that luxuriates in an softly oiled and delicate peatiness. Other grassy malts also abound and makes for a mouth-watering experience; f22 plenty of vanilla and a curious bitter cherry sharpness amid the smoke and cocoa; **b**22 there is an appealing youthfulness to this whisky and no little complexity, nose apart. An enjoyable and rewarding journey. **42.8%**. *McDowell & Co Ltd, India.*

# NEW ZEALAND
## THE SOUTHERN DISTILLING CO LTD

⠿ **The Coaster Single Malt Whiskey** Batch No. 2356 **(85)** **n**20 **t**22 **f**21 **b**22 Distinctly small batch and sma' still with the accent very much on honey. Nosed blind I might have mistaken as Blue Mouse whisky from Germany: certainly European in style. Recovers well from the wobble on the nose and rewards further investigation. **40%**

⠿ **The MacKenzie Blended Malt Whiskey** **(85)** **n**20 **t**22 **f**21 **b**22 A vaguely spicier, chalkier, mildly less honeyed version of Coaster. Quite banana-laden nose. I have flown over Timeru many times, half way as it is between Christchurch and Dunedin. By the time you read this, there is more than even chance I shall have driven there and visited this distillery. I'll let you know on the website. **40%**

## WILSON DISTILLERY

**Milford Aged 10 Years** Batch 321M42, dist 93, bott 04 db **(89)** **n**20 less than impressive with a touch of soap; **t**23 fresh, grassy barley with a mildly metallic hardness; **f**23 waves of vanilla, soft spices and that continuing grassy, metallic theme; **b**23 what a shame that the Wilson distillery is not still extant and rich new make was being filled into some high quality bourbon casks. **43%**. *4780 bottles.*

**Milford Aged 10 Years Limited Edition** dist 91 bott Aug 02 batch no. F9/0/08 **(89)** **n**22 mildly minty, dry oak suppressing slightly the barley-sugar sweetness; gentle peat adds lovely depth; **t**23 rich, clean malt then that superb, trademark Wilson distillery fizz accompanying that delicate smoke; **f**21 softer oaky notes but some brittle peat offers some length to an otherwise abrupt finish; **b**23 charming yet always busy on the palate. **43%** *New Zealand Malt Whisky Co. 5573 bottles.*

**Milford Aged 12 Years Limited Edition** dist 90 bott Oct 02 batch no. E50/0 **(88)** **n**22 firm, crisp barley; the oak is dry despite a faint burbony character; a slight shake of black pepper; **t**24 beautifully mouth-watering and rich, the malt is stunningly intense and its usual ultra-clean self. A little bite and fizz towards the middle; **f**20 quite light, short and a touch thin; **b**22 the mouth arrival and barley lift-off is the stuff of New Zealand whisky legend; only the closed finish prevents this being a major classic. Excellent whisky. **43%**. *New Zealand Malt Whisky Co. 2840 bottles.*

**Milford Aged 15 Years** Batch 89M414, dist 88, bott 04 db **(91)** **n**21 battling, lively vanilla with the barley. Even the most distant hint of coal smoke; **t**24 beautiful barley delivery that shows remarkable freshness and zest. Lubeck marzipan offers a mild nutty sweetness, bringing with it some soft oaks which cranks up the complexity towards the middle; **f**23 light with strands of vanilla and a touch of citrus; **b**23 quality whisky though slightly flattened by age but shows enough early on to confirm its class. **43%**.

**Lammerlaw Aged 12 Years Peated Malt Sherry Cask Finishing** **(85)** **n**22 **t**19 **f**23 **b**21. Gets over the hurdle of the rough start to finish how it began on the nose: wonderfully! **50%. nc ncf.** *From Wilson Distillery, though it says Willowbank on the label.*

**Cadenhead's Lammerlaw 10 Years Old** **(88)** **n**22 big, fresh malt with a drying, chalky oak influence; **t**23 mouthwatering, clean, juicy malt. A touch of salt seasons it; complexity is further aided by warming spices and the most subtle hints of citrus; **f**21 back to that drying, chalky oak; **b**22 seriously sensuous and complex malt from a tragically lost distillery. Pure New Zealand, but Speyside in style, and its complexity puts a good number of Speysiders to shame. **48.2%**

**Cadenhead's World Whiskies Lammerlaw Aged 10 Years** bott May 06 **(90)** **n** 21 very slightly soapy; fabulous citrus tries to lift it; **t**22 rich, juicy barley overcomes that soap; **f**24 beautiful orangey notes link heavenly with the barley; **b**23 not even a sub-standard bourbon cask can ruin this beautiful malt. **47.3%**.

**Cadenhead's World Whiskies Lammerlaw Aged 10 Years** Bourbon, bott Sept 06 **(90)** **n**22 dry oak forms an elegant structure on which the crisp barley hangs; **t**23 sensuous and mouth-watering dovetailing of crystal-clear, fruity malt and balancing oak; **f**22 as dry as the nose with the usual cocoa-oak suspects; **b**23 one could almost weep for the loss of this unique distillery. The malt, in this classy and delicate form, is comparable with Speyside's finest. **47.7%**. *222 bottles.*

**Meenan's Lammerlaw 12 Years Old (90) n**23 beautifully honeyed, with lavender and a very distant rumble of peat: the oak suggests something older; **t**23 an outstanding delivery of soft, fruity malts, a layer of sweet honey and some oak and distant smoke; **f**21 heaps of vanilla and soft spice and a gradual build-up of something peaty; **b**23 this is a genuinely complex, beautifully made malt where the oak makes a wonderful divergence. A classic from any continent. **50%**. *Available only in New Zealand.*

## Blends

**Kiwi Whisky (37) n**2 **t**12 **f**11 **b**12. Strewth! I mean, what can you say? Perhaps the first whisky containing single malt offering virtually no nose at all and the flavour appears to be grain neutral spirit plus lashings of caramel and (so I am told) some Lammerlaw single malt. The word bland has been redefined. As has whisky. **40%**. *Ever-Rising Enterprises, NZ, for the Asian market.*

**Wilson's Superior Blend (89) n**22 stupendously clean and malt rich. Imperiously mouthwatering and enticing; **t**23 brilliant, almost dazzling clean malt arrival sharpened even further with mildly though distant crisp grain. One of the world's maltiest, most salivating blends, perhaps a touch simplistic but the charm of the malt endures while the ultra-delicate oak offers a teasing weight; **f**21 loses marks only because of a caramel-induced toffee arrival, but still the malt and grain are in perfect sync while the drying oak offers balance; **b**23 apparently has a mixed reception in its native New Zealand but I fail to see why: this is unambiguously outstanding blended whisky. On the nose you expect a mouthwatering mouthful and it delivers with aplomb. Despite this being a lower priced blend it is, intriguingly, a marriage of 60% original bottled 10-y-o Lammerlaw and 40% old Wilson's blend, explaining the high malt apparent. Dangerous and delicious and would be better still at a fuller strength...and with less caramel. **37.5%**. *Continental Wines and Spirits, NZ.*

## SOUTH AFRICA
### Single malt
#### JAMES SEDGWICK DISTILLERY

**Three Ships 10 Years Old** db **(83) n**21 **t**21 **f**20 **b**21. Seems to have changed character, with more emphasis on sherry and natural toffee. The oak offers a thrusting undercurrent. **43%**

### Blends

**Harrier (87) n**20 bit of a culture clash but is pretty tactile; **t**22 sweet and silky with a wonderful spice development; **f**23 more cotton and silk but with stunning smoke guaranteeing length, weight and style; **b**22 this guy is getting better and better. An extra dose of smoke has given it great poise and body. Harrier is taking off. **43%**.

**Knights (77) n**19 **t**20 **f**19 **b**19. Sweet, pleasant, but a little flat. **43%**.

**Three Ships Bourbon Cask Finish** db **(91) n**22 sweet, biscuity malt and the mildest glazed ginger; **t**23 the best arrival of any South African whisky: the softness and sheen is exemplary, and the follow-through is of wonderfully gentle malt-oak complexity; **f**23 just so many layers of delicate oak, yet never over-dries or appears too old; **b**23 a minor classic here, with the emphasis being on a mouthwatering lushness. **43%**

**Three Ships 5 Years Old (89) n**22 sweet gristy peat and a unique hint of mildly roasted Colombian (coffee...!); **t**22 young, chewy, sweet peat of a Bowmore variety, softened and thinned by the trademark velvet grain; **f**23 long, spiced and elegant; **b**22 first-rate blending: it is as if they are beginning to understand the balancing values of their own whiskies. **43%**. *South African/Scotch Whisky.*

**Three Ships Original (82) n**19 **t**22 **f**21 **b**20. Not sure if this is meant to be the 3-yo. Certainly has different character, being smokeless save perhaps some late, late spice. Great grains, though. **43%**

## MISCELLANEOUS

**Jaburn & Co Pure Grain & Malt Spirit (53) n**14 **t**13 **f**13 **b**13. Tastes like neutral grain and caramel to me. Some shop keepers, I hear, are selling it as whisky though this is not claimed on the label. Trust me: it isn't. **37.5%**. *Jaburn & Co, Denmark.*

**House of Westend Blended Whisky (67) n**17 **t**18 **f**16 **b**16. No more than OK if you are being generous; some tobacco-dirty notes around. Doesn't mention country of origin anywhere on the label. **40%**. *Bernkasteler Burghof, Germany*.

**Prince of Wales Welsh Whisky (69) n**17 **t**18 **f**17 **b**17. A syrupy aroma is compounded by an almost liqueurish body. Thin in true Scotch substance, probably because it claims to be Welsh but is really Scotch with herbs diffused in a process that took place in Wales. Interestingly, my "liqueur" tasting notes were written before I knew exactly what it was I was tasting, thus proving the point and confirming that, with these additives, this really isn't whisky at all. **40%**

**Shepherd's Export Finest Blend (46) n**5 **t**16 **f**12 **b**13. A dreadful, illdefined grain-spirit nose is softened on the palate by an early mega-sweet kick. The finish is thin and eventually bitter. Feeble stuff. **37.2%**. *"A superb blend of Imported Scotch Malt whiskies and Distilled N.Z. grain spirit", claims the label which originally gives the strength as 40%, but has been over-written. Also, the grain, I was told, was from the USA. Southern Grain Spirit, NZ.*

## CROSS-COUNTRY VATTED MALT

⫶⫶⫶ **Celtic Nations** (Bruichladdich 1994 & Cooley Irish 1999) **(82) n**20 **t**22 **f**20 **b**20 Pleasant enough, very softly smoked, but a degree of inter-country bickering. **46%**. *Bruichladdich Distillery.*

**Cradle Mountain db (77) n**19 **t**21 **f**18 **b**19. Doesn't quite gel for me, though it has some delicious malty moments. **46%**. *This is a vatting of Aussie malt from Cradle Mountain and Springbank single malt scotch.*

**Cradle Mountain Double db (88) n**20 no shortage of fruit with tangerines and diced green apples to the fore; **t**23 in your face malt of almost awesome intensity. Lashings of clean barley, grassy notes showing both age and youth; **f**23 lingers at first, then the Cradle Mountain signature of fruit and nuts descends. Also the cocoa is back with some serious oak present but always in control; **b**22 this appears to be a different vatting to the 46% with greater Tasmanian whisky evident – although it isn't! Much more poise and zest and no shortage of charisma. Brilliant stuff. **54.4%**. *This is a vatting of Aussie malt from Cradle Mountain and single malt scotch from Springbank.*

**Jon, Mark and Robbo's The Smooth Sweeter One** a vatting of Scottish and Irish malt **(92) n**24 a real citrus and grassy kick to this with soft vanilla offering only a background noise. So delicate, you feel it might shatter if you nose too hard; **t**22 fresh and fruity; **f**23 long with some genuine complexity on the gently-spiced waves;controlled barley sweetness but drier vanillas dominate with those spices at the end; **b**23 a beautiful whisky. Intriguing as it may be, claims I have heard of this being the first such whisky of its type are way off mark – not to mention Jon and Robbo. A hundred years ago and more it was not uncommon to find bottled malt whisky being a combination of Scotch and Irish. It would have come under the general title "whisky" and brought together by merchants procuring whiskies at the best prices they could get. In my library somewhere I have old labels of these forebears. That said, those whiskies of a century ago would have been hard pushed to better it. **40%**. *Edrington.*

⫶⫶⫶ **Premium Bottlers Pure Malt Whisky Aged 11 Years** BLAT cask no. 1011 (marriage of Blair Athol Single Malt and Canadian Single malt) **(84) n**19 **t**22 **f**21 **b**22 After a disaster at the first fence, picks itself up for a deliciously malty comeback. **46%. nc ncf.**

⫶⫶⫶ **Premium Bottlers Pure Malt Whisky Aged 12 Years** BRIN cask no. 1009 (marriage of Benrinnes Single Malt and Canadian Single Malt) **(76) n**18 **t**20 **f**19 b19 A tad feinty and falls at the first hurdle. **46%. nc ncf.**

⫶⫶⫶ **Premium Bottlers Pure Malt Whisky Aged 10 Years** LINK cask no. 1013 (marriage of Linkwood Single Malt and Canadian Single Malt) **(86) n**21 **t**23 **f**21 **b**21 Gallops off at a brisk, juicy, malty pace but tires as the natural caramels take hold. **46%. nc ncf.**

⫶⫶⫶ **Premium Bottlers Pure Malt Whisky Aged 11 Years** RLOC cask no. 1015 (marriage of Royal Lochnagar Single Malt and Canadian Single Malt) **(89) n**21 heavy barley and firm, metallic notes; **t**22 stodgy barley at first but begins to lighten as some honey bursts through; **f**23 goes into honey-barley overdrive, again with a sharp metallic bite, but so delicious.... **b**23 after a slow, cumbersome start finishes the course with surprising strength and grace. **46%. nc ncf.**

**Premium Bottler Vatted Malt Whisky Aged 10 Years** ACHN 102 (99% Auchentoshan Scotch, 1% Glenora Canadian) **(84) n**21 **t**22 **f**20 **b**21. Very young, enormously citrussy effort with all the usual Auchtoshan foibles. Coming from a third fill makes for interesting dramming. **46%. nc ncf.**

**Premium Bottler Vatted Malt Whisky Aged 12 Years** GLLS 101 (99% Glen Lossie Scotch, 1% Glenora Canadian) **(86) n**21 **t**22 **f**22 **b**21. Very drinkable, pre-pubescent Lossie. Beware the false finale: it appears to vanish for a short finish and then reappears even more intensely than before. **46%. nc ncf.**

**Premium Bottler Vatted Malt Whisky Aged 12 Years** MRTL 101 (99% Mortlach Scotch, 1% Glenora Canadian) **(83) n**21 **t**20 **f**21 **b**21. Very decent heavyweight despite the lack of oak involvement. Excellent natural oils. **46%. nc ncf**

**Premium Bottler Vatted Malt Whisky Aged 10 Years** SCAP 101 (99% Scapa Scotch, 1% Glenora Canadian) **(90) n**23 stewing apples form the centre ground of this astonishingly young, new make-coated aroma. As refreshing as a face full of driven rain; **t**23 that glorious freshness now turns into something so salivating you'll have to drink a pint of water ahead of time to survive. Rarely is barley this concentrated; **f**22 layering of intense barley continues, with just a drying coffee to offer the required balance; **b**22 absolutely amazing malt. This Scapa, from a third-fill bourbon cask one assumes, appears half its age and simply glories in its natural brilliance. If this doesn't prove what world-great whisky this distillery conjures up in its most simple form, nothing will. **46%. nc ncf.**

**Premium Bottler Vatted Malt Whisky Aged 10 Years** STRT 101 (99% Strathisla Scotch, 1% Glenora Canadian) **(86) n**20 **t**22 **f**23 **b**21. Early evidence, on the nose particularly, of an over-tired cask but the natural exuberance and lustre of the distillate carries it through. Wonderfully chewy in part. **46%. nc ncf.**